MSU LIBRARIES
W9-BRZ-445

INDEX TO PERIODICAL FICTION IN ENGLISH, 1965-1969

compiled and edited, and with an introduction by

Douglas Messerli

and

Howard N. Fox

The Scarecrow Press, Inc.
Metuchen, N.J. & London
1977

Library of Congress Cataloging in Publication Data

Messerli, Douglas, 1947-
Index to periodical fiction in English, 1965-1969.

1. English fiction--Indexes. 2. American fiction--Indexes. 3. English fiction--Translations from foreign languages--Indexes. 4. Fiction--Translations into English--Indexes. 5. Periodicals--Indexes. I. Fox, Howard N., joint author. II. Title.

Z2014.F5M475 [PR821] 016.813 76-42288
ISBN 0-8108-0952-4

ACKNOWLEDGMENTS

The following libraries were the sources of our research, and thus our appreciation goes to their officers and staff:

Battelle-Tompkins Memorial Library, American University, Washington, D.C.

Founders Library, Howard University, Washington, D.C.

Fred Lewis Pattee Library, Pennsylvania State University, University Park.

Hugh M. Morris Library, University of Delaware, Newark.

John K. Mullen of Denver Memorial Library, Catholic University of America, Washington, D.C.

Library of Congress, Washington, D.C.

McKeldin Library, University of Maryland, College Park.

Milton S. Eisenhower Library, Johns Hopkins University, Baltimore.

New York Public Library.

University of Pennsylvania Libraries, University of Pennsylvania, Philadelphia.

Our thanks also go to Dr. Robert L. Beare, Assistant Director of Libraries, University of Maryland, and to Lawrence Shifreen.

And finally, our especial gratitude goes to Jerry and Sandy Fox, whose financial and moral support made this index possible.

CONTENTS

INTRODUCTION

The Index to Periodical Fiction was first conceived in 1973 while we were doing research for a bibliography. What had been made clear during that research was that it was immensely difficult to uncover primary source material which did not appear in book form. For collected short fiction there was the selective Short Story Index, but for uncollected fiction, poetry and drama published in periodicals it was primarily a hit-or-miss proposition. True, the Index to Little Magazines listed the contents of approximately 49 little magazines for the years 1920-1967,* and the Readers' Guide to Periodical Literature further listed 161 magazines,† but most periodical literature remained unindexed. Also in 1973 Sander W. Zulauf and Irwin H. Weiser began the Index of American Periodical Verse (an annual; also published by Scarecrow Press), which was the first real attempt to fill this research gap. Since our interest lay mostly in fiction, we decided to compile an index to periodical fiction.

As is often the case, the project immediately escalated once underway. Although we had to impose an obvious limitation on the years covered in one volume, we had determined that we would try to be as inclusive as possible within the five-year period chosen, in order to benefit all forms of research. Thus we perceived quite early that we could not limit ourselves to American journals. We realized that the international exchange of fiction is one of the most vital aspects of periodical literature, and, indeed, is essential in

*Information is based on the 1966-67 edition; 40 of these magazines published fiction. The Index to Commonwealth Magazines further indexed 41 British Commonwealth magazines (based on the 1968-69 ed.).

†Information is based on vol. 33 (March 1973-Feb. 1974); only 16 of these magazines published fiction.

evaluating intercultural relationships. We therefore chose journals published in English throughout the world. Obviously we could not cover all foreign periodicals, but we could and did choose a variety of large and small journals outside of the United States. Simultaneously, we attempted to index all American magazines which published fiction that we could obtain except those which were highly localized or parochial in subject matter. In other words, all American periodicals obtainable were indexed except university or college publications which published only their own students' work, and those publications with highly specialized subjects such as mystery, fantasy and science fiction.

Again to be as helpful to the researcher as possible, we defined fiction in the broadest sense. For the most part we indexed those works which were described as fiction by the periodical itself, but when such descriptions were not given, or when we felt that a particular work had a "fictional tone," we indexed it. Similarly, whenever the distinctions between fiction and poetry or between fiction and essay were vague--as in prose poetry or as in reminiscences--we listed the work. The result is an index of 11,077 entries from 405 magazines published from January 1965 through December 1969.

Our bibliographical form is a standard one: author, title, periodical title, volume or issue number, date, and complete page numbers. However, because of the varying formats of individual periodicals, there are many exceptions, a few of which are worth noting.

Authors: Authors are indexed by last name. Stories written by more than one author are fully cited under each. Japanese, Chinese, Spanish and other such names are entered as they would be in the author's home country whenever such information is available. Works by authors who have changed their names since the publication of their fiction and by authors known also by pseudonyms are fully cited under the alternate form whenever possible. Finally, authors whose work is signed only by initials are listed under the last initial given.

Titles: Whenever possible, the titles indexed are those which appeared on the first page of the fiction proper, not those listed in the table of contents. In the titles we included information concerning the book source if that information appeared as part of the title on the title page. For example, if it was noted that a selection was from a novel already published, about to be published, or in progress, the name of that novel is also included. Similarly, if a story or novel was serialized, and the installment number of the serialization was noted with the title, then that number is included. Slashes are used to indicate type changes and/or line breaks which separated the title from its source or separated the title from its installment number. Where the selection is obviously from a novel, but was not indicated as such within the title itself, we have not noted it. We feel that although we may recognize many such cases, it would be inconsistent to note some and not others. Those stories for which no author was listed (13 in all) are entered by title and appear in alphabetical order at the very beginning. (Five legends (i.e., entries 14-18) then follow before the author sequence begins.) A listing of titles indexed to entry numbers follows the listing of translators at the back of the book.

Translators: The name of a translator or adapter is given as part of the entry in the main sequence (the author listing); an alphabetical listing of translators, indexed to entry numbers, follows the main author listing. Authors who translated their own works are not included in this list.

Periodicals: All periodicals are named without abbreviations. Wherever two or more periodicals have the same name, the place of publication is included in parentheses after the periodical name. These periodicals are indicated by the underlining of the place of publication on the master list of periodicals which precedes the main author list.

Volume, issue number and dates: Volume numbers are indicated whenever available. When the periodical does not note a volume number, issue numbers are given. Dates are listed by month and year, or season and year, or by year alone, depending upon the information supplied by the periodical. Where periodicals have not indicated month or season we have noted both volume and issue numbers whenever possible. If no volume, issue or year is given by the periodical, approximate dates have been indicated.

Page numbers: All page numbers are given. When the first page of the text is preceded by an illustration which is clearly related to the text, then that page is given as the first page of the story or novel. Since this is somewhat arbitrary there are deviations, but every page of text is listed in all cases. We have indicated non-paginated periodicals by the abbreviation "n.p.," followed by a count, enclosed in brackets, of the pages, starting with the first page of text of the story.

Notes and emendations: All notes and emendations follow the page numbers and are enclosed in brackets. All of these should be self-explanatory.

Understandably, working with such a large number of periodicals--many of which have become rare collectors' items--we were unable to obtain every issue of every periodical we indexed. However, we felt it preferable to list the fiction in those issues we did find, rather than to strike the periodical from our list. In the master list of periodicals we have noted, when ascertainable, which issues we are missing from those journals we believe to be incomplete. In many cases we have noted that we have no further issues after a particular date. Our coverage of several of these periodicals may actually be complete, but since they have stopped publication without notification we have not always been able to certify this. Any information on the fiction of the missing issues will be appreciated, and will be indexed into future volumes.

Finally, in working with such a large number of entries, we are bound to have introduced a few inconsistencies. We hope that in subsequent volumes of this Index such inconsistencies may be eliminated. We believe, however, that in all cases we have achieved one of our aims: to send the reader to the proper source. If the Index also helps the researcher to discover new writers and periodicals of interest, and if it can attest to the quality and variety of fiction being published in English language periodicals, then it has fulfilled the hopes which sustained its compilation.

Douglas Messerli
Howard N. Fox

College Park, Maryland

PERIODICALS INDEXED*

Abraxas. 1969- . New Paltz, N. Y.

Abyss. 1967- . Dunkirk, N. Y.

Accent. 1969- . New Delhi, India.

Adam International Review. 1929- . Bucharest, Rumania; London, England.

Aesop's Feast. 1968- . West Lafayette, Ind.

Alaska Review. 1963- . Anchorage, Alas.

Aldebaran Review. 1967- . Berkeley, Calif.

Alphabet. 1960- . London, Ont., Canada.

Alta. 1966- . Birmingham, England.

Ambience. 1968- . London, England.

Ambit. 1959- . London, England.

American. 1965- . Washington, D. C. (no further issues after IV, 1 (Spring 1968)).

American Dialog. 1964- . New York, N. Y.

American Judaism. 1951-1967. New York, N. Y.

American P. E. N. 1969- . New York, N. Y.

American Scandinavian Review. 1913- . New York, N. Y.

Américas. 1949- . Washington, D. C.

Analecta. 1967- . Demarest, N. J.

Angel Hair. 1966-1969. Williamstown, Mass.

Anglo-Welsh Review. 1949- . Pembroke Dock, England; Temby, Wales.

Ann Arbor Review. 1967- . Ann Arbor, Mich.

Ante. 1964-1968. Los Angeles, Calif.

Antioch Review. 1941- . Yellow Springs, O.

---

*Where a date of commencement of publication is missing, it was simply not available.

Ant's Forefoot. 1967- . Toronto, Ont., Canada (missing nos. 1 & 2).

Aphra. 1969- . Springtown, Pa.

Appalachian Review. 1966-1968. Morgantown, W. Va.

Approach. 1947-1967. Alburtis, Pa.

Ararat. 1960- . New York, N.Y.

The Archive. 1887- . Durham, N.C. (missing all issues of 1965, and no further issues after LXXX, 4 (1968)).

Arena. 1961- . London, England.

Ariel. 1962- . Jerusalem, Israel.

Arizona Quarterly. 1945- . Tucson, Ariz.

Arlington Quarterly. 1967- . Arlington, Tex.

Armenian Review. 1948- . Boston, Mass.

Art and Literature. 1964-1967. Lausanne, Switzerland.

Arx. 1967- . Austin, Tex. (missing I, 1 (1967)).

Aspects. 1964- . Eugene, Ore.

Assay. 1945- . Seattle, Wash.

Athanor. 1967- . New York, N.Y. (missing all issues after I, 1 (1967)).

Athene. 1940-1967. Chicago, Ill.

Atlantic. 1857- . Boston, Mass.

Audience. 1968; 1971- . Boston, Mass.

Australian Letters. 1957- . Melbourne, Australia (missing all issues except VII, 1 (1968)).

Avant Garde. 1968- . New York, N.Y.

Ave Maria. 1965-1914; 1915- . Notre Dame, Ind.

Avenues. 1968- . New Delhi, India (no further issues after II, 6-7 (1969)).

Aylesford Review. 1955-1968. Aylesford, Kent, England.

Ball State University Forum (previously Ball State Teachers College Forum). 1960- . Muncie, Ind.

Bengali Literature. 1966- . Calcutta, India (no further issues after II, 1 (1967)).

Bennington Review. 1966-1970. Bennington, Vt.

Beyond Baroque. 1968- . Venice, Calif.

Bhubaneswar Review. 1968- . Bhubaneswar, India.

Bim. 1944- . St. Michael, Barbados (missing nos. 40-41 (1965)).

Blackbird. 1963-1966. Chicago, Ill.

Blacklist. 1965- . New York, N.Y. (no issues after 1965).

Bones. 1967- . New York, N.Y.

Boss. 1966-1970. New York, N.Y.

Boston Review. 1966- . Cambridge, Mass. (no further issues after no. 1 (1966)).

Brigham Young University Studies. 1959- . Provo, Utah.

California Review. 1967- . Santa Barbara, Calif.

Cambridge Review. 1879- . Cambridge, England.

Canadian Forum. 1920- . Toronto, Ont., Canada.

The Cantuarian. Canterbury, England.

Caribbean Review. 1969- . Hato Rey, Puerto Rico.

Carleton Miscellany. 1960- . Northfield, Minn.

Carolina Quarterly. 1948- . Chapel Hill, N.C.

Caterpillar. 1967- . New York, N.Y.

Catholic World. 1865- . New York, N.Y.

Caught. 1969- . Davis, Calif. (no further issues after I, 1 (1969)).

Cavalier. 1952- . Greenwich, Conn. (missing May-June & Aug.-Dec. 1966 and all of 1967-1969).

Chelsea. 1958- . New York, N.Y.

Chicago Review. 1946- . Chicago, Ill.

Cimarron Review. 1967- . Stillwater, Okla.

The Circle. 1968- . Washington, D.C. (missing nos. 1-2; no further issues after no. 3).

The Classic. 1963- . Johannesburg, South Africa.

Colorado Quarterly. 1952- . Boulder, Colo.

Columbia. 1921- . New York, N.Y.

Columbia Review. 1815- . New York, N.Y.

Commentary. 1945- . New York, N.Y.

Compass. Aptos, Calif. (no issues except June 1965).

Confrontation. 1968- . Greenvale, N.Y.

Consumption. 1967-1970. Seattle, Wash.

Contemporary Literature in Translation. 1968- . Vancouver, B.C., Canada.

Contrast. 1960- . Cape Town, South Africa.

Contrast. 1968- . Oxford, England.

Coraddi. 1918- . Greensboro, N.C. (missing all issues of 1965-1966; possibly missing issues of 1967-1969).

Cornhill Magazine. 1860- . London, England.

El Corno Emplumado (The Plumed Horn). 1962- . Mexico.

Corral. 1961- . Austin, Tex. (no further issues after 1966).

Cosmopolitan. 1886- . New York, N.Y.

Courier. 1936-1965. London, England.

Coyotes Journal. 1964- . Eugene, Ore.; San Francisco, Calif.

Crucible. 1956- . Richmond, Ind.

Dalhousie Review. 1921- . Halifax, Nova Scotia, Canada.

Damascus Road. 1961-1967. Allentown, Pa.

Dare. 1963- . Cleveland, O. (no further issues after VI, 3 (October 1968)).

Dasein. 1961- . New York, N.Y.; Washington, D.C.

December. 1957- . Iowa City, Ia; Chicago, Ill.

DeKalb Literary Arts Journal. 1966- . Clarkston, Ga.

Delos. 1968- . Austin, Tex.

Delta. 1958- . Amsterdam, Netherlands.

Delta. 1953- . Cambridge, England.

Delta. Louisiana.

Delta Review. 1963-1969; 1970- . Greenville, Miss. (missing vols. II & III (1965-1966), except for III, 1 (1966)).

Denver Quarterly (The University of Denver Quarterly). 1966- . Denver, Colo.

Dialogue. 1965- . Nairobi, Kenya (no further issues after no. 3 (1966)).

Diliman Review. 1953- . Quezon City, Philippines.

Dimension. 1968- . Austin, Tex.

Discourse. 1958-1970. Moorhead, Minn.

Domestic Pair. ? Pittsburgh, Pa.

Dublin Magazine. 1961- . Dublin, Ireland.

Duel. 1969- . Montreal, Quebec, Canada.

Dust. 1964- . El Cerrito, Calif.

East-West Review. 1964- . Kyoto, Japan.

Eastern Horizon. 1960- . Hong Kong.

Edge. 1963-1969. Edmonton, Alberta, Canada.

Encounter. 1953- . London, England.

Enigma. 1969- . Leicester, England.

Epoch. 1947- . Ithaca, N. Y.

Era. 1964-1968. Philadelphia, Pa.

Esquire. 1933- . Chicago, Ill.

Evergreen Review. 1957- . New York, N. Y.

Evidence. 1961-1967. Toronto, Ont., Canada.

Expression. 1968- . Limbe, Malawi.

Extensions. 1968- . New York, N. Y.

The Fair. 1966-1968. Terre Haute, Ind.

The Fiddlehead. 1953- . Fredericton, N. B., Canada.

Fire. 1967- . London, England (missing no. 1 (1967); no further issues after no. 2 (1968)).

Floating Bear. 1961- . New York, N. Y.

Florida Quarterly. 1967- . Gainesville, Fla.

Focus. 1961- . Singapore (missing scattered issues of 1965-1966; no further issues after no. 2 (new series) (1968)).

For Now. 1966-1968. New York, N. Y.

Forum. 1956- . Houston, Tex.

Four Quarters. 1951- . Philadelphia, Pa.

Foxfire. 1967- . Rabun Gap, Ga.

Free Lance. 1953- . Cleveland, Ohio.

Freelance. 1965- . St. Louis, Mo. (missing all issues before VII, 2 (1969)).

Gato Magazine. 1966- . Los Gatos, Calif. (no further issues after II, 1 (1967)).

The Gauntlet. 1966?- . Bronx, N. Y. (missing all issues except I, 4 (1967)).

Genesis: Grasp. 1968- . New York, N. Y.

Genesis West. 1962-1965. Burlingame, Calif.

Georgia Review. 1947- . Athens, Ga.

Gnomon. 1965- . Lexington, Ky. (no further issues after no. 2 (1967)).

Goddard Journal. 1967- . Plainfield, Vt. (missing I, 1 (1967) and II, 1 (1968); no further issues after II, 2 (1968)).

Good Housekeeping. 1885- . Holyoke, Mass.

Goodly Co. 1964- . West Lafayette, Ind.; Kalamazoo, Mich.; Sewell, N.J.

Grande Ronde Review. 1964- . La Grande, Ore. (missing nos. 4 & 5 (1965-66)).

Grecourt Review. 1957- . Northampton, Mass. (missing scattered issues of 1965, 1967 & 1968; no further issues after XI, 2 (1968)).

Green River Review. 1968- . Owensboro, Ky.

Greensboro Review. 1966- . Greensboro, N.C.

El Grito. 1967- . Berkeley, Calif.

Grok. 1966- . New York, N.Y. (no further issues after I, 2 (1967)).

Haravec. 1966- . Lima, Peru (missing no. 1; no further issues after no. 3 (1967)).

Harper's Bazaar. 1867- . New York, N.Y.

Harper's Magazine. 1850- . New York, N.Y.

Harvard Advocate. 1866- . Cambridge, Mass.

Hemisphere. 1957- . Sydney, Australia.

Hudson Review. 1948- . New York, N.Y.

Human Voice (Human Voice Quarterly). 1965- . Homestead, Fla. (missing I, 1 & I, 2 (1965)).

Husson Review. 1968- . Bangor, Me.

Idea and Image. 1967-1968. New York, N.Y.

Ikon. 1964-1966. Leeds, England (missing I, 5 (1966)).

Ikon. 1967- . New York, N.Y. (missing I, 1 (1967); no further issues after I, 3 (1967)).

Illuminations. 1965- . San Francisco, Calif. (missing no. 2; no further issues after no. 3 (1967)).

Imprint. 1961- . Bombay, India (no issues before April 1968).

Indian Literature. 1957- . New Delhi, India.

Intrepid. 1964- . New York, N.Y.; Buffalo, N.Y.

Intro. 1968- . New York, N.Y.

Io Magazine. 1966- . Ann Arbor, Mich.; Amherst, Mass., etc.

Japan Quarterly. 1954- . Tokyo, Japan.

Jeopardy. 1966- . Bellingham, Wash. (missing no. 2).

Jewish Frontier. 1933- . New York, N.Y. (no further issues after 1966).

Jewish Life. 1933- . New York, N.Y.

Joglars. 1964-1966. Providence, R.I.

Kansas Magazine. 1950-1968. Manhattan, Kans.

Kansas Quarterly. 1968- . Manhattan, Kans.

Kenyon Review. 1939-1970. Gambier, O.

Kulcher. 1960-1965. New York, N.Y.

Ladies' Home Journal. 1883- . Philadelphia, Pa.

Lance. Worcester, Mass. (no further issues after V, 2 (1965)).

Landfall. 1947- . Christchurch, New Zealand.

Latitudes. 1967-1972. Houston, Tex. (no issues except II, 1 (1968)).

Lillabulero. 1967- . Chapel Hill, N.C.

Limbo. 1964-1967. Vancouver, B.C., Canada.

Lines. 1964-1965. New York, N.Y.

The Lit. Notre Dame, Ind. (no issues except no. 7).

Lit (Lambda Iota Tau). 1957- . Jackson, Tenn; Hays, Kans.; Vermillion, S.D., etc.

Literary Half Yearly. 1960- . Mysore, India.

Literary Magazine of Tufts University. 1966- . Medford, Mass. (missing I, 1 (1966); no further issues after III, 2 (1968)).

Literary Review. 1957- . Teaneck, N.J.

Literature East and West. 1954- . New Paltz, N.Y.

Little Magazine. See The Quest.

Little Review of the Pacific Northwest. 1965- . Portland, Ore. (no issues except no. 1 (1965)).

Little Square Review. 1966- . Santa Barbara, Calif.

Lituanus. 1954- . Chicago, Ill.

London Magazine. 1961- . London, England.

Long View Journal. 1968- . Raleigh, N.C.

Lotus. 1968- . Athens, O.

Lugano Review. 1965-1966. Lugano, Switzerland.

Mad River Review. 1964-1967. Dayton, O.

Mademoiselle. 1935- . New York, N.Y.

Magazine. 1964-1966. New York, N.Y.

Maguey. 1968- . El Cerrito, Calif. (no further issues after no. 2 (1968)).

Malahat Review. 1967- . Victoria, B.C., Canada.

Man About Town. 1967- . Chattanooga, Tenn. (no further issues after II, 1 (1968)).

Mandala. 1968- . Madison, Wis.; Iowa City, Ia. (missing no. 2; no further issues after no. 5 (1969)).

Manhattan Review. 1966-1967. New York, N.Y.

Manuscript. Northfield, Minn.

Massachusetts Review. 1959- . Amherst, Mass.

McCall's. 1870- . Dayton, O.

Meanjin Quarterly. 1941- . Brisbane, Australia.

Mexico Quarterly Review. 1962- . Mexico City, Mexico.

Michigan Quarterly Review. 1962- . Ann Arbor, Mich.

Midstream. 1955- . New York, N.Y.

Midwestern University Quarterly. 1965-1967. Wichita Falls, Tex.

Mill Mountain Review. 1969- . Roanoke, Va.

Minnesota Review. 1960- . Minneapolis, Minn.

Miscellaneous Man. 1968- . Los Angeles, Calif.

Modern Age. 1957- . Chicago, Ill.

Montparnasse Review. 1964- . Paris, France. (no further issues after no. 2 (1966)).

Moonlight Review. 1967- . Brooklyn, N.Y. (no further issues after I, 2 (1968)).

Mother. 1964-1967. Dallas, Tex.

Mt. Adams Review. Cincinnati, O. (no further issues after II, 4 (1967-68)).

Mundus Artium. 1967- . Athens, O.

Negro Digest (now Black World). 1942- . Chicago, Ill. (missing Sept.-Oct. 1967).

New American Review. 1967- . New York, N.Y.

New Campus Review. 1966- . Denver, Colo.

New Campus Writing. 1955- . New York, N.Y.

New Directions. 1947- . New York, N.Y.

New Frontiers. 1955- . Fairfield, Conn. (no further issues after XI, 2 (1966)).

New Hungarian Quarterly. 1959- . Budapest, Hungary.

New Leaven. 1951- . Xavier, Kans. (missing vols. 15, 17 & 18).

New Letters. See University Review.

New Mexico Quarterly. 1931-1968. Albuquerque, N.M.

New Orleans Review. 1968- . New Orleans, La.

New Renaissance. 1968- . Arlington, Mass.

New Worlds. 1946- . London, England (missing all issues before no. 174, and missing nos. 175-180, 182, 184, 186-187, and all issues after 188).

New Writers. 1961- . London, England.

New Writing from Zambia. 1964- . Lusaka, Zambia (missing 1965 & nos. 2 of both 1967 & 1969).

New Yorker. 1925- . New York, N.Y.

New Zealand Listener. 1939- . Wellington, New Zealand (missing all issues after Aug. 15, 1969, and missing scattered issues throughout).

Nexus. 1969- . Lafayette, La.

Nexus. 1966-1968. Nairobi, Kenya (no further issues after II, 1 (1967)).

Nexus. 1963-1967. San Francisco, Calif.

Niagara Frontier Review. 1964-1966. Buffalo, N.Y.

Nigerian Students Voice. 1963- . Baltimore, Md. (no further issues after III, 3 (1966)).

Nimrod. 1956- . Tulsa, Okla.

Niobe. 1965-1966. Brooklyn Heights, N.Y.

North American Mentor. 1964- . Conesville, Ia.; Davenport, Ia. (no issues before III, 1 (1965)).

North American Review. 1964- . Cedar Falls, Ia.

North Dakota Quarterly. 1910- . Grand Forks, N.D.

Northwest Review. 1957- . Eugene, Ore.

Nova. 1965- . London, England (missing April 1965-March 1966, Aug. & Nov. 1966, March 1967 and Sept. 1969).

Now. 1969- . Jerusalem, Israel.

Obzor. 1967- . Sofia, Bulgaria (missing nos. 2-4 of 1969).

Occident. 1948-1966, old series; 1967- , new series. (missing 1966).

Ohio University Review (now Ohio Review). 1959- . Athens, O.

Okyeanne. 1961- . Accra, Ghana (no issues except IV, I (1968)).

Old Lady of Treadneedle Street. 1921- . London, England.

Once Series. 1966-1967.

Open Space. 1963-1965. California.

Origin. 1966- . Kyoto, Japan.

Out of Sight. 1966- . San Francisco, Calif.

The Outsider. 1961-1969. Tucson, Ariz.

Overflow. 1967- . Ann Arbor, Mich. (missing I, 1, II, 2; no further issues after II, 3 (1969)).

Overland. 1954- . Melbourne, Australia.

PS. 1953-1965. Denver, Colo.

PS. 1966. New York, N.Y.

Pakistan Review. 1953- . Lahore, Pakistan.

Pan-African Journal. 1968- . New York, N.Y.

Panache. 1965- . New York, N.Y.

Parallel. 1966-1967. Montréal, Canada.

Paris Review. 1953- . Paris, France; New York, N.Y.

The Park (previously Wivenhoe Park Review). 1968- . Colchester, England (no further issues after nos. 4 & 5 (1969)).

Pegasus. 1962- . Bloomington, Ind. (no further issues after V, 1 (1967)).

Penthouse. 1969- . New York, N.Y.

Per/Se. 1966-1969. Stanford, Calif.

Perspective. 1947- . Louisville, Ky.

The Phoenix. 1965- . Charleston, S.C. (missing all of 1966; no further issues after 1967).

Phylon. 1940- . Atlanta, Ga.

Plaintiff. 1965- . Mankato, Minn. (no issues before 1968; no further issues after V, 3 (1969)).

Playboy. 1953- . Chicago, Ill.

Plume & Sword. Charlottesville, Va. (VII, 1 (1966) only issue indexed).

The Pluralist. 1962- . Sydney, Australia (no further issues after no. 6 (1966)).

Poetmeat. ? -1967. Lancashire, England.

Prairie Schooner. 1927- . Lincoln, Neb.

Prism International. 1959- . Vancouver, B.C., Canada.

The Prolog. Lancaster, Pa. (VII, 1 & VII, 2 (1969) only issues indexed).

Prospero's Cell. 1966-1967. Seattle, Wash.

Purple Renoster. Johannesburg, South Africa (no. 9 (1969) only issue indexed).

Pyramid. 1968- . Waltham, Mass.

Quadrant. 1956- . Sydney, Australia.

Quarry. 1952- . Kingston, Ont., Canada (missing vol. XVI).

Quarterly. New Rochelle, N.Y. (missing 1965; no further issues after 1968).

Quarterly Review of Literature. 1943- . Chapel Hill, N.C.

Quartet. 1962- . Lafayette, Ind.

Queen. 1861- . London, England (missing scattered nos. throughout).

Queen's Quarterly. 1893- . Kingston, Ontario, Canada.

Quest. 1965- . London, England (no. 1 (1965) only issue indexed).

The Quest. 1965- . New York, N.Y.

Radcliffe Quarterly. 1916- . Cambridge, Mass.

Radix. 1964-1965. Somerville, Mass.

Ramparts. 1962- . Menlo Park, Calif.

Readers & Writers. 1966- . Jamaica, N.Y. (no further issues after II, 1 (1968)).

Red Cedar Review. 1963- . East Lansing, Mich.

Red Clay Reader. 1964- . Charlotte, N.C.

Redbook. 1903- . Chicago, Ill.; Dayton, O.

Response. 1967- . New York, N.Y.

Review. 1967- . Rawalpindi, Pakistan (no further issues after II, 3 (1969)).

Riverrun. 1967- . New York, N.Y. (no further issues after no. 2 (1968)).

Riverside Quarterly. 1964- . Saskatoon, Sask., Canada.

Roanoke Review. 1967- . Salem, Va. (III, 1 (1969) only issue indexed).

Rocky Mountain Review. 1963- . Billings, Mont.

Rolling Stone. 1967- . San Francisco, Calif.

Sage. 1952-1968. Laramie, Wyo.

Salmagundi. 1965- . Flushing, N.Y.

Salted Feathers. 1964- . Portland, Ore. (nos. 8, 9 & 10 (1967) only issues indexed).

Salzberg Village Idiot. ?. Ann Arbor, Mich. (1967 only issue indexed).

San Francisco Earthquake. 1967-1968. San Francisco, Calif.

Saturday Evening Post. 1821-1969. Philadelphia, Pa.

Saturday Night. 1887- . Toronto, Ont., Canada.

Scala International. 1961- . Frankfort am Main, Germany.

Scottish International. 1968- . Edinburgh, Scotland.

Second Coming Magazine. 1961-1965.

Sequoia. 1956- . Stanford, Calif. (no further issues after XIII, 1 (1968)).

Seventeen. 1942- . Philadelphia, Pa.

Sewanee Review. 1892- . Sewanee, Tenn.

Shenandoah. 1950- . Lexington, Va.

Signature. 1966- . New York, N.Y.

Silo. 1962- . Bennington, Vt. (no further issues after no. 13 (1968)).

The Smith. 1964- . New York, N.Y.

Solidarity. 1966- . Manila, Philippines.

Solstice. 1966- . Cambridge, England.

Some/Thing. 1965-1966; 1968- . New York, N.Y.

Soundings. 1964- . Stony Brook, N.Y. (no further issues after IV (1967)).

South Carolina Review. 1968- . Greenville, S.C.

South Dakota Review. 1963- . Vermillion, S.D.

Southerly. 1939- . Sydney, Australia.

Southern Humanities Review. 1967- . Auburn, Ala.

Southern Review. 1965- . Baton Rouge, La.

Southwest Review. 1915- . Austin, Tex.

Sou'wester. 1967- . Edwardsville, Ill.

Soviet Literature. 1931- . Moscow, U.S.S.R.

Spectrum. 1957- . Goleta, Calif.

Spero. 1965-1966. Chicago, Ill., etc.

Stand. 1952- . London, England.

Stanford Chaparral. 1899- . Stanford, Calif. (1968 only issue indexed).

Statement. 1950- . Los Angeles, Calif.

Status (Status and Diplomat). 1965- . New York, N.Y. (no further issues after XVIII, 229 (1970)).

Stony Brook. 1968- . Stony Brook, N.Y.

Story. 1967. New York, N.Y.

Story Yearbook. 1968- . New York, N.Y.

Sumac. 1968- . Fremont, Mich.

Sundial. 1966- . New York, N.Y. (missing I, 2 and all of vol. II).

Tamarack Review. 1956- . Toronto, Ont., Canada.

Texas Quarterly. 1958- . Austin, Tex.

Things. 1964-1966. New York, N.Y.

Threshold. 1957- . Belfast, Ireland.

Trace. 1952- . London, England; Hollywood, Calif.

Transatlantic Review. 1959- . Rome, N.Y.; London, England.

Transition. 1961- . Kampala, Uganda.

TransPacific (formerly Colorado State Review). 1969- . Laport, Colo.

Tri-Quarterly. 1958-1964; 1965- . Evanston, Ill.

Triveni. 1928- . Machilipatnam & Madras, India.

Tropix. 1966- . Calcutta, India (no further issues after II, 4 (1967)).

Turk's Head Review. Urbana, Ill. (1969 only issue indexed).

Twentieth Century. 1877- . London, England.

25. 1968- . Washington, D.C. (no further issues after I, 2 (1968)).

Twigs. 1965- . Pikeville, Ky. (missing nos. 3 & 4).

UMD Humanist. 1952- . Duluth, Minn. (missing XIII, 1 (1965) & XVI, 2 (1968)).

US. 1969. New York, N.Y.

U.S. Catholic Magazine and Jubilee. 1963- . Chicago, Ill. (no issues before Oct. 1968).

Unicorn Journal. 1968- . Santa Barbara, Calif.

University of Portland Review. 1965- . Portland, Ore. (no issues before 1969).

University of Windsor Review. 1965- . Windsor, Ont., Canada.

University Review (formerly University of Kansas City Review and now New Letters). 1934-1970. Kansas City, Mo.

VDRSVPVDRSVPVDRSVP. 1969. San Francisco, Calif.

Vagabond. 1965-1967. Munich, Germany.

Vincent the Mad Brother of Theo. 1966-1968. New York, N.Y.

Virginia Quarterly Review. 1925- . Charlottesville, Va.

Vision. 1952- . Karachi, Pakistan.

Vogue. 1892- . New York, N.Y.

Voyages. 1967-1973. Washington, D.C.

WIN. 1965- . New York, N.Y. (II, 14 & 15 (1966) only issues indexed before III, 8 (1967)).

Wascana Review. 1966- . Regina, Sask., Canada.

Washington and Jefferson Literary Journal. 1966- . Washington, Pa.

Washington Square Review. 1965- . New York, N.Y. (no further issues after II, 1 (1966)).

Weekend Telegraph (Daily Telegraph Magazine). 1964- . London, England (missing July 1967-Sept. 1968 and scattered issues elsewhere).

West Coast Review. 1966- . Burnaby, B.C., Canada.

Westerly. 1956- . Nedlands, Australia, etc.

Western Humanities Review. 1947- . Salt Lake City, Utah.

Western Review. 1964- . Silver City, N.M. (missing 1965).

Whe're. 1966. Detroit, Mich.

Wild Dog. 1963- . Pocatello, Id.; Salt Lake City, Utah; San Francisco, Calif.

William and Mary Review. 1962- . Williamsburg, Va.

Wisconsin Review. 1962- . Oshkosh, Wis. (no issues before II, 2 (1967)).

Wivenhoe Park Review (later, Park Review). 1965-1968. Colchester, England.

Woman's Day. 1937- . New York, N.Y.

Work. 1965-1968. Detroit, Mich.

Works. 1967- . New York, N.Y.

The World. 1967-1968. New York, N.Y.

Wormwood Review. 1960- . Storrs, Conn.
Writer's Forum. 1965- . New York, N.Y.

Yale Literary Magazine (Yale Lit). 1836- . New Haven, Conn.
Yale Review. 1911- . New Haven, Conn.

0 to 9. 1967-1969. New York, N.Y.

THE INDEX

Entries by Title

01 "Les Arenes," The Cantuarian, (December 1966), 295-296.

02 "Aszy's Worshippers," Riverrun, (May 1967), 57-67.

03 "The Death of the Hare, Koro Sonsan [Malian Stories]," Sou'-wester, (Spring 1969), 75.

04 "Excerpts," Abyss, II (January-February 1968), 47-48.

05 "A Family Tragedy," New Writing from Zambia, no. 2 (1968), 9-16.

06 "The Farmer Who Tricked the Devil [Malian Stories]," Sou'-wester, (Spring 1969), 78-79.

07 "From the Skin In," Salzberg Village Idiot, (Autumn 1967), 19.

08 "The Hunter and the Crocodile [Malian Stories]," Sou'wester, (Spring 1969), 76-78.

09 "El Ojo del Culo," (By a Spanish lady/student/author), Anthony Kerrigan, trans., December, X (1968), 22.

10 "The Round Trip of Ice/from Nehalem Tillamook Tales," 0 to 9, no. 1 (April 1967), 4-11.

11 "A Story of the Year One," Prairie Schooner, XLIII (Spring 1969), 63-65.

12 "A Traditional Tale from Turkey," Vision, XV (January 1966), 11.

13 "Why the Sky Is So High [Malian Stories]," Sou'wester, (Spring 1969), 74.

14 Arabian Legend. "To Please God," Adam International Review, nos. 325-327 (1968), 237.

15 Legends of Palestine (collected by Zev Vilnay). "Messiah among the Arabs," Adam International Review, nos. 325-327 (1968), 167.

16 from Tain Bo Cuailnge. "Cuchulainn's Boyhood Deeds," Thomas Kinsella, trans., Malahat Review, no. 8 (October 1968), 91-104.

17 Talmudic Legend. "God's Arrow," Adam International Review, nos. 325-327 (1968), 44-46.

18 Talmudic Legend. "The Song of the Night," Adam International Review, nos. 325-327 (1968), 18-19.

THE INDEX

Entries by Author

19 Aaron, Joann. "The Sudra," Washington Square Review, II (Winter 1966), 28-30.

20 Abastilla, Rodolfo. "Tarantula," New Campus Writing, (1966), 31-38.

21 Abbas, Ghulam. "The Overcoat," Abul Khair Kashfi and Janet M. Powers, trans., Arizona Quarterly, XXII (Autumn 1966), 209-216.

22 Abbas, Khwaja Ahmad. "All That Two Hands Can Carry," Imprint, VIII (January 1969), 27-32.

23 ———. "The 13th Victim," Imprint, VIII (August 1968), 35-37, 39, 41, 43, 45, 47.

24 Abbas, Muzaffar. "Echo," Pakistan Review, XIII (February 1965), 11-13.

25 ———. "Lost Generations," Pakistan Review, XIII (May 1965), 7-8, 35.

26 Abbaszade, Gusein. "One Night in Spring," Alice Ingman, trans., Soviet Literature, (no. 12, 1969), 46-51.

27 Abbe, George. "Day of Rest," Trace, no. 66 (Fall 1967), 387-395.

28 ———. "The Non-Conformist," The Smith, no. 6 (1965), 6-22.

29 Abbey, Edward. "Sunflowers," Western Review, IV (Summer 1967), 17-21.

30 Abbott, Dwight. "The Incident at Hymes Ford," University Review, XXXI (June 1965), 305-310.

31 ———. "Sex and Major Gwynne," Kansas Magazine, (1966), 78-83.

32 Abbott, Nell S. "Overlappings," DeKalb Literary Arts Journal, III (Spring 1969), 39-44.

33 Abbott, William. "---before the sun sets---" Trace, no. 57 (Summer 1965), 171-173.

34 Abdou, Elias. "Beauty Is Truth, Truth Beauty," Quartet, no. 21 (Winter 1968), 1-6.

35 _____. "The Pitchman," Midwestern University Quarterly, II, no. 1 (1966), 74-84.

36 Abdullah, Mohsin. "Paradise Gained," Eastern Horizon, V (March 1966), 55-60.

37 Abdullah, Omer Bin. "Discotheque Resolution," Vision, XVIII (August 1969), 23-24.

38 _____. "Zero on the Precipice," Vision, XVIII (June 1969), 19-21.

39 Abe Kōbō. "Red Cocoon," John Nathan, trans., Japan Quarterly, XIII (April-June 1966), 217-219.

40 _____. "Stick," John Nathan, trans., Japan Quarterly, XIII (April-June 1966), 214-217.

41 Abelman, Paul. "The Bay Area," Transatlantic Review, no. 26 (Autumn 1967), 71-80.

42 Abernathy, Ila Lea. "Riff," Grecourt Review, VIII (May 1965), 11-13.

43 Abu-Bakar, Akhmedkhan. "The Snow Men," Margaret Wettlin, trans., Soviet Literature, (no. 7, 1968), 3-96.

44 Achebe, Chinua. "Uncle Ben's Choice," Meanjin Quarterly, XXV (June 1966), 175-178.

45 Achterhof, Carole. "Charlie," UMD Humanist, XIII (Spring 1965), 11-14.

46 Ackerley, J. R. "A Summer's Evening," London Magazine, IX (October 1969), 39-46.

47 Ackerson, Duane. "The Accident," Midwestern University Quarterly, II, no. 1 (1966), 1-7.

48 _____. "The Dust of August," Phylon, XXVII (Summer 1966), 188-191.

49 Ackley, David. "All of You, All of Us," Greensboro Review, II (December 1966), 80-90.

50 ______. "Halt: Who Brinser?" *Greensboro Review,* III (Summer-Fall 1968), 62-77.

51 Adamich, Maida. "Judas Kiss at Dawn," *Trace*, no. 70 (1969), 113-116.

52 Adams, Alice. "Gift of Grass," *New Yorker*, XLV (November 8, 1969), 58-62.

53 ______. "Henry and the Pale-Faced Redskin," *Cosmopolitan*, CLXIII (October 1967), 146-148, 150.

54 ______. "Sea Gulls Are Happier Here," *Cosmopolitan*, CLXII (January 1967), 108-111.

55 ______. "Young Couple with Class," *Redbook,* CXXIX (September 1967), 72-73, 121-123, 126-128.

56 Adams, Alvin. "Ice Tea," *Negro Digest*, XV (March 1966), 70-79.

57 Adams, Dock Wilson. "Death on the River," *Lillabulero*, I (Summer 1967), 36-43.

58 ______. "Preachers Work on Sunday," *Carolina Quarterly*, XX (Spring 1968), 49-67.

59 Adams, Jerome R. "Omar," *Red Clay Reader,* no. 4 (1967), 20-23.

60 Adams, Junius. "Some Thoughts on the Meaning of Life," *Esquire*, LXV (February 1966), 90-93, 46, 48, 50, 52.

61 Adarkar, Vivek B. "The Examination," *Seventeen,* XXIV (April 1965), 154, 238, 240, 242, 244, 246-247.

62 ______. "Girl as Pretty as the Taj," *Seventeen,* XXV (February 1966), 124-125, 236-239, 244-245, 249.

63 ______. "Let's Just Say I've Been Around," *Seventeen,* XXVI (April 1967), 148-149, 246-248.

64 ______. "The Squealer," *Seventeen,* XXV (April 1966), 146-147, 226, 228, 230, 232.

65 ______. "We Could Be Happy Together," *Seventeen,* XXVII (March 1968), 146-147, 224, 226, 228-229.

66 Adcock, Betty. "Pattern with Beast," *Red Clay Reader*, no. 5 (1968), 109-111.

67 Addington, Luther F. "Oldtime Christmas on Critical," *Arizona Quarterly,* XXII (Winter 1966), 319-327.

68 Adkins, Gil. "The Rosewood Piano," Green River Review, II (Fall 1969), 25-34.

69 Adler, Carl. "The Ghost," Perspective, XIV (Spring 1966), 179-192.

70 Adler, Carol. "Minhag," Midstream, XIV (March 1968), 45-50.

71 Adler, Hans. "To a Water Lily, a Wild Rose, To an Ear of Wheat," Abyss, I (September-October 1967), 29-31.

72 Adler, Renata. "The Beagle Reflex," Harper's Bazaar, XCIX (September 1966), 281, 352.

73 _____. "Will You Speak to Anyone Who Answers?" Harper's Bazaar, XCVIII (April 1965), 166, 224.

74 Adler, Robert. "The Dying," Queen's Quarterly, LXXIV (Spring 1967), 159-173.

75 Adler, Stan Gwaine. "Disappearing Cross/(two selections from an unpublished novel)," Trace, no. 70 (1969), 101-104.

76 Adrian, Allan Aaron. "The Grotesque Agonies of Illumination/ noli me tangere," Beyond Baroque 692, I (July 1969), 6-9.

77 Agîrbiceanu, Ion. "The Icon Candle," Literary Review, X (Summer 1967), 457-464.

78 Agnon, S. Y. "The Doctor's Divorce," Robert Alter, trans., Midstream, XIV (February 1968), 44-60.

79 _____. "From Lodging to Lodging," Jules Harlow, trans., Midstream, XIII (February 1967), 27-35.

80 _____. "The Good Years," Curt Leviant, trans., Ariel, no. 17 (Winter 1966/67), 129-140.

81 _____. "'Iddo' and 'Eynam'," Curt Leviant, trans., Ariel, no. 11 (Summer 1965), 26-68.

82 _____. "The Lady and the Pedlar," G. S., trans., Ariel, no. 17 (Winter 1966/67), 116-126.

83 _____. "Me´oyev Le´ohev--From Foe to Friend," Joel Blocher, trans., Adam International Review, nos. 307-309 (1966), 13-16.

84 _____. "The Orchestra," Rabbi Jules Harlow, trans., Ariel, no. 17 (Winter 1966/67), 109-115.

85 _____. "A Pot Story," I. M. Lask, trans., Jewish Frontier,

XXXIII (December 1966), 6-9.

86 ______. "The Tale of the Scribe," Isaac Frank, trans., Midstream, XIII (February 1967), 16-26.

87 ______. "Tehilla," Walter Lever, trans., Ariel, no. 17 (Winter 1966/67), 75, 108.

88 ______. "Three Stories/Fable of the Goat," Barney Rubin, trans., Commentary, XLII (December 1966), 42-43.

89 ______. "Three Stories/First Kiss," Neal Kozodoy, trans., Commentary, XLII (December 1966), 35-37.

90 ______. "Three Stories/The Lady and the Peddler," Robert Alter, trans., Commentary, XLII (December 1966), 37-42.

91 ______. "Two Stories/From Enemy to Friend," Carol Hymer, trans., Spectrum, VIII (Summer 1966), 148-151.

92 ______. "Two Stories/To Father's House," Carol Hymer, trans., Spectrum, VIII (Summer 1966), 152-155.

93 Aguallo, Thomaline. "Celebration," Seventeen, XXVIII (November 1969), 138-139, 208, 211-213.

94 ______. "David's Friend," Seventeen, XXVII (October 1968), 130-131, 185-187, 195.

95 ______. "The Loudest Noise in the World," Seventeen, XXVII (April 1968), 158-159, 236, 238, 240, 242.

96 ______. "The World's Mirror," Seventeen, XXVIII (October 1969), 120-121, 195-196.

97 Aharonian, Avedis. "Judgement," Sarkis Ashjian, trans., Ararat, IX (Fall 1968), 34-37.

98 Ahlin, Lars. "After Years of Silence," Frederic Fleisher, trans., Adam International Review, nos. 304-306 (1966), 30-37.

99 ______. "Polluted Zone," Walter Johnson, trans., Literary Review, IX (Winter 1965-66), 221-236.

100 Ahmad, Abul Mansur. "The Prophet's Deputy," Manzoor Ahmad, trans., Pakistan Review, XVI (May 1968), 42-45.

101 Ahmad, Humaira. "Hold Back the Hand," Pakistan Review, XVII (October 1969), 27-29, 36.

102 Ahmad, Iqbal. "Grandma," Literary Review, XII (Summer 1969), 445-453.

103 _____. "The Kumbh Fair," The Fiddlehead, no. 80 (May-July 1969), 44-52.

104 _____. "Time to Go," Canadian Forum, XLVI (April 1966), 302-304.

105 Ahmad, Shahran. "Hush, Hush Winter's Coming," Pakistan Review, XVI (January 1968), 24-25.

106 Ahmadzadeh, J. "Story," The Cantuarian, (August 1966), 214-215.

107 Ahmed, Khaled. "Kafka and Lucky Rahim," Pakistan Review, XIII (July 1965), 12-17.

108 Aibek. "First Joys, First Sorrows/(Excerpts from the Novel Childhood)," Peggy Brown, trans., Soviet Literature, (no. 12, 1967), 11-33.

109 Aichinger, Ilse. "The Lake Spirits," George Raymond Selden, trans., Scala International, (June 1967), 35-37.

110 _____. "Where I Live," Alisa Weinreich, trans., Vogue, CLIII (May 1969), 259, 263-264.

111 _____. "The Young Lieutenant," James Alldridge, trans., Mundus Artium, I (Winter 1967), 28-33 [in German and English on alternate pages].

112 Aidoo, Ama Ata. "Other Versions," Literary Review, XI (Summer 1968), 459-466.

113 Ailisli, Akram. "The Old Cherry Tree," Eve Manning, trans., Soviet Literature, (no. 12, 1969), 83-92.

114 Aini, Sadriddin. "Memories of the Past," Margaret Wettlin, trans., Soviet Literature, (no. 9, 1967), 5-20.

115 Aitmatov, Chinghiz. "Farewell, Gyulsary," Eve Manning, trans., Soviet Literature, (no. 1, 1967), 2-124.

116 Ajtony, Árpád. "Kázmér Rákóczi," New Hungarian Quarterly, X (Spring 1969), 75-81.

117 Akhmad, Said. "The Cranes," Alice Ingman, trans., Soviet Literature, (no. 12, 1967), 105-110.

118 Akhtar, Fehmida. "Revenge," Pakistan Review, XV (January 1967), 35-38.

119 Akinari Ueda. "'Shiramine' from Ugetsu Monogatari," Leon M. Zolbrod, trans., Literature East and West, XI (December 1967), 402-414.

120 Aksyonov, Vasili. "On the Square and Across the River," Soviet Literature, (no. 4, 1967), 207-216.

121 ______. "Two Stories/Little Whale, A Born Varnisher of Reality," Avril Pyman, trans., Soviet Literature, (no. 9, 1965), 90-101.

122 ______. "Two Stories/The Queer One," Thomas Botting, trans., Soviet Literature, (no. 9, 1965), 67-89.

123 Akutagawa, Ryunosuke. "The Cogwheel," Beongcheon Yu, trans., Chicago Review, XVIII, no. 2 (1965), 31-53.

124 ______. "A Fool's Life," Will Petersen, trans., Caterpillar, nos. 3-4 (April-July 1968), 4-54.

125 ______. "The Marshland," Beongcheon Yu, trans., Chicago Review, XVIII, no. 2 (1965), 60-62.

126 ______. "The Mirage," Beongcheon Yu, trans., Chicago Review, XVIII, no. 2 (1965), 54-59.

127 Alba, Nanina. "The Satin-Back Crepe Dress," Negro Digest, XIV (May 1965), 36-39.

128 ______. "A Scary Story," Negro Digest, XV (July 1966), 65-68.

129 Alberts, Will. "Selection from a Novel in Progress," Red Cedar Review, IV (Spring 1966), 15-18, 21-28.

130 Albertson, Margery. "Love Is Just Some Kind of Unpaid Work," Redbook, CXXXII (November 1968), 78-79, 127-128.

131 Aldecoa, Ignacio. "Poor Men's Calling," Arena, no. 23 (April 1965), 3-9.

132 Alderton, Eileen. "The Perfect Wife," Woman's Day, (June 1967), 28-29, 88-89.

133 Aldiss, Brian W. "... And the Stagnation of the Heart," New Worlds, no. 185 (December 1968), 4-9.

134 ______. "A Difficult Age," Nova, (December 1967), 114-115, 117.

135 ______. "Down the Up Escalation," London Magazine, VI February 1967), 58-65.

136 ______. "The Humming Heads," Solstice, no. 8 (1968), 31-32, 34-35.

137 ______. "Multi-Valve Motorway," New Worlds, no. 174

(1967), 47-53.

138 ______. "Randy's Syndrome," Nova, (March 1969), 94, 96, 98-99, 101, 104.

139 ______. "The Village Swindler," Queen, CDXXXIV (September 17-30, 1969), 82-85, 122.

140 ______. "Wonder Weapon," Nova, (December 1967), 119, 120, 122-123.

141 Aldo, J. L. "Picnic," Prospero's Cell, II (Spring 1967), 5-19.

142 Aldrich, Michael. "Dive off the Mountain," South Dakota Review, IV (Spring 1966), 3-26.

143 Aldridge, James. "A Braver Time," Redbook, CXXIX (May 1967), 149, 151-173.

144 ______. "The Unfinished Soldiers," Playboy, XVI (March 1969), 76-78, 159-164, 166-167.

145 Alexander, Floyce M. "Body & Soul," Dust, III (Fall 1967), 31-34.

146 Alexander, James. "The Greater Happiness," Open Space, no. 12 (1965?), n.p. [7-8].

147 Alexander, R. W. "Don't Ever Change," Good Housekeeping, CLXVII (November 1968), 104-105.

148 ______. "The House That Love Built," Good Housekeeping, CLXVI (March 1968), 116-117.

149 ______. "In a Woman's Heart," Good Housekeeping, CLXIII (September 1966), 98-99.

150 ______. "The Morning Kind," Good Housekeeping, CLXII (March 1966), 106-107.

151 ______. "My Young and True Love," Good Housekeeping, CLXII (May 1966), 102-103.

152 ______. "A Safe Little House," Good Housekeeping, CLXI (October 1965), 80-81, 148, 150, 152, 154, 156.

153 ______. "So Dear to My Heart," Good Housekeeping, CLX (May 1965), 88-89, 148, 150.

154 ______. "A Sudden Silence," Good Housekeeping, CLX (April 1965), 90-91, 166, 169-170.

155 ______. "This Small Stranger," Good Housekeeping, CLX

(March 1965), 94-95, 168, 170.

156 _____. "When It Really Counts," Good Housekeeping, CLXIV (June 1967), 84-85, 150, 152-154.

157 _____. "With These Words," Good Housekeeping, CLXVI (June 1968), 96-97.

158 Alexander, Robert. "Under Those Bermuda Palms," North American Review, II (May 1965), 23-31.

159 Alexander, V. C. "The Magic Stairway/from Story Games for Everybody," 0 to 9, no. 1 (April 1967), 74-79.

160 Alexander, Walter F. "The Moon and Her Lute: A Chagall," New Campus Writing, (1966), 39-43.

161 Alexandrova, Veronika. "Siskin Takes an Exam," Bryan Bean, trans., Soviet Literature, (no. 12, 1968), 156-160.

162 Alexeyev, Mikhail. "Karyukha," Eve Manning, trans., Soviet Literature, (no. 6, 1968), 3-54.

163 _____. "Once Having Lied," Undine Wilson, trans., Ambit, no. 29 (1966), 33-42.

164 Alexin, Anatoli. "A Tale of Terror/The Detective Story Alik Detkin Wrote," Eve Manning, trans., Soviet Literature, (no. 7, 1969), 3-93.

165 Alger, Thomas. "The Betrothed," Plaintiff, IV (Spring-Summer 1968), 7.

166 Algren, Nelson. "Decline & Fall of Dingdong--Daddyland," Commentary, XLVIII (September 1969), 69-76.

167 _____. "Home to Shawneetown," Atlantic Monthly, CCXXII (August 1968), 41-47.

168 _____. "A Ticket on Skoronski," Saturday Evening Post, CCXXXIX (November 5, 1966), 48-49, 52-56.

169 Ali, Ahmed. "The Castle," Eastern Horizon, IV (October 1965), 47-56.

170 _____. "A Feudal House," Eastern Horizon, V (November 1966), 56-62.

171 Ali, Mohammed. "By God," Pakistan Review, XIII (April 1965), 33-34.

172 Alimzhanov, Anuar. "The Spring," D. Efremova, trans., Soviet Literature, (no. 1, 1965), 120-126.

173 Allen, Bill. "Tomorrow," Delta Review, IV (November 1967), 30-33, 66, 69.

174 Allen, Elizabeth. "Age of Innocence," Good Housekeeping, CLXII (May 1966), 94-95, 152, 154, 156-157.

175 ______. "A Dancer in the Dark," Redbook, CXXVII (August 1966), 139, 141-156.

176 ______. "The Hidden Heart," Good Housekeeping, CLX (February 1965), 84-85.

177 ______. "The Pink Pagoda," Seventeen, XXVIII (October 1969), 124-125, 161-162, 164.

178 ______. "The Wrong Road," Seventeen, XXVIII (February 1969), 142-143, 172-174, 176, 178.

179 Allen, John Houghton. "Horse Cavalry," Southwest Review, LI (Spring 1966), 161-166.

180 ______. "The Long Ride," Southwest Review, LIII (Autumn 1968), 417-422.

181 Allen, Leroy B. "Mammy and the Moccasin," Delta Review, VI (September 1969), 22-25, 57-58, 60.

182 Allen, Richard. "April Is the Cruellest Month," Plaintiff, IV (Spring-Summer 1968), 11-13.

183 Allen, Woody. "A Little Louder, Please," New Yorker, XLII (May 28, 1966), 39-41.

184 ______. "The Metterling Lists," New Yorker, XLV (May 10, 1969), 34-35.

185 ______. "My Philosophy," New Yorker, XLV (December 27, 1969), 25-26.

186 ______. "Notes from the Overfed," New Yorker, XLIV (March 16, 1968), 38-39.

187 ______. "Spring Bulletin," New Yorker, XLIII (April 29, 1967), 38-39.

188 ______. "Viva Vargas! / Excerpts from the Diary of a Revolutionary," Evergreen Review, XIII (August 1969), 24-27.

189 ______. "Yes, But Can the Steam Engine Do This?" New Yorker, XLII (October 8, 1966), 52-53.

190 Alley, Henry. "The Festival," University Review, XXXVI (Autumn 1969), 75-80.

191 Allgaier, Alice. "A Room of One's Own," New Leaven, XIX (1969), 13-16.

192 Allison, P. "The Fulfilling of the Law," Transatlantic Review, no. 20 (Spring 1966), 113-122.

193 Allman, John. "The Tip," Epoch, XVII (Spring 1968), 278-294.

194 Allman, T. D. "Dawn of the Super-Renaissance," Harvard Advocate, C (March 1966), 20-27.

195 Al-Masu, Issa Salim. "The Rebellious One," Maliha Ansari, trans., Vision, XV (December 1966), 28-50.

196 Alnaes, Finn. "Prelude," Nancy Coleman, trans., Literary Review, XII (Winter 1968-69), 203-212.

197 Alper, Gerald. "The Mechanical Sweetheart," Trace, no. 66 (Fall 1967), 396-401.

198 Alper, Sandra. "5-R," The World, no. 9 (December 1967), n.p. [51-53].

199 Alsahimi, Abd Aljabbar. "Hamdan," Maliha Ansari, trans., Vision, XV (December 1966), 23-24, 52.

200 Altena, Ina. "Elizabeth," Contrast (Cape Town, South Africa), no. 15 (March 1967), 11-17.

201 Altendorf, Wolfgang. "Dancing Lessons--Reminiscences," Margaret D. Howie, trans., Scala International, (February 1969), 34-37.

202 Alter, Robert Edmund. "The Gentlemen from Caximas," Signature, II (February 1967), 23.

203 Altman, Laurence. "Laury Oh, Laury Apple," Readers & Writers, I (October-November 1966), 33-41.

204 ______. "Swim," Writer's Forum, II (Summer 1966), 11-14.

205 Altshuler, Jeffrey A. "Thoughts that Run Through an Idle Mind," Lance, V (Spring 1965), 55-56.

206 Álvarez, Jacinto. "I Remember Beau Geste," Américas, XIX (November 1967), 28-31.

207 Alvarez, Joan Maxwell. "The Recital," Virginia Quarterly Review, XLIII (Winter 1967), 107-122.

208 Alvaro, Corrado. "The Job," Charles Fantazzi, trans., Western Humanities Review, XXIII (Spring 1969), 129-133.

209 Amansec, Lilia Pablo. "Loverboy," Solidarity, I (January-March 1966), 71-79.

210 Ambler, Eric. "Dirty Story (Part I)," Saturday Evening Post, CCXL (August 26, 1967), 23-27, 58, 60-65.

211 ______. "Dirty Story (Part II)," Saturday Evening Post, CCXL (September 9, 1967), 50-61.

212 ______. "Dirty Story (Conclusion)," Saturday Evening Post, CCXL (September 23, 1967), 70-72, 78, 80, 82-84, 85.

213 ______. "The Intercom Conspiracy," Cosmopolitan, CLXVII (November 1969), 174-191, 195-197, 200-203.

214 Ambrose, David. "The Making of Unman," Westerly, no. 4 (December 1969), 32-35.

215 Amen, Grover. "The Scholar of Bourbon Street," New Yorker, XL (February 13, 1965), 32-38.

216 Ames, Bernice. "New Shoes," Arizona Quarterly, XXXIII (Spring 1967), 16-26.

217 ______. "A Pair of Hands," Cimarron Review, no. 8 (June 1969), 95-99.

218 Amft, M. J. "At Auntie Lou's," Seventeen, XXVIII (September 1969), 152-153, 210, 213-214.

219 ______. "Becky and I," Seventeen, XXIV (November 1965), 128-129, 182, 186.

220 ______. "Calm Makes the World Go Round," Seventeen, XXVI (October 1967), 126-127, 172-174.

221 ______. "Come Live with Me Off Campus," Seventeen, XXVII (September 1968), 148-149, 234-236.

222 ______. "Forget It Ever Happened," Seventeen, XXVI (June 1967), 116-117, 161-162, 165.

223 ______. "Franny," Seventeen, XXVIII (February 1969), 138-139, 220-222.

224 ______. "The Giant Sex Riot," Seventeen, XXV (February 1966), 140-141, 227-229.

225 ______. "Good-by," Seventeen, XXV (November 1966), 166-167, 229-231.

226 ______. "The Holly Green," Seventeen, XXVIII (December 1969), 112, 179-180.

227 ______. "In Due Time," Seventeen, XXVII (November 1968), 122-123, 187-188.

228 ______. "The Injured Party," Seventeen, XXVI (November 1967), 146-147, 222, 224, 228.

229 ______. "Is It a Vice or a Talent?" Seventeen, XXIV (May 1965), 136-137, 204, 206, 208, 211.

230 ______. "A Little Learning," Seventeen, XXVI (August 1967), 306-307, 389.

231 ______. "The Long Winter," Seventeen, XXVII (February 1968), 140-141, 177-178.

232 ______. "Memento, Memento," Seventeen, XXV (April 1966), 158-159, 246, 248, 250, 252, 254.

233 ______. "Michael I and Michael II," Seventeen, XXIV (August 1965), 228-229, 348, 350, 352, 358, 364.

234 ______. "My Most Unforgettable Experience of Last Summer," Seventeen, XXIV (February 1965), 140, 185-187.

235 ______. "The Poet Lies," Seventeen, XXVII (June 1968), 100-101, 168-169.

236 ______. "Something Else," Seventeen, XXVI (September 1967), 154-155, 200, 202, 204.

237 ______. "Thank You," Seventeen, XXVII (July 1968), 78-79, 123.

238 ______. "To Keep Your Cool," Seventeen, XXVI (February 1967), 152-153, 246-248.

239 ______. "To Protect the Innocent," Seventeen, XXVII (April 1968), 168-169, 254-257.

240 ______. "When the Two Hands Are Up," Seventeen, XXVII (August 1968), 268-269, 392, 394, 398, 400.

241 ______. "Where Will All the Bluebirds Go?" Seventeen, XXV (June 1966), 114-115, 144, 146.

242 ______. "Yes ( ) No ( ) Check One," Seventeen, XXVIII (May 1969), 158-159, 210, 212, 214, 216.

243 Amichai, Yehuda. "Nina of Ashkelon," Ada Hameirit-Sarell, trans., Commentary, XLIV (July 1967), 40-47.

244 Aminuddin, M. "The Cobra Dance," Pakistan Review, XIII (August 1965), 21-22.

245 _____. "Darkness and Light," Pakistan Review, XIII (March 1965), 12-14.

246 _____. "The Melody of a Dream" Pakistan Review, XV (February 1967), 30-32.

247 _____. "The Prized Mango," Pakistan Review, XVI (December 1968), 33-35.

248 _____. "The Re-Awakening," Pakistan Review, XV (June 1967), 13-15, 24.

249 _____. "A Taste of Money," Pakistan Review, XVII (June 1969), 35-37.

250 _____. "A Timely Miracle," Pakistan Review, XVI (June 1968), 21-23.

251 _____. "Two Is Company," Pakistan Review. XV (November 1967), 38-40.

252 Amir, S. Javed. "The Addict," Pakistan Review, XVI (January 1968), 27-28.

253 _____. "Ha! Ha! Ha!" Pakistan Review, XIII (May 1965), 9-10.

254 _____. "'Here My Spirit Dwells'," Pakistan Review, XIII (January 1965), 13-14.

255 _____. "The Mask," Pakistan Review, XVII (November 1969), 19-20.

256 Amis, Kingsley. "I Want It Now," Cosmopolitan, CLXVI (March 1969), 148-151.

257 _____. "I Want It Now," Nova, (October 1968), 126, 131, 133, 141, 143-144.

258 Anand, Mulk Raj. "At What Price, My Brothers," Indian Literature, X (January-March 1967), 52-60.

259 _____. "Birth," Literary Review, XI (Autumn 1967), 5-12.

260 _____. "A Fool's Cap," Eastern Horizon, V (July 1966), 57-60.

261 _____. "The Gold Watch," Eastern Horizon, VIII (September-October 1969), 55-60.

262 Ananda. "The Girl I Murdered," V. K. J. Iyengar, trans., Triveni, XXXVII (April 1968), 25-38.

263 Ananian, Vakhtang. "Huntsman Vatchag's Adventures," Ararat, VIII (Winter 1967), 26-32.

264 _____. "Two Stories/A Meeting in the Reeds," Darya Efremova, trans., Soviet Literature, (no. 3, 1966), 115-120.

265 _____. "Two Stories/Moufflons," Darya Efremova, trans., Soviet Literature, (no. 3, 1966), 121-122.

266 Anar. "The Last Night of the Old Year," Eve Manning, trans., Soviet Literature, (no. 12, 1969), 93-102.

267 Anastas, Peter. "A Confluence of Things," Niobe, no. 2 (1966), 67-73.

268 _____. "One October at the Gateway," Niobe, no. 1 (1965), 11-21.

269 Andersch, Alfred. "Lord Glouster," George Raymond Selden, trans., Scala International (March 1966), 32-34.

270 Andersen, Benny. "Tarzan. The Government. Refrigerators." Ken Tindall, trans., Evergreen Review, X (June 1966), 42-45.

271 Andersen, C. R. "With Respect to the Boskops," Epoch, XIV (Winter 1965), 130-143.

272 Andersen, Hans. "Frames of a Story," Origin (Kyoto, Japan), no. 12 (January 1969), 38-39 [from "The Snow Queen"].

273 Anderson, David. "Bernadette of Lourdes," Columbia Review, XLVIII, no. 2 (1968), 18-22.

274 _____. "Lee Harvey Oswald," Columbia Review, XLVIII, no. 1 (1967), 6-13.

275 _____. "The Oil Murders," Columbia Review," XLVIII, no. 3 (1969), 51-62.

276 _____. "Smoke," Columbia Review, XLVII, no. 1 (1966), 23-24.

277 _____ and Johnny Stanton. "Time Is on Our Side," Columbia Review, XLIX, no. 2 (1969), 65-89.

278 Anderson, Hesper. "If Winter Comes," McCall's, XCV (March 1968), 102-103, 130-133.

279 _____. "Summer Days, Summer Nights," Cosmopolitan, CLXVI (June 1969), 136-137.

280 Anderson, Jack. "Shakespeare," The World, no. 7 (October

1967), n.p. [12].

281 _____. "Three Little Stories," Epoch, XVI (Winter 1967), 181-182.

282 Anderson, Jani. "The Castle," Seventeen, XXVII (January 1968), 93, 124-125.

283 Anderson, Kenneth. "Harness Bells," Delta, XXI (1967), 10-17.

284 Anderson, LaVere. "Mrs. Lincoln's Hat," Woman's Day, (April 1965), 54-55, 120, 122-124, 126, 126B, 131.

285 Anderson, Nels. "The Private and Last Frontier," Sewanee Review, LXXVII (January-March 1969), 25-90.

286 Anderson, Paul. "Among Thieves," New Campus Review, I (Fall 1967), 30-39.

287 Anderson, Robert. "The Elevator," UMD Humanist, XIV (Spring 1966), 25-26.

288 Anderson, Sherwood. "The Rabbit-Pen," Readers & Writers, I (April 1968), 32-37.

289 Anderson, Stanley. "Life's Picnic," UMD Humanist, XIV (Winter 1966), 38-40.

290 Anderson Imbert, Enrique. "The Ghost," Donald A. Yates, trans., in "The 'Microtale': An Argentine Specialty," by Donald A. Yates, Texas Quarterly, XII (Summer 1969), 18-21.

291 Andres, Stefan. "The Bridge of Justice," J. Bennett, Jr., trans., Vagabond, I, no. 2 (1966), 31-32.

292 _____. "The Cows," George Raymond Selden, trans., Scala International, (February 1965), 32-35.

293 _____. "The Pigeon Shoot," Margaret D. Howie, trans., Scala International, (December 1969), 35-37.

294 Andrews, Irma. "Tent Show," Literary Review, XIII (Winter 1969-70), 158-166.

295 Andrews, Isobel. "Another Part of the Forest," New Zealand Listener, (August 26, 1966), 10, 18.

296 Andreyev, Leonid. "In the Garden of Geth-Semane," Walter Morrison, trans., Adam International Review, nos. 325-327 (1968), 108-109.

297 Andric, Ivo. "Children," Stanley Frye, trans., Jewish Life,

XXXIV (March-April 1967), 43-47.

298 _____. "Thirst," Joseph Hitrec, trans., Esquire, LXIV (December 1965), 205, 255, 258, 260.

299 _____. "Thirst," Aleksander Stefanovic, trans., Kenyon Review, XXVIII (September 1966), 459-469.

300 Andriušis, Pulgis. "He Wasn't Allowed to See," Clark Mills, trans., Literary Review, VIII (Spring 1965), 335-340.

301 Andrzejewski, Jerzy. "The Court Hearing," Cecylia Wojewoda, trans., Literary Review, X (Spring 1967), 285-298.

302 Angell, Olav. "The Hidden Meaning of Life," Cheryl D. Schmidt, trans., Literary Review, XII (Winter 1968-69), 241-244.

303 Angell, Roger. "Keeping Up with the Outs," New Yorker, XLI (May 29, 1965), 24-27.

304 Angoff, Charles. "Katya," Southwest Review, L (Summer 1965) 270-283.

305 _____. "My First Trip to New York City," Quartet, no. 11 (Summer 1965), 12-20.

306 _____. "The Steamer," Literary Review, XII (Summer 1969), 505-511.

307 Anjou, Robert. "Francine," Western Humanities Review, XXII (Autumn 1968), 315-322.

308 _____. "Princeton and Parslow," Western Humanities Review, XXI (Autumn 1967), 299-309.

309 Annis, Cindy. "What Are Little Girls Made Of?" Florida Quarterly, II (October 1969), 75-86.

310 Annixter, Paul. "The Lord of Alder Run," Columbia, XLVII (April 1967), 23-27.

311 Ansell, Jack. "Can't We Come Back Yesterday," American Judaism, XV (Spring 1966), 12-13, 54-55.

312 Ansen, Alan. "Professor Joe: A Candidate for the Presidency," VDRSVPVDRSVPVDRSVPVDRSVP, (1969), n.p. [front page].

313 _____. "A Routine," VDRSVPVDRSVPVDRSVP, (1969), n.p. [front page].

314 Ansen, David. "The Sentimental Journey of Arthur Friedberg," Harvard Advocate, C (November 1965), 15-17, 19-23.

315 Anthem, Jack. "Theft," Epoch, XV (Fall 1965), 61-70.

316 Antin, David. "Autobiography 2," Some/Thing, nos. 4 & 5 (Summer 1968), 5-13.

317 Anstiss, N. L. "The Wreckers," New Zealand Listener, LIII (August 6, 1965), 4, 16.

318 Antonides, Chris. "The Day of the Barber," Red Cedar Review, VI (January 1968), n.p. [3-20].

319 Antonov, Sergei. "In the Morning," Soviet Literature, (no. 4, 1967), 166-173.

320 ______. "Running Empty," Eve Manning, trans., Soviet Literature, (no. 6, 1965), 49-84.

321 Anvery, F. A. "Dead Man's Shoes," Vision, XVI (February 1967), 6, 24.

322 ______. "The Flame Flower," Vision, XVI (January 1968), 9-10, 26.

323 Apollinaire, Guillaume. "The Art of Touch," David Coxhead, trans., Contemporary Literature in Translation, no. 4 (Spring 1969), 37-38.

324 ______. "A Good Film," Remy Inglis Hall, trans., Status, I (November 1965), 38-39.

325 Appelfield, Aharon. "Cold Spring," Now, no. 1 (1969), 29-39.

326 ______. "In the Wilderness," Edward Zarrit, trans., Response, I (Winter 1968), 39-44.

327 ______. "The Road from Drovna to Drovitch," A. Levinston, trans., Ariel, no. 16 (Autumn 1966), 26-38.

328 Apperly, Fairlie. "Grey & Green," Westerly, no. 4 (December 1968), 17-19.

329 Årads, Eva. "The Canal," Signhild V. Gustafson, trans., American Scandinavian Review, LIV (September 1966), 275-280.

330 Aramyan, Raphael. "Tale about a Little Boy and a Big Lorry-Driver," Darya Efremova, trans., Soviet Literature, (no. 3, 1966), 123-127.

331 Araya, Enrique. "Requiescat in Pace," Américas, XVIII (March 1966), 29-31.

332 Arcaro, Anne. "The Picture," Arx, III (July 1969), 3-4.

333 Archibald, Irene Presson. "Call Me Old Man," Red Clay Reader, no. 4 (1967), 112-117.

334 Arditi, Abraham A. "Hands," Yale Literary Magazine, CXXXIV (January 1966), 28-31.

335 Argüedas, José María. "Death of Arangos," Matthew Shipman and Marisa Valencia, trans., Haravec, no. 2 (March 1967), 69-74.

336 Arias-Mission, Alain. "Confessions of a Concrete Poet or You Gotta Talk," Chicago Review, XX (June 1968), 93-96.

337 _____. "The Garden of Manahatta, or Henry & the Bishop," Chicago Review, XIX, no. 2 (1967), 35-51.

338 _____. "Requiem to Me," Chicago Review, XIX, no. 1 (1966), 78-82.

339 Ariniello, Doreen. "The Driver and the Rider," Ave Maria, CI (June 5, 1965), 22-23.

340 _____. "Show and Tell Time," Ave Maria, CIII (January 1, 1966), 22-25.

341 Arlen, Michael. "Shelmerdene," Ararat, VII (Autumn 1966), 20-24.

342 Armah, Ayi Kwei. "The Offal Kind," Harper's Magazine, CCXXXVIII (January 1969), 79-84.

343 _____. "Yaw Manu's Charm," Atlantic Monthly, CCXXI (May 1968), 89-95.

344 Armen, Mkrtich. "A Song about My Town/Howling for the Moon," Tom Botting, trans., Soviet Literature, (no. 3, 1966), 108-110.

345 _____. "A Song about My Town/The Winged Horse Pegasus," Tom Botting, trans., Soviet Literature, (no. 3, 1966), 110-114.

346 Armfelt, Nicholas. "Catching Up," Delta (Cambridge, England), no. 40 (Winter 1967), 10-14.

347 _____. "The Lord's Work," Delta (Cambridge, England), no. 35 (Spring 1965), 18-20.

348 Armitage, Jack "They Were Only Human/Part One," Ambience, no. 2 (Spring 1969), 29-35.

349 _____. "They Were Only Human/Part Two," Ambience, no. 3 (Summer 1969), 27-36.

350 Armstead, Dolores. "A Day's Living," Negro Digest, XV (June 1966), 72-75.

351 Armstrong, Judy. "Arabella," Nimrod, XIII (Winter 1969), 23-26. ["The Editors of Nimrod apologize for a printing error. The contents of page 23 should be read after page 24" (editor's note bound into issue).].

352 Armstrong, Marion. "Communion," Intro, no. 2 (September 1969), 141-152.

353 Armstrong, Velma. "The Garden of Delight," Trace, nos. 62 & 63 (Fall-Winter 1966-67), 449-450.

354 Arnér, Sivar. "Lee," P. M. Fullinwider, trans., Literary Review, IX (Winter 1965-66), 209-220.

355 _____. "Obedience," Ian Macphail, trans., Adam International Review, nos. 304-306 (1966), 38-51.

356 Arnet, Robert. "McDonogh and the Goblin," Columbia, XLV (September 1966), 24-26, 44.

357 von Arnim, Achim. "Gentry by Entailment," Alan Brown, trans., Art and Literature, no. 11 (Winter 1967), 9-44.

358 Arnold, Elliott. "The Accident," Redbook, CXXIV (February 1965), 54-55, 86-89.

359 Arnold, Lyn. "Three for a Wedding," Cosmopolitan, CLIX (July 1965), 80-83.

360 Arrabal. "The Stone of Madness/From Panic Stories," F. Castillo, trans., Transatlantic Review, no. 26 (Autumn 1967), 37-38.

361 Arreola, Juan José. "The Crows of Zapotlán," Mexico Quarterly Review, II (July 1965), 135, 137 [in Spanish and English on alternate pages].

362 _____. "The Owl," George D. Schade, trans., Maguey, no. 1 (May 1968), 30, 34 [in Spanish and English on alternate pages].

363 _____. "The Switchman," Ben Belitt, trans., Tri-Quarterly, nos. 13-14 (Fall-Winter 1968-69), 185-192.

364 Artaud, Antonin. "Letter to the Legislator of the Drug Act," Victor Corti, trans., Transatlantic Review, no. 27 (Winter 1967-68), 5-8.

365 _____. "Nerve Scales," Victor Corti, trans., Transatlantic Review, no. 27 (Winter 1967-68), 8-11.

366 Arthur, Lew. "Come Back Valery or A Long Day Demonstrating," Panache, no. 3 (1969), 3-12.

367 Arthur, Thomas. "The Pattern," Pegasus, IV, no. 1 (1966), 33-43.

368 Arzhak, Nikolai [Yuli Daniel]. "The Hands," David Floyd, trans., Weekend Telegraph, no. 76 (March 11, 1966), 41-42, 44, 46.

369 Asanovic, Stefan. "Bitter Fragrance," Blazo & Gail Sredanovic, trans., Prism International, IX (Summer 1969), 57-60.

370 Asch, Sholem. "The Rabbi," Maurice Samuel, trans., Adam International Review, nos. 325-327 (1968), 100-102.

371 Ash, N. A. "Deutscher Kaffee," The Cantuarian, (April 1965), 336-337.

372 Ashbery, John and James Schuyler. "At Mrs. Kelso's," Art and Literature, no. 12 (Spring 1967), 73-85.

373 ______ and James Schuyler. "Further Adventures," Paris Review, XI (Summer 1968), 32-54.

374 Asher, Ansurya. "The Window," Denver Quarterly, I (Summer 1966), 96-101.

375 Asher, Don. "Far Above Cayuga's Waters--g--chung, g--chung," Saturday Evening Post, CCXXXIV (November 5, 1966), 64-68, 70.

376 Ashford, Bob. "One's a Crowd," Sequoia, XI (Spring 1966), 30-35.

377 Ashk, Upendranath. "The Dark Saahabs," Edith Irwin, trans., Arizona Quarterly, XXV (Winter 1969), 304-312.

378 Asimov, Isaac. "Fantastic Voyage Into the Human Brain/(Part I)," Saturday Evening Post, CCXXXIX (February 26, 1966), 40-44, 46-51, 53, 57-58, 60-61.

379 ______. "Fantastic Voyage Into the Human Brain/(Conclusion)," Saturday Evening Post, CCXXXIX (March 12, 1966), 56-60, 62-68, 70, 73-77.

380 Askildsen, Kjell. "Meeting," John Weinstock, trans., Literary Review, XII (Winter 1968-69), 223-232.

381 Aspinwall, Alice. "Last Walk to the River," California Review, no. 1 (Spring 1967), 5-15.

382 Aspittle, Stanley E., Jr. "The City: A Fable," Trace, no. 65

(Summer 1967), 249-251.

383 _____. "Of Love and Slags," Minnesota Review, V (October-December 1965), 281-291.

384 _____. "The Quest of Sam Sagittus," Ante, IV (Summer-Fall 1968), 105-121.

385 de Assis, Machado. "Chapters from Esau and Jacob," Helen Caldwell, trans., Shenandoah, XVI (Spring 1965), 8-15.

386 Astafyev, Victor. "Three Stories/A Troubled Dream," Robert Daglish, trans., Soviet Literature, (no. 10, 1969), 76-91.

387 _____. "Three Stories/Wild Onions," Hilda Perham, trans., Soviet Literature, (no. 10, 1969), 100-121.

388 _____. "Three Stories/The Wild Stag," Margaret Wettlin, trans., Soviet Literature, (no. 10, 1969), 92-99.

389 _____. "Whether by Daylight," Vladimir Talmy, trans., Soviet Literature, (no. 4, 1968), 85-107.

390 Astpórsson, Gísli J. "Child Overboard," Lawrence F. Beste, trans., American Scandinavian Review, LXI (March 1968), 66-70.

391 Astrachan, Samuel. "Katherine Weaver," Carleton Miscellany, IX (Summer 1968), 30-38.

392 Asturias, Miguel Angel. "from Strong Wind," Gregory Rabassa, trans., Tri-Quarterly, nos. 13-14 (Fall-Winter 1968-69), 393-405.

393 Atarov, Nikolai. "Summer Is Brief in the Mountains," Anthony Wixley, trans., Soviet Literature, (no. 2, 1967), 52-142.

394 Athas, Daphne. "The Hitchhiker," Carolina Quarterly, XXI (Spring 1969), 42-55.

395 Athill, Diana. "Poor Little Renata," Transatlantic Review, no. 31 (Winter 1968-69), 34-50.

396 Atkinson, Brooks. "American Mobile--Age 9," Woman's Day, (May 1966), 38-39, 95-96.

397 Atkinson, Hugh. "A Boy in a Ford," Weekend Telegraph, no. 54 (October 1, 1965), 51, 53-54.

398 _____. "A Day on the Diggings," Weekend Telegraph, no. 83 (April 29, 1966), 45, 47-48.

399 _____. "A Job for Moses," Meanjin Quarterly, XXIX (December

1965), 462-472.

400 ______. "Johnny and the Viking Helmet," Quadrant, XII (July-August 1968), 70-73.

401 ______. "Stop Loving Me," Quadrant, XI (July-August 1967), 76-79.

402 Atwood, Margaret. "Going to Bed," Evidence, no. 9 (1965), 5-10.

403 ______. "Testament Found in a Bureau Drawer," Prism International, V (Autumn 1965), 58-65.

404 Aub, Max. "Some Exemplary Crimes," Keith Botsford, trans., Quarterly Review of Literature, XIV (1967), 252-260.

405 Aucamp, Hennie. "When the Saints Go Marching In," Contrast (Cape Town, South Africa), no. 14 (November 1966), 66-74.

406 Auchincloss, Louis. "The Cathedral Builder," McCall's, XCVI (May 1969), 88-89, 142-146.

407 ______. "Collector of Innocents," McCall's, XCIV (April 1967), 102-103, 149-151.

408 ______. "The Money Juggler," Yale Literary Magazine, CXXXV (September 1966), 3-13.

409 ______. "Sabina and the Herd," Saturday Evening Post, CCXXXIX (January 29, 1966), 70-75.

410 ______. "The Secret Journal of Waring Stohl," Saturday Evening Post, CCXXXIX (April 23, 1966), 76-80, 82, 84.

411 ______. "The Wagnerians," McCall's, XCIII (July 1966), 88-89, 111-115.

412 ______. "The Waiver," Cosmopolitan, CLXVII (December 1969), 154-156, 158.

413 ______. "The World of Profit," Imprint, IX (June 1969), 77, 79, 81, 83, 85, 87, 89, 91, 93, 95, 97, 99, 101, 103, 105, 107, 109, 111, 113, 115.

414 ______. "A World of Profit," Ladies' Home Journal, LXXXVI (January 1969), 113-120, 124-126, 128.

415 Auer, John. "A Man from the Toy Factory," Pegasus, III (Winter 1965), 33-45.

416 ______. "When They Don't Bend," Pegasus, III (Spring 1965), 18-30.

417 Aukema, Charles. "Climbing Jacob's Ladder," Intro, no. 1 (September 1968), 34-40.

418 _____. "Frozen Voices," Quarterly Review of Literature, XVI, nos. 3-4 (1969), 274-294.

419 _____. "Get with Child a Mandrake Root," North American Review, V (September-October 1968), 26-31.

420 _____. "The Receiver," Bennington Review, III (Winter 1969), 53-58.

421 Ausanka, Jacqueline. "Caprice Macabre," Quarterly, LXIII, no. 1 (1966), 4-7.

422 Aussant, Mary. "The Balaam Fire," Crucible, V (Fall 1968), 13-15.

423 _____. "Ice Classic," Crucible, III (Fall 1966), 41-43.

424 _____. "Revenant," Crucible, II (Fall 1965), 34-35.

425 Austin, Alex. "Something About Heaven," Mademoiselle, LXIV (March 1967), 176-177, 222-227.

426 Avakian, Apik. "Three or Four Hours Ago," Armenian Review, XVIII (Winter 1965), 51-55.

427 Avaliani, Lado. "Zuloaga's Hat," Vakhtang Eristavi, trans., Soviet Literature, (no. 8, 1969), 120-138.

428 Averchenko, Arkady. "A Fatal Winning," G. C. Schellhorn and Arkady Rossol, trans., North Dakota Quarterly, XXXIV (Winter 1966), 12-16.

429 _____. "Wolfskin Coat," G. C. Schellhorn and Arkady Rossol, trans., South Dakota Review, V (Autumn 1967), 50-55.

430 Avrett, Robert. "A Brace of Grouse," North American Mentor, IV (Summer 1966), 11-13.

431 Awooner, Kofi. "from This Earth, My Brother/An Allegorical Tale of Africa," Stony Brook, nos. 3-4 (1969), 231-232.

432 Awoonor-Williams, George. "The Funeral," Eastern Horizon, IV (May 1965), 56-60.

433 _____. "The Reverend," Eastern Horizon, IV (June 1965), 49-54.

434 Ayala, Jose V. "Bestiary," Solidarity, III (December 1968), 48-52.

435 Ayalti, Hanan J. "Grandmother's 'Best Seller'," Jewish Frontier, XXXII (December 1965), 22-24.

436 Ayer, Ethan. "The Promise of Heat," New Yorker, XLII (September 3, 1966), 30-35.

437 ______. "The Treasure Dream," New Yorker, XLIII (March 11, 1967), 167-168, 171-175.

438 Azam, Ikram. "My Name-Sake," Pakistan Review, XIV (January 1966), 13-14.

439 ______. "My Son," Pakistan Review, XIII (May 1965), 3-4.

440 ______. "Sons of the Soil," Pakistan Review, XIII (August 1965), 17-18.

441 Azhayev, Vasili. "Odd Man Out," Alice Ingman, trans., Soviet Literature, (no. 8, 1968), 57-71.

442 GGB. "You Know/(a mirroric essay)," Twigs, no. 2 (1966), 50-53.

443 M. B. "A Nice Garden," New Zealand Listener, LVIII (October 4, 1968), 10.

444 Ba, Vivian. "The Rainbow Story," Hemisphere, XII (January 1968), 35-36.

445 Babb, Sanora. "Daft," Southwest Review, LIV (Winter 1969), 72-78.

446 ______. "An Owl on Every Post," Prairie Schooner, XLIII (Spring 1969), 87-94.

447 ______. "Run, Sheepy, Run!" Kansas Magazine, (1966), 19-25.

448 ______. "A Scandalous History," Northwest Review, IX (Spring 1968), 79-99.

449 Babel, Isaac. "Awakening," Soviet Literature, (no. 4, 1967), 73-78.

450 ______. "Berestechko," Nova, (November 1969), 43, 48.

451 ______. "The Blind," Max Hayward, trans., Harper's Bazaar, CII (December 1968), 164-165.

452 ______. "The Certificate of Merit," Ann Barlow, trans., Stand, X, no. 3 (1969), 2-4.

453 ______. "Forgotten Stories/Elya Isaakovich and Margarita Prokofievna," Antony Wood, trans., Stand, VII, no. 2 (1965),

33-35.

454 ______. "Forgotten Stories/An Evening at the Empress's," Antony Wood, trans., Stand, VII, no. 2 (1965), 29-30.

455 ______. "Forgotten Stories/Inspiration," Antony Wood, trans., Stand, VII, no. 2 (1965), 31-32.

456 ______. "Forgotten Stories/Rimma, Alla and Mamma," Antony Wood, trans., Stand, VII, no. 2 (1965), 20-26.

457 ______. "Forgotten Stories/Sulak," Antony Wood, trans., Stand, VII, no. 2 (1965), 27-28.

458 ______. "Grishchuk," Max Hayward, trans., Harper's Bazaar, C (November 1967), 113.

459 ______. "The Jewess," Max Hayward, trans., New Yorker, XLIV (August 31, 1968), 26-29.

460 ______. "Line and Colour," Moura Budberg, trans., London Magazine, IX (July/August 1969), 84-86.

461 ______. "Mosaic," Max Hayward, trans., Harper's Bazaar, CII (December 1968), 165.

462 ______. "My First Fee," Max Hayward, trans., Ararat, IX (Summer 1968), 42-45.

463 ______. "'No Iron Can Stab the Heart with Such Force as a Period Put Just at the Right Place'," Max Hayward, trans., Harper's Bazaar, CII (December 1968), 164.

464 ______. "The Public Library," Max Hayward, trans., Harper's Bazaar, C (October 1967), 266.

465 ______. "Shabos Nahamu," Max Hayward, trans., Atlantic Monthly, CCXVII (March 1966), 79-81.

466 ______. "Sunset," Antony Wood, trans., Stand, VII, no. 4 (1965), 7-16.

467 ______. "Two Stories/The Deserter," Max Hayward, trans., Commentary, XLV (January 1968), 45-46.

468 ______. "Two Stories/The Quaker," Max Hayward, trans., Commentary, XLV (January 1968), 46-47.

469 ______. "You Must Know Everything," Max Hayward, trans., New Yorker, XLII (April 9, 1966), 36-38.

470 Baber, Asa, Jr. "My Sister and Me," Transatlantic Review, no. 24 (Spring 1967), 37-54.

471 _____. "Revelations," Playboy, XVI (October 1969), 123, 130, 230-231.

472 Bablyak, Vladimir. "Matei Rozmarina," Eve Manning, trans., Soviet Literature, (no. 9, 1968), 73-84.

473 Bacchus, Ataur. "The Professor," Alphabet, no. 17 (December 1969), 47-52.

474 Bache, William B. "The Four-time Loser," Discourse, XI (Spring 1968), 195-198.

475 _____. "The Gnomic Muse," Discourse, XI (Summer 1968), 335-340.

476 _____. "A Guest of the Management," Discourse, XII (Spring 1969), 170-189.

477 _____. "On the Road to Innsbruck and Back," University Review, XXXIV (Spring 1968), 181-186.

478 _____. "Our Sincerest Laughter," Discourse, XII (Autumn 1969), 480-492.

479 Bachmann, Ingeborg. "A Place for Incidents," Paul O'Hearn, trans., Dimension, II, no. 3 (1969), 586-591 [in German and English on alternate pages].

480 Baer, Stan. "Notes on Goons, Slip-backs and Mechografts," Second Coming, I (January 1965), 16-19.

481 _____. "The Statue of Liberty/As Seen from an Elevated Stop in Brooklyn," Literary Review, IX (Autumn 1965), 37-41.

482 Bagchi, Shantonu. "The Message in the Meteorite," Tropix, II, no. 3 (1967), 41-51.

483 Bahler, Beth Fellman. "A Blue Pass," Quartet, no. 17 (Winter 1967), 22-28.

484 Băiescu, Ion. "The Bear," London Magazine, VII (April 1967), 51-55.

485 _____. "A Disease Without a Name," Literary Review, X (Summer 1967), 537-543.

486 Bail, Jay. "Lament," North American Review, III (March 1966), 5-9.

487 _____. "The Mannequins," Trace, no. 69 (1968), 446-456.

488 _____. "One Night in March," Canadian Forum, XLV (October 1965), 156-158.

489 ______. "Period of Time," Trace, no. 64 (Spring 1967), 65-74.

490 ______. "Variations," Ante, IV (Summer-Fall 1968), 21-36.

491 Bail, Murray. "Albie," Westerly, no. 3 (October 1969), 5-9.

492 ______. "The Dog Show," Meanjin Quarterly, XXV (June 1966), 211-214.

493 ______. "Life of the Party," Meanjin Quarterly, XXVIII (Winter 1969), 232-237.

494 ______. "The Silence," Westerly, no. 3 (1967), 50-53.

495 Bailey, A. J. "The Information Bureau," The Cantuarian, (August 1966), 209.

496 Bailey, Anthony. "Fog," Redbook, CXXVII (July 1966), 59, 107-110.

497 Bailey, C. P. "The Barbed Wire," Michigan Quarterly Review, V (Summer 1966), 209-213.

498 ______. "The Sail Boat," DeKalb Literary Arts Journal, I (Fall 1966), 33-42.

499 Bailey, Don. "If You Hum Me a Few Bars, I Might Remember the Tune," Quarry, XVIII (Spring 1969), 4-12.

500 Bailey, Hilary. "Dr. Gelabius," New Worlds, no. 181 (April 1968), 4-5.

501 Bailey, Norman A. "The Temple," Ararat, VII (Winter 1966), 7-9.

502 Bailey, Paul. "Trespasses," London Magazine, IX (November 1969), 45-63.

503 Bails, John. "Housekeeper," South Dakota Review, IV (Spring 1966), 65-87.

504 Bakhnov, Vladlen. "Three Stories/The Robniks," Vladimir Talmy, trans., Soviet Literature, (no. 5, 1968), 138-139.

505 ______. "Three Stories/Speaking of Demonology," Vladimir Talmy, trans., Soviet Literature, (no. 5, 1968), 141-144.

506 ______. "Three Stories/The Story of a Man Who Was Once a Genius," Vladimir Talmy, trans., Soviet Literature, (no. 5, 1968), 140-141.

507 Bakounts, Axel. "Lar-Markar," Mischa Kudian, trans., Ararat,

VIII (Summer 1967), 24-28.

508 _____. "The Mountain Cyclamen," Anthony Wixley, trans., Soviet Literature, (no. 3, 1966), 67-74.

509 Balaskas, Mina. "My Name," The Classic, II, no. 4 (1968), 20-22.

510 _____. "Rats/From a work in progress," The Classic, II, no. 4 (1968), 19-20.

511 Balchin, Nigel. "In the Absence of Mrs. Petersen," Good Housekeeping, CLXIII (July 1966), 69-71, 128, 130, 132-134, 136, 140, 142, 144-146, 148, 150, 152-156.

512 Baldwin, Brooks and B. F. Gorham. "Just before Dawn," Good Housekeeping, CLXI (August 1965), 66-67, 179-183.

513 Baldwin, James. "Going to Meet the Man," Status, I (October 1965), 47-49, 69-72.

514 _____. "The Man Child," Playboy, XIII (January 1966), 101-102, 211-214.

515 _____. "Tell Me How Long the Train's Been Gone," McCall's, XCIV (February 1967), 118-119, 154, 156, 158-160, 162, 164, 166.

516 Baldwin, Marlene. "Untitled," Plume & Sword, VII (Fall 1966), 11-12.

517 Baldwin, Michael. "The Capitalists," Nova, (April 1968), 100-102, 104, 109-110.

518 Balfour, John. "Morry's Boots," New Zealand Listener, (September 23, 1966), 7, 15.

519 Ball, John. "Johnny Get Your Gun," Good Housekeeping, CLXIX (September 1969), 73-75, 206, 208-214, 216, 218-220, 222-228, 230, 232-234, 236, 238, 240, 242, 244, 246, 250, 252.

520 Ball, Pasco C. "A Matter of Principle," Appalachian Review, II (Winter 1968), 31-36.

521 Ballard, Holley. "The Beautiful Accomplishment," Redbook, CXXXI (August 1968), 119-121.

522 Ballard, J. G. "The Atrocity Exhibition," Encounter, XXVIII (March 1967), 3-9.

523 _____. "The Dead Astronaut," Playboy, XV (May 1968), 118-120, 166, 168.

524 ______. "The Draining Lake," Ambit, no. 23 (1965), 34-40.

525 ______. "The Generations of America," New Worlds, no. 183 (October 1968), 13-14.

526 ______. "The Killing Ground," New Worlds, no. 188 (March 1969), 47-50.

527 ______. "Plan for the Assassination of Jacqueline Kennedy," Ambit, no. 31 (1966-67), 9-11.

528 ______. "Souvenir," Playboy, XII (May 1965), 98-99, 108, 192, 194-195.

529 ______. "Tolerances of the Human Face," Encounter, XXXIII (September 1969), 3-14.

530 ______. "The University of Death," Transatlantic Review, no. 29 (Summer 1968), 68-79.

531 ______. "You: Coma: Marilyn Monroe," Ambit, no. 27 (1966), 3-6.

532 Ballard, James. "A Bargain," Massachusetts Review, VI (Autumn-Winter 1964-65), 73-90.

533 ______. "Jordan River, Deep and Wide," Northwest Review, VII (Spring-Summer 1965), 5-16.

534 ______. "A Season and a Time," Northwest Review, VII (Fall-Winter 1965-66), 52-114.

535 ______. "Wild Honey," Atlantic Monthly, CCXVII (January 1966), 63-67.

536 Ballvé, Julieta. "Night Walk," Américas, XVII (December 1965), 34-36.

537 Baloy, Cleotide. "Mother and Son," Diliman Review, XIII (October 1965), 348-354.

538 Balsey, Eugene D. "Count Three and Stick Your Foot In It," Saturday Evening Post, CCXXXVIII (February 13, 1965), 64-65, 68, 70-71.

539 Baltensperger, Peter. "Reflections," Limbo, II (November 1967), 42-43, 46-47.

540 Bamberg, Estelle G. "The Hypnotist," Phylon, XXIX (Winter 1968), 403-409.

541 ______. "Yuletide Greetings," Phylon, XXVIII (Summer 1967), 209-211.

542 Banaphool. "Name," L. I. F., trans., Bengali Literature, I (May 1967), 20-23.

543 Banda, George N. "The Road to Ndola," New Writing from Zambia, no. 1 (1969), 16-20.

544 Bandopadhyaya, Swaraj. "Two Worlds," Mavelikara Ramachandran, trans., Accent, I (March 1969), 18-19, 21.

545 ______. "Two Worlds [Part II]," Mavelikara Ramachandran, trans., Accent, I (April 1969), 16-18.

546 ______. "Two Worlds [Part III]," Mavelikara Ramachandran, trans., Accent, I (May 1969), 26-29.

547 ______. "Two Worlds [Part IV]," Accent, I (June 1969), 34-36, 40.

548 Bandyopadhyay, Tarashankar. "The Woman and the Serpent," Mahasveta Devi, trans., Indian Literature, XII (March 1969), 80-85.

549 Bank, Marvin. "Aguardiente Reverie," Mexico Quarterly Review, II (July 1965), 175-178.

550 ______. "The Golem," Mexico Quarterly Review, II (Fall 1967), 24-31.

551 Bankier, William. "The Replacement," Ladies' Home Journal, LXXXV (January 1968), 98-100.

552 Banks, Carolyn. "Idyll," Voyages, II (Fall 1968), 46.

553 Banks, Loy Otis. "The Calliope Voice," Wisconsin Review, III (Spring 1968), 6-9.

554 ______. "The Explicitress," Human Voice Quarterly, II (February 1966), 3, 24-25.

555 ______. "The Great Communication Plague," Limbo, II (November 1966), 40-42.

556 ______. "Grief Mask," Discourse, X (Autumn 1967), 440-445.

557 ______. "Junction," Montparnasse Review, no. 1 (1965), 12-18.

558 ______. "Passage," Perspective, XV (Autumn 1967), 109-116.

559 ______. "The Secret Orange," The Fiddlehead, no. 71 (Spring 1967), 36-40.

560 ______. "The Sunder Score," Four Quarters, XVIII (March 1969), 13-18.

561 _____. "Two Islands," South Dakota Review, III (Autumn 1965), 21-31.

562 _____. "Walter," North Dakota Quarterly, XXXIII (Winter 1965), 14-17.

563 Banks, Lynne Reid. "Miss Daviot's Vice," Cornhill Magazine, CLXXVI (Spring 1967), 56-69.

564 _____. "Only Son," Ladies' Home Journal, LXXXIV (May 1967), 100-101, 142, 144, 146-147.

565 _____. "The Thirtieth Birthday of Clara Hawkins," McCall's, XCII (March 1965), 118-119, 146, 148, 150-152.

566 _____. "Zalman's Galatea," Cosmopolitan, CLX (April 1966), 106-115.

567 Banks, Russell. "The Adjutant Bird," Lillabulero, I (Fall 1967), 7-10.

568 _____. "A Circle of Clowns," Carolina Quarterly, XVIII (Fall 1965), 65-80.

569 _____. "The Drive Home," New American Review, no. 4 (August 1968), 66-84.

570 _____. "Krump Pays through the Nose, and Yet Comes Back for More," Dust, IV (Summer 1969), 29-31.

571 _____. "Lyman Burdette's Hegira," Lillabulero, no. 6 (Fall-Winter 1968), 14-20.

572 _____. "from Musgrave's Book," Ann Arbor Review, nos. 5 & 6 (1969), 42-46.

573 _____. "My Name Is Legion," Carolina Quarterly, XX (Winter 1968), 23-46.

574 _____. "To Give the Lie," Trace, no. 68 (1968), 277-284.

575 Banville, John. "Sanctuary," Transatlantic Review, no. 31 (Winter 1968-69), 83-90.

576 _____. "Summer Voices," Transatlantic Review, no. 28 (Spring 1968), 99-107.

577 _____. "Wild Wood," Dublin Magazine, VIII (Spring-Summer 1969), 25-30.

578 Barba, Harry. "God's Friends--The Moonflyers," Ararat, IX (Summer 1968), 34-37.

579 ______. "Hello, To the Light," Ararat, X (Winter 1969), 10-13.

580 ______. "A Letter to the Corinthians," North American Review, V (November-December 1968), 21-26.

581 ______. "A Triangle Compounded," Ararat, VI (Spring 1965), 28-36.

582 Barber, Patricia. "Flagstop," Intro, no. 1 (September 1968), 52-61.

583 Barbu, Eugen. "The Sea Has Shores," Pakistan Review, XVI (October 1968), 32-33.

584 Barker, Rubin. "The King of the Tuppsbury Fair," Lillabulero, I (Spring 1967), 10-13.

585 Barkin, Haskell and Harlan Ellison. "Do It for a Penny?" Playboy, XIV (October 1967), 127, 179-182, 184.

586 Barksdale, Richard K. "The Last Supper," Phylon, XXVII (Spring 1966), 91-94.

587 Barnebey, Clyde. "You Can't Come Back," Prism International, VI (Spring 1967), 75-81.

588 ______. "The Voice of the Turtle," Prism International, VIII (Autumn 1968), 109-116.

589 Barnebey, Karl. "The Chelonophile," The Fair, II (Winter 1967), 31-60.

590 ______. "A Mixture," The Fair, I (March 1966), 53-63.

591 ______. "On the Playground," The Fair, I (May 1966), 2-5.

592 Barnes, Charlene. "A Pillar of Salt," William and Mary Review, IV (Spring 1966), 53-58.

593 Barnes, Gregory. "Faith, Hope, Love," Grecourt Review, VIII (April 1965), 9-18.

594 ______. "People to People," University Review, XXXIII (December 1966), 124-128.

595 Baronas, Aloyzas. "In the Morning/(Excerpt from a novel The Third Woman), Nola M. Zobarskas, trans., Lituanus, XV (Spring 1969), 76-81.

596 Barraclough, Robert. "A Visit to the Last Objective," Readers & Writers, I (April-May 1967), 14-16.

597 Barraco Mármol, Mario. "Not Even Dead," Américas, XX

(July 1968), 11-13.

598 Barrett, B. L. "The Passion of Daisy Hall," Saturday Evening Post, CCXXXVIII (November 6, 1965), 66-68, 70-73.

599 ______. "A Time for Everything," Ave Maria, CIV (November 12, 1966), 26-28.

600 ______. "A Well Brought Up Girl," Redbook, CXXXIII (June 1969), 155-177.

601 Barrett, Lindsey. "The Hunger Brings Bread, Also Honey Eyes," Montparnasse Review, no. 2 (1966), 5-10.

602 Barrett, Mary Ellin. "Castle Ugly/Part I," Ladies' Home Journal, LXXXIII (October 1966), 167-174, 184-185.

603 ______. "Castle Ugly/Conclusion," Ladies' Home Journal, LXXXIII (November 1966), 147-154, 164-170.

604 Barrington, Theodore. "Seascape," Nimrod, XI (Spring 1967), 37-41.

605 Barrio, Raymond. "Greed," Gato Magazine, I (Autumn 1966), 9-11.

606 ______. "If You Can, Insure with Ameri-can," Dust, IV (Summer 1969), 2-6.

607 ______. "Just What the Doctor Ordered," Dust, II (Spring-Summer 1965), 37-39.

608 ______. "The Master Peace," December, VII (1965), 15-19.

609 ______. "The Ordeal of Mr. Quill," Midwestern University Quarterly, I, no. 4 (1966), 1-19.

610 ______. "Sortie," Trace, no. 58 (Autumn 1965), 279-280.

611 Barrow, Jonathan. "Two Stories/1. Rats," London Magazine, IX (September 1969), 75-77.

612 ______. Two Stories/2. The Embankment," London Magazine, IX (September 1969), 78-80.

613 Barry, Barbara D. "Herby," December, VII (1965), 168-180.

614 Barry, Jeanne. "The Brussels Sprout," Signature, II (November 1967), 34.

615 Barry, P. S. "The Civilising Influence," Edge, no. 4 (Spring 1965), 52-54.

616 Barsamian, Kenneth J. "'The Transgressor'," Armenian Review, XVIII (Spring 1965), 52-59.

617 _____. "The Water Spigot's Niece," Armenian Review, XIX (Spring 1966), 41-49.

618 Barshay, Bernard. "Home from the Hospital," Moonlight Review, I (June 1967), 36-46.

619 Barth, John. "Autobiography: A Self-Recorded Fiction," New American Review, no. 2 (January 1968), 72-75.

620 _____. "Lost in the Funhouse," Atlantic Monthly, CCXX (November 1967), 73-82.

621 _____. "Night-Sea Journey," Esquire, LXV (June 1966), 82-83, 147-148.

622 _____. "Petition," Esquire, LXX (July 1968), 68-71, 135.

623 _____. "Title," Yale Review, LVII (Winter 1968), 213-221.

624 Barthel, Thomas Hanley. "A Saturday at the Lake," Greensboro Review, III (Winter 1967), 48-58.

624a Bartheleme, Steve. "Aspirin," Massachusetts Review, X (Autumn 1969), 681-684.

625 Barthelme, Donald. "The Affront," Harper's Bazaar, XCIX (November 1965), 169, 229-230.

626 _____. "Alice," Paris Review, XI (Summer 1968), 25-31.

627 _____. "At the Tolstoy Museum," New Yorker, XLV (May 24, 1969), 32-37.

628 _____. "The Balloon," New Yorker, XLII (April 16, 1966), 46-48.

629 _____. "Can We Talk," Art and Literature, no. 5 (Summer 1965), 148-150.

630 _____. "City Life," New Yorker, XLIV (January 18, 1969), 31-32.

631 _____. "City Life II," New Yorker, XLV (June 21, 1969), 32-37.

632 _____. "The Dolt," New Yorker, XLIII (November 11, 1967), 56-58.

633 _____. "Edward and Pia," New Yorker, XLI (September 25, 1965), 46-49.

634 ______. "Eugénie Grandet," New Yorker, XLIV (August 17, 1968), 24-25.

635 ______. "The Explanation," New Yorker, XLIV (May 4, 1968), 44-46.

636 ______. "The Falling Dog," New Yorker, XLIV (August 3, 1968), 28-29.

637 ______. "A Few Moments of Sleeping and Waking," New Yorker, XLIII (August 5, 1967), 24-26.

638 ______. "Game," New Yorker, XLI (July 31, 1965), 29-30.

639 ______. "Games Are the Enemies of Beauty, Truth and Sleep, Amanda Said," Mademoiselle, LXIV (November 1966), 136, 212-213.

640 ______. "The Indian Uprising," New Yorker, XLI (March 6, 1965), 34-37.

641 ______. "Kierkegaard Unfair to Schlegel," New Yorker, XLIV (October 12, 1968), 53-55.

642 ______. "Mouth," Paris Review, XII (Fall 1969), 189-202.

643 ______. "On Angels," New Yorker, XLV (August 9, 1969), 29.

644 ______. "Paraguay," New Yorker, XLV (September 6, 1969), 32-34.

645 ______. "Philadelphia," New Yorker, XLIV (November 30, 1968), 56-58.

646 ______. "The Policeman's Ball," New Yorker, XLIV (June 8, 1968), 31.

647 ______. "Report," New Yorker, XLIII (June 10, 1967), 34-35.

648 ______. "Robert Kennedy Saved from Drowning," New American Review, no. 3 (1968), 107-116.

649 ______. "See the Moon?" New Yorker, XLII (March 12, 1966), 46-50.

650 ______. "Several Garlic Tales," Paris Review, X (Spring 1966), 62-67.

651 ______. "Snap Snap," New Yorker, XLI (August 28, 1965), 108-111.

652 ______. "Snow White," New Yorker, XLII (February 11, 1967), 38-50, 52, 57-58, 60, 63, 66, 68, 70, 75-77, 80, 82, 87-89,

92, 94, 99-100, 102, 104, 106, 109-110, 112, 117-118, 120, 122-124, 126, 128-131.

653 ______. "This Newspaper Here," New Yorker, XLI (February 12, 1966), 28-29.

654/5 ______. "Views of My Father Weeping," New Yorker, XLV (December 6, 1969), 56-60.

656 Bartholomeusz, Mark. "The Brainwave," Hemisphere, XIII (December 1969), 30-33.

657 ______. "Of Love and Squalor," Hemisphere, IX (April 1965), 30-34.

658 Bartlett, Paul Alexander. "Raincoat," Forum, IV (Fall 1966), 42-46.

659 Bartov, Hanoch. "A Distant Sister," Hillel Halkin, trans., Midstream, XIII (January 1967), 32-52.

660 Bart-Williams, Gaston. "My Friend," Prism International, VIII (Summer 1968), 40-42.

661 ______. "My Friend," West Coast Review, I (Fall 1966), 4-6.

662 Baruzdin, Sergei. "They Call Her Yolka," Vladimir Talmy and Tom Botting, trans., Soviet Literature, (no. 2, 1966), 44-77.

663 ______. "Tasya," Margaret Wettlin, trans., Soviet Literature, (no. 2, 1968), 3-47.

664 Basak, Subimal. "Calcutta & Calcutta," D. S. Klein, trans., Salted Feathers, nos. 8 & 9 (March 1967), n.p. [111-114].

665 ______. "from Guerilla Indignance," Subimal Basak and Carl Weissner, trans., Intrepid, no. 10 (Spring 1968), n.p. [29-32].

666 ______. "3 Episodes from 'Chhatha Matha'," Subimal Basak and Carl Weissner, trans., Intrepid, no. 10 (Spring 1968), n.p. [26].

667 Bassett, Mary. "The Jasmine Seed," DeKalb Literary Arts Journal, III (Winter 1969), 38-60.

668 Basu, Manoj. "Revenge," Manoj Basu, trans., Triveni, XXXVI (October 1967), 45-49.

669 ______. "The Truth He Couldn't Tell," Sachindra Lal Ghosh, trans., Indian Literature, IX (April-June 1966), 67-74.

670 Bataille, Georges. "The Dead Man," Austryn Wainhouse, trans., Works, II (Fall/Winter 1969), 70-98.

671 Bates, Arthenia J. "Home X and Me," Negro Digest, XIV (September 1965), 43-47.

672 ______. "Lost Note," Delta, XIX (1965), 46-52.

673 Bates, Darrell. "A Dark Sown Seed," Queen, CDXXV (Christmas Issue, 1965), 118-121.

674 ______. "The Husband," Cosmopolitan, CLIX (July 1965), 88-94.

675 ______. "Seven Years Is a Long Time," Cosmopolitan, CLVIII (January 1965), 89-90, 92-93.

676 ______. "The Third Wife," Cosmopolitan, CLVIII (April 1965), 89-90, 92.

677 Bates, H. E. "The Triple Echo," Daily Telegraph Magazine, no. 269 (December 5, 1969), 64-65, 67-68, 70.

678 ______. "The Triple Echo/Part Two," Daily Telegraph Magazine, no. 270 (December 12, 1969), 77-78, 82-83, 86.

679 ______. "The Triple Echo/Conclusion," Daily Telegraph Magazine, no. 271 (December 19, 1969), 53-54, 56, 59.

680 ______. "The Winter Sound," Weekend Telegraph, no. 35 (May 21, 1965), 41, 43, 45-46.

681 Bates, Paulette. "The Enemy," Intro, no. 2 (September 1969), 108-122.

682 ______. "The Sounds of Silence," South Carolina Review, I (May 1969), 20-29.

683 Bates, Randy. "A Spectre of Innocence," Cimarron Review, no. 7 (March 1969), 57-59.

684 Bates, Richard. "The Trout," Queen, CDXXIX (July 19, 1967), 42-45.

685 Batie, Jean. "Good Friday," Assay, XXII (Spring 1966), 17-22.

686 Batinski, Virginia C. "Concerning Two Who Recanted," University Review, XXXII (March 1966), 204-206.

687 Batistich, A. E. "Champion of the Northern Wairoa," New Zealand Listener, LII (June 18, 1965), 4.

688 Batten, Loring W., 3rd. "So Long at the Fair," New Frontiers, X, no. 2 (1965), 69-72.

689 Batty, Harry. "Dime Novel," Assay, XXV (Spring 1969), 18-23.

690 Baudelaire, Charles. "The Parisian Spleen," Peter Schlaifer, trans., Carolina Quarterly, XVIII (Fall 1965), 4-26.

691 Bauer, Josef Martin. "For Man Needs Warmth," George Raymond Selden, trans., Scala International, (May 1967), 35-37.

692 Bauer, W. A. "Pig-of-the-Wind: A Fragment from the Archives," The Fiddlehead, no. 78 (January-February 1969), 32-41.

693 Baugh, Sue. "Land," Greensboro Review, IV (Spring 1969), 22-34.

694 Baum, E. R. "Fate," Ave Maria, CIV (October 1, 1966), 24-26.

695 Baum, Philip. "My Normal Development," Era, II (Spring 1967), 31-35.

696 Baum, Thomas. "A Friend in Need," Transatlantic Review, no. 30 (Autumn 1968), 101-115.

697 Baumbach, Jonathan. "Code of Honor," Michigan Quarterly Review, IV (Summer 1965), 166-173.

698 Baumgart, Reinhard. "Memoriam," Silas O. Hughes, Jr., trans., Dimension, II, no. 1 (1969), 128-141 [in German and English on alternate pages].

699 Bax, Martin and Michael Foreman. "On, At or About America," Ambit, no. 39 (1969), 2-8.

700 _____. "Seconds out of the Ring," Ambit, no. 31 (1966-67), 27-30.

701 _____. "The Turned-in, Broken-up and Gone World," Ambit, no. 34 (1968), 5-13.

702 Baxt, George. "Swing Low, Sweet Harriet," Cosmopolitan, CLXIII (September 1967), 144-150, 152, 154-161, 166-173.

703 Baydo, James Richard. "The Friends," Prospero's Cell, I (Winter 1967), 7-24.

704 Bayer, Ann. "The Eye of the Needle," Mademoiselle, LXIX (October 1969), 204-208.

705 _____. "The Goddess of Aisle E," Mademoiselle, LXIII (May 1966), 168-169.

706 _____. "My Heart Belongs to (A), (B), (C), (D), (Other)," Saturday Evening Post, CCXXXIX (December 31, 1966), 57-59.

707 ______. "The Secret Infidelity of Arthur Nydes," Saturday Evening Post, CCXXXVIII (September 25, 1965), 70-71, 73-75

708 ______. "The Woman Who Gave of Herself," Saturday Evening Post, CCXL (May 20, 1967), 62-64, 66-67.

709 Beach, Mary. "Who's in Charge Here?" VDRSVPVDRSVP-VDRSVP, (1969), n.p. [front and back pages].

710 Beagle, Peter. "My Daughter's Name Is Sarah," Ladies' Home Journal, LXXXIII (February 1966), 62-63, 106-107.

711 Beal, M. F. "The End of Days," New American Review, no. 7 (August 1969), 191-200.

712 ______. "Joining Up," Atlantic Monthly, CCXVIII (December 1966), 102, 105-108.

713 ______. "Survival," New American Review, no. 3 (1968), 188-200.

714 Beattie, Ann. "Dear Professor," American, I (Fall 1965), 34.

715 ______. "Performance," American, II (Spring 1966), 18-21, 46-47.

716 ______. "Sea Monsters and Philosophers from Trenton, New Jersey: A Parable in Between," American, II (Fall 1966), 16-17.

717 ______. "Stuck with the Flag and Other Items/Alvin and the Parade," American, IV (Spring 1968), 31.

718 ______. "Stuck with the Flag and Other Items/Clara Like Every Other Girl," American, IV (Spring 1968), 28-29.

719 ______. "Stuck with the Flag and Other Items/Edmund in the Family," American, IV (Spring 1968), 27-28.

720 ______. "Stuck with the Flag and Other Items/Ernest in the School," American, IV (Spring 1968), 30.

721 ______. "Stuck with the Flag and Other Items/Sol and Uncle Irving," American, IV (Spring 1968), 29.

722 ______. "Whoever Heard of Fitzgerald," American, III (Spring 1967), 57-63.

723 Beaufort, Bowman. "The Game," Greensboro Review, II (December 1966), 58-66.

724 ______. "'The Projectionist'," Greensboro Review, IV (Winter

1968), 52-66.

725 de Beauvoir, Simone. "Les Belles Images," Patrick O'Brien, trans., Ladies' Home Journal, LXXXV (March 1968), 125-132, 134-139.

726 Beberfall, Lester. "Dreams," North American Mentor, V (Summer 1967), 25-29.

727 Becerra de Jenkins, Lyll. "Saúl," Américas, XXI (February 1969), 34-36.

728 Becker, Jürgen. "Margins," A. Leslie Willson, trans., Dimension, I, no. 2 (1968), 198-217 [in German and English on alternate pages].

729 Beckett, Samuel. "The Calmative," Evergreen Review, XI (June 1967), 47-49, 93-95.

730 _____. "Imagination Dead Imagine," Evergreen Review, X (February 1966), 48-49.

731 _____. "Ping," Encounter, XXVIII (February 1967), 25-26.

732 _____. "Ping," Harper's Bazaar, C (June 1967), 120, 140.

733 _____. "Texts for Nothing: VI," London Magazine, VII (August 1967), 47-50.

734 _____. "Texts for Nothing/XII," Transatlantic Review, no. 24 (Spring 1967), 115-116.

735 Bedford, Ian. "In Darkest Hungary," The Pluralist, no. 4 (May 1965), 11-15.

736 Bedi, Rajinder Singh. "Give Me Your Sorrows," Karen Leonard and G. C. Narang, trans., Indian Literature, XI (April-July 1968), 20-47.

737 Beggs, Christina. "A Diminished Seventh," Westerly, no. 3 (1967), 33-35.

738 Beghtol, Clare. "There's Been a Death," Queen's Quarterly, LXXVI (Winter 1969), 681-691.

739 Begum, Rabiunissa. "The Meeting Point," Pakistan Review, XVII (November 1969), 10-12.

740 _____. "The Second Chance," Pakistan Review, XIII (January 1965), 17-18, 16.

741 Beiles, Sinclair and Annie Rooney. "Alice in Progress," San Francisco Earthquake, I (Summer-Fall 1968), 60.

742 ______ and Annie Rooney. "Bones," San Francisco Earthquake, I, (Summer-Fall 1968), 60-61.

743 ______ and Annie Rooney. "From 'Breakout'--A Study of One Year Olds in the Paris Literary World," San Francisco Earthquake, I (Summer-Fall 1968), 61-63.

744 ______ and Annie Rooney. "Collectors Corner," VDRSVPVDRSVPVDRSVP, (1969), n.p. [front page].

745 ______ and Annie Rooney. "Extract from a Speech on the Cuban Problem," San Francisco Earthquake, I (Summer-Fall 1968), 63-64.

746 ______. "Invasions (Scenes from the Jazz Age)," VDRSVPVDRSVPVDRSVP, (1969), n.p. [front page].

747 ______. "Notes from a Tour," VDRSVPVDRSVPVDRSVP, (1969), n.p. [back page].

748 ______ and Annie Rooney. "Radio Cairo Reporting," San Francisco Earthquake, I (Summer-Fall 1968), 64-65.

749 ______ and Annie Rooney. "Where to Find Alice in Progress," San Francisco Earthquake, I (Summer-Fall 1968), 65-66.

750 Beja, Morris. "The Churches, Chapels and/or Shrines of Mykonos," Cimarron Review, no. 7 (March 1969), 60-66.

751 Belcher, Victor. "Only One Eye," Transatlantic Review, no. 24 (Spring 1967), 129-136.

752 Bell, Margaret "Fly in Amber," New Zealand Listener, LIII (August 13, 1965), 4.

753 Bellocchio, Piergiorgio "Not Guilty," Raymond Rosenthal, trans., Chelsea, nos. 18-19 (June 1966), 19-36.

754 Bellow, Saul. "Mosby's Memoirs," New Yorker, XLIV (July 20, 1968), 36-42, 44-49.

755 ______. "Mr. Sammler's Planet/Part I," Atlantic Monthly, CCXXIX (November 1969), 95-150.

756 ______. "Mr. Sammler's Planet/Part II," Atlantic Monthly, CCXXIV (December 1969), 99-142.

757 ______. "The Old System," Playboy, XV (January 1968), 140-142, 144, 240, 242, 244-247, 249-250.

758 Belov, Vasili. "Lyuba-Lyubushka," Gladys Evans, trans., Soviet Literature, (no. 3, 1965), 112-123.

759 _____. "That's How It Is," Eve Manning, trans., Soviet Literature, (no. 1, 1969), 3-131.

760 Belyaev, Alexander. "Amba," Eve Manning, trans., Soviet Literature, (no. 5, 1968), 55-73.

761 Benchley, Nathaniel. "First Snow," New Yorker, XLI (November 20, 1965), 194, 196-198.

762 _____. "A Funny Thing Happened...," New Yorker, XLI (January 15, 1966), 78-80, 82-83.

763 _____. "The Hour of the Wolf," Signature, II (September 1967), 42-43, 70-71.

764 _____. "Now the Fun Starts," Saturday Evening Post, CCXLII (December 28, 1968-January 11, 1969), 56-58, 60-61.

765 _____. "The Ombudsman," New Yorker, XLIII (July 1, 1967), 33-35.

766 _____. "Settling In," McCall's, XCIV (November 1966), 100+.

767 _____. "The Visitors," Cosmopolitan, CLIX (August 1965), 106-121, 125-129, 131-133.

768 _____. "Welcome to Xanadu," Redbook, CXXXI (July 1968), 133-155.

769 Bender, Eleanor. "The Judgment of Madame Charpentier," Carleton Miscellany, VII (Fall 1966), 2-12.

770 Bender, Hans. "The Screech Owl in the Country," George Raymond Selden, trans., Scala International, (November 1965), 34-37.

771 _____. "Sheep's Blood," Christopher Middleton, trans., Stand, VII, no. 4 (1965), 28-31.

772 Benedictus, David. "Eat Me!" Status, XVIII (November 1968), 32-33.

773 _____. "Extract from Hump," Solstice, no. 3 (1966), 8-9.

774 _____. "The Unworthiness of Caspar," Queen, CDXXV (September 1, 1965), 64-65, 84.

775 Benesch, Walter. "Palingenesy," Pyramid, no. 4 (1969), 35-37.

776 Benich, John D. "Thanksgiving Day," North American Review, II (November 1965), 23-24.

777 Benjamin, Ella. "Father Was Held in High Esteem," New Frontiers, X, no. 1 (1965), 11-19.

778 Bennett, Henry. "Wild Dogs," Arizona Quarterly, XXII (Winter 1966), 347-363.

779 Bennett, J., Jr. "The Night of the Great Butcher," December, IX (1967), 185-192.

780 ______. "Of Banjos and Flowers," Transatlantic Review, no. 30 (Autumn 1968), 14-19.

781 Bennett, John Z. "The Coil," North American Review, V (September-October 1968), 22-25.

782 Bennett, Paul L. "The Peduncle of the Rose," University Review, XXXIII (March 1967), 234-240.

783 Bennett, Penelope Agnes. "The Littlest Christmas Tree," Queen, CDXXIX (December 13, 1967), 48-49.

784 Bennett, Warren. "The Long Journey," Wascana Review, II, no. 1 (1967), 21-30.

785 Bense, Max. "Grignan," Anselm Hollo, trans., Damascus Road, no. 2 (1965), 27-29.

786 Bense, Robert. "A Miracle Down in the Second Platoon," Massachusetts Review, IX (Spring 1968), 231-240.

787 ______. "A Report from Jerusalem," William and Mary Review, V (Winter 1967), 39-53.

788 Benson, Arnold. "Knight On a Bicycle," Redbook, CXXXI (May 1968), 64-65, 136, 138, 140-144.

789 ______. "The Upper Hand," Redbook, CXXIX (July 1967), 84-85.

790 Benson, Ingatz. "Genre Story," Yale Literary Magazine, CXXXVIII (January 1969), 18-24.

791 Bentham, Josephine. "With Love and Cold Water Soap," McCall's, XCII (August 1965), 90-91, 148-151.

792 Berckman, Evelyn. "A Case of Nullity," Cosmopolitan, CLXIII (July 1967), 124-130, 132, 134-140, 146-153.

793 Berczeller, Richard. "The Morphinist," New Yorker, XLII (April 16, 1966), 141-142, 144, 146-153.

794 Bereman, Loujen. "Bucephalus," Sage, XII (Spring 1968), 77-84.

795 Berestov, Valentin. "Grains of Stone," Vladimir Talmy, trans.,

Soviet Literature, (no. 10, 1969), 40-74.

796 _____. "Hullo, Parnassus! /A Humoresque," Vladimir Talmy, trans., Soviet Literature, (no. 5, 1968), 134-137.

797 Berg, H. M. "Two Worlds," H. R. Meyer, trans., American Scandinavian Review, LIII (March 1965), 73-77.

798 Bergé, Carol. "The Neighbors: Hannah, the King, Ruby the Chicken Lady, and All the Others," For Now, no. 8 (c. 1966-68), 77-84.

799 Bergelson, David. "The Hole through Which Life Slips," Reuben Bercovitch, trans., Art and Literature, no. 10 (Autumn 1966), 181-190.

800 _____. "Der Kabron," Cynthia Ozick, trans., Antioch Review, XXV (Fall 1965), 430-445.

801 Berger, Phil. "Lose Like a Man," Dare, III (May-June 1965), 35.

802 _____. "Two Sons," New Campus Writing, (1966), 44-54.

803 Berger, Thomas. "Application to Elysium," Esquire, LXVIII (December 1967), 214-216, 270-276.

804 _____. "Controversy: The Arthur Badger Show," Esquire, LXXI (March 1969), 90, 92-93, 134, 140-141.

805 _____. "A Monkey of His Own," Saturday Evening Post, CCXXXVIII (May 22, 1965), 66-70, 73, 76.

806 Berges, Ruth. "Biedermeier Souvenir," Discourse, XII (Summer 1969), 283-290.

807 _____. "Innocence a Child," Discourse, XI (Spring 1968), 205-211.

808 _____. "The Last Day," University Review, XXXIV (Winter 1967), 140-144.

809 _____. "Stopover," University Review, XXXII (December 1965), 137-142.

810 Bergson, Lucy. "Peter and Ramon," Harvard Advocate, CII (March 1968), 2-7.

811 Bergstein, Eleanor. "The Ideal Woman," Redbook, CXXXI (June 1968), 74-75, 125-130.

812 _____. "Winter Fragments," Cosmopolitan, CLXVII (December 1969), 148-153.

813 Berkley, S. "The Actor," Literary Review, XII (Spring 1969), 317-323.

814 Berkman, Sylvia. "Hail to Hugo!" Southern Review, III (April 1967), 416-424.

815 _____. "An Unfamiliar Guest," Radcliffe Quarterly, LII (February-March 1968), 13-17.

816 Berland, Alwyn. "Preparations for a War," Queen's Quarterly, LXXI (Winter 1965), 494-508.

817 Bernanos, George. "A Selection from L'Imposture," Donald Phelps, trans., For Now, no. 3 (c. 1966-68), 37-50.

818 Bernard, Kenneth. "A Dog Named Tim," Discourse, IX (Summer 1966), 338-344.

819 _____. "Firm Ground," Minnesota Review, IX (1969), 159-160.

820 _____. "The Noon Butterfly," Discourse, X (Summer 1967), 343-344.

821 Bernard, Sidney. "Night of the Warhawks," The Smith, no. 7 (1966), 26-29.

822 Berne, Stanley. "From The Unconscious Victorious and Other Stories/All that the Eye Can See," South Dakota Review, IV (Winter 1966), 25-30.

823 _____. "From The Unconscious Victorious and Other Stories/ Heaven Above, Hell Below," South Dakota Review, IV (Winter 1966), 30-33.

824 _____. "From The Unconscious Victorious and Other Stories/ The Indian Signs of Hope," South Dakota Review, IV (Winter 1966), 33-37.

825 Bernlef, Jan. "For Whom the Bell Tolls," Ina Rike, trans., Delta (Amsterdam), XI (Summer 1968), 55-68.

826 Berriault, Gina. "Anna Lisa's Nose," Esquire, LXIII (June 1965), 74-75, 132-135.

827 _____. "The Cove," Esquire, LXXI (January 1969), 81-82.

828 _____. "Lonesome Road," Genesis West, III (Winter 1965), 41-46.

829 _____. "The Science of Life," Redbook, CXXVI (April 1966), 86-87.

830 _____. "The Search for J. Kuper," Esquire, LXVI (October 1966), 104-105, 163, 164, 166-167.

831 Berrigan, Ted and Ron Padgett. "Big Travel Dialogues," Kulcher, no. 20 (Winter 1965-66), 2-29.

832 _____. "Chapter 28 from Clear the Range," Bones, no. 2 (Winter 1968-69), 23-26.

833 _____. "from Clear the Range," Angel Hair, no. 2 (Fall 1966), n. p. [38-39].

834 _____. "from Clearing the Range: Chapter 25," The Once Series (Vice), I (1966-67), n. p. [19].

835 _____. "A Cranny of Life," The Once Series (Ice), I (1966-67), n. p. [16].

836 _____. "Don't Forget Anger," Mother, no. 5 (Summer 1965), 24.

837 _____. "Great Stories of the Chair," Mother, no. 5 (Summer 1965), 24.

838 _____. "Great Stories of the Chair/The Conscience of a Conservative," Angel Hair, no. 4 (Winter 1967-68), n. p. [54].

839 _____. "Great Stories of the Chair/Don't Forget Anger," Angel Hair, no. 4 (Winter 1967-68), n. p. [54].

840 _____. "Great Stories of the Chair/Great Stories of the Chair," Angel Hair, no. 4 (Winter 1967-68), n. p. [51].

841 _____. "Great Stories of the Chair/July," Angel Hair, no. 4 (Winter 1967-68), n. p. [55].

842 _____. "Great Stories of the Chair/A Letter from Dick Gallup," Angel Hair, no. 4 (Winter 1967-68), n. p. [56].

843 _____. "Great Stories of the Chair/Mother Cabrini," Angel Hair, no. 4 (Winter 1967-68), n. p. [51-52].

844 _____. "Great Stories of the Chair/Richard Gallup at 30," Angel Hair, no. 4 (Winter 1967-68), n. p. [53].

845 _____. "Great Stories of the Chair/Some Trips to Go On," Angel Hair, no. 4 (Winter 1967-68), n. p. [55].

846 _____. "Great Stories of the Chair/The Sunset Hotel," Angel Hair, no. 4 (Winter 1967-68), n. p. [52].

847 _____. "Great Stories of the Chair/Tulsa Rose Gardens," Angel Hair, no. 4 (Winter 1967-68), n. p. [52].

848 ______. "Great Stories of the Chair/What's the Racket," Angel Hair, no. 4 (Winter 1967-68), n.p. [54].

849 ______. "Great Stories of the Chair/Who I Am and What I Think," Angel Hair, no. 4 (Winter 1967-68), n.p. [53].

850 ______. "Gus," The World, no. 4 (June 1967), n.p. [60-62].

851 ______ and Ron Padgett. "Inner Landscapes," 0 to 9, no. 3 (January 1968), 79-81.

852 ______. "Life with the Woods," The World, no. 4 (June 1967), n.p. [60].

853 ______. "from Looking for Chris," Art and Literature, no. 11 (Winter 1967), 84-89.

854 ______. "from Looking for Chris," Mother, no. 6 (Thanksgiving 1965), 34-35.

855 ______. "Looking for Chris--Part I," The Once Series (Spice), I (1966-67), n.p. [1-6].

856 ______ and Ron Padgett [Ronald and Edmund Beaumont, (pseud.)]. "A Pink Valentine," Mother, no. 5 (Summer 1965), 71-78.

857 ______, Mike Brownstein and Dick Gallup. "A Story," The World, no. 4 (June 1967), n.p. [62].

858 ______ and Ron Padgett. "Tristan Unsalted," The World, no. 2 (March 1967), n.p. [5-9].

859 ______. "Tulsa Rose Gardens," Mother, no. 5 (Summer 1965), 25.

860 Berry, Newton. "Goodbye, McHowe," Writer's Forum, I (Fall 1965), 36-43.

861 ______. "Whore Is Just a Cuss Word!" Dust, III (Fall 1967), 9-19.

862 Berry, Wendell. "A Day in the History of Old Jack's Place," Texas Quarterly, IX (Winter 1966), 107-127.

863 ______. "from A Place on Earth," Mad River Review, II (Summer 1966), 71-76.

864 Bertolino, James. "Ten Fingers," Wisconsin Review, III (Fall 1967), 16-17.

865 Berton, Pierre. "11:30 A.M.," Parallel, no. 2 (May-June 1966), 54-58.

866 _____. "9:45 A.M.," Parallel, no. 1 (March-April 1966), 4-11.

867 Besch, Lutz. "Jagiello," George Raymond Selden, trans., Scala International, (December 1965), 34-37.

868 Bessie, Alvah. "Susan Aldridge, Requiescat," American Dialog, III (November-December 1966), 28-33.

869 Beteta, Ramón. "La Cucaracha," Coley Taylor, trans., Mexico Quarterly Review, III, no. 1 (1968), 27-37.

870 Betti, Ugo. "The Dream House," Michael Bullock, trans., Prism International, VII (Summer 1967), 4-8.

871 _____. "Isabella in Love," Michael Bullock, trans., Malahat Review, no. 7 (July 1968), 21-25.

872 _____. "The New Hat," Michael Bullock, trans., Malahat Review, no. 7 (July 1968), 17-21.

873 _____. "The People of the Via Lungagna," Michael Bullock, trans., Prism International, VIII (Summer 1968), 81-85.

874 _____. "A Strange Evening," Michael Bullock, trans., Malahat Review, no. 7 (July 1968), 26-42.

875 _____. "A Theft of Washing," Michael Bullock, trans., London Magazine, VII (December 1967), 48-52.

876 Bettis, Berkley. "Strays," Red Cedar Review, V (January 1967), 1-17.

877 Betts, Doris. "The Bald Pigeon," Carolina Quarterly, XXI (Winter 1969), 27-44.

878 _____. "Burning the Bed," South Carolina Review, I (May 1969), 49-64.

879 _____. "Put Them All Together," Greensboro Review, IV (Winter 1968), 4-20.

880 _____. "The Ugliest Pilgrim," Red Clay Reader, no. 6 (1969), 33-41.

881 Beuchler, James. "The Second-Best Girl," Redbook, CXXVI (January 1966), 36-37, 97-100.

882 Bezbaroa, Lakshminath. "'No I Won't ...'," Prafulladatta Goswami, trans., Indian Literature, XI (April-July 1968), 37-42.

883 Bharadwaja, Ravoori. "The Heirs of Circumstances,"

K. Vixwanadham, trans., Triveni, XXXIV (July 1965), 63-74.

884 Bhattacharya, Bhabani. "The Baleful Planet," Eastern Horizon, VI (October 1967), 62-64.

885 ______. "The Faltering Pendulum," Hemisphere, X (March 1966), 17-19.

886 ______. "Glory at Twilight," Eastern Horizon, V (August 1966), 54-60.

887 ______. "Image of 1943/The Boat-wreckers," Eastern Horizon, V (April 1966), 51-55.

888 ______. "Image of 1943/A Fistful of Figs," Eastern Horizon, V (April 1966), 55-57.

889 ______. "Image of 1943/No Human Feeling!" Eastern Horizon, V (April 1966), 57-59.

890 ______. "Latest Design," Eastern Horizon, VI (January 1967), 59-62.

891 ______. "My Brave Great-Uncle," Hemisphere, XIII (February 1969), 34-36.

892 ______. "Public Figure," Hemisphere, XII (March 1968), 30-32.

893 Bhattacharya, Swarnkamal. "'Khoka' Goes to School," N. R. Deobhankar, adapt., Avenues, I (May 1968), 20-25.

894 Bialik, Chayim Nachman. "The Destruction," Michael Harari, trans., Adam International Review, nos. 325-327 (1968), 55.

895 Bianciardi, Luciano. "The Same Old Soup," Melton Davis, trans., Evergreen Review, XII (June 1968), 17-21, 74-75.

896 Bibb, Louise. "The Doll," The Archive, LXXIX (May 1967), 9-11.

897 ______. "Remembering Aunt Lucy," The Archive, LXXIX (April 1967), 17-22.

898 Bice, C. E. "The Collected Lyrics of Tenient e Robles," University Review, XXXIII (October 1966), 61-66.

899 Bichsel, Peter. "The Animal-Lover," Michael Hamburger, trans., Queen, CDXXX (May 22, 1968), 41.

900 ______. "The Game of Cards," Michael Hamburger, trans., Queen, CDXXX (May 22, 1968), 41.

901 ______. "Really Frau Blum Would Like to Get to Know the

Milkman/The Daughter," Michael Hamburger, trans., Audience, Pilot Issue (Spring 1968), 88.

902 _____. "Really Frau Blum Would Like to Get to Know the Milkman/Herr Gigon," Michael Hamburger, trans., Audience, Pilot Issue (Spring 1968), 87.

903 _____. "Really Frau Blum Would Like to Get to Know the Milkman/The Knife," Michael Hamburger, trans., Audience, Pilot Issue (Spring 1968), 85.

904 _____. "Really Frau Blum Would Like to Get to Know the Milkman/The Lions," Michael Hamburger, trans., Audience, Pilot Issue (Spring 1968), 89.

905 _____. "Really Frau Blum Would Like to Get to Know the Milkman/The Milkman," Michael Hamburger, trans., Audience, Pilot Issue (Spring 1968), 84.

906 _____. "Really Frau Blum Would Like to Get to Know the Milkman/Musical Boxes," Michael Hamburger, trans., Audience, Pilot Issue (Spring 1968), 86.

907 _____. "A Table Is a Table/A Children's Story," A. Leslie Willson, trans., Dimension, I, no. 2 (1968), 312-319 [in German and English on alternate pages].

908 _____. "Wood Shavings," Michael Hamburger, trans., Queen, CDXXX (May 22, 1968), 41.

909 Bieler, Manfred. "My Father's Birthday," Christopher Middleton, trans., Dimension, II, no. 3 (1969), 720-729 [in German and English on alternate pages].

910 _____. "Wedding March," Christopher Middleton, trans., Evergreen Review, X (April 1966), 54-55.

911 Bienek, Horst. "The Cell/Seven Excerpts from a Novel," Ursula Mahlendorf, trans., Unicorn Journal, no. 3 (1969), 74-96.

912 _____. "Voices in the Dark," Michael Bullock, trans., Contemporary Literature in Translation, no. 4 (Spring 1969), 22-26.

913 Bier, Jesse. "Indian Rug," Epoch, XIV (Winter 1965), 144-149.

914 _____. "The Whiskey Rebellion," Carleton Miscellany, VIII (Winter 1967), 48-63.

915 Bierds, Linda. "Footprints," Assay, XXV (Spring 1969), 43-52.

916 Bilbrough, Norman. "The Apprentice's Story," Landfall, no. 78

917 _____. "The Black Stick," New Zealand Listener, LIII (September 3, 1965), 8, 17.

918 Bill, Kenneth. "D. G.," Mother, no. 7 (Mother's Day, 1966), 70-71.

919 Bims, Hamilton. "United States Congressman," Negro Digest, XV (March 1966), 80-87.

920 Binding, Norman. "House in the Valley," Anglo-Welsh Review, XVIII, no. 41 (Summer 1969), 102-104.

921 Binford, Bonnie Wright. "A Silver Shroud for Grandma," Corral 1965, 41-51.

922 _____. "Thursday Born," Corral 1965, 27-39.

923 Bingham, Sallie. "Bare Bones," Radcliffe Quarterly, LI February-March 1967), 9-13.

924 _____. "Bare Bones," Redbook, CXXIV (March 1965), 52-53, 112, 114-116.

925 _____. "The New Place," Transatlantic Review, no. 18 (Spring 1965), 60-69.

926 Bingham, Samuel. "Epitaph for Lewis Green of Jackson County," Yale Literary Magazine, CXXXVI (September 1967), 16-19.

927 _____. "The Heart's Blood," Yale Literary Magazine, CXXXIV, (March 1966), 14-20.

928 Binney, James. "A Modern Little View," Kansas Magazine, (1965), 1-5.

929 _____. "Night of Love," University Review, XXXV (Autumn 1968), 75-80.

930 _____. "Visitor," Arizona Quarterly, XXV (Summer 1969), 157-168.

931 Birkás, Endre. "The Dog," New Hungarian Quarterly, IX (Summer 1968), 104-113.

932 Birkett, John, "How I Spent 4 Days of My Summer Vacation by Esther Williams Johnson," Twigs, no. 5 (Fall 1969), 59-81.

933 _____. "Misdemeanors Don't Count," Red Clay Reader, no. (June 1966), 134-142.

4 (1967), 40-44.

934 Birstein, Ann. "'Young and You're Nervous'," Vogue, CXLVII (March 15, 1966), 124-125, 159.

935 Biryukov, Nikolai. "Through Whirlwinds of Hostility," Tom Botting, trans., Soviet Literature, (no. 2, 1966), 118-141.

936 Bischoff, Friedrich. "Sit, Jessica," George Raymond Selden, trans., Scala International, (May 1965), 32-36.

937 Bishop, Christopher. "A Point of Navigation," Sewanee Review, LXXVI (October-December 1968), 597-607.

938 Bishop, Glade M. "Rain ... Dust," Prairie Schooner, XLI (Summer 1967), 244-245.

939 Bittle, Camilla. "A Divorce for Rob Phillips," Good Housekeeping, CLXIV (February 1967), 76-77, 129, 131-135.

940 _____. "The Scent of Roses," Good Housekeeping, CLXIII (September 1966), 90-91, 148-150, 152.

941 _____. "The Survivor," Redbook, CXXXII (December 1968), 147-169.

942 Bitts, Jerry A. "The Teachers' Party," Trace, no. 67 (1968), 90-96.

943 Biyani, Brijlal. "Nartaki," R. C. Gupta, trans., Triveni, XXXIV (October 1965), 25-29.

944 Björneboe, Jens. "Moment of Freedom," John Weinstock, trans., Literary Review, XII (Winter 1968-69), 197-202.

945 Black, Kyra. "Incommunicado," Literary Review, XI (Spring 1968), 373-390.

946 Blackburn, Mark. "Two Stories/The Bricks in Brooklyn," Carolina Quarterly, XIX (Winter 1967), 60-63.

947 _____. "Two Stories/A Fit Morning in," Carolina Quarterly, XIX (Winter 1967), 58-59.

948 _____. "Two Stories/Under the Table with Alice," Carolina Quarterly, XIX (Fall 1967), 64-66.

949 _____. "Two Stories/Weatherman," Carolina Quarterly, XIX (Fall 1967), 62-64.

950 Blackburn, Paul. "Translations from the Provençal of Bertran de Born," Works, II (Fall/Winter 1969), 32-44, 46-57.

951 Blackburn, Sara. "Mrdr'd in Full Kitch., Acc. to Grdn," New Yorker, XLIII (November 25, 1967), 205-207.

952 _____. "Taxi!" New Yorker, XLIV (February 8, 1969), 102-104.

953 Blackburn, Thomas. "Patronized by Royalty," London Magazine, VI (March 1967), 19-28.

954 Blais, Marie-Claire. "A Season in the Life of Emmanuel," Derek Coltman, trans., Tamarack Review, no. 39 (Spring 1966), 6-14.

955 Blaise, Clark L. "Burning Man," Minnesota Review, VII (1967), 133-141.

956 _____. "Extractions and Contractions," Tri-Quarterly, no. 16 (Fall 1969), 125-135.

957 _____. "The Mayor," Tamarack Review, no. 42 (Winter 1967), 14-32.

958 _____. "Notes Beyond a History," Shenandoah, XIX (Autumn 1967), 3-15.

959 _____. "Relief," Shenandoah, XVII (Autumn 1965), 82-92.

960 _____. "A Scholar's Work Speaks for Itself," Colorado Quarterly, XIV (Summer 1965), 41-47.

961 _____. "Thibidault et Fils," Prism International, V (Winter-Spring 1966), 26-42.

962 Blake, George. "'As It Appears in Translation'," Prism International, VI (Autumn 1966), 108-112.

963 _____. "'Dear Mr. President'," Canadian Forum, XLVI (February 1967), 255-256.

964 _____. "The Heart-Line," December, VIII (1966), 145-151.

965 _____. "I Now Pronounce You," Aspects, no. 8 (October 1966), 2-5.

966 _____. "Man in a Movement," Canadian Forum, XLVII (December 1967), 207-209.

967 _____. "A Modern Development," Kansas Quarterly, I (Winter 1968), 9-16.

968 _____. "A Place Not on the Map," Literary Review, IX (Summer 1966), 564-574.

969 _____. "A Resemblance to Butterflies," Canadian Forum, XLV (October 1965), 155-156.

970 Blake, Ian. "The Spring Game," Dublin Magazine, V (Autumn/ Winter 1966), 62-73.

Blake, Nicholas. See C. Day Lewis

971 Blakely, Roger. "The Stag at Eve," Minnesota Review, IX (1969), 143-147.

972 _____. "Wooden Feet," Minnesota Review, VIII (1968), 3-6.

973 Blakeston, Oswell. "There's Candy Still to Go with It," Ambit, no. 32 (1967), 32-34.

974 Blakiston, Noel. "The Funeral," Cornhill Magazine, no. 1043 (Spring 1965), 322-334.

975 _____. "The Regans," Cornhill Magazine, CLXXVII (Summer 1969), 323-331.

976 Blanchard, Lucile. "Like Clockwork," Cimarron Review, no. 8 (June 1969), 70-75.

977 _____. "Scavenger," Antioch Review, XXVII (Summer 1967), 249-259.

978 Blankenship, W. D. "Troubadour," Statement, no. 21 (Spring 1965), 3-6.

979 Blei, Norbert. "At the Counter," Aspects, no. 11 (April 1968), 8-11.

980 _____. "The Basement," Minnesota Review, VII (1967), 199-207.

981 _____. "Deathbed," Arx, III (September 1969), 26-27.

982 _____. "The Hour of the Sunshine Now," Minnesota Review, VIII (1968), 99-116.

983 _____. "The Letter Carrier," Trace, no. 67 (1968), 97-105.

984 _____. "The Old Woman's Preserves," December, IX (1967), 21-25.

985 _____. "The White Balloon," Midwestern University Quarterly, II, no. 4 (1967), 49-54.

986 Bleibtreau, John N. "Resurrection," Ararat, VIII (Autumn 1967), 65-71.

987 Block, Libbie. "The Fourth Sarah," Redbook, CXXVI (March 1966), 58-59, 124-128, 130.

988 _____. "Where Did All the Flowers Go?" McCall's, XCII (March 1965), 90-91, 189-192.

989 Bloom, Theodore. "A Four-Day Wait," Quarterly Review of Literature, XIV (1967), 261-268.

990 _____. "Road-Runner," Transatlantic Review, no. 23 (Winter 1966-67), 86-94.

991 Bloomfield, Mitchell. "Auction on Lincoln Street," Red Cedar Review, VI (May 1968), 33-47.

992 Blosten, Louise. "No Sweat," Ave Maria, CIV (December 31, 1966), 27-28.

993 Bluestone, George. "Racoon in the Zinnia Bed," Northwest Review, IX (Fall-Winter 1967-68), 78-95.

994 Bluitt, Ben. "Bus No. 51," Negro Digest, XV (May 1966), 73-75.

995 _____. "Gift," Negro Digest, XIV (May 1965), 53-55.

996 Blum, Ralph. "The Carp," New Yorker, XL (February 6, 1965), 30-36.

997 _____. "In Thursday Country," Mademoiselle, LXVI (March 1968), 170-171, 220-224.

998 Blyth, Myrna. "Baby's Home," Redbook, CXXXI (August 1968), 50, 52.

999 _____. "The Company of Women," Redbook, CXXX (March 1968), 70-71, 121, 123, 125.

1000 _____. "Do You Remember, James Dean?" McCall's, XCV (September 1968), 70-71, 139-142.

1001 _____. "An Irresistible Case of Motherhood," Redbook, CXXXII (November 1968), 88-89.

1002 _____. "The Lovers," Redbook, CXXVIII (November 1966), 64-65, 141-142, 144.

1003 _____. "No One But Me," Redbook, CXXVI (March 1966), 66-67, 121-123.

1004 _____. "A Tall and Fascinating Stranger," Redbook, CXXIX (July 1967), 78-79, 123, 126-128.

1005 _____. "The Wife-Eater," Cosmopolitan, CLXVII (October 1969), 158-163.

1006 Bobrowski, Johannes. "Two Stories/Owlet," Ruth and Matthew Mead, trans., Art and Literature, no. 8 (Spring 1966), 210-211.

1007 _____. "Two Stories/Tansy," Ruth and Matthew Mead, trans., Art and Literature, no. 8 (Spring 1966), 206-209.

1008 Bochénski, Jacek. "Tabu," Marcus Wheeler, trans., Tri-Quarterly, no. 9 (Spring 1967), 79-103.

1009 Bocock, Maclin. "The Journey," Denver Quarterly, II (Autumn 1967), 71-80.

1010 Bode, Elroy. "End of Spring," Redbook, CXXXI (May 1968), 70-71, 134-135.

1011 _____. "How Will I Know My True Love?" Redbook, CXXIX (August 1967), 36-37.

1012 _____. "Life and Harry Burns," South Dakota Review, IV (Autumn 1966), 28-40.

1013 _____. "A Visit Home," Redbook, CXXV (August 1965), 48-49.

1014 Bode, Winston. "Back Home," Southwest Review, LI (Autumn 1966), 361-370.

1015 _____. "Summer Skies," Southwest Review, LI (Winter 1966), 87-93.

1016 Body, Andrew. "Security," Courier, XLIV (May 1965), 64-68.

1017 Boetie, Dugmore. "Three Cons/From a novel to be published," The Classic, II, no. 4 (1968), 26-37.

1018 Boewe, Charles. "Elton's Flight from Reality," Vision, XIV (March 1965), 17-22.

1019 _____. "Parallax of Time," Vision, XIV (September-October 1965), 9-11, 22.

1020 Bogomolov, Vladimir. "First Love," Soviet Literature, (no. 4, 1967), 182-184.

1021 _____. "Zosia," Eve Manning and Tom Botting, trans., Soviet Literature, (no. 2, 1966), 3-43.

1022 Boissonneau, Alice. "John," Alphabet, no. 14 (December 1967), 66-80.

1023 Boles, Paul Darcy. "The Animal Kingdom," Seventeen, XXV (October 1966), 148-149, 195-199.

1024 ______. "April Trombone," Seventeen, XXVI (April 1967), 160-161, 233-235.

1025 ______. "The Big Beast," Saturday Evening Post, CCXXXVIII (August 14, 1965), 48-51.

1026 ______. "The Girl at the Plaza," Seventeen, XXVII (September 1968), 132-133, 228, 230-231.

1027 ______. "The Holiday Rider," Seventeen, XXVII (December 1968), 96-97, 174-176.

1028 ______. "A Million Guitars," Seventeen, XXVI (October 1967), 134-135, 166-168.

1029 ______. "Miss Rose," Seventeen, XXVIII (August 1969), 326-327, 457-461.

1030 ______. "The Most Beautiful Race in the World," Playboy, XII (August 1965), 56-58, 60, 66, 154.

1031 ______. "The Night Watch," Seventeen, XXIV (April 1965), 160, 248-253.

1032 ______. "The Running of the Deer," Seventeen, XXIV (July 1965), 86-87, 134-137.

1033 ______. "The Somewhere Music," Seventeen, XXVI (July 1967), 82-83, 128-129.

1034 ______. "Swinger," Seventeen, XXV (May 1966), 180-181, 264, 266-269.

1035 ______. "The Telephone Artist," McCall's, XCVI (November 1968), 102-103, 142-144.

1036 ______. "Today Is My Sister's Wedding," Good Housekeeping, CLXIX (October 1969), 110-111, 190, 192-196.

1037 ______. "A Verray Parfit Gentil Knight," Seventeen, XXV (September 1966), 182-183, 259-262.

1038 Bolger, Margaret. "Pride Is Put in a Cradle," Plaintiff, IV (Fall-Winter 1967-68), 45-46.

1039 Bolitho, Hector. "The Twist of the Knife," Texas Quarterly, X (Summer 1967), 186-192.

1040 Böll, Heinrich. "The Adventure," Leila Vennewitz, trans., Harper's Bazaar, XCVIII (October 1965), 216, 290-291.

1041 _____. "The Church in the Village," Leila Vennewitz, trans., Delos, no. 2 (1968), 132-152.

1042 _____. "Like a Bad Dream," Leila Vennewitz, trans., Harper's Magazine, CCXXXI (October 1965), 61-64.

1043 _____. "No Tears for Schmeck," Leila Vennewitz, trans., Encounter, XXXII (May 1969), 3-13.

1044 _____. "Pale Anna," Michael Bullock, trans., Mundus Artium, I (Spring 1968), 42-51 [in German and English on alternate pages].

1045 _____. "Peace," Leila Vennewitz, trans., Saturday Evening Post, CCXXXVIII (August 28, 1965), 50-57.

1046 _____. "The Secret of the Box," Leila Vennewitz, trans., Saturday Evening Post, CCXXXVIII (July 17, 1965), 60-63.

1047 _____. "So Ward Abend und Morgen," J. Bennett Jr. and Abraham van der Meulen, trans., Vagabond, I (January-March 1966), 10-19 [in German and English on alternate pages].

1048 _____. "The Thrower Away," Leila Vennewitz, trans., Harper's Bazaar, XCIX (August 1966), 114-115, 179.

1049 Bollock, Shirley. "The Brief, Wonderful Blossoming of Gertrude Silverman," Per/Se, III (Winter 1968/69), 32-36.

1050 _____. "Seretta Glassman's Wild Heart," Prairie Schooner, XLII (Spring 1968), 35-43.

1051 Bolton, Muriel Roy. "Drop in Any Mailbox," Ladies' Home Journal, LXXXVI (May 1969), 108-109, 163-164.

1052 Bonazzi, Robert. "Cowper and the Sun Rising," Minnesota Review, IX (1969), 42-43.

1053 _____. "Light Casualties," Transatlantic Review, no. 28 (Spring 1968), 46-51.

1054 _____. "The Man Who Painted Christmas Trees," Arx, II (November 1968), 8-12.

1055 _____. "Straw Purse Filled with Ice, Dripping," Work, no. 4 (Summer/Fall/Winter 1966), 77-79.

1056 _____. "Under the Dome," Minnesota Review, IX (1969), 40-41.

1057 Bond, George L. "The Human Preying Mantis Case," Tropix, I (January 1966), 43-46.

1058 _____. "The Human Preying Mantis Case [Part II]," Tropix, I, no. 2 (1966), 35-39, 77.

1059 _____. "The Human Preying Mantis Case [Part III]," Tropix, I, no. 3 (1966), 36-38, 40.

1060 _____. "The Human Preying Mantis Case [Part IV]," Tropix, I, no. 4 (1966), 68-73.

1061 _____. "The Human Preying Mantis Case [Part V]," Tropix, I, no. 5 (1966), 75-80.

1062 _____. "The Human Preying Mantis Case [Part VI]," Tropix, II, no. 1 (1967), 71-76.

1063 _____. "The Human Preying Mantis Case [Conclusion]," Tropix, II, no. 2 (1967), 29-37.

1064 Bond, Ruskin. "Panther's Moon," Imprint, IX (December 1969), 128, 131, 133, 135, 139, 141, 143, 145, 149, 151, 153, 155, 157, 159-160.

1065 Bondarenko, W. C. "The Big Pencil," New Directions 19 (1966), 254-256.

1066 _____. "Candy Fever," Ball State University Forum, VII (Winter 1966), 70-71.

1067 _____. "Candy Fever," Dust, I (Winter 1965), 77-79.

1068 _____. "The Great Talker," Midwestern University Quarterly, I, no. 4 (1966), 111-113.

1069 _____. "A Job Well Done," Nexus (San Francisco, Calif.), II (May-June 1965), 33-38.

1070 _____. "Knots Untied," Ball State Teachers College Forum, VI (Winter 1965), 54-59.

1071 _____. "Knots Untied," New Directions 19 (1966), 257-259.

1072 _____. "Op-Choo," Edge, no. 6 (Spring 1967), 61-64.

1073 _____. "The Pea-Shooters," Aspects, no. 6 (January 1965), 11-13.

1074 _____. "The Pea-Shooters," Midwestern University Quarterly, I, no. 3 (1966), 33-35.

1075 _____. "A Summer Rose," Edge, no. 6 (Spring 1967), 65-66.

1076 Bonellie, Janet. "Why Are the People Staring?" Tamarack

Review, no. 44 (Summer 1967), 13-31.

1077 _____. "Why Are the People Staring? (Two)," Tamarack Review, no. 48 (Summer 1968), 15-24.

1078 _____. "Why Are the People Staring? (Three)," Tamarack Review, no. 48 (Summer 1968), 45-56.

1079 Bongartz, Roy. "I Can Always Stop," Esquire, LXVI (December 1966), 201, 336.

1080 _____. "The Steel Ball," Saturday Evening Post, CCXXXVIII (January 16, 1965), 60-62, 64-65.

1081 _____. "The Whoo-ee Egg," Transatlantic Review, no. 23 (Winter 1966-67), 56-70.

1082 Bonham, Margaret. "Wish For An Afternoon," Good Housekeeping, CLXV (August 1967), 62-65.

1083 Bonnet, Leslie. "The Best-Kept Village," Old Lady of Threadneedle Street, XLII (June 1966), 74-78.

1084 _____. "Brace of Pheasants," Old Lady of Threadneedle Street, XLV (December 1969), 226-231.

1085 _____. "In Bed with a Rat Goblin," Old Lady of Threadneedle Street, XLI (June 1965), 92-96.

1086 _____. "One Tiger Was Riderless," Old Lady of Threadneedle Street, XLIII (June 1967), 84-85.

1087 Bontempelli, Massimo. "The Ten O'Clock," W. L. Dale, trans., Cornhill Magazine, no. 1044 (Summer 1965), 375-382.

1088 Boode, Clint. "The Bastard," December, IX (1967), 193-194.

1089 _____. "Funny that Way," Illuminations, no. 3 (Summer 1967), 14.

1090 _____. "Some People: A Fable," Quartet, no. 16 (Fall 1966), 19-20.

1091 Boon, Louis Paul. "The Bird of Paradise," James S. Holmes and Hans van Marle, trans., Delta (Amsterdam), X (Spring/Summer 1967), 94-97.

1092 Booth, Luella. "Man in the Mirror," The Fiddlehead, no. 66 (Fall 1965), 28-35.

1093 Borchers, Elisabeth. "Murder or This Story Is No Proof," James A. Hayes, trans., Dimension, II, no. 2 (1969), 452-

459 [in German and English on alternate pages].

1094 Borenstein, A. Farrell. "A Fragment of Glass," Arlington Quarterly, I (Autumn 1967), 75-83.

1095 _____. "An Heir for Horowitz," North American Review, II (Spring 1965), 45-50.

1096 _____. "The Natural History of a Friendship," Nimrod, XI (Winter 1967), 5-27.

1097 _____. "Parting Gift," University Review, XXXII (June 1966), 268-274.

1098 Borenstein, Walter. "The Dark Gods of Healing," Maguey, no. 2 (Autumn 1968), 12-24 [in English and Spanish on alternate pages].

1099 _____. "The Other Cheek," Phylon, XXVII (Summer 1966), 180-187.

1100 Borgen, Johan. "The Honeysuckle Vine," Mary Kay Norseng and Faith Ingwersen, trans., Literary Review, XII (Winter 1968-69), 180-187.

1101 _____. "The Swan," Miranda Cavanagh, trans., American Scandinavian Review, LV (June 1967), 170-177.

1102 Borges, Jorge Luis. "Everything and Nothing," Donald A. Yates, trans. [in "The 'Microtale': An Argentine Specialty," by Donald A. Yates], Texas Quarterly, XII (Summer 1969), 17-18.

1103 _____ and Margarita Guerrero. "Imaginary Beings," Thomas di Giovanni, Jorge Luis Borges and Margarita Guerrero, trans., New Yorker, XLV (October 4, 1969), 39-46.

1104 _____. "The Implausible Imposter Tom Castro," James E. Irby, trans., Quarterly Review of Literature, XV (1968), 231-237.

1105 _____. "The Intruder," Donald A. Yates, trans., Atlantic Monthly, CCXXII (October 1968), 78-80.

1106 _____. "The Intruder," Alastair Reid, trans., Encounter, XXXII (April 1969), 15-17.

1107 _____. "The Intruder," Ronald Christ and Paschal Cantatore, trans., Tri-Quarterly, nos. 13/14 (Fall/Winter 1968-69), 224-228.

1108 _____. "The Masked Dyer Hakim of Merv," James E. Irby, trans., Quarterly Review of Literature, XV (1968), 238-242.

1109 ______. "The Other Death," Thomas di Giovanni and Jorge Luis Borges, trans., Encounter, XXXII (April 1969), 32-35.

1110 ______. "The Other Death," Thomas di Giovanni, trans., New Yorker, XLIV (November 2, 1968), 52-55.

1111 ______. "Three Stories/I-Biography of Tadeo Isidoro Cruz (1829-74)," Anthony Kerrigan, trans., New Yorker, XLII (January 7, 1967), 23-24.

1112 ______. "Three Stories/II-The Dead Man," Anthony Kerrigan, trans., New Yorker, XLII (January 7, 1967), 24-27.

1113 ______. "Three Stories/III-The Aleph," Anthony Kerrigan, trans., New Yorker, XLII (January 7, 1967), 27-33.

1114 ______. "A Vindication of the Cabala," L. A. Murillo, trans., Gnomon, no. 2 (1967), 23-26.

1115 ______. "A Vindication of the Counterfeit Basilides," Anthony Kerrigan, trans., Transatlantic Review, no. 27 (Winter 1967-68), 14-17.

1116 Borgese, Elisabeth Mann. "Insan Adam," Unicorn Journal, no. 1 (1968), 18-25.

1117 ______. "The Mongol," New Directions 19 (1966), 175-190.

1118 Borneman, Ernest. "Cable from Mr. Menzies," Playboy, XV (March 1968), 75, 78, 171-172, 174-178.

1119 Borowski, Tadeusz. "The People Who Walked," Miwa Zielinski, trans., Commentary, XLIII (February 1967), 65-69.

1120 Boscardin, Kathy. "The Breaking Point," Grecourt Review, XI (May 1968), 35-38.

1121 Bosker, Noel. "Guest Speaker," New Zealand Listener, LIV (April 22, 1966), 6.

1122 Bosse, M. J. "The Boy Who Loved Shakespeare," North American Review, III (November 1966), 16-19.

1123 Boston, Bruce. "Carmichal and the City," Occident, III (Spring/Summer 1969), 77-88.

1124 Bostwick, Sally. "The Animal Boy," Ave Maria, CII (August 21, 1965), 22-25, 27.

1125 ______. "Marcus," Ave Maria, CI (May 22, 1965), 22-25.

1126 ______. "My Aunt's Harmonica," Ave Maria, CII (November 27, 1965), 24-26.

1127 _____. "The Princess with the Gold Teeth," Ave Maria, CII (October 2, 1965), 22-25.

1128 _____. "Send Me No Zithers," Ave Maria, CII (October 30, 1965), 22-25.

1129 _____. "Young Ladies of Virtue," Ave Maria, CI (March 20, 1965), 18-22.

1130 Botsford, Keith. "A Member of the Delegation," Paris Review, XII (Summer 1969), 63-82.

1131 Boughton, Anna. "The Arrangement," McCall's, XCIV (February 1967), 94-95, 176-180.

1132 Boughton, Audrey A. "The Visitor," Saturday Evening Post, CCXXXVIII (July 3, 1965), 66-67, 70-71.

1133 Bourgoyne, J. E. "Jules, Patrice, and Me," Delta, XXII (1968), 40-45.

1134 _____. "Sculpture without Leaves," Delta, XX (1966), 13-14.

1135 Bourjaily, Vance. "In the Summer of the Valve Trombone/ from The Man Who Knew Kennedy," Ladies' Home Journal, LXXXIV (February 1967), 93-98, 147-148.

1136 _____. "A Lover's Mask," Saturday Evening Post, CCXL (May 6, 1967), 84-86, 88, 90.

1137 Bourne, St. Clair T. "Authority by Pigmentation," Southwest Review, L (Autumn 1965), 378-387.

1138 Bovasso, Julie. "Out of the Mouths of Minstrels," Status, II (March 1966), 30-33, 85-86.

1139 Bowell, Don. "February," Quarry, XV (September 1965), 35-42.

1140 Bowen, Robert O. "The Minuteman," Prism International, V (Summer 1965), 36-47.

1141 _____. "Recognition," Wascana Review, I, no. 1 (1966), 15-22.

1142 Bowen, Russell. "The Sacred Rite of the New Year," Readers & Writers, I (January-February 1967), 23-25.

1143 Bowering, George. "Ebbe & Hattie," Quarry, XVIX (Fall 1969), 11-21.

1144 _____. "The Elevator," Tamarack Review, no. 40 (Summer 1966), 21-29.

1145 _____. "Flycatcher," The Fiddlehead, no. 64 (Spring 1965), 30-36.

1146 _____. "The Gamin on the Island Ferry," Queen's Quarterly, LXXII (Summer 1965), 347-354.

1147 _____. "The Hayfield," Dalhousie Review, XLV (Summer 1965), 182-188.

1148 _____. "The House on Tenth," Canadian Forum, XLV (March 1966), 275-278.

1149 _____. "Looking for Ebbe," The Fiddlehead, no. 72 (Summer 1967), 6-18.

1150 _____. "Ricardo and the Flower," West Coast Review, II (Winter 1968), 12-21.

1151 _____. "Time and Again," Quarry, XV (November 1965), 7-14.

1152 _____. "Two Grave News Stories/The Deputy Sheriff," Edge, no. 5 (Fall 1966), 69-71.

1153 _____. "Two Grave News Stories/The Towers," Edge, no. 5 (Fall 1966), 68-69.

1154 _____. "The Valley," Parallel, II (June-July 1967), 42-45.

1155 _____. "The White Coffin," Quarry, XVII (Fall 1967), 16-30.

1156 Bowers, Ed. "Bells," Work, no. 5 (1968), 23-25.

1157 Bowes, Barry and Adrian Henri. "Biography," Ambit, no. 26 (1965/66), 6-15.

1158 _____. "The Various Solitudes," Ambit, no. 24 (1965), 19-21.

1159 Bowler, Christine. "Between the Broken Glass the People Play," New Writers, no. 8 (1968), 7-42.

1160 Bowles, Jane. "Everything Is Nice," London Magazine, VI (June 1966), 5-11.

1161 _____. "Two Serious Ladies," Queen, CDXXIII (January 27, 1965), 38-41, 68.

1162 Bowles, Jerry. "The War and Pvt. Miller," Appalachian Review, I (Spring 1967), 32-35.

1163 Bowles, Paul. "Pages from Cold Point," Nova, (April 1968), 132-133, 135, 137, 139, 141.

1164 ______. "The Spring," trans. from Mohammed Mrabet, Transatlantic Review, no. 21 (Summer 1966), 53-57.

1165 Bowness, Charles. "When the Circus Came," Courier, XLIV (April 1965), 44-46.

1166 Boyars, Marion. "Last Exit to Wonderland," Twentieth Century, CLXXVI (1967/68), 46-47.

1167 Boyd, Catherine. "An Endless Chain," Redbook, CXXIV (March 1965), 68-69.

1168 ______. "In the Face of Life," McCall's, XCII (May 1965), 96-97, 174, 178-179.

1169 ______. "The More the Merrier," Redbook, CXXVI (December 1965), 44-45, 141-142, 144-145.

1170 Boyd, John. "The Air Gun," Threshold, no. 20 (Winter 1966/67), 5-21.

1171 Boyd, Martin. "Expatriates Dine," Meanjin Quarterly, XXVIII (Winter 1969), 173-176.

1172 Boyd, Sue Abbott. "Second Comings," Dust, III (Fall 1967), 37-38.

1173 Boyd, Susan Kuehn. "Encounter with a Stranger," Redbook, CXXIV (April 1965), 70-71, 128-130.

1174 Boyle, Kay. "Fire in the Vineyards," Saturday Evening Post, CCXXXIX (July 2, 1966), 76-77, 79-81.

1175 ______. "One Sunny Morning," Saturday Evening Post, CCXXXVIII (July 3, 1965), 60-62, 64.

1176 ______. "One Sunny Morning," Solidarity, I (April-June 1966), 98-102.

1177 ______. "The Wild Horses," Saturday Evening Post, CCXXXIX (April 9, 1966), 60-65.

1178 Boyle, Patrick. "The Betrayers," Sewanee Review, LXXIII (April-June 1965), 239-280.

1179 ______. "Blessed Are the Meek," Dublin Magazine, VII (Spring 1968), 29-37.

1180 ______. "Dialogue," Queen, CDXXIX (September 1, 1969), 42-44.

1181 ______. "The Pishogue," Dublin Magazine, IV (Summer 1965), 56-62.

1182 ______. "Rise Up, My Love, and Come Away," Queen, CDXXVIII (January 18, 1967), 28-30.

1183 ______. "Sally," Threshold, no. 22 (Summer 1969), 8-24.

1184 ______. "Shaybo," Evergreen Review, XI (February 1967), 21-23, 106, 108.

1185 Bracho, Diana. "Improvisations," Quarterly, LXIII, no. 1 (1966), 20-22.

1186 Brackenridge, Judge Hugh Henry. "The Trial of Mamachtaga, a Delaware Indian, the First Person Convicted of Murder West of the Alleghany Mountains, and Hanged for His Crime," Whe're, no. 1 (Summer 1966), 1-6.

1187 Brackett, Leigh. "The True Death of Juanito Rodriguez," Cosmopolitan, CLVIII (February 1965), 98, 101-102.

1188 Brackman, Jacob. "Dance with a Stranger," Playboy, XIV (December 1967), 208-210, 301-302, 304-306, 308-309.

1189 ______. "In New York, I Only Shoot Straight," Ramparts, V (February 1967), 47-50.

1190 Bradbury, Malcolm. "The Adult Education Class," Transatlantic Review, no. 21 (Summer 1966), 59-67.

1191 ______. "Dodos among the Elephants," Transatlantic Review, no. 29 (Summer 1968), 5-9.

1192 ______. "Fritz," Transatlantic Review, no. 18 (Spring 1965), 13-18.

1193 Bradbury, Ray. "The Beautiful One Is Here!" McCall's, XCVI (August 1969), 62-63, 114-120.

1194 ______. "The Best of Times," McCall's, XCIII (December 1966), 60-63, 121-123.

1195 ______. "Downwind from Gettysburg," Playboy, XVI (June 1969), 98-100, 110, 112, 241.

1196 ______. "The Lost City of Mars," Playboy, XIV (January 1967), 86-90, 92, 260, 262-264, 266-267.

1197 ______. "The Man in the Rorschach Shirt," Playboy, XIII (October 1966), 82-84, 92, 210-211.

1198 ______. "The Year the Glop-Monster Won the Golden Lion at Cannes," Cavalier, XVI (July 1966), 26-28, 88-91.

1199 Bradford, James C. "The Youngest Wise Man," Ave Maria,

CII (December 25, 1965), 22-26.

1200 Bradley, Ardyth. "The Gift," Quarterly Review of Literature, XV (1968), 243-254.

1201 Bradley, Nicholas H. "Eddy Freeman," Red Cedar Review, IV (Spring 1966), 5-8.

1202 Bradshaw, George. "The Gay Hearts," Saturday Evening Post, CCXXXIX (August 27, 1966), 62-67.

1203 ______. "The Privileged Class," Saturday Evening Post, CCXXXIX (December 3, 1966), 74-76, 79-80, 82-83.

1204 Bradshaw, Graham. "The Ladybird," Old Lady of Threadneedle Street, XLV (September 1969), 166-167.

1205 Brady, Bruce. "Daniel Was a Bulldog," Delta Review, VI (June 1969), 38-41.

1206 Bragdon, David. "Footnote to a Crusade," Approach, no. 59 (Spring 1966), 9-16.

1207 Brainard, Joe. "Alice," Art and Literature, no. 11 (Winter 1967), 82-83.

1208 ______. "Aug. 29, 1967," Angel Hair, no. 5 (Spring 1968), n.p. [45-46].

1209 ______. "The China Sea," The World, no. 10 (February 1968), n.p. [47].

1210 ______. "January 26th, 1967," The World, no. 4 (June 1967), n.p. [41].

1211 ______. "Life," The Once Series, (Nice), I (1966-67), n.p. [1].

1212 ______. "Pat," The World, no. 4 (June 1967), n.p. [41].

1213 ______. "Polly," Lines, no. 3 (February 1965), 8.

1214 ______. "Sunday, July the 30th, 1964," Kulcher, no. 18 (Summer 1965), 56-58.

1215 ______. "Sunday, July the 30th, 1964," Lines, no. 3 (February 1965), 47-49.

1216 Brand, Peter. "Bobby Shaftoe," Carleton Miscellany, VI (Winter 1965), 90-99.

1217 Branda, Eldon. "The Dark Days of Christmas," Texas Quarterly, IX (Summer 1966), 124-132.

1218 _____. "Death in New Orleans," Antioch Review, XXV (Summer 1965), 313-332.

1219 Brandys, Kazimierz. "Joker/(excerpts)," Edward Rothert, trans., Literary Review, X (Spring 1967), 361-364.

1220 Branner, H. C. "At the End of August," Victoria Nott, trans., American Scandinavian Review, LIV (September 1966), 281-287.

1221 Brannon, Michael. "Chastain on the X-Axis, Stebbins on the Y-Axis," Story: the Yearbook of Discovery, (1968), 67-74.

1222 Branson, Branley Allan. "The Elected," North Dakota Quarterly, XXXV (Autumn 1967), 104-113.

1223 Brashers, H. C. "Crack, Crash Orange Flare," South Dakota Review, V (Autumn 1967), 28-35.

1224 _____. "Growing Pains," Michigan Quarterly Review, VII (Summer 1968), 166-170.

1225 Brata, Sasthi. "In Search of a Wife," Cornhill Magazine, CLXXVI (Spring 1967), 30-41.

1226 _____. "Wake No False Dawn," Cornhill Magazine, no. 1054 (Winter 1967/68), 269-281.

1227 Braunstein, Elliott B. "Susie and the Imperial Mutant," Columbia, XLVIII (March 1968), 24-28.

1228 Brautigan, Richard. "The Armored Car," The Once Series, (Nice), I (1966-67), n. p. [8].

1229 _____. "A Complete Movie of Germany and Japan," Rolling Stone, no. 33 (May 17, 1969), 12.

1230 _____. "Crazy Old Women Are Riding the Buses of America Today," Rolling Stone, no. 24 (December 21, 1968), 24.

1231 _____. "Elmira," Rolling Stone, no. 30 (April 5, 1969), 8.

1232 _____. "Ernest Hemingway's Typist," Rolling Stone, no. 48 (December 13, 1969), 40.

1233 _____. "Fame in California," Rolling Stone, no. 24 (December 21, 1968), 24.

1234 _____. "Forgiven," Rolling Stone, no. 29 (March 15, 1969), 25.

1235 _____. "A High Building in Singapore," Rolling Stone, no. 48 (December 13, 1969), 40.

1236 ______. "I Was Trying to Describe You to Someone," Rolling Stone, no. 27 (February 15, 1969), 10.

1237 ______. "A Long Time Ago People Decided to Live in America," Rolling Stone, no. 34 (May 31, 1969), 37.

1238 ______. "Memory of a Girl," Rolling Stone, no. 39 (August 9, 1969), 37.

1239 ______. "A Need for Gardens," Rolling Stone, no. 24 (December 21, 1968), 24.

1240 ______. "1/3, 1/3, 1/3," Ramparts, VI (December 1967), 43-45.

1241 ______. "Pale Marble Movie," Rolling Stone, no. 42 (August 20, 1969), 25.

1242 ______. "A Short History of Religion in California," Rolling Stone, no. 37 (July 12, 1969), 37.

1243 ______. "Two Stories/Revenge of the Lawn," Tri-Quarterly, no. 5 (Winter 1966), 55-57.

1244 ______. "Two Stories/A Short History of Religion in California," Tri-Quarterly, no. 5 (Winter 1966), 58-59.

1245 ______. "The Weather in San Francisco," Vogue, CLIV (October 1, 1969), 126.

1246 ______. "What Are You Going to Do With 390 Photographs of Christmas Trees?" Evergreen Review, XII (December 1968), 24-26.

1247 ______. "The Wild Birds of Heaven," Parallel, I (July-August 1966), 10-12.

1248 Brawley, Ernest. "The Chicken," Story: the Yearbook of Discovery, (1968), 59-66.

1249 Braybrooke, Neville. "The Dead Nag," Ave Maria, CVII (February 10, 1968), 26-28.

1250 Brean, Herbert. "The Traces of Merrilee," Cosmopolitan, CLXI (September 1966), 122-132, 138-144, 146-153.

1251 Brecon, Hunter. "Kin," New Zealand Listener, (February 9, 1968), 6, 23.

1252 Bredin, Hugh. "The White Flower," Threshold, no. 22 (Summer 1969), 50-57.

1253 Bremser, Bonnie. "The Is Salvation," Spero, I, no. 2 (1966), 27-28.

1254 Bremson, Edward. "Bull of the Woods," Long View Journal, I (Spring 1969), 165-172.

1255 _____. "Mister Lackey," Long View Journal, I (Winter 1968), 93-97.

1256 Brennan, Christopher. "A Massacre of Innocents," Queen, CDXXVII (December 7, 1966), 77-79.

1257 Brennan, Maeve. "The Children Are There, Trying Not to Laugh," New Yorker, XLIII (January 13, 1968), 24-25.

1258 _____. "The Door on West Tenth Street," New Yorker, XLIII (October 7, 1967), 54-57.

1259 _____. "The Eldest Child," New Yorker, XLIV (June 29, 1968), 30-33.

1260 _____. "I See You, Bianca," New Yorker, XLII (June 11, 1966), 32-36.

1261 _____. "The Shadow of Kindness," New Yorker, XLI (August 14, 1965), 30-36.

1262 _____. "A Snowy Night on West Forty-ninth Street," New Yorker, XLII (January 21, 1967), 28-34.

1263 _____. "The Sofa," New Yorker, XLIV (March 2, 1968), 39-43.

1264 _____. "Stories of Africa," New Yorker, XLIV (August 10, 1968), 24-32.

1265 _____. "The Twelfth Wedding Anniversary," New Yorker, XLII (September 24, 1966), 60-66.

1266 Brent, P. L. "Ritual," Weekend Telegraph, no. 25 (March 12, 1965), 41, 43, 45.

1267 Brenton, Howard. "In the Garden," Solstice, no. 2 (1966), 4-10.

1268 Breslow, Paul. "Before the Operation," Transatlantic Review, no. 24 (Spring 1967), 105-114.

1269 _____. "Notes on Obtaining a Divorce from a Woman Who Is Fatally Ill," Transatlantic Review, no. 27 (Winter 1967-68), 134-137.

1270 Bretnor, R. "The Other Way," Riverside Quarterly, II (November 1966), 171-174.

1271 Breton, André. "The Jacques Vaché Story," Sandra Berrigan, trans., Mother, no. 4 (February-March 1965), 44-45.

1272 Brett, David. "Waiting for the Ferry," Cornhill Magazine, CLXXVI (Spring 1968), 359-365.

1273 Brett, Peter. "Blum's Moment," Overflow, II, no. 1 (1968), 9-12.

1274 Brewer, Robert. "Three Pots," Green River Review, I (November 1968), 46-48.

1275 Brewster, Elizabeth. "Between the Fall and the Flood," Canadian Forum, XLIX (June 1969), 68-71.

1276 _____. "Moving to Moss Lake," The Fiddlehead, no. 78 (January-February 1969), 15-22.

1277 _____. "Visiting Hours," Canadian Forum, XLV (August 1965), 107-109.

1278 Brewster, Harry C. "The Marquis and the Crocodile," Sewanee Review, LXXIII (October-December 1965), 535-586.

1279 _____. "Philomena," Sewanee Review, LXXIV (July-September 1966), 571-588.

1280 _____. "Sappho's Leap," Sewanee Review, LXXVI (July-September 1968), 382-414.

1281 _____. "Where the Trout Sing," Sewanee Review, LXXV (January-March 1967), 159-189.

1282 Breyten. "Expulsion," Montparnasse Review, no. 2 (1966), 30-31.

1283 _____. "The Fascist Pumpkin," Montparnasse Review, no. 2 (1966), 30.

1284 _____. "My Illusion," Montparnasse Review, no. 2 (1966), 31-32.

1285 Brian, Lee. "Changing of the Guard," Arx, III (July 1969), 8-12.

1286 _____. "The Debate Team," Midwestern University Quarterly, II, no. 1 (1966), 40-48.

1287 _____. "An Egregious Affair," Kansas Magazine, (1966), 29-35.

1288 _____. "An Interval of Mourning," North Dakota Quarterly, XXXVI (Summer 1968), 55-59.

1289 ______. "The Last Place," Husson Review, I (1968), 96-103.

1290 ______. "Young Harry," Arx, II (April 1969), 11-16.

1291 Bridges, Joan. "The Prisoner," Old Lady of Threadneedle Street, XLIV (March 1968), 18-21.

1292 ______. "Toile de Jouy," Cornhill Magazine, CLXXVII (Autumn 1969), 365-379.

1293 ______. "The Ward in Chancery," Old Lady of Threadneedle Street, XLV (September 1969), 154-159.

1294 Bridges, Thomas. "Music to Lay Eggs By," Transatlantic Review, no. 30 (Autumn 1968), 19-31.

1295 Briggs, William D. "You Gotta Go...," Nimrod, XIV (Fall 1969), n.p. [16-18].

1296 Brikman, S. "Up, Up and Away," Penthouse, I (December 1969), 104-106.

1297 Brill, Noah. "Sunday, May the Seventh," New Campus Review, II (Spring 1969), 43.

1298 Brillantes, Gregorio F. "Faith, Love, Time, and Dr. Lazaro," Literature East and West, IX (March 1965), 64-74.

1299 Briskin, Jacqueline. "The Captive," Seventeen, XXVI (February 1967), 148-149, 232, 234.

1300 ______. "How Will I Know?" Seventeen, XXVIII (April 1969), 178-179, 202, 204.

1301 ______. "Knight in Unshining Armor," Seventeen, XXVI (September 1967), 148-149, 251-254.

1302 ______. "Rimoftheworld," Seventeen, XXVII (August 1968), 238-239, 406, 408, 410-411.

1303 ______. "Saints, Zaddikim, and Fictional Characters," Southwest Review, LII (Summer 1967), 290-302.

1304 ______. "Tsunami," Seventeen, XXIV (July 1965), 108-109, 112, 114-115.

1305 Britting, Georg. "Cain," Peter Paul Fersch, trans., Mundus Artium, II (Spring 1969), 82-85 [in German and English on alternate pages].

1306 ______. "Dance of Death," Peter Paul Fersch, trans., Contemporary Literature in Translation, no. 2 (Fall 1968), 3-4.

1307 _____. "The Death of Don Quixote," Peter Paul Fersch, trans., Prism International, VII (Autumn 1967), 9-10.

1308 _____. "The Duel of Two Horses," Peter Paul Fersch, trans., Prism International, VII (Autumn 1967), 4-8.

1309 _____. "Madness," Peter Paul Fersch, trans., Contemporary Literature in Translation, no. 1 (1968), 4.

1310 _____. "Two Stories/The Feast of the Four Hundred," Peter Paul Fersch, trans., Prism International, IX (Autumn 1969), 48-50.

1311 _____. "Two Stories/The Mosquito Battle," Peter Paul Fersch, Prism International, IX (Autumn 1969), 50-51.

1312 Brobowski, Johannes. "Stranded in a Capital," Ruth and Matthew Mead, trans., Transatlantic Review, no. 23 (Winter 1966-67), 50-52.

1313 Brock, Robert. "No. 1," Nexus (San Francisco, Calif.), II (March-April 1965), 39.

1314 Brodeur, Paul. "Blue Lawns," Seventeen, XXV (March 1966), 154-155, 233-237.

1315 _____. "Hydrography," New Yorker, XL (February 13, 1965), 28-31.

1316 _____. "The Salt Marsh Caper," Seventeen, XXV (August 1966), 300-301, 430-437.

1317 _____. "The Secret," Seventeen, XXIV (December 1965), 104-105, 168, 170, 174.

1318 _____. "The Siphon," Michigan Quarterly Review, V (Spring 1966), 107-112.

1319 _____. "The Ski Lesson," Seventeen, XXVII (February 1968), 130-131, 166, 168, 170, 173, 175.

1320 _____. "The Snow in Petrograd," New Yorker, XLII (February 11, 1967), 136, 138-141.

1321 _____. "The Spoiler," New Yorker, XLI (January 8, 1966), 28-34.

1322 _____. "Surveillance," Michigan Quarterly Review, VIII (Winter 1969), 15-20.

1323 _____. "The Toll," Michigan Quarterly Review, VI (Summer 1967), 211-216.

1324 ______. "The Turtle," Saturday Evening Post, CCXXXVIII (March 27, 1965), 42-44, 48, 50.

1325 Brodey, Jim. "First Evening in San Francisco," San Francisco Earthquake, I (Fall 1967), 3-4.

1326 ______. "A Poem & Prose/from: The Horrible, part one, Mah Heart," The World, no. 1 (1967), n.p. [39].

1327 Brodkey, Harold. "Bookkeeping," New Yorker, XLIV (April 27, 1968), 44-50, 52, 54, 59, 62, 65-66, 68, 73, 76, 78, 80, 83.

1328 ______. "Hofstedt and Jean--and Others," New Yorker, XLIV (January 25, 1969), 26-36.

1329 ______. "On the Waves," New Yorker, XLI (September 4, 1965), 24-27.

1330 ______. "The Shooting Range," New Yorker, XLV (September 13, 1969), 46-54, 56, 61-62, 64, 66, 68, 71-72, 74, 76, 78, 83-84, 86, 88-90, 93-94, 96-98, 100.

1331 Brody, Alan. "A Cup of Coffee at Walgreens'," Carleton Miscellany, X (Fall 1969), 4-27.

1332 Brody, Rick. "The Iliad: An Allegory," Washington and Jefferson Literary Journal, III, no. 1 (1969), 21-26.

1333 Bromhead, Freda. "Holiday," Cornhill Magazine, CLXXVII (Spring 1969), 250-256.

1334 Broner, E. M. "Each Face Extinct," Mad River Review, I (Spring-Summer, 1965), 3-10.

1335 ______. "A Magic Thing that Fixes," Ante, III (Winter 1967), 39-46.

1336 ______. "The New Nobility," Epoch, XVI (Winter 1967), 147-178.

1337 ______. "Remember, Daughter, Remember the Tale," Midstream, XV (August/September 1969), 29-36.

1338 ______. "The Woman Who Lived for Ten," Ante, II (Fall 1966), 20-28.

1339 ______. "'The Woman Who Lived for Ten'," Epoch, XVI (Fall 1966), 3-13.

1340 Brontë, Charlotte. "The Search for Happiness," Daily Telegraph Magazine, no. 265 (November 7, 1969), 38-39, 41, 43, 46.

1341 Brooke, Richard. "The Flowers and the Fire," Evergreen Review, XIII (January 1969), 50-53, 68.

1342 Brooke-Rose, Christine. "George and the Seraph," Quarterly Review of Literature, XIII (1965), 277-284.

1343 ______. "Red Rubber Gloves," Quarterly Review of Literature, XIII (1965), 284-293.

1344 Brookhouse, Christopher. "If Lost, Return," Carolina Quarterly, XXI (Spring 1969), 33-37.

1345 ______. "from Running Out," Carolina Quarterly, XX (Fall 1968), 83-92.

1346 Brooks, Bill. "The Best of Jud," Arx, I (July-August 1967), 23-28.

1347 Brooks, Colleen. "Open and Shut," New Yorker, XLV (July 5, 1969), 34-35.

1348 Brooks, Dorothy. "Joe's Niche," Arx, I (September 1967), 17-18, 38-40.

1349 ______. "A Point of Knowledge," Arx, I (February 1968), 32-40.

1350 ______. "Stella Tabor," Arx, II (September 1968), 7-14.

1351 ______. "A Visiting Celebrity," Arx, II (March 1969), 37-38.

1352 Brooks, James. "Five Vignettes," Wisconsin Review, III (Fall 1967), 12-13.

1353 Brooks, Karen Ann. "Tereu," Minnesota Review, VI (1967), 282-292.

1354 Brooks, T. E. "The Nothing Box," Seventeen, XXIV (November 1965), 132-133, 218, 220, 222, 225-226, 230.

1355 Brophy, Brigid. "The Woodcutter's Upright Son," Atlantic Monthly, CCXXII (November 1968), 96-98.

1356 Brossard, Chandler. "The Peculiar Husband," Cavalier, XV (December 1965), 52-53, 77-78, 80.

1357 Broughton, T. Alan. "Imperfect Enjoyment," Cimarron Review, no. 3 (March 1968), 19-36.

1358 Brower, Brock. "Quick Hop," Playboy, XVI (August 1969), 76-78, 90, 176-178.

1359 ______. "Rockabye," Esquire, LXIX (April 1968), 94-97, 182-187.

1360 _____. "Storm Still," Tri-Quarterly, no. 8 (Winter 1967), 91-109.

1361 Brown, Clark. "Love on the Far Shore," Occident, I (Spring/Summer 1967), 10-42.

1362 Brown, George Mackay. "The Ferryman," Cornhill Magazine, no. 1049 (Autumn 1966), 310-313.

1363 _____. "Fine Green Waves," Atlantic Monthly, CCXXI (April 1968), 107-110, 112-113.

1364 _____. "Merrag and her Sons," Scottish International, no. 3 (August 1968), 38-39.

1365 _____. "The Story of Jorkel Hayforks," Atlantic Monthly, CCXVII (May 1966), 87-88, 91-92.

1366 _____. "A Time to Keep," Cornhill Magazine, CLXXVI (Summer 1968), 433-452.

1367 _____. "Witch," Weekend Telegraph, no. 82 (April 22, 1966), 39-40, 42, 45-46.

1368 Brown, Gifford. "A Game of Chess," New Yorker, XLI (June 12, 1965), 37-46.

1369 Brown, Guillermo. "Spell of the Rainbow," Américas, XVII (August 1965), 32-34.

1370 Brown, Harry. "A Small Buffet in Maldita," Playboy, XIV (September 1967), 102-104, 110, 248-252, 254-256.

1371 _____. "The Truth," Playboy, XVI (October 1969), 102-104, 244, 246, 248, 250, 252, 254, 256, 258, 260, 262-264, 266, 268.

1372 Brown, J. Edward. "The Breakfast Food Boy," New Zealand Listener, (December 8, 1967), 6.

1373 _____. "The Diamond," New Zealand Listener, LXI (June 13, 1969), 12.

1374 _____. "Katikana Ken," New Zealand Listener, LVIII (August 16, 1968), 10.

1375 _____. "The Old Sharkey," New Zealand Listener, LX (February 7, 1969), 10.

1376 _____. "Uncle Harvey," New Zealand Listener, LVIII (June 14, 1968), 10.

1377 Brown, Jane. "As If We Were God's Spies," Mademoiselle,

LXII (March 1966), 128-129, 205, 207-213, 232.

1378 _____. "Away from Home," Art and Literature, no. 7 (Winter 1965), 110-121.

1379 _____. "Buildings," Shenandoah, XVII (Spring 1966), 43-61.

1380 _____. "Looking at Pictures," Shenandoah, XVII (Autumn 1965), 25-29.

1381 Brown, Jeff. "Incident on the Tenth Floor," Saturday Evening Post, CCXXXIX (July 30, 1966), 58-63.

1382 _____. "The Secret By the Pond," Redbook, CXXVI (April 1966), 70-71, 118, 120, 122.

1383 Brown, Julian. "Fable and Fancy," Riverside Quarterly, II (November 1966), 179.

1384 Brown, Kay. "Schnec," Overland, no. 40 (Summer 1968-69), 5-10.

1385 _____. "She Let Them Know," Overland, no. 31 (Autumn 1965), 5-8.

1386 Brown, Laurel. "By George!" Limbo, II (March 1965), 23-28.

1387 Brown, Lennie. "Enclosure," Nimrod, XII (Spring 1968), 42-45.

1388 Brown, Margery Finn. "Christmas Journey," McCall's, XCIV (December 1966), 94-95, 160-164.

1389 _____. "The Long Flight of Stairs," Redbook, CXXVII (September 1966), 82-83, 142-145.

1390 _____. "A String of Popcorn," McCall's, XCVI (December 1968), 78-79, 128-129.

1391 Brown, Michael A. "The Menagerie Business," Chicago Review, XX & XXI (May 1969), 74-76.

1392 Brown, Robert V. N. "Coming Home Baby," Carolina Quarterly, XVIII (Fall 1965), 56-64.

1393 Brown, T. K., III. "The Goblin of Curtery Sink," Playboy, XII (November 1965), 108-109, 120, 173-174, 176.

1394 _____. "Midnight Snack," Playboy, XVI (February 1969), 95, 180-181.

1395 Brown, William. "In Honeytown/(part of a novel, The Way

To the Uncle Sam Hotel)," Coyote's Journal, no. 3 (1965), 1-107 [complete issue].

1396 _____. "9 June 1945," Coyote's Journal, nos. 5-6 (1966), 110-115.

1397 _____. "From the First Part of The Way to the Uncle Sam Hotel," Wild Dog, no. 18 (1965), 7-10.

1398 Brownstein, Michael. "The Plot to Save the World," Paris Review, XII (Fall 1969), 115-120.

1399 _____, Ted Berrigan and Dick Gallup. "A Story," The World, no. 4 (June 1967), n.p. [62].

1400 Brú, Hedin. "Emanuel," Hedin Brønner, trans., American Scandinavian Review, LV (June 1967), 178-181.

1401 _____. "The White Church," Hedin Brønner, trans., American Scandinavian Review, LIV (December 1966), 392-396.

1402 Brubaker, Bill R. "It Was Christmas," Southern Humanities Review, III (Summer 1969), 233-241.

1403 Bruce, Michael T. "Weeds," Southerly, XXV, no. 2 (1965), 108-113.

1404 Bruce, Sylvia. "El Dorado," Alta, no. 7 (Winter 1968-69), 30-31.

1405 _____. "Extracts from her second novel--The Wonderful Garden," Alta, no. 7 (Winter 1968-69), 25-26.

1406 _____. "Extracts from 'The Wonderful Garden'," Aylesford Review, IX (Autumn 1967), 10-15.

1407 Brucker, Gerald. "Tres Avisos," Forum, IV (Summer 1966), 39-42.

1408 Brunot, James. "The M. Team," Evergreen Review, XI (October 1967), 80-85.

1409 Bryan, C. D. B. "The Best of Friends at Farmington," Mademoiselle, LXIII (October 1966), 136-137, 208-210.

1410 Bryan, Elizabeth. "Rag and Bone Man," California Review, no. 2 (Spring 1968), 5-11.

1411 Bryan, J. Y. "Tea and Treason," Southwest Review, LII (Summer 1967), 225-234.

1412 _____. "To Lure the Wolves," Southwest Review, L (Summer 1965), 225-242.

1413 Bryant, C. M. "Obituary," Michigan Quarterly Review, IV (Spring 1965), 106-108.

1414 Bryant, Dorothy M. "No End to It," Four Quarters, XIX (November 1969), 34-40.

1415 Brycht, Andrzej. "Dry Grass," Jerzy Hummel, trans., Literary Review, XI (Spring 1968), 335-340.

1416 Bryl, Yanka. "Short Stories/Dark of Night," Margaret Wettlin, trans., Soviet Literature, (no. 10, 1969), 122-128.

1417 _____. "Short Stories/Look at the Green Grass," Margaret Wettlin, trans., Soviet Literature, (no. 10, 1969), 129-137.

1418 _____. "Short Stories/You Are Alive," Margaret Wettlin, trans., Soviet Literature, (no. 10, 1969), 137-142.

1419 Bryson, D. D. "Swing of the Pendulum," Dust, II (Fall 1965), 49-56.

1420 Buchan, Perdita. "It's Cold Out There," New Yorker, XLIV (September 14, 1968), 48-56.

1421 _____. "Winter in the Spare-Parts Yard," New Yorker, XLV (March 22, 1969), 38-44.

1422 Buchan, Stuart. "The Dead Sea Shell," Prism International, V (Autumn 1965), 36-46.

1423 Buchanan, Cynthia. "The Charley," North American Review, VI (Spring 1969), 52-55.

1424 _____. "The Wind Chandelier," Epoch, XVII (Winter 1968), 183-192.

1425 Buchanan, Dodds. "Quality of Mercy," Dare, IV (September 1966), 22-23.

1426 Buchanan, Evelyn. "At the Lake," New Zealand Listener, LIV (May 27, 1966), 6.

1427 Buchwald, Art. "The Unfaithful Executive," Imprint, VIII (June 1968), 58-60.

1428 Buck, Pearl S. "All the Days of Love and Courage," Good Housekeeping, CLXIX (December 1969), 72-73, 204, 206, 208, 210.

1429 _____. "Matthew, Mark, Luke and John," Good Housekeeping, CLXIII (December 1966), 93-95, 227-231, 239, 241-246.

1430 _____. "Secrets of the Heart," Good Housekeeping, CLXVII

(December 1968), 70-71, 166-170.

1431 _____. "Stranger, Come Home," Good Housekeeping, CLXV (December 1967), 84-85, 213-220.

1432 Buckle, Daphne. "For Hortense," Wild Dog, no. 21 (March 1966), 36-37.

1433 Buckley, Fergus Reid. "East of New York, South of Madrid, Down to Kenya," Vogue, CXLIX (April 1, 1967), 82-85.

1434 Budrys, Algis. "The Master of the Hounds," Saturday Evening Post, CCXXXIX (August 27, 1966), 46-47, 49-54, 56-60.

1435 _____. "The Ultimate Brunette," Playboy, XII (September 1965), 120-122, 208, 211-212.

1436 Buechler, James. "The Ambulance Driver," Saturday Evening Post, CCXXXVIII (April 24, 1965), 64-71.

1437 Buettner, Wayne. "The Man Who Couldn't Die," Discourse, XII (Spring 1969), 232-247.

1438 Buitrago, Fanny. "The Dirty Heron," Américas, XVII (March 1965), 30-32.

1439 _____. "Quo Vadis?" Américas, XX (March 1968), 36-39.

1440 _____. "The West Side of the Island," Américas, XVIII (April 1966), 36-38.

1441 Bukowski, Charles. "The Birth, Life and Death of an Underground Newspaper," Evergreen Review, XIII (September 1969), 41-43, 67-72.

1442 Bulgakov, Mikhail. "From The Notes of a Young Doctor/ The Blizzard," Robert Daglish, trans., Soviet Literature, (no. 8, 1968), 102-112.

1443 _____. "From The Notes of a Young Doctor/An Egyptian Darkness," Robert Daglish, trans., Soviet Literature, (no. 8, 1968), 112-124.

1444 _____. "From The Notes of a Young Doctor/The Towel with the Cock," Avril Pyman, trans., Soviet Literature, (no. 8, 1968), 90-101.

1445 Bullins, Ed. "The Absurd One," Wild Dog, no. 14 (February 1965), 12-13.

1446 _____. "An Ancient One," Illuminations, no. 1 (Summer 1965), 7.

1447 ______. "The Beacon," Illuminations, no. 1 (Summer 1965), 7.

1448 ______. "The Helper," Dust, II (Fall 1965), 63-70.

1449 ______. "The Hungered One," Nexus (San Francisco, Calif.), II (January-February 1965), 12-14.

1450 ______. "The Lonely Host," Wild Dog, no. 15 (March 1965), 16.

1451 ______. "The Messenger/(from a novel in progress: Absurd)," Trace, no. 57 (Summer 1965), 167-170.

1452 ______. "The Saviour," Dust, I (Winter 1965), 35-42.

1453 ______. "The Storekeeper," Negro Digest, XVI (May 1967), 55-58.

1454 ______. "Support Your Local Police," Negro Digest, XVII (November 1967), 53-58.

1455 ______. "Travel from Home," Manhattan Review, no. 2 (1966), 11-16.

1456 Bullock, Michael. "A Man, A Girl and a Door," Prism International, VIII (Summer 1968), 92-95.

1457 ______. "The Net," Prism International, VIII (Spring 1969), 27-29.

1458 ______. "To the Top of the Tower," Mundus Artium, II (Spring 1969), 36-38.

1459 ______. "Two Girls and a Man Coming and Going," Prism International, VII (Summer 1967), 10-13.

1460 Bumpus, Jerry. "Adolph Hitler, Judy Mauritz, and the Clear Blue Sky of Japan," December, VIII (1966), 79-84.

1461 ______. Anaconda, December, IX (1967), 1-136.

1462 ______. "The Conspiracy Against Mister Mann," The Fair, II (Summer 1968), 14-29.

1463 ______. "A Day in a Life," Washington and Jefferson Literary Journal, II (Winter 1968), 25-30.

1464 ______. "A Father," The Fair, II (Spring 1968), 40-47.

1465 ______. "In the Cold," TransPacific, no. 2 (Fall 1969), 33-45.

1466 _____. "The Man Who Looked Like Peter Sellers and Other Problems," Mandala, no. 4 (1969), 17-29.

1467 _____. "Mister Mann in Madrid," Midwestern University Quarterly, I, no. 3 (1966), 43-53.

1468 _____. "A New World," Washington and Jefferson Literary Journal, II (Winter 1968), 45-47.

1469 _____. "The Season of Deep Water," Minnesota Review, IX (1969), 11-18.

1470 _____. "Song of the Tiger," December, X (1968), 60-63.

1471 _____. "The Soul's Most Natural Kingdom," Midwestern University Quarterly, II, no. 1 (1966), 155-172.

1472 _____. "Why the Afternoons Are Long," December, VII (1965), 29-35.

1473 Bunao, G. Bruce. "The Roof," Solidarity, IV (October 1969), 47-51.

1474 _____. "Two Stories/ 1. Doors," Solidarity, III (January 1968), 42-47.

1475 _____. "Two Stories/ 2. The Vigil," Solidarity, III (January 1968), 47-55.

1476 Bunch, David R. "The Fable of the Moonshooter and the Indifferent Undergraduate," Dare, V (October 1967), 36-39.

1477 _____. "Losing at Home," Nexus (San Francisco, Calif.), II (March-April 1965), 40-43.

1478 _____. "The Miracle of the Flowers," The Smith, no. 7 (1966), 11-23.

1479 _____. "Sad Case #1 (Many-Too-Many)," Dare, V (March 1967), 26-27.

1480 _____. "Taking Leave," The Smith, no. 10 (December 1968), 86-93.

1481 _____. "The Time Battler," The Smith, no. 5 (1965), 62-72.

1482 _____. "Two Pessimists and a Pigeon," Aspects, no. 11 (April 1968), 1-3.

1483 _____. "When It Comes to Bascarts, I'll Take a Full One," Aspects, no. 12 (January 1969), 18-20.

1484 _____. "When It Comes to Bascarts, I'll Take a Full One,"

Grand Ronde Review, no. 6 (1966), n.p. [101-105].

1485 Buonaugurio, S. J. "A Writer's Picnic," Ave Maria, CVI (August 12, 1967), 28-30.

1486 Buquoi, Nancy J. "Wave a White Flag," Delta, XXIII (1969), 1-8.

1487 Burch, Emil. "The Children's Game," Vagabond, I (January-March 1966), 33-34.

1488 Burgess, Anthony. "An American Organ," Mad River Review, I (Winter 1964-65), 33-39.

1489 _____. "A Benignant Growth," Transatlantic Review, no. 32 (Summer 1969), 10-15.

1490 _____. "From It Is the Miller's Daughter--a novel in progress," Transatlantic Review, no. 24 (Spring 1967), 5-15.

1491 _____. "The Muse," Hudson Review, XXI (Spring 1968), 109-126.

1492 Burgess, Jackson. "Snakes," New Orleans Review, I (Fall 1968), 65-68.

1493 Burgess, William Vincent. "Today Is Your Day," Kenyon Review, XXXI (1969), 329-347.

1494 Burgess, Yvonne. "If You Swallow You're Dead," Contrast (Cape Town, South Africa), no. 21 (August 1969), 11-24.

1495 _____. "Outeniqua Holiday," Purple Renoster, no. 9 (Spring 1969), 8, 29.

1496 _____. "Requiescat in Pace," Contrast (Cape Town, South Africa), no. 18 (July 1968), 49-52.

1497 Burk, James E. "Fruits of the Lemon," Arx, I (September 1967), 12-13, 35-37.

1498 Burke, Betsy. "Message from Another Planet," Ave Maria, CII (November 6, 1965), 24-26.

1499 _____. "Miss Hallam," Ave Maria, CIV (September 10, 1966), 24-27.

1500 Burke, Ruth. "Ten Minutes at the Bus Stop," Negro Digest, XIV (January 1965), 70-75.

1501 Burmeister, Peter. "The Student," Columbia Review, XLV (Spring 1965), 62-65.

1502 Burnam, Tom. "Act of Love," Little Review of the Pacific Northwest, I (Fall 1965), 80-85.

1503 _____. "The Dummy," Georgia Review, XX (Summer 1966), 182-187.

1504 _____. "A Wallet at His Back," Texas Quarterly, IX (Winter 1966), 145-156.

1505 Burns, Alan. "from Europe After the Rain," New Directions 20, (1968), 75-95.

1506 Burns, Carol. "Infatuation," New Writers, no. 6 (1967), 7-98.

1507 Burns, Jim. "Blow Mr. Dexter," Poetmeat, nos. 9 & 10 (Summer 1965), 72-74.

1508 Burr, Dan. "The Grim Reapers/A Sketch on Hip-Rock," Wisconsin Review, III (Spring 1968), 36.

1509 _____. "Neenah," Wisconsin Review, II (May 1967), 17.

1510 Burris, Jack. "Judah's a Two-Way Street Running Out," Negro Digest, XV (January 1966), 64-73.

1511 Burrough, Loretta. "The Sand Castle," Ladies' Home Journal, LXXXVI (July 1969), 58-59, 98, 104-105.

1512 Burroughs, William S. [untitled], Lines, no. 5 (May 1965), 15.

1513 _____. [untitled], Lines, no. 5 (May 1965), 22-23.

1514 _____. "Academy 23," Wormwood Review, IX, no. 4 (1969), 19-26.

1515 _____. "The Coldspring News," San Francisco Earthquake, I (Summer/Fall 1968), 54-57.

1516 _____. "Day the Records Went Up," Evergreen Review, XII (November 1968), 46-50, 76-77.

1517 _____. "Exterminator!" Evergreen Review, XI (April 1967), 54-55.

1518 _____. "'Johnny 23'," Evergreen Review, XII (March 1968), 26-27.

1519 _____. "Last Awning Flaps on the Pier," Intrepid, no. 5 (March 1965), n.p. [21].

1520 _____. "Last Awning Flaps on the Pier," San Francisco

Earthquake, I (Winter 1968), 38-40.

1521 _____. "The Last Post," Lines, no. 6 (November 1965), 31.

1522 _____. "Mother and I Would Like to Know," Evergreen Review, XIII (June 1969), 34-37.

1523 _____. "The Moving Times," VDRSVPVDRSVPVDRSVP, (1969), n.p. [front and back pages].

1524 _____. "The Perfect Servant," London Magazine, VII (December 1967), 8-12.

1525 _____ and Brion Gysin. "Pieces," Mother, no. 5 (Summer 1965), 63-67.

1526 _____. "The 'Priest' They Call Him," Weekend Telegraph, no. 132 (April 14, 1967), 46.

1527 _____. "Salt Chunk Mary," Intrepid, no. 6 (1966), n.p. [15-17].

1528 _____. "Salt Chunk Mary," San Francisco Earthquake, I (Winter 1968), 35-38.

1529 _____. "'Speaking Clock' Speaking in Present Time/June 18, 1964. 12:45 P.M.," Transatlantic Review, no. 21 (Summer 1966), 99-102.

1530 _____. "They Do Not Always Remember," Esquire, LXV (May 1966), 95.

1531 _____. "23 Skiddoo," Transatlantic Review, no. 25 (Summer 1967), 93-96.

1532 _____. "23 Skiddoo Eristic Elite," Florida Quarterly, I (Fall 1967), 14-20.

1533 _____. "Wind Die, You Die, We Die," Esquire, LXX (August 1968), 56-57, 120, 122.

1534 _____. "'Word Authority More Habit Forming Than Heroin'," San Francisco Earthquake, I (Fall 1967), 25-31.

1535 Busch, Frederick. "Grass Comes Up on the BMT," Quarterly Review of Literature, XIV (1967), 269-281.

1536 _____. "How Does That Garden Grow," New American Review, no. 7 (August 1969), 162-168.

1537 _____. "Hunt Them Where They Live and Kill Them Dead," Transatlantic Review, no. 31 (Winter 1968-69), 140-144.

1538 _____. "I Guarantee: You Are My Man," New American Review, no. 5 (January 1969), 144-153.

1539 _____. "People, We Are Called," Transatlantic Review, no. 21 (Summer 1966), 155-161.

1540 _____. "Something Is Moving Just under the Skin," Goddard Journal, II (Winter 1968), 2-16.

1541 Butler, Dorothy. "The Darkness," Overland, no. 40 (Summer 1968-69), 14-16.

1542 Butler, Gerald. "After School," West Coast Review, I (Winter 1967), 31-39.

1543 Butler, Guy. "Portrait of an Artist as a Young South African," Contrast (Cape Town, South Africa), no. 13 (December 1965), 10-19.

1544 Butler, John. "Snow in the Tropics," Transition, VII, no. 34 (December/January 1968), 31-33.

1545 _____. "The Ward," Riverrun, no. 2 (1968), 50-59.

1546 Butler, William. "Kindling," Transatlantic Review, no. 29 (Summer 1968), 90-94.

1547 Butor, Michel. "The Library/from Portrait of the Artist as a Young Monkey," Frederick Brown, trans., Harper's Bazaar, CI (April 1969), 124, 128, 219, 221, 227.

1548 Butson, Barry. "Ups and Downs," The Fiddlehead, no. 82 (November-December 1969), 12-15.

1549 Butterfield, Stephen. "Bloodsuckers," Goodly Co., no. 12 (July 1968), 3-7.

1550 _____. "The Honorable Estate," University Review, XXXIV (Autumn 1967), 38-44.

1551 Butters, Dorothy Gilman. "Uncertain Voyage," Cosmopolitan, CLXIII (August 1967), 130-134, 136-143, 148-149, 152-155.

1552 Butterworth, Michael. "Concentrate 1," New Worlds, no. 174 (1967), 57-58.

1553 _____. "Concentrate 2," New Worlds, no. 181 (April 1968), 38-41.

1554 _____. "Sergeant Peppers Postatomic Skull," Ambit, no. 36 (1968), 13-15.

1555 _____. "The Soundless Scream," Cosmopolitan, CLXIII

(November 1967), 150-154, 156, 158-167, 170-175, 176-177, 180-183.

1556 _____. "The Uneasy Sun," Cosmopolitan, CLXVI (June 1969), 142-146, 148-157, 160-163, 166-170.

1557 Buzzati, Dino. "The Epidemic," Frances Frenaye, trans., The Quest, I (Spring 1966), 19-26.

1558 _____. "Triumph," Frances Frenaye, trans., The Quest, II (Spring 1967), 21-25.

1559 Bye, Judith. "Experiment in Birth," UMD Humanist, XIV (Spring 1966), 31-32.

1560 _____. "Justice," UMD Humanist, XIV (Winter 1966), 3-11.

1561 Byers, L. "And Thus a Man," Dare, IV (May-June 1966), 18-19.

1562 Bygrave, Mike. "Extract from New Yorkers," Solstice, no. 5 (1967), 12-17.

1563 Byram, George. "The Chronicle of the 656th," Playboy, XV (March 1968), 64-66, 74, 124, 126-130, 132-134.

1564 Byrd, Malley J. "The Day We Doctored Webster McLendon's Cow," Delta Review, IV (January-February 1967), 20-23.

1565 Byrd, Scott. "The Withering Away of Mrs. Manderville," Carolina Quarterly, XIX (Spring 1967), 23-31.

1566 Byrne, Johnny. "Stopcock," Transatlantic Review, no. 31 (Winter 1968-69), 64-71.

1567 E. C. "The Jump Show," Origin (Kyoto, Japan), no. 2 (July 1966), 38-42.

1568 Cabbell, Edward J. "The Soul's Sting," Phylon, XXX (Winter 1969), 413-419.

1569 Caceres, Andres. "Premonition," H. E. Francis, trans., DeKalb Literary Arts Journal, I (Fall 1966), 45-48.

1570 Cade, Toni. "The Hammer Man," Negro Digest, XV (February 1966), 54-60.

1571 _____. "Maggie of the Green Bottles," Prairie Schooner, XLI (Winter 1967), 384-391.

1572 Cadell, Elizabeth. "The Golden Collar," Redbook, CXXXI (October 1968), 167-189.

1573 _____. "The Third Surprise," Redbook, CXXXIII (July 1969), 167-189.

1574 Cady, Jack. "The Burning," Atlantic Monthly, CCVI (August 1965), 53-57.

1575 _____. "The Constituent," Twigs, no. 5 (Fall 1969), 35-42.

1576 _____. "The Shark," Yale Review, LVII (Spring 1968), 386-393.

1577 _____. "With No Breeze," Carolina Quarterly, XXI (Fall 1969), 57-75.

1578 Cain, Jocelyn. "The Coffee Urn," Kansas Magazine, (1967), 26-28.

1579 Cairns, A. T. "Visitant," Dalhousie Review, XLVI (Autumn 1966), 348-355.

1580 Calabro, Louis. "A Bagatelle of the Mind," Silo, no. 10 (Fall 1966), 16-27.

1581 Caldwell, Price. "John Deere," Delta Review, V (November 1968), 64-67, 71.

1582 _____. "A Sense of Family," New Orleans Review, I (Summer 1969), 353-356.

1583 Calin, Anne A. "The Adventure," Literary Review, X (Autumn 1966), 20-32.

1584 _____. "Auld Lang Syne," Ararat, IX (Spring 1968), 28-32.

1585 _____. "A Better Time of Day," Ararat, VI (Summer 1965), 36-41.

1586 _____. "Night in Another Country," South Dakota Review, V (Winter 1967-68), 14-22.

1587 _____. "The Portrait," Ararat, IX (Winter 1968), 46-49.

1588 Calin, Harold. "A Cleaner Greener Land," Ararat, VIII (Summer 1967), 48-54.

1589 Calisher, Hortense. "Fathers and Satyrs," Evergreen Review, X (December 1966), 24-27, 72-79.

1590 _____. "Gargantua," Harper's Bazaar, XCVIII (February 1965), 130-131, 183-185, 187, 192.

1591 _____. "A Summer Psychosis," Harper's Bazaar, C (September 1967), 326-329, 240, 242, 244, 248, 252, 254, 256-

258, 268, 270, 274.

1592 Callender, Timothy. "A Farewell," Bim, XI (January-June 1966), 122-127.

1593 ______. "The Man Who Saw Visions," Bim, XII (July-December 1967), 53-56.

1594 ______. "Obeah for the Obeah Man," Bim, XII (January-June 1969), 224-229.

1595 ______. "One Day with Uncle," Bim, XI (July-December 1966), 168-175.

1596 ______. "Painting Sold," Bim, XII (July-December 1968), 141-144.

1597 ______. "Peace and Love," Bim, XI (January-June 1967), 259-266.

1598 ______. "Romantic Interlude," Bim, XIII (July-December 1969), 9-13.

1599 ______. "The Steel Donkey," Bim, XII (January-June 1968), 84-89.

1600 Callison, Cleve. "Boss Man," The Archive, LXXIX (April 1967), 24-26.

1601 ______. "Time Passes," The Archive, LXXIX (December 1966), 11-12.

1602 Caltofen Segura, Rodolfo. "The Girl in the Harbor," Human Voice, IV, no. 4 (1968), 41-43.

1603 ______. "A Little Notebook," Ave Maria, CVII (February 24, 1968), 26-27.

1604 Calvino, Italo. "The Night Driver," William Weaver, trans., Mademoiselle, LXIX (September 1969), 174-175, 212-213.

1605 ______. "The Origin of Everything/All at One Point," Playboy, XV (March 1968), 80-82, 179.

1606 ______. "The Origin of Everything/Games Without End," Playboy, XV (March 1968), 179-180.

1607 Cameron, Donald. "Justice," Canadian Forum, XLIX (July 1969), 93-95.

1608 ______. "Love by the Book," The Fiddlehead, no. 78 (January-February 1969), 54-63.

1609 Cameron, Eric. "The Abyss," Queen's Quarterly, LXXIV (Winter 1967), 701-706.

1610 ______. "The Red Bikini," Queen's Quarterly, LXXVI (Summer 1969), 239-249.

1611 ______. "Thorn in the Flesh," Queen's Quarterly, LXXV (Autumn 1968), 476-481.

1612 ______. "The Turning Point," Queen's Quarterly, LXXIII (Autumn 1966), 398-420.

1613 Campbell, Colin. "Lizard without a Tail," Westerly, (August 1965), 7-10.

1614 Campbell, Haldane. "For Richer ... For Poorer ... For Better ... For Faith," Good Housekeeping, CLXII (March 1966), 98-99, 192, 194.

1615 ______. "A Summer of Tender Dreams," Good Housekeeping, CLXVII (August 1968), 64-65, 126, 128-130.

1616 Campbell, Joan. "The Essence of Ovel," Red Cedar Review, III (Spring 1965), 43-47.

1617 Campert, Remco. "A Trip to Zwolle," Sheila Vuijsje, trans., Delta (Amsterdam), XII (Autumn 1969), 35-40.

1618 Campos, George. "The Attempt," Arena, no. 23 (April 1965), 9-16.

1619 Canary, Glenn. "The Greenbrier Hut," Ave Maria, CVI (September 23, 1967), 28-30.

1620 Cannon, Marie. "Three To Make Ready," Red Clay Reader, no. 6 (1969), 100-102.

1621 Canson, Jack. "The Surprise," Atlantic Monthly, CCXXII (August 1968), 74-77, 82-83.

1622 Cantor, Harold. "The Shoo-in," Michigan Quarterly Review, IV (Winter 1965), 23-31.

1623 Canzoneri, Robert. "The Extended Hand," Southern Review, IV (April 1968), 447-457.

1624 ______. "The Prodigal Uncle," Southern Review, III (January 1967), 155-170.

1625 Capote, Truman. "A Christmas Memory," Ladies' Home Journal, LXXXIII (December 1966), 86-87, 133-138.

1626 ______. "A Curious Gift," Redbook, CXXV (June 1965),

52-53, 92-94.

1627 ______. "Miriam," Mademoiselle, LXV (October 1967), 142-143, 207-210.

1628 ______. "The Thanksgiving Visitor," McCall's, XCV (November 1967), 75, 155-162.

1629 Cardwell, Guy A. "Blow Bugles: Answer Echoes," Shenandoah, XVII (Spring 1966), 3-18.

1630 ______. "The Captain's Gala," Shenandoah, XIX (Autumn 1967), 19-30.

1631 ______. "Did You Once See Shelley?" Carleton Miscellany, X (Fall 1969), 36-68.

1632 ______. "Pig and Mouse," Carleton Miscellany, VII (Fall 1966), 13-28.

1633 ______. "Starling's Nest," Carleton Miscellany, VI (Summer 1965), 86-107.

1634 ______. "Time of Fermeture," Shenandoah, XIX (Spring 1968), 3-17.

1635 ______. "Transparent English," Quarterly Review of Literature, XVI, nos. 3-4 (1969), 295-310.

1636 Carling, Finn. "Blind World," Nancy Coleman, trans., Literary Review, XII (Summer 1969), 526-527.

1637 Carlson, Judith. "Mr. Namura," Ball State University Forum, X (Autumn 1969), 35-38.

1638 Carlson, Mary. "The Last Wild Horse," South Dakota Review, IV (Spring 1966), 34-59.

1639 Carlson, William K. "Moon Wine," Carleton Miscellany, X (Winter 1969), 22-45.

1640 Carmiggelt, Simon. "Collage," Elizabeth Willems-Treeman, trans., Delta (Amsterdam), XII (Winter 1969-70), 106.

1641 ______. "Fulfilment," Elizabeth Willems-Treeman, trans., Delta (Amsterdam), XI (Autumn 1968), 45-46.

1642 ______. "Genius," Elizabeth Willems-Treeman, trans., Delta (Amsterdam), VIII (Autumn 1965), 24-25.

1643 ______. "Happy Holiday," Elizabeth Willems-Treeman, trans., Delta (Amsterdam), VIII (Summer 1965), 63-64.

1644 _____. "High Style," Elizabeth Willems-Treeman, trans., Delta (Amsterdam), XI (Summer 1968), 39-40.

1645 _____. "Highly Obscene," Elizabeth Willems-Treeman, trans., Delta (Amsterdam), XI (Spring 1968), 57-58.

1646 _____. "The Horse," Elizabeth Willems-Treeman, trans., Delta (Amsterdam), VIII (Winter 1965-66), 65-66.

1647 _____. "Hunger, "Elizabeth Willems-Treeman, trans., Delta (Amsterdam), VIII (Spring 1965), 81-85.

1648 _____. "Orange on High," Elizabeth Willems-Treeman, trans., Delta (Amsterdam), IX (Spring/Summer 1966), 67-69.

1649 _____. "Out from Under," Elizabeth Willems-Treeman, trans., Delta (Amsterdam), X (Autumn 1967), 89-90.

1650 _____. "Punishment," Elizabeth Willems-Treeman, trans., Delta (Amsterdam), X (Winter 1967-68), 63-64.

1651 _____. "Sympathy," Elizabeth Willems-Treeman, trans., Delta (Amsterdam), XI (Winter 1968-69), 38-40.

1652 _____. "Triumph," Elizabeth Willems-Treeman, trans., Delta (Amsterdam), IX (Winter 1966-67), 71-72.

1653 Caro, Ronald. "The Triangle," Washington Square Review, I (Winter 1965), 8-11.

1654 Carossa, Hans. "Freckles," Margaret D. Howie, trans., Scala International, (January 1969), 34-37.

1655 Carper, Charles. "The Land of the Free," Story: the Yearbook of Discovery, (1969), 116-122.

1656 Carpluk, Nicholas. "Voyage," Abraxas, I (December 1969), 35-36, 48.

1657 Carr, John. "The Botleas," Intro, no. 2 (September 1969), 44-52.

1658 _____. "In the Pines, in the Pines," Red Clay Reader, no. 5 (1968), 19-25.

1659 Carr, Judy. "A Goal Scored," Jewish Frontier, XXXIII (January 1966), 28-29, Section 2.

1660 Carra, Paolo. "The Score," Ursule Molinaro, trans., Chelsea, nos. 18/19 (June 1966), 62-73.

1661 Carrega, Ugo. "Encephalitis," Ursule Molinaro, trans.,

Chelsea, nos. 18/19 (June 1966), 137-144.

1662 Carrier, Warren. "Angel Food," Quarterly Review of Literature, XV (1968), 255-258.

1663 Carroll, Jim. "From the Basketball Diary," The World, no. 11 (April 1968), n.p. [83].

1664 Carroll, Megan. "The Sense of the Sun," Grecourt Review, IX (May 1966), 20-27.

1665 Carson, Anthony. "The Swedish South," Queen, CDXXIV (May 19, 1965), 82-83.

1666 Carson, Josephine. "First Man, Last Man," Ante, II (Summer 1966), 5-21.

1667 _____. "The Taste of Spice," Ante, II (Spring 1966), 9-18.

1668 Carson, Robert E. "A Family Affair," Columbia, XLIX (March 1969), 26-29.

1669 _____. "The Stranger," Columbia, XLVIII (February 1968), 24-27.

1670 Carter, Angela. "The Beautiful Gun Lady," Nova, (August 1968), 78, 80.

1671 _____. "The Empress of Cockaigne," Queen, CDXXX (January 17, 1968), 48-50.

1672 Carter, Harriet. "Ecclesiastes/Or The Preacher," Pegasus, IV, no. 1 (1966), 30-32.

1673 _____. "Prelude," Pegasus, III (Spring 1965), 11-13.

1674 _____. "Visions," Pegasus, III (Spring 1965), 13-16.

1675 Carter, John Stewart. "Enter on a Monument," Encounter, XXIV (February 1965), 3-15.

1676 Carter, Margaret. "'Darling,' Said Amanda," Ladies' Home Journal, LXXXII (September 1965), 56-57, 115-116.

1677 Carter, Mary. "The Face of the Moon," McCall's, XCIII (November 1965), 108-109, 178-180.

1678 _____. "Polar Zone," McCall's, XCIV (July 1967), 84-85, 138-139.

1679 _____. "Sound and Light," McCall's, XCV (October 1967), 88, 157-161.

1680 Carter, Ron. "Come Again Some Other Day," Per/Se, III (Spring 1968), 33-36.

1681 Carvajal, Gabriel. "Across the Forest," Américas, XX (June 1968), 37-38.

1682 Carver, Raymond. "Bright Red Apples," Gato Magazine, II (Spring-Summer 1967), 8-13.

1683 _____. "Dummy," Discourse, X (Summer 1967), 241-256.

1684 _____. "The Father," December, X (1968), 32.

1685 _____. "Sixty Acres," Discourse, XII (Winter 1969), 117-127.

1686 _____. "Will You Please Be Quiet, Please?" December, VIII (1966), 9-27.

1687 Carver, Wayne. "A Child's Christmas in Utah," Carleton Miscellany, VII (Winter 1966), 66-75.

1688 _____. "With Voice of Joy and Praise," Western Humanities Review, XIX (Autumn 1965), 301-315.

1689 Cary, Joyce. "New Boots," Threshold, no. 21 (Summer 1967), 107-112.

1690 Casares, Adolfo Bioy. "Fable (In Memoriam A. P.)," Donald A. Yates, trans. in "The 'Microtale': An Argentine Specialty" by Donald A. Yates, Texas Quarterly, XII (Summer 1969), 15-16.

1691 Casewit, Curtis W. "The Important Man," Man About Town, I (June 1968), 14-18.

1692 _____. "Last Ski Race," Four Quarters, XVII (March 1968), 1-7.

1693 Casey, Isabelle. "Sure, Mama, Sure," North American Review, II (November 1965), 8-10.

1694 Casey, John. "Mandarins in a Farther Field," New Yorker, XLV (June 14, 1969), 34-42.

1695 _____. "A More Complete Cross-Section," New Yorker, XLIV (October 19, 1968), 55-64.

1696 Casey, Juanita. "Breed Unknown," Weekend Telegraph, no. 110 (November 4, 1966), 57-58, 61.

1697 Cashen, Eric. [untitled], Dust, III (Fall 1967), 28.

1698 _____. "Closet Without Walls," The Smith, no. 4 (1965), 43.

1699 _____. "The Fugue of Age," Blackbird, I, no. 3 (1966), 63-64.

1700 _____. "Hector," The Smith, no. 4 (1965), 44-45.

1701 _____. "The Rising Sun," El Corno Emplumado, no. 15 (July 1965), 139-140.

1702 _____. "The Sausage Turned," Aspects, no. 7 (September 1965), n.p. [1-2].

1703 _____. "A Yellow Ghost," El Corno Emplumado, no. 15 (July 1965), 139.

1704 Caspary, Vera. "Ruth," Good Housekeeping, CLXVI (February 1968), 67-69, 192-205, 213-218.

1705 Casper, Leonard. "The Left-handed Honeycomb," Southwest Review, LIV (Autumn 1969), 354-366.

1706 Casper, Linda T. "The Convert," New Mexico Quarterly, XXXV (Spring 1965), 29-38.

1707 _____. "The Transparent Sun," New Mexico Quarterly, XXXVII (Autumn 1967), 281-288.

1708 _____. "Two Stories /1. Cogon Full of Quail," Solidarity, III (September 1968), 74-80.

1709 _____. "Two Stories/2. The Dream of Cain," Solidarity, III (September 1968), 80-84.

1710 Cassel, William and Joan. "Justification for an Application for Federal Funds Under Public Law 8910," Plaintiff, V (Winter 1969), 47-48.

1711 Cassidy, George. "Tranquility," UMD Humanist, XIV (Spring 1966), 33-36.

1712 Cassill, R. V. "And in My Heart," Paris Review, IX (Winter-Spring 1965), 97-156.

1713 _____. "The Covenant," Saturday Evening Post, CCXXXVIII (April 10, 1965), 66-68, 70-71, 75-76, 78.

1714 _____. "The Gadfly," Jeopardy, no. 5 (Spring 1969), 165-176.

1715 _____. "My Brother, Wilbur," Northwest Review, VII (Spring-Summer 1965), 30-38.

1716 _____. "The Rationing of Love," New American Review, no. 3 (1968), 257-275.

1717 Castagnera, Jim. "Fat Lou," Prolog, VII (Winter 1969), 8-11.

1718 Castelain, Daniel. "An Unlikely Meeting," Patrick Bowles, trans., New Writers, no. 5 (1966), 7-63.

1719 Castille. "Dream Girl," Nexus (Lafayette, La.), I (1969), 1-2.

1720 Castree, D. "Monday," New Zealand Listener, LIII (December 17, 1965), 17.

1721 Casty, Alan. "The Winged Life Destroy," Perspective, XIV (Winter 1967), 225-241.

1722 Catalina, Don. "Buck Fever," Transatlantic Review, no. 25 (Spring 1967), 104-118.

1723 _____. "The End of Summer for Lickety Split," Transatlantic Review, no. 31 (Winter 1968-69), 114-130.

1724 Cather, Willa. "Peter," Readers & Writers, I (January-February 1967), 30-31.

1725 Catling, Patrick Skene. "The Exterminator," Nova, (April 1969), 128-130, 133, 141.

1726 Cato, Nancy. "The Olive-Stealers," Quadrant, X (January-February 1966), 70-72.

1727 Caudill, Rebecca. "A Certain Small Shepherd," Woman's Day, (December 1965), 27-32, 70, 72.

1728 Cavalier, Richard. "Arrivederci Roma," Man About Town, II (July 1968), 20-23.

1729 Cavalieri, Grace. "Major Pettigrew," Freelance (St. Louis, Mo.), VIII, no. 1 (1969), n.p. [1-4, 7, 9].

1730 Cavanaugh, Arthur. "Catherine and the Sparrows," Ladies' Home Journal, LXXXV (November 1968), 98-99, 173-175.

1731 _____. "The Children Are Gone," Ladies' Home Journal, LXXXIII (February 1966), 71-78.

1732 _____. "A Girl for Robert," Redbook, CXXX (March 1968), 78-79, 130-132.

1733 _____. "The Journey from Home," Ladies' Home Journal, LXXXVI (August 1969), 64-65, 91-94.

1734 _____. "Miss Awful," McCall's, XCVI (April 1969), 82-83, 179-182.

1735 _____. "The Offering," McCall's, XCIII (December 1965), 90-91, 150, 152-153.

1736 _____. "The Twenty-Five-Cent Job," McCall's, XCIV (August 1967), 58-59, 128-129.

1737 _____. "The Wonderful Prize," Redbook, CXXVI (December 1965), 64-65, 133.

1738 _____. "A Yearling No More," Woman's Day, (June 1969), 40-41, 82-84.

1739 Cave, Hugh. "Believe in Me," Good Housekeeping, CLXVIII (March 1969), 96-97, 161-164, 166.

1740 _____. "Change of Heart," Good Housekeeping, CLXI (September 1965), 84-85.

1741 _____. "Come Live with Me," Good Housekeeping, CLXVI (March 1968), 102-103, 156, 158, 160, 162.

1742 _____. "Double Wedding," Good Housekeeping, CLXI (July 1965), 88-89.

1743 _____. "End of the Road," Good Housekeeping, CLX (March 1965), 100-101.

1744 _____. "A Forever Kind of Thing," Good Housekeeping, CLXIX (August 1969), 72-73, 162-165.

1745 _____. "The Girl in Apartment 3-A," Good Housekeeping, CLXVIII (January 1969), 70-71, 120, 122, 124, 126.

1746 _____. "He Loves Me!" Good Housekeeping, CLXI (October 1965), 102-103.

1747 _____. "The Island of Eve," Good Housekeeping, CLXV (October 1967), 87-89, 214-220, 222, 224, 226, 228-230, 232, 234, 236, 238-240, 242-244, 251-252, 254, 256, 260-262, 264-267, 271-272.

1748 _____. "My Brand New Mother-in-Law," Good Housekeeping, CLXII (March 1966), 94-95, 199-200.

1749 _____. "The Search for Little Mary," Good Housekeeping, CLXVIII (June 1969), 73-75, 182-200, 204-212, 214-217.

1750 _____. "Second Baby," Good Housekeeping, CLXII (April 1966), 102-103.

1751 _____. "Something Wonderful," Good Housekeeping, CLXIII (July 1966), 84-85.

1752 _____. "Summer Serenade," Good Housekeeping, CLXV (July 1967), 72-73, 140-142, 146-147.

1753 _____. "To Trust in Andy," Good Housekeeping, CLX (April 1965), 102-103.

1754 Cavrell, Jean. "I Haven't Danced in Years," Redbook, CXXXI (June 1968), 78-79, 130-133, 137-138.

1755 _____. "Rock-a-Bye Baby," Redbook, CXXXII (December 1968), 78-79, 132-134.

1756 Cegledy, S. "The Fight," New Zealand Listener, LVIII (June 21, 1968), 10.

1757 Cela, Camilo José. "The Orange Is a Winter Fruit," John W. Kronik, trans., Prairie Schooner, XXXIX (Summer 1965), 148-155.

1758 Céline, Louis-Ferdinand. "The Colleague," Ralph Manheim, trans., Paris Review, XI (Winter 1968), 125-131.

1759 _____. "The Nymphettes of Siegmaringen/A Reminiscence," Ralph Manheim, trans., Evergreen Review, XII (November 1968), 36-40, 72-76.

1760 Cendrars, Blaise. "A Curious Virgin," Nina Zootes, trans., Queen, CDXXXII (April 30-May 13, 1969), 91, 94, 99, 103.

1761 Chadwick, Charles. "The Immensity of a Setting," Wascana Review, IV, no. 1 (1969), 5-18.

1762 Chaffin, Lillie D. "Ambiguous Season," Prairie Schooner, XLI (Spring 1967), 57-63.

1763 _____. "Beyond the Curve," North American Review, V (September-October 1968), 32-36.

1764 Chaikin, Nancy. "A Sense of Order," Colorado Quarterly, XV (Spring 1967), 319-336.

1765 Chaitanya. "The School Teacher," Accent (New Delhi, India), 11-13.

1766 Chaloner, David. "Friend," Solstice, no. 6 (1967), 30.

1767 _____. "Hung Up," Solstice, no. 6 (1967), 29.

1768 Chalpin, Lila. "The Hussy," Ball State Teachers College

Forum, VI (Winter 1965), 48-53.

1769 Chambers, George. "The Old Man," Sou'wester, (Summer 1968), 25-26.

1770 Chambers, Gray. "The Grudge Match," Stanford Chaparral, LXVIII (Winter 1968), 38-39.

1771 Chamblee, Robert. "Pig and the Wind," North American Review, II (July 1965), 35-40.

1772 Chan, Ronald. "The Modern Hermit," Focus (Singapore), III, no. 3, 15-16.

1773 Chanco, Rouben. "Second Generation," North American Review, IV (March 1967), 36-37.

1774 Chandramouli. "The Relative," Chamdramouli, trans., Triveni, XXXV (April 1966), 33-37.

1775 Chandrasekharan, K. "'Mother'!" K. Chandrasekharan, trans., Triveni, XXXVI (January 1968), 31-40.

1776 Chaney, Pomme. "The Reflection," Quarterly, LXV (Autumn 1968), 18-19.

1777 Chang, Suyong. "Mother of Spring," Eastern Horizon, V (June 1966), 53-62.

1778 Chapin, Victor. "Amy Evans Street," Four Quarters, XIV (March 1965), 1-22.

1779 Chaplin, Patrice. "Da Souza and the Dinosaur," London Magazine, IX (July/August 1969), 132-151.

1780 _____. "Wedding," London Magazine, VIII (October 1968), 56-58.

1781 Chaplin, Sid. "The Big Heap," Stand, IX, no. 3 (1968), 21-31.

1782 _____. "Burden of Proof," Queen, CDXXIII (March 10, 1965), 86-88.

1783 Chapman, Frank M. "The Tan and the Black," Ante, II (Fall 1966), 39-48.

1784 Chappell, Fred. "The Conscript," Carolina Quarterly, XVIII (Fall 1966), 12-25.

1785 _____. "The Crawling Eye," Malahat Review, no. 6 (April 1968), 73-97.

1786 _____. "Fragment from Dagon," Red Clay Reader, no. 2 (1965), 72-75.

1787 _____. "Gothic Perplexities," Red Clay Reader, no. 3 (1966), 44-49.

1788 Chappell, Jack. "The Girl on the Swing," Stand, X, no. 1 (1968), 56-63.

1789 _____. "Sewn-up," Stand, X, no. 4 (1969), 48-54.

1790 Char, K. T. Narasimha. "Atonement," Triveni, XXXIII (January 1965), 45-51.

1791 Char, René. "Lettera Amorosa," Lane Dunlop, trans., Harper's Bazaar, XCVIII (September 1965), 200-202.

1792 Charles, Gerda. "A Mixed Marriage," Quest, no. 1 (September 1965), 10-14.

1793 Charlton, Thomas. "Nithio," Manuscript, XIX (Spring 1966), 10-14.

1794 _____. "Undine Spirit," Manuscript, XIX (Spring 1966), 8-9.

1795 Charnock, Graham. "The Death Layout," New Worlds, no. 188 (March 1969), 25-27.

1796 Charteris, Hugo. "The Day of the Dance," London Magazine, VIII (March 1969), 34-39.

1797 _____. "Hairdriers for Belleburn," London Magazine, V (October 1965), 9-23.

1798 Charteris, Leslie. "The Gadget Lovers," Imprint, IX (July 1969), 59-65, 67, 69, 71, 73, 75, 77, 79, 81, 83, 85, 87, 89, 91, 93, 95, 97, 99, 101, 103, 105, 107, 109, 111, 113, 115-116.

1799 Charyn, Jerome. "The Changeling," Transatlantic Review, no. 27 (Winter 1967-68), 81-92.

1800 _____. "The Man Who Grew Younger," Paris Review, X (Spring 1966), 93-102.

1801 _____. "'Sing, Shaindele, Sing!'" Transatlantic Review, no. 22 (Autumn 1966), 139-148.

1802 Charyn, Marlene. "Last One Home," Ararat, VIII (Autumn 1967), 35-44.

1803 Chase, Virginia. "Not Even Solomon in All His Glory," Woman's Day, (March 1966), 44-45, 105-106.

1804 ______. "The Nut," Seventeen, XXVI (July 1967), 86-87, 122-123.

1805 Chatain, Robert. "The Adventure of the Mantises," New American Review, no. 7 (August 1969), 150-158.

1806 ______. "Notes on the Present Configuration of the Red-Blue Conflict," Tri-Quarterly, no. 16 (Fall 1969), 41-44.

1807 Chatfield, Hale. "Prose V," Minnesota Review, IX (1969), 244-247.

1808 Chauhan, Vijay. "Departure," Eastern Horizon, IV (December 1965), 57-60.

1809 Chauncey, William. "One Summer," Crucible, III (Spring 1967), 16-17.

1810 Chavchavadze, Paul. "Scheherazade," New Yorker, XLIV (May 11, 1968), 41-45.

1811 Chay, Marie. "At Least We Were Spared That," Discourse, X (Autumn 1967), 416-420.

1812 ______. "Everything in Season," Modern Age, XII (Spring 1968), 169-172.

1813 ______. "Fourteen Times Fourteen," Modern Age, IX (Winter 1964-65), 77-81.

1814 ______. "I Like It Better That Way," Southwest Review, LIII (Winter 1968), 65-73.

1815 ______. "Justice Is All," Arizona Quarterly, XXII (Spring 1966), 67-77.

1816 ______. "Like Water from a Well," Arizona Quarterly, XXV (Winter 1969), 349-359.

1817 ______. "My Grandmother and the Ant," Modern Age, X (Fall 1966), 366-369.

1818 ______. "Round Instead of Flat," Modern Age, XIII (Winter 1968-69), 62-66.

1819 ______. "So Many You's to Remember," Arizona Quarterly, XXI (Winter 1965), 357-363.

1820 ______. "Someone's Up at the Machados," Arizona Quarterly, XXIV (Winter 1968), 342-349.

1821 ______. "That, You Can Count On," Approach, no. 57 (Fall 1965), 29-37.

1822 ______. "Then You'll Be Left Behind," Arizona Quarterly, XXI (Summer 1965), 146-158.

1823 ______. "They're Not All Stars," Modern Age, X (Winter 1965-66), 78-80.

1824 ______. "You're Right. There Won't Be Any Next Time," Arizona Quarterly, XXIII (Autumn 1967), 259-267.

1825 Cheever, John. "Another Story," New Yorker, XLIII (February 25, 1967), 42-48.

1826 ______. "Bullet Park," New Yorker, XLIII (November 25, 1967), 56-59.

1827 ______. "The Geometry of Love," Saturday Evening Post, CCXXXIX (January 1, 1966), 34-39.

1828 ______. "Playing Fields," Playboy, XV (July 1968), 76-78, 84, 164-165.

1829 ______. "Reunion," Weekend Telegraph, no. 20 (February 5, 1965), 25.

1830 ______. "The World of Apples," Esquire, LXVI (December 1966), 216-219.

1831 ______. "The Yellow Room," Playboy, XV (January 1968), 86-90, 92, 217, 219-222, 224.

1832 Chekhov, Anton. "A Letter from the Don Landowner Stepan Vladimirovich N. to His Learned Neighbor Dr. Friedrich," Readers & Writers, II (Summer 1968), 36-40.

1833 ______. "Two Unpublished Short Stories/The Conspirators, an Eye-Witness Account," Leona Eisele, trans., Adam International Review, no. 300 (1963-65), 45-48.

1834 ______. "Two Unpublished Short Stories/To Speak or Keep Silent, a Fairy Tale," Leona Eisele, trans., Adam International Review, no. 300 (1963-65), 44-45.

1835 Cheney, Brainard. "Get on Board Little Children," Sewanee Review, LXXVI (July-September 1968), 437-447.

1836 Cherici, P. Raoul. "In Barren Meadows," North American Mentor, VII (Winter 1969), 1-3.

1837 Cherney, David. "Aftermath," Dust, IV (Summer 1969), 44-51.

1838 ______. "The Escape," Nexus (San Francisco, Calif.), II (November-December 1965), 20-23.

1839 Chernoff, Sanford. "'Evelyn's People'," Epoch, XIX (Fall 1969), 89-100.

1840 _____. "Not My Animal," New Directions 21, (1969), 206-212.

1841 Cherry, Kelly. "The Ruins of Athens Revisited," Greensboro Review, no. 7 (Summer-Fall 1969), 60-71.

1842 _____. "Tycho Brahe's Gold and Silver Nose," Red Clay Reader, no. 4 (1967), 30-37.

1843 Cherrytree, E. F. "The Fly," Evergreen Review, XII (September 1968), 42-47.

1844 _____. "Hello Out There!" Evergreen Review, XI (December 1967), 72-81.

1845 Chester, Alfred. "Glory Hole/(Nickel views of the Infidel in Tangiers)," Evergreen Review, IX (March 1965), 53-59.

1846 _____. "Ismael," Queen, CDXXIV (April 21, 1965), 78-80.

1847 Chetwin, Derek. "Alf and the Red Umbrella," Old Lady of Threadneedle Street, XLIII (September 1967), 161-165.

1848 Chew, Shirley. "Trying Times," Focus (Singapore), III, no. 3, 26-32.

1849 Chiara, Piero. "Giuditta," Sigfrid Walter de Rachewiltz, trans., Transatlantic Review, no. 29 (Summer 1968), 50-52.

1850 Chidambarananda. "The Beggar's Gift," Yashoda N. Bhat, trans., Literary Half-Yearly, VI (January 1965), 43-50.

1851 Chidester, Ann. "The Big Girl," Good Housekeeping, CLXVI (January 1968), 66-69.

1852 _____. "The Frenchwoman," McCall's, XCIII (May 1966), 80-81, 158-160.

1853 _____. "Jennaver," Redbook, CXXV (October 1965), 80-81.

1854 _____. "The Scent of Ginger," McCall's, XCIV (March 1967), 112-113, 184, 188.

1855 Chieffet, George. "Five Years Ago," Greensboro Review, no. 7 (Summer-Fall 1969), 4-13.

1856 _____. "Looking Up to the Dead," Greensboro Review, III (Winter 1967), 5-16.

1857 _____. "Nothing Like It in the World," Greensboro Review,

III (Summer-Fall 1968), 25-48.

1858 _____. "The Well," Red Clay Reader, no. 5 (1968), 34-37.

1859 Childers, Bob. "About the Tree," Wild Dog, no. 17 (June 1965), 37-38.

1860 Childers, Robert. "Cherub's Garden," Mexico Quarterly Review, III, no. 1 (1968), 70-76.

1861 Childress, William. "Charley," Human Voice, IV, no. 5 (1968), 14-21.

1862 _____. "The Doll," Human Voice, V, nos. 1-4 (1969), 23-31.

1863 _____. "The Roast Duck," Human Voice, V, nos. 1-4 (1969), 32-39.

1864 _____. "The Tractor," Southern Review, IV (January 1968), 182-191.

1865 _____. "Uncle Roman," Southern Review, I (October 1965), 896-905.

1866 _____. "Uncle Roman," Story: the Yearbook of Discovery, (1969), 99-106.

1867 Childs, James. "The Rose Glass," The Fair, II (Winter 1967), 25-30.

1868 Chin Ching-mai. "The Song of Ouyang Hai," Colin Mackerras and Paul Lowenstein, trans., Eastern Horizon, V (September 1966), 6-13.

1869 _____. "The Song of Ouyang Hai," Colin Mackerras and Paul Lowenstein, trans., Eastern Horizon, V (October 1966), 49-56.

1870 Chisholm, Scott. "Priscilla," Quartet, no. 10 (Spring 1965), 17-19.

1871 _____. "A Rose by Any Alexander," The Fair, II (Spring 1968), 29-37.

1872 _____. "Silence and Salami," The Fair, II (Summer 1968), 39-44.

1873 Chittister, Sister Mary. "Sharper than a Serpent's Tooth," Ave Maria, CIII (April 16, 1966), 25-27.

1874 _____. "Till Death Do Us Part," Ave Maria, CIII (March 5, 1966), 20-24.

1875 Chivilikhin, Vladimir. "The Story of Klava Ivanova," Margaret Wettlin, trans., Soviet Literature, (no. 11, 1966), 22-101.

1876 Chobanian, Peter. "A Birthday for Panoz," The Fiddlehead, no. 79 (March-April 1969), 93-98.

1877 Choi, Sivanandan. "How I Spent a Day at the University of Singapore," Focus (Singapore), New Series, no. 1 (1967), 35-39.

1878 Choly, R. "Two Point Three," Analecta, no. 1 (Fall 1967), 65-69.

1879 Choonara, I. "A View from the Window," Contrast (Cape Town, South Africa), no. 22 (December 1969), 9-16.

1880 _____. "A View from the Window," Transatlantic Review, no. 25 (Summer 1967), 123-129.

1881 Chopping, Richard. "The Gardeners," Queen, CDXXVIII (June 21, 1967), 74-77.

1882 Choudhuri, Pradip. "From My Rapid Activities," Intrepid, no. 10 (Spring 1968), n.p. [24].

1883 Choudhuri, Ramapada. "Birth and Death of a Hospital," Saroj Acharya, trans., Bengali Literature, I (October/December 1966), 41-51.

1884 Chowdhary, Omar. "The Ten-Minute President," Vision, XV (April 1966), 12-13.

1885 Chraïbi, Driss. "Four Trunks," Dorothy S. Blair, trans., The Classic, II, no. 2 (1966), 46-60.

1886 Christensen, Paul Norman. "Joachim and I," William and Mary Review, IV (Winter 1966), 37-43.

1887 Christesen, C. B. "The Ash-Blonde Benefactress," Meanjin Quarterly, XXIX (December 1965), 506-524.

1888 _____. "Grey Day, White Night," Westerly, (May 1966), 30-37.

1889 _____. "The Long-stemmed Chalice," Meanjin Quarterly, XXVIII (Autumn 1969), 80-84.

1890 _____. "The Troubled Eyes of Women," Meanjin Quarterly, XXV (December 1966), 465-474.

1891 Christie, Agatha. "At Bertram's Hotel/(Part I)," Good Housekeeping, CLXII (March 1966), 87-89, 208, 211-214, 216,

218, 224, 226-227, 231-235, 242, 244, 246, 252-261.

1892 _____. "At Bertram's Hotel/(Conclusion)," Good Housekeeping, CLXII (April 1966), 92-93, 230-232, 236, 238-239, 241, 246-258, 263, 270-271.

1893 _____. "By the Pricking of My Thumbs," Cosmopolitan, CLXVII (July 1969), 124-130, 132-138, 140-141, 144-151.

1894 _____. "Endless Night," Imprint, VIII (September 1968), 49, 51, 53, 55, 57, 59, 61, 63, 65, 67, 69, 71, 73, 75, 77, 79, 81, 83, 85, 87, 89, 91, 93, 95, 97, 99, 101, 103, 105, 107, 109, 111, 113-114.

1895 _____. "Endless Night (Part I)," Saturday Evening Post, CCXLI (February 24, 1968), 58-60, 62-68, 70, 72-73.

1896 _____. "Endless Night (Conclusion)," Saturday Evening Post, CCXLI (March 9, 1968), 50-59.

1897 _____. "Hallowe'en Party," Cosmopolitan, CLXVII (December 1969), 160-164, 166-168, 170-177, 180-183, 185-189.

1898 _____. "The Third Girl," Redbook, CXXVIII (April 1967), 139, 141-171.

1899 Christie, Michael. "George and Lisbeth," Edge, no. 8 (Fall 1968), 35-40.

1900 _____. "Rolling Down the Bowling Green," Prism International, IV (Spring 1965), 22-31.

1901 _____. "What Has Wings but Cannot Fly?" Prism International, V (Autumn 1965), 4-11.

1902 Christie, Philippa. "What the Neighbors Did," Twentieth Century, CLXXV (First Quarter 1967), 28-31.

1903 Christopher, John. "Rendezvous," Playboy, XIII (September 1966), 123, 148, 230-231.

1904 Christou, B. "Alone," Westerly, no. 3 (October 1968), 28-29.

1905 _____. "Evening," Westerly, no. 1 (March 1968), 18-20.

1906 Chu Po. "Taking Tiger Mountain by Surprise," Sidney Shapiro, trans., Eastern Horizon, VI (March 1967), 7-20.

1907 _____. "Taking Tiger Mountain by Surprise," Sidney Shapiro, trans., Eastern Horizon, VI (April 1967), 46-60.

1908 Chughtai, Mirza Azim Baig. "The Examiner's Betel-Leaf," Abdul Qayyum, trans., Pakistan Review, XVI (February 1968), 22-24.

1909 Chukovsky, Nikolai. "The Fifth Day/29 October 1917, Old Style," George Iankovsky, trans., Soviet Literature, (no. 11, 1968), 94-106.

1910 ______. "Little Girl Life," Vladimir Talmy, trans., Soviet Literature, (no. 2, 1965), 44-63.

1911 Chung Yee Chong. "On the Beach in the Rain," Focus (Singapore), New Series, no. 2 (1968/69), 10-11.

1912 Church, Marilyn Jakes. "Crisis at Kindergarten Corners," Columbia, LXVIII (September 1968), 24-28.

1913 ______. "The Importance of Squirrels," Columbia, XLVIII (January 1968), 24-27.

1914 ______. "Involvement," Ave Maria, CVII (January 13, 1968), 26-30.

1915 Chute, B. J. "January Thaw," Redbook, CXXIV (January 1965), 42-43, 85-88.

1916 ______. "The Temptation of Mrs. Logan," Good Housekeeping, CLXIII (August 1966), 72-73, 126-128, 130-131.

1917 Čingo, Živko. "The Medal," Donald Davenport, trans., Literary Review, XI (Winter 1967), 236-242.

1918 Ciobanu, Ion C. "Blackthorn," Margaret Wettlin, trans., Soviet Literature, (no. 11, 1965), 48-53.

1919 Citkovitz, Caroline. "Please Baby Don't Cry," London Magazine, IX (December 1969), 32-46.

1920 Clancy, R. "Boy against the Wall," Dare, IV (April 1966), 22-23.

1921 Clark, Brynda. "Destination Unknown," Foxfire, I (Fall 1967), 29.

1922 ______. "Going, Going, Gone," Foxfire, I (Spring 1967), 39-41.

1923 Clark, Charles C. "Plato and the Swing of Pleiades," Arlington Quarterly, I (Spring 1968), 223-240.

1924 Clark, Don. "Silent Song," McCall's, XCIV (October 1966), 128-129, 148, 150, 157-158, 160.

1925 Clark, Eleanor. "At the Falls at Nine," Yale Review, LVIII (Summer 1969), 572-577.

1926 Clark, Florence A. "Passenger Pigeons," Epoch, XVIII

(Fall 1968), 61-68.

1927 _____. "Since Saturday," Epoch, XIV (Winter 1965), 171-177.

1928 Clark, I. E. "God Sees Us Naked," Arx, II (April 1969), 34-38.

1929 Clark, J. Wesley. "The Twenty-First Annual Dance," Midwestern University Quarterly, I, no. 4 (1966), 57-63.

1930 Clark, Manning. "The Discovery," Quadrant, X (January-February 1966), 49-56.

1931 Clark, Naomi. "Eyes: A Fable," Quartet, no. 18 (Spring 1967), 20-23.

1932 Clark, Thomas. "Baseball," The Once Series, (Slice, no. 1), I (1966-67), n.p. [13].

1933 _____. "from Cluttering the Ranch:/Chapter 90," The Once Series (Vice), I (1966-67), n.p. [20-21].

1934 _____. "from Cluttering the Ranch/Chapter 2," The Once Series (Vice), I (1966-67), n.p. [24-25].

1935 _____. "The Fire-Dance," The Once Series, (Slice, no. 1), I (1966-67), n.p. [13].

1936 _____. "A Hundred Locomotives in the Roundhouse," Rolling Stone, no. 47 (November 29, 1969), 40.

1937 _____. "Mudball Gathering," The Once Series, (Slice, no. 1), I (1966-67), n.p. [13].

1938 _____. "Pancakes," The Once Series, (Slice, no. 1), I (1966-67), n.p. [13].

1939 _____. "from The Riot at the Garrick Theatre," The Once Series, (Nice), I (1966-67), n.p. [9-10].

1940 _____. "from The Riot at the Garrick Theatre," The World, no. 12 (June 1968), n.p. [83-85].

1941 _____. "Spectacles," The Once Series, (Slice, no. 1), I (1966-67), n.p. [13].

1942 _____. "The Trial," The Once Series, (Slice, no. 1), I (1966-67), n.p. [13].

1943 Clarke, Arthur C. "Dial 'F' for Frankenstein," Playboy, XII (January 1965), 148-149, 215-216.

1944 _____. "The Light of Darkness," Playboy, XIII (June 1966), 113, 174-176.

1945 _____. "Maelstrom II," Playboy, XII (April 1965), 84-86, 90, 178, 180.

1946 _____. "Playback," Playboy, XIII (December 1966), 220, 277.

1947 Clarke, Austin C. "The Collector," Transatlantic Review, no. 24 (Spring 1967), 24-37.

1948 _____. "Four Stations in His Circle," Saturday Night, LXXX (December 1965), 23-27.

1949 _____. "Give Us This Day; And Forgive Us," Tamarack Review, no. 38 (Winter 1966), 21-34.

1950 _____. "A Wedding in Toronto," Tamarack Review, no. 45 (Autumn 1967), 54-58, 60, 62-64.

1951 _____. "Why Didn't You Use a Plunger?" Tamarack Review, no. 52 (1969), 51-57, 60-62.

1952 _____. "Why Didn't You Use the Plunger?" Yale Literary Magazine, CXXXVIII (Fall 1969), 26-30.

1953 Clarke, Dick. "The Interview," Ave Maria, CII (October 16, 1965), 22-23.

1954 _____. "The Sheepshead," Ave Maria, CII (October 16, 1965), 24-25.

1955 Clarke, Harry. "The Drawing Lesson," Old Lady of Threadneedle Street, XLIII (March 1965), 14-15.

1956 _____. "'Every Nice Girl...'," Old Lady of Threadneedle Street, XLV (March 1969), 28-29.

1957 Clarke, Iole. "The Weatherman," New Zealand Listener, LII (June 18, 1965), 4.

1958 Clarke, John Hendrik. "How Many Were Going to St. Ives?" North American Review, IV (March 1967), 18-19.

1959 Clarke, Judith. "Ruth," Westerly, no. 2 (1967), 5-9.

1960 _____. "Thank You Mrs. Greenberger," Westerly, no. 1 (March 1968), 23-25.

1961 _____. "The Wisdom of Mrs. Greenberger," Westerly, no. 3 (October 1968), 5-8.

1962 Clarke, Linda. "The Child," Little Review of the Pacific Northwest, I (Fall 1965), 70-72.

1963 Clarke, Neva. "The Cat Who Cleaned House," Redbook, CXXX (March 1968), 82-83.

1964 _____. "Holiday Job," New Zealand Listener, (April 28, 1967), 6.

1965 _____. "The Slippery Damn Mat," New Zealand Listener, (September 22, 1967), 6.

1966 Claus, Hugo. "After the Movies," London Magazine, IX (October 1969), 5-8.

1967 Clay, George R. "Bird in the Hand," Ladies' Home Journal, LXXXIV (March 1967), 96-97, 174.

1968 _____. "The Management Is Not Responsible," Seventeen, XXVI (February 1967), 144-145, 218.

1969 _____. "The Paperweight Snowstorm," Seventeen, XXV (December 1966), 120-121, 182-183.

1970 Clays, Gino. "Omnia Mea Mecum Porto," Wild Dog, no. 17 (June 1965), 19-20.

1971 Clayton, Jay. "Tautology," Arx, II (October 1968), 5-8.

1972 Clayton, John J. "The Cave Is Full of Soldiers," Massachusetts Review, X (Spring 1969), 231-243.

1973 Cleaver, Eldridge. "The Flashlight," Playboy, XVI (December 1969), 120-124, 287-290, 292, 296, 298, 301-302.

1974 Cleaver, Gerald. "Never Press the Lapels," Playboy, XV (May 1968), 107, 162, 164-165.

1975 Cleaver, Vera and Bill. "I Reckon I Love You," Woman's Day, (August 1966), 38-39, 83-87.

1976 _____. "The Quiet Girl," McCall's, XCIII (February 1966), 84-85, 162-165.

1977 Cleeve, Brian. "Foxer," Saturday Evening Post, CCXXXVIII (December 18, 1965), 48-49, 52-54, 58-59.

1978 Clifford, Frances. "The Naked Runner," Cosmopolitan, CLX (January 1966), 98-115, 119-121, 123-129.

1979 _____. "Time Is an Ambush," Cosmopolitan, CLXI (December 1966), 142-148, 150-157, 161-166, 168-171.

1980 Clifford, Francis. "Another Way of Dying," Playboy, XV (December 1968), 110-112, 114, 248-250, 252, 254-256, 258, 261-262.

1981 _____. "Another Way of Dying/Part II," Playboy, XVI (January 1969), 154-156, 208, 210, 212-214, 217-219.

1982 _____. "Another Way of Dying/Conclusion," Playboy, XVI (February 1969), 140-142, 148, 167-169, 171-176, 178-179.

1983 _____. "Third Side of the Coin," Cosmopolitan, CLVIII (January 1965), 98-126.

1984 Clifton, Lucille. "The Magic Mama," Redbook, CXXXIV (November 1969), 88-89.

1985 Clinton, Sister Mary Frances. "Desert Hunt," New Leaven, XIX (1969), 4-9.

1986 Cloar, Carroll. "Two Fables/The Little Girl Who Got Smaller and Smaller," Delta Review, VI (November-December 1969), 89-90.

1987 _____. "Two Fables/The Little Girl Who Lost Her Name," Delta Review, VI (November-December 1969), 88-90.

1988 Clover, M. E. "Fool's Ransom," North American Review, V (July-August 1968), 35-38.

1989 Coates, Robert M. "The Setting-in of Winter," New Yorker, XLIII (December 9, 1967), 60-68, 70, 72, 75-76, 78, 81-82, 84, 87, 90.

1990 Coates, Rodney [Minkey]. "Essay on Tongues and Frustration," Work, no. 2 (Fall 1965), 43-44.

1991 Coates, Ruth Allison. "The Mailbox," Minnesota Review, VII (1967), 3-10.

1992 Cobb, William. "The Hunted," Arlington Quarterly, I (Summer 1968), 5-15.

1993 Coburn, Andrew. "From a Novel in Progress," Transatlantic Review, no. 26 (Autumn 1967), 111-117.

1994 _____. "The Heir," Transatlantic Review, no. 20 (Spring 1966), 80-84.

1995 Cochran, F. L. "The Box of Irony," Phylon, XXVI (Fall 1967), 282-285.

1996 Cochran, John R. "Two Leaves," Discourse, VIII (Autumn 1965), 331-335.

1997 Cochran, S. Vadah, Jr. "The Circus Lady," Delta Review, V (September 1968), 16-18.

1998 Cochrane, Shirley Graves. "Remember Charlie Mock?" Ladies' Home Journal, LXXXIII (March 1966), 82-83, 160-164.

1999 Cocteau, Jean. "Rose and Alfred," Margaret Crosland, trans., London Magazine, VIII (February 1969), 56-61.

2000 Coffer, Helene Lewis. "The Message of the Bells," Good Housekeeping, CLXVII (December 1968), 74-75, 201, 203-209.

2001 _____. "A Saint on Earth," Good Housekeeping, CLXII (April 1966), 98-99, 205, 210, 212, 214, 216, 218, 221.

2002 _____. "The True and Lasting Kind," Good Housekeeping, CLXV (November 1967), 94-95, 161-164, 166-168.

2003 Cogswell, Fred. "An Evening with Emily," Trace, no. 61 (Summer 1966), 186-189.

2004 Cohen, Cecilia. "Missy Discontent," Man About Town, I (April 1967), 61-62.

2005 Cohen, Edward M. "Fishman Paper Box Co., Inc.," Evergreen Review, IX (September 1965), 27-29, 85-87.

2006 Cohen, Florence Chanock. "Confessions from a Seashell About a Writer in Wales," Epoch, XVII (Fall 1967), 91-96.

2007 _____. "The Promise," Epoch, XV (Spring 1966), 219-234.

2008 Cohen, Gerald. "Life Class," Quartet, no. 24 (Fall 1968), 6-8.

2009 Cohen, Keith. "At the Inlet," Paris Review, XI (Fall 1968), 108-118.

2010 _____. "The Balustrade," Paris Review, XII (Spring 1969), 61-85.

2011 _____. "Grecian Dreams," Columbia Review, XLVII, no. 1 (1966), 26-33.

2012 _____. "Grecian Dreams," Paris Review, XI (Fall 1968), 119-128.

2013 _____. "Part II of a Novel," Columbia Review, XLVII, no. 2 (1967), 12-29.

2014 _____. "Strands Growing Downward," Columbia Review,

XLVI, no. 1 (1965), 2-7.

2015 _____. "You Froze the Light and Flew," Columbia Review, XLVI, no. 2 (1966), 20-23.

2016 _____. "Vizcaya," Art and Literature, no. 7 (Winter 1965), 51-55.

2017 _____. "Water," Art and Literature, no. 10 (Autumn 1966), 34-40.

2018 Cohen, Leonard. "Luggage Fire Sale," Parallel, no. 2 (May-June 1966), 40-44.

2019 Cohen, Marvin. "The Bedtime Story that Ends in One Peace," Chelsea, no. 27 (December 1969), 106-118.

2020 _____. "Dialogues," Transatlantic Review, no. 27 (Winter 1967-68), 92-95.

2021 _____. "Hounded by an Author into a Second Identity," Extensions, no. 2 (1969), 60-65.

2022 _____. "Five Stories/How the Precious Human Instrument of Truth Failed to Survive in the Crude Accidents of Evolution," Salmagundi, no. 9 (Spring 1969), 91-95.

2023 _____. "Five Stories/A Jewelled Discourse on Brevity's Permanent Master," Salmagundi, no. 9 (Fall 1969), 90-91.

2024 _____. "Five Stories/The Law of Internal Dynamics," Salmagundi, no. 9 (Spring 1969), 95-98.

2025 _____. "Five Stories/The Selfishness to Survive; and No Gain without Ruthlessness," Salmagundi, no. 9 (Fall 1969), 88-89.

2026 _____. "Five Stories/A Surprise Turn," Salmagundi, no. 9 (Spring 1969), 94-95.

2027 _____. "The Imperishable Container of All Current Pasts," Transatlantic Review, no. 22 (Autumn 1966), 119-120.

2028 _____. "Love by Proxy of Solitude," New Directions 21, (1969), 219-238.

2029 _____. "The Monday Rhetoric of the Love Club," New Directions 19, (1966), 263-287.

2030 _____. "Paintings on Museum Walls," Chelsea, no. 27 (December 1969), 66-73.

2031 _____. "Plays and Things from Marvin Cohen," Ambit,

no. 39 (1969), 13-20.

2032 _____. "from The Self-Devoted Friend," Quarterly Review of Literature, XIII (1965), 375-380.

2033 _____. "Stories/The Blood of a Dentist," Ambit, no. 32 (1967), 11.

2034 _____. "Stories/Charles' Courtship, Engagement, and Marriage with Irene His Happy Bride," Ambit, no. 32 (1967), 9-10.

2035 _____. "Stories/How Barry Tamed the Past, and Brought It Up to Date," Ambit, no. 32 (1967), 8-9.

2036 _____. "Stories/Listening to Herman," Ambit, no. 32 (1967), 12-16.

2037 _____. "Stories/The Art of Concealed Abortion," Ambit, no. 34 (1968), 38-39.

2038 _____. "Stories/The Comments Aroused by a House; About It and the Disputative Commentators," Ambit, no. 34 (1968), 40-42.

2039 _____. "Stories/How Never to Be Able to Tell Bob Apart from Peter," Ambit, no. 34 (1968), 39.

2040 _____. "Stories/How to Cultivate Decadence in One Easy Dialogue," Ambit, no. 34 (1968), 42.

2041 Cohen, Matt. "Nihilism or Insanity: The Strange Life of Ichabod Oise," Freelance (St. Louis, Mo.), VII, no. 2 (1969), 9-14.

2042 Cohen, Mike. "The Bright Young Man," Redbook, CXXVI (February 1966), 155-181.

2043 Cohn, Nik. "The Art of Klaus Antonio," Nova, (September 1966), 133-134, 139-140.

2044 Cohoe, Grey. "The Promised Visit," South Dakota Review, VII (Summer 1969), 45-56.

2045 Coker, Elizabeth B. "The Wishing Bone," South Carolina Review, II (November 1969), 23-35.

2046 Colby, Vineta. "The Flexible Shadow," University Review, XXXI (March 1965), 195-198.

2047 Cold, John O. "The Rime of the Efficient Dog Grinder," Ante, III (Spring 1967), 27-39.

2048 _____. "'Say, Mister Cuthbert: Why Don't You Give a Dime or Two to Some Nice Worthy Cause'," Crucible, IV (Spring 1968), 8, 10-14.

2049 Cole, Frances. "The Return," William and Mary Review, IV (Winter 1966), 81-85.

2050 Cole, Tom. "On the Edge of Arcadia," Atlantic Monthly, CCXVI (September 1965), 81-88.

2051 _____. "Saint John of the Hershey Kisses: 1964," Kenyon Review, XXXI (1969), 17-53.

2052 Colebatch, Hal. "Under the Wharf," Westerly, no. 4 (December 1968), 15-16.

2053 Coleman, Earl. "Model of a Sage Man," Esquire, LXIX (January 1968), 77, 79, 38.

2054 Coleman, Emily. "A Step-Father," Art and Literature, no. 4 (Spring 1965), 236-243.

2055 Coleman, James. "The Yes Man," December, XI (1969), 57-61.

2056 Coleman, Thomas. "Hunting I," Plaintiff, V (Fall 1968), 17.

2057 _____. "Hunting II," Plaintiff, V (Fall 1968), 17.

2058 _____. "Painters," Plaintiff, V (Winter 1969), 52-53.

2059 Colette. "The Shackle," Mademoiselle, LXIX (July 1969), 110-129, 131-138.

2060 Colladay, Winter. "The Coulters," Quarterly Review of Literature, XIV (1967), 282-333.

2061 Collett, Walter G. "The Committal," Massachusetts Review, VIII (Winter 1967), 98-120.

2062 _____. "Hanging Around," Jeopardy, no. 5 (Spring 1969), 177-181.

2063 Collier, Eugenia W. "Marigolds," Negro Digest, XIX (November 1969), 54-62.

2064 Collier, Zena. "The Chimney," University Review, XXXIV (Summer 1968), 258-266.

2065 Collins, David M. "Guadalupe," Discourse, XII (Autumn 1969), 522-527.

2066 Collins, Dennis. "Spinach Will Give You Muscles," Wisconsin

Review, III (Fall 1967), 22-24.

2067 Collman, Richard F. "Portrait of a Boy," UMD Humanist, XIII (Spring 1965), 15.

2068 Collymore, Frank A. "The Diaries," Bim, XI (July-December 1966), 217-221.

2069 _____. "To Meet Her Mother," Bim, XI (January-June 1967), 290-295.

2070 Colquhoun, Keith. "A Military Memorandum," Stand, X, no. 4 (1969), 11-17.

2071 Colter, Cyrus. "Black for Dinner," Chicago Review, XVIII, no. 2 (1965), 82-97.

2072 _____. "A Gift," Northwest Review, VIII (Fall-Winter 1966-67), 50-63.

2073 _____. "from The Hippodrome," Chicago Review, XIX (June 1967), 37-45.

2074 _____. "A Man in the House," Prairie Schooner, XLI (Fall 1967), 267-277.

2075 Colum, Padraic. "In Pilver Park There Walks a Deer," New Yorker, XLV (May 31, 1969), 35-38.

2076 _____. "The Tradition that Existed in My Grandmother's House," New Yorker, XLIII (December 23, 1967), 28-31.

2077 Colvin, Michael. "A Moment at Christmas," Delta, XXII (1968), 13-16.

2078 Colwell, Robert. A Nameless Scow, The Smith, Special Issue no. 3 (1969), n.p. [2-18].

2079 _____. "One More Time, Sweet Baby," DeKalb Literary Arts Journal, III (Spring 1969), 79-85.

2080 _____. "Tilley Tuning Out," Pyramid, no. 3 (1969), 15-22.

2081 Colwin, Laurie. "The Man Who Jumped into the Water," New Yorker, XLV (December 20, 1969), 38-42.

2082 Comber, Leon, trans. "The Strange Cases of Magistrate Pao/Chinese Tales of Crime and Detection/The Case of the Passionate Monk," Imprint, VIII (April 1968), 91-100.

2083 _____, trans. "The Strange Cases of Magistrate Pao/Chinese Tales of Crime and Detection/The Key," Imprint, VIII (April 1968), 107-108, 111-115, 117, 119, 121-122.

2084 _____, trans. "The Strange Cases of Magistrate Pao/Chinese Tales of Crime and Detection/The Temple by the River," Imprint, VIII (April 1968), 101-106.

2085 Como, Joseph. "The Old Established Firm," Signature, I (December 1966), 68-69, 104, 106, 110.

2086 Compton, D. G. "A Turning off the Minch Park Road," Art and Literature, no. 10 (Autumn 1966), 41-54.

2087 Conaway, Frank, Jr. "Rilke, Rainer Maria: The Confessions of a Younger Poet," The Fair, II (Winter 1967), 2-10.

2088 Conaway, James. "The Abecedarian," Texas Quarterly, VIII (Winter 1965), 126-131.

2089 _____. "The Outsider," Lillabulero, II (Winter 1968), 5-8.

2090 Conaway, Ray. "If You Need Me, Let Me Know," Saturday Evening Post, CCXXXIX (July 16, 1966), 64-66, 68, 70-71.

2091-2099 [numbering gap]

2100 _____. "A Matter of Style," Redbook, CXXXII (February 1969), 76-77, 120-123.

2101 Congdon, Kirby. "Selections from Dream Work," Boss, (Spring 1967), 76-78.

2102 _____. "Jaganath," Nexus (San Francisco, Calif.), III (January-February 1967), 32-33.

2103 Conger, Lesley. "Heart of the Family," Good Housekeeping, CLXIV (April 1967), 106-107.

2104 Coningham, John. "Circe and the Bristolian," Old Lady of Threadneedle Street, XLI (September 1965), 162-164.

2105 Conly, Jane. "Etude," Grecourt Review, XI (February 1968), 25-33.

2106 Connell, Evan S., Jr. "Leon & Berbert Aloft," Carolina Quarterly, XIX (Winter 1967), 9-20.

2107 _____. "Mr. Bridge," Esquire, LXXI (May 1969), 173-176, 178, 184, 186, 189, 194, 198, 202-204, 206, 208.

2108 _____. "Puig's Wife," New Mexico Quarterly, XXXVII (Summer 1967), 129-156.

2109 _____. "St. Augustine's Pigeon," Saturday Evening Post, CCXXXVIII (March 13, 1965), 52-53, 56, 58, 60-63, 65-66, 68, 70, 72, 74-78.

2110 ______. "The Scriptwriter," Paris Review, XII (Fall 1969), 12-18.

2111 ______. "The Voyeur," Lillabulero, I (Winter 1967), 27-28.

2112 ______. "The Undersigned, Leon & Bébert," Esquire, LXXII (December 1969), 232-233, 294, 296, 298-300, 302-303.

2113 Connell, Graeme K. "A Number to Ring," New Zealand Listener, (September 16, 1966), 6.

2114 Connor, Jack. "An Escape," Prolog, VII (Spring 1969), 16-22.

2115 Connor, Thomas. "Mixing," New Frontiers, XI, 2 (1966), 25.

2116 Connor, Tony. "A Sunday Morning Drive," The Archive, LXXIX (December 1966), 19-22.

2117 Connors, Burton. "Delilah," Twentieth Century, CLXXVII (First Quarter, 1968), 51-53.

2118 ______. "Tale of a Mountain Town," Anglo-Welsh Review, XVII (Winter 1969), 116-119.

2119 Connors, Thomas E. "Big Game," Modern Age, XI (Summer 1967), 294-299.

2120 ______. "The Couple," December, XI (1969), 63-65.

2121 ______. "Death and the Man," North American Review, V (September-October 1968), 13-18.

2122 ______. "Dies Irae," Chelsea, no. 17 (August 1965), 84-89.

2123 ______. "Eden Flowering," Western Humanities Review, XX (Winter 1966), 13-20.

2124 ______. "The Immanence of Loss," Modern Age, X (Spring 1966), 173-178.

2125 ______. "The Silence of Skin," December, VIII (1966), 165-169.

2126 ______. "Weekend Retreat," Western Humanities Review, XXIII (Spring 1969), 135-154.

2127 Conrad, Barnaby. "The Night-Runner," Signature, I (November 1966), 46-47, 94, 96, 98.

2128 Conroy, Frank. "Hanging On," New Yorker, XLII (December 10, 1966), 58-63.

2129 _____. "Nights Away from Home," New Yorker, XLII (October 22, 1966), 56-66, 68, 73, 75-76, 78, 80.

2130 _____. "Please Don't Take My Sunshine Away," Paris Review, X (Winter-Spring 1967), 72-92.

2131 _____. "A Yo-Yo Going Down," London Magazine, VII (March 1968), 27-38.

2132 Constable, Antoinette. "The Dollar Fifty Farewell," New Campus Review, I (Winter/Spring 1968), 12-13.

2133 Constant, Nicholas. "The Gar Pool," Georgia Review, XXI (Fall 1967), 330-344.

2134 Constantino, E. O. "The Phantom," Solidarity, I (July-September 1966), 35-40.

2135 Contoski, Victor. "Journal of a Masked Man," North American Review, IV (July 1967), 6-8.

2136 _____. "The Visitation," The Quest, II (Spring 1966), 301-305.

2137 Conversi, Leonard. "The Portable D. L. Marston," North American Review, III (September 1966), 8-10.

2138 Cook, Bruce. "The Goyische Garfield," December, X (1968), 64-69.

2139 _____. "The Jew of Frankfort," Trace, no. 69 (1968), 474-486.

2140 Cook, Richard. "Casa Chace," William and Mary Review, VII (Winter 1969), 78-85.

2141 Cook, Whitfield. "Only Women Can Be Wives," Redbook, CXXXII (March 1969), 70-71, 142, 144, 146.

2142 Coolidge, Clark. "The Breaks," Joglars, no. 3 (1966), n.p. [28].

2143 Cooper, Edmund. "Five to Twelve," Cosmopolitan, CLXVI (April 1969), 160-166, 168, 170-174, 176-178, 180-183, 186-188.

2144 Cooper, Marc. "When I Am Seven...," Analecta, II (Spring 1968), 47-50.

2145 Cooper, Parley J. "'The Crop'," Signature, II (March 1967), 36-39, 60.

2146 Cooper, Pat Outlaw. "Goodbye Soldier," Crucible, IV (Spring 1968), 37-39.

2147 ______. "The Goshen Girl," Crucible, II (Fall 1965), 37-41.

2148 ______. "The Gravedigger," Crucible, VI (Fall 1969), 40, 42-43.

2149 ______. "Only the Wind Is Free," Crucible, III (Spring 1967), 41-44.

2150 ______. "Soldier Gone Away," Crucible, I (Spring 1965), 42-45.

2151 Cooper, Peter V. H., Jr. "Waste," Delta, XXI (1967), 44-47.

2152 Coorey, Alfred. "A Singular Person," Quarto, (Fall 1965), 15-16.

2153 Coover, Robert. "The Cat in the Hat for President," New American Review, no. 4 (August 1968), 7-45.

2154 ______. "The Gingerbread House," New American Review, no. 6 (April 1969), 113-123.

2155 ______. "The Hat Act," Playboy, XV (February 1968), 127, 170-172.

2156 ______. "Incident in the Streets of the City," Playboy, XVI (January 1969), 80-86, 88, 238-239.

2157 ______. "The Magic Poker," Esquire, LXXII (July 1969), 87-91, 20, 22, 24, 26.

2158 ______. "The Mex Would Arrive in Gentry's Junction at 12:10...," Evergreen Review, XI (June 1967), 62-65, 98-102.

2159 ______. "Romance of the Thin Man and the Fat Lady," Bennington Review, III (Fall 1969), 3-9.

2160 ______. "That the Door Opened," Quarterly Review of Literature, XVI, nos. 3-4 (1969), 311-316.

2161 ______. "Three Stories by Robert Coover/J's Marriage," Quarterly Review of Literature, XIV (1967), 428-435.

2162 ______. "Three Stories by Robert Coover/The Milkmaid of Samaniego," Quarterly Review of Literature, XIV (1967), 436-440.

2163 ______. "Three Stories by Robert Coover/Scene for 'Winter'," Quarterly Review of Literature, XIV (1967), 422-427.

2164 ______. "The Wayfarer," New American Review, no. 2

(January 1968), 144-148.

2165 Cope, Jack. "The Castaway," Contrast (Cape Town, South Africa), no. 22 (December 1969), 70-81.

2166 ______. "Kathy's Papa," New Yorker, XLII (October 8, 1966), 207-208, 210, 213-216, 219-222, 225-226.

2167 ______. "The Name of Patrick Henry," Contrast (Cape Town, South Africa), no. 11 (March 1965), 52-65.

2168 ______. "The Name of Patrick Henry," Meanjin Quarterly, XXIV (June 1965), 201-213.

2169 ______. "The Name of Patrick Henry," New Yorker, XLI (October 16, 1965), 55-61.

2170 ______. "A Place of Safety," London Magazine, VIII (November 1968), 45-57.

2171 ______. "A Pound of Flesh," Contrast (Cape Town, South Africa), no. 15 (March 1967), 21-32.

2172 ______. "Power," Mademoiselle, LXII (December 1965), 144-147.

2173 ______. "They Broke the String," Contrast (Cape Town, South Africa), no. 17 (November 1967), 73-85.

2174 Ćopić, Branko. "Love and Jealousy," Donald Davenport, trans., Literary Review, XI (Winter 1967), 187-192.

2175 Corbett, Martyn. "Home Again," Delta (Cambridge, England), no. 39 (Summer 1966), 12-17.

2176 Corcoran, Barbara. "The Man in the Bicycle Cap," Redbook, CXXVIII (November 1966), 92-93.

2177 ______. "The Man of Your Choice," Woman's Day, (November 1966), 46-47, 126-130.

2178 ______. "You Can't Put a Black Jack on a Black Queen," Redbook, CXXIX (August 1967), 40-41.

2179 ______. "What Ever Became of Maggie?" Woman's Day, (April 1969), 56-57, 76-78.

2180 Cordero-Fernando, Gilda. "A Harvest of Humble Folk," Literature East and West, IX (March 1965), 27-42.

2181 ______. "The Visitation of the Gods," Hemisphere, XI (September 1967), 9-14.

2182 Cordes, Jim. "The Dropout," Dare, IV (July-August 1966), 30-31.

2183 _____. "The Matter with Howard," Dare, IV (October 1966), 18-19.

2184 Cordier, Robert. "from Artoise," Genesis: Grasp, I, no. 3 (1969), 23-28.

2185 Cording, John. "A Visit to the Botanical Gardens," Arx, III (June 1969), 14.

2186 Corfman, Eunice. "Art Alopie Epidures," Texas Quarterly, X (Winter 1967), 220-234.

2187 _____. "To Be an Athlete," Harper's Magazine, CCXXXV (November 1967), 86-94, 97.

2188 _____. "The Wife Syndrome," McCall's, XCV (February 1968), 81, 155, 162.

2189 Corke, Hilary. "Arrived," Quarterly Review of Literature, XIII (1965), 294-313.

2190 _____. "The Still Sea," Kenyon Review, XXVII (Winter 1965), 73-93.

2191 Corliss, Allene. "A Girl to Remember," Good Housekeeping, CLXVIII (February 1969), 70-71, 134, 136, 138-139.

2192 Corman, Patrick. "The King Is Dead, Long Live the King," Occident, (Fall 1965), n.p. [9-22].

2193 Cormier, Robert. "Bunny Berigan--Wasn't He a Musician or Something?" Redbook, CXXVI (January 1966), 40-41, 95-97.

2194 _____. "Charlie Mitchell, You Rat, Be Kind to My Little Girl," McCall's, XCVI (April 1969), 106-107, 192.

2195 _____. "Mine On Thursdays," Woman's Day, (October 1968), 50-51, 108-110.

2196 _____. "President Cleveland, Where Are You?" Redbook, CXXV (May 1965), 48-49, 139, 151-152.

2197 Corn, Hilda. "First Lady," Redbook, CXXX (November 1967), 90-91.

2198 Cornillon, John. "Journal Entry--September 24," Wormwood Review, V, no. 4 (1965), 19.

2199 Cornish, Sam. "Winters/(from Lobster for Breakfast)," Ann Arbor Review, no. 3 (Spring 1968), 5-6.

2200 Cornwell, Anita R. "And Save a Round for Jamie Brown," Negro Digest, XV (April 1966), 83-92.

2201 ______. "Between the Summers," Phylon, XXVII (Fall 1966), 292-300.

2202 ______. "The Rope on the Steps," Negro Digest, XIV (May 1965), 56-68.

2203 Cornwell, Ethel F. "Nunc Dimittis," The Fiddlehead, no. 74 (Winter 1968), 34-41.

2204 Corodimas, Peter. "The Circle," Prairie Schooner, XLIII (Summer 1969), 143-150.

2205 Corrigan, Matthew. "Danae," Canadian Forum, XLV (September 1965), 133-134.

2206 ______. "Night Wait," Forum, IV (Winter-Spring 1967), 32-38.

2207 Corrington, John William. "First Blood," Georgia Review, XIX (Spring 1965), 16-39.

2208 ______. "The Lonesome Traveller," Arlington Quarterly, I (Winter 1967-68), 5-59.

2209 ______. "The Night School," Massachusetts Review, IX (Summer 1968), 463-482.

2210 ______. "The Retrievers," Arlington Quarterly, I (Spring 1968), 183-206.

2211 ______. "A Time to Embrace," Denver Quarterly, II (Winter 1968), 43-85.

2212 ______. "To Carthage Then I Came," Southwest Review, LI (Spring 1966), 110-121.

2213 Corse, Murray. "Sick Leave," Edge, no. 5 (Fall 1966), 35-43.

2214 Corson, Martha. "A Girl to Marry," Good Housekeeping, CLXII (January 1966), 52-53, 167-170.

2215 Cortázar, Julio. "I Am an Axolotl," Paul Blackburn, trans., Vogue, CXLIX (February 15, 1967), 124-125.

2216 ______. "The Night Face Up," Paul Blackburn, trans., New Yorker, XLIII (April 22, 1967), 49-52.

2217 ______. "Unusual Occupations," Paul Blackburn, trans., Tri-Quarterly, no. 15 (Spring 1969), 184-199.

2218 Corwin, Stanley. "Area Code 202," Signature, I (March 1966), 27.

2219 Corydon, Jeff, III. "The Reluctant Chess Man," North American Review, III (March 1966), 20-25.

2220 Cosgrove, Fred. "A Statement from the Dean," Limbo, II (October 1965), 12-17.

2221 Coshin, Eric. "Po-Chek," Mt. Adams Review, II (Winter 1965), 32-33.

2222 Costa, Richard Hauer. "When the Bus Came to Thorofare," The Goodly Co., no. 6 (August 1966), 23-33.

2223 Costello, Mark. "Murphy in Missouri," North American Review, III (March 1966), 14-18.

2224 ______. "Murphy's Xmas," Transatlantic Review, no. 27 (Winter 1967-68), 55-67.

2225 ______. "Strong Is Your Hold O Love," Epoch, XIV (Winter 1965), 99-109.

2226 Costigan, Madeleine. "The Day of the Daffodils," Georgia Review, XXI (Fall 1967), 311-318.

2227 ______. "It's Different Now," Ave Maria, CII (November 13, 1965), 24-25.

2228 ______. "Rosabel," Ave Maria, CVI (October 7, 1967), 26-27, 29-30.

2229 ______. "A Short Walk for Jeremy Cole," Ave Maria, CI (June 26, 1965), 22-25.

2230 ______. "They're Very Undependable," Ave Maria, CIV (September 24, 1966), 22-24.

2231 Cotich, Felicia. "Old Bull," Antioch Review, XXVI (Fall 1966), 385-397.

2232 ______. "Target," Ante, III (Winter 1967), 57-65.

2233 ______. "What a Lovely Dream," Colorado Quarterly, XVII (Summer 1968), 83-95.

2234 Coulter, Stephen. "Embassy," Ladies' Home Journal, LXXXVI (August 1969), 99-106, 108-109.

2235 Coulton, S. R. "Two of a Kind," Literary Review, IX (Autumn 1965), 42-64.

2236 Coursen, Herbert R., Jr. "Hunting Accident," Sage, XI (Fall 1967), 281-287.

2237 Courtney, W. Peter. "Sin," Nexus (San Francisco, Calif.), II (July-August 1965), 14-20.

2238 Cousins, Margaret. "A Band of Angels," McCall's, XCIV (December 1966), 78-79, 139-143, 145.

2239 _____. "The Gifted Child," Ladies' Home Journal, LXXXVI (December 1969), 32, 122-124.

2240 _____. "The Incident at Versailles," McCall's, XCII (May 1965), 114-115, 192-197.

2241 _____. "O. J. Hazeltine," Ladies' Home Journal, LXXXIII (May 1966), 90-91, 161-163.

2242 _____. "Still Waters," Good Housekeeping, CLXII (April 1966), 90-91, 160, 162, 164, 166, 168.

2243 Covel, Thomas. "Firethorn," Voyages, II (Fall 1968), 96-100.

2244 Covert, Alice Lent. "The Lost and Lonely Heart," Good Housekeeping, CLXIII (August 1966), 68-69, 194-196, 201, 205-209.

2245 Cowan, James. "The Atheist Next Door," New Zealand Listener, (November 4, 1966), 6.

2246 _____. "The Betrayed," New Zealand Listener, (November 24, 1967), 6, 14.

2247 _____. "The Bullfight," New Zealand Listener, (November 3, 1967), 6, 24.

2248 _____. "The Longest Day," New Zealand Listener, (July 7, 1967), 6, 14.

2249 _____. "The New State," New Zealand Listener, (September 9, 1966), 6.

2250 _____. "The Road to Quarzazate," New Zealand Listener, (November 8, 1968), 10, 14-15.

2251 Cowan, Peter. "The Rock," Meanjin Quarterly, XXIX (December 1965), 421-435.

2252 _____. "The Tins," Meanjin Quarterly, XXIV (June 1965), 159-178.

2253 Coward, Noel. "Bon Voyage," McCall's, XCII (June 1965),

86-87, 128, 130-152.

2254 ______. "Echo of Laughter," McCall's, XCIII (February 1966), 98-99, 174-176.

2255 Cowasjee, Saros. "The General Secretary," Indian Literature, XII (March 1969), 40-46.

2256 Cowell, M. A. "Poetic Justice," The Cantuarian, (April 1966), 108-110.

2257 Cowell, Mark S. "Trapeze Artist," Four Quarters, XIX (November 1969), 9-13.

2258 Cowley, Joy. "House with a View," New Zealand Listener, LIII (October 22, 1965), 4, 13.

2259 ______. "Like Christmas," New Zealand Listener, (December 17, 1965), 8-9.

2260 ______. "A Place to Go," New Zealand Listener, (September 1, 1967), 6.

2261 ______. "The Scapegoat," New Zealand Listener, (November 25, 1966), 6, 17.

2262 ______. "The Silk," New Zealand Listener, March 5, 1965), 8, 16.

2263 ______. "Sunday Dinner," New Zealand Listener, (May 20, 1966), 6, 23.

2264 Cox, Arthur Jean. "Work in Progress," Riverside Quarterly, II (January 1966), 5-34.

2265 Cox, William. "The Magi Hangup," New Yorker, XLIII (December 23, 1967), 44-46.

2266 Coxhead, Nona. "The Bracelet," Cosmopolitan, CLXIII (December 1967), 126-130.

2267 Crabtree, Peter. "The Forgotten Ones," Arizona Quarterly, XXII (Summer 1966), 115-135.

2268 Craft, Commodore. "Under the Snow-White Earth," Twigs, no. 1 (1965), 35-40.

2269 Crane, Stephen. "Stephen Crane's 'Apache Crossing'/The Text of an Unfinished Story," Prairie Schooner, XLIII (Summer 1969), 184-185.

2270 ______. "Four Men in a Cave," Readers & Writers, I (April-May 1967), 32-33.

2271 Crawford, Betty Anne. "The Worms," Seventeen, XXVIII (January 1969), 82-83, 128.

2272 Crawford, Constance. "Far from Blue Earth," Seventeen, XXVIII (April 1969), 166-167, 216, 218, 220, 222.

2273 Crayder, Dorothy and Helen McCully. "The Christmas Pony," Woman's Day, (December 1966), 34-37, 78-80, 85-87.

2274 Crayton, Pearl. "The Day the World Came to an End," Negro Digest, XIV (August 1965), 54-60.

2275 _____. "The Gold Fish Monster," Texas Quarterly, X (Summer 1967), 199-203.

2276 Creal, Margaret. "Lifeline," McCall's, XCVI (August 1969), 54-55, 121-122.

2277 Creed, Richard. "Midway through the Second Spin," American, IV (Spring 1968), 14-25.

2278 Cremeens, Carlton. "The Lord God Bird," Georgia Review, XXII (Fall 1968), 400-415.

2279 _____. "To Weep into Stones," Southern Review, V (October 1969), 1183-1191.

2280 Cremer, Jan. "French Fries without a Pickle," Evergreen Review, XII (December 1968), 54-56, 89-92.

2281 Cresswell, Helen. "The Cuckoo," Cornhill Magazine, CLXXVII (Autumn-Winter 1968-69), 169-180.

2282 _____. "A Hole in the Sand," Cornhill Magazine, no. 1043 (Spring 1965), 345-352.

2283 Cretan, Gladys Yessayan. "Dali Haig," Ararat, VI (Summer 1965), 23-25.

2284 Crews, Harry. "The Player Piano," Florida Quarterly, I (Fall 1967), 30-36.

2285 Crichton, Robert. "The Day Mussolini Died in Santa Vittoria," Saturday Evening Post, CCXXXIX (December 17, 1966), 44-46, 50, 52, 54-55.

2286 _____. "To Honor the Harvest/from The Secret of Santa Vittoria," Ladies' Home Journal, LXXXIV (January 1967), 97-100.

2287 Criner, Calvin. "Private Drive," Long View Journal, I (Spring 1969), 61-71.

2288 ______. "Without Malice," Long View Journal, I (Winter 1968), 37-40.

2289 Criswell, Marianne. "My Mother and Joey," Seventeen, XXIV (June 1965), 96-97, 157-158, 160.

2290 ______. "The Pickup," Seventeen, XXVII (October 1968), 140-141, 172, 174.

2291 Crittenden, Jordan. "The Man Who Made His Home in the Los Angeles International Airport," Saturday Evening Post, CCXXXIX (September 24, 1966), 60-61.

2292 ______. "The Man Who Was a Little on the Heavy Side," Harper's Bazaar, XCIX (November 1965), 166.

2293 ______. "Mary Chaffee," Harper's Bazaar, C (August 1967), 46.

2294 ______. "Mr. Schellenberg and the Thing He Couldn't Explain Over the Phone," Harper's Bazaar, CI (August 1968), 136-137.

2295 ______. "Mrs. Laura Hamilton Reese," Harper's Bazaar, C (September 1967), 174.

2296 ______. "Phil Stacey and Why He Feels the Way He Does about Oxnard, California," Harper's Bazaar, XCIX (March 1966), 139-143, 146.

2297 ______. "Susan Crosby," Harper's Bazaar, CI (April 1968), 206-207.

2298 ______. "Three Stories/Beverly Snodgrass," New Yorker, XLII (March 19, 1966), 178-180.

2299 ______. "Three Stories/George Pierce," New Yorker, XLII (March 19, 1966), 180, 183.

2300 ______. "Three Stories/Jerome Mossbacher," New Yorker, XLII (March 19, 1966), 177-178.

2301 Crome, Nicholas. "All Things Rare," University of Windsor Review, IV (Fall 1968), 61-73.

2302 Cross, James. "Pin Money," Playboy, XIV (June 1967), 103-104, 195-199.

2303 Crossman, Patricia R. "Boy in a Box," Redbook, CXXVI (November 1965), 74-75.

2304 ______. "The Gold-Headed Cane," McCall's, XCIV (March 1967), 118-119.

2305 ______. "A Life to Live," Good Housekeeping, CLXVIII (March 1969), 112-113.

2306 ______. "Time Out of Yesterday," Good Housekeeping, CLX (June 1965), 78-79, 220-226, 231-233, 238-240.

2307 ______. "The Very Nature of Love," Woman's Day, (February 1967), 50-51, 113.

2308 ______. "Walk Toward Tomorrow," Good Housekeeping, CLXIII (October 1966), 96-97, 174, 176-178.

2309 Crowe, Cecily T. "Kilraven Castle," Redbook, CXXVI (December 1965), 147, 149-175.

2310 ______. "Northwater," Ladies' Home Journal, LXXXV (July 1968), 87-94, 120-124.

2311 Crowe, Patricia. "Wang Tay," William and Mary Review, IV (Spring 1966), 47-48.

2312 Cruz, Andres Cristobal. "The Old Well," Patricia Melendrez, trans., Literature East and West, XIII (December 1969), 281-290.

2313 Csák, Gyula. "The Lord Chamberlain," New Hungarian Quarterly, VII (Summer 1966), 213-219.

2314 Cseres, Tibor. "Cold Days/Part of a novel," New Hungarian Quarterly, VII (Spring 1966), 59-85.

2315 Csurka, István. "The Barge Pilot," Literary Review, IX (Spring 1966), 347-352.

2316 Cuervo Delgado, Herminio. "Any Other Sunday," William and Mary Review, VI (Spring 1968), 15-23.

2317 ______. "Avanzada," William and Mary Review, V (Winter 1967), 21.

2318 Cuevas, Ernesto. "Organization," Canadian Forum, XLVIII (November 1968), 188-190.

2319 Culff, Robert. "Citadels of Hard Glass," Works, I (Autumn 1967), 30-37.

2320 Cullen, John B. "When Giants Fell," Georgia Review, XXI (Fall 1967), 397-406.

2321 Cullinan, Elizabeth. "The Old Priest," New Yorker, XLI (December 18, 1965), 52-58.

2322 ______. "A Sunday Like the Others," New Yorker, XLIII

(August 26, 1967), 26-33.

2323 _____. "A Swim," New Yorker, XLI (June 5, 1965), 41-48.

2324 Culver, Monty. "The Chance of a Lifetime," Saturday Evening Post, CCXXXIX (January 15, 1966), 58-63.

2325 Cumbie, Wylie. "Revival," Harper's Bazaar, XCIX (November 1965), 144, 146, 148, 152, 156.

2326 Cunningham, E. V. "Penelope," Cosmopolitan, CLVIII (May 1965), 124-135, 138-145, 148-153.

2327 Cuomo, George. "And He Shall Have Music," Malahat Review, no. 11 (July 1969), 17-26.

2328 _____. "The Deliverance of the Pure," Tamarack Review, no. 35 (Spring 1965), 47-61.

2329 _____. "A Real Good Price," Malahat Review, no. 11 (July 1969), 5-16.

2330 Curewitz, Richard. "Then and Now, Here and Now," Sundial, I (Spring 1966), 6-14.

2331 Curley, Daniel. "The Gingerbread Man," Texas Quarterly, X (Winter 1967), 111-128.

2332 _____. "The Moth, the Bear and the Shivering Stars," U.S. Catholic and Jubilee, XXIV (May 1969), 33-36.

2333 _____. "Where You Wouldn't Want to Walk," Hudson Review, XXII (Autumn 1969), 442-448.

2334 Curley, Edmund C. "The Barbarians," Ave Maria, CVII (March 30, 1968), 26-28.

2335 Curnow, Wystan. "The Emergence of Herman Threshold," Landfall, no. 86 (June 1968), 127-138.

2336 _____. "A Seminal Occasion," Landfall, no. 77 (March 1966), 63-75.

2337 Curran, Dolores. "To Sell a Soul," Ave Maria, CV (March 25, 1967), 24-26.

2338 _____. "Visitation Saturday," Ave Maria, CIV (November 19, 1966), 24-26.

2339 Curran, Mary Doyle. "The Devil's Advocate," Massachusetts Review, VI (Autumn-Winter 1964-65), 113-117.

2340 _____. "Mrs. Reardon's Gamble," Massachusetts Review,

VII (Winter 1966), 47-56.

2341 Currey, Stella Martin. "To Live the Dream," Good Housekeeping, CLXIX (November 1969), 90-91, 159-161, 163-164, 166.

2342 Currier, Elizabeth. "Tenderly Arrogant," UMD Humanist, XV (Winter 1967), 16-20.

2343 Currier, John. "Billy Grout Griff," Mill Mountain Review, I (1969), 56.

2344 Curtis, Jean-Louis. "Time after Death," John Jolliffe, trans., Adam International Review, nos. 310-312 (1966), 73-114.

2345 Curtis, Margaret E. "One Summer There Were Dragons," Good Housekeeping, CLXIX (August 1969), 68-69, 165-166, 168.

2346 Curtiss, Ursula. "Danger: Hospital Zone," Good Housekeeping, CLXII (May 1966), 85-87, 194, 196, 198, 200, 206-208, 210-212, 217-231, 237-239.

2347 Curtler, Douglas Carrick. "Poor Little Upside-Down Cake," William and Mary Review, V (Spring 1967), 39-55.

2348 _____. "This Child Is Not for Burning," William and Mary Review, VI (Winter 1968), 33-37.

2349 Cusack, Isabel Langis. "The Girl from Endsville," Ladies' Home Journal, LXXXV (November 1968), 116-117, 176-178, 180.

2350 _____. "A Lot to Learn," Redbook, CXXXIII (June 1969), 76-77, 146-147, 150-153.

2351 _____. "A Mother of Kindness," Good Housekeeping, CLXVIII (May 1969), 104-105, 179-183.

2352 _____. "The Shell Game," Saturday Evening Post, CCXL (December 2, 1967), 58-61.

2353 _____. "What a Lovely Way to Go!" McCall's, XCV (October 1967), 104-105, 174-176.

2354 Cushman, John. "When It Began," Sundial, I (Spring 1966), 23.

2355 Cusick, Robert Sherman. "Inheritance," The Smith, no. 8 (March 1968), 144-150.

2356 Cutten, H. A. "Another World," New Zealand Listener, (October 14, 1966), 6, 26.

2357 _____. "Just Shifting Thanks," New Zealand Listener, (June 23, 1967), 6.

2358 Czeszko, Bohdan. "Troubles of the Authority," Jerzy Hummel, trans., Literary Review, X (Spring 1967), 386-392.

2359 D'Abate, Richard. "Home and Away," Epoch, XIX (Fall 1969), 16-17.

2360 Dabney, Richard. "A Trip to the Blue Room," Dasein, nos. 7 & 8 (1968), 16, 18-25.

2361 Dabrowska, Maria. "The Winter Coat," Literary Review, XIII (Winter 1969-70), 262-265.

2362 Dagerman, Stig. "Two A. M. in Klara," Mary Sandbach, trans., Adam International Review, nos. 304-306 (1966), 26-27.

2363 _____. "Why Must Children Do What They Are Told?" Mary Sandbach, trans., Adam International Review, nos. 304-306 (1966), 27-28.

2364 Dahl, Roald. "The Last Act," Avant Garde, no. 6 (January 1969), 52-59.

2365 _____. "The Last Act," Playboy, XIII (January 1966), 82-84, 86, 215-218, 220, 222-223.

2366 _____. "The Visitor," Avant Garde, no. 2 (March 1968), 58-72.

2367 _____. "The Visitor," Playboy, XII (May 1965), 78-80, 82, 114, 116, 154-156, 159-162, 164.

2368 Daiber, Hans. "The Candidate For Life," Irma Saffold, trans., Western Review, III (Winter 1966), 55-57.

2369 Daisne, Johan. "Death on a Motorcycle," Joseph Kadijk, trans., Delta (Amsterdam), IX (Spring/Summer 1966), 118-125.

2370 Dallas, Michael J. "Limbo," Limbo, II (October 1965), 3-6.

2371 Dal Masetto, Antonio. "Romeo and Juliet," Américas, XVII (January 1965), 32-35.

2372 Dalon, Richard L. "Vanquished," Trace, nos. 62 & 63 (Fall-Winter 1966-67), 336-344.

2373 Dalton, Elizabeth. "A Child of the Sacred Heart," New Yorker, XLI (October 23, 1965), 59-66, 68, 71-72, 74, 76, 78, 83-84, 86, 88, 90, 93.

2374 Dalton, Gregory. "The Beard Lady," Boston Review, I (Fall 1966), 21-31.

2375 Daly, Conway. "Intrigue, Ontario Style," Canadian Forum, XLV (May 1965), 41-43.

2376 Daly, Cyril. "The Bribe," Ave Maria, CIII (January 15, 1966), 24-28.

2377 Daniels, R. Balfour. "Far Away and Long Ago," Forum, VI (Fall-Winter 1968), 18-21.

2378 Danielson, Gudmundur. "A Lost Battle," Peter Kidson, trans., American Scandinavian Review, LIII (September 1965), 288-295.

2379 Danielson, Larry W. "The Encounter," Kansas Magazine, (1966), 1-7.

2380 Danilov, Ivan. "The Alliance of Great Pathfinders/(From the Book Song of Yakutia)," Vladimir Leonov, trans., Soviet Literature, (no. 4, 1969), 128-135.

2381 Darío, Rubén. "The Song of Gold," Coley Taylor, trans., Mexico Quarterly Review, II (Fall 1967), 59-65 [with Spanish text on facing columns].

2382 Darland, Jane. "Windigo Jones and the Royal Jelly Soap Salesman," The Archive, LXXVIII (April 1966), 34-37.

2383 Das, Kishori Charan. "Million Birds," Kishori Charan Das, trans., Bhubaneswar Review, no. 2 (Winter 1968-69), 74-81.

2384 Dash, Joan. "Bagnio De Novia," Michigan Quarterly Review, VIII (Summer 1969), 169-175.

2385 _____. "The Cover-up," Seventeen, XXVII (May 1968), 130-131, 226-228.

2386 _____. "Herself in Red," Minnesota Review, VI (1966), 171-181.

2387 _____. "Nothing to Hide," Seventeen, XXVIII (July 1969), 84-85, 133-135.

2388 _____. "The Other One," Denver Quarterly, II (Autumn 1967), 81-91.

2389 _____. "The Rockery," University Review, XXXV (Summer 1969), 262-270.

2390 Daskalov, Stoyan Ts. "Autumn Hay," Roussi Roussev, trans.,

Obzor, (Summer 1968), 16-34.

2391 Daugherty, Fred. "Another Room in the Castle," The Archive, LXXVIII (April 1966), 14-17.

2392 _____. "Wind/or A Piece, Perhaps from the Novel, or Perhaps for the Page which Charlie, the Wicked Editor, Who Ran Off to Mexico, Left Blank," The Archive, LXXX (September 1967), 14, 26.

2393 Daughtridge, Mary Fond. "The Joke," Coraddi, (Winter 1969), 17-20.

2394 Davenport, Guy. "The Aeroplanes at Brescia," Hudson Review, XXII (Winter 1969-70), 567-585.

2395 Davenport, Gwen. "The Practical Joker," Saturday Evening Post, CCXXXIX (January 1, 1966), 40-45.

2396 Davey, Frank. "The Mural," The Fiddlehead, no. 69 (Summer 1966), 23-29.

2397 _____. "The Room in the Garden," Tamarack Review, no. 49 (1969), 60-63.

2398 Davids, Frances. "They Don't Make It Easy," Discourse, XI (Winter 1968), 122-128.

2399 Davidson, Avram. "The Invasion," Playboy, XII (July 1965), 75, 78.

2400 Davidson, John H., Jr. "The Black Sons-of-Bitches," Story: the Yearbook of Discovery, (1969), 123-126.

2401 Davie, Elspeth. "Allergy," Cornhill Magazine, no. 1050 (Winter 1966/67), 378-384.

2402 _____. "The Day the Bridges Burned," Canadian Forum, XLVII (April 1967), 15-18.

2403 _____. "Out of Hand," Scottish International, no. 2 (April 1968), 40-44.

2404 _____. "The Spark," London Magazine, V (July 1965), 8-20.

2405 _____. "The Stamp," Scottish International, no. 6 (April 1969), 7-10.

2406 _____. "Traveller," Transatlantic Review, no. 23 (Winter 1966-67), 24-30.

2407 Davies, Lloyd. "The Holiday," Westerly, no. 3 (October 1968), 20-26.

2408 _____. "The Milk Round," Overland, no. 35 (Summer 1966-67), 37-39.

2409 _____. "Past Master," Westerly, (Summer 1966), 12-14.

2410 Davies, Rhys. "The Chosen One," New Yorker, XLII (June 4, 1966), 36-44, 46, 48, 51-52, 54, 57-58, 60, 63-64, 66, 69-70, 72.

2411 _____. "The Fugutive," Saturday Evening Post, CCXXXIX (March 26, 1966), 94-96, 98, 100, 102-103.

2412 Davin, Dan. "Bluff Retrospect," Landfall, no. 82 (June 1967), 163-167.

2413 _____. "First Flight," Landfall, no. 89 (March 1969), 12-33.

2414 _____. "Goosey's Gallic War," Landfall, no. 88 (December 1968), 387-396.

2415 _____. "Roof of the World," Malahat Review, no. 10 (April 1969), 89-95.

2416 Davis, Angela. "House of Gifts," Carolina Quarterly, XIX (Spring 1967), 5-17.

2417 _____. "Mr. Rudishill," Greensboro Review, I (May 1966), 5-14.

2418 Davis, Brenda. "Ring Around the Family," Twigs, no. 1 (1965), 41-50.

2419 Davis, Carmyn. "Those Were the Days," Arizona Quarterly, XXV (Winter 1969), 319-333.

2420 Davis, Caroline G. Ratliff. "A Measure of Love," Corral 1965, 15-23.

2421 Davis, Christopher. "A Man of Affairs," Esquire, LXIII (May 1965), 70, 128-129, 131-132, 134.

2422 Davis, Dale. "The Just and the Unjust," The Phoenix, (First Semester 1967-68), 16-39.

2423 Davis, George B. "Like a Piece of Blues," Negro Digest, XVI (July 1967), 55-63.

2424 Davis, Gloria. "The Wall," Negro Digest, XV (August 1966), 59-62.

2425 Davis, John A. "The Love Game," Redbook, CXXXIII (September 1969), 84-85.

2426 Davis, Mildred. "The Third Half," Redbook, CXXXII (January 1969), 143-165.

2427 ______. "A World of Strangers," Redbook, CXXVIII (January 1967), 125, 127-153.

2428 Davis, Nolan. "Object Lesson," Stanford Chaparral, LXVIII (Winter 1968), 18-21.

2429 Davis, Olivia. "Briholme in Winter," Kenyon Review, XXVIII (June 1966), 339-351.

2430 ______. "Constance," Virginia Quarterly Review, XLII (Autumn 1966), 587-600.

2431 ______. "Girl Bathing," Virginia Quarterly Review, XLV (Summer 1969), 413-429.

2432 ______. "The Lodge Pin," Four Quarters, XV (January 1966), 7-15.

2433 ______. "Loss and Chaos," Kenyon Review, XXIX (January 1967), 39-53.

2434 ______. "The Other Child," Prairie Schooner, XLIII (Fall 1969), 252-262.

2435 ______. "Sappho in Wales," Kenyon Review, XXVII (Autumn 1965), 625-644.

2436 ______. "The Scent of Apples," Queen's Quarterly, LXXVI (Spring 1969), 101-112.

2437 ______. "Stained Glass," Vagabond, I, no. 2 (1966), 4-8.

2438 Davis, Rik. "Queen of a Very Strange Country," Beyond Baroque 692, I (July 1969), 29-32.

2439 Dawson, Fielding. "The American," El Corno Emplumado, no. 15 (July 1965), 142-143.

2440 ______. "from The Dream," Lines, no. 5 (May 1965), 31-32.

2441 ______. "from The Dream," Work, no. 2 (Fall 1965), 10.

2442 ______. "The Firm Grip," Joglars, no. 3 (1966), n.p. [27].

2443 ______. "The Fundamentals," For Now, no. 7 (c. 1966-68), 15-17.

2444 ______. "Hernando's Hideaway," The Once Series (Frice), I (1966-67), n.p. [1].

2445 _____. "The King and the Burning Boy," Harper's Bazaar, C (August 1967), 54, 60.

2446 _____. "The King and the Burning Boy," Wild Dog, no. 17 (June 1965), 25-26.

2447 _____. "Little Women/Lost Horizon," Wild Dog, nos. 19 & 20 (December 8, 1965), 38-39.

2448 _____. "The Mandalay Dream," The Park, nos. 4 & 5 (Summer 1969), 112-119.

2449 _____. "Moebius Strip," For Now, no. 6 (c. 1966-68), 21-24.

2450 _____. "November Dreams," Art and Literature, no. 12 (Spring 1967), 97-106.

2451 _____. "Oblivion Calling," The Once Series (Frice), I (1966-670, n.p. [2].

2452 _____. "Ship o' Fools," For Now, no. 5 (c. 1966-68), 25.

2453 _____. "Some History," The Once Series (Ice), I (1966-67), n.p. [7-10].

2454 _____. "The Split-Second/(Different People #6)," Wild Dog, no. 21 (March 1966), 5.

2455 _____. "Spring Sequence," The Once Series (Slice, no. 2), I (1966-67), n.p. [1-5].

2456 _____ and Drew Wagnon. "Test," Wild Dog, no. 21 (March 1966), 1-4.

2457 _____. "Urbana, Illinois," Domestic Pair, n.d., n.p. [3-4].

2458 _____. "Webster Chicago," Damascus Road, no. 2 (1965), 39-40.

2459 _____. "West Side Story," Lines, no. 4 (March 1965), 9-10.

2460 Day, R. C. "No Hard Feelings," Kenyon Review, XXVII (Spring 1965), 239-257.

2461 Dazai Osamu. "Leaves," Eric Gangloff, trans., Chicago Review, XX, no. 1 (1968), 30-41.

2462 _____. "Romanesque," John Nathan, trans., Japan Quarterly, XII (July-September 1965), 331-346.

2463 _____. "A Sound of Hammering," Frank T. Motofuji, trans., Japan Quarterly, XVI (April-June 1969), 194-202.

2464 Deacove, J. "Granny," Limbo, II (April 1965), 29-39.

2465 Deal, Babs H. "Catch Me A Star," Good Housekeeping, CLXV (September 1967), 84-85, 144-145, 147.

2466 _____. "Lemmings Are Lonely," Cosmopolitan, CLX (May 1966), 98-102.

2467 _____. "Night-Blooming Cereus," Ladies' Home Journal, LXXXIII (March 1966), 80-81, 154, 156-158.

2468 _____. "To Ride an Elephant," Redbook, CXXV (August 1965), 50-51.

2469 _____. "The Tree," Woman's Day, (October 1965), 40-41, 102, 104-108.

2470 Deal, Borden. "The Award," Southwest Review, LIII (Winter 1968), 25-35.

2471 _____. "A Long Way to Go," Good Housekeeping, CLXI (July 1965), 65-66, 165-169, 175-182, 186-196.

2472 De Andrade, Mario. "Do the Li'l Chil' Grieve? He Do." Jack E. Tomlins, trans., Prism International, IX (Summer 1969), 28-41.

2473 Deasy, Mary. "Manogue Territory," Minnesota Review, VII (1967), 99-115.

2474 _____. "Slade Mahone Day in Lexington, Kentucky," Redbook, CXXXI (September 1968), 68-69, 124-125.

2475 _____. "Woman Thoughts," Redbook, CXXXIII (July 1969), 88-89, 164-166.

2476 _____. "Yesterday, Saturday, Tomorrow," Redbook, CXXXIII (October 1969), 90-91, 148, 150, 152-153.

2477 De Bus, David. "Cavalcade of the Areopagite," Beyond Baroque 691, I (December 1968), 3.

2478 De Chabrillan, Celeste. "Extracts from The Gold Thieves," Jean & Leonie Garagnon, trans., Meanjin Quarterly, XXVIII (Winter 1969), 202-207.

2479 de Chirico, Georges. "from Hebdomeros," John Ashbery, trans., Art and Literature, no. 4 (Spring 1965), 9-36.

2480 Deck, David. "The Man Who Could," Cavalier, XV (January 1965), 58-60.

2481 Deck, John. "Greased Samba," Atlantic Monthly, CCXX

(September 1967), 76-80, 85-86.

2482 ______. "One Sunday in Spain: A Condensation of a Longer Life," Paris Review, XII (Fall 1969), 37-64.

2483 ______. "Preface to Anonymous Max," Atlantic Monthly, CCXXIV (September 1969), 91-95.

2484 de Elizalde, Fernando. "The Gate," Américas, XIX (January 1967), 27-28.

2485 Deemer, Charles. "The Scrapbook," Northwest Review, IX (Spring 1968), 46-57.

2486 ______. "The Teacher," Colorado Quarterly, XVIII (Summer 1969), 86-96.

2487 ______. "The Thing at 34° 03'15"N, 118° 15'23"W," Colorado Quarterly, XVII (Spring 1969), 359-369.

2488 De Feo, Ronald. "Board Off," Transatlantic Review, no. 30 (Autumn 1968), 126-132.

2489 ______. "Dust to Dust," Massachusetts Review, VIII (Summer 1967), 411-418.

2490 ______. "Snap," North American Review, VI (Fall 1969), 38-40.

2491 DeFoe, Mark. "A Friend of Truman Fletcher," Florida Quarterly, I (October 1968), 33-44.

2492 ______. "My Grandmother's Aberrations," Cimarron Review, no. 8 (June 1969), 16-20.

2493 Degnan, James P. "An Existential Experience," Virginia Quarterly Review, XLII (Summer 1966), 434-441.

2494 Dego, Giuliano. "About Milan," London Magazine, IX (May 1969), 5-11.

2495 de Grys, Francy. "The Night of the Frogs," Westerly, (May 1965), 25-32.

2496 Deighton, Len. "An Expensive Place to Die/Part I," Nova, (May 1967), 161-172.

2497 ______. "An Expensive Place to Die/Part II," Nova, (June 1967), 129-140.

2498 ______. "An Expensive Place to Die," Playboy, XIII (December 1966), 126-130, 132, 144, 328-332, 334, 336-338, 340.

2499 _____. "An Expensive Place to Die/Part II," Playboy, XIV (January 1967), 110-112, 118, 235-239, 241-250.

2500 _____. "An Expensive Place to Die/Part III," Playboy, XIV (February 1967), 86-88, 106, 178-182, 184-190, 192-193.

2501 _____. "An Expensive Place to Die/Conclusion," Playboy, XIV (March 1967), 100-102, 108, 173-174, 176-178, 180-184, 186-188.

2502 Deiss, Joseph Jay. "Promotion in Baccodoro," Cosmopolitan, CLIX (October 1965), 101-103.

2503 de Jesus, Alma. "Drizzle," Solidarity, I (April-June 1966), 88-97.

2504 de Joie, Norman. "'On,' the Charm of Harry Jones," Negro Digest, XVI (August 1967), 73-78.

2505 DeJong, David Cornel. "Ars Domestica," Carleton Miscellany, IX (Winter 1968), 3-12.

2506 _____. "In the Merry Month of Jay," Southern Review, II (January 1966), 179-188.

2507 _____. "The Yellow Door," Southwest Review, LII (Winter 1967), 13-23.

2508 Délano, Poli. "The Boarding House," Carlyn Baraona, trans., Arizona Quarterly, XXIII (Summer 1967), 171-183.

2509 De Lanux, Eyre. "Cot No. 11," New Yorker, XLIV (October 26, 1968), 62-63.

2510 Delany, Samuel R. "Time Considered As a Helix of Semi-Precious Stones," New Worlds, no. 185 (December 1968), 40-56.

2511 DeLattre, Pierre Henri. "Dark Angel," Texas Quarterly, IX (Autumn 1966), 89-101.

2512 DeLaurentis, Louise Budde. "Dry Rain," Midwestern University Quarterly, II, no. 4 (1967), 27-38.

2513 _____. "The Eyes of Home," Kansas Quarterly, I (Winter 1968), 51-56.

2514 _____. "Temporary Trellis," Kansas Magazine, (1965), 40-44.

2515 Delbanco, Nicholas. "from Consider Sappho Burning," Bennington Review, III (Summer 1969), 59-74.

2516 Delibes, Miguel. "On a Night Like This," Arena, no. 23 (April 1965), 27-34.

2517 DeLillo, Don. "Baghdad Towers West," Epoch, XVII (Spring 1968), 195-217.

2518 _____. "Spaghetti and Meatballs," Epoch, XIV (Spring 1965), 244-250.

2519 Delios, George. "Electra," George Christopoulos, trans., Athene, XXVII (Winter 1967), 18-19.

2520 Delius, Anthony. "How Much for Charon?" Contrast (Cape Town, South Africa), no. 11 (March 1965), 8-17.

2521 _____. "Nothing Personal," New Yorker, XLII (March 19, 1966), 47-52.

2522 Delman, David. "In All the Treasured Ways," Good Housekeeping, CLXVII (June 1969), 78-79, 176-181.

2523 _____. "The Jilting," Redbook, CXXIX (June 1967), 62-63, 102, 104-105.

2524 _____. "Mama Napoleon," Redbook, CXXX (April 1968), 70-71, 103-104, 106, 108-109.

2525 _____. "Sam's Ways," Woman's Day, (June 1968), 50-51, 93-95.

2526 _____. "Triangle," Redbook, CXXVII (June 1966), 145, 147-173.

2527 Delmar, Viña. "The Enchanted," McCall's, XCII (February 1965), 102-105, 186-196.

2528 _____. "The Enchanted [Part 2]," McCall's, XCII (March 1965), 88-89, 154-156, 158-166.

2529 _____. "The Enchanted [Part 3]," McCall's, XCII (April 1965), 132-133, 168-172, 176-177.

2530 Demas, Corinne. "A Case of Camembert," Literary Magazine of Tufts University, II, no. 1 (1967), 16-19.

2531 _____. "Collage I: Athens," Literary Magazine of Tufts University, I, no. 2 (1966), 52-57.

2532 _____. "Collage II: Amphilochia," Literary Magazine of Tufts University, III (Winter 1968), 16-21.

2533 _____. "In-Shore," Literary Magazine of Tufts University, II (Spring 1967), 30-33.

2534 Demirchyan, Derenik. "Merkeh," Avril Pyman, trans., Soviet Literature, (No. 3, 1966), 60-64.

2535 _____. "Miniatures/The Inventor," Avril Pyman, trans., Soviet Literature, (No. 3, 1966), 65.

2536 _____. "Miniatures/Laughter," Avril Pyman, trans., Soviet Literature, (no. 3, 1966), 66.

2537 _____. "Miniatures/The Old Woman," Avril Pyman, trans., Soviet Literature, (no. 3, 1966), 65-66.

2538 De Mott, Benjamin. "An Eye on the Weather," Hudson Review, XVIII (Autumn 1965), 359-369.

2539 _____. "How to Win at Cocktails," Saturday Evening Post, CCXXVIII (August 14, 1965), 52-55.

2540 _____. "The Other Man," Massachusetts Review, VII (Winter 1966), 12-20.

2541 Denevi, Marco. "The Ant," George McWhirter, trans., Contemporary Literature in Translation, no. 5 (Fall 1969), 10-11 [attributed by Denevi to Pavel Vodnik].

2542 _____. "The Apocalypse," Susan Herman Price, trans., Contemporary Literature in Translation, no. 3 (Winter 1968), 10.

2543 _____. "Apocalypse," in "The 'Microtale': An Argentine Specialty," by Donald A. Yates, Donald A. Yates, trans., Texas Quarterly, XII (Summer 1969), 14-15.

2544 _____. "Dulcinea of the Toboso," Susan Herman Price, trans., Contemporary Literature in Translation, no. 3 (Winter 1968), 9.

2545 _____. "Fragments from an Intimate Diary," George McWhirter, trans., Contemporary Literature in Translation, no. 4 (Spring 1969), 15-17 [attributed by Denevi to Rene Vico].

2546 _____. "The God of the Flies," George McWhirter, trans., Contemporary Literature in Translation, no. 5 (Fall 1969), 10 [attributed by Denevi to Alfonso Sayarte].

2547 _____. "The Master Betrayed," Susan Herman Price, trans., Contemporary Literature in Translation, no. 3 (Winter 1968), 9.

2548 _____. "The Rose Girl," George McWhirter, trans., Contemporary Literature in Translation, no. 5 (Fall 1969), 12-13 [attributed by Denevi to Ludovico Strozzi].

2549 _____. "Some Falsifications," George McWhirter, trans., Prism International, IX (Autumn 1969), 83-91.

2550 _____. "The Virgin Queen," George McWhirter, trans., Contemporary Literature in Translation, no. 5 (Fall 1969), 11 [attributed by Denevi to an anonymous N. N.].

2551 Denholtz, Elaine. "Nothing Comes Easy," Quartet, no. 9 (Winter 1965), 5-10.

2552 _____. "Rachmonis," Literary Review, XIII (Winter 1969-70), 167-178.

2553 Denigan, Mary Gerard. "Nancy," Ave Maria, CIII (May 21, 1966), 26-29.

2554 Denman, Alan. "The Adamatine Dream," Alta, no. 9 (Autumn 1969), 181-183.

2555 Dennis, Patrick. "The Joyous Season," Ladies' Home Journal, LXXXII (January 1965), 44-45, 68-75, 77-79.

2556 Dennis, Ralph. "The Son of the Sad Fat Wordman Goes North," Lillabulero, I (Fall 1967), 33-40.

2557 _____. "Wind Sprints," Lillabulero, I (Spring 1967), 1-3.

2558 Dennison, George. "Alleys, Fields," WIN, IV (August 1968), 8-9.

2559 Deobhankar, N. R. "The Curse of the Gods," Avenues, II (July 1969), 23-26, 30.

2560 _____. "The Yellow Scarf," Avenues, I (August-September 1968), 24-30, 33.

2561 Depew, W. M. "The Case of the Peeping Thomist," Dust, III (Fall 1966), 28-29.

2562 De Ramus, Betty. "Voices," Literary Review, XII (Spring 1969), 399-403.

2563 de Ransart, Robert. "Lidice under Snow," Dublin Magazine, V (Summer 1966), 50-60.

2564 Derleth, August. "The White Stars," Minnesota Review, VI (1966), 123-128.

2565 Dermoût, Maria. "The Buddha Ring," James Brockway, trans., Harper's Bazaar, CI (January 1968), 76, 140-141.

2566 _____. "Kwan Yin's Snake," James Brockway, trans., Harper's Bazaar, XCIX (April 1966), 148-149, 214-215, 217.

2567 ______. "Mary," James Brockway, trans., Harper's Bazaar, C (February 1967), 166-167, 222, 233.

2568 ______. "The Shark-Fighter," James Brockway, trans., Harper's Bazaar, XCIX (January 1966), 116, 165.

2569 ______. "The South Sea," James Brockway, trans., Harper's Bazaar, XCVIII (January 1965), 150-151.

2570 Déry, Tibor. "Behind the Brick Wall," John Sakerford, trans., Literary Review, IX (Spring 1966), 353-366.

2571 ______. "A Gift from the Stag/(From the cycle 'Capriccios')," New Hungarian Quarterly, VIII (Winter 1967), 63-66.

2572 ______. "The Portuguese Princess," Kathleen Szasz, trans., Tri-Quarterly, no. 9 (Spring 1967), 21-36.

2573 Deryaev, Khidyr. "Truth Travels on Foot, Guile in the Saddle/(An Excerpt from the Novel Fate)," Tom Botting, trans., Soviet Literature, (no. 7, 1966), 82-92.

2574 DeSade, D. A. F. "From: Justine," Austryn Wainhouse and Richard Seaver, trans., Evergreen Review, IX (June 1965), 57-60, 89-92.

2575 Desmond, John F. "Tender Years," Michigan Quarterly Review, VII (Summer 1968), 199-205.

2576 Desnica, Vladan. "Justice," Jan Dekker, trans., Literary Review, XI (Winter 1967), 163-166.

2577 Desnos, Robert. "All that Is Visible Is Gold," Michael Benedikt, trans., Art and Literature, no. 9 (Summer 1966), 148-157.

2578 Dessart, Gina. "The Balloon Race," Arizona Quarterly, XXI (Spring 1965), 21-28.

2579 ______. "Nemesis in the Cornfield," Literary Review, X (Autumn 1966), 36-43.

2580 Dethier, Vincent G. "The Burning Mill," Catholic World, CCII (December 1965), 171-175.

2581 ______. "The Decapitated Snowmen," Era, III (Fall 1966), 15-22.

2582 ______. "Mpanda, the Beggar," Catholic World, CC (February 1965), 307-311.

2583 Detweiler, David. "Silvia," Yale Literary Magazine, CXXXVI (May 1968), 38-43.

2584 Deutsch, Robert. "Supply and Demand," Riverrun, no. 2 (1968), 35-41.

2585 Devereux, Sean. "Mud between His Toes," The Archive, LXXX (May 1968), 5-13.

2586 _____. "Samsâra," The Archive, LXXX (September 1967), 7-13.

2587 de Villiers, Marq. "Dribble," Contrast (Cape Town, South Africa), no. 17 (November 1967), 21-28.

2588 Devine, James F. "The Emissary," Long View Journal, I (Winter 1968), 73-77.

2589 _____. "The Weapon," Long View Journal, I (Spring 1969), 55-63.

2590 De Voti, William. "Summer Dust," Arx, II (September 1968), 15-21.

2591 _____. "Summer Is a Lifetime," Moonlight Review, I (June 1967), 20-28.

2592 de Vries, Abraham. "Brood," Contrast (Cape Town, South Africa), no. 12 (July 1965), 73-80.

2593 De Vries, Peter. "Journey to the Center of the Room," New Yorker, XLIV (October 5, 1968), 56-57.

2594 _____. "Nothing to Write Home About," Harper's Magazine, CCXXXV (August 1967), 68-72.

2595 De Vries, Theun. "Imperial Blood," Theun De Vries, trans., Delta (Amsterdam), VIII (Summer 1965), 24-33.

2596 De Wet, Andre. "The Temptation of Saint Anthony," The Classic, II, no. 4 (1968), 38-39.

2597 De Witte, Dirk. "Isabelle 1940," Elisabeth Eybers, trans., Delta (Amsterdam), VIII (Autumn 1965), 59-67.

2598 Dey, Richard. "That's My Boy (A Vignette)," Pyramid, no. 2 (1968), 61-62.

2599 Diaz, Manuel S. "Requiem for Grandfather," Literature East and West, XIII (December 1969), 314-324.

2600 Diaz, Robert John. "Where Gomes Is On Trial," Man About Town, I (Winter 1967), 16-17.

2601 Díaz de León, Martha. "The Red Flower," Américas, XXI (March 1969), 30-32.

2602 Dibble, Warren. "Genesis 38," Landfall, no. 85 (March 1968), 15-23.

2603 _____. "In It," Landfall, no. 81 (March 1967), 91-95.

2604 _____. "A Way of Love," Landfall, no. 81 (March 1967), 89-90.

2605 Dickson, J. W. "The Wall," Denver Quarterly, III (Summer 1968), 49-60.

2606 _____. "The Water Carriers," Prairie Schooner, XLI (Spring 1967), 28-38.

2607 Didion, Joan. "The Welfare Island Ferry," Harper's Bazaar, XCVIII (June 1965), 82-83, 105, 107.

2608 _____. "When Did the Music Come this Way? Children Dear, Was It Yesterday," Denver Quarterly, I (Winter 1967), 54-62.

2609 Di Donato, Pietro. "The Fireplace," Playboy, XII (October 1965), 93, 178, 180-181.

2610 _____. "The Hayloft," Playboy, VIII (May 1966), 127, 152, 170, 173.

2611 _____. "O'Hara's Love," Playboy, XIII (March 1966), 72-74, 131-132.

2612 Diespecker, Don. "Big Day at Olympus," Overland, no. 38 (Summer 1968), 4-8.

2613 Dietrich, Luc. "Apprentice of the City," Idea and Image, I, no. 2 (1968), 18-23.

2614 Diez de Medina, Fernando. "The White Llama," Américas, XXI (August 1969), 31-35.

2615 Diggs, Jeff. "Both My Girls," Negro Digest, XIV (October 1965), 79-82.

2616 Dik, Iosif. "The Lucky Pen," Margaret Wettlin, trans., Soviet Literature, (no. 12, 1968), 103-104.

2617 Dikeman, May. "The Peak," Atlantic Monthly, CCXV (January 1965), 55-60.

2618 _____. "The Tour," Atlantic Monthly, CCXVII (February 1966), 82-84, 87-89.

2619 Dillard, Leona M. "The Brothers," Kansas Quarterly, I (Winter 1968), 83-88.

2620 Dillon, Jack. "The Grizzly," Saturday Evening Post, CCXLI (July 27, 1968), 42-51.

2621 _____. "'Tom Says It's that Kids Have More Freedom These Days'," McCall's, XCIII (August 1966), 90-91, 111-115.

2622 _____. "'Wasn't He Nice, Pete? Wasn't He Nice?'," McCall's, XCIV (September 1967), 82-83, 147-150.

2623 Dillon, Millicent G. "Induce," Encounter, XXXII (June 1969), 14-18.

2624 Dimov, Dimiter. "Achilles' Heel/(Excerpt from His Last, Unfinished Novel)," Svetoslaw Piperov, trans., Obzor, (Spring 1969), 23-37.

2625 Dineen, John E. "The Gods of Rome," Transatlantic Review, no. 20 (Spring 1966), 152-166.

2626 Dinges, Ricka Leonhardt. "Paris, London, Berlin," Red Cedar Review, IV (Spring 1966), 35-42.

2627 Dion, Grace. "French Revolution," Prospero's Cell, I (Summer 1966), 9-21.

2628 Dionne, Joe. "The Great Ten Day Legume War," Red Cedar Review, VI (September 1968), 9-19.

2629 Diop, Birago. "Sarzan," Dorothy S. Blair, trans., The Classic, II, no. 2 (1966), 11-20.

2630 Di Pego, Gerald. "It's Never Cold in Daydreams," Redbook, CXXXIII (September 1969), 80-81, 141-142, 143.

2631 _____. "Sunday." Redbook, CXXXIII (August 1969), 78, 142.

2632 di Prima, Diane. "The Christmas Section/from Spring and Autumn Annals," Niagara Frontier Review, (Fall 1965), 20-25.

2633 _____. "from her book:/Spring and Autumn Annals: A Celebration of the Seasons for Freddie," The Outsider, nos. 4 & 5 (1968-69), 45-50.

2634 DiSalvo, Jacqueline. "Blind Man's Bluff," New Campus Writing, (1966), 55-69.

2635 Disch, Anabel. "The Grave Plot," Discourse, XI (Winter 1968), 15-22.

2636 Disch, Thomas M. "Camp Concentration/Part Two," New Worlds, no. 174 (1967), 6-25, 58.

2637 ____. "Casablanca," New Worlds, no. 183 (October 1968), 24-30, 42-44.

2638 ____. "Cephalotron," Playboy, XIII (December 1966), 222, 279.

2639 ____. "The Colours," New Worlds, no. 185 (December 1968), 28-31.

2640 ____ and John Sladek. "Danny's New Friends from Deneb," Mademoiselle, LXVII (September 1968), 58, 76, 100.

2641 ____. "The Master of the Milford Altarpiece," Paris Review, XII (Spring 1969), 12-27.

2642 ____. "1-A," New Worlds, no. 181 (April 1968), 6-11.

2643 ____. "Slaves," Transatlantic Review, no. 26 (Autumn 1967), 121-131.

2644 Disraeli, Benjamin. "David Alroy Beholds Jerusalem," Adam International Review, nos. 325-327 (1968), 173.

2645 ____. "Sabbath in the City," Adam International Review, nos. 325-327 (1968), 191-192.

2646 Distler, Alan. "White and Fast Water," New American Review, no. 4 (August 1968), 105-113.

2647 Dixon, Christine. "The Clover Ring," Seventeen, XXVI (January 1967), 84-85, 103.

2648 Dixon, Stephen. "Berry-Smashing Day at the C & L," Playboy, XVI (May 1969), 115, 156, 178-182.

2649 ____. "The Bussed," Bennington Review, III (Winter 1969), 62-68.

2650 ____. "The Neighbors," Atlantic Monthly, CCXVII (April 1966), 96-102.

2651 ____. "Pale Cheeks of a Butcher's Boy," Per/Se, I (Spring 1966), 51-56.

2652 ____. "What Is All This?" Playboy, XVI (November 1969), 143, 233-234, 236, 238, 240, 242.

2653 ____. "The Young Man Who Read Brilliant Books," Playboy, XV (August 1968), 56-58, 68, 118, 120, 122-123.

2654 Djumayev, Nariman. "The Quiet Daughter-in-Law," Margaret Wettlin, trans., Soviet Literature, (no. 7, 1966), 9-45.

2655 D'lott, Barry. "One of the Intimate Memoirs/of Alvin Edward Cooper," Trace, no. 68 (1968), 285-291.

2656 D'Monte, Vincent, O. F. M. "The Queen's Friend," Imprint, VIII (January 1969), 19-20.

2657 Dneprov, Anatoli. "Crabs Take Over the Island," George Yankovsky, trans., Soviet Literature, (no. 5, 1968), 91-111.

2658 _____. "The Purple Mummy," Vision, XVII (July 1968), 6-12, 26-28, 30.

2659 Doar, Harriet. "The Fighting Cocks," Red Clay Reader, no. 2 (1965), 27-30.

2660 Dobbs, Kildare. "Afternoon in Manhattan," Saturday Night, LXXXIII (August 1968), 20-22.

2661 _____. "One Day in the Life of a Semi-private Room," Saturday Night, LXXXIV (March 1969), 34-36.

2662 _____. "Studies of the Ilanga District," Tamarack Review, no. 41 (Autumn 1966), 22-41.

2663 _____. "Trial of a Lesser Magistrate," London Magazine, V (September 1965), 80-86.

2664 Dobinson, Frank. "The Master Copy," Playboy, XIII (May 1966), 101, 184-185.

2665 Döblin, Alfred. "A Summer Romance," George Raymond Selden, trans., Scala International, (July 1967), 34-37.

2666 Dobreva, Irina. "A Dumb Story," The Goodly Co., no. 5 (April 1966), 22.

2667 _____. "Three Bodies in a Picture," The Goodly Co., no. 5 (April 1966), 23.

2668 Dockry, Margaret M. "A Crown to Her Husband," Ave Maria, CVI (August 5, 1967), 28-30.

2669 Doctorow, E. L. "The Songs of Billy Bathgate," New American Review, no. 2 (January 1968), 54-69.

2670 Dodd, Bill. "When Babies Think," Montparnasse Review, no. 2 (1966), 16-18.

2671 Dodge, Thomas. "Speaking of Angels," Redbook, CXXXI (May 1968), 68-69, 123-126.

2672 Dohan, Mary Helen. "End of Innocence," Redbook, CXXVII (August 1966), 44-45, 116, 125-127.

2673 Dokey, Richard. "Crazy Woman of Wales Hotel," Quartet, no. 28 (Fall 1969), 3-9.

2674 _____. "Sanchez," Southwest Review, LII (Autumn 1967), 354-367.

2675 Dolinsky, Lewis. "My Kind of Town," Occident, (Fall 1965), n.p. [30-36].

2676 H. D. [Hilda Dolittle]. "The Death of Martin Presser," Quarterly Review of Literature, XIII (1965), 241-261.

2677 Dollarhide, Louis. "The Gift," Georgia Review, XXIII (Spring 1969), 32-35.

2678 _____. "Heat," Southern Review, II (January 1966), 149-165.

2679 Dolson, Charles W. "Passage to the Day," Intro, no. 2 (September 1969), 97-107.

2680 Dolujanoff, Emma. "The Story of Tatán," Jed Linde, trans., Maguey, no. 1 (May 1968), 4-15 [in Spanish and English on alternate pages].

2681 Domb, Cyril. "The Secret Life of Velvel Mittstein," Jewish Life, XXXIV (January-February 1967), 37-43.

2682 Donahey, Scott. "A Time of the Flesh," Sequoia, XII (Autumn 1966), 13-18.

2683 Donahue, Geraldine. "And the Meek Shall...," DeKalb Literary Arts Journal, III (Fall 1968), 72-81.

2684 Donald, Elsie Burch. "Five Acres and a Mule," Delta Review, VI (October 1968), 20-23, 58-61.

2685 Donis, Miles. "The Madness of Us Alone," Mademoiselle, LXV (September 1967), 146-147, 179-171, 191-193, 201-204.

2686 Donleavy, J. P. "The Beastly Beatitudes of Balthazar B," Nova, (January 1969), 84-87.

2687 _____. "A Fair Festivity," Playboy, XV (November 1968), 92-94, 198, 200, 202, 204, 206, 208-211.

2688 _____. "A Friend," Queen, CDXXIV (April 7, 1965), 88.

2689 _____. "In My Peach Shoes," Queen, CDXXIV (April 7, 1965), 88.

2690 _____. "Rite of Love," Playboy, XV (October 1968), 86-88, 90, 98, 187-188, 190, 193-195.

2691 _____. "A Small Human Being," Saturday Evening Post, CCXLI (November 16, 1968), 33-38, 43-48, 72.

2692 Donnelly, John F. "Hop Sing," Queen's Quarterly, LXXV (Summer 1968), 330-337.

2693 _____. "A Promise of Silence," The Fiddlehead, no. 73 (Fall 1967), 18-27.

2694 Donohue, H. E. F. "Joe College," Carleton Miscellany, X (Summer 1969), 58-79.

2695 Donohue, Patrick. "Mrs. Malloy," Ave Maria, CV (February 18, 1967), 26-27.

2696 Donoso, José. "Paseo," Lorraine O'Grady Freeman, trans., Tri-Quarterly, nos. 13/14 (Fall/Winter 1968-69), 307-324.

2697 Dooher, Gerald. "Indians in Raincoats," Blacklist, no. 1 (1965), 16-19.

2698 Dooley, J. A. "The Class Incident," Lugano Review, I, no. 2 (1965), 20-23.

2699 _____. "A Golden Haired Little Fellow," Lugano Review, I, no. 2 (1965), 17-19.

2700 _____. "The Road," New Writers, no. 6 (1967), 169-224.

2701 Dooley, Roger B. "A Pint of Bitter," The Gauntlet, I (Fall 1967), 23-31.

2702 Doran, Jeffrey. "Rider," Harvard Advocate, CI (May 1967), 14-25.

2703 _____. "Under Another's Sky," Atlantic Monthly, CCXXI (December 1968), 68-75.

2704 Dorcas, Alice E. "Camel Configurations," Harvard Advocate, CII (March 1968), 10-17.

2705 Dority, Vale. "The Wake," Prairie Schooner, XLI (Summer 1967), 226-228.

2706 Dorland, Keith R. "The Greatest Thing," Quarry, XVII (Winter 1968), 24-27.

2707 Dorman, Sonya. "The Art of Living," Redbook, CXXXI (July 1968), 64-65, 128-132.

2708 _____. "A Cup of Tea," Ladies' Home Journal, LXXXVI (January 1969), 84-85, 130, 132.

2709 _____. "The Dancer," Redbook, CXXXI (September 1968), 157-179.

2710 _____. "The Desperate Choice," Redbook, CXXVII (August 1966), 157-167.

2711 _____. "Harry the Tailor," Cosmopolitan, CLX (May 1966), 110-113.

2712 _____. "Some of the Time, All of the Time," Saturday Evening Post, CCXXXVIII (February 27, 1965), 50-52, 54-56, 58.

2713 _____. "Subject to Change," Cosmopolitan, CLIX (November 1965), 114-117.

2714 _____. "Voyage to the Stars," Saturday Evening Post, CCXXIX (December 31, 1966), 44-45, 47-48.

2715 _____. "Zero on the Compass," Saturday Evening Post, CCXXXVIII (May 8, 1965), 58-66, 68-74, 76-77.

2716 Dorn, Edward. "A Trip," Niagara Frontier Review, (Spring-Summer 1965), 24-28.

2717 Dorr, Anne. "I Do Not Mark the Passing of Summer," Quarterly, LXIII, no. 1 (1966), 10-16.

2718 Dorr, Lawrence. "An Act of Admiration," Florida Quarterly, II (April 1969), 41-56.

2719 _____. "Curfew," Florida Quarterly, I (Summer 1967), 95-99.

2720 _____. "Once You Were No People," Virginia Quarterly Review, XLIII (Winter 1967), 96-106.

2721 Dos Ramos, I. "Water in a Basket," Kansas Quarterly, I (Winter 1968), 113-129.

2722 Douglas, Gilean. "Moment In Adolescence," Human Voice Quarterly, II (Winter 1966), 223.

2723 Dowling, Tom. "The Untouched One," Columbia, XLIX (August 1969), 24-27.

2724 Downey, Harris. "The Cukoo's Nest," Southern Review, II (July 1966), 607-618.

2725 _____. "Polly," Southern Review, IV (April 1968), 396-414.

2726 _____. "The Vicar-General and the Wide Night," Southern Review, I (January 1965), 142-166.

2727 Dowty, Leonhard. "The Dearest One of All," Good Housekeeping, CLXIII (December 1966), 100-101.

2728 _____. "Good-Bye Too Soon," Good Housekeeping, CLXIX (October 1969), 118-119.

2729 _____. "Pride and Joy," Good Housekeeping, CLXVII (December 1968), 82-83.

2730 _____. "The Trouble with Carol and Ellen," Good Housekeeping, CLXIX (July 1969), 80-81.

2731 _____. "When the Heart Remembers," Good Housekeeping, CLXI (December 1965), 84-85, 259-262.

2732 Doxey, William S. "In the Days of Joseph," Cimarron Review, no. 4 (June 1968), 52-66.

2733 _____. "The Quality of Love," Michigan Quarterly Review, VIII (Fall 1969), 229-233.

2734 _____. "The Racer," Southwest Review, LIII (Winter 1968), 46-55.

2735 _____. "Sailing Westward," DeKalb Literary Arts Journal, II (Spring 1968), 53-61.

2736 _____. "Tell It Not in Gath," Readers & Writers, I (November-January 1968), 18-23.

2737 Draayer, Ken. "Rainy Days," Quarry, XVIII (Summer 1969), 30-34.

2738 Drabble, Margaret. "Faithful Lovers," Saturday Evening Post, CCXLI (April 6, 1968), 62-65.

2739 _____. "Hassan's Tower," Nova, (June 1966), 100, 102, 104, 106, 108.

2740 _____. "A Pyrrhic Victory," Nova, (July 1968), 80, 84, 86.

2741 _____. "A Voyage to Cythera," Mademoiselle, LXVI (December 1967), 98-99, 148-150.

2742 Draffin, Peter. "Too Merry a Christmas by Half," Penthouse, I (December 1969), 58-59, 98, 100, 103.

2743 _____. "Vee-8," Penthouse, I (November 1969), 88-91, 93.

2744 Dragunsky, Victor. "Independent Gorbushka," Vladimir Talmy, trans., Soviet Literature, (no. 12, 1968), 149-153.

2745 Drake, Alan. "Eight Sketches of Change/(or Join Me If You

Want To 'Cause It's All a Game," Abraxas, I (December 1969), 7-9, 45.

2746 Drake, Albert. "The Breakage," South Dakota Review, VI (Autumn 1968), 119-122.

2747 _____. "Directory of Absit Omen," Quartet, no. 14 (Spring 1966), 26-28.

2748 _____. "Father to Son," Redbook, CXXXIII (August 1969), 77, 153.

2749 _____. "Friday Night at the Place," Ante, III (Winter 1967), 25-35.

2750 _____. "The Hem of Harvest," December, XI (1969), 75-85.

2751 _____. "In the Time of Surveys," Northwest Review, VIII (Summer 1966), 100-113.

2752 _____. "Odyssey: Corinthos to Patras by Train," Ante, II (Fall 1966), 5-15.

2753 _____. "Overtures to Motion: A Portrait of a Writer," Chicago Review, XXI (December 1969), 5-15.

2754 _____. "The Schrams at Waterloo," West Coast Review, II (Fall 1967), 5-11.

2755 _____. "A Spanish Parable," North American Review, II (September 1965), 22-26.

2756 _____. "Traveler's Log," Quartet, no. 19 (Summer 1967), 21-23.

2757 Drake, Barbara. "Cats and Rabbits," North American Review, IV (July 1967), 35-39.

2758 _____. "Night Out," Red Cedar Review, VI (September 1968), 57-62.

2759 _____. "Short Flight," Northwest Review, VII (Spring-Summer 1965), 40-47.

2760 Drake, Robert. "The Loner," Texas Quarterly, IX (Winter 1966), 61-63.

2761 _____. "Saint Peter Right in the Eye," Delta Review, VI (April 1969), 40-43.

2762 _____. "She Was Strangely Affected," Delta Review, VI (November-December 1969), 55, 114-118.

2763 _____. "The Tower and the Pear Tree," Georgia Review, XXI (Fall 1967), 381-385.

2764 _____. "Will the Merchant Prince's Son Come Down the Sawdust Trail?" Delta Review, VI (November-December 1969), 52-54, 113-114.

2765 Drake-Brockman, H. "Desert Journey," Westerly, no. 4 (1967), 32-36.

2766 Drayton, Geoffrey. "The Moon and the Fisherman," Bim, XII (July-December 1967), 17-20.

2767 Dresner, Samuel H. "A Yom Kipper Tale," Jewish Frontier, XXXIII (September 1966), 32-33.

2768 Dressel, Holly. "Unicorn," Pegasus, III (Spring 1965), 6-9.

2769 Drew, George. "The Tree," Jeopardy, no. 5 (Spring 1969), 67-69.

2770 Drexler, Rosalyn. "Dear," Paris Review, X (Summer 1966), 42-56.

2771 _____. "Like...," New American Review, no. 7 (August 1969), 36-63.

2772 Driskell, Leon V. "He Heard the Nickel Go Down," Phylon, XXVIII (Winter 1967), 426-433.

2773 _____. "The Note," Georgia Review, XXII (Summer 1968), 201-207.

2774 Drought, James. "The Enemy," Cavalier, XV (February 1965), 36-38, 74-76.

2775 _____. "The Enemy: Part II," Cavalier, XV (March 1965), 54-56, 58-59, 94.

2776 _____. "The Enemy: Part III," Cavalier, XV (April 1965), 36-37, 62-63.

2777 _____. "Robinson Crusoe in the American Literary Desert!" December, X (1968), 187-189.

2778 Drury, Michael. "In Her Wisdom," Good Housekeeping, CLXVIII (January 1969), 74-75, 148-152.

2779 _____. "The Miracle," Good Housekeeping, CLXIV (April 1967), 100-101, 268-269, 271-275.

2780 _____. "Portrait of a Gentle Lady," Good Housekeeping, CLXVI (March 1968), 96-97, 178-183.

2781 Dryer, Stan. "The Fully Automated Love Life of Henry Keanridge," Playboy, XV (July 1968), 86-88, 92, 148-151.

2782 Dryland, Gordon. "A Recital of French Songs," New Zealand Listener, LIV (March 25, 1966), 4, 13.

2783 Dubois, Kinney. "An Afternoon Trip to the Museum," Harvard Advocate, CIII (December 1969), 24-26.

2784 Dubuisson, Laura. "Of Gray and Gold," Lit (Lambda Iota Tau), IX (Autumn 1968), 21-27.

2785 Dubus, Andre. "Andromache," New Yorker, XLIII (January 6, 1968), 22-31.

2786 _____. "The Cross Country Runner," Midwestern University Quarterly, I, no. 4 (1966), 25-42.

2787 _____. "The Doctor," New Yorker, XLV (April 26, 1969), 38-39.

2788 _____. "If They Knew Yvonne," North American Review, VI (Fall 1969), 18-27.

2789 _____. "Love Is the Sky," Midwestern University Quarterly, II, no. 2 (1966), 18-32.

2790 _____. "Madeline Sheppard," Midwestern University Quarterly, II, no. 4 (1967), 1-12.

2791 _____. "Over the Hill," Sage, XI (Fall 1967), 255-266.

2792 Duchemin, Dorothy. "In the Dark No Lamp," Georgia Review, XIX (Summer 1965), 219-225.

2793 Duckworth, Marilyn. "Among Strangers," New Zealand Listener, LIX (November 15, 1968), 10.

2794 _____. "The Troglodyte," New Zealand Listener, LIX (December 13, 1968), 10.

2795 Duda, Margaret. "The Living and the Dead," Ave Maria, CIII (June 25, 1966), 24-26.

2796 _____. "Mancika," Ave Maria, CIII (January 29, 1966), 22-25.

2797 _____. "The Patriarch," University Review, XXXIV (Spring 1968), 227-232.

2798 _____. "The Robbery," Green River Review, I (May 1969), 51-56.

2799 Dudley, A. E. "A Kind of Compassion," The Fiddlehead, no. 66 (Fall 1965), 14-18.

2800 _____. "The Translators," Anglo-Welsh Review, XVI (Winter 1967), 41-43.

2801 Dueker, Joyce. "An Unconventional Teacher," Ave Maria, CV (March 4, 1967), 22-24.

2802 Dufeck, Jerry. "Travesty," UMD Humanist, XIV (Winter 1966), 41-43.

2803 Duff, Gerald. "The Apple and the Aspirin Tablet," Florida Quarterly, II (October 1969), 1-11.

2804 Du Fresne, Yvonne. "A Walk by the Sea," Landfall, no. 91 (September 1969), 213-221.

2805 Duggal, Kartar Singh. "The Sins of Thy Fathers...," N. Iqbal Singh, trans., Indian Literature, X (July-September 1967), 48-52.

2806 Duggan, Maurice. "An Appetite for Flowers," Landfall, no. 83 (September 1967), 227-250.

2807 _____. "O'Leary's Orchard," Landfall, no. 81 (March 1967), 3-50.

2808 Duggin, Richard. "Gamma Gamma Gamma," Playboy, XV (June 1968), 118-120, 202, 204-206, 208, 210-212.

2809 Duhrssen, Alfred. "from Memoir of an Aged Child," Harper's Bazaar, XCVIII (April 1965), 171, 231.

2810 _____. "The Swiss Interlude," Harper's Bazaar, XCVIII (September 1965), 334-335, 337, 340.

2811 Dulany, Harris. "Mamma's Boy," Genesis: Grasp, I, no. 2 (1969), 22-26, 28-32, 34-36.

2812 Dumas, H. "The Lake," Trace, no. 69 (1968), 439-441.

2813 Dumas, Henry. "The Crossing," Negro Digest, XV (November 1965), 80-86.

2814 _____. "Rain God," Negro Digest, XVII (January 1968), 54-57.

2815 _____. "Will the Circle Be Unbroken," Negro Digest, XVI (November 1966), 76-80.

2816 du Maurier, Daphne. "The Breakthrough," Ladies' Home Journal, LXXXIII (March 1966), 101-108.

2817 _____. "The Flight of the Falcon (Part 1)," Good Housekeeping, CLX (February 1965), 65-74, 196-200, 205-214.

2818 _____. "The Flight of the Falcon (Part 2)," Good Housekeeping, CLX (March 1965), 85-87, 202, 204, 206, 208, 210-212, 214, 216, 218-219, 222, 224, 226-227, 238-241, 248-250, 255-256.

2819 _____. "The Flight of the Falcon (Part 3)," Good Housekeeping, CLX (April 1965), 94-95, 222, 224, 226, 228, 230, 232, 238-240, 242, 244, 246, 248, 250, 252, 254, 256-257, 264, 266, 268-269, 275-276, 278.

2820 _____. "The Flight of the Falcon (Conclusion)," Good Housekeeping, CLX (May 1965), 100-102, 214, 216-224, 226-230, 235-241, 246-254.

2821 Dumonte, Ed. "The Spanish Prisoner Routine," Signature, I (October 1966), 30.

2822 Duncan, Lawrence. "The Death of Bugs Bunny," Sou'wester, (Fall 1967), 29-34.

2823 Duncan, Lois. "True Believer," Redbook, CXXV (August 1965), 52.

2824 Dundy, Elaine. "The Sound of a Marriage," Cosmopolitan, CLXII (February 1967), 116-123.

2825 Dunford, Nelson James. "Teams of Many Men," Chelsea, nos. 22/23 (June 1968), 129-133.

2826 _____. "True Believer," Carolina Quarterly, XVII (Winter 1965), 3-13.

2827 Dunham, J. E. "My Brother Mary," Red Clay Reader, no. 5 (1968), 104-108.

2828 Dunlavy, Marjorie. "The Window," Arlington Quarterly, I (Summer 1968), 66-83.

2829 Dunn, Harold. "Walls of Quandary," Per/Se, III (Spring 1968), 2-7.

2830 Dunn, Si. "Bars," Arx, III (November 1969), 11.

2831 Dunne, John J. "Bait," Ave Maria, CVI (August 19, 1967), 26-28.

2832 Dunning, Lawrence. "After the Wedding," University Review, XXXV (Autumn 1968), 21-28.

2833 _____. "The Baxters in Kiddieland," Discourse, XI (Autumn

1968), 421-427.

2834 ______. "The Black Lamb of God," New Campus Review, I (May 1966), 21-32.

2835 ______. "End of the Game," Colorado Quarterly, XV (Summer 1966), 87-94.

2836 ______. "Night Song," New Campus Review, I (Fall 1967), 3-10.

2837 Dunovan, Cass. "Fair Is for Games," McCall's, XCIII (April 1966), 112-113, 177-178, 180.

2838 ______. "The Voyage of the Lollipop," Redbook, CXXV (August 1965), 160-169.

2839 Duprey, Jean-Pierre. "By Way of a Prologue," Mary Beach, trans., Extensions, no. 3 (1969), 43-50.

2840 ______. "Solution H or The Second Imagined Voyage of Mr. H," Mary Beach, trans., San Francisco Earthquake, I (Spring 1968), 7-13.

2841 Duprey, Richard A. "Recessional," Catholic World, CCIII (July 1966), 239-242.

2842 Durant, Mary. "Messenger, What Tidings?" Esquire, LXV (February 1966), 72-73, 52.

2843 Durham, John. "Foxes at the Bridge," Cosmopolitan, CLVIII (March 1965), 84, 86-87.

2844 Durk, Barbara G. "The Spanish Galleon," Confrontation, no. 1 (Spring 1968), 33-38.

2845 Durrell, Gerald. "Rosy Is My Relative," Cosmopolitan, CLXV (October 1968), 146-150, 152.

2846 Durrell, Lawrence. "All to Scale," Playboy, XIII (September 1966), 159, 194.

2847 ______. "The Little Affair in Paris," Saturday Evening Post, CCXXXIX (June 4, 1966), 64-66, 68, 70.

2848 ______. "Taking the Consequence," Mademoiselle, LXIV (December 1966), 131, 142.

2849 ______. "Tunc," Nova, (March 1968), 120-122, 124.

2850 Dürrenmatt, Friedrich. "The Picture of Sisyphus," Michael Bullock, trans., Mundus Artium, I (Summer 1968), 52-69 [in German and English on alternate pages].

2851 Dursin, Margaret. "An Off-Campus Love Story," Harper's Magazine, CCXXXII (January 1966), 60-64.

2852 Durston, P. E. H. "Mortissimo," Cosmopolitan, CLXII (March 1967), 146-152, 154-163, 167-169, 171-175.

2853 Dusenbery, Gail Chiarello. "Viet Nam, Viet Nam, Viet Nam," VDRSVPVDRSVPVDRSVP, (1969), n.p. [back page].

2854 du Toit, Marcelle. "The Thoughts of a Modern Bushman," Contrast (Cape Town, South Africa), no. 16 (June 1967), 21-28.

2855 Dworkin, Martin. "In a Park of the Old French Royalty: August 1944," Transatlantic Review, no. 26 (Autumn 1967), 117-120.

2856 _____. "The Rocket Guns," Transatlantic Review, no. 19 (Autumn 1965), 116-121.

2857 Dworkin, Stan. "The Love Experts," Redbook, CXXVII (June 1966), 56-57, 114-116, 118.

2858 Dygat, Stanisław. "A Fragment," Jerzy Hummel, trans., Literary Review, X (Spring 1967), 339-344.

2859 Dyson, Lindsay. "Green on the River," Westerly, no. 3 (October 1968), 42-43.

2860 Early, Jubal. "Homeward," The Archive, LXXX (April 1968), 27-31.

2861 Early, Sandra. "Rhododendroms," Literary Review, IX (Summer 1966), 592-603.

2862 _____. "The Sagrada Familia Demands It," Antioch Review, XXV (Fall 1965), 361-371.

2863 Earnshaw, Anthony and Eric Thacker. "Musrum," Evergreen Review, XIII (February 1969), 46-49, 69-74.

2864 East, Charles. "Evensong and Requiem," Per/Se, II (Summer 1967), 57-60.

2865 _____. "Fisherman's Wife," New Mexico Quarterly, XXXV (Summer 1965), 118-127.

2866 _____. "Stopover," Weekend Telegraph, no. 130 (March 31, 1967), 31, 33, 38.

2867 _____. "The Summer of the White Collie," Red Clay Reader, no. 2 (1965), 25-26.

2868 Eastlake, William. "The Bamboo Bed," Evergreen Review, XIII (September 1969), 24-27, 63-66.

2869 ______. "The Biggest Thing Since Custer," Atlantic Monthly, CCXXII (September 1968), 92-97.

2870 ______. "The Hanging at Prettyfields," Evergreen Review, XIII (February 1969), 28-31, 67-68.

2871 ______. "Jack Armstrong in Tangier," Evergreen Review, X (August 1966), 24-27, 82-84.

2872 ______. "The Last Frenchman in Fez," Evergreen Review, XI (December 1967), 44-46, 93-95.

2873 ______. "Now Lucifer Is Not Dead," Evergreen Review, XII (November 1968), 22-25, 69-71.

2874 ______. "There's a Camel in My Cocktail," Harper's Magazine, CCXXXII (April 1966), 63-68.

2875 Eastlund, Madelyn. "Before the Tiger Got Loose," University Review, XXXV (Winter 1968), 144-148.

2876 Eastwood, James. "The Chinese Visitor," Cosmopolitan, CLIX (October 1965), 110-146, 148-151.

2877 Eaton, Charles Edward. "The Girl from Ipanema," University Review, XXXIV (Spring 1968), 163-174.

2878 ______. "The Mandarin," Discourse, XII (Autumn 1969), 436-448.

2879 ______. "The Ugly Duckling," Southwest Review, LII (Summer 1967), 235-248.

2880 Eaton, Elizabeth. "Then," Grecourt Review, XI (May 1968), 52-53.

2881 Echewa, Thomas O. "The Bride Price," Ave Maria, CII (September 11, 1965), 22-27.

2882 ______. "Candidates for Matrimony," Ave Maria, CV (April 15, 1967), 28-30.

2883 ______. "Her Majesty vs. Okorobia Ezedike," Ave Maria, CIII (June 11, 1966), 26-29.

2884 Eckhoff, Jo. "The Proposal," American, I (Spring 1965), 28-30, 37, 42.

2885 Eclov, Shirley. "The Accident," Redbook, CXXIX (May 1967), 60-61, 114-116.

2886 _____. "Not Any More," Redbook, CXXXII (November 1968), 173-195.

2887 Eden, Dorothy. "The Shadow Bride," Redbook, CXXIX (October 1967), 169, 171-193.

2888 Edkins, Anthony. "A Distant Prospect of Greek Pyramids," Ante, IV (Summer-Fall 1968), 11-16.

2889 _____. "More and More and More and More," Ante, III (Winter 1967), 19-24.

2890 Edler, Peter. "Combat Nurse," Nexus (San Francisco, Calif.), III (January-February 1967), 19-21.

2891 _____. "One-Hundred-and-Fifteenth Part of a Second from the Shallow Life of a Photograph," Nexus (San Francisco, Calif.), II (March-April 1965), 47-49.

2892 Edschmid, Kasimir. "The Winner at Holmenkollen," G. R. Selden, trans., Scala International, (February 1967), 35-37.

2893 Edson, Russell. "The Bride of Dream Man," Wormwood Review, VI, no. 1 (1966), 4.

2894 _____. "The Cult," The Outsider, nos. 4 & 5 (1968-69), 19.

2895 _____. "The Death of a Young Tree," Wormwood Review, VI, no. 1 (1966), 5.

2896 _____. "The Delicate Matter," Some/Thing, nos. 4 & 5 (Summer 1968), 21.

2897 _____. "The Ending," Some/Thing, nos. 4 & 5 (Summer 1968), 22.

2898 _____. "Four Fables/The Dead," Lugano Review, I, no. 2 (1965), 42.

2899 _____. "Four Fables/The Dog," Lugano Review, I, no. 2 (1965), 41.

2900 _____. "Four Fables/The Old Man and the Dog," Lugano Review, I, no. 2 (1965), 42-43.

2901 _____. "Four Fables/Toward the Writing," Lugano Review, I, no. 2 (1965), 41.

2902 _____. "The Pattern," Some/Thing, nos. 4 & 5 (Summer 1968), 21.

2903 _____. "The Prophylactic," Wormwood Review, VI, no. 1 (1966), 4.

2904 _____. "The Toad Father," Some/Thing, nos. 4 & 5 (Summer 1968), 22.

2905 _____. "The Toy Maker," The Outsider, nos. 4 & 5 (1968-69), 19.

2906 _____. "The Wedding Night/from The Horsecock Chair," New Directions 20, (1968), 170-177.

2907 Edwards, Anne. "The Survivors," Cosmopolitan, CLXV (July 1968), 118-122, 124, 126-132, 134, 136, 138-148.

2908 Edwards, B. J. "At the End of the Line," New Zealand Listener, (October 28, 1966), 6.

2909 Edwards, Jorge. "Family Orders," John Cameron Murchison, trans., Tri-Quarterly, nos. 13/14 (Fall/Winter 1968-69), 413-434.

2910 Edwards, Sally. "Color Me Loving," Redbook, CXXVIII (April 1967), 66-67, 104-107.

2911 Efendiev, Ilyas. "The Roofer and the Red Flower," Alice Ingman, trans., Soviet Literature, (no. 12, 1969), 15-22.

2912 Effendie, T. B. Darwin. "Alfatihah," M. A. Jaspan, trans., Westerly, (October 1966), 92-93.

2913 Efremov, Ivan. "Cor Serpentis," Vladimir Talmy, trans., Soviet Literature, (no. 5, 1968), 3-54.

2914 Eggers, Arnold. "The Bailiwick Congruent with the Cucumber Field," Columbia Review, XLVII, no. 2 (1967), 5-9.

2915 _____. "The Bouquet of Faded Flowers and the Christmas Tree," Columbia Review, XLVII, no. 1 (1966), 2-6.

2916 _____. "Hansel and Gretel," Columbia Review, XLVIII, no. 2 (1968), 27-30.

2917 _____. "A Quick Victory Parade Between Battles," Columbia Review, XLVI, no. 2 (1966), 64-66.

2918 _____. "The Wax City," Columbia Review, XLVI, no. 1 (1965), 69-72.

2919 Ehrenburg, Ilya. "The Communard's Pipe," Soviet Literature, (no. 4, 1967), 43-52.

2920 Eigerman, Daniel. "Girl and the Island," Quartet, no. 26 (Spring 1969), 9-14.

2921 _____. "Someone Else," Trace, no. 69 (1968), 487-488.

2922 Eigner, Larry. [untitled], Wivenhoe Park Review, no. 1 (Winter 1965), 21-22.

2923 _____. "Qt," Domestic Pair, n.d., n.p. [5-7].

2924 Einstein, Charles. "Man on the Bridge," Signature, II (January 1967), 25.

2925 Eisenberg, Larry. "The Ifrit's Gift," Cavalier, XV (February 1965), 20, 23, 92-95.

2926 Eisenreich, Herbert. "The Toughest Steeplechase in the World," Astrid Ivask, trans., Literary Review, IX (Summer 1966), 605-611.

2927 Eisenstein, Samuel. "All the Monkeys," TransPacific, no. 1 (Summer 1969), 8-21.

2928 _____. "County Jail, June 2, 1964," Prism International, V (Summer 1965), 22-24.

2929 _____. "Gabriel," Ante, III (Summer 1967), 33-39.

2930 _____. "The Inner Garden," Ante, IV (Summer-Fall 1968), 7-9.

2931 _____. "Jacob," Beyond Baroque 692, I (July 1969), 44-45.

2932 _____. "Jezebel and Joseph," Trace, no. 59 (Winter 1966), 379-383.

2933 _____. "Letters to a Nun," Voyages, II (Fall 1968), 49-53.

2934 Elder, Gary. "In Beautiful Devonian Slime," Dust, II (Spring-Summer 1965), 9-14.

2935 _____. "One Fast Life with Final Judgment," Dust, IV (Summer 1969), 19-23.

2936 _____. "Rabbit Dance," North American Review, IV (January 1967), 22-27.

2937 Eldridge, Marian. "Maternity," Westerly, (August 1965), 14-17.

2938 _____. "Paterson's Flats," Westerly, no. 1 (1967), 21-25.

2939 Elevitch, M. D. "A Revival of Blood/(from an unpublished novel)," Trace, no. 58 (Autumn 1965), 276-278.

2940 Eliot, Alexander. "The White Heifer," Texas Quarterly, X (Summer 1967), 90-94.

2941 Elkin, Sam. "Ikey the Gun," Dare, IV (May-June 1966), 38-39.

2942 _____. "How to Die While Growing Up," Ararat, VIII (Summer 1967), 43-45.

2943 _____. "Prisoner of War," University Review, XXXI (March 1965), 184-190.

2944 _____. "Washed Up," Columbia, XLVII (September 1967), 24-27.

2945 Elkin, Stanley. "Everything Must Go!" Saturday Evening Post, CCXXXVIII (July 31, 1965), 50-54, 56-57.

2946 _____. "The Garbage Dump," Saturday Evening Post, CCXL (April 22, 1967), 60-62.

2947 _____. "The Guest," Paris Review, IX, no. 34 (Spring-Summer 1965), 43-77.

2948 _____. "The Merchant of New Desires," Saturday Evening Post, CCXL (May 6, 1967), 70-72, 74, 76.

2949 _____. "Perlmutter at the East Pole," Saturday Evening Post, CCXXXVIII (February 13, 1965), 46-49, 52, 54, 56-58, 60, 62-63.

2950 _____. "A Poetics for Bullies," Esquire, LXIII (April 1965), 66-68, 128, 132.

2951 Ellin, Stanley. "The Specialty of the House," Nova, (December 1969), 82-85, 102.

2952 Ellingham, Lewis. "Nightmare and Dream," Open Space, no. 9 (1965?), n.p. [16-18].

2953 _____. "Psyche," Open Space, no. 11 (1965?), n.p. [22].

2954 Ellingson, Marnie. "I Felt Sorry for Rosemary," Ladies' Home Journal, LXXXV (June 1968), 84-85, 103-104.

2955 _____. "Mark and the Rest of the World," Ladies' Home Journal, LXXXIII (July 1966), 56-57, 92-94.

2956 _____. "Slay Me No Dragons," Ladies' Home Journal, LXXXVI (June 1969), 64-65, 116-119.

2957 Elliot, Bruce. "A Place to Start From," Prairie Schooner, XLIII (Fall 1969), 263-269.

2958 Elliott, George P. "The Boy with U-V Eyes," Northwest Review, VII (Spring-Summer 1965), 49-58.

2959 ______. "In a Hole," Tri-Quarterly, no. 5 (Winter 1966), 73-78.

2960 ______. "Into the Cone of Cold," Esquire, LXVIII (December 1967), 149, 151, 223-224, 237-238, 240, 242, 246, 248, 250, 252-254, 256-258.

2961 ______. "Nikki for a Couple of Months," Esquire, LXXI (June 1969), 95, 97, 154-156, 158, 160, 164, 166.

2962 ______. "Something to Want," Northwest Review, VII (Spring 1966), 6-45.

2963 ______. "Tourist and Pilgrim," Harper's Magazine, CCXXXVI (April 1968), 67-73.

2964 Elliott, Janice. "Body and Soul," Queen, CDXXVIII (May 24, 1967), 50-52.

2965 ______. "The Interior of Henry," Queen, CDXXIX (November 8, 1967), 96-97, 99.

2966 Elliott, Lee. "The Testimonial," Mill Mountain Review, I (1969), 59-62.

2967 Elliott, Richard. "His Feet Were in There," Art and Literature, no. 6 (Autumn 1965), 182-195.

2968 Elliott, William D. "In Flight," Twigs, no. 5 (Fall 1969), 218-229.

2969 ______. "People Are Too Sentimental," South Dakota Review, VI (Winter 1968-69), 44-52.

2970 ______. "Stopping Off in Switzerland," Ann Arbor Review, no. 3 (Spring 1968), 27-29.

2971 Ellis, A. E. "Happily Ever After," London Magazine, VI (February 1967), 7-15.

2972 ______. "Spring in a Handful of Mirrors," London Magazine, VI (September 1966), 67-72.

2973 Ellis, Dianne. "Sundays with Jason," Carleton Miscellany, IX (Spring 1968), 70-89.

2974 Ellis, Peter. "A Cat in the Metro," Paris Review, IX, no. 34 (Spring-Summer 1965), 157-162.

2975 Ellison, Harlan and Haskell Barkin. "Do It for a Penny?" Playboy, XIV (October 1967), 127, 179-182, 184.

2976 Ellison, Jerome. "Night of the Raging Waters," University

Review, XXXII (June 1966), 243-255.

2977 Ellison, Ralph. "Juneteenth/(from work in progress)," Quarterly Review of Literature, XIII (1965), 262-276.

2978 ______. "Night-Talk," Quarterly Review of Literature, XVI (1969), 317-329.

2979 Elman, Richard M. "The Kerensky Complex," Evergreen Review, X (February 1966), 44-47, 80.

2980 ______. "Law 'n Order Day," Bennington Review, III (Winter 1969), 13-18.

2981 ______. "The Memorial," Evergreen Review, IX (March 1965), 44-50.

2982 ______. "The Smithy in His Soul/from a new novel in progress," Bennington Review, II (Spring 1968), 3-13.

2983 ______. "Tit for Tat," Transatlantic Review, no. 18 (Spring 1965), 69-76.

2984 ______. "Turn on Guatemala," Evergreen Review, XII (October 1968), 20-23, 66-68.

2985 Elmslie, Kenward. "An Afternoon Visit with Mrs. Kruger," Mother, no. 6 (Thanksgiving 1965), 72-73.

2986 ______. "An Idea that Backfired," Mother, no. 5 (Summer 1965), 8-12.

2987 ______. "The Orchid Stories," Paris Review, XI (Summer-Fall 1967), 54-77.

2988 El-Saadani, Mahmoud. "The African," Vision, XVII (May 1968), 8-10, 24.

2989 Elsdon, John. "The Consultation," Canadian Forum, XLIX (September 1969), 132-134.

2990 El Seba'i, Youssef. "I Have Been Here Before," Vision, XVII (January 1969), 21-22, 24.

2991 Elsner, Gisela. "The Eighth," Joel Carmichael, trans., Evergreen Review, IX (June 1965), 19-23, 79-84.

2992 ______. "A Pastoral/from The Giant Dwarves," Joel Carmichael, trans., Paris Review, IX, no. 34 (Spring-Summer 1965), 12-17.

2993 Ely, David. "The Academy," Playboy, XII (June 1965), 113, 126, 196-198.

2994 _____. "An Angel of Mercy," Playboy, XII (November 1965), 130-131, 188, 190.

2995 _____. "The Assault on Mount Rushmore," Cavalier, XVI (July 1966), 42-43, 57-58, 63-64.

2996 _____. "Creatures of the Sea," Cosmopolitan, CLIX (August 1965), 86-89.

2997 _____. "Dolly Madison in Peru," Cosmopolitan, CLVIII (June 1965), 97-100.

2998 _____. "Living in Sin," Massachusetts Review, VI (Winter-Spring 1965), 273-283.

2999 Embiricos, Andreas. "Two Stories/Samuel Harding," Nikos Strangos, trans., London Magazine, V (November 1965), 38-44.

3000 _____. "Two Stories/The Texts," Nikos Stangos, trans., London Magazine, V (November 1965), 37-38.

3001 Emerson, Jonathan. "Widow's Walk," Sequoia, X (Winter 1965), 36-46.

3002 Emery, Thomas A. "The Kill," Georgia Review, XXII (Fall 1968), 372-391.

3003 Emswhiller, Carol. "Eohippus," Transatlantic Review, no. 24 (Spring 1967), 145-151.

3004 _____. "I Love You," Epoch, XIX (Fall 1969), 30-34.

3005 _____. "White Dove," New Worlds, no. 188 (March 1969), 21-24.

3006 Engberg, Susan. "Lambs of God," Kenyon Review, XXX (1968), 351-383.

3007 Engelmann, Ruth. "Election Day," Literary Half-Yearly, VIII (January & July 1967), 85-90.

3008 _____. "Occupation Forces," Literary Half-Yearly, VII (January 1966), 67-77.

3009 _____. "The Rose Tulip," Literary Half-Yearly, VI (January 1965), 35-41.

3010 Engh, Calvin H. "Chickens for Sale," UMD Humanist, XVII (Spring 1969), 5-9.

3011 Engle, Allan. "The Interruption," Four Quarters, XVIII (March 1969), 19-22.

3012 Engle, Katherine. "The Different One," Redbook, CXXIX (June 1967), 74-75, 134-137.

3013 _____. "The Right Man," Good Housekeeping, CLXVIII (May 1969), 92-93, 206, 208, 210, 212.

3014 Engleman, Roberta. "The Garden," Coraddi, (Fall 1967), 14, 16-18.

3015 _____. "The Mighty Men Which Were of Old," Coraddi, (Arts Festival 1969), 19-22.

3016 English, Isobel. "Nobody Came," Art and Literature, no. 6 (Autumn 1965), 175-181.

3017 Ennis, Julian. "The Day I Had Pneumonia," Anglo-Welsh Review, XV (Spring 1967), 116-120.

3018 _____. "Number 44," Anglo-Welsh Review, XVI (Winter 1967), 137-139.

3019 Enright, Elizabeth. "An Hour in September," Ladies' Home Journal, LXXXIII (September 1966), 80-81, 131.

3020 _____. "The Little Citadel," Ladies' Home Journal, LXXXVI (March 1969), 84-85, 140, 142.

3021 Enriquez, Antonio. "The Iguana," Solidarity, III (August 1968), 29-38.

3022 Ensana, Joel A. "Mady Goes Home," Quartet, no. 14 (Spring 1966), 18-22.

3023 Enslin, Theodore. "New Sharon's Prospect & Journals," Coyote's Journal, no. 7 (1966), 1-67 [complete issue].

3024 Epstein, Florence. "The Family," Beyond Baroque 692, I (July 1969), 3-4.

3025 Epstein, Leslie. "The Disciple of Bacon," New American Review, no. 4 (August 1968), 140-161.

3026 _____. "Playground," Yale Review, LVII (Winter 1968), 222-235.

3027 Epstein, Seymour. "Chapter One of a New Novel," New Orleans Review, I (Fall 1968), 43-48.

3028 _____. "The Home," Antioch Review, XXV (Winter 1965-66), 525-539.

3029 _____. "In the Deep Sea," Redbook, CXXV (September 1965), 62-63, 100, 102, 104, 106.

3030 _____. "In the Place of Angels," Redbook, CXXIV (February 1965), 137-162.

3031 _____. "Think of Green," Harper's Magazine, CCXXXVII (July 1968), 75-81.

3032 Ernst, Paul. "Emergency Ward," Good Housekeeping, CLXVII (September 1968), 74-77, 192-198, 200, 202-206, 208, 210, 212-214, 220-228, 232.

3033 _____. "The Long Way Home," Redbook, CXXVI (April 1966), 173, 175-201.

3034 _____. "Once Upon a Midnight," Good Housekeeping, CLXII (January 1966), 58-59, 160-162, 166.

3035 Erskine, J. S. "The Little Siren," Dalhousie Review, XLVI (Spring 1966), 63-66.

3036 Escarlata, L. R. "Beauty and the Beast," Limbo, II (November 1966), 23-25.

3037 Eshleman, Clayton. "On Mules Sent from Chavin," Some/Thing, nos. 4 & 5 (Summer 1968), 42-71.

3038 _____. "Theseus Ariadne," The Lit, no. 7 (May 1968), 2-5.

3039 Espey, John. "B. J. R. Con Amore," Arizona Quarterly, XXI (Winter 1965), 308-314.

3040 Espino, Federico Licsi, Jr. "The Children of Miguel Ruiz," Solidarity, IV (June 1969), 66-69.

3041 Espinosa, Rafeal. "Pachuko," Rolling Stone, no. 44 (October 18, 1969), 28.

3042 Espinosa, Rudy. "Little Eagle and the Rainbow," El Grito, II (Winter 1969), 78-80.

3043 Espy, Hilda Cole. "My Phony Valentine," McCall's, XCV (February 1968), 94-95, 132-133.

3044 _____. "Those Wonderful Shots of Killarney," Redbook, CXXIX (May 1967), 56-57, 138, 140-141.

3045 Esslinger, Pat M. "Desire Is a Bus," Phylon, XXVIII (Fall 1967), 312-317.

3046 _____. "Progress Report--Candelaria Project," Southern Review, V (October 1969), 1205-1213.

3047 _____. "El Santa," New Mexico Quarterly, XXXVI (Winter 1966-67), 339-345.

3048 Essop, A. "Gerty's Brother," Purple Renoster, no. 9 (Spring 1969), 31-32.

3049 Estrada, Ezequiel. "A Crime with No Reward," J. David Danielson, trans., South Dakota Review, VII (Autumn 1969), 19-30.

3050 Estrada, Ricardo H. "The Osprey and the Sparrowhawk," Robert Coover, trans., Quarterly Review of Literature, XV (1968), 259-262.

3051 Etchison, Dennis. "Sitting in the Corner, Whimpering Quietly," Statement, no. 24 (Spring 1968), 1-4.

3052 Eustis, Helen. "Miss Bird and I," Redbook, CXXXII (November 1968), 74-75, 119-123.

3053 Evans, Alan. "The Scrapper," Weekend Telegraph, no. 65 (December 17, 1965), 47-50.

3054 Evans, Alton N., Jr. "Part Three," Delta, XXII (1968), 33-36.

3055 Evans, B. E. "The Answer Obviously Is No," Transatlantic Review, no. 20 (Spring 1966), 105-112.

3056 Evans, Dan. "The Wedding Gift," New Yorker, XLII (October 15, 1966), 219-220, 222, 225-226, 228.

3057 Evans, Eleanor. "En Route," Confrontation, no. 2 (Spring 1969), 3-4.

3058 Evans, Jane M. "Minners and Eskimos," Mademoiselle, LX (April 1965), 199-200, 237-242, 252.

3059 Evans, Joan. "White Roses," Washington Square Review, I (Spring 1965), 8-12.

3060 Evans, Max. "The Call," South Dakota Review, VI (Spring 1968), 52-55.

3061 ______. "The Ultimate Giver," South Dakota Review, IV (Autumn 1966), 43-54.

3062 Evans, Robert O. "A Visit to Lily," Virginia Quarterly Review, XLII (Winter 1966), 108-130.

3063 Evart, Carlos. "Horses, to the Horizon," Texas Quarterly, VIII (Spring 1965), 105-117.

3064 Even, Bill. "23¢," Ave Maria, CVI, 26-28.

3065 Everson, Grace. "The Fly in the Parlor," Ave Maria, CIII

(June 18, 1966), 26-29.

3066 Ewart, Sybil. "The Wax Doll," New Zealand Listener, (October 6, 1967), 6.

3067 Ewen, Lois Stuart. "Come Back to San Francisco," Good Housekeeping, CLXIV (June 1967), 78-79, 243-247.

3068 _____. "The Shining Moment," Good Housekeeping, CLXVIII (March 1969), 90-91, 182-185.

3069 Ezell, Madelon K. "When Is a Captain," Mademoiselle, LXI (August 1965), 270-271, 339-343.

3070 Faecke, Peter. "When Elizabeth Arden Was Nineteen," Ingeborg McCoy, trans., Dimension, II, no. 2 (1969), 356-363 [in German and English on alternate pages].

3071 Faessler, Shirley. "A Basket of Apples," Atlantic Monthly, CCXXIII (January 1969), 70-76.

3072 _____. "Intercede For Us, Auntie Chayele," Tamarack Review, no. 46 (Winter 1968), 53-72.

3073 _____. "Maybe Later It Will Come Back To My Mind," Atlantic Monthly, CCXIX (April 1967), 101-104, 107-110.

3074 Faik, Sait. "Two Stories/Encounter," Ayseli Usluata & Edgar Wolfe, trans., Prairie Schooner, XXXIX (Winter 1965/66), 307-311.

3075 _____. "Two Stories/May Day Come, May There Be Harvest," Ayseli Usluata & Edgar Wolfe, trans., Prairie Schooner, XXXIX (Winter 1965/66), 307-311.

3076 Fainlight, Ruth. "Daylife and Nightlife," Transatlantic Review, no. 26 (Autumn 1967), 39-47.

3077 Fair, Ronald R. "Life with Red Top," Negro Digest, XIV (July 1965), 65-72.

3078 Fairbains, Zoe. "Strictest Confidence," Nova, (December 1968), 108-109, 111, 113, 115, 117.

3079 Fallow, Thomas Lee. "Like a Photograph Inviting You," Harvard Advocate, CI (May 1967), 34-37.

3080 Fallowsward, Murval Shirley. "Death Dies Hard," Mandala, no. 3 (1968), 41-43.

3081 Fardoulis-Lagrange, Michel. "In Benoni's Time," Bernard Frechtman, trans., Lugano Review, I, no. 1 (1965), 18-42.

3082 Fariña, Richard. "American Afternoon," Mademoiselle, LXIII (September 1966), 166-167, 216-218.

3083 ______. "Long Time Coming and a Long Time Gone," Playboy, XIV (February 1967), 123, 174-176.

3084 ______. "Ringing Out the Old in Happy Havana," Esquire, LXXII (September 1969), 130-131, 156, 158, 160, 164, 166.

3085 Farlow, Betty. "The Trespassers," Corral 1966, 83-85.

3086 Farnase, Alexander. "The Well-Built Nest," Mt. Adams Review, II, no. 3 (1966), 40.

3087 Faroese legend. "Upsala-Pætur's Christmas," Hedin Brønner, trans., American Scandinavian Review, LVII (December 1969), 397-399.

3088 Farr, Judith. "The Butterfly," Minnesota Review, V (August-October 1965), 195-199.

3089 ______. "The Dead Woman," Minnesota Review, VI (1966), 100-103.

3090 Farr, Roberta. "A Ride on the Esplande," Shenandoah, XVIII (Autumn 1966), 33-64.

3091 Farrell, James T. "An American Student in Paris," Southern Review, III (October 1967), 958-989.

3092 ______. "How Our Day Began," The Smith, no. 8 (March 1968), 8-25.

3093 ______. "How Our Day Began/Part 2," The Smith, no. 10 (December 1968), 148-160.

3094 ______. "Sunday Evening," The Smith, no. 6 (1965), 41-58.

3095 ______. "The Vast Present," Voyages, II (Spring 1969), 46-48.

3096 Farrell, Patricia. "It's the Duty of the Young to Be Happy," Redbook, CXXIX (October 1967), 68-69, 138, 140, 144, 146.

3097 ______. "Quetzalcoatl and the Lady," Redbook, CXXVI (April 1966), 74-75, 129-132.

3098 Farrelly, John. "My Devil," Ambit, no. 41 (1969), 18-19.

3099 Farrington, Connor. "Tar," Dublin Magazine, IV (Spring 1965), 52-56.

3100 Farris, John. "When Michael Calls," Good Housekeeping,

CLXV (November 1967), 85-87, 218-220, 222, 224, 226, 228, 230, 232, 234-236, 238, 240, 242, 244, 246-252, 254, 256-258, 260-262.

3101 Farzan, Massud. "The Plane Reservation," Literary Review, XIII (Winter 1969-70), 236-242.

3102 Fatka, James. "George's Place," North American Review, III (September 1966), 29-31.

3103 Fatow, Ilyana B. "What? No Balalaika?" Arizona Quarterly, XXIV (Autumn 1968), 240-251.

3104 Faucheux, Linda Anne. "The Symposium," Delta, XXIII (1969), 31-35.

3105 Faulk, Odie B. "Old Willie's Revenge," Arizona Quarterly, XXII (Winter 1966), 338-346.

3106 Faulkner, William. "Mr. Acarius," Saturday Evening Post, CCXXXVIII (October 9, 1965), 26-31.

3107 _____. "Once Aboard the Lugger," Lillabulero, I (Spring 1967), 20-23.

3108 _____. "The Wishing Tree," Saturday Evening Post, CCXL (April 8, 1967), 48-53, 57-58, 60-63.

3109 Faust, Irvin. "The Double Snapper," Esquire, LXIV (December 1965), 180, 182, 304-308.

3110 _____. "Gary Dis-Donc," Northwest Review, IX (Summer 1967), 6-18.

3111 _____. "Simon Girty Go Ape," Transatlantic Review, no. 21 (Summer 1966), 67-75.

3112 _____. "The World's Fastest Human," Queen, CDXXII (February 10, 1965), 36-39.

3113 Faust, Seymour. "From Place to Place," Origin (Kyoto, Japan), no. 7 (October 1967), 13-14.

3114 Fay, Robert. "To Find a Mountain," Dust, II (Fall 1965), 19-25.

3115 Fazl, Abul. "Rahu," Mesbahuddin Ahmed, trans., Review, I (July 1968), 39-49.

3116 Fedin, Konstantin. "The Bonfire," Margaret Wettlin, trans., Soviet Literature, (no. 8, 1965), 3-139.

3117 _____. "A Drawing of Lenin," Soviet Literature, (no. 4,

1967), 64-72.

3118 Fedo, Michael W. "A Life In a Day of Price Loughery," Twigs, no. 5 (Fall 1969), 51-58.

3119 Fedoseyev, Grigori. "The Last Campfire," Margaret Wettlin, trans., Soviet Literature, (no. 8, 1969), 3-119.

3120 Feeley, Constance. "On the Edge," New Yorker, XLI (October 2, 1965), 52-56.

3121 Fein, Richard J. "The Mountain and the Caves," Abraxas, I (December 1969), 28-29.

3122 Fejes, Endre. "Engagement," Literary Review, IX (Spring 1966), 369-373.

3123 Fekete, Irene. "Feast before Winter," Cornhill Magazine, no. 1047 (Spring 1966), 161-174.

3124 Feld, Bernard. "A Dying," Shenandoah, XX (Summer 1969), 46-51.

3125 Feld, Michael. "Living in London--II," London Magazine, VIII (December 1968), 20-28.

3126 _____. "The Short Cut Life of Bacchus Pocock," London Magazine, VII (February 1968), 5-30.

3127 Feld, Ross. "Tale," For Now, no. 7 (c. 1966-68), 9.

3128 Felderman, Eric. "Two Sections from a novel called/Black's Theme," Columbia Review, XLV (Spring 1965), 11-26.

3129 Feldman, Alan. "The Divorce: Or How To Get Out of Woodmere/a Ghost Story," Columbia Review, XLV (Spring 1965), 78-92.

3130 _____. "Living In the Sea," Columbia Review, XLVI, no. 1 (1965), 73-95.

3131 Feldman, Brandyn DeLynne. "Sybil," Aspects, no. 10 (August 1967), 7-9.

3132 Feldman, Herbert. "Four Voices/The First Voice Zanda," Abyss, II (January-February 1968), 8-14.

3133 _____. "Four Voices/Part Two/A Novel," Abyss, II, no. 2 (1969), 37-56.

3134 _____. "Four Voices/The Second Voice Pauline," Abyss, II (January-February 1968), 14-28.

3135 Feldman, Steve. "Resolutions: Part Two/Towards a Novelette," Duel, no. 1 (Winter 1969), 51-55.

3136 Fellner, I. W. "The First Skirmish," Jewish Frontier, XXXIII (March 1966), 20-21.

3137 Fennerton, William. "The Lucifer Cell," Ladies' Home Journal, LXXXV (February 1968), 67-74, 105-111.

3138 Fenstermaker, Vesle. "Human Beings, Bring Your Parents," McCall's, XCVI (November 1968), 118-119, 158-160.

3139 Fenton, Brian. "The Fat Woman at the Fountain," Ave Maria, CIV (November 5, 1966), 21-23.

3140 Fenton, James. "Down the Pipe," New Zealand Listener, LII (January 22, 1965), 4, 11.

3141 Fenway, H. E. "Calling Dr. Kildare, He Should Live So Long," Quarterly Review of Literature, XIV (1967), 334-344.

3142 _____. "Calling Dr. Kildare, He Should Live So Long," Yale Literary Magazine, CXXXIV (October 1965), 4-12.

3143 Ferard, Nancy. "A Perfect Punishment," Redbook, CXXIX (August 1967), 66-67, 136-139.

3144 Fereva, Anton. "Brother John," Ararat, IX (Winter 1968), 30-35.

3145 Ferguson, Joseph. "The Tears of Things," New Campus Review, I (Winter 1967), 9-20.

3146 Ferlinghetti, Lawrence. "Where Is Vietnam?" New Directions 19, (1966), 201-202.

3147 Fernandez, Lynn. "The Living Dead," New Writing from Zambia, no. 1 (1968), 24-28.

3148 Fernando, Lloyd. "Paid in Full," Literature East and West, X (December 1966), 362-367.

3149 Ferretti, Massimo. "Racket," Ursule Molinaro, trans., Chelsea, nos. 18/19 (June 1966), 118-126.

3150 Fetler, Andrew. "Afternoon of a Sleepwalker," Epoch, XVI (Fall 1966), 77-82.

3151 _____. "The Demons of Nikolai," Kenyon Review, XXIX (September 1967), 475-492.

3152 _____. "In Line for Lemonade," Malahat Review, no. 1 (January 1967), 55-61.

3153 _____. "The Pillow from Niagara Falls," Antioch Review, XXVIII (Fall 1968), 341-352.

3154 Fetler, James. "The Blum Invitation," Story, I (May 1967), 68-73.

3155 _____. "The Dust of Yuri Serafimovich," Atlantic Monthly, CCXVII (June 1966), 63-69.

3156 _____. "Mutability and the Meat Loaf," Prairie Schooner, XLI (Spring 1967), 13-24.

3157 Fiedler, Leslie. "Bad Scene at Buffalo Jump," Esquire, LXIII (March 1965), 100-101, 117-118, 122.

3158 _____. "The Last Jew in America," Ramparts, IV (November 1965), 45-60.

3159 Field, Andrew. "Fractions," Tri-Quarterly, no. 10 (Fall 1967), 203-219.

3160 Field, Eugene. "The Temptation of Friar Gonsol/A Story of the Devil, Two Saints and a Booke," New Mexico Quarterly, XXXV (Autumn 1965), 196-203.

3161 Field, Frances. "Farewells," Voyages, II (Fall 1968), 35-38.

3162 Field, Michael. "The Accident," Four Quarters, XIV (January 1965), 28-36.

3163 Fields, Curtis. "A Commercial Venture," Greensboro Review, I (May 1966), 15-26.

3164 Fields, Frederick. "Before They Went," Boston Review, I (Fall 1966), 97-116.

3165 Fields, Jeff. "We'll Be in Touch. Okay?" McCall's, XCVI (February 1969), 86-87, 135-138.

3166 Fields, Julia. "The Equalizer Supreme," Negro Digest, XVI (August 1967), 79-82.

3167 _____. "The Hypochondriac," Negro Digest, XVII (July 1968), 61-65.

3168 _____. "Not Your Singing, Dancing Spade," Negro Digest, XVI (February 1967), 54-59.

3169 _____. "Ten to Seven," Negro Digest, XV (July 1966), 79-81.

3170 Fields, Richard. "At the Silver Rail," New Directions 20, (1968), 97-113.

3171 Fifield, William. "Bottled Worlds," London Magazine, VII (July 1967), 46-55.

3172 _____. "Et tu, Neanderthal," Kenyon Review, XXVII (Winter 1965), 135-151.

3173 _____. "Second Fiddle," Texas Quarterly, VIII (Spring 1965), 81-95.

3174 Figi, J. B. "Hassan," December, X (1968), 9-14.

3175 Figueroa, John. "The Practice of Education," Bim, XII (July-December 1968), 175-186.

3176 Filipowicz, Kornel. "A Quiet Afternoon," Edward Rothert, trans., Literary Review, X (Spring 1967), 332-337.

3177 Finch, Christopher. "from As a Goose or a Gull," Art and Literature, no. 6 (Autumn 1965), 53-66.

3178 Finch, Constance. "Fin de Siècle," Grecourt Review, VIII (May 1965), 15-19.

3179 Findley, Timothy. "Chronicle of the Nightmare," Esquire, LXXI (April 1969), 140-142, 158, 160, 162, 166, 172, 174.

3180 Fineman, Morton. "Are You Ready for Egyptland?" Saturday Evening Post, CCXXXVIII (January 30, 1965), 56-58, 60, 63-64.

3181 _____. "Distress Signals," Saturday Evening Post, CCXXXIX (December 31, 1966), 50-52, 54.

3182 _____. "The Games that Husbands Play," Saturday Evening Post, CCXXXIX (April 9, 1966), 52-58.

3183 _____. "Journey to the Fishing Waters," Saturday Evening Post, CCXLI (July 13, 1968), 42-44, 46-47.

3184 _____. "Sunday Is a Narrow Place," Saturday Evening Post, CCXLI (March 23, 1968), 68-70, 72, 74-76.

3185 Finn, Frank. "A Door in the Wall," William and Mary Review, VII (Spring 1969), 36-44.

3186 Finn, Seamus. "History of a Novel," Arx, II (January 1969), 42-45.

3187 _____. "Waiting for the Bus," Pyramid, no. 5 (1969), 17.

3188 _____. "Who Is My Leader When--," Midwestern University Quarterly, II, no. 3 (1967), 59-65.

3189 Finnegan, Joan. "'Some of the Street In'," Literary Review, VIII (Summer 1965), 456-467.

3190 Finney, Ernest J. "The Investigator," Epoch, XV (Winter 1966), 136-151.

3191 Finney, Jack. "Double Take," Playboy, XII (April 1965), 111-112, 114, 140-141, 143.

3192 Fiore, Peter. "For Three Dead Astronauts," Red Cedar Review, VI (January 1968), n.p. [29].

3193 _____. "from Journeys & Other Things/Chicago East," Red Cedar Review, V (April 1967), 48.

3194 _____. "from Journeys & Other Things/The Pilgrims," Red Cedar Review, V (April 1967), 45.

3195 _____. "from Journeys & Other Things/Round Midnight," Red Cedar Review, V (April 1967), 47.

3196 _____. "from Journeys & Other Things/Slides," Red Cedar Review, V (April 1967), 46.

3197 _____. "Milestones," Red Cedar Review, VI (January 1968), n.p. [30].

3198 _____. "These Foolish Things," Red Cedar Review, VI (January 1968), n.p. [28].

3199 Fireall, Pat. "The Transgressor," Statement, no. 25 (Spring 1969), 14-17.

3200 Fischl, Sara. "Veil of Dirty Glass," Red Cedar Review, III (Spring 1965), 69-72.

3201 Fish, Daniel. "The Appointment," Soundings, II (Spring 1965), 48-50.

3202 Fisher, Elizabeth. "My Wife," Aphra, I (Fall 1969), 55-72.

3203 Fisher, Franklin. "Normal," Western Humanities Review, XXII (Autumn 1968), 297-304.

3204 Fisher, M. F. K. "The Changeover," New Yorker, XLII (May 14, 1966), 43-45.

3205 _____. "The Lost, Strayed, Stolen," New Yorker, XLI (March 20, 1965), 47-52, 54, 56, 59-60, 62, 65-66, 68, 71-72, 74, 77-78, 80.

3206 _____. "Two Kitchens in Provence," New Yorker, XLII (August 27, 1966), 29-36.

3207 _____. "What Happened to Miss Browning," Carleton Miscellany, VIII (Summer 1967), 92-120.

3208 Fisk, Michael David. "Virgil's Love Story," Washington and Jefferson Literary Journal, I, no. 1 (1966), 52-56.

3209 Fitch, Harry. "The Colonel's Colors," Western Humanities Review, XXI (Winter 1967), 13-20.

3210 _____. "The Venetian Blind," Per/Se, I (Spring 1966), 12-15.

3211 FitzGerald, Bill. "The Midnight Movie Director," Saturday Evening Post, CCXLI (May 4, 1968), 56-58, 60-62, 64-65.

3212 FitzGerald, Gregory. "The Summer Tenant," The Quest, II (Spring 1966), 261-271.

3213 Fitzgerald, James. "A Small Room," Washington and Jefferson Literary Journal, I, no. 2 (1967), 42-45.

3214 Fitzgerald, Zelda. "The Party that Never Stopped," Queen, CDXXXII (December 18, 1968), 64, 70, 73, 75.

3215 Fitzpatrick, James. "The Dream of Reason," December, VIII (1966), 85-102.

3216 Flamm, Dudley. "The Ball," Minnesota Review, VIII (1968), 30-36.

3217 _____. "Philip and the UFO," Minnesota Review, IX (1969), 194-199.

3218 Flannery, Jack. "Don't Bother to Call," Redbook, CXXV (July 1965), 68-69.

3219 _____. "A Limited Lone Ranger," Redbook, CXXV (June 1965), 58-59.

3220 Flannery, Margaret. "His & Hers," Queen, CDXXVIII (March 1, 1967), 40-41.

3221 Flaubert, Gustave. "Carnac," R. M. Dunne, trans., 0 to 9 no. 3 (January 1968), 35-45.

3222 Flavell, Wayne. "Mask for a Bus-ride," Landfall, no. 79 (September 1966), 233-243.

3223 Fleisher, Michael L. "Collage for One-Ear," Spero, I, no. 2 (1966), 31-37.

3224 Fleming, Ian. "The Man with the Golden Gun," Playboy, XII (April 1965), 64+.

3225 ______. "The Man with the Golden Gun/Part II," Playboy, XII (May 1965), 86-88, 165-170, 172-174.

3226 ______. "The Man with the Golden Gun/Part III," Playboy, XII (June 1965), 106-108, 210-216, 218, 220-222.

3227 ______. "The Man with the Golden Gun/Conclusion," Playboy, XII (July 1965), 88-90, 138-142, 144-149.

3228 ______. "Octopussy," Playboy, XIII (March 1966), 60-62, 118-120.

3229 ______. "Octopussy/Conclusion," Playboy, XIII (April 1966), 102-104, 170, 173-176.

3230 ______. "Quantum of Solace," Cosmopolitan, CLX (May 1966), 103-108.

3231 Fleming, Thomas. "The Iron Girls," Cavalier, XV (November 1965), 22-23, 88.

3232 ______. "The Nude Dummy," Cavalier, XV (April 1965), 26-27, 93.

3233 Fleming, Wray. "The Kitchen," Crucible, II (Spring 1966), 11-12.

3234 Flick, A. J. "A Case for the Defence," The Cantuarian, (April 1965), 330-332.

3235 ______. "In My End Is My Beginning," The Cantuarian, (December 1965), 36-37.

3236 Flood, Cynthia. "On California Street," Wascana Review, III, no. 2 (1968), 5-25.

3237 Flower, Pat. "Watching Barbara Stanwyck," Overland, no. 41 (Winter 1969), 5-6.

3238 Flowers, Paul. "An Endowment Dilemma," Delta Review, VI (November-December 1969), 94-95.

3239 Floyd, Patty. "The Net," Nimrod, XI (Autumn 1966), 1-12.

3240 Flynn, Robert. "Babe in the Wilderness," Saturday Evening Post, CCXL (April 22, 1967), 48-50, 54, 56, 58, 59.

3241 ______. "The Boy from Chillicothe," Yale Review, LIV (Summer 1965), 567-577.

3242 ______. "Stampede!" Saturday Evening Post, CCXL (March 25, 1967), 52-56, 58, 60.

3243 Flythe, Starkey. "The Creative Impulse," Quartet, no. 27 (Summer 1969), 11-15, 18-19.

3244 Fogel, Aaron. "The Turtle Hunt," Columbia Review, XLVI, no. 1 (1965), 34-62.

3245 Fogelin, Maria Bontempi. "Who Do You Love?" Redbook, CXXVII (May 1966), 155, 157-183.

3246 Fokkema, Boukje. "Semi-Detached," James S. Holmes and Hans van Marle, trans., Delta (Amsterdam), VIII (Winter 1965-66), 21-25.

3247 Forbeck, Jesse. "Confirmation, Confirmation," University Review, XXXII (June 1966), 297-302.

3248 Forbes, Stanton. "Relative to Death," Cosmopolitan, CLIX (September 1965), 112-125, 129-133, 135-139.

3249 Ford, Edsel. "Mrs. Colville's First Husband, and Others," New Mexico Quarterly, XXXV (Summer 1965), 101-104.

3250 _____. "Some Glad Morning," New Mexico Quarterly, XXXVI (Autumn 1966), 228-240.

3251 Ford, Jesse Hill. "An Act of Self-defense," Atlantic Monthly, CCXIX (April 1967), 72-76.

3252 _____. "The Bee Tree," Atlantic Monthly, CCXVII (April 1966), 60-63.

3253 _____. "The Britches Thief," Atlantic Monthly, CCXVI (November 1965), 87-89.

3254 _____. "Business as Usual," Delta Review, V (July 1968), 43-44.

3255 _____. "The Collector," Atlantic Monthly, CCXXI (February 1968), 77-80, 85-87.

3256 _____. "Destruction," Esquire, LXXII (July 1969), 96-98, 34.

3257 _____. "The Doctor," Atlantic Monthly, CCXXIII (January 1969), 86-88, 90-92.

3258 _____. "Duplicate Monday Nights," Georgia Review, XX (Spring 1966), 45-49.

3259 _____. "Emma," Cosmopolitan, CLIX (August 1965), 84-85.

3260 _____. "Gudliev," Delta Review, V (January 1968), 11-13.

3261 _____. "The Highwayman," Paris Review, X, no. 38 (Summer 1966), 130-139.

3262 _____. "The Messenger," Atlantic Monthly, CCVI (July 1965), 60-63.

3263 _____. "Monday Morning, Mazatlan," Shenandoah, XVII (Autumn 1965), 31-44.

3264 _____. "The Rabbit," Delta Review, IV (October 1967), 30-35, 61.

3265 _____. "The Savage Sound," Atlantic Monthly, CCXX (July 1967), 41-44.

3266 _____. "The Sherwood Forest Papers," Delta Review, IV (December 1967), 29.

3267 _____. "Whenever I Left Carver Hill," Delta Review, III (Spring 1966), 38, 62-63, 66-68.

3268 _____. "Winterkill," Esquire, LXVIII (September 1967), 112-113, 184-185, 187-188.

3269 Ford, John. "A Noble Art," Westerly, (May 1966), 20-27.

3270 Forde, A. N. "A Baby for Berry," Bim, XI (January-June 1966), 86-89.

3271 _____. "The Coachman and the Cab," Bim, XI (January-June 1967), 231-236.

3272 _____. "Home," Bim, XI (July-December 1966), 154-157.

3273 Foreman, Michael and Martin Bax. "On, At or About America," Ambit, no. 39 (1969), 2-8.

3274 Forest, Léonard. "The Struggles of Alexander," Saturday Night, LXXXIII (April 1968), 37-42.

3275 Forester, C. S. "Hornblower During the Crisis/(Part I)," Saturday Evening Post, CCXXXIX (July 16, 1966), 50-52, 54, 56-60, 62-63.

3276 _____. "Hornblower During the Crisis/(Part II)," Saturday Evening Post, CCXXXIX (July 30, 1966), 40-45, 48, 50-54, 56-57.

3277 Foronda, Marcelino, A., Jr. "The Avocado Tree," Literature East and West, XIII (December 1969), 325-334.

3278 _____. "The Avocado Tree," Solidarity, III (February 1968), 39-44.

3279 Forrer, Eric. "Two Stories by Eric Forrer/Muskrat," Prism International, IX (Autumn 1969), 54.

3280 _____. "Two Stories by Eric Forrer/Seal," Prism International, IX (Autumn 1969), 55.

3281 Forrest, Leon R. "That's Your Little Red Wagon," Blackbird, I, no. 3 (1966), 12-22.

3282 Forsberg, David P. "The Padre," Lance, V (Spring 1965), 49-50.

3283 Forshaw, Thelma. "The Mateship Syndrome," Meanjin Quarterly, XXIX (September 1965), 291-297.

3284 _____. "The Pawn," Quadrant, XI (March-April 1967), 43-46.

3285 _____. "The Welding Ridge," Southerly, XXVII, no. 2 (1967), 109-115.

3286 Forsyth, Judy. "A Chicken from the Farm," Westerly, no. 1 (March 1968), 31-33.

3287 _____. "For the Good of the People," Westerly, (August 1966), 5-10.

3288 Forsyth, Malcolm. "Sergeant Sykes," Michigan Quarterly Review, VII (Spring 1968), 114-118.

3289 Fort, Keith. "The Coal Shoveller," Sewanee Review, LXXVII (October-December 1969), 630-653.

3290 Fortescue, M. D. "Jenks," Nexus (San Francisco, Calif.), II (November-December 1965), 8-9.

3291 Forthman, Susan. "In the Dorm," Human Voice Quarterly, II (Winter 1966), 170-172.

3292 Foster, Charles. "Genesis," Wild Dog, no. 16 (April 1965), 22-26.

3293 Foster, Elma Wilkins. "The Marriageable Daughter," Human Voice Quarterly, I (November 1965), 153-167.

3294 Foster, Irene. "Heart of the Family," Good Housekeeping, CLXII (January 1966), 62-63, 156-160.

3295 Foster, Martha Standing. "'Hosanna!' I Said," Redbook, CXXV (June 1965), 44-45, 86, 88-89.

3296 Foster, Ruel E. "'A Good Bootlegger Is Hard To Find'," Spero, I, no. 1 (1965), 56-61.

3297 Fouch, Betty. "I Am Not What I Am," Epoch, XVII (Fall 1967), 88-90.

3298 Fowler, Douglas. "Scenario of a Fable," Chelsea, no. 16 (March 1965), 76-83.

3299 Fowler, Gene. "Rider in a Barrel," Nexus (San Francisco, Calif.), III (January-February 1967), 22-24.

3300 _____. "Solomon," Dust, III (Spring 1969), 3-4.

3301 _____. "Still Life," Gato Magazine, I (Autumn 1966), 15-17.

3302 Fowler, Will. "The Red Carpet Treatment," Prairie Schooner, XLII (Summer 1968), 127-136.

3303 Fowles, Jib. "Babe the Blue Ox," Atlantic Monthly, CCXIX (February 1967), 54-59.

3304 Fowles, John. "The Magus," Cosmopolitan, CLX (March 1966), 114-123.

3305 _____. "The Woman in the Reeds," Michigan Quarterly Review, IV (Spring 1965), 131-145.

3306 Fox, Caryn. "The Dress," UMD Humanist, XIV (Spring 1966), 3-6.

3307 Fox, George. "Kessler, the Inside Man," Esquire, LXVIII (October 1967), 124-125, 155, 157.

3308 _____. "The Need," Cavalier, XV (June 1965), 18-19, 78, 80, 82-84.

3309 Fox, Hugh B. "At the Rootbeer Stand," Wisconsin Review, III (Spring 1968), 17.

3310 _____. "Filaments and Vacuums--Burn," Ann Arbor Review, no. 2 (Winter 1967), 35-38.

3311 Fox, Janet. "A Fine Day for a Funeral," Kansas Magazine, (1965), 62-63.

3312 _____. "Just for Kicks," Riverside Quarterly, II (November 1966), 185-187.

3313 Fox, Paula. "The Living," Negro Digest, XVII (September/October 1968), 22-26.

3314 _____. "Lord Randal," Negro Digest, XIV (July 1965), 60-63.

3315 Fox, R. S. "The Last Train," Old Lady of Threadneedle

Street, XLIII (December 1967), 227-229.

3316 Fox, Robert. "All the Little Children," December, VII (1965), 20-22.

3317 _____. "A Fable," Midwestern University Quarterly, I, no. 4 (1966), 71-74.

3318 _____. "Joey," Prism International, IX (Summer 1969), 68-71.

3319 _____. "Linda," Midwestern University Quarterly, I, no. 4 (1966), 75-78.

3320 _____. "She Wrote:" Midwestern University Quarterly, I, no. 4 (1966), 68-70.

3321 _____. "Some of Them Were Boys," December, X (1968), 86-88.

3322 Fox, William Price. "I'm in Great Shape," Saturday Evening Post, CCXL (July 15, 1967), 56-61.

3323 _____. "Jack Driscoll's Revenge," Saturday Evening Post, CCXL (May 20, 1967), 30-33, 68, 70, 74-76, 78, 80, 82-83.

3324 _____. "Just a Friendly Little Game," Saturday Evening Post, CCXXXVIII (October 23, 1965), 54-56, 58, 71-74.

3325 Foxe, Andrew. "The Hard Times of a Hollywood Squaw Man," Cavalier, XVI (April 1966), 30-31, 33, 76, 78, 80-82.

3326 Fradin, D. "Waiting," Dare, IV (April 1966), 16.

3327 Frame, Janet. "The Bath," Landfall, no. 75 (September 1965), 225-230.

3328 _____. "The Bath," Weekend Telegraph, no. 102 (September 9, 1966), 29-32.

3329 _____. "The Birds of the Air," Harper's Bazaar, CII (June 1969), 102-105.

3330 _____. "A Boy's Will," Landfall, no. 80 (December 1966), 314-323.

3331 _____. "In Alco Hall," Harper's Bazaar, XCIX (November 1966), 166-167, 225, 228.

3332 _____. "You Are Now Entering the Human Heart," Cornhill Magazine, CLXXVII (Autumn 1969), 401-404.

3333 _____. "You Are Now Entering the Human Heart," New

Yorker, XLV (March 29, 1969), 134, 137-138.

3334 Francis, H. E. "All the Carnivals in the World," Southern Review, V (April 1969), 531-548.

3335 _____. "All the People I Never Had," Transatlantic Review, no. 21 (Summer 1966), 83-93.

3336 _____. "The Deepest Chamber," Four Quarters, XV (March 1966), 10-18.

3337 _____. "Does He Treat You All Right?" Four Quarters, XIV (May 1965), 1-4.

3338 _____. "Don't Stay Away Too Long," Southwest Review, LIV (Autumn 1969), 379-397.

3339 _____. "Going West," Transatlantic Review, no. 28 (Spring 1968), 70-80.

3340 _____. "Her," Georgia Review, XXIII (Fall 1969), 388-394.

3341 _____. "In Transit," Arlington Quarterly, I (Spring 1968), 129-151.

3342 _____. "The Listener," University Review, XXXV (Autumn 1968), 55-67.

3343 _____. "The Man Who Made People," DeKalb Literary Arts Journal, I (Spring 1967), 1-19.

3344 _____. "The Moment," North American Review, III (May 1966), 20-23.

3345 _____. "Moments in the Definition of Space," DeKalb Literary Arts Journal, III (Fall 1968), 37-52.

3346 _____. "One of the Boys," Southwest Review, LI (Spring 1966), 131-147.

3347 _____. "The Rate of Decomposition in a Cold Climate," Southwest Review, LIII (Summer 1968), 236-256.

3348 _____. "Something Just over the Edge of Everything," Four Quarters, XIX (November 1969), 25-33.

3349 _____. "Summer Is the Suffering Time Here," North American Review, IV (May 1967), 9-13.

3350 _____. "3," Virginia Quarterly Review, XLIV (Autumn 1968), 611-625.

3351 Francis, Robin. "The Message of Will," Transatlantic Review, no. 29 (Summer 1968), 124-126.

3352 Franco, Marjorie. "The Eye of Love," Redbook, CXXIX (August 1967), 72-73, 140, 142, 144-148.

3353 _____. "I Am a Gentle, Peaceful Man," Redbook, CXXIX (June 1967), 70-71, 111-114.

3354 _____. "A Mile to Walk," Redbook, CXXXI (September 1968), 88-89.

3355 _____. "Shy Emily," Redbook, CXXXII (March 1969), 74-75, 126, 128, 130, 132.

3356 Franco, Natalia. "The Revolving Door," Mexico Quarterly Review, III, no. 2 (1968), 13-23.

3357 Frank, Jeffrey. "Admissions," Mademoiselle, LXVI (January 1968), 84-85, 128-129.

3358 Frank, Leonhard. "Breathe," George Raymond Selden, trans., Scala International, (September 1967), 34-37.

3359 Frankau, Pamela. "Colonel Blessington," Cosmopolitan, CLXVII (August 1969), 132-145, 147-149, 152-156.

3360 Frankel, Zygmunt. "Mr. Finkelstein's Ulcer," London Magazine, VII (October 1967), 24-29.

3361 _____. "The Peasant and the Snake," Transatlantic Review, no. 27 (Winter 1967-68), 96-98.

3362 Franklin, Edward. "All that Sunday Madness," Transatlantic Review, no. 20 (Spring 1966), 19-29.

3363 _____. "The Girl with the Monica Vitti Nose," Nexus (San Francisco, Calif.), II (January-February 1965), 35-36.

3364 _____. "Hope City," Transatlantic Review, no. 24 (Spring 1967), 138-144.

3365 _____. "The Infinity Question," Nexus (San Francisco, Calif.), III (March-April 1967), 9-12.

3366 _____. "The Mad Doctor of Market Street," Nexus (San Francisco, Calif.), II (May-June 1965), 39-43.

3367 _____. "Sunday Games," Dust, III (Winter-Spring 1967), 41-45.

3368 _____. "Three Hole Harper," Transatlantic Review, no. 32 (Summer 1969), 76-81.

3369 _____. "Vignettes by an Ex-Wife," Dust, I (Winter 1965), 49-68.

3370 Franklin, F. K. "Nigger Horse," Southwest Review, LII (Winter 1967), 68-82.

3371 Franklin, Ronni. "The Frump Queen," Redbook, CXXXI (October 1968), 78-79, 161, 164-166.

3372 Franzen, Byron. "Behold the Birds," Discourse, X (Autumn 1967), 385-392.

3373 Fraser, Malcolm. "The Goddess," Landfall, no. 84 (December 1967), 348-352.

3374 Fraser, Raymond. "Chatham's Flying Saucer," The Fiddlehead, no. 79 (March-April 1969), 23-33.

3375 _____. "Renting a TV," Canadian Forum, XLVIII (November 1968), 191.

3376 Frater, Alexander. "An Autumn Sortie," New Yorker, XLIII (October 21, 1967), 52-56.

3377 _____. "The Corporal," New Yorker, XLIV (January 4, 1969), 33-37.

3378 _____. "The Drummer," New Yorker, XLI (November 27, 1965), 54-55.

3379 _____. "The Matriarch," New Yorker, XLII (April 16, 1966), 53-56.

3380 _____. "The Practitioner," New Yorker, XLIII (April 1, 1967), 42-45.

3381 Frayn, Michael. "Dyson on the Box," Playboy, XIV (April 1967), 125, 130, 132, 178, 180-182, 184.

3382 Frazer, Chris. "Phantasmagoria," Seventeen, XXVII (May 1968), 142-143.

3383 Frazier, Willard. "A Table for Two," Good Housekeeping, CLXIV (January 1967), 66-67.

3384 Fredd, Eric. "A Character Introduction to the Individuals Involved in The Affairs of Town II," Manuscript, XIX (Spring 1966), 42-47.

3385 Frede, Richard. "The Secret Circus," Ramparts, V (June 1967), 36-45.

3386 Frederick, K. C. "All the Shortstops in Ohio," Sage, XI

(Fall 1967), 271-280.

3387 _____. "Eugene and Me," Epoch, XIV (Spring 1965), 251-263.

3388 _____. "Extra Innings: A Short Story," Epoch, XIX (Fall 1969), 36-48.

3389 _____. "Suitors, Shooters," University Review, XXXI (June 1965), 265-272.

3390 _____. "'Whose Country Have I Come to Now?'," Epoch, XVII (Winter 1968), 109-134.

3391 Frederick, Stephenie. "Hint," Statement, no. 23 (Spring 1967), 31-39.

3392 Free, Barbara. "Dear Mary Maude," New Zealand Listener, LII (January 29, 1965), 5.

3393 _____. "A Foreign Language," New Zealand Listener, LIII (November 19, 1965), 4, 21.

3394 _____. "Love and Marriage," New Zealand Listener, LX (February 21, 1969), 12.

3395 _____. "The Magpies," New Zealand Listener, (September 29, 1967), 6, 15.

3396 _____. "Mother of the Bride," New Zealand Listener, (December 9, 1966), 6, 25.

3397 Free, William J. "Caleb and the Iron Monster," Georgia Review, XX (Winter 1966), 413-424.

3398 Freedman, Morris. "The Earring," New Mexico Quarterly, XXXVII (Spring 1967), 14-19.

3399 Freeman, Anne Hobson. "What Ever Became of Agnes Mason?" McCall's, XCVI (January 1969), 76-77, 112.

3400 Freeman, Gary. "No Exit," Ave Maria, CIX (June 14, 1969), 13-15.

3401 Freeman, Jean Todd. "Games Children Don't Play," Ladies' Home Journal, LXXXVI (March 1969), 100-101, 158, 166.

3402 _____. "Panther," Redbook, CXXXI (August 1968), 72-73, 103-106.

3403 _____. "The Thirty-sixth Brick," Redbook, CXXVIII (December 1966), 54-55, 140-141, 144-145.

3404 _____. "Who Am I?" Redbook, CXXXII (April 1969), 88-89, 137-139.

3405 Freeman, R. A. "Indoro Bush College," Literary Review, XI (Summer 1968), 435-441.

3406 Freeman, Seth. "Mouse," Prospero's Cell, I (Winter 1967), 25-36.

3407 Freitag, George H. "Dear Anybody in the World:" Quartet, no. 13 (Winter 1966), 2-4.

3408 _____. "An Old Man and His Act," Harper's Magazine, CCXXXIV (June 1967), 96-97.

3409 _____. "Something No One Ever Sees," New Yorker, XLIV (March 23, 1968), 33-34.

3410 Fremantle, Anne. "Antepenultimate," New Yorker, XLII (March 12, 1966), 52-57.

3411 _____. "Balm in Gilead," New Yorker, XLV (September 13, 1969), 41-45.

3412 _____. "Christmas Eve," New Yorker, XL (February 13, 1965), 110-112, 115-116, 118, 121-122, 124, 125.

3413 _____. "Dear Casper," The Quest, II (Spring 1966), 243-247.

3414 _____. "Siesta," The Quest, I (Winter 1965-66), 23-28.

3415 Fremlin, Celia. "The Jealous One," Cosmopolitan, CLVIII (March 1965), 94-111, 114-119, 122-129.

3416 French, John T. "Barzak's Way," William and Mary Review, III (Winter 1965), 77-93.

3417 French, Marilyn. "The Sinking of the Golden Boat," Southern Humanities Review, III (Spring 1969), 138-144.

3418 French, Warren. "The Butterfly Boxing Club," Little Review of the Pacific Northwest, I (Fall 1965), 45-46.

3419 Friday, Nancy. "Mixed-up Time," Cosmopolitan, CLXIV (March 1968), 162-167.

3420 Fried, Eric Wolf. "Worship to Greenland," Epoch, XVII (Fall 1967), 8-49.

3421 Fried, Sister Sharon, O. S. B. "Phoebe Reviewed," Catholic World, CCIII (April 1966), 40-41.

3422 Friedland, R. L. "The Elevator," The Gauntlet, I (Fall 1967), 2-5.

3423 Friedman, Alan. "Willy-Nilly," New American Review, no. 2 (January 1968), 15-38.

3424 Friedman, B. H. "Did You Know Gorky? Kline? Pollock?" Evergreen Review, XI (June 1967), 27, 85.

3425 ______. "Museum," Quarterly Review of Literature, XV (1968), 263-315.

3426 ______. "Whispers," New American Review, no. 5 (January 1969), 235-267.

3427 Friedman, Bruce Jay. "Brazzaville Teen-Ager," Esquire, LXIV (July 1965), 78, 108.

3428 ______. "A Change of Plan," Esquire, LXV (January 1966), 96-97, 111-112.

3429 ______. "A Different Ball Game," Esquire, LXXII (December 1969), 229, 231, 282.

3430 ______. "The Hero," Cavalier, XVI (January 1966), 36-37, 78-81.

3431 ______. "The Humiliation," Cavalier, XVI (April 1966), 42-43, 88-90.

3432 ______. "The Neighbors," Cavalier, XV (July 1965), 20-21+.

3433 ______. "The Operator," Cavalier, XV (April 1965), 22-23, 88-93.

3434 ______. "The Partners," Esquire, LXXII (August 1969), 72-74, 150-152.

3435 ______. "The Pledges," Esquire, LXVIII (September 1967), 133, 156.

3436 ______. "The Punch," Esquire, LXIII (February 1965), 116, 118-119.

3437 ______. "The Scientist," Esquire, LXVII (April 1967), 105, 107.

3438 ______. "The Subversive," Queen, CDXXIV (June 2, 1965), 66-68.

3439 Friedman, Paul. "An Afternoon by the Pool," Delta (Cambridge, England), no. 39 (Summer 1966), 29-33.

3440 _____. "An Evening of Fun," Perspective, XV (Autumn 1968), 244-270.

3441 _____. "The Forecast," Arlington Quarterly, II (Autumn 1969), 59-70.

3442 _____. "Home Is Where the Heart Is," Wisconsin Review, II (May 1967), 7-9, 23.

3443 _____. "A Matter of Survival," Four Quarters, XVI (March 1967), 16-19.

3444 _____. "Portrait: My American Man, Fall, 1966," New Directions 20, (1968), 63-69.

3445 _____. "A View of the Poet," North American Review, IV (July 1967), 10-14.

3446 _____. "The White Man's Burden," Prism International, VI (Autumn 1966), 21-33.

3447 _____. "Why Mrs. Barron Perspires," Florida Quarterly, I (Winter 1968), 27-40.

3448 Friedman, Robert. "The Candy Store Job," Greensboro Review, I (May 1966), 33-39.

3449 Friedman, S. L. "Bond-Paper Gardenia: A Profile," Quartet, no. 16 (Fall 1966), 21-22.

3450 Friedman, Thomas. "The Dying Gaul," Riverrun, no. 2 (1968), 60-67.

3451 Friel, Brian. "Among the Ruins," Threshold, no. 21 (Summer 1967), 117-128.

3452 _____. "The Gold in the Sea," New Yorker, XLI (July 31, 1965), 32-37.

3453 Friesen, Victor Carl. "Fence," Canadian Forum, XLIX (December 1969), 214-215.

3454 Frings, Ketti. "To Paris--with All My Heart," Good Housekeeping, CLXVII (November 1968), 86-87, 193-197.

3455 Frisbie, Johnny. "Mama Tala," Atlantic Monthly, CCXV (February 1965), 69-74.

3456 Frisch, A. "Yes John Do Have a Good Night's Sleep," Dare, IV (July-August 1966), 22-23.

3457 Fritz, Jean. "Catch a Falling Star," Seventeen, XXVI (December 1967), 90-91, 154-157.

3458 ______. "Kelly's Girl," Seventeen, XXIV (December 1965), 96-97, 181-185.

3459 ______. "Little Christmas," Seventeen, XXV (December 1966), 112-113, 178, 180-181.

3460 ______. "Mr. Sterling, Darling," Seventeen, XXVII (December 1968), 112-113, 166-169.

3461 ______. "Season of Renewal," McCall's, XCV (December 1967), 126-127, 158-161.

3462 Froscher, Wingate. "A Letter from Nueva York," New Mexico Quarterly, XXXVII (Spring 1967), 59-67.

3463 Frumkes, Roi. "On Age," Nexus (San Francisco, Calif.), II (May-June 1965), 62-70.

3464 Fudoli, M. "The Old Man and the Dove," Damayanti Soebiarto, trans., Solidarity, III (November 1968), 16-21.

3465 Fuentes, Carlos. "A Change of Skin," Audience, Pilot Issue (Spring 1968), 4-11.

3466 ______. "The Doll Queen," Agnes Moncy, trans., Tri-Quarterly, no. 15 (Spring 1969), 264-279.

3467 ______. "The Two Elenas," Elaine Cameron, trans., Tamarack Review, no. 44 (Summer 1967), 41-51.

3468 Fuhrman, Jim. "Diggin' for Coxey's Army in a Murky Min'," The Circle, no. 3 (1968), 1-17, 19-29.

3469 Fuller, Hoyt W. "The Drowning Man," North American Review, II (May 1965), 43-48.

3470 Fulton, Bart. "Flight," Columbia, XLVI (August 1966), 24-27.

3471 Furlong, Joan. "Lonely Hearts," Modern Age, XII (Fall 1968), 395-397.

3472 Furman, Laura. "The Light," Silo, no. 8 (Fall 1965), 60-67.

3473 Fytton, Francis. "Assassination," Stand, VII, no. 1 (1965), 8-47.

3474 ______. "Interrogation," Stand, VII, no. 3 (1965), 43-69.

3475 ______. "My Barbouze," Ambit, no. 30 (1966/67), 8-19.

3476 ______. "We Shall Hear Bugles," Ikon (Leeds, England), I

(March 1966), 12-23.

3477 Gabbard, Andrea. "The Companion," Seventeen, XXV (January 1966), 84-85, 131-132.

3478 Gabel, Margaret. "The Custard Dispute," Carolina Quarterly, XX (Winter 1968), 5-12.

3479 _____. "See How It Goes," Intro, no. 1 (September 1968), 80-86.

3480 Gabour, Jim. [untitled], Delta, XXIII (1969), 15-16.

3481 Gaffron, Carole. "The Choice," Woman's Day, (May 1967), 38-39, 94-97, 100.

3482 _____. "The French Teacher," Cosmopolitan, CLVIII (May 1965), 108, 110-114.

3483 _____. "The Girl in the Camel's-Hair Coat," Redbook, CXXV (October 1965), 76-77, 112, 114, 116, 118.

3484 _____. "The Girl Who Knew Everything," Redbook, CXXVIII (November 1966), 171, 173-199.

3485 Gagen, Joseph F. "The Going Away," Ave Maria, CIII (May 7, 1966), 26-27, 29.

3486 Gailor, Denis. "Gweal," London Magazine, VI (May 1966), 63-70.

3487 _____. "Two Incidents/Apple," London Magazine, VI (December 1966), 35-39.

3488 _____. "Two Incidents/The Interview," London Magazine, VI (December 1966), 30-35.

3489 Gaines, Charles. "The Recruitment," Harper's Magazine, CCXXXV (December 1967), 92-98.

3490 Gaines, Diana. "The Legacy," Redbook, CXXVIII (March 1967), 165, 167-189.

3491 _____. "No Game for Children," Redbook, CXXV (May 1965), 161, 163-185.

3492 Gaines, Ernest J. "My Grandpa and the Haint," New Mexico Quarterly, XXXVI (Summer 1966), 149-160.

3493 Gair, Lucy. "The Ceremony," Transatlantic Review, no. 27 (Winter 1967-68), 124-133.

3494 Gaiser, Carolyn. "Differences," Paris Review, X (Winter-

Spring 1967), 179-183.

3495 Gaiser, Gerd. "But Deliver Us from Evil," George Raymond Selden, trans., Scala International, (June 1966), 34-37.

3496 Galban, Eugenio Suarez. "The Net," Ave Maria, CV (January 28, 1967), 26-27.

3497 Galbraith, John Kenneth. "The Triumph," Imprint, VIII (October 1968), 82-84, 87-91, 93, 95, 97, 99, 101-102, 105, 107, 109, 111, 113, 115, 117, 119, 121, 123, 125, 127, 129, 131, 133-134.

3498 _____. "The Triumph," Saturday Evening Post, CCXLI (April 20, 1968), 32-35, 54-57, 60-65, 68-75.

3499 Gale, Vi. "Ultimately Primroses," Midwestern University Quarterly, II, no. 2 (1966), 55-61.

3500 Galey, John H. "The Jawbone," New Directions 19, (1966), 102-127.

3501 Galgóczi, Erzsébet. "Alien in the Village," New Hungarian Quarterly, VII (Spring 1967), 82-106.

3502 _____. "It's a Million Miles to Budapest," New Hungarian Quarterly, X (Autumn 1969), 94-111.

3503 Gallagher, Theresa Bond. "A Kind of Fury," Assay, XXIV (Spring 1968), 23-28.

3504 Gallagher, Thomas. "Oona O'," Redbook, CXXVI (March 1966), 161, 163-185.

3505 Gallant, Gerald. "Crumpdinker/Chapter Five of Quagmire, a Novel in Progress," For Now, no. 5 (c. 1966-68), 39-53.

3506 _____. "The Mirror," Epoch, XVIII (Spring 1969), 292-305.

3507 _____. "Quagmire: A Novel in Progress," For Now, no. 1 (c. 1966-68), 21-39.

3508 Gallant, Mavis. "The Accident," New Yorker, XLIII (October 28, 1967), 55-59.

3509 _____. "April Fish," New Yorker, XLIII (February 10, 1968), 27-28.

3510 _____. "Bonaventure," New Yorker, XLII (July 30, 1966), 34-38, 40, 45, 48, 50, 54, 56-63.

3511 _____. "The Captive Niece," New Yorker, XLIV (January 4, 1969), 28-32.

3512 _____. "The End of the World," New Yorker, XLIII (June 10, 1967), 36-39.

3513 _____. "Good Deed," New Yorker, XLV (February 22, 1969), 35-41.

3514 _____. "In Transit," New Yorker, LXI (August 14, 1965), 24-25.

3515 _____. "Malcolm and Bea," New Yorker, XLIV (March 23, 1968), 35-43.

3516 _____. "The Old Friends," New Yorker, XLV (August 30, 1969), 27-30.

3517 _____. "Orphans' Progress," New Yorker, XLI (April 3, 1965), 49-51.

3518 _____. "Paola and Renata," Southern Review, I (January 1965), 199-209.

3519 _____. "The Prodigal Parent," New Yorker, XLV (June 7, 1969), 42-44.

3520 _____. "Questions and Answers," New Yorker, XLII (May 28, 1966), 33-38.

3521 _____. "The Rejection," New Yorker, XLV (April 12, 1969), 42-44.

3522 _____. "A Report," New Yorker, XLII (December 3, 1966), 62-65.

3523 _____. "Saturday," New Yorker, XLIV (June 8, 1968), 32-40.

3524 _____. "The Statues Taken Down," New Yorker, XLI (October 9, 1965), 53-56.

3525 _____. "The Sunday after Christmas," New Yorker, XLIII (December 30, 1967), 35-36.

3526 _____. "Vacanes Pax," New Yorker, XLII (July 16, 1966), 26-29.

3527 _____. "Virus X," New Yorker, XL (January 30, 1965), 29-40, 42, 44, 47-48, 50, 53-54, 56, 59-61.

3528 _____. "The Wedding Ring," New Yorker, XLV (June 28, 1969), 41-42.

3529 Gallico, Paul. "Mrs. 'Arris Goes to Parliament," Ladies' Home Journal, LXXXII (March 1965), 80-81, 119-135.

3530 _____. "The Poseidon Adventure," Redbook, CXXXIII (August 1969), 157-187.

3531 Gallo, Louis. "I Begin This Year," Abyss, (January-February 1967), n.p. [1-20].

3532 Gallo, Marilyn. "Pellegrino and the Professor," Mademoiselle, LXI (August 1965), 262-263, 344-347.

3533 Gallup, Dick. "The Abductors," Mother, no. 7 (Mother's Day, 1966), 65.

3534 _____. "A Celebration," Mother, no. 5 (Summer 1965), 60.

3535 _____. "A Chinese Murder," Mother, no. 7 (Mother's Day, 1966), 64.

3536 _____. "Homage to Fran," Mother, no. 5 (Summer 1965), 61.

3537 _____. "Homage to Fran," Mother, no. 7 (Mother's Day, 1966), 62.

3538 _____. "An Idea that Reaches the Moon," The Once Series, (Nice), I (1966-67), n.p. [17].

3539 _____. "More Life," Mother, no. 7 (Mother's Day, 1966), 67.

3540 _____. "A Self-Contained Actress," Mother, no. 7 (Mother's Day, 1966), 66.

3541 _____, Ted Berrigan and Mike Brownstein. "A Story," The World, no. 4 (June 1967), n.p. [62].

3542 _____ and Tom Veitch. "Strawberries/from The Planetary Route," Yale Literary Magazine, CXXXVIII (May 1969), 29-32.

3543 _____. "Tips to Go On," Mother, no. 7 (Mother's Day, 1966), 63.

3544 Gambee, Ruth. "Sunday Visitors," Crucible, V (Fall 1968), 17-20.

3545 Gamzatov, Rasul. "My Daghestan/(Chapters from the Book)," Avril Pyman, trans., Soviet Literature, (no. 11, 1968), 3-93.

3546 Gangemi, Kenneth. "The Appointment," Transatlantic Review, no. 27 (Winter 1967-68), 108-115.

3547 _____. "The Snow-Lobsters," Art and Literature, no. 8

(Spring 1966), 184-191.

3548 Gangopadhyay, Narayan. "Three Men and the Fourth," Bhabani P. Ghost, trans., Bengali Literature, I (May 1967), 31-40.

3549 Ganly, Andrew. "The Story of Artemis and Actaeon Retold," Dublin Magazine, VI (Spring 1967), 13-18.

3550 Gant, Phyllis. "All Stained with Yellow Mud," New Zealand Listener, LIV (June 17, 1966), 23.

3551 _____. "A Sense Of ...," New Zealand Listener, LX (March 14, 1969), 12.

3552 Ganz, Earl. "Genesis," Occident, III (Spring/Summer 1969), 59-66.

3553 _____. "Rosegarden Revisited," Minnesota Review, VIII (1968), 132-137.

3554 _____. "The Swastika Painter," Malahat Review, no. 12 (October 1969), 92-99.

3555 Garber, Eugene K. "Philo Castratus," December, IX (1967), 41-46.

3556 García Márquez, Gabriel. "Balthazar's Marvelous Afternoon," J. S. Bernstein, trans., Atlantic Monthly, CCXXI (May 1968), 52-55.

3557 _____. "Tuesday Siesta," J. S. Bernstein, trans., Tri-Quarterly, nos. 13/14 (Fall/Winter 1968-69), 209-215.

3558 Gardien, Kent. "Lola, Lola, Lola," Quarterly Review of Literature, XIII (1965), 425-439.

3559 _____. "Rush," Quarterly Review of Literature, XIII (1965), 412-425.

3560 Gardiner, Norman. "Skin Job," Meanjin Quarterly, XXVIII (Summer 1969), 479-484.

3561 Gardner, Fred. "The Whereabouts of Mr. Haber," Transatlantic Review, no. 28 (Spring 1968), 131-136.

3562 Gardner, Herb. "Guess Who Died?" Playboy, XIV (April 1967), 97, 186-188.

3563 _____. "Who Is Harry Kellerman and Why Is He Saying Those Terrible Things About Me?" Saturday Evening Post, CCXL (March 11, 1967), 54-56, 58, 62, 66, 68-69.

3564 Gardner, John. "Amber Nine," Mademoiselle, LXIII (July 1966), 89-120.

3565 _____. "Nickel Mountain," Southern Review, II (April 1966), 374-418.

3566 _____. "The Spike in the Door," Ball State University Forum, VIII (Autumn 1967), 52-55.

3567 Gardner, Leonard. "An Arkansas Traveler," Genesis West, III (Winter 1965), 46-47.

3568 _____. "Flea Circus," Southwest Review, L (Autumn 1965), 337-344.

3569 _____. "From the Chair Car," Red Clay Reader, no. 4 (1967), 55-58.

3570 Garen, Robert. "The Forces," University of Windsor Review, I (Winter 1965), 236-238.

3571 _____. "The Old Woman," University of Windsor Review, III (Spring 1968), 30-32.

3572 Garner, Hugh. "The Sound of Hollyhocks," Tamarack Review, no. 52 (1969), 5-18.

3573 _____. "You Never Ast Me Before," Tamarack Review, no. 35 (Spring 1965), 3-12.

3574 Garner, Robert. "Screams Are Ears Trying to Hear," Nexus (San Francisco, Calif.), III (March-April 1967), 37-39.

3575 _____. "The War Machine," Evergreen Review, XII (March 1968), 45-46, 91-95.

3576 Garoogian, Lawrence E. "The Carriage," Armenian Review, XIX (Spring 1966), 62-67.

3577 Garrard, Christopher. "The Inheritance of Emmy One Horse," South Dakota Review, VI (Spring 1968), 3-12.

3578 Garrett, George. "Bread from Stones," Queen, CDXXIV (June 16, 1965), 71-75.

3579 _____. "Poison Pen," Per/Se, II (Summer 1967), 30-37.

3580 _____. "Fragment from the Unpublished Novel--'Poison Pen, or The Triumph of Shinola'," Mill Mountain Review, I (1969), 25.

3581 _____. "To Whom Shall I Call Now in My Hour of Need?"

Red Clay Reader, no. 2 (1965), 4-15.

3582 Garrett, Leslie. "The Only Man in Paris without a Woman," Evergreen Review, XIII (July 1969), 22-25, 72-77.

3583 Garvey, Bart. "The Wednesday Warriors Take a Bum Trip," William and Mary Review, VII (Spring 1969), 4-6.

3584 Garvin, Tim. "Fire Tower," Delta, XXII (1968), 1-7.

3585 _____. "A Gray Jay in the Sun," Delta, XXII (1968), 61-65.

3586 _____. "Patriot," Delta, XXIII (1969), 53-63.

3587 de la Garza, Beatriz. "The Birds Are Still Singing," Corral 1966, 8-17.

3588 _____. "The Wanderer," Corral 1966, 22-31.

3589 Gaskin, Howard. "An Old Man's Summer Evening," Westerly, no. 1 (1967), 17-20.

3590 Gasner, Beverly. "Girls' Rules," Redbook, CXXXII (March 1969), 177-199.

3591 _____. "Nina Upstairs," McCall's, XCII (January 1965), 64-73.

3592 Gasper, B. G. and Brue Woodford. "The Rope, a Fugue from Hell," Aesop's Feast, I (January 1969), 9-19.

3593 Gass, William H. "The Clairvoyant," Aesop's Feast, I (May 1968), 14-29.

3594 _____. "In the Heart of the Heart of the Country," New American Review, no. 1 (1967), 259-283.

3595 _____. "The Sugar Crock," Art and Literature, no. 9 (Summer 1966), 158-171.

3596 _____. "We Have Not Lived the Right Life," New American Review, no. 6 (April 1969), 7-32.

3597 Gasser, Larry. "The Fall of Dark," Jeopardy, no. 1 (1966), 3-10.

3598 _____. "The Water Tank," Jeopardy, no. 3 (Spring 1967), 3-15.

3599 Gathorn-Hardy, Jonathan. "The Picnic," Nova, (October 1969), 136, 139, 141, 144, 149.

3600 Gatruboi, David N. "A Child of Sin," Nexus, II (July 1968), 32-40.

3601 Gatten, Thomas. "The Density of Green," Art and Literature, no. 12 (Spring 1967), 208-224.

3602 ______. "The Voyage," The Quest, III (Summer-Fall 1968), 13-20.

3603 Gauer, Harold. "The 100-Volt Monkey," Dare, V (February 1967), 30-31.

3604 Gayle, Addison, Jr. "There Is No Other Way," Negro Digest, XVI (May 1967), 60-70.

3605 Gebhart, Rosalyn. "The Sisters," North American Review, II (September 1965), 27-31.

3606 Gebler, Ernest. "The Power over a Woman," Queen, CDXXXII (January 22, 1969), 41-43.

3607 Gecau, James K. "Dr. Sole's Case," Nexus, II (July 1968), 18-22.

3608 ______. "Just Like Jane," Nexus, I (August 1967), 12-13.

3609 ______. "The Ridge," Nexus, I (1966), 8-14.

3610 Gee, June. "A Short Story/An adaption of J. D. Salinger's style in Catcher in the Rye," UMD Humanist, XVII (Winter 1969), 33-36.

3611 Gee, Maurice. "The Champion," Landfall, no. 78 (June 1966), 113-125.

3612 ______. "Down in the World," Landfall, no. 83 (September 1967), 296-302.

3613 ______. "A Retired Life," Landfall, no. 90 (June 1969), 101-116.

3614 Geeraerts, Jef. "The Troglodytes," Christopher Levenson, trans., Delta (Amsterdam), XI (Spring 1968), 72-88.

3615 Geeslin, Hugh, Jr. "Time of Life," Georgia Review, XIX (Winter 1965), 426-435.

3616 Geiser, Steffi. "Buildings Should Speak," Readers & Writers, I (April 1968), 26-29.

3617 Gelléri, Andor Endre. "Drunk," New Hungarian Quarterly, X (Winter 1969), 55-60.

3618 Gellhorn, Martha. "The Lowest Trees Have Tops," Ladies' Home Journal, LXXXIV (August 1967), 43-50.

3619 Gellis, Willard. "Cocoon," Analecta, II (Spring 1968), 40-42.

3620 Genet, Jean. "From: Funeral Rites," Bernard Frechtman, trans., Evergreen Review, XIII (July 1969), 46-49, 78-81.

3621 Gengenbach, Linda. "The Empty House," Twigs, no. 1 (1965), 59-62.

3622 George, Gerald. "The Cold," Kansas Magazine, (1968), 15-19.

3623 Georgiev, Kolyo. "Solitaries," Svetoslaw Piperov, trans., Obzor, (Spring 1969), 65-68.

3624 Gerard, Charles. "The Fire Broom," Ball State University Forum, VII (Winter 1966), 38-41.

3625 _____. "The Great Shitepoke Slough," Minnesota Review, VI (1966), 185-193.

3626 Gerard, John Bart. "Alabama Jacks," Ararat, VIII (Autumn 1967), 88-94.

3627 _____. "Blood Letting," Atlantic Monthly, CCXXIII (May 1969), 88-90.

3628 _____. "The Catch," Texas Quarterly, XI (Spring 1968), 139-146.

3629 _____. "Walking Wounded," Harper's Magazine, CCXXXVII (August 1968), 45-50.

3630 Gerasimov, Iosif. "Five Days' Rest," Eve Manning, trans., Soviet Literature, (no. 9, 1969), 43-109.

3631 Gerber, Merrill Joan. "Approval," Redbook, CXXIV (February 1965), 44-45, 128, 133-134, 136.

3632 _____. "Baby Blues," Redbook, CXXVI (November 1965), 60-61, 104-105, 107.

3633 _____. "The Bargain," Redbook, CXXXI (June 1968), 70-71, 105-108.

3634 _____. "Chipping," Redbook, CXXV (May 1965), 56-57, 153, 158-159.

3635 _____. "Explain That to a Baby Sitter," Redbook, CXXXI (July 1968), 72-73, 103, 105-106.

3636 _____. "Invitation to the Dance," Redbook, CXXVII (October 1966), 58-59, 139-143.

3637 _____. "The Stork Is a Wonderful Bird," Redbook, CXXVIII (February 1967), 84-85, 151-153.

3638 _____. "Ten Cents' Worth of Love," Redbook, CXXVII (July 1966), 66-67.

3639 _____. "What Do I Want to Do Today?" Redbook, CXXXIV (December 1969), 100-101, 144, 146.

3640 _____. "Yom Kippur," Florida Quarterly, I (Fall 1967), 1-9.

3641 Gerber, Phil. "Amid the Alien Corn," Prairie Schooner, XLIII (Summer 1969), 209-220.

3642 Geringer, Laura. "The Raspberries," Sundial, I (Spring 1967), 8-11.

3643 Gersh, Gabriel. "The Fire Walkers," Ararat, VIII (Autumn 1967), 95-100.

3644 _____. "Samson," Ararat, VII (Summer 1966), 11-16.

3645 Gershon, Karen. "The Tenth of November," Midstream, XIV (March 1968), 17-23.

3646 _____. "Two Stories/On Mount Zion," Midstream, XIII (March 1967), 38-43.

3647 _____. "Two Stories/Shelter," Midstream, XIII (March 1967), 43-49.

3648 Ghanem, Fathi. "Dunya," Vision, XVIII (May 1969), 6-9.

3649 Ghani, Mahboob. "That T.V. Set," Pakistan Review, XIV (December 1966), 16, 26.

3650 Ghaznavi, Khatir. "Mahbuba Jalaat," Parveen Qazi, trans., Pakistan Review, XIV (October 1966), 40-42.

3651 Gherman, Yuri. "The Ambush," Bryan Bean, trans., Soviet Literature, (no. 10, 1968), 92-96.

3652 Ghilia, Alecu Ivan. "Negostina," Literary Review, X (Summer 1967), 545-552.

3653 Ghose, Ashis. "I Committed a Sin," Sajal Basu, trans., Bengali Literature, I (June/August 1966), 35-40.

3654 Ghose, Subhash. "My Hypnotism/(from My Key)," D. S. Klein, trans., Salted Feathers, nos. 8 & 9 (March 1967), n.p. [108-110].

3655 _____. "Red Road from Aamaar Chaabi," Intrepid, no. 10

(Spring 1968), n.p. [17-18].

3656 Ghosh, Santosh Kumar. "They Are Three," Enakshi Chatterjee, trans., Bengali Literature, I (October/December 1966), 13-18.

3657 Giacalone, Margaret LoMonaco. "The Bingo Prize Walked In," Columbia, XLVI (June 1966), 26-29.

3658 Gibbs, Donna Alyce. "Ashes," Yale Literary Magazine, CXXXV (November 1966), 28-29.

3659 Gibran, Khalil. "The Ambitious Violet," Maliha Ansari, trans., Vision, XV (December 1966), 18-19, 50, 52.

3660 Gibson, Freda. "Alone Upstairs," Old Lady of Threadneedle Street, XLI (March 1965), 9-14.

3661 _____. "Fools' Paradise," Old Lady of Threadneedle Street, XLI (September 1965), 146-150.

3662 Gibson, Margaret. "Old Maids," Georgia Review, XXIII (Summer 1969), 214-233.

3663 _____. "Trainride," Shenandoah, XXI (Autumn 1969), 48-62.

3664 Gibson, McNeill. "Buddy of Mine," The Archive, LXXIX (April 1967), 13-14.

3665 Gibson, Miles. "Bedsitters," Daily Telegraph Magazine, no. 241 (May 23, 1969), 29-30, 33.

3666 _____. "Death of an Angel," Daily Telegraph Magazine, no. 261 (October 10, 1969), 73.

3667 Gichangi, Duncan M. "A Homecoming," Nexus, I (January 1968), 20-21.

3668 _____. "Nyakiemo," Nexus, II (July 1968), 10-12.

3669 Gicomoya, D. M. "Gathondu," Nexus, II (July 1968), 7-8.

3670 Gifford, William. "The Cliffs," Quarterly Review of Literature, XIV (1967), 345-350.

3671 _____. "A Long Illness," Colorado Quarterly, XV (Autumn 1966), 143-152.

3672 Gifkins, Michael. "Artist," Landfall, no. 73 (March 1965), 33-36.

3673 _____. "The Visit," Landfall, no. 80 (December 1966), 341-345.

3674 _____. "The Weathercock," Landfall, no. 84 (December 1967), 319-325.

3675 Gijsen, Marnix. "Game and Wildfowl," Elisabeth Eybers, trans., Delta (Amsterdam), IX (Winter 1966-67), 31-39.

3676 Gilbert, Christopher. "Nose Bleed," Nexus (San Francisco, Calif.), III (March-April 1967), 23-26.

3677 Gilbert, Elliot L. "Eight One-Page Novels: Upstairs and Downstairs," Epoch, XVII (Winter 1968), 169-176.

3678 Gilbert, Sister Mary. "Purple," Virginia Quarterly Review, XLI (Winter 1965), 92-101.

3679 _____. "The View from the Oregon Side," Malahat Review, no. 2 (April 1967), 21-34.

3680 Gilbert, Sandra. "The Noisemaker," Mademoiselle, LXVIII (November 1968), 174-175, 205-209.

3681 Gildner, Gary. "The Crush," North American Review, V (March-April 1968), 32-38.

3682 _____. "Pearl," Cimarron Review, no. 7 (March 1969), 9-14.

3683 _____. "Shake the Dew," December, XI (1969), 116-119.

3684 Gilkey, Linda. "Victory Number Three," Seventeen, XXVI (January 1967), 91, 106.

3685 Gill, Brendan. "People of Property," New Yorker, XLII (June 11, 1966), 37-41.

3686 Gilles, Albert S., Sr. "Not Yet," Kansas Quarterly, I (Winter 1968), 95-102.

3687 _____. "Prologue to a Novel," Yale Literary Magazine, CXXXV (September 1966), 15-17.

3688 Gillespie, Alfred. "The Evil Eye," Saturday Evening Post, CCXXXIX (January 15, 1966), 48-57.

3689 _____. "The Sheep Killer," Saturday Evening Post, CCXL (December 16, 1967), 56-60, 62-64, 66-69.

3690 _____. "Tonight at Nine Thirty-six," Redbook, CXXXII (March 1969), 78-79, 153, 155, 157-164.

3691 _____. "The Witness," Saturday Evening Post, CCXL (August 12, 1967), 42-44, 46-48, 50-51.

3692 Gillespie, Charles. "Jack Learns His Lesson," Western Humanities Review, XXII (Summer 1968), 201-205.

3693 _____. "Life," Ball State University Forum, VIII (Autumn 1967), 3-5.

3694 _____. "Roxanna Street Revenge," DeKalb Literary Arts Journal, II (Winter 1968), 1-7.

3695 Gillespie, Gerald. "The Appointed Season," North American Mentor, V (Spring 1967), 13, 15, 17-18, 21-22, 24.

3696 _____. "Wrath of Lionell," Northwest Review, IX (Summer 1967), 70-82.

3697 Gillette, Gene L. "In the Beginning," Plaintiff, V (Spring-Summer 1969), 12-13.

3698 _____. "The Observer," Cimarron Review, no. 5 (September 1968), 4-13.

3699 Gilliatt, Penelope. "Albert," New Yorker, XLIV (October 1968), 46-54.

3700 _____. "Come Back If It Doesn't Get Better," Cornhill Magazine, CLXXVII (Autumn-Winter 1968-69), 149-161.

3701 _____. "Come Back If It Doesn't Get Better," New Yorker, XLIII (October 21, 1967), 57-62.

3702 _____. "Fred and Arthur," New Yorker, XLIV (June 15, 1968), 30-38, 40, 43-44, 46, 49, 52, 54, 56, 61-62.

3703 _____. "Known for Her Frankness," London Magazine, VIII (July 1968), 8-21.

3704 _____. "Known for Her Frankness," New Yorker, XLIII (February 3, 1968), 26-31.

3705 _____. "The Last To Go," New Yorker, XLV (April 19, 1969), 38-46.

3706 _____. "Living on the Box," New Yorker, XLII (December 17, 1966), 48-52.

3707 _____. "The Nuisance," London Magazine, VI (October 1966), 45-48.

3708 _____. "The Redhead," Transatlantic Review, no. 18 (Spring 1965), 5-13.

3709 _____. "The Tactics of Hunger," New Yorker, XLIV (April 6, 1968), 40-44.

3710 _____. "Was I Asleep?" New Yorker, XLIV (April 20, 1968), 46-55.

3711 _____. "What's It Like Out?" New Yorker, XLIV (October 26, 1968), 52-61.

3712 Ginger, John. "Caroline on the Rivers," London Magazine, V (January 1966), 13-25.

3713 _____. "The Classical-Romantic-Expressionism of Cesare Beppo," London Magazine, VIII (August 1968), 24-42.

3714 Gingrass, H. L. "A Dog for Martha," Washington Square Review, I (Winter 1965), 27-34.

3715 _____. "Georgia," Washington Square Review, I (Spring 1965), 59-78.

3716 Gins, Madeline. "Word Rain/or A Discursive Introduction to the Intimate Philosophical Investigations of G, R, E, T, A, G, A, R, B, O, It Says," Extensions, no. 3 (1969), 74-94.

3717 Ginsberg, Morton. "That's It," Man About Town, I (Winter 1967), 63.

3718 Ginsberg, Robert. "Leaves from a Western Journal," Montparnasse Review, no. 1 (1965), 39-43.

3719 Ginzburg, Natalia. "My Job," Walter Clemons, trans., Transatlantic Review, no. 20 (Spring 1966), 126-136.

3720 Giovanni, Nikki. "A Revolutionary Tale," Negro Digest, XVII (June 1968), 70-83.

3721 Girae, David. "The Ladies of Loughmoron," Cavalier, XV (October 1965), 28-29, 52, 54, 56-58.

3722 Gisser, Marv. "StdOilNJ Up One Employee Down One," Dare, IV (November 1966), 33.

3723 Giteck, Ronald. "Charlie I," Analecta, no. 1 (Fall 1967), 71-83.

3724 _____. "The Fat Boy Is Dead (II)," For Now, no. 6 (c. 1966-68), 46-48.

3725 Gizycka, Felicia. "I Am the Celebrant," Prairie Schooner, XLII (Winter 1968/69), 283-293.

3726 Glaeser, Ernst. "The Cherry Festival," Margaret D. Howie, trans., Scala International, (October 1968), 34-37.

3727 Glanville, Brian. "Greenberg," London Magazine, VII (April 1967), 16-22.

3728 Glascock, Ellen L. "Three Far-Fetched Fata Tales (For Far-Out Children--And Otherwise)/Alexander's Bigtime Egg," Human Voice, IV, no. 5 (1968), 27-28.

3729 ______. "Three Far-Fetched Fata Tales (For Far-Out Children--And Otherwise)/An Animal Story," Human Voice, IV, no. 5 (1968), 22-24.

3730 ______. "Three Far-Fetched Fata Tales (For Far-Out Children--And Otherwise)/An Uncommon Afternoon," Human Voice, IV, no. 5 (1968), 25-26.

3731 Glaser, Robert S. "Kopek," December, IX (1967), 102-108.

3732 Glaskin, G. M. "The Asking Price," Westerly, no. 1 (March 1968), 5-11.

3733 ______. "Coconuts Are Better Green," Eastern Horizon, IV (February 1965), 60-67.

3734 ______. "Small World," Westerly, no. 4 (December 1968), 24-30.

3735 ______. "Tail End of Winter," Westerly, no. 4 (1967), 14-18.

3736 Glasser, P. William. "Barney and the Ants," Riverrun, no. 2 (1968), 42-45.

3737 Glaze, Eleanor. "The Longest Time," Redbook, CXXVII (June 1966), 64-65, 102-106.

3738 ______. "One of Those Days," Redbook, CXXV (September 1965), 78-79, 130-131, 133, 136.

3739 ______. "Shadows," Redbook, CXXXIII (July 1969), 86-87, 142, 144-147, 149.

3740 ______. "Success Story," McCall's, XCIV (May 1967), 98-99, 151-154.

3741 ______. "The Telephone," Redbook, CXXX (November 1967), 88-89, 151, 154-156.

3742 ______. "You're at My Island," Delta Review, IV (December 1967), 38-39, 53-54, 59.

3743 Gleason, Gail. "The Courtship of Mary Alice Applewhite," Mademoiselle, LXVII (May 1968), 178-179, 237, 239-240.

3744 Glenday, Alice. "Beginning," New Zealand Listener, (August 11, 1967), 6, 25.

3745 _____. "Exit, Pursued by Pancakes," Redbook, CXXX (November 1967), 82-83, 118, 120, 123.

3746 _____. "The Homecoming," New Zealand Listener, (June 9, 1967), 6, 18.

3747 _____. "Hot Summer Night," New Zealand Listener, LII (January 8, 1965), 5.

3748 _____. "The Party," New Zealand Listener, (October 21, 1966), 6, 23.

3749 _____. "A Perfect Day in Spring," Good Housekeeping, CLXVIII (April 1969), 94-95, 192, 194-199.

3750 _____. "So Dark a Night," Ladies' Home Journal, LXXXIV (June 1967), 72-73, 129-130.

3751 _____. "Unhappy Returns," Redbook, CXXVI (March 1966), 68-69.

3752 Glendinning, Peter. "Flight of the Golden Swans," Penthouse, I (November 1969), 38-40, 42.

3753 Glenn, Michael L. "The Room," Hudson Review, XVIII (Winter 1965-66), 506-522.

3754 _____. "The Schedule," Antioch Review, XXVI (Winter 1966-67), 459-467.

3755 Glennon, Maurade. "My True Love's Face," Texas Quarterly, IX (Spring 1966), 171-182.

3756 Glenny, Mollie G. "Shall We Play My Records?" Delta (Cambridge, England), no. 46 (Winter 1969), 4-10.

3757 _____. "The Two Cheerful Men," Delta (Cambridge, England), no. 43 (June 1968), 4-10.

3758 Glimm, Adele. "Richard's Wife," Redbook, CXXX (February 1968), 153-174.

3759 Glynn, Thomas. "Except for the Sickness I'm Quite Healthy Now. You Can Believe That," Paris Review, XI (Winter-Spring 1968), 72-88.

3760 Goda, Gábor. "Solitary Voyage," New Hungarian Quarterly, VII (Summer 1966), 96-103.

3761 Godden, Rumer. "The Kitchen Madonna," Ladies' Home Journal, LXXXIII (April 1966), 39-46.

3762 Godfrey, Dave. "The First Encountering of Mr. Basa-Basa and His Excellency, Ling Huo," Tamarack Review, no. 41 (Autumn 1966), 113-118.

3763 _____. "The Hard-Headed Collector," Tamarack Review, no. 40 (Summer 1966), 3-14.

3764 _____. "Images. From A Moving Railway Car," Genesis West, III (Winter 1965), 51-66.

3765 Godwin, Gail. "Liza's Leaf Tower," North American Review, VI (Fall 1969), 41-44.

3766 _____. "St. George," Cosmopolitan, CLXVII (September 1969), 152-158.

3767 Goff, Richard J. "The Subway," Lance, V (Spring 1965), 3-4.

3768 Goins, Melinda. "The Exhibitor's Dance," Greensboro Review, III (Summer-Fall 1968), 5-21.

3769 _____. "The Polo Match," Red Clay Reader, no. 4 (1967), 118-123.

3770 Gold, Herbert. "The Ancient Company," Playboy, XIII (November 1966), 98-100, 102, 210, 212-214, 216.

3771 _____. "City of Light '65," Playboy, XII (October 1965), 84-86, 92, 215-218.

3772 _____. "The Crippler," Midstream, XII (June/July 1966), 36-40.

3773 _____. "Down the Ladder Awhile," Evergreen Review, X (February 1966), 28-32.

3774 _____. "The Elsewhere People," Harper's Bazaar, CIII (December 1969), 182-183.

3775 _____. "The Game of Hide and Seek," Playboy, XIII (July 1965), 97, 118-119, 121.

3776 _____. "Girl Getting Educated at Noon on Sunday," Playboy, XV (June 1968), 80-82, 84, 90.

3777 _____. "Green Love Later," Cosmopolitan, CLXV (July 1968), 112-117.

3778 _____. "A Haitian Gentleman," Hudson Review, XVIII (Spring 1965), 54-66.

3779 _____. "How to Find Out if You Are Rich or Poor without Actually Having Any Money," Harper's Bazaar, CII (August

1969), 197, 199.

3780 _____. "The Lid," Evergreen Review, XIII (March 1969), 38-40, 66-69.

3781 _____. "The Little Treasury of WASP Folklore," Transatlantic Review, no. 32 (Summer 1969), 63-71.

3782 _____. "Love Potion Number Last," Ladies' Home Journal, LXXXV (November 1968), 72.

3783 _____. "Marriage, Food, Money, Children, Ice Skating," Playboy, XIII (April 1966), 127, 162, 164-169.

3784 _____. "My Father and His Gangsters," Playboy, XIII (June 1966), 95, 106, 186-188.

3785 _____. "My Father, His Father and Ben," Playboy, XIII (August 1966), 97, 100, 140, 142-143.

3786 _____. "Nicholas in Exile," American Judaism, XV (Fall 1965), 18-19, 58-61.

3787 _____. "Peacock Dreams," Playboy, XIV (June 1967), 137, 170-171.

3788 _____. "A Selfish Story," Harper's Magazine, CCXXXIV (May 1967), 88-92, 96-97.

3789 _____. "An Unevenness of Blessings," Playboy, XII (September 1965), 112-113, 138, 212-216.

3790 Gold, John D., Jr. "Within a Wall," Crucible, I (Spring 1965), 34-36.

3791 Goldberg, Gerald Jay. "The Courting of Mendelbaum," Lugano Review, I (Summer 1966), 60-66.

3792 _____. "The Education of Martin Fogle," Art and Literature, no. 12 (Spring 1967), 184-197.

3793 _____. "The Loving Tongue," Harper's Bazaar, XCIX (February 1966), 174-175, 186-188, 204.

3794 _____. "A Sign of Favor," Shenandoah, XVI (Winter 1965), 13-21.

3795 Goldberg, Peter. "The Bench," Limbo, I (February 1965), 26-28.

3796 Goldhurst, Richard. "From Doweries," Red Clay Reader, no. 2 (1965), 75-78.

3797 Golding, William. "Inside a Pyramid," Esquire, LXVI (December 1966), 165-169, 286-288, 290-294, 296-300, 302.

3798 _____. "On the Escarpment," Kenyon Review, XXIX (June 1967), 311-400.

3799 Goldknopf, David. "Hannah," Prairie Schooner, XLI (Winter 1967), 423-436.

3800 _____. "The Playwright at Home," North American Review, IV (March 1967), 38-39.

3801 _____. "The President of the Family," University Review, XXXIV (Winter 1967), 114-120.

3802 _____. "Rabbits," Discourse, XI (Autumn 1968), 460-463.

3803 Goldman, Annette. "A Rabbi in Winter," Silo, no. 11 (Spring 1967), 62-95.

3804 Goldman, Hannah Stern. "Something to Warm the Soul," Denver Quarterly, I (Winter 1967), 63-68.

3805 Goldman, Hazel. "Just One Room," Canadian Forum, XLVIII (November 1968), 190.

3806 Goldman, Miriam. "Doctor Sifer," Massachusetts Review, X (Winter 1969), 39-45.

3807 _____. "Fireflies," Massachusetts Review, VI (Spring-Summer 1965), 485-490.

3808 Goldreich, Gloria. "First Year," McCall's, XCIII (July 1966), 58-59, 117-118.

3809 _____. "A Gradual Joy," McCall's, XCIII (October 1965), 102-103, 203-205.

3810 _____. "The Heart Attack of Morris Fishkin," Midstream, XIII (November 1967), 32-40.

3811 Goldrosen, Donald J. "Who Needs It?" Lance, V (Winter 1965), 6-8.

3812 Goldschmidt, Jean. "The Testament of Uncle George," Story, I (May 1967), 4-7, 89-93.

3813 Goldstein, Michael. "By Balloon," Transatlantic Review, no. 24 (Spring 1967), 54-57.

3814 _____. "The Self-Contained Compartment," Transatlantic Review, no. 21 (Summer 1966), 103-104.

3815 _____. "Two Short Pieces," Transatlantic Review, no. 26 (Autumn 1967), 106-107.

3816 [No entry.]

3817 Goldstein, Sanford. "The Charcoal Crane," Arizona Quarterly, XXV (Summer 1969), 134-149.

3818 _____. "The White and the Black," Literature East and West, XII (December 1968), 199-215.

3819 Gollata, James A. "Donna with Child," Wisconsin Review, III (Fall 1967), 28.

3820 Gollschewsky, E. A. "The Cat on the Hearth," Quadrant, X (September-October 1966), 63-72.

3821 _____. "Innocent Party," Southerly, XXV, no. 3 (1965), 183-191.

3822 _____. "Jibber," Overland, no. 35 (Summer 1966-67), 17-20.

3823 _____. "Ultimate Summer," Meanjin Quarterly, XXVI (Summer 1967), 435-442.

3824 _____. "Where's Grandpa?" Quadrant, IX (November-December 1965), 52-58.

3825 _____. "The White Goshawk," Southerly, XXVII, no. 3 (1967), 199-217.

3826 Gombrowicz, Witold. "The Banquet," Felica Krance and Alice De Barcza, trans., Evergreen Review, X (December 1966), 41-43, 62-64.

3827 _____. "Ferdydurke: an excerpt," Eric Mosbacher, trans., Tri-Quarterly, no. 9 (Spring 1967), 43-50.

3828 _____. "On the Backstairs," Richard Seaver, trans., Evergreen Review, IX (March 1965), 26-31, 83-85.

3829 _____. "from Pornografia," Alastair Hamilton, trans., Art and Literature, no. 10 (Autumn 1966), 9-21.

3830 Gonchar, Oles. "A Man in the Steppe," Anthony Wixley, trans., Soviet Literature, (no. 4, 1968), 75-84.

3831 _____. "The Sandy Spit," Anthony Wixley, trans., Soviet Literature, (no. 9, 1968), 85-95.

3832 González, Fernando. "The Schoolteacher," Barbara de la

Cuesta, trans., Quarterly Review of Literature, XVI, nos. 3-4 (1969), 330-359.

3833 Gonzalez, N. V. M. "Another Shore, a Rising Wind," Literature East and West, IX (March 1965), 79-82.

3834 _____. "Porta Pinciana," Solidarity, I (April-June 1966), 82-87.

3835 González Ledo, Liliana. "The Crystal Ball," Américas, XXI (June 1969), 37-38.

3836 Goodfriend, Mark Serge. "Mommy, Mommy," DeKalb Literary Arts Journal, II (Summer 1968), 1-5.

3837 Goodman, J. Carol. "A Disturbance," North American Review, II (May 1965), 35-42.

3838 _____. "The Pot of Gold," North American Review, II (May 1965), 49-52.

3839 Goodman, Joseph. "Blood," Transatlantic Review, no. 26 (Autumn 1967), 132-141.

3840 Goodman, Kathy. "The Train," New Leaven, no. 16 (1966), 38-42.

3841 Goodstein, Jack. "An Orange Jacket," Works, I (Summer 1968), 34-38.

3842 Goodwin, Inge. "Champ du Moulin," Quarterly Review of Literature, XV (1968), 316-322.

3843 Goodwin, Stephen. "Veteran's Evening Song," Shenandoah, XX (Summer 1969), 28-41.

3844 Gooler, Dennis. "Rally for Unity," UMD Humanist, XIII (Spring 1965), 3-6.

3845 Göransson, Lars. "Nureddin's Nose," Marion Marzolf, trans., Literary Review, IX (Winter 1965-66), 202-208.

3846 Gorbellone-Kindlieber, Diego. "'How's Come' Story No. 7," Salzberg Village Idiot, (Autumn 1967), 16-17.

3847 Gordimer, Nadine. "Abroad," Southern Review, IV (July 1968), 725-744.

3848 _____. "The Bride of Christ," Atlantic Monthly, CCXX (August 1967), 58-64.

3849 _____. "The Bride of Christ," Nova, (July 1967), 88-91, 93.

3850 ______. "Inkalamu's Place," Contrast (Cape Town, South Africa), no. 18 (July 1968), 13-23.

3851 ______. "Inkalamu's Place," Harper's Bazaar, XCIX (June 1966), 76-77, 134-135, 138.

3852 ______. "The Late Bourgeois World," Encounter, XXVI (June 1966), 19-26.

3853 ______. "The Life of the Imagination," New Yorker, XLIV (November 9, 1968), 61-67.

3854 ______. "Livingstone's Companions," Kenyon Review, XXXI (1969), 181-214.

3855 ______. "Not for Publication," Contrast (Cape Town, South Africa), no. 12 (July 1965), 14-29.

3856 ______. "A Meeting in Space," Cornhill Magazine, CLXXVI (Summer 1967), 122-135.

3857 ______. "Open House," Encounter, XXXII (February 1969), 8-14.

3858 ______. "Otherwise Birds Fly In," Cornhill Magazine, CLXXVII (Summer 1969), 296-308.

3859 ______. "Out of the Walls," New Yorker, XLII (February 11, 1967), 34-37.

3860 ______. "Praise," Atlantic Monthly, CCXV (April 1965), 99-105.

3861 ______. "The Proof of Love," Ladies' Home Journal, LXXXII (February 1965), 80-81, 90, 93-94, 96.

3862 ______. "Rain Queen," Cosmopolitan, CLXVI (March 1969), 142-147.

3863 ______. "A Satisfactory Settlement," Atlantic Monthly, CCXXI (January 1968), 54-58.

3864 ______. "Say Something African," New Yorker, XLII (August 20, 1966), 34-40.

3865 ______. "Some Monday for Sure," Transition, IV, no. 18 (1965), 9-15.

3866 ______. "A Third Presence," Cosmopolitan, CLIX (July 1965), 95-96, 98-99.

3867 ______. "A Third Presence," London Magazine, VI (September 1966), 75-84.

3868 ______. "Vital Statistics," Kenyon Review, XXVII (Winter 1965), 27-48.

3869 ______. "The Worst Thing of All," London Magazine, IV (February 1965), 3-21.

3870 Gordon, C. "The Upholsterer," Dare, IV (January-February 1966), 20-21.

3871 Gordon, Caroline. "Cloud Nine," Sewanee Review, LXXVII (October-December 1969), 591-629.

3872 ______. "Cock-Crow," Southern Review, I (July 1965), 554-569.

3873 ______. "A Walk with the Accuser (Who Is God of This World)/(an extract from a novel in progress)," Transatlantic Review, no. 31 (Winter 1968-69), 96-113.

3874 Gordon, Daniel. "Hiding from Walter," New Yorker, XLII (May 21, 1966), 159-162, 164-165.

3875 Gordon, Ethel Edison. "The Boy Who Wanted to Be Somebody," Redbook, CXXVI (February 1966), 54-55, 118-120, 122.

3876 ______. "A House by the Water," Redbook, CXXXIII (October 1969), 179-201.

3877 ______. "Legacy," McCall's, XCIII (April 1966), 106-107, 159-163.

3878 ______. "Make Me No Match," McCall's, XCIV (May 1967), 80-81, 133-137.

3879 ______. "My Enemy," Redbook, CXXVI (January 1966), 50-51, 88-91.

3880 ______. "New Neighbors," Redbook, CXXVI (November 1965), 173, 175-201.

3881 ______. "So Far from Home," Redbook, CXXXI (August 1968), 155, 157-179.

3882 ______. "The Summer Husband," Redbook, CXXIV (January 1965), 111-138.

3883 ______. "Where Did the Summer Go?" Redbook, CXXIX (July 1967), 129, 131-137.

3884 ______. "Wife in Orbit," Woman's Day, (April 1966), 38-39, 88-90, 99-102.

3885 Gordon, Giles. "The Enemy," Stand, IX, no. 2 (1967), 38-42.

3886 _____. "The Man/the House/the Egg," Stand, X, no. 3 (1969), 58-61.

3887 _____. "from The Mission," Ambit, no. 25 (1965), 37-48.

3888 _____. "The Scorpion," Scottish International, no. 2 (April 1968), 55-57.

3889 _____. "Two Women, Two Eyes," Transatlantic Review, no. 20 (Spring 1966), 36-40.

3890 Gordon, Ilya. "A Misunderstanding," Tom Botting, trans., Soviet Literature, (no. 4, 1966), 126-129.

3891 Gordon, Lorraine. "Not Ungentle," New Leaven, XIX (1969), 49-53.

3892 Gordon, Margaret. "Washday in Waihi," New Zealand Listener, LII (December 3, 1965), 4.

3893 Gordon, Mildred and Gordon. "The Night Before the Wedding," Imprint, IX (August 1969), 49-73, 75, 77, 79, 81, 83, 85, 87, 89, 91, 93, 95, 97, 99, 101, 103, 105, 107, 109, 111, 113, 115, 117, 119-120.

3894 _____. "The Night Before the Wedding/(Part I), Good Housekeeping, CLXVIII (March 1969), 85-87, 206, 208, 210, 212, 221-222, 230, 232, 234-236, 238, 241-247, 249-250, 252, 260.

3895 _____. "The Night Before the Wedding/(Conclusion)," Good Housekeeping, CLXVIII (April 1969), 98-99, 214, 216, 218, 220, 222, 224, 226, 228, 242-251, 253, 256, 258, 268.

3896 Gordon, Noah. "The Rabbi," Ladies' Home Journal, LXXXII (July 1965), 56-59, 105-106, 108-111.

3897 Gordon, Robert. "About Chicken Little," Western Humanities Review, XX (Summer 1966), 191-202.

3898 _____. "The Brave Feat of Ida Finney," Discourse, VIII (Autumn 1965), 339-347.

3899 _____. "The Case of Miss Harford's New Title," Western Humanities Review, XXIII (Winter 1969), 43-47.

3900 _____. "The Last of the Frontier," Prism International, VI (Autumn 1966), 34-48.

3901 _____. "A Lovely Ring," Transatlantic Review, no. 22

(Autumn 1966), 122-129.

3902 ______. "Satisfaction," Literary Review, X (Autumn 1966), 47-54.

3903 ______. "Something Like a Temple," Ball State University Forum, VIII (Autumn 1967), 32-41.

3904 Gorham, B. F. and Brooks Baldwin. "Just Before Dawn," Good Housekeeping, CLXI (August 1965), 66-67, 179-183.

3905 Gorky, Maxim. "The Life of Klim Samgin/(Excerpt from the Novel)," Vladimir Talmy, trans., Soviet Literature, (no. 3, 1968), 25-45.

3906 ______. "Makar Chudra," Margaret Wettlin, trans., Soviet Literature, (no. 3, 1968), 4-15.

3907 ______. "A Man Is Born," Joseph Fineberg, trans., Soviet Literature, (no. 3, 1968), 15-24.

3908 ______. "The Saltmine," Selig O. Wassner, trans., Forum, IV (Winter-Spring 1965), 27-31.

3909 ______. "Song of the Stormy Petrel," Margaret Wettlin, trans., Soviet Literature, (no. 3, 1968), 3-4.

3910 ______. "Stories about Heroes," Soviet Literature, (no. 4, 1967), 5-15.

3911 Gorman, Brian. "Afternoon Among Flowers," Overland, no. 33 (Summer 1965-66), 5-8.

3912 Gorman, Michael. "A Salute for Paddy," Ambience, no. 1 (October 1968), 24-27.

3913 Gormley, Rita. "Fire from a Fanbelt," Columbia, XLVIII (July 1968), 24-29.

3914 Goulart, Ron. "A Man's Home Is His Castle," Playboy, XVI (March 1969), 119, 217-220.

3915 ______. "The Trouble with Machines," Playboy, XV (August 1968), 105, 124-126, 128-129.

3916 Gould, F. J. "A Boat Almost Finished," Nexus (San Francisco, Calif.), II (September-October 1965), 11-13.

3917 ______. "An Explanation," Carolina Quarterly, XIX (Fall 1967), 45-47.

3918 ______. "Panto's Place," Nexus (San Francisco, Calif.), II (September-October 1965), 10-11.

3919 Goulet, John. "Captain Robin," Intro, no. 1 (September 1968), 134-154.

3920 Govan, Christine Noble. "High Heel Henry," Man About Town, I (Winter 1967), 49-50.

3921 Gowans, Helen. "An Awfully Mature Person," Canadian Forum, XLVI (August 1966), 100-102.

3922 Grace, Nancy. "The Thief," Carleton Miscellany, VII (Spring 1966), 106-113.

3923 Gracer, Gene B. "Shadows of Dawn," Dust, II (Winter 1966), 29-34.

3924 Graham, Andrew Jay. "The Inheritance," Minnesota Review, VI (1966), 16-24.

3925 Graham, Bernard. "The Booby," Bim, XII (January-June 1969), 255-258.

3926 _____. "Cry For the Innocent," Bim, XII (July-December 1968), 204-207.

3927 _____. "'In Never-Ending Line'," Bim, XI (July-December 1966), 214-216.

3928 _____. " Soliloquy," Bim, XI (January-June 1966), 134-138.

3929 _____. "When You Were Very Young," Bim, XII (January-June 1968), 98-100.

3930 Graham, David. "Contrecoup," Transatlantic Review, no. 28 (Spring 1968), 81-90.

3931 Graham, Elizabeth W. "For the Love of Stephanie," Seventeen, XXV (July 1966), 108-109, 120, 122, 128.

3932 Graham, George. "Go Tell, Aunt Rodi," William and Mary Review, VI (Winter 1968), 29-31.

3933 Graham, Henry. "The Piano," Transatlantic Review," no. 29 (Summer 1968), 132-137.

3934 Graham, S. J. "The Monkey King's Wish," Eastern Horizon, IV (August 1965), 56-57.

3935 Gramm, Gene. "The Typewriter Repairman," Mademoiselle, LXIV (March 1967), 20, 40, 53, 56.

3936 Grana, Edgar. "The Glass Eye," Washington and Jefferson Literary Journal, I, no. 2 (1967), 27-34.

3937 Granat, Robert. "The Old Lineman," New Mexico Quarterly, XXXVI (Autumn 1966), 222-227.

3938 Granin, Daniil. "The First Visitor/A Film Story," Vladimir Talmy, trans., Soviet Literature, (no. 4, 1966), 38-91.

3939 ______. "The House on the Fontanka," Vladimir Talmy, trans., Soviet Literature, (no. 6, 1968), 55-66.

3940 Granite, Harvey. "Mr. Weinberg and the Deluge," Antioch Review, XXV (Fall 1965), 411-428.

3941 Grant, L. T. "Dead End," Soundings, IV (Spring 1967), 107-122.

3942 ______. "The Insured," Soundings, IV (Spring 1967), 1-22.

3943 Grant, Marcus. "Endor Burton Waits His Chance," Cambridge Review, LXXXIX (February 16, 1968), 286-288.

3944 ______. "The (St. Michael & All Angels) Massacre," Cambridge Review, LXXXIX (May 17, 1968), 476-478.

3945 Gration, Gwen. "Teacher," Four Quarters, XVI (March 1967), 1-9.

3946 Gratus, Jack. "The Day King Lost His Fear," Queen, CDXXVII (September 1, 1966), 32-37.

3947 ______. "Did You Hear About Mrs. Kagan?" Queen, CDXXVI (April 27, 1966), 92-96.

3948 Grau, Shirley Ann. "The Beach Party," Redbook, CXXV (September 1965), 54-55, 147-148, 155, 160.

3949 ______. "The Burglar," Saturday Evening Post, CCXLI (October 19, 1968), 68-71, 74.

3950 ______. "The Condor Passes," Atlantic Monthly, CCXIX (January 1967), 62-67, 71-73.

3951 ______. "Sea Change," Atlantic Monthly, CCXX (November 1967), 105-109.

3952 ______. "The Way Back," Southern Review, III (April 1967), 407-415.

3953 ______. "Wind Shifting West," Cosmopolitan, CLXI (August 1966), 90-94, 128-129.

3954 ______. "The Young Men," Redbook, CXXX (April 1968), 64-65, 134, 136-138.

3955 Graubart, Rose. "Cereal," Chelsea, no. 26 (May 1969), 77-81.

3956 Gravage, Dorothy. "Three Paragraph Story," Trace, no. 59 (Winter 1966), 393.

3957 Graves, Jack. "The Aisles of Grease," Sage, XI (Spring 1966), 5-15.

3958 _____. "Oh, Come, All You Faithfull," Prism International, VII (Summer 1967), 14-26.

3959 Graves, John. "The Dreamer," Readers & Writers, I (May-June 1966), 25-32.

3960 Graves, Marlene L. "Memoirs of a Fallen Woman," Jeopardy, no. 3 (Spring 1967), 49-53.

3961 Graves, Robert. "No, Mac, It Just Wouldn't Work," Playboy, XIV (January 1967), 117, 195.

3962 Graves, T. W., Jr. "Charlie's Place," William and Mary Review, III (Winter 1965), 9-16.

3963 _____. "A Time of the Good Working," William and Mary Review, III (Spring 1965), 23-28.

3964 Gray, Alasdair. "The Comedy of the White Dog," Scottish International, no. 8 (October 1969), 18-21.

3965 Gray, Betty Lee. "The Square," Crucible, II (Spring 1966), 55.

3966 Gray, Patrick W. "Too Soon Solos," Georgia Review, XX (Summer 1966), 198-206.

3967 Gray, Simon. "The Autobiography of James Haydon-Sprigg/ Episode from a novel in progress," Delta (Cambridge, England), no. 41 (September 1967), 37-42.

3968 _____. "The Autobiography of James Haydon-Sprigg/Further Extracts," Delta (Cambridge, England), no. 42 (February 1968), 20-23.

3969 Gray, Stephen. "The Colossus of Rhodes," North American Review, VI (Spring 1969), 21-28.

3970 _____. "The Largest Dam in the World," Contrast (Cape Town, South Africa), no. 20 (March 1969), 20-25, 27-38.

3971 _____. "White Spaces," Solstice, no. 1 (1966), 9-16.

3972 Greeley, John. "Michael," Jeopardy, no. 4 (Spring 1968), 10-16.

3973 _____. "The Pride of Italy," Jeopardy, no. 3 (Spring 1967), 18-22.

3974 Green, Charmian. "The Burial," The Phoenix, (Fall 1968), 42-48.

3975 Green, Douglas J. "Beware of False Prophets," Lance, V (Spring 1965), 5-7.

3976 _____. "It's a Good Life," Lance, V (Spring 1965), 31.

3977 _____. "Laissez-moi Tranquille," Lance, V (Winter 1965), 23.

3978 Green, Ely. "Aristocratic Mouse," Sewanee Review, LXXVI (January-March 1968), 1-22.

3979 Green, Gerald. "The Dispatcher," Playboy, XIV (August 1967), 60-62, 64, 76, 170-172.

3980 Green, Hannah. "The Dead of the House," New Yorker, XLV (October 11, 1969), 54-60, 62, 64, 68, 70, 73-74, 76, 79-80, 82.

3981 _____. "The Sphinx and the Pyramid," New Yorker, XLII (April 2, 1966), 130, 132, 134, 136-137.

3982 Green, James. "Devices," 25, I (October 1968), 18-21, 52-55.

3983 Green, James, Jr. "Three Naked Ladies Standing on a Bridge," William and Mary Review, IV (Winter 1966), 59-69.

3984 Green, Martin. "Criseyde," Radix, I (Spring 1965), 38-54.

3985 Green, R. "The Morning the Phone Rang," Dare, IV (March 1966), 38-39.

3986 Green, Tom. "The Judgment," Arx, I (June 1967), 2-3.

3987 Greenbaum, Everett. "A Fine Piece of Machinery," Saturday Evening Post, CCXL (March 25, 1967), 62-64.

3988 _____. "There Were Pigeons in the Square," Harper's Magazine, CCXXX (April 1965), 94-97.

3989 Greenberg, Barbara. "Golden Worms," Yale Review, LVIII (Spring 1969), 408-413.

3990 Greenberg, Joanne. "A Cry of Silence," Good Housekeeping, CLXIV (March 1967), 88-89, 170, 172, 186-188.

3991 ______. "How Beautiful with Feet," American Judaism, XV (Summer 1966), 9, 27.

3992 ______. "Hunting Season," McCall's, XCIII (June 1966), 74-75.

3993 ______. "No Happier Time," Redbook, CXXXI (August 1968), 76-77, 137-138, 140, 142-144, 146-147.

3994 ______. "L'Olom and White Shell Woman," Denver Quarterly, I (Spring 1966), 117-129.

3995 ______. "Timekeeper," McCall's, XCVI (January 1969), 70-71, 99-100.

3996 Greenberg, Judith Ann. "Color of a Gray Winter's Day," Minnesota Review, IX (1969), 30-34.

3997 Greenburg, Dan. "'Was It Good For You, Too?'," Avant Garde, no. 3 (May 1968), 22-25.

3998 Greene. "And What Did You Find There?" Stanford Chaparral, LXIX (Election 1968), 34-38.

3999 Greene, Alexander. "The Water-Colour," Soviet Literature, (no. 4, 1967), 26-30.

4000 Greene, Charles R. "Paul and Helene," Confrontation, no. 2 (Spring 1969), 54-64.

4001 Greene, David. "A Formal Absolution," Sou'wester, (Summer 1968), 43-49.

4002 Greene, George. "One of the Street People," Forum, IV (Summer 1965), 41-46.

4003 Greene, Graham. "Awful When You Think of It," Cosmopolitan, CLXIII (August 1967), 116.

4004 ______. "Beauty," Nova, (April 1967), 163, 166.

4005 ______. "The Blessing," Harper's Magazine, CCXXXII (March 1966), 91-94.

4006 ______. "Chagrin in Three Parts," Cosmopolitan, CLXIII (August 1967), 114-115.

4007 ______. "Chagrin in Three Parts," Weekend Telegraph, no. 109 (October 28, 1966), 55, 57-58.

4008 ______. "Crook's Tour," Playboy, XVI (November 1969), 114-116, 192, 194, 196, 199-200, 202-203, 206-208.

4009 ______. "Crook's Tour/Part II," Playboy, XVI (December 1969), 144-146, 150, 339-340, 342, 344-347.

4010 ______. "Doctor Crombie," Status, I (December 1965), 36, 92, 94.

4011 ______. "The Invisible Japanese Gentlemen," Saturday Evening Post, CCXXXVIII (November 20, 1965), 60-61.

4012 ______. "The Overnight Bag," Status, I (October 1965), 36-38.

4013 ______. "The Secret," Vogue, CXLIX (January 1, 1967), 94-95, 144, 151.

4014 ______. "A Shocking Accident," Nova, (April 1967), 160-161.

4015 ______. "Two Gentle People," Weekend Telegraph, no. 127 (March 10, 1967), 41-42, 45.

4016 ______. "The Worm Inside the Lotus Blossom," Daily Telegraph Magazine, no. 221 (January 3, 1969), 6-7, 9, 11.

4017 Greene, Jonathan. "Trickster Tales/1. How Kittiwake Learned Justice before Food," Joglars, no. 3 (1966), n.p. [16].

4018 ______. "Trickster Tales/2. Breathing Exercise," Joglars, no. 3 (1966), n.p. [17].

4019 ______. "Trickster Tales/3. Ohandu & Spirit," Joglars, no. 3 (1966), n.p. [17].

4020 ______. "Trickster Tales/4. [untitled]," Joglars, no. 3 (1966), n.p. [18].

4021 Greene, Philip L. "Establish Your Credentials," Transatlantic Review, no. 26 (Autumn 1967), 91-103.

4022 Greene, Robert. "A Pleasant Tale of a Man that Was Maryed to Sixteen Wiues, and How Courteously His Last Wife Intreated Him," 0 to 9, no. 3 (January 1968), 15-21.

4023 Greenfield, Eloise. "Karen's Spring," Negro Digest, XV (January 1966), 59-62.

4024 ______. "Noblesse Oblige," Negro Digest, XV (July 1966), 82-86.

4025 ______. "Not Any More," Negro Digest, XVIII (August 1969), 62-66.

4026 Greenlee, Rush. "An Addict in the Street," Chelsea, no. 16 (March 1965), 84-88.

4027 Greenlee, Sam. "Autumn Leaves," Negro Digest, XVI (January 1967), 69-73.

4028 _____. "The D. C. Blues," Negro Digest, XVIII (June 1969), 86-92.

4029 _____. "The Sign," Negro Digest, XV (February 1966), 61-63.

4030 _____. "Summer Sunday," Negro Digest, XV (September 1966), 60-61.

4031 _____. "Yes, We Can Sing," Negro Digest, XV (December 1965), 65-69.

4032 Greenspan, Elaine. "Tea," Western Humanities Review, XXI (Spring 1967), 103-116.

4033 Gregor-Dellin, Martin. "Visit to an Exhibition," Brian L. Harris, trans., Dimension, II, no. 2 (1969), 248-255 [in German and English on alternate pages].

4034 Gregory, Serge V. "Viktor Oblinsky," William and Mary Review, VI (Winter 1968), 67-77.

4035 Greig, Desmond. "Landscape with Rhino," Contrast (Cape Town, South Africa), no. 12 (July 1965), 64-72.

4036 Gresham, David. "Anxious Days," Epoch, XVII (Spring 1968), 235-244.

4037 Gresser, Seymour. "Liborio," Trace, no. 70 (1969), 126-135.

4038 Grieve, Gordon. "Fugitive from Reality--Excerpts," Alphabet, no. 14 (December 1967), 49-65.

4039 Griffith, Patricia Browning. "Brief Legacy," Colorado Quarterly, XVI (Winter 1968), 287-292.

4040 _____. "The Man," Overflow, II, no. 1 (1968), 65-70.

4041 _____. "Nights at O'Rear's," Harper's Magazine, CCXXXVIII (March 1969), 81-84, 86, 88, 90.

4042 Griffith, Thomas. "The Election Fiesta in Ultra," Atlantic Monthly, CCXIX (February 1967), 80-86.

4043 Griffiths, Sally. "Ferrets for Friends," Transatlantic Review, no. 20 (Spring 1966), 99-105.

4044 Grimes, C. "The Shortest Day of the Week," Dare, IV (January-February 1966), 42.

4045 Grimes, Sally. "Obit," US, no. 1 (June 1969), 167-187.

4046 Grimm, Cherry. "A Trip Overseas," Quadrant, XI (March-April 1967), 47-49.

4047 Grinstead, David. "A Day in Operations," Literary Review, XII (Autumn 1968), 103-115.

4048 Grissom, Bob. "The Big Kill," Delta Review, VI (August 1969), 54-56.

4049 Gronowicz, Antoni. "The Grease of Power," DeKalb Literary Arts Journal, II (Fall 1967), 14-27.

4050 Gropman, Donald. "The Heart of This or That Man," Literary Review, XI (Autumn 1967), 27-38.

4051 Groppe, John. "A Shred of Decency," Western Humanities Review, XXII (Spring 1968), 143-159.

4052 Groshong, James W. "The Blackiston Legend," Malahat Review, no. 12 (October 1969), 5-15.

4053 _____. "This Newman," Antioch Review, XXIX (Winter 1969-70), 561-572.

4054 Gross, Sandra. "The Octangular House," Arx, I (April 1967), 20-23.

4055 _____. "Thessalonika," Arx, III (August 1969), 7-8.

4056 _____. "The Thief," Arx, II (March 1969), 15-17.

4057 Grosser, Morton. "The Fabulous Fifty," Saturday Evening Post, CCXXXIX (October 8, 1966), 78-82, 86, 88, 90, 92-95.

4058 Grossinger, Richard. "Astrological Sections," Literary Magazine of Tufts University, III (Winter 1968), 33-39.

4059 _____. "Baseball," Io Magazine, no. 6 (Summer 1969), 111-116.

4060 _____. "from Book of the Earth and Sky," Io Magazine, no. 6 (Summer 1969), 142-159.

4061 _____. "Dream Lover," Ann Arbor Review, no. 2 (Winter 1967), 25-29.

4062 _____. "The Game," Caterpillar, nos. 8 & 9 (October 1969), 72-75.

4063 _____. "from Oecological Sections," Io Magazine, no. 6

(Summer 1969), 159-165.

4064 ______. "Psychological Sections," Sou'wester, II (Fall 1968), 70-72.

4065 ______. "Scorpio," For Now, no. 8 (c. 1966-68), 27-34.

4066 ______. "Solar Journal/(excerpt) Alchemical Sections," Io Magazine, no. 4 (Summer 1967), 83-105.

4067 ______. "A Story," Io Magazine, no. 1 (1966), n.p. [26-28].

4068 ______. "Talismans," Io Magazine, no. 6 (Summer 1969), 197-210.

4069 Grossman, Alfred. "The Beauty Contest," Transatlantic Review, no. 23 (Winter 1966-67), 120-133.

4070 Grossman, Arnold. "Buttered Toast and Coffee," The Quest, I (Summer 1966), 20-31.

4071 Grossman, Carol Z. "Dream Cottage," Redbook, CXXXI (June 1968), 80-81, 121-124.

4072 ______. "The New Boy," Discourse, X (Autumn 1967), 429-435.

4073 ______. "Respect, Respect," Discourse, X (Spring 1967), 195-204.

4074 ______. "Where All Is Venture," Discourse, IX (Winter 1966), 58-66.

4075 Grossman, Sylvia. "A Throne In Heaven," Redbook, CXXVII (May 1966), 54-55, 132-135.

4076 Grossman, Vasili. "The Road," Soviet Literature, (no. 4, 1967), 137-143.

4077 Grostein, Sonia. "The Fly and I," The Gauntlet, I (Fall 1967), 11-15.

4078 Grove, Walt. "Oh Danny Boy," Playboy, XII (March 1965), 100-102, 153-155.

4079 Grubb, Davis. "A Tree Full of Stars," Ladies' Home Journal, LXXXII (December 1965), 62-63, 118-119, 121-124.

4080 Grusenberg, Mikhail M. "Une Vrai Femme du Monde," Curt Johnson, trans., Analecta, II (Spring 1968), 11-15.

4081 Guarino, Steve. "Svevo," Spero, I, no. 2 (1966), 9-15.

4082 Guerard, Albert J. "On the Operating Table," Denver Quarterly, I (Autumn 1966), 58-70.

4083 _____. "The Vanishing Anarchists: A Memory," Sewanee Review, LXXVII (July-September 1969), 440-462.

4084 Guerrero, Margarita and Jorge Luis Borges. "Imaginary Beings," Thomas di Giovanni, Jorge Luis Borges and Margarita Guerrero, trans., New Yorker, XLV (October 4, 1969), 39-46.

4085 Guittar, Lee J. "Candystripe Barn," Columbia, XLVI (November 1966), 26-29.

4086 _____. "His Doggonedest Moment," Columbia, XLV (November 1965), 24-26, 45-46.

4087 _____. "The St. Francis Heist," Columbia, XLVI (January 1966), 24-28.

4088 Gulia, Georgi. "The Kittens/(A Page from a Family Chronicle)," Eve Manning, trans., Soviet Literature, (no. 3, 1969), 129-133.

4089 Gulyam, Gafur. "Uzbek Folk Tales/The Cauldron and the Beetroot," Alice Ingman, trans., Soviet Literature, (no. 12, 1967), 111.

4090 _____. "Uzbek Folk Tales/Madaminbek Wanted to Be Merry," Alice Ingman, trans., Soviet Literature, (no. 12, 1967), 113-114.

4091 _____. "Uzbek Folk Tales/The Skinflint," Alice Ingman, trans., Soviet Literature, (no. 12, 1967), 111-113.

Gunnarson, Karl. See 10808.

4092 Gunnette, Don. "A Fatal Gift of Beauty," Prospero's Cell, I (April-June 1966), 9-12.

4093 Gunning, Allegram. "Tedoro," California Review, no. 2 (Spring 1968), 25-56.

4094 Guntekin, Reshat Nuri. "The Cold Hearth," Nancy C. Dorian, Helen E. Thomas and David N. Weinman, trans., Literature East and West, XI (June 1967), 162-168.

4095 Gunther, John. "Dinner for Three," Esquire, LXVI (December 1966), 238-239, 340-342.

4096 Gupta, Basudeb Das. "from The Disturbed," Dick Bakken, trans., Salted Feathers, no. 8 & 9 (March 1967), n.p. [104-107].

4097 Guralnick, Peter. "Down Child," Transatlantic Review, no. 27 (Winter 1967-68), 33-55.

4098 Gusein, Mekhti. "A Legend of Kerem," Alice Ingman, trans., Soviet Literature, (no. 12, 1969), 10-14.

4099 Guseinov, Chinghiz. "From Autumn Musings," Alice Ingman, trans., Soviet Literature, (no. 12, 1969), 103-106.

4100 Gusewelle, G. W. "The Lion Makers," Virginia Quarterly Review, XLIII (Autumn 1967), 614-628.

4101 _____. "Robert Melendez: Retrospect," Texas Quarterly, XI (Summer 1968), 155-167.

4102 Gustafson, Ralph. "The Tangles of Neaera's Hair," Prism International, IV (Winter 1965), 24-29.

4103 Guthrie, A. B., Jr. "Loco," Esquire, LXVIII (November 1967), 122-123, 165.

4104 Guthrie, D. J. "Shorn Lamb in a Sharkskin Suit," Little Review of the Pacific Northwest, I (Fall 1965), 62-69.

4105 Gutterson, Herbert. "JT," Cosmopolitan, CLIX (October 1965), 98-100.

4106 Guy, Georges. "The Logic of Death/Four Synopses," Diana Clemmons and Richard Tristman, trans., Bennington Review, II (Winter 1968), 26-31.

4107 Gyllensten, Lars. "Sunday Outing," Literary Review, IX (Winter 1965-66), 267-271.

4108 Gyory, Anne. "Summer's End," Seventeen, XXVII (January 1968), 80-81, 118-120.

4109 Gysin, Brion and William Burroughs. "Pieces," Mother, no. 5 (Summer 1965), 63-67.

4110 Haavardsholm, Espen. "Two Stories/The Dive," Elizabeth Rokkan, trans., Literary Review, XII (Winter 1968-69), 251-253.

4111 _____. "Two Stories/Ramparts," Elizabeth Rokkan, trans., Literary Review, XII (Winter 1968-69), 254-257.

4112 Haber, Leo. "Beatitude in Brooklyn," Ararat, VIII (Autumn 1967), 8-13.

4113 _____. "The Heretic," Jewish Frontier, XXXII (January 1965), 19-25.

4114 Hacikyan, Hagop. "Gigo Dies," Ararat, X (Summer 1969), 43-44.

4115 Hackel, Gloria. "Williamsburg," North American Review, III (September 1966), 32-36.

4116 Hadow, Lyndall. "A Day in the Life of Mrs. Aubrey Campbell," Westerly, no. 4 (December 1969), 80-87.

4117 _____. "Rilla," Westerly, (May 1966), 4-10.

4118 _____. "Summer Afternoon," Westerly, no. 4 (1967), 38-43.

4119 Haehlen, Jeanne. "The Hat," Focus (Singapore), New Series, no. 1 (1967), 5-8.

4120 Haenke, Helen. "The Chosen Child," Southerly, XXVII, no. 2 (1967), 75-81.

4121 _____. "Lament for a Death by Euthanasia," Southerly, XXVII, no. 4 (1967), 227-231.

4122 Haensel, Carl. "A Splash in a Pool," Margaret D. Howie, trans., Scala International, (March 1968), 34-37.

4123 Haerdter, Robert. "The Operation," George Raymond Selden, trans., Scala International, (September 1966), 34-36.

4124 Hagglund, Ben. "The Famous Trip to Duluth, the Iron Range and Grand Forks," Carleton Miscellany, VIII (Fall 1967), 62-76.

4125 Haig, Ross. "Men Who Travel," Westerly, (May 1966), 52-55.

4126 Haigaz, Aram. "Tolls of the Massacres," Armenian Review, XVIII (Winter 1965), 40-42.

4127 Haigler, Robert. "As It Should Be," Plaintiff, V (Winter 1969), 34-36.

4128 Hailey, Arthur. "Airport," Imprint, VIII (January 1969), 35-50, 53-81, 83, 85, 87, 89, 91, 93, 95, 97, 99, 101, 103, 105, 107, 109, 111, 113, 115-116.

4129 _____. "Airport/(Part I)," Good Housekeeping, CLXVI (March 1968), 87-94, 207-208, 210, 212, 217-218, 220, 222-224, 226, 228, 230-232, 234-241, 250.

4130 _____. "Airport/(Part II)," Good Housekeeping, CLXVI (April 1968), 93-95, 257-258, 260-272, 278, 280-283, 290, 292-296.

4131 ______. "Airport/(Conclusion)," *Good Housekeeping*, CLXVI (May 1968), 96-97, 202, 204, 206, 208, 210-219, 221, 223-224, 226, 228, 230-232.

4132 Haimowitz, Benjamin. "The General and the Liver," *Ararat*, VIII (Autumn 1967), 72-81.

4133 Halberstam, David. "One Very Hot Day," *Saturday Evening Post*, CCXLI (January 13, 1968), 40-54.

4134 Hale, Nancy. "An Age for Action," *Ladies' Home Journal*, LXXXII (March 1965), 92-93, 138.

4135 ______. "All Anybody," *Georgia Review*, XX (Spring 1966), 30-34.

4136 ______. "Animals in the House," *Harper's Magazine*, CCXXXIII (September 1966), 94-100.

4137 ______. "An Arrangement in Parents," *New Yorker*, XLIV (June 22, 1968), 27-31.

4138 ______. "Eyes and No Eyes; or, The Art of Seeing," *New Yorker*, XLI (November 20, 1965), 52-59.

4139 ______. "Family Ties," *Southern Review*, II (April 1966), 419-426.

4140 ______. "A Good Light," *New Yorker*, XLIV (September 28, 1968), 100, 102, 107-108, 110, 112, 114, 119-120.

4141 ______. "Inheriting a Garden," *New Yorker*, XLIV (May 18, 1968), 112, 114, 117, 118, 120, 122.

4142 ______. "The Innocent," *Virginia Quarterly Review*, XLIII (Spring 1967), 281-296.

4143 ______. "Joyous Gard," *New Yorker*, XLIV (October 12, 1968), 175-176, 178, 181-182, 184, 187-190.

4144 ______. "The Most Elegant Drawing Room in Europe," *New Yorker*, XLII (September 17, 1966), 55-64.

4145 ______. "My Mother's Solitudes," *New Yorker*, XLI (March 6, 1965), 38-42.

4146 ______. "The Other Side," *New Yorker*, XLV (March 1, 1969), 82, 84, 86-93.

4147 ______. "The Signorina," *Transatlantic Review*, no. 19 (Autumn 1965), 45-51.

4148 ______. "Sunday Lunch," *New Yorker*, XLI (May 8, 1965), 44-49.

4149 _____. "Waiting," Virginia Quarterly Review, XLII (Autumn 1966), 574-586.

4150 _____. "What Haunts Thee in Fond Shapes," New Yorker, XLIII (August 5, 1967), 27-29.

4151 _____. "The World, the Flesh, and the Devil," New Yorker, XLIV (April 27, 1968), 38-42.

4152 Halio, Jay L. "Sic Transit," University Review, XXXII (December 1965), 101-106.

4153 Hall, Donald. "Mr. Schwartz," Esquire, LXIV (October 1965), 88.

4154 Hall, James B. "Getting Married," Virginia Quarterly Review, XLIII (Summer 1967), 421-434.

4155 _____. "God Cares, but Waits," Virginia Quarterly Review, XLV (Spring 1969), 294-314.

4156 _____. "I Like It Better Now," Atlantic Monthly, CCXXIV (August 1969), 80-84.

4157 _____. "A Kind of Savage," Saturday Evening Post, CCXL (February 11, 1967), 60-67.

4158 _____. "While Going North," Virginia Quarterly Review, XLIV (Winter 1968), 90-97.

4159 Hall, Larue. "The Mule Master," Mexico Quarterly Review, III, no. 4 (1969), 35-45.

4160 Hall, Maxwell. "The Ancestral Urn," Literature East and West, X (December 1966), 357-361.

4161 Hall, Rodney. "The Birdcage Man," Meanjin Quarterly, XXVII (Spring 1968), 336-342.

4162 Hallam, F. S. "The Car," The Cantuarian, (August 1966), 212-213.

4163 _____. "Eastward Ho or The Mid-London Mock," The Cantuarian, (April 1967), 373-374.

4164 _____. "The Wall," The Cantuarian, (December 1966), 298-299.

4165 Hallmann, Hopkins. "Anna and David," Delta, XXI (1967), 75-85.

4166 Halperin, Irving. "Home, Sweet Home," Phylon, XXVI (Summer 1965), 186-194.

4167 _____. "The Jew and the Easter Eggs," Phylon, XXIX (Spring 1968), 81-87.

4168 _____. "Masha's Rabbit," Ante, III (Summer 1967), 20-21.

4169 Halpin, Maureen. "Afternoon at Fifth and Plum," Sou'wester, (Spring 1968), 18-20.

4170 Hamblem, Abigail Ann. "The Pal," University Review, XXXIV (Autumn 1967), 8-12.

4171 Hamburger, Michael. "Zombie's Notebook," Stony Brook, nos. 3-4 (1969), 179-181.

4172 Hamburger, Philip. "The Diaries and Letters of Sir Gerald Woolton," New Yorker, XLIII (October 28, 1967), 52-53.

4173 _____. "The Double Bollix," New Yorker, XLIV (June 22, 1968), 24-26.

4174 _____. "Indulgence in Games/By Dirk Arndt, M.D.," New Yorker, XLIV (February 24, 1968), 36-37.

4175 Hamilton, Bob. "The Blackberry Pit," Negro Digest, XIV (March 1965), 57-61.

4176 Hamilton, Carol. "Stanley's Girl," Discourse, XII (Summer 1969), 414-418.

4177 _____. "Water's Edge," Roanoke Review, III (Fall 1969), 11-18.

4178 Hamilton, Dorothy. "The Runaway," Ball State University Forum, X (Autumn 1969), 39-45.

4179 Hamilton, Rosemary. "Winds of Love," Cosmopolitan, CLXVII (November 1969), 170-173.

4180 Hamilton-Staite, Barrie. "The Landing," Courier, XLIV (May 1965), 61-63.

4181 Hammer, Nicholas. "The Ruler," Transatlantic Review, no. 27 (Winter 1967-68), 116-123.

4182 Hammer, Roger. "Birthday in Bedlam," Art and Literature, no. 5 (Summer 1965), 169-173.

4183 Hammond, Anthony. "Majora Non Credunt," Solstice, no. 5 (1967), 36-39.

4184 Hampe, Walter. "Einstein's Dilemma," Chelsea, no. 16 (March 1965), 131-141.

4185 Hancock, Anson Uriel. "John Auburntop, Novelist," Prairie Schooner, XLIII (Spring 1969), 46-58.

4186 Hand, Mary. "Lost Boy," New Zealand Listener, LIII (December 31, 1965), 5.

4187 Handa, R. L. "The Potato Grower of Kufri," R. L. Handa, trans., Accent (New Delhi, India), 21-22, 24, 20.

4188 Hanko, Beverly [Wisloski]. "On the Fauna and the Flora," Manuscript, XIX (Spring 1966), 51-55.

4189 _____. "The Ride," Manuscript, XVIII (Spring 1965), 50-57.

4190 _____. "Who Rode the Red Scooter to Banbury Cross?" Manuscript, XVIII (Spring 1965), 9-10.

4191 Hanley, Ruth Ann. "Come with Me to Prairie Town," Ave Maria, CVI (December 9, 1967), 28-30.

4192 _____. "Neighbor Boy," Ave Maria, CVII (March 9, 1968), 26-27.

4193 _____. "The Ride," Ave Maria, CII (September 18, 1965), 22-25.

4194 Hannah, Barry. "The Crowd Punk-Season Drew," Intro, no. 1 (September 1968), 3-19.

4195 Hansard, Peter. "Happy Breakfast, Please Come Back," New Zealand Listener, (November 10, 1967), 6.

4196 Hansen, Joseph. "Mourner," South Dakota Review, V (Spring 1967), 25-34.

4197 Hansen, Norvin. "Prairie Sketches/The Boy," South Dakota Review, VI (Spring 1968), 30-32.

4198 _____. "Prairie Sketches/The Field," South Dakota Review, VI (Spring 1968), 32-33.

4199 _____. "Prairie Sketches/The Road," South Dakota Review, VI (Spring 1968), 33-36.

4200 _____. "Prairie Sketches/The Stream," South Dakota Review, VI (Spring 1968), 29-30.

4201 Hansen, Richard. "The Beach," William and Mary Review, VII (Spring 1969), 20-22.

4202 Haqqani, Basit. "Casanova," Pakistan Review, XIII (May 1965), 5-6.

4203 Haqqi, Yehia. "We Are Three Orphans," Vision, XVI (June 1967), 10-11, 28-29.

4204 Hara, Stocker O. "Mundo," Expression, no. 2 (n.d.), 17-19.

4205 Harbinson, Robert. "The Spit of the Ould Da," Threshold, no. 21 (Summer 1967), 33-40.

4206 Hardie, Jack. "The Dark Water," Manuscript," XVIII (Spring 1965), 63-71.

4207 Hardie, Richard. "Search of an American," Grecourt Review, XI (May 1968), 39-41.

4208 Hardin, Mary Frances. "Repeat for Credit," U. S. Catholic and Jubilee, XXIV (October 1969), 29-31.

4209 Hardwick, Adam. "For God's Sake, Angela," Ambit, no. 38 (1969), 23-27.

4210 Hardy, Thomas. "The Model of the City," Adam International Review, nos. 325-327 (1968), 222-223.

4211 Haresnape, Geoffrey. "The Tomb," The Classic, II, no. 4 (1968), 48-57.

4212 _____. "The Tomb," Evergreen Review, X (August 1966), 42-44, 87-88, 90-93.

4213 Har'even, Shulamith. "Accident at Bernima Pass," Midstream, XV (May 1969), 61-67.

4214 Harington, Donald. "Artificial Respiration," Esquire, LXX (November 1968), 108-111, 161, 164-167.

4215 _____. "Down in the Dumps," Esquire, LXVII (February 1967), 106-107, 124, 126, 128-129.

4216 _____. "A Second Career," Esquire, LXVII (January 1967), 117, 119, 154.

4217 Haris, Petros. "Death of a God," Mary P. Gianos, trans., Athene, XXVII (Winter 1967), 5-6, 22.

4218 Harlow, Jean. "Today Is Tonight," Mademoiselle, LXI (July 1965), 90-117.

4219 Harman, Barbara Leah. "Chrism," Literary Magazine of Tufts University, III (Winter 1968), 26-31.

4220 _____. "The Clew," Literary Magazine of Tufts University, II, no. 1 (1967), 40-45.

4221 _____. "Love Story (to a man unknown)," Literary Magazine of Tufts University, III (Winter 1968), 80-81.

4222 Harnack, Curtis. "Feed the Starving Armenians," Ararat, IX (Summer 1968), 17-23.

4223 _____. "The Mistake," North American Review, III (July 1966), 9-13.

4224 _____. "Voice of the Town," Tri-Quarterly, no. 16 (Fall 1969), 51-64.

4225 Harper, Edward. "The Day Uncle Marvin Died," Georgia Review, XIX (Winter 1965), 437-445.

4226 Harper, Richard C. "Cry 'Warlock' Softly Angel," West Coast Review, I (Fall 1966), 17-19.

4227 Harriet, Sidney. "Imbeciles," Arx, II (October 1968), 13-14.

4228 Harrington, Evans. "The Sweet Man," Southern Review, IV (April 1968), 423-436.

4229 _____. "Under the Sun," Delta Review, IV (January-February 1967), 24-26, 44-48.

4230 Harrington, William. "Pillar of Salt," Stand, X, no. 3 (1969), 54-56.

4231 Harris, Barbara A. "A Bad Angel Made Me," Human Voice Quarterly, III (Spring 1967), 5-8.

4232 Harris, Bertha. "Catching Saradove," Greensboro Review, II (December 1966), 44-57.

4233 _____. "Catching Saradove," Greensboro Review, III (Winter 1967), 41-47.

4234 _____. "Confessions of Cherubino/from an unfinished novel," Red Clay Reader, no. 5 (1968), 93-95.

4235 _____. "Confessions of Cherubino (Section from the novel)," Greensboro Review, III (Summer-Fall 1968), 52-56.

4236 Harris, Bill. "The Price," Work, no. 4 (Summer/Fall/Winter 1966), 127-138.

4237 Harris, Derek. "A Time for Reason," Story: the Yearbook of Discovery, (1968), 92-99.

4238 Harris, Elizabeth. "An Afternoon of a Middle Class Madwoman: Perfect Whoredom," Epoch, XIX (Fall 1969), 49-61.

4239 _____. "Home One Winter," Colorado Quarterly, XVIII (Summer 1969), 65-72.

4240 Harris, Emily Katharine. "The Legend of Gray Mountain," Anglo-Welsh Review, XV (Spring 1967), 63-69.

4241 Harris, Gladys. "Grow Gently," Ave Maria, CII (October 9, 1965), 22-25.

4242 Harris, J. K. "Egg," The Cantuarian, (April 1968), 102.

4243 _____. "The Raincoat," The Cantuarian, (December 1966), 293-294.

4244 Harris, Joel. "The Twenty-Fifth Hour," Prairie Schooner, XLII (Winter 1968/69), 327-335.

4245 _____. "Who Shot the Runner?" Transatlantic Review, no. 26 (Autumn 1967), 108-111.

4246 Harris, MacDonald. "Ammazzafiori," Western Humanities Review, XXII (Spring 1968), 101-113.

4247 _____. "Snow and Lilac," Redbook, CXXV (August 1965), 72-73, 119-122.

4248 _____. "Trepleff," Harper's Magazine, CCXXXIII (December 1966), 61-68.

4249 _____. "Vooz Etts a Merry Can?" Cosmopolitan, CLX (January 1966), 84-89.

4250 Harris, Marilyn. "The Clay Man," Trace, nos. 62 & 63 (Fall-Winter 1966-67), 309-322.

4251 _____. "'Icarus Again'," Malahat Review, no. 2 (April 1967), 95-105.

4252 _____. "The Man in the Rosebush," Red Clay Reader, no. 3 (1966), 75-82.

4253 Harris, Mark. "At Prayerbook Cross," Cimarron Review, no. 6 (December 1968), 6-13.

4254 Harrison, D. "A Friend for a Season," Moonlight Review, I (Winter 1967-68), 9-25.

4255 Harrison, Deloris. "A Friend for a Season," Redbook, CXXXIII (August 1969), 74-75, 144-145, 148-150.

4256 Harrison, Harry. "The Greatest Car in the World," Status, II (January/February 1966), 54-55, 99-101, 103.

4257 Harrison, Lorena. "The Square of the Hypotenuse," Statement, no. 23 (Spring 1967), 22-24.

4258 Harrison, R. P. "Shepherd's Cloak," Columbia, XLIX (December 1969), 24-27.

4259 Harrison, William. "The Amateur," Cosmopolitan, CLVIII (January 1965), 76, 78-79.

4260 ______. "The Chameleons," Cosmopolitan, CLXV (November 1968), 146-148, 150.

4261 ______. "A Cook's Tale," Cosmopolitan, CLX (January 1966), 90-97.

4262 ______. "The Direct Approach," Redbook, CXXXIII (September 1969), 88-89, 128, 130, 132-133.

4263 ______. "The Hermit," New Orleans Review, I (Fall 1968), 20-25.

4264 ______. "January Graduation," Cosmopolitan, CLXI (October 1966), 110-112.

4265 ______. "Money," Cosmopolitan, CLXII (February 1967), 110-112, 114-115.

4266 ______. "The Pinball Machine," Saturday Evening Post, CCXL (April 22, 1967), 64-68.

4267 ______. "The Snooker Shark," Saturday Evening Post, CCXL (July 29, 1967), 56-58, 60-61.

4268 Harrity, Rory. "The Amorous Armadillo," Penthouse, I (September 1969), 53.

4269 ______. "A Bear and His Honey," Penthouse, I (November 1969), 53.

4270 ______. "The Incredible Singing Dog," Penthouse, I (October 1969), 53.

4271 ______. "The Overweight Fox," Penthouse, I (December 1969), 57.

4272 Hart, Carl. "from The Miser/A Novel in Progress," Beyond Baroque 691, I (December 1968), 42-43.

4273 Hart, Newell. "The Abstract Maiden," Tràce, no. 64 (Spring 1967), 100-106.

4274 Harter, Evelyn. "Bosom of the Family," Virginia Quarterly Review, XLII (Spring 1966), 279-289.

4275 _____. "Greet You with Garlands," Southwest Review, LIII (Autumn 1968), 349-358.

4276 _____. "In My Next Incarnation," North American Review, II (November 1965), 32-36.

4277 _____. "A Kingly Exit," Prairie Schooner, XL (Fall 1966), 250-260.

4278 _____. "Renegade," Antioch Review, XXVI (Fall 1966), 357-369.

4279 Hartley, Lodwick. "Daphne," South Carolina Review, I (November 1968), 39-51.

4280 Hartwell, George. "The Sustenance of Tail," Jeopardy, no. 5 (Spring 1969), 70-71.

4281 Harvey, Francis. "The Mystery Tour," Dublin Magazine, VI (Spring 1967), 79-93.

4282 Harvey, Ruth. "The Pleasure of Your Company," Seventeen, XXIV (February 1965), 112, 188-190, 192-193, 195.

4283 Hasnat, Abul. "Thirst," Mesbahuddin Ahmed, trans., Review, I (December 1967), 58-65.

4284 Hassan, Riffat. "Rahiman," Pakistan Review, XVI (December 1968), 21-22, 24.

4285 Hassler, Donald. "Darling," The Fiddlehead, no. 67 (Winter 1966), 18-24.

4286 Hastings, Anne. "K/Kalimera," Harper's Bazaar, CI (March 1968), 178, 114.

4287 _____. "Lunch," Harper's Bazaar, CI (September 1968), 240, 244, 246.

4288 Hatch, James. "It's Hysterical," Ararat, VII (Spring 1966), 42-47.

4289 _____. "Unofficial Leave of Absence," Ararat, VI (Autumn 1965), 65-67.

4290 Hathaway, John F. "Barrel," Story: the Yearbook of Discovery, (1968), 75-78.

4291 Hathaway, Stephen. "The Revival Meeting," Red Cedar Review, VI (September 1968), 27-29.

4292 Hatherley, Mary. "Rosie," Westerly, no. 4 (1967), 26-29.

4293 _____. "The Valour of Mr. Charters," Westerly, no. 4 (December 1968), 20-23.

4294 Hauser, Marianne. "Mimoun of the Mellah," Harper's Bazaar, XCIX (December 1966), 114-115, 178, 182.

4295 _____. "The Seersucker," Carleton Miscellany, IX (Fall 1968), 2-14.

4296 Hausmann, Manfred. "Demeter," George Raymond Selden, trans., Scala International, (April 1966), 30-36.

4297 Hawes, Evelyn. "A Madras-Type Jacket," Redbook, CXXIX (June 1967), 155, 157-179.

4298 Hawkins, Robert. "Two Epidemics from Zero, a Novel in Progress," Nexus (San Francisco, Calif.), II (March-April 1965), 22-36.

4299 Hawley, Cameron. "The Hurricane Years," Imprint, VIII (March 1969), 59-75, 77, 79, 81, 83, 85, 87, 89, 91, 93, 95, 97, 99, 101, 103, 105, 107, 109, 111, 113, 115-116.

4300 _____. "The Hurricane Years," Ladies' Home Journal, LXXXV (September 1968), 135-142, 144-146.

4301 _____. "The Hurricane Years/Conclusion," Ladies' Home Journal, LXXXV (October 1968), 153-160, 166-168.

4302 Hayden, Elizabeth Ann. "'Twas Brillig and the Slithy Toves ...'," Nimrod, IX (Spring 1965), 23-28.

4303 Hayes, D. "The Cobber," New Zealand Listener, (March 1, 1968), 6.

4304 Hayes, Peter. "The Muse of Newark," Atlantic Monthly, CCXXIII (April 1969), 76-80.

4305 _____. "The Muse of Newark," Harvard Advocate, CI (October 1967), 4-7.

4306 Hayes, Philip T. "The Stubborn Old Lady," Redbook, CXXIX (August 1967), 70-71, 120-122.

4307 Haynes, Colin. "The Really Christmas," Queen, CDXXVII (Christmas Issue, 1966), 108.

4308 Hays, Doris. "Munich Melody/Number Two," Wisconsin Review, II (May 1967), 11.

4309 Hayward, Jack R. "Burning Cats," Win, II, nos. 14 & 15 (August 1966), 38-39.

4310 Haywood, Mike. "The Rose Garden," Solstice, no. 4 (1966), 51-54.

4311 Hazaz, Hayyim. "The Hidden Puzzle," Ariel, no. 20 (Autumn 1967), 36-50.

4312 _____. "Yaish Meets the Angels/(An Extract)," Ariel, no. 20 (Autumn 1967), 51-57.

4313 Hazel, Robert. "White Anglo-Saxon Protestant," Hudson Review, XIX (Winter 1966-67), 551-584.

4314 Hazeldine, Peggy. "A Matter of Importance," New Zealand Listener, LIV (March 4, 1966), 5, 20.

4315 Hazzard, Shirley. "Canton More Far," New Yorker, XLIII (December 16, 1967), 42-49.

4316 _____. "The Evening of the Holiday," New Yorker, XLI (April 17, 1965), 44-52, 54, 56, 59-60, 62, 64, 66, 69, 71-72, 74, 76, 79-80, 82, 84, 86, 89-90, 92, 94, 96, 101-102, 104, 106, 108, 111-112, 114, 116, 118, 121-122, 124, 126, 128, 131-132, 134, 136-138, 141-142, 144-157.

4317 _____. "The Everlasting Delight," New Yorker, XLIII (August 19, 1967), 32-37.

4318 _____. "The Meeting," New Yorker, XLII (July 23, 1966), 26-31.

4319 _____. "Nothing in Excess," New Yorker, XLII (March 26, 1966), 48-57.

4320 _____. "Official Life," New Yorker, XLIII (June 24, 1967), 24-30.

4321 _____. "Out of Itea," New Yorker, XLI (May 1, 1965), 125-126, 128, 131-132, 134, 137-138.

4322 _____. "A Sense of Mission," New Yorker, XLIII (March 4, 1967), 40-46.

4323 _____. "The Separation of Dinah Delbanco," New Yorker, XLIII (July 22, 1967), 31-34.

4324 _____. "Swoboda's Tragedy," New Yorker, XLIII (May 20, 1967), 39-48.

4325 Head, Ann. "End of Innocence," Good Housekeeping, CLXV (October 1967), 92-93, 168, 170, 172, 174, 176, 178, 180, 182-183.

4326 _____. "Mr. and Mrs. Bo Jo Jones," Good Housekeeping,

CLXIII (October 1966), 87-89, 198, 200, 202, 204, 206, 208-209, 211-212, 214, 216-218, 238, 242, 244-246, 248-252, 254, 256, 258-259.

4327 _____. "Requiem for a Bachelor," McCall's, XCIV (June 1967), 82-83.

4328 Head, Barney. "Sorrow Food," Transition, VI, no. 30 (April/May 1967), 47-48.

4329 Head, Barry. "A Special Vision," Redbook, CXXXIII (June 1969), 80-81, 141-142.

4330 Heahlen, Jeanne. "The Name," Focus (Singapore), V, no. 1 (1967), 18-19.

4331 Healey, Kathleen. "Ethel," New Zealand Listener, (October 7, 1966), 6, 18.

4332 Healy, Rose Million. "Whatever Happened to Dixie Dumbar?" Cosmopolitan, CLX (February 1966), 98-103.

4333 Heanue, James. "Argorillo," Chelsea, no. 26 (May 1969), 95-108.

4334 Hearon, Shelby. "The World of Clara Blue," McCall's, XCV (August 1968), 56-57, 98-109.

4335 Hearst, James. "A Box of Candy," The Fiddlehead, no. 72 (Summer 1967), 67-76.

4336 _____. "The Confidant," Kansas Magazine, (1966), 11-16.

4337 _____. "The Speech," Discourse, VIII (Summer 1965), 219-229.

4338 Hearsum, John. "Death-Mask," Stand, X, no. 3 (1969), 17-32.

4339 _____. "Nucleus," London Magazine, IX (May 1969), 70-74.

4340 Hebert, H. V. "Screw," Transatlantic Review, no. 28 (Spring 1968), 120-126.

4341 Hecht, Florence. "Good-by to Molly," Redbook, CXXV (October 1965), 68-69, 142-146.

4342 _____. "That's Your Story, Baby," New Orleans Review, I (Spring 1969), 221-225.

4343 _____. "The Women Come and Go," Esquire, LXVI (September 1966), 164-167, 202, 204-206.

4344 Hecox, Robert A. "Without End," Denver Quarterly, III (Spring 1968), 57-65.

4345 Hedayat, Sadegh. "The Mongol's Shadow," D. A. Shojai, trans., Chicago Review, XX & XXI (May 1969), 95-104.

4346 Hedges, Morris. "Thanksgiving," Commentary, XLVIII (July 1969), 33-49.

4347 Hedin, Mary. "The Peculiar Vision of Mrs. Winkler," Redbook, CXXXIII (May 1969), 82-83, 142, 144, 147.

4348 _____. "Places We Lost," McCall's, XCIII (October 1965), 120-121, 206-212.

4349 Hedrick, F. M. "Cony-Catching Simplified," Human Voice, III (Summer-Fall 1967), 126-132.

4350 _____. "The Face of a Stranger," Human Voice Quarterly, II (May 1966), 62-63.

4351 Heeresma, Heere. "How Those Two Met," Elisabeth Eybers, trans., Delta (Amsterdam), X (Winter 1967-68), 66-80.

4352 Heflin, Lee. "A Rose Is a Rose," Aspects, no. 6 (January 1965), 3-4.

4353 Heidlebaugh, Tom. "The Spring in Far Kashmir," Nexus, I (January 1968), 24-28.

4354 Heimer, Mel. "Two More Days," Ladies' Home Journal, LXXXII (February 1965), 102d-102f, 102h-102j.

4355 Heineman, Nancy. "The Great Auk/A Bird Now Extinct," Saturday Evening Post, CCXLI (January 27, 1968), 46-49.

4356 Heinemann, Arthur. "Doctor Putney's Darkest Hour," McCall's, XCII (July 1965), 76-77, 131-135.

4357 _____. "The Family Man," Redbook, CXXV (June 1965), 48-49, 97-98, 100-103.

4358 _____. "I Love You, Charley, Please Come Back," McCall's, XCII (September 1965), 76-77, 185-186, 188.

4359 _____. "The Longest Day in the Year," Ladies' Home Journal, LXXXV (December 1968), 92-93, 136, 138-140, 142.

4360 _____. "The Magic Touch," Redbook, CXXVII (July 1966), 46-47, 86-91.

4361 _____. "The Vandal," Saturday Evening Post, CCXXXIX (May 21, 1966), 72-79.

4362 _____. "The Visible Surface," McCall's, XCIII (March 1966), 106-107, 145-149.

4363 Heiserman, Arthur. "A Short Story about Saints, Priests, Races, etc., Kenyon Review, XXVII (Summer 1965), 463-475.

4364 Heist, Jerry. "The Maddening Funk-Funk-Funk of the Foo-Foo," Harvard Advocate, CI (October 1967), 9-10.

4365 Hekkanen, Ernest. "The Disarrayed," Literary Review, XII (Summer 1969), 477-484.

4366 _____. "Do Not Decry," Carolina Quarterly, XXI (Fall 1969), 77-84.

4367 _____. "Sharp Edge of the Knife," Consumption, II (Winter 1969), 22-28.

4368 Helbemäe, Gerd. "Still Life," Literary Review, VIII (Spring 1965), 373-382.

4369 Heller, Joseph. "Love, Dad," Playboy, XVI (December 1969), 180-182, 348.

4370 _____. "Something Happened," Esquire, LXVI (September 1966), 136-141, 212-213.

4371 Hellman, Robert. "The World and Weehawken," Ararat, VII (Autumn 1966), 32-36.

4372 Hellyer, Jill. "That's the Way It Goes," Westerly, no. 2 (1967), 27-31.

4373 Helmer, Pat. "Marie," Arx, I (July-August 1967), 2-5.

4374 Helprin, Mark Henry. "Because of the Waters of the Flood," New Yorker, XLV (September 27, 1969), 35.

4375 Helwig, David. "After School," Quarry, XV (November 1965), 27-29.

4376 _____. "Among the Trees of the Park," Canadian Forum, XLVIII (May 1968), 42-43.

4377 _____. "In Exile," The Fiddlehead, no. 80 (May-July 1969), 64-70.

4378 _____. "The Small Rain," Quarry, XVII (Spring 1968), 16-20.

4379 _____. "Something for Olivia's Scrapbook I Guess," Saturday Night, LXXXIII (March 1968), 33-38.

4380 Hemenway, Robert. "I Am Waiting," New Yorker, XLV (September 6, 1969), 35-40.

4381 Hemesath, James. "The Box," Dare, V (December 1967), 20-22.

4382 Hen, Joseph. "Death and the Boxer," Thad Kowalski, trans., Literary Review, XI (Autumn 1967), 111-143.

4383 Henderson, Dion. "The Last Day of Shooting," Signature, II (October 1967), 44-45, 82, 84, 86.

4384 Henderson, Michael. "Change," Landfall, no. 89 (March 1969), 55-60.

4385 Henderson, Natalie Gaudet. "And One to Grow on," Georgia Review, XXII (Spring 1968), 97-105.

4386 _____. "Red Is for Ribbons, Apples and Cheeks," Ave Maria, CIII (May 28, 1966), 26-29.

4387 Henderson, Robert. "Aftermath," New Yorker, XLV (March 8, 1969), 33-37.

4388 _____. "Avizandum," New Yorker, XLIII (September 2, 1967), 28-32.

4389 _____. "Cockcrow," New Yorker, XLIV (July 6, 1968), 22-27.

4390 _____. "Codicils," New Yorker, XLII (December 24, 1966), 32-36.

4391 _____. "Community Spirit," New Yorker, XLIII (July 22, 1967), 28-30.

4392 _____. "Cradle Song," New Yorker, XLII (October 29, 1966), 56-59.

4393 _____. "Driftwood," New Yorker, XLIV (November 9, 1968), 56-60.

4394 _____. "The Fipple Flute," New Yorker, XLIII (April 22, 1967), 44-47.

4395 _____. "The House that Jerry Built," New Yorker, XLI (November 20, 1965), 48-51.

4396 _____. "The Intruder," Saturday Evening Post, CCXXXVIII (March 13, 1965), 44-46, 50-51.

4397 _____. "The Long Letter," New Yorker, XLII (June 18, 1966), 36-40.

4398 _____. "The Unknown Rooms," New Yorker, XLI (June 5, 1965), 36-40.

4399 Henderson, Stephen. "The Magic Word," Negro Digest, XVIII (June 1969), 58-67.

4400 Hendrickson, Robert. "The Electric Chair Salesman & Co.," North American Review, V (September-October 1968), 19-21.

4401 Hendrie, Don. " Saint Jones/[Chapter I of a novel-in-progress," Silo, no. 11 (Spring 1967), 30-49.

4402 Hening, W. "Weehawken Rhapsody," Yale Literary Magazine, CXXXIV (September 1965), 16-23.

4403 Henri, Adrian and Barry Bowes. "Biography," Ambit, no. 26 (1965/66), 6-15.

4404 Henricksen, Bruce. "Reflection," Aspects, no. 6 (January 1965), 9-10.

4405 _____. "Snowscape," Little Review of the Pacific Northwest, I (Fall 1965), 37, 39.

4406 Henry, Vera. "The Glass World in June," Seventeen, XXIV (June 1965), 90-91, 122, 124, 127.

4407 Henson, Robert. "Father Says," Shenandoah, XVII (Winter 1966), 55-68.

4408 _____. "The Land of Beginning Again," Michigan Quarterly Review, VII (Winter 1968), 44-56.

4409 _____. "Lykaon," Epoch, XVIII (Winter 1969), 203-225.

4410 Hentoff, Margot. "Oh Hegeman, My Love," Harper's Bazaar, C (March 1967), 142, 284.

4411 _____. "Where Do the Detectives Eat," Harper's Magazine, CCXXXVI (February 1968), 73-74, 78.

4412 Herbert, Jack. "The Disturbance of the Magpie," Edge, no. 5 (Fall 1966), 83-91.

4413 Herbst, Josephine. "Watcher with the Horn/(section of her Novel)," Lotus, no. 1 (1968), 35-45.

4414 Herburger, Günter. "A Monotonous Landscape," Esquire, LXIX (May 1968), 110-111, 114, 150, 152, 154, 156, 158.

4415 _____. "Where Ancestors Lived," D. C. Travis, trans., Dimension, I, no. 2 (1968), 226-245 [in German & English on alternate pages].

4416 Herlihy, James Leo. "The Day of the Seventh Fire," Florida Quarterly, I (Summer 1967), 109-127.

4417 ______. "The Fright of Mrs. Yeager," Esquire, LXIV (October 1965), 108-109, 157-159.

4418 ______. "Laughs, etc.," Playboy, XIV (July 1967), 67, 152-154.

4419 Herman, Jan Jacob. "The Cards of Say," San Francisco Earthquake, I (Summer/Fall 1968), 81-87.

4420 ______. "A Dangerous Opiate," VDRSVPVDRSVPVDRSVP, (1969), n.p. [front page].

4421 ______. "Yes, Prince, Clear Surprise!" VDRSVPVDRSVP-VDRSVP, (1969), n.p. [front and back pages].

4422 Hermann, John. "The Legacy," Perspective, XV (Spring-Summer 1967), 3-15.

4423 Hermans, Willem Frederik. "The House of Refuge," Estelle Debrot, trans., Delta (Amsterdam), IX (Autumn 1966), 31-66.

4424 Hernández, Juan José. "The Favorite," John Cameron Murchison, trans., Tri-Quarterly, nos. 13/14 (Fall/Winter 1968-69), 356-361.

4425 ______. "Julian," H. E. Francis, trans., Massachusetts Review, X (Summer 1969), 483-490.

4426 ______. "Like You Were Playing," H. E. Francis, trans., Texas Quarterly, XI (Spring 1968), 147-151.

4427 ______. "Lord Nelson," H. E. Francis, trans., Malahat Review, no. 8 (October 1968), 81-82.

4428 ______. "The Widow," H. E. Francis, trans., Harper's Bazaar, CI (June 1968), 140, 66.

4429 Herrickson, L. M. "The Minor Canon," Anglo-Welsh Review, XV (Summer 1965), 124-128.

4430 ______. "A Slave's Affair. Melodrama for Speaker and Bassoon Consort," Poetmeat, nos. 9 & 10 (Summer 1965), 79.

4431 Herring, Robert. "The Sound of Hounds," Epoch, XVI (Spring 1967), 261-274.

4432 ______. "Varnel," Colorado Quarterly, XIV (Winter 1966), 259-275.

4433 Herrmann, John. "Aliwar and His Angel," Montparnasse Review, no. 1 (1965), 1-7.

4434 _____. "All the Way to the Tigers," Nexus (San Francisco, Calif.), II (March-April 1965), 10-17.

4435 _____. "F," Northwest Review, X (Summer 1968), 68-71.

4436 _____. "Penates," Virginia Quarterly Review, XLIV (Spring 1968), 246-264.

4437 _____. "The Sky Above, the Sea Around and Nothing Else," South Dakota Review, IV (Winter 1966), 9-21.

4438 _____. "Where Are You? I Can't Find You," North American Review, V (July-August 1968), 22-26.

4439 Hersch, Burton. "The Out-of-Doors and Solomon Eichorn," Transatlantic Review, no. 25 (Summer 1967), 129-138.

4440 Hertz, K. V. "The Last Canadian Dreidle Maker," Midstream, XIV (December 1968), 37-45.

4441 Herzel, Roger. "The Pool," Soundings, III (Spring 1966), 63-64.

4442 Hesse, Herman. "Autumn in Tesslin," K. W. Maurer, trans., The Fiddlehead, no. 77 (Fall 1968), 35-40.

4443 _____. "A Fairy Tale," Thomas Nadar and Daniel Wire, trans., Overflow, II, no. 1 (1968), 17-22.

4444 _____. "Little Mohr," K. W. Maurer, trans., The Fiddlehead, no. 67 (Winter 1966), 38-42.

4445 Hessell, Dora. "Double Patience," New Zealand Listener, (January 12, 1968), 4.

4446 Hester, Mary. "Sweet William," Prairie Schooner, XL (Summer 1966), 95-117.

4447 Hewett, Dorothy. "The Awakening of Miss Huggett," Westerly, (August 1965), 20-28.

4448 _____. "You Can't Come Home Again," Meanjin Quarterly, XXVI (Autumn 1967), 29-40.

4449 Heym, Stefan. "The Survivor," Meanjin Quarterly, XXV (June 1966), 200-207.

4450 Heyman, Arlene. "Freedom Now," New American Review, no. 5 (January 1969), 190-209.

4451 _____. " Something that Would Grow," Epoch, XVII (Fall 1967), 62-86.

4452 _____. "Strains of Iris," New American Review, no. 2 (January 1968), 110-131.

4453 Hickey, Margaret Condon. "The Bishop's Banquet," Columbia, XLVII (January 1967), 24-27.

4454 Hicks, Mabel. "Artie," University Review, XXXIV (Winter 1967), 101-106.

4455 _____. "Bright Saturday," Discourse, VIII (Winter 1965), 70-75.

4456 _____. "The Odd Ones," Ball State University Forum, VII (Autumn 1966), 49-53.

4457 _____. "Show and Tell," Discourse, IX (Spring 1966), 227-229.

4458 _____. "Three to Five," North American Review, III (March 1966), 26-31.

4459 Hider, Mitchell. "Cleo," Four Quarters, XVIII (January 1969), 25-30.

4460 Hiehle, Patrice. "Good Morning, Pretty Girl," Kansas Magazine, (1965), 29-31.

4461 Higgins, Aidan. "Balcony of Europe," London Magazine, V (June 1965), 7-29.

4462 _____. "Balcony of Europe-2," London Magazine, VII (September 1967), 20-39.

4463 _____. "The Bathing Girls and other Receding Images," Dublin Magazine, VII (Autumn/Winter 1968), 43-47.

4464 _____. "from Langrishe, Go Down," Art and Literature, no. 8 (Spring 1966), 9-21.

4465 _____. "from Langrishe, Go Down," Paris Review, IX (Winter 1966), 131-143.

4466 Higgins, Anne. "The Wood Burning Stove," Red Clay Reader, no. 4 (1967), 105-111.

4467 Higgins, Bella. "The Duels and the Green Man," Scottish International, no. 6 (April 1969), 49-52.

4468 Higgins, Daniel. "It Beats Hell Out of the Other Thing," Aspects, no. 12 (January 1969), 1-2.

4469 Higgins, George V. "Mass in Time of War," Cimarron Review, no. 9 (September 1969), 73-81.

4470 ______. "Something Dirty You Could Keep," Massachusetts Review, X (Autumn 1969), 631-644.

4471 Higgins, Judith. "The Only People," Atlantic Monthly, CCXIX (June 1967), 96-98, 101-108.

4472 ______. "The Only People," Cornhill Magazine, CLXXVI (Summer 1968), 394-418.

4473 Higgins, Kurt. "The Coward," Jeopardy, no. 4 (Spring 1968), 17-22.

4474 Highsmith, Patricia. "The Snail Watcher," Nova, (April 1966), 155, 157, 159-160.

4475 ______. "The Snails," Saturday Evening Post, CCXL (June 17, 1967), 44-45, 48, 50, 52, 54-55.

4476 ______. "Those Who Walk Away," Cosmopolitan, CLXII (April 1967), 154-169, 176-183.

4477 Hildebrand, T. "The Foggy, Foggy Dew," Mandala, no. 1 (1968), 12-15.

4478 Hildesheimer, Wolfgang. "The Apartment in the Attic," Ernestine Schlant, trans., Harper's Bazaar, CIII (November 1969), 184-185.

4479 ______. "A Slightly Bigger Acquisition," Ernestine Schlant, trans., Harper's Bazaar, CIII (November 1969), 240.

4480 ______. "The Studio Party," A. P. Schroeder, trans., Extensions, no. 2 (1969), 51-56.

4481 Hildreth, Gabrielle. "The Red Shirt," New Zealand Listener, (April 14, 1967), 6, 24.

4482 ______. "Stingray," New Zealand Listener, LIV (May 13, 1966), 6.

4483 Hildt, Robert. "Jefe/from Yes, But Do You Come From a Good Family, a novel," Chelsea, no. 26 (May 1969), 128-140.

4484 Hill, C. D. "The Shameless Shiksa," Playboy, XVI (September 1969), 173-174, 176.

4485 Hill, Dave. "Christmas 1965," Ave Maria, CII (December 11, 1965), 22-24, 26.

4486 Hill, Edwin L. "Morgan's Mouse," North American Review, IV (May 1967), 17-18.

4487 Hill, Elizabeth Starr. "Someone Missing at the Manger," Good Housekeeping, CLXV (December 1967), 108-109, 160-163.

4488 Hill, Eugenie. "I Don't Really Care," Daily Telegraph Magazine, no. 216 (November 22, 1968), 61, 63, 66-67.

4489 Hill, Judith Brenner. "The Health Scheme," Literary Review, X (Autumn 1966), 55-69.

4490 Hill, Mary Antonnette. "Fox at Noon," Corral 1966, 33-43.

4491 Hill, Richard F. "The Air Conditioner Hat," New Campus Review, I (Winter/Spring 1968), 5-9.

4492 _____. "Mrs. Marosky's Vigil," Florida Quarterly, I (October 1968), 49-55.

4493 Hill, Robert. "Homer," Greensboro Review, IV (Spring 1969), 5-14.

4494 _____. "The Little Deli," Greensboro Review, no. 7 (Summer-Fall 1969), 16-19.

4495 Hill, Weldon. "Orvil Smith Was Here," Nimrod, XI (Autumn 1966), 30-40.

4496 Hillerman, Tony. "The Replacement," New Mexico Quarterly, XXXVII (Autumn 1967), 276-280.

4497 Hillman, Daphne. "Return," Westerly, no. 1 (April 1969), 17-19 [mistakenly attributed to Natalie Scott, but corrected in following issue].

4498 Hillman, Gerald. "Willy," Harvard Advocate, C (November 1965), 2-4.

4499 Hills, Peter Bennett. "Thicker Than Water," Overland, no. 36 (Winter 1967), 10-15.

4500 Himber, Alan. "The Buried Life," Sewanee Review, LXXIV (April-June 1966), 489-496.

4501 Himes, Chester. "Pinktoes," Evergreen Review, IX (March 1965), 16-18, 72-74, 76-78, 80-83.

4502 Hinchman, Jane. "A Clue of Daffodils," Redbook, CXXIX (October 1967), 62-63, 128, 131, 133-134.

4503 Hindmarsh, Thomas. "The Little War," New Zealand Listener,

LIV (April 1, 1966), 4.

4504 ______. "May I Take a Message," New Zealand Listener, (July 8, 1966), 6.

4505 ______. "Pattern of Anger," New Zealand Listener, LXI (May 16, 1969), 12.

4506 ______. "Rockbottom," New Zealand Listener, (April 21, 1967), 6.

4507 ______. "See You Tomorrow," New Zealand Listener, (August 18, 1967), 6.

4508 ______. "A Woman to Aspire to," New Zealand Listener, (November 11, 1966), 6.

4509 Hiner, James. "At Once the Summary and Climax," Minnesota Review, VIII (1968), 12-24.

4510 ______. "Caribbean Cruise," Human Voice, III (Summer-Fall 1967), 41-50.

4511 ______. "The Gunmen of Buffalo Mills," El Corno Emplumado, no. 15 (July 1965), 74-80.

4512 ______. "The Gunmen of Buffalo Mills," Human Voice Quarterly, II (February 1966), 11-12.

4513 ______. "The Price of Admission," Minnesota Review, IX (1969). 103-107.

4514 Hines, James and E. M. Lake. "Aftermath," Minnesota Review, V (October-December 1965), 274-280.

4515 ______. "Dawn of a Remembered Summer," Arizona Quarterly, XXII (Summer 1966), 146-156.

4516 ______. "For the Love of Sadie May," University Review, XXXII (June 1966), 307-310.

4517 ______. "Hill Neighbors," University Review, XXXIII (Summer 1967), 286-292.

4518 ______. "The Transgressing Woman," Arizona Quarterly, XXI (Winter 1965), 346-356.

4519 Hinton, Susan. "Rumble Fish," Nimrod, XIII (October 1968), 4-8. [This issue of Nimrod appeared as a special supplement to The University of Tulsa Alumni Magazine. It resumed publication as a separate entity with its next issue, Winter 1969.]

4520 Hirsch, Miryam Aber. "A Small, Small Story," Solidarity, III (February 1968), 55.

4521 Hirsh, Rita. "Arthur Mencken," Writer's Forum, II (Summer 1966), 22-24.

4522 Hirshleifer, Phyllis. "Madame Has Bought the Paradis," Discourse, XI (Winter 1968), 94-97.

4523 Hise, Jesse, Jr. "A Tighter Clasp: A Story," Kansas Magazine, (1968), 41-46.

4524 Hitchens, Dolores. "A Collection of Strangers," Redbook, CXXXIII (September 1969), 159-181.

4525 _____. "Postscript to Nightmare," Cosmopolitan, CLXII (June 1967), 150-163, 167-175.

4526 _____. "The Unloved," Redbook, CXXV (October 1965), 173, 175-205.

4527 Hlasko, Marek. "Amor 43," Teresa Fand, trans., Tri-Quarterly, no. 9 (Spring 1967), 183-188.

4528 Hoag, Helen I. "The Final Boat," Columbia, XLVI (March 1966), 24-27.

4529 Hoag, M. de Koning. "Gina Between," Seventeen, XXVII (November 1968), 134-135, 191-192, 194, 196.

4530 _____. "The Involvement," Seventeen, XXVII (July 1968), 82-83, 112.

4531 _____. "Liar, Liar," Seventeen, XXVI (November 1967), 154-155, 191, 193-194.

4532 _____. "Summer Hang-up," Seventeen, XXVI (June 1967), 92-93, 182-183.

4533 _____. "The Whole Cookie," Seventeen, XXVIII (June 1969), 118-119, 180-182.

4534 Hoaglund, Edward. "The Colonel's Power," New American Review, no. 2 (January 1968), 230-251.

4535 _____. "A Fable of Mammas," Transatlantic Review, no. 32 (Summer 1969), 106-114.

4536 _____. "The Final Fate of the Alligators," New Yorker, XLV (October 18, 1969), 52-57.

4537 _____. "Kwan's Coney Island," New American Review, no. 5 (January 1969), 106-116.

4538 _____. "The Witness," Paris Review, XI (Summer-Fall 1967), 141-178.

4539 Hobbs, Jenny. "Compensation," Contrast (Cape Town, South Africa), no. 19 (November 1968), 78-81.

4540 Hobhouse, Christina. "Camellias," Queen, CDXXX (March 13, 1968), 50-53.

4541 Hobson, Laura Z. "Single, Age Twenty-Five," Good Housekeeping, CLXII (June 1966), 87-89, 192, 194-196, 198, 200, 202, 210, 212, 214, 216, 218, 220-224, 227-228, 230-233.

4542 Hoch, Edward D. "The Dying Knight," Signature, II (June 1967), 20.

4543 _____. "The Fifth Victim," Signature, I (May 1966), 36.

4544 _____. "A Girl Like Cathy," Signature, I (October 1966), 45-47, 80, 84, 88, 90.

4545 _____. "The Only Girl in His Life," Signature, I (February 1966), 38-39, 68, 70, 72, 75-77.

4546 Hochberg, Matthew. "Throne," December, X (1968), 70-71.

4547 Hochhuth, Rolf. "The Berlin Antigone," Robert David Macdonald, trans., Daily Telegraph Magazine, no. 239 (May 9, 1969), 46-48, 50, 54.

4548 Hochman, Sandra. "The Kid and Benny Bassoon at Miami Beach," Harper's Bazaar, CII (December 1968), 156-157, 72, 74, 76.

4549 Hochstein, Rolaine. "The Affirming Flame of Ardith Manners," Redbook, CXXXIII (October 1969), 100-101, 158, 160.

4550 _____. "Child of Delight," Redbook, CXXVII (October 1966), 80-81, 104, 106-108, 110.

4551 Hodges, D. M. "... Louder Than Words," UMD Humanist, XIV (Spring 1966), 9-12.

4552 Hodges, William. "The Seventh Stage," Delta Review, VI (April 1969), 46-48, 50.

4553 Hodgetts, Craig. "Pottsworth," Mt. Adams Review, II (Winter 1967-68), 26-28.

4554 Hodgins, Jack. "Every Day of His Life," Northwest Review, IX (Spring 1968), 108-120.

4555 _____. "The God of Happiness," Westerly, no. 4 (December

1968), 5-9.

4556 ______. "Promise of Peace," North American Review, VI (Winter 1969), 27-31.

4557 Hodgkin, Righton. "Of God and the Hunter," DeKalb Literary Arts Journal, II (Fall 1967), 49-56.

4558 Hodson, Mary Lou. "The Beauty and the Big Time," Signature, I (August 1966), 18.

4559 Hodson, Tom. "Cold Canvassing," Signature, I (December 1966), 40.

4560 Hoeft, Robert D. "One Thousand Three Hundred and Twelve Games of Tic-Tac-Toe," Readers & Writers, II (Summer 1968), 41-44.

4561 Hoffman, A. C. "The Edge of the Sea," Quarterly Review of Literature, XV (1968), 323-342.

4562 ______. "The Landmarks," Literary Review, XII (Autumn 1968), 116-123.

4563 ______. "The Sisters," Ball State University Forum, VIII (Autumn 1967), 60-65.

4564 ______. "The Skirmish," Epoch, XVI (Spring 1967), 238-242.

4565 Hoffman, Charles. "A Door Opened," Ladies' Home Journal, LXXXVI (February 1969), 78-79, 134-136.

4566 Hoffman, Margaret. "A Cure-All for Mortality," Coraddi, (Fall 1967), 7-9.

4567 ______. "Full Fathoms Deep," Coraddi, (Fall 1968), 6-7.

4568 Hoffman, Michael J. "Call Me Ishmael," Era, III (Spring 1966), 55-64.

4569 Hoffman, William. "The Lifeguard," McCall's, XCV (August 1968), 70-71, 94-96.

4570 ______. "Mother Wants to Meet You," McCall's, XCVI (July 1969), 68-69, 109-112.

4571 ______. "Sea Tides," McCall's, XCIII (September 1966), 86-87, 150-154.

4572 ______. "The Waters of Stingray," Playboy, XII (March 1965), 107, 156, 158.

4573 ______. "Where the Boys Are," Status & Diplomat, XVIII

(January 1967), 54-57, 66.

4574 Hoffmann, Charles G. "My Brother Paul," Ball State University Forum, VIII (Autumn 1967), 71-77.

4575 Hoffmann, Rita. "Hello, Good-by, Hello Again," McCall's, XCVI (October 1968), 106-107, 150-154.

4576 _____. "The Moving Finger Writes," McCall's, XCVI (March 1969), 72-73, 146-150.

4577 Hofmann, Kitzia. "Old Adelina," Anne Fremantle, trans., The Quest, I (Spring 1966), 31-39.

4578 Hoggard, James. "London Bridge and Searcy Gassman," Southwest Review, LI (Summer 1966), 272-284.

4579 _____. "Mesquite," Southwest Review, LIV (Spring 1969), 175-186.

4580 _____. "One-Legged Dancer," Southwest Review, LII (Summer 1967), 274-289.

4581 Hohoff, Curt. "Dangerous Crossing," Margaret D. Howie, trans., Scala International, (June 1969), 35-37.

4582 Holbrook, Bruce. "A Breach in Our Existence," Transatlantic Review, no. 27 (Winter 1967-68), 25-32.

4583 _____. "Kauskas," Transatlantic Review, no. 29 (Summer 1968), 53-56.

4584 Holbrook, Jean R. "Penelope and the Pituitary Gland," Delta Review, IV (July-August 1967), 82-85, 111-112, 114, 116-117.

4585 Holditch, Kenneth. "In November the Nights Come Early," Phylon, XXVII (Fall 1966), 286-291.

4586 _____. "One of These Mornings," Phylon, XXVI (Spring 1965), 80-90.

4587 Holiday, A. "The Headache," Contrast (Cape Town, South Africa), no. 14 (November 1966), 61-64.

4588 Holland, Barbara. "The Backward Heart," McCall's, XCV (January 1968), 82-83, 114-115.

4589 _____. "Daffodil and the Man," Cosmopolitan, CLX (June 1966), 106-108, 110.

4590 _____. "The Dreams of Rosemary," McCall's, XCIII (January 1966), 52-53, 138, 140.

4591 ______. "A Gift of Dolphins," Redbook, CXXVI (March 1966), 62-63, 100-102.

4592 ______. "The Rescue," McCall's, XCVI (July 1969), 58-59, 115-117.

4593 ______. "Someone In the Kitchen," McCall's, XCIII (June 1966), 64-65, 134-136.

4594 ______. "The World Outside," Redbook, CXXIV (March 1965), 56-57, 102, 104-105.

4595 Holland, Jay. "Valerie," Queen, CDXXX (March 27, 1968), 96, 98-99.

4596 Holland, William. "So Quick, So Clean an Ending," Prairie Schooner, XLI (Summer 1967), 253-258.

4597 Hollander, Robert. "The Starving Girl," Cimarron Review, no. 5 (September 1968), 50-58.

4598 Holloway, Kirby. "The Jabberwock Died on Thursday Last," Coraddi, (Fall 1968), 12-13.

4599 Holloway, Sister Marcella M., C. S. J. "The Fable of the Phoebe Bird," Catholic World, CCII (January 1966), 224-227.

4600 Holmes, Edward M. "Island Hunt," Husson Review, I (1968), 132-136.

4601 ______. "Monday through Friday," Husson Review, II (1969), 106-110.

4602 Holmes, Nancy. "The Greatness of the World in Tears," Quartet, no. 16 (Fall 1966), 1-9.

4603 Holmes, Theodore. "A Futuristic Tale," December, XI (1969), 95-105.

4604 Holmes, William. "The Wasting of Father Fallon," Columbia, XLVII (July 1967), 24-27.

4605 Holrel, F. Tuy. "The Confessions of George Washington," Negro Digest, XVII (July 1968), 66-73, 95-98.

4606 Holst, Spencer. "Another Imposter," Sou'wester, II (Fall 1968), 67-68.

4607 ______. "Truant," Sou'wester, II (Fall 1968), 69.

4608 ______. "True Confessions Party," El Corno Emplumado, no. 18 (April 1966), 150-155.

4609 _____. "Wisher," Win, II, nos. 14 & 15 (August 1966), 7-8.

4610 Holstun, Barry. "Beneath," Ave Maria, CVII (March 2, 1968), 28-29.

4611 Holt, Kåre. "The Bird," Thelma Martin, trans., American Scandinavian Review, LVII (September 1969), 289-292.

4612 Holt, Victoria. "The King of the Castle/(Part I)," Good Housekeeping, CLXIV (May 1967), 81-83, 204, 206, 208-212, 214, 216-220, 222, 224, 226, 228, 230, 233-234, 236, 238-241, 248-249, 255-256.

4613 _____. "The King of the Castle/(Conclusion)," Good Housekeeping, CLXIV (June 1967), 96-97, 206, 208, 210, 212, 214, 216, 218, 220, 222, 224-234, 236-237.

4614 Hon, David. "Crumbs of May," Prospero's Cell, I (Winter 1967), 37-45.

4615 _____. "Last Ball," Nimrod, IX (Winter 1965), 9-14.

4616 Honeycutt, J. C. "A Time to Keep Silence, and a Time to Speak," The Archive, LXXIX (December 1966), 27-28.

4617 Honwana, Luis Bernardo. "Papa Snake and I," The Classic, II, no. 3 (1967), 5-16.

4618 Hood, Hugh. "Around Theaters," Parallel, I (July-August 1966), 47-50.

4619 _____. "Brother Andre, Pere Lamarche, & My Grandmother Eugenie Blagdon," Alphabet, no. 13 (June 1967), 34-49.

4620 _____. "The Fruit Man, the Meat Man, and the Manager," Canadian Forum, XLVIII (August 1968), 104-106.

4621 _____. "A Game of Touch," Tamarack Review, nos. 50-51 (1969), 73-83.

4622 _____. "Getting to Williamstown," Tamarack Review, no. 34 (Winter 1965), 3-14.

4623 _____. "The Holy Man," Tamarack Review, no. 37 (Autumn 1965), 3-18.

4624 _____. "It's a Small World/Paradise Retained?" Tamarack Review, no. 46 (Winter 1968), 101-108.

4625 _____. "One Way North and South," Tamarack Review, no. 41 (Autumn 1966), 82-94.

4626 _____. "Scenes from Montreal Life/(VI: Looking Down from Above)," Prism International, VI (Autumn 1966), 4-13.

4627 _____. "A Sherbrooke Street Man," Parallel, I (November-December 1966), 50-54.

4628 _____. "A Solitary Ewe," Literary Review, VIII (Summer 1965), 468-483.

4629 _____. "The Tolstoy Pitch," The Fiddlehead, no. 79 (March-April 1969), 44-59.

4630 Hookens, W. E. "The Little More...," Trevini, XXXVIII (July 1969), 34-46.

4631 _____. "The Woman and the Dog," Triveni, XXXVI (April 1967), 40-44.

4632 Hooper, Peter. "A Banner with a Strange Device," New Zealand Listener, LIV (March 18, 1965), 4, 21.

4633 _____. "Too Wide Is the World," New Zealand Listener, LII (February 5, 1965), 5.

4634 Hoornik, Ed. "The Last Word," Elisabeth Eybers, trans., Delta (Amsterdam), X (Spring/Summer 1967), 64-83.

4635 _____. "Petronella," Elisabeth Eybers, trans., Delta (Amsterdam), XI (Winter 1968-69), 53-84.

4636 Hoover, Carol. "A Murmur of Doves," Denver Quarterly, I (Autumn 1966), 71-89.

4637 Hoover, Dwight W. "You Can't Get There from Here," Ball State Teachers College Forum, VI (Winter 1965), 60-64.

4638 Hopkins, J. F. "Dear Harry," Four Quarters, XVIII (March 1969), 1-12.

4639 _____. "The Sign Painter," Four Quarters, XVI (January 1967), 7-14.

4640 _____. "The Threat," Four Quarters, XVII (May 1968), 5-10.

4641 Hopkins, John. "The Pig Scene," Art and Literature, no. 11 (Winter 1967), 90-105.

4642 _____. "The Up and the Down," Transatlantic Review, no. 21 (Summer 1966), 105-110.

4643 Hopkins, William. "Jimmy's Gone Days," Aspects, no. 12 (January 1969), 6-8.

4644 Hopkinson, Tom. "Bare Bones," London Magazine, VI (April 1966), 35-40.

4645 Hora, Jan. "Still Life with Fear," Quadrant, XIII (July-August 1969), 56-63.

4646 Hornberger, Marian. "The Apple Tree," Michigan Quarterly Review, VIII (Spring 1969), 83-85.

4647 Horne, Lewis B. "When Dry Summers End," Discourse, XII (Winter 1969), 42-53.

4648 Hornsby, Walter C. "The Fish that Swim by the Strand," Yale Literary Magazine, CXXXV (March 1967), 14-17.

4649 Horowitz, Floyd Ross. "A Visit to Chiah," Kansas Magazine, (1967), 7-17.

4650 Horowitz, Gloria Goldreich. "Schechter's Daughter," Colorado Quarterly, XIII (Winter 1965), 261-269.

4651 Horvath, Adam. "A Slice of Cake," Sundial, I (Spring 1967), 42-51.

4652 Hosie, J. S. "The Devil with Uncle," Westerly, (August 1965), 31-34.

4653 Hotta Yoshie. "Shadow Pieces/The Beach," P. G. O'Neill, trans., Japan Quarterly, XIII (July-September 1966), 357-365.

4654 _____. "Shadow Pieces/The Old Man," P. G. O'Neill, trans., Japan Quarterly, XIII (July-September 1966), 348-352.

4655 _____. "Shadow Pieces/The Younger Man," P. G. O'Neill, trans., Japan Quarterly, XIII (July-September 1966), 352-357.

4656 Houboult, Jan. "People Are Dying," American, I (Fall 1965), 40-41.

4657 Houlston, Margaret. "Something in Common," Westerly, (Summer 1966), 26-31.

4658 Household, Geoffrey. "Exiles," Saturday Evening Post, CCXLI (December 14, 1968), 52-53.

4659 _____. "Keep Walking," Good Housekeeping, CLXVI (January 1968), 70-72.

4660 _____. "Secret Police," Atlantic Monthly, CCXVI (December 1965), 57-61.

4661 Houston, James D. "The Native Sons of the Golden West," Compass, (Summer 1965), 10-19.

4662 _____. "On His Way to Epley's Bike Shop," Playboy, XVI (February 1969), 149, 187-192.

4663 _____. "The Shadow Cast," Per/Se, I (Winter 1966), 38-43.

4664 _____. "Straightaway," Compass, (Summer 1965), 7-9.

4665 _____. "Waiting for the Curtain," Illuminations, no. 3 (Summer 1967), 46-47.

4666 Houston, Linda. "Fallen Apples," Western Humanities Review, XX (Spring 1966), 125-134.

4667 Houston, Robert. "Within the Skin," Ante, III (Spring 1967), 57-67.

4668 Hovde, A. J. "A Great Campus for Dogs," Jeopardy, no. 4 (Spring 1968), 42-47.

4669 _____. "Picnic at the Lake," December, IX, nos. 2/3 (1967), 83-88.

4670 _____. "Prisoner's Choice," Arx, III (May 1969), 22-23.

4671 Howard, Quentin R. "Gate Fixers," Twigs, no. 1 (1965), 4-14.

4672 _____. "Something for Remembering," Twigs, no. 2 (1966), 43-48.

4673 Howard, R. G. "The Garden," Westerly, (Summer 1966), 5-10.

4674 Howard, Roger. "The Threshold," Solstice, no. 2 (1966), 44-45.

4675 Howe, Fanny. "The Other Side of Lethe," Mademoiselle, LXVII (June 1968), 104-105, 159-160, 166-167, 169.

4676 Howell, Claire. "People and Flowers," Silo, no. 8 (Fall 1965), 48-52.

4677 Howell, Robert. "from Ten Great Poetry Readings: VI," The Once Series (Twice), I (1966-67), n.p. [1-4].

4678 Hower, Edward. "Euthanasia," Epoch, XV (Fall 1965), 8-35.

4679 Howland, Mary. "Spring in a Strange Land," California

Review, no. 2 (Spring 1968), 61-68.

4680 Hoyer, Linda Grace. "The Burning Bush," New Yorker, XLII (October 1, 1966), 50-55.

4681 _____. "Hindsight and Foresight," New Yorker, XLIV (February 1, 1969), 30-37.

4682 _____. "The Predator," New Yorker, XLIII (May 13, 1967), 53.

4683 _____. "A Predisposition to Enchantment," New Yorker, XLI (March 13, 1965), 40-43.

4684 Hoyland, Michael. "The Beach," London Magazine, V (December 1965), 9-23.

4685 Hrabal, Bohumil. "A Breath of Fresh Air," Marian Wilbraham, trans., Literary Review, XIII (Fall 1969), 30-38.

4686 _____. "The Imposters," Edith Pargeter, trans., Stand, X no. 2 (1969), 22-26.

4687 _____. "The Kafkorium," Walter L. Solberg, trans., Tri-Quarterly, no. 9 (Spring 1967), 155-163.

4688 _____. "Uncle's Funeral," London Magazine, VII (November 1967), 12-16.

4689 Hsia Mien-ts'un. "The Long Idleness," J. P. Seaton, trans., Literature East and West, XII (December 1968), 255-262.

4690 Hsia, T. A. "The Birth of a Son," Literature East and West, IX (December 1965), 291-309.

4691 Hu Shih-chih. "The Biography of Mr. Just About," The Fair, II (Summer 1968), 30-31.

4692 Hubbard, Jan. "The Woman Who Ate Garbage," Focus, (Spring 1967), 27-33.

4693 Huber, Kathleen. "Now, Tell Me Pray, and Tell Me True," Seventeen, XXV (January 1966), 101, 119, 121.

4694 _____. "A Very Narcissus," Seventeen, XXVI (May 1967), 158-159, 244-248.

4695 Hubly, Erlene. "Henrietta and the Non-Lorelei Song of the Housepainter," Readers & Writers, I (November-January 1968), 44-48.

4696 _____. "The Woman Who Lived in Grand Central Station," Colorado Quarterly, XVIII (Summer 1969), 41-49.

4697 Huddle, David. "Rosie, Baby," Georgia Review, XXIII (Fall 1969), 323-342.

4698 Huddleston, Blanche. "Sundays Were the Worst," Kansas Magazine, (1965), 17-21.

4699 Hudson, Helen. "Hofmannstahl," Northwest Review, IX (Summer 1967), 38-53.

4700 _____. "The Listener," Antioch Review, XXVII (Summer 1967), 167-179.

4701 _____. "Mr. Thistle's Last Supper," Quarterly Review of Literature, XIV (1967), 351-372.

4702 _____. "Send a Patrol Car to Spartanburg," Mademoiselle, LXIII (June 1966), 118-119, 153, 163.

4703 _____. "The Tenant," Virginia Quarterly Review, XLIII (Autumn 1967), 629-643.

4704 Hudson, Jeffery. "How Does That Make You Feel?" Playboy, XV (November 1968), 115, 156, 158-159.

4705 Hugdahl, Vicky. "The Funeral," UMD Humanist, XV (Winter 1967), 40-42.

4706 Hughes, Cledwyn. "Merioneth," Anglo-Welsh Review, XV (Spring 1967), 19-28.

4707 Hughes, Gail. "The Head," Edge, no. 8 (Fall 1968), 111-116.

4708 Hughes, James. "Papa Krumpke," Readers & Writers, I (November-January 1968), 50-54.

4709 Hughes, Langston. "Bodies in the Moonlight," Readers & Writers, I (November-January 1968), 38-41.

4710 Hughes, Lawrence Patrick. "Easter in Tunisia," Prospero's Cell, I (Summer 1966), 23-28.

4711 Hughes, Mary Gray. "The Foreigner in the Blood," Esquire, LXIX (February 1968), 80, 82-83, 36, 42, 44.

4712 _____. "Welcome, Strangers--And Others Too," Redbook, CXXV (June 1965), 54-55, 125, 128, 130.

4713 Hughes, Philip. "Another Christ," Saturday Night, LXXXI (December 1966), 29-32.

4714 Hughes, Riley. "Brother Barnabas Sounds His 'A'," Columbia, XLV (January 1965), 24-27, 35-37.

4715 Hughes, Robert. "Flying the Black Mamba," London Magazine, IX (November 1969), 5-17.

4716 ______. "The Gift," Scottish International, no. 4 (October 1968), 18-26.

4717 Hughes, Tom. "It May Not Be Love, but She's My Baby," Jeopardy, no. 1 (1966), 49-50.

4718 Hulcoop, John. "A Fable for James," The Fiddlehead, no. 75 (Spring 1968), 25-40.

4719 Hull, E. M. "The Sheik," Cosmopolitan, CLX (February 1966), 104-109.

4720 Huma, Humayun. "Mahwa," Pakistan Review, XIV (July 1966), 29, 33.

4721 Humason, S. W. M. "And Be My Love," Ladies' Home Journal, LXXXII (October 1965), 78-80, 163-165.

4722 ______. "Mrs. Ambrose and Several Other People," Woman's Day, (September 1968), 50-51, 101-105.

4723 Humes, Harry. "From Here to There Isn't Far," Greensboro Review, II (December 1966), 5-14.

4724 Humphrey, James E. " Something Important," North American Mentor, IV (Summer 1966), 39-41.

4725 Humphrey, William. "The Gaudiest Thing on Wheels," Saturday Evening Post, CCXXXVIII (August 28, 1965), 60-64, 66-67.

4726 ______. "A Home away from Home," Saturday Evening Post, CCXLI (September 7, 1968), 56-59.

4727 ______. "The Human Fly," Esquire, LXX (September 1968), 128-130, 152, 156-157.

4728 ______. "A Job of the Plains," Quarterly Review of Literature, XIII (1965), 440-461.

4729 ______. "The Last of the Caddos," Esquire, LXX (October 1968), 189-192, 213, 222-223, 227.

4730 ______. "Mrs. Shumlin's Cow Trixie," Esquire, LXXII (December 1969), 246-247, 277-278, 280, 282.

4731 ______. "The Rainmaker," Saturday Evening Post, CCXL (December 2, 1967), 62-64, 66-67, 70, 74-77.

4732 Humphreys, J. R. "Dolf and the Outre Silence," Chelsea, no. 27 (December 1969), 9-47.

4733 _____. "The Young Soldier Shows His Wounds," Chelsea, no. 26 (May 1969), 45-46.

4734 Humphreys, Josephine. "All My Lovely Daughters," The Archive, LXXIX (May 1967), 5-7.

4735 _____. "Nightingales and Wine," The Archive, LXXIX (April 1967), 5-6.

4736 Humphreys, Kaki. "The Garden," The Archive, LXXX (April 1968), 7-10, 31.

4737 _____. "Weekend Home," The Archive, LXXX (May 1968), 23-27.

4738 Humphreys, Larry G. "No More Worthy," Corral 1966, 45-56.

4739 _____. "Tanya," Corral 1966, 70-81.

4740 _____. "Tanya," Story: the Yearbook of Discovery, (1969), 107-115.

4741 Huncke, Herbert. "Beware of Fallen Angels," Niagara Frontier Review, (Spring-Summer 1965), 43-53.

4742 _____. "Johnny I," Intrepid, no. 5 (March 1965), n.p. [15-17].

4743 _____. "A New Orleans Scene," San Francisco Earthquake, I (Winter 1968), 47-49.

4744 _____. "Sea Voyage," Niagara Frontier Review, (Spring-Summer 1965), 5-13.

4745 Huneeus, Cristián. "Couple with a Grant," Delta (Cambridge, England), no. 39 (Summer 1966), 23-28.

4746 _____. "The House at Algarrobo," Gordon Brotherston, trans., Stand, VIII, no. 2 (1966), 46-58.

4747 Hungerford, T. A. G. "The Budgerigar," Westerly, (May 1965), 12-22.

4748 _____. "Final Round," Westerly, no. 1 (April 1969), 5-9.

4749 _____. "Over the Garden Wall," Westerly, no. 4 (December 1969), 12-27.

4750 _____. "The Voyager," Westerly, no. 4 (1967), 5-11.

4751 Hunt, Chris. "Wind and Window Flower," William and Mary Review, IV (Spring 1966), 9-12.

4752 Hunt, Helen. "The Cry," Southerly, (1969), 63-68.

4753 _____. "Miss Carroll," Westerly, no. 4 (December 1968), 31-34.

4754 Hunt, Hugh Allyn. "Acme Rooms and Sweet Marjorie Russell," Transatlantic Review, no. 20 (Spring 1966), 5-19.

4755 _____. "Ciji's Gone," Transatlantic Review, no. 30 (Autumn 1968), 74-84.

4756 _____. "A Mole's Coat," Transatlantic Review, no. 32 (Summer 1969), 130-134.

4757 _____. "Rebuilding in a Brittle World," Perspective, XIV (Winter 1966), 119-128.

4758 Hunt, Jane. "Sarah Waiting/Part 1," Seventeen, XXV (June 1966), 108-109, 167-175.

4759 _____. "Sarah, Waiting/Part 2," Seventeen, XXV (July 1966), 96-97, 129-130, 132-133.

4760 Hunter, David. "Goodbye Dinosaur," Plaintiff, IV (Fall-Winter 1967-68), 47-48.

4761 _____. "Herb's Dumb Story," Plaintiff, IV (Spring-Summer 1968), 3-4.

4762 _____. "It Was a Good Dream, Wasn't It?" Plaintiff, V (Fall 1968), 8-12.

4763 Hunter, E. N. "A Novel in Progress," Statement, no. 22 (Fall 1966), 47-57.

4764 Hunter, Evan. "Beginnings," Playboy, XVI (July 1969), 76-78, 90, 192-196, 200-202.

4765 _____. "The Birthday Party," Playboy, XII (December 1965), 168-172, 246, 248.

4766 _____. "A Horse's Head," Playboy, XIV (July 1967), 60-62, 156-158, 160-164.

4767 _____. "A Horse's Head/Part II," Playboy, XIV (August 1967), 98-100, 104, 158, 160-164, 166-168.

4768 _____. "Last Summer," Ladies' Home Journal, LXXXV (May 1968), 143-150, 152-156.

4769 _____. "The Paper Dragon," Ladies' Home Journal, LXXXIII (June 1966), 89-96, 136-138, 140.

4770 _____. "The Sharers," Playboy, XIV (November 1967), 90-92, 206-208, 210.

4771 _____. "Wilt Thou Have This Woman?" McCall's, XCVI (August 1969), 58-59, 123, 128.

4772 Hunter, Kristin. "Debut," Negro Digest, XVII (June 1968), 62-69.

4773 Hunter, Robert. "Erebus," Evergreen Review, XIII (June 1969), 22-25, 66-72.

4774 Hunting, Constance. "Downwards to Morning," Quartet, no. 20 (Fall 1967), 1-4.

4775 Huntington, E. G. "Katey Darling," Redbook, CXXIX (October 1967), 66-67, 135-137.

4776 Huntley, Christopher N. "Your Seaward Demarcation," Michigan Quarterly Review, VI (Fall 1967), 292-295.

4777 Huntley, Timothy Wade. "Bum," Evergreen Review, XIII (July 1969), 66-68.

4778 Hupp, Sandra. "Intaglio," Arx, II (June 1968), 2-22.

4779 _____. "Matadors in Paradise," Arx, II (September 1968), 2-6.

4780 _____. "An Ordinary Malady," Arx, I (March 1968), 25-26, 28-32.

4781 _____. "A Proper Gypsy," Arx, I (December 1967), 4-17.

4782 Hurd, Douglas and Andrew Osmond. "The Smile on the Face of the Tiger," Imprint, IX (May 1969), 21-29, 31, 33, 35, 37, 39, 41, 43, 45, 47, 49, 51, 53, 55, 57, 59, 61, 63, 65, 67, 69, 71, 73, 75, 77, 79, 81, 83, 85, 87, 89, 91, 93-116.

4783 Hurlburt, Kaatje. "The Secret," Redbook, CXXXI (July 1968), 50-52, 100-102.

4784 Hurreh, Ismael. "I, You, the Whorehouse," Intro, no. 1 (September 1968), 170-194.

4785 Hurst, James. "The Summer of Two Figs," Transatlantic Review, no. 20 (Spring 1966), 136-152.

4786 Hurt, Henry. "The Chumbleys and the Law," Southern Review,

II (January 1966), 134-148.

4787 Husain, Mir Abul. "The Third Man," Mesbahuddin Ahmed, trans., Review, I (March-April 1968), 76-83.

4788 Hussain, Sagheer. "The Lonely Scholar," Pakistan Review, XIII (December 1965), 35-37.

4789 Hutchins, Maude. "Blood on the Doves," Ramparts, IV (February 1966), 51-65.

4790 Hutchinson, Duane. "The Open Door," Prairie Schooner, XLI (Summer 1967), 185-187.

4791 Huth, P. A. D. "Introduction and Allegro," The Cantuarian, (August 1967), 458-459.

4792 Hutsalo, Evgen. "Inna and Mudrik," Anthony Wixley, trans., Soviet Literature, (no. 9, 1968), 111-123.

4793 Hutter, Donald. "Valedictory," Esquire, LXV (May 1966), 110-111, 144, 148, 150, 154, 156-158.

4794 Hutton, Bill. "Billy Ziegfeld Is Not My Name," Intrepid, no. 8 (June 1967), n.p. [19].

4795 ______. "The Declaration of Independence," Work, no. 5 (1968), 93.

4796 ______. "The Musicians Are Out in the Snow," Work, no. 3 (Winter 1965-1966), 70-74.

4797 ______. "Peach Melba Atomic Bastard Insane," Wild Dog, no. 21 (March 1966), 19-22.

4798 ______. "'Saloon'," Work, no. 1 (Summer 1965), 36-39.

4799 ______. "Squaw Creek Orgy," Work, no. 2 (Fall 1965), 50-56.

4800 ______. "The Strange Odyssey of Howard Pow!" Work, no. 4 (Summer/Fall/Winter 1966), 107-112.

4801 ______. "'Who's Your Pal?'," Art and Literature, no. 11 (Winter 1967), 196-207.

4802 Huu, Mai. "Wings," Stephen Wang and Brian Fisher, trans., Eastern Horizon, V (December 1966), 54-64.

4803 Hyde, Eleanor. "Footsteps on the Roof," Arizona Quarterly, XXII (Autumn 1966), 223-231.

4804 ______. "The Winner," December, VIII (1966), 54-61.

4805 Hyde, Robert McKee. "Wind in the Papyrus," California Review, no. 1 (Spring 1967), 28-32.

4806 Hyde, Wayne F. "I Know You from Someplace," Dare, III (November-December 1965), 20-21.

4807 Hyman, Sarah G. J. "Autumn Leaves," Silo, no. 10 (Fall 1966), 7-15.

4808 Hyman, Susan. "A Mon Seul Désir," Grecourt Review, VIII (April 1965), 29-31.

4809 Hymer, Robert. "Fighting Back," Spectrum, VIII (Winter 1965), 66-68.

4810 _____. "My Uncle's Marriage," Spectrum, VIII (Spring 1965), 41-49.

4811 _____. "Walter Milestone," Spectrum, VIII (Winter 1965), 69-71.

4812 Hyry, Antti. "Cloudberries," John R. Pitkin, trans., American Scandinavian Review, LV (December 1967), 391-392.

4813 Iaquinto, Lorraine. "Roses Are Blue," Columbia, XLVI (April 1966), 24-27.

4814 Ibbotson, Eva. "The Bellingham Baby," Ladies' Home Journal, LXXXV (August 1968), 66-67, 115-116.

4815 _____. "The Girl Who Liked Houses," Woman's Day, (January 1966), 36-37, 78-82.

4816 _____. "A Most Essential Marriage," Ladies' Home Journal, LXXXVI (July 1969), 70-71, 121-122, 128.

4817 _____. "Why Weep for Otto?" Ladies' Home Journal, LXXXVI (September 1969), 104-105, 166, 168-169, 171.

4818 _____. "With Love from Dominic," McCall's, XCVI (October 1968), 90-91, 139-141.

4819 Ibragimbekov, Maksud. "The Aroma of Life," Alice Ingman, trans., Soviet Literature, (no. 12, 1969), 52-82.

4820 Ibsen, Brian P. "Monica," Yale Literary Magazine, CXXXV (March 1967), 27-29.

4821 Ibuse Masjui. "At Mr. Tange's," Sadamichi Yokoo and Sanford Goldstein, trans., Literature East and West, XIII (June 1969), 167-181.

4822 _____. "Black Rain," John Bester, trans., Japan Quarterly,

XIV (April-June 1967), 187-215.

4823 _____. "Black Rain II," John Bester, trans., Japan Quarterly, XIV (July-September 1967), 333-357.

4824 _____. "Black Rain III," John Bester, trans., Japan Quarterly, XIV (October-December 1967), 469-489.

4825 _____. "Black Rain IV," John Bester, trans., Japan Quarterly, XV (January-March 1968), 69-98.

4826 _____. "Black Rain V," John Bester, trans., Japan Quarterly, XV (April-June 1968), 194-223.

4827 _____. "Black Rain VI," John Bester, trans., Japan Quarterly, XV (July-September 1968), 330-359.

4828 _____. "Kuro, the Fighting Cock," Yokichi Miyamoto and Frederic Will, trans., Chicago Review, XIX, no. 1 (1966), 83-89.

4829 _____. "The Salamander," Yokoo Sadamichi and Sanford Goldstein, trans., Japan Quarterly, XIII (January-March 1966), 71-75.

4830 _____. "Swan on the Roof," Yokichi Miyamoto and Frederic Will, trans., Chicago Review, XIX, no. 1 (1966), 51-54.

4831 Idrees, Hafiz Muhammad. "Elopement," Ahsan Tahir, trans., Pakistan Review, XVI (February 1968), 35-36.

4832 Idriss, Yussef. "The Aorta," Vision, XVII (September 1968), 7-8, 18.

4833 Iglauer, Edith. "The Beautiful Day," New Yorker, XLII (March 19, 1966), 53-56.

4834 Ignatow, Rose Graubert. "The Brown Duck," Carleton Miscellany, VIII (Fall 1967), 36-39.

4835 _____. "Colors," Carleton Miscellany, VII (Fall 1966), 37-41.

4836 Igo, John. "The Gesture," Epoch, XVIII (Spring 1969), 247-256.

4837 Ik, Kim Young. "From Here You Can See the Moon," Texas Quarterly, XI (Summer 1968), 201-208.

4838 Ilf, Ilya and Evgeni Petrov. "A Man of Many Parts," Soviet Literature, (no. 4, 1967), 93-96.

4839 Illés, Endre. "The Lieutenant's Wife," New Hungarian Quarterly, VI (Summer 1965), 96-103.

4840 Illyés, Gyula. "Orator in the Night," New Hungarian Quarterly, VIII (Winter 1967), 15-21.

4841 Il Tedesco, Gino. "Fog Ducking," Wild Dog, no. 14 (February 1965), 17-18.

4842 _____. "Fog Ducking," Wild Dog, no. 15 (March 1965), 24-25.

Imamu Amiri Baraka. See LeRoi Jones.

4843 Imbrie, Nora. "French Leave," Queen's Quarterly, LXXIII (Winter 1966), 573-578.

4844 Ingalls, Susan. "The Ideal Couple," Seventeen, XXVIII (November 1969), 130-131, 172, 175-178.

4845 _____. "A Perverse Madonna in Love," Seventeen, XXVIII (June 1969), 124-125, 134-135.

4846 Ingler, James. "Monkeys of the Temple," Southwest Review, LII (Summer 1967), 262-272.

4847 Ingram, Alyce. "The Blue Madonna," North American Review, IV (May 1967), 26-28.

4848 _____. "Madame Butterfly," North American Review, VI (Fall 1969), 65-66.

4849 _____. "The Original Investment," North American Review, II (Spring 1965), 24-27.

4850 _____. "The Pocahontas Part," North American Review, III (July 1966), 24-26.

4851 _____. "The Tinkle-Bell," North American Review, VI (Spring 1969), 49-51.

4852 Iniguez, Maria L. "The Man Who Hated Violence," Ante, IV (Summer-Fall 1968), 47-51.

4853 _____. "The Tightrope," Ante, III (Summer 1967), 11-15.

4854 Inman, Robert. "I'll Call You," Quarterly Review of Literature, XVI, nos. 3-4 (1969), 360-389.

4855 Innerst, Ivan. "That Spring," Southwest Review, LIV (Summer 1969), 120-131.

4856 Ionesco, Eugène. "Slime," Robert Lamont, trans., Evergreen Review, X (June 1966), 22-27, 69-70.

4857 Iorio, John J. "Jacob," Arizona Quarterly, XXII (Autumn 1966), 253-257.

4858 _____. "The Man in the Black Apron," Southern Review, III (October 1967), 990-1000.

4859 _____. "Rahab," The Quest, II (Fall 1967), 169-186.

4860 _____. "The Recognition," Southern Review, II (January 1966), 166-178.

4861 _____. "A Well Ordered Life," Colorado Quarterly, XIV (Summer 1965), 72-77.

4862 _____. "The White Wall," Prairie Schooner, XXXIX (Spring 1965), 42-52.

4863 _____. "Woman on an Island," Four Quarters, XVIII (November 1968), 9-21.

4864 Iqbal, N. Najmuddin. "The Atonement," Pakistan Review, XIII (June 1965), 27-29.

4865 Irbe, Andrejs. "Tale of a Return," Ruth Speirs, trans., Literary Review, VIII (Spring 1965), 423-429.

4866 Irshad-Ul-Hassan. "The Doll," Pakistan Review, XIII (February 1965), 23-24.

4867 Irvine, Connie. "The Fool," Prism International, VII (Summer 1967), 82-94.

4868 Irving, John. "A Winter Branch," Redbook, CXXVI (November 1965), 56-57, 143-146.

4869 Isaksson, Ulla. "Gift of God," Sven Karell and Edith Aney Davidson, trans., Literary Review, IX (Summer 1966), 612-621.

4870 Ishmael. "Sleeping Beauty," Transatlantic Review, no. 26 (Autumn 1967), 61-70.

4871 Ishman, Robert T. "Things Are Getting a Little Dull Around Here, Anyway," Human Voice, IV, no. 3 (1968), 36-38.

4872 Iskander, Fazil. "Old Crooked Arm," Robert Daglish, trans., Soviet Literature, (no. 6, 1968), 67-92.

4873 Ismail, Taufiq. "Robbers, Robbers," Yanti Soebiakto, trans., Solidarity, III (November 1968), 3-15.

4874 Israel, Charles E. "The Hostages," Redbook, CXXVII (July 1966), 129, 131-161.

4875 Israel, Peter. "In Praise of Solitary Constructs," New Orleans Review, I (Winter 1969), 125-127.

4876 _____. "Scoring on Big Blonde," Esquire, LXIX (February 1968), 102-103, 120-121.

4877 Iverson, Jim. "Stanley," UMD Humanist, XV (Winter 1967), 29-31.

4878 Iwaszkiewicz, Jarosław. "The Badger," Ilona Ralf Sues, trans., Literary Review, X (Spring 1967), 267-271.

4879 Jabotinsky, Vladimir. "A Tale of the Dark Ages," Midstream, XII (August-September 1966), 26-36.

4880 Jackel, Karen. "Down They Go," Bennington Review, III (Fall 1969), 37-50.

4881 _____. "Their Meeting," Harper's Bazaar, CI (August 1968), 78, 96, 99, 116.

4882 Jackson, Bill. "And Did He Smile," American, I (Spring 1965), 23-25.

4883 Jackson, Carlton. "Wergild," Southern Humanities Review, I (Summer 1967), 151-157.

4884 Jackson, Charles. "The Lady Julia," McCall's, XCII (April 1965), 110-111, 160-164, 166-167.

4885 Jackson, Glenn F. "The Money Tree," Discourse, XII (Summer 1969), 368-375.

4886 _____. "Gibraltor," Literary Review, X (Winter 1966-67), 231-240.

4887 _____. "How Much Do You Love Me?" Quartet, no. 20 (Fall 1967), 9-13.

4888 _____. "Seven Days and One Night," Twigs, no. 5 (Fall 1969), 43-50.

4889 Jackson, Mae. "I Remember Omar," Negro Digest, XVIII (June 1969), 83-85.

4890 Jackson, Shirley. "The Bus," Saturday Evening Post, CCXXXVIII (March 27, 1965), 62-63, 65-67.

4891 _____. "Come Along with Me," McCall's, XCVI (February 1969), 72-73, 118-126.

4892 _____. "Home," Ladies' Home Journal, LXXXII (August 1965), 64-65, 116, 118.

4893 _____. "The Possibility of Evil," Saturday Evening Post, CCXXXVIII (December 18, 1965), 61-64, 68-69.

4894 Jackson, William Dean. "Book of Matches," American, II (Spring 1966), 42-45.

4895 _____. "Strategic Target," American, II (Fall 1966), 28-31.

4896 Jacob, Frances. "Joey," Colorado Quarterly, XVI (Spring 1968), 353-369.

4897 Jacob, Max. "Adventure Story," Ron Padgett, trans., The Once Series (Frice), I (1966-67), n.p. [7].

4898 _____. "Christmas Story," Ron Padgett, trans., The Once Series (Frice) I (1966-67), n.p. [7].

4899 _____. "The Enemy of the Citadel," Ted Berrigan, trans., The Once Series (Slice), I (1966-67), n.p. [16].

4900 _____. "Genre Biographie," Ted Berrigan, trans., The Once Series (Slice, no. 1), I (1966-67), n.p. [16].

4901 _____. "The Key," Ron Padgett, trans., The Once Series (Frice), I (1966-67), n.p. [7].

4902 _____. "Literary Ways," Tom Clark, trans., The World, no. 4 (June 1967), n.p. [36].

4903 _____. "The Name," Serge Gavronsky, trans., Chicago Review, XVIII, nos. 3 & 4 (1966), 83-90.

4904 _____. "The Non-Solitary Walker," Serge Gavronsky, trans., Chicago Review, XVIII, nos. 3 & 4(1966), 91-94.

4905 _____. "Spanish Generosity," Armand Schwerner, trans., Damascus Road, no. 2 (1965), 48.

4906 _____. "Symbolic Egyptienne," Ted Berrigan, trans., The Once Series (Slice, no. 1), I (1966-67), n.p. [16].

4907 _____. "Urgency," Armand Schwerner, trans., Damascus Road, no. 2 (1965), 47.

4908 _____. "Valiant Warrior on Foreign Soil," Ron Padgett, trans., The Once Series (Frice), I (1966-67), n.p. [7].

4909 _____. "The War," Ted Berrigan, trans., The Once Series (Slice, no. 1), I (1966-67), n.p. [16].

4910 _____. "Z False News! New Graves!" Michael Brownstein, trans., The World, no. 13 (November 1968), n.p. [21].

4911 Jacobs, Harvey. "A Break in the Weather," Cosmopolitan, CLXV (December 1968), 144-148.

4912 _____. "The Death of an Onlooker," Esquire, LXIX (June 1968), 96, 182.

4913 _____. "Disturbance of the Peace," New Worlds, no. 183. (October 1968), 4-12, 18.

4914 _____. "The Girl Who Drew the Gods," Mademoiselle, LXI (May 1965), 174-175, 222-228.

4915 _____. "The Negotiators," Esquire, LXXI (April 1969), 128, 44, 48, 50, 52, 54.

4916 _____. "Sideshow," Status, II (January/February 1966), 40-41, 92, 94, 96.

4917 Jacobs, Judith. "And Waking, the Dream Goes on...," Harvard Advocate, CI (December 1967), 4-7.

4918 Jacobs, Marjorie K. " Sins of Fathers," Phylon, XXIX (Summer 1968), 199-207.

4919 Jacobs, R. Bradley. "The Lady in Tweed," Lance, V (Winter 1965), 4-5.

4920 _____. "The Old Man and the Bear," Lance, V (Spring 1965), 18-23.

4921 Jacobsen, Jens Peter. "Dr. Faust," Peter H. Salus, trans., The Quest, I (Winter 1965-1966), 57-59.

4922 _____. "The Plaque in Bergamo," Peter H. Salus, trans., The Quest, I (Winter 1965-1966), 47-56.

4923 _____. "There Should Have Been Roses," Peter H. Salus, trans., American Scandinavian Review, LV (December 1967), 393-396.

4924 Jacobsen, Josephine. "The Glen," Epoch, XVI (Spring 1967), 275-287.

4925 _____. "The Jungle of Lord Lion," Epoch, XIX (Fall 1969), 18-28.

4926 _____. "On the Island," Kenyon Review, XXVII (Autumn 1965), 675-691.

4927 _____. "The Taxi," Prairie Schooner, XLI (Winter 1967), 398-409.

4928 Jacobson, Dan. "Boaz and the Israelites," Commentary, XLV

(February 1968), 40-52.

4929 _____. "Led Astray," New Yorker, XL (January 23, 1965), 34-39.

4930 _____. "Sonia," Commentary, XXXIX (May 1965), 47-50.

4931 _____. "Sonia," Weekend Telegraph, no. 51 (September 10. 1965), 43-44, 47, 49.

4932 _____. "Two Israeli Scenes," Quest, no. 1 (September 1965), 6-9.

4933 Jaffe, Rona. "Rose White and Rose Red," Saturday Evening Post, CCXXXIX (September 10, 1966), 66-68, 70.

4934 Jagendorf, Zvi. "The House in Jerusalem," Midstream, XV (March 1969), 40-48.

4935 Jahnn, Jans Henny. "A Master Chooses His Manservant," Art and Literature, no. 8 (Spring 1966), 161-178.

4936 Jain, Sunita. "The Princes Are Pawned," Prairie Schooner, XLIII (Fall 1969), 276-280.

4937 _____. "A Woman Is Dead," Sunita Jain, trans., Arizona Quarterly, XXII (Winter 1966), 313-318.

4938 Jalil, Rakhim. "Pulat and Gulru/(Chapters from the Novel)," Alice Ingman, trans., Soviet Literature, (no. 9, 1967), 21-34.

4939 James, Alan. "Beyond Chicago Someone Sleeps," Negro Digest, XVI (March 1967), 67-72.

4940 James, Betty Payne. "Let Fall No Burning Leaf," Story: the Yearbook of Discovery, (1969), 63-74.

4941 _____. "A Winter's Tale," Intro, no. 2 (September 1969), 3-8.

4942 James, Sinzer. "The End," Dust, II (Winter 1966), 55-56.

4943 _____. "The Funeral and the Funeral-Baked Meats," Nexus (San Francisco, Calif.), II (January-February 1965), 49-57.

4944 _____. "Marine with Moray," Dust, I (Winter 1965), 69-71.

4945 Jameson, F. A. "Growing Up in Patterson, N.J., 1945," Queen's Quarterly, LXXIV (Spring 1967), 176-181.

4946 Jameson, Fredric. "Living the Dead Life in America," Tri-Quarterly, no. 15 (Spring 1969), 71-87.

4947 Jamieson, Michael. "Parties," Ambit, no. 28 (1966), 29-32.

4948 Janigian, Charles J. "Journey Around the Camel Hairs," Armenian Review, XVIII (Winter 1965), 46-48.

4949 Janus, Christopher G. "Sacha's Prize Possessions," Athene, XXVIII (Spring-Summer 1967), 14-16.

4950 Japrisot, Sebastien. "The Lady in the Car," Cosmopolitan, CLXIV (June 1968), 140-146, 148-155, 160-162, 164, 166-172.

4951 Jarasandha. "The Price of Revolution," Basudha Chakravarty, trans., Triveni, XXXV (July 1966), 27-42.

4952 Jarrett, Ann. "The Thyme Snails," Epoch, XVIII (Winter 1969), 149-164.

4953 Jašik, Rudolf. "White Stones," Káča Poláčková, trans., Literary Review, XIII (Fall 1969), 90-97.

4954 Jasudowicz, Dennis. "Diarrhoea," VDRSVPVDRSVPVDRSVP, (1969), n.p. [front and back pages].

4955 _____. "Mammyduke's Ghost," San Francisco Earthquake, I (Winter 1968), 52-54.

4956 Jazmines, Alan. "Chinatown: Impressions," Diliman Review, XIII (October 1965), 355-358.

4957 Jegerings, R. "The Raise Manipulator," Northwest Review, VIII (Fall-Winter 1966-67), 68-82.

4958 Jenkins, Lee. "Sherrie," Texas Quarterly, X (Summer 1967), 48-56.

4959 Jenning, Michael. "Arithmetic," Man About Town, I (June/July 1967), 30-31, 44.

4960 _____. "Kissing Jamie Carey," Seventeen, XXV (November 1966), 158-159, 219-220.

4961 _____. "A Prone and Speechless Dialect," Seventeen, XXV (January 1966), 77, 109.

4962 Jennings, Michael S. "The Ball Field," Carolina Quarterly, XIX (Fall 1967), 33-37.

4963 Jennings, Murray. "Blues for Crowley," Westerly, no. 2 (July 1968), 9-13.

4964 Jensen, Eileen. "First Love, the Second Time," Ladies' Home Journal, LXXXIII (April 1966), 90-91, 131-132, 133-134.

4965 _____. "Touch of Magic," Good Housekeeping, CLXV (November 1967), 98-99.

4966 _____. "Wife and Mother," Good Housekeeping, CLXVIII (January 1969), 82-83.

4967 _____. "The Wisdom of the Heart," Good Housekeeping, CLXIX (September 1969), 80-81, 135-139.

4968 Jensen, James B. "It Makes a Difference," Delta, XX (1966), 17-25.

4969 Jensen, Johannes V. "The Moon City," Lee M. Hollander, trans., Literary Review, XII (Spring 1969), 360-366.

4970 Jensen, Margaret Mary. "Alison," Ave Maria, CV (February 25, 1967), 26-28.

4971 _____. "The Likes of MacAdee," Ave Maria, CV (March 11, 1967), 22-25.

4972 Jepsen, Hans Lyngby. "The Blackbird," David Stoner, trans., American Scandinavian Review, LVI (March 1968), 60-65.

4973 _____. "Jezebel and the Shoemaker," Eva Schweizer Vogel, trans., American Scandinavian Review, LVII (September 1969), 283-288.

4974 Jerome, Judson. "Sunday with Sally," Epoch, XV (Winter 1966), 169-181.

4975 Jerrard, Margot. "Long Honeymoon," Redbook, CXXXIII (October 1969), 94-95, 212-214, 216.

4976 Jespersen, Ruth. "High Dudgeon," Prism International, V (Winter-Spring 1966), 94-117.

4977 _____. "Mildred," Quartet, no. 26 (Spring 1969), 3-8.

4978 Jhabvala, R. Prawer. "A Bad Woman," London Magazine, VI (September 1966), 13-30.

4979 _____. "A Course of English Studies," Cornhill Magazine, CLXXVII (Autumn-Winter 1968-69), 35-36.

4980 _____. "A Course of English Studies," Kenyon Review, XXX (1968), 43-66.

4981 _____. "Foreign Wives," London Magazine, VII (January 1968), 12-22.

4982 _____. "In Love with a Beautiful Girl," New York, XLI (January 15, 1966), 31-39.

4983 ______. "An Indian Citizen," New Yorker, XLIII (September 30, 1967), 38-46.

4984 ______. "The Man with the Dog," New Yorker, XLII (November 19, 1966), 52-60.

4985 ______. "Passion," New Yorker, XLIII (December 2, 1967), 56-64.

4986 ______. "A Spiritual Call," Cornhill Magazine, no. 1049 (Autumn 1966), 335-354.

4987 ______. "The Young Couple," London Magazine, VI (January 1967), 11-24.

4988 ______. "A Young Man of Good Family," Cornhill Magazine, no. 1053 (Autumn 1967), 168-188.

4989 Jobes, Lavon Mattes. "The Minority," Phylon, XXIX (Spring 1968), 76-80.

4990 Johannes, R. "A Tanglewood Tale," Antioch Review, XXVI (Summer 1966), 171-183.

4991 Johnson, Arnold. "The Deep Woods," Human Voice, IV, nos. 1 & 2 (1968), 86-91.

4992 Johnson, B. S. "Aren't You Rather Young to Be Writing Your Memoirs?" Transatlantic Review, no. 25 (Summer 1967), 83-87.

4993 ______. "These Count as Fictions," Encounter, XXX (February 1968), 46-50.

4994 ______. "from Trawl," Ambit, no. 29 (1966), 27-29.

4995 ______. "Extract from 'Trawl'," Transatlantic Review, no. 21 (Summer 1966), 25-29.

4996 ______. "Extract from The Unfortunates," Transatlantic Review, no. 28 (Spring 1968), 23-27.

4997 Johnson, Curt. "Able, Baker, Automation," Vagabond, no. 5 (Summer 1967), 22-24.

4998 ______. "Appointment with the Photographer," Arx, II (December 1968), 2-11.

4999 ______. "Blue Bird," Midwestern University Quarterly, I, no. 3 (1966), 55-61.

5000 ______. "Bottle of Wine," Jeopardy, no. 5 (Spring 1969), 182-192.

5001 _____. "Circus," Minnesota Review, VII (1967), 254-271.

5002 _____. "An End to Abléphary/A Story in Five Chapters from a Novel of the Same Name in Endless Progress," Midwestern University Quarterly, II, no. 1 (1966), 130-148.

5003 _____. "Gasserpod, Gasserpod!" Minnesota Review, VIII (1968), 291-308.

5004 _____. "Jaquar," Sou'wester, (Spring 1969), 72-73.

5005 _____. "A Question of Ethics," Aspects, no. 10 (August 1967), 1-3.

5006 _____. "Story," Vagabond, I, no. 3 (1966), 21-24.

5007 _____. "Turn the C, Make an E," Pyramid, no. 6 (1969), 15-18.

5008 Johnson, Doris. "Somebody," Negro Digest, XVII (November 1967), 75-77.

5009 Johnson, Dorothy M. "The Ten-Pound Box of Candy," McCall's, XCIII (April 1966), 92-93, 194-196.

5010 Johnson, Eyvind. "'Interruption in Marshland'," May Broman and Basil Ashmore, trans., Adam International Review, nos. 304-306 (1966), 16-24.

5011 Johnson, James A. "Super Sauna or a Trip to New Helsinki 1967," UMD Humanist, XVII (Spring 1969), 17-19.

5012 Johnson, James William. "Von Doom Comes at Night," Ball State University Forum, VI (Spring 1965), 11-20.

5013 Johnson, Kay. "The Emerald City," The Outsider, nos. 4 & 5 (1968-69), 188-190.

5014 Johnson, Lemuel. "Melon Flowers," Literary Review, XII (Spring 1969), 334-356.

5015 Johnson, Mary Eugenia. "The Ring," New Leaven, no. 16 (1966), 44-52.

5016 Johnson, Myron. "A Boy, a Girl and a Sunday," Edge, no. 6 (Spring 1967), 67-72.

5017 _____. "The Hitchiker," Alphabet, no. 12 (August 1966), 22-25.

5018 Johnson, Patricia. "The Confidant," New Zealand Listener, (October 20, 1967), 6.

5019 _____. "In Memoriam," New Zealand Listener, LVIII (July 5, 1968), 10, 24.

5020 Johnson, Paul. "December Snow," Athanor, I (Spring 1967), 33-51.

5021 _____. "December Snow," Win, II, nos. 14 & 15 (August 1966), 9-16.

5022 Johnson, Raymond. "Rainbow Bridge," Minnesota Review, VII (1967), 117-126.

5023 _____. "The Stuff of History," Four Quarters, XVII (November 1967), 15-21.

5024 _____. "A Trip Beyond the Bay," Texas Quarterly, IX (Autumn 1966), 51-60.

5025 Johnson, Richard. "Prelude in Black and White," Discourse, XI (Spring 1968), 215-219.

5026 _____. "The Red-Haired Boy," North American Review, IV (July 1967), 9-10.

5027 _____. "The Temple to God," Four Quarters, XVI (January 1967), 24-31.

5028 Johnson, Robert C. "Elizabeth," The Archive, LXXX (September 1967), 19-21.

5029 Johnson, Sikes. "The Loser," Denver Quarterly, III (Autumn 1968), 39-72.

5030 Johnson, Steve. "The Song," December, XII (1965), 181-185.

5031 Johnson, Victor H. "The Case of the Sunday Morning Woodpecker," Texas Quarterly, IX (Spring 1966), 137-139.

5032 _____. "The Clothespin Birds," Texas Quarterly, IX (Spring 1966), 139-142.

5033 _____. "The Militant Mockers," Texas Quarterly, IX (Spring 1966), 142-145.

5034 Johnston, Arnold. "Marginal," Colorado Quarterly, XVIII (Autumn 1969), 145-165.

5035 Johnston, Tod. "A Tree Not Named," Crucible, I (Spring 1965), 16.

5036 _____. "The Visit," Crucible, II (Fall 1965), 52-53.

5037 Johnston, Velda. "The Phantom Cottage," Redbook, CXXXIV

(December 1969), 169-191.

5038 Johnstone, Rick. "nunc dimittis," Quarry, XV (March 1966), 31-32.

5039 ______. "Two Pages from a Journal," Quarry, no. 14 (1964-65), 27-28.

5040 Joiner, Ron. "The Dead Cow," Assay, XXV (Spring 1969), 5-10.

5041 Jókai, Anna. "Hungarian Lesson," New Hungarian Quarterly, X (Spring 1969), 64-65.

5042 Jolas, Eugene. "While Dreaming Mexico," R. C. Robichaud, trans., Wormwood Review, VI, no. 3 (1966), 10.

5043 Jolley, Elizabeth. "A Hedge of Rosemary," Westerly, no. 2 (1967), 18-22.

5044 ______. "The Rhyme," Westerly, no. 4 (1967), 46-49.

5045 ______. "The Sick Vote," Quadrant, XII (September-October 1968), 43-46.

5046 Jonas, Gerald. "The Prince," Commentary, XLII (October 1966), 55-68.

5047 ______ and Jean Marple. "The Stand-in," Paris Review, XII (Summer 1969), 98-104.

5048 Jones, Ben. "Before I Split for Oklahoma I'd Like to Say that...," Carolina Quarterly, XXI (Spring 1969), 30-32.

5049 Jones, Dedwydd. "The Thinker," Limbo, I (February 1965), 18-20.

5050 Jones, Eleanor. "The Green Whale," Woman's Day, (February 1966), 38-39, 81, 85-86.

5051 ______. "The Heart's Call," Woman's Day, (September 1965), 46-47, 102-104.

5052 Jones, Ita. "The Creator," Arx, I (October 1967), 2-3.

5053 Jones, J. Jeffrey. "It Takes Guts to Play a Fiddle," Transatlantic Review, no. 24 (Spring 1967), 124-129.

5054 ______. "Motorcycle Appassionata," Transatlantic Review, no. 29 (Summer 1968), 98-103.

5055 Jones, LeRoi. "The Alternative," Transatlantic Review, no. 18 (Spring 1965), 46-60.

5056 _____. "Answers in Progress," Umbra, (1967-1968), 37-39.

5057 _____. "The Death of Horatio Alger," Evergreen Review, IX (June 1965), 28-29, 92-93.

5058 _____. "Doing Down Slow," Evergreen Review, X (October 1966), 41-43, 93-96.

5059 Jones, Madison. "An Exile," Sewanee Review, LXXV (January-March 1967), 25-158.

5060 _____. "Home Is Where the Heart Is," Arlington Quarterly, I (Spring 1968), 12-69.

5061 _____. "A Modern Case," Delta Review, VI (August 1969), 42-44, 72-75.

5062 Jones, Margaret. "Free Association," Cornhill Magazine, CLXXVI (Spring 1968), 343-348.

5063 _____. "The Trophy," Queen, CDXXIX (December 1, 1967), 97-99, 101, 103.

5064 Jones, Mary Lange. "A New and Gentle Light," Good Housekeeping, CLXIX (July 1969), 66-67, 132, 134, 136-137.

5065 Jones, Michael L. "The Youth and the Old Man," DeKalb Literary Arts Journal, II (Fall 1967), 1-2, 4-6.

5066 Jones, Raphael. "Ducks Don't Fly on a Cloudless Day," Shenandoah, XVIII (Spring 1967), 52-63.

5067 Jones, Roy. "The Conversion of Uncle Elwyn," Twentieth Century, CLXXV (First Quarter 1967), 26-28.

5068 Jones, Thomas G. "A Family Privation," Georgia Review, XXII (Spring 1968), 37-41.

5069 Jones, Violet. "A Bed for Nettie," Human Voice, IV, no. 4 (1968), 73-82.

5070 Jonker, Ingrid. "The Goat," Jack Cope, trans., London Magazine, VI (December 1966), 7-18.

5071 Jordan, Eileen Herbert. "The Bed Elizabeth Taylor Once Slept In," Redbook, CXXVII (May 1966), 50-51, 110-115.

5072 _____. "The Car-Sitter," McCall's, XCII (June 1965), 74-75, 156-159.

5073 _____. "'It's Not a Ranch,' Mr. Bertram Said, 'It's Not a Split-Level'," Ladies' Home Journal, LXXXVI (May 1969), 114-115, 173-177.

5074 _____. "The Man Who Stopped the Square Dance," Ladies' Home Journal, LXXXIV (August 1967), 70-71, 101-102, 104.

5075 _____. "O Come, O Come, Emmanuel," McCall's, XCVI (December 1968), 92-93, 134-136.

5076 _____. "Santa Claus and the Boy-Who-Knew-Everything," Woman's Day, (December 1968), 50-51, 74, 76-79, 83, 85.

5077 _____. "The Wanderer," McCall's, XCII (February 1965), 124-125, 197-201.

5078 _____. "The Weekends," Redbook, CXXXII (January 1969), 63, 119-122, 124.

5079 Jose, F. Sionil. "Something Is Wrong with My Hearing," Solidarity, III (May 1968), 59-70.

5080 Josephus. "David's Capture of Jerusalem, the Royal City," Adam International Review, nos. 325-327 (1968), 19-20.

5081 Joth, Gerald. "The Dwarf's Table," Works, II (Spring 1969), 53-56.

5082 Joyce, James. "Giacomo Joyce," Harper's Magazine, CCXXX-VI (January 1968), 27-30.

5083 Joyce, Larry. "Set 'em Up Again," Jeopardy, no. 1 (1966), 28-32.

5084 Joyce, William. "Rats," Story: the Yearbook of Discovery, (1969), 51-62.

5085 Jump, Barbara. "Babes in the Woods/A Romance," Malahat Review, no. 3 (July 1967), 5-15.

5086 _____. "The Fool Discovered," Malahat Review, no. 7 (July 1968), 46-61.

5087 _____. "A Haunt of Storks," Malahat Review, no. 12 (October 1969), 50-63.

5088 Jünger, Friedrich Georg. "The Button," Margaret D. Howie, trans., Scala International, (October 1967), 34-37.

5089 Junghanns, G. "No Vacancy," Arizona Quarterly, XXII (Spring 1966), 19-26.

5090 Jurale, Joan. "The Wooden Sparrow," Carolina Quarterly, XVIII (Winter 1966), 63-69.

5091 Jurkowski, John. "The More Things Change," Redbook, CXXXIII (August 1969), 73, 139, 141-142.

5092 I. A. K. "Under a Bed at Midnight," Pakistan Review, XIII (July 1965), 22-23.

5093 Kabak, Abraham Aba. "Jesus' First Visit to Jerusalem," Ronnie Greenberg, trans., Adam International Review, nos. 325-327 (1968), 113-114.

5094 Kadzako, E. B. "Hogo and Lenna," Expression, no. 1 (1968), 12-14.

5095 Kagan, Dona. [untitled], Focus, (Spring 1967), 5-6.

5096 ______. "Thoughts for Sara," Focus, (1968), 11.

5097 Kahiga, Samuel and Bernard Mbui. "Cops and Robbers," Nexus, I (August 1967), 9-11.

5098 ______. "In Silent Shadows," Nexus, I (January 1968), 12-14.

5099 ______ and Bernard Mbui. "The Oat," Nexus, I (1966), 5-7.

5100 Kahn, E. J., Jr. "The Raffle," Playboy, XIV (February 1967), 75, 177-178.

5101 Kain, Mary. "Miss Amy and the Magic Beans," Assay, XXI (Spring 1965), 5-10.

5102 Kaiser, Barbara. "Bring a Rose for Gentian," Florida Quarterly, I (Summer 1967), 34-44.

5103 Kakhar, Abdulla. "The Girls," Vladimir Talmy, trans., Soviet Literature, (no. 12, 1967), 34-37.

5104 Kalb, Jeffrey. "The Deli on Second Avenue," Washington Square Review, II (Winter 1966), 8-10.

5105 Kaleb, Vjekoslav. "The Arch of Triumph," Donald Davenport, trans., Literary Review, XI (Winter 1967), 167-172.

5106 Kalechofsky, Roberta. "Epiphany," Works, I (Spring 1968), 88-96, 98-102.

5107 Kalki. "Kedari's Mother," Santha Rangachari, trans., Indian Literature, IX (January-March 1966), 33-42.

5108 Kalumba, Larry Yoma. "Other Side," New Writing from Zambia, no. 1 (1968), 8-11.

5109 Kalyanasundaram, M. S. "Retrogressive?" Triveni, XXXV (October 1966), 54-61.

5110 Kamarck, Lawrence. "The Last Dinosaur," Cosmopolitan, CLXIV (March 1968), 168-172, 174-185, 187-188, 190-193.

5111 Kaminski, Gerald. "Keys," University Review, XXXIII (October 1966), 39-42.

5112 _____. "A Woman's Miscellany," December, X (1968), 89-93.

5113 Kaminsky, Akiva. "Upon the Graves," Literary Magazine of Tufts University, II, no. 1 (1967), 78-91.

5114 _____. "Watch at the Gritz," Literary Magazine of Tufts University, III (Winter 1968), 80-91.

5115 Kaminsky, Stuart M. "Drup Number One," New Mexico Quarterly, XXXV (Spring 1965), 63-75.

5116 Kaminsky, Wallace. "The Sound-Machine," University Review, XXXI (March 1965), 163-174.

5117 Kamiya, Taeko. "The Day of Miai," Literary Review, XII (Summer 1969), 459-471.

5118 Kanin, Garson. "Buddy-Buddy," Playboy, XIII (September 1966), 114-116, 122, 244-246, 248-249.

5119 _____. "Girl Overboard," Cosmopolitan, CLXVI (January 1969), 108-113.

5120 _____. "Money Man," McCall's, XCII (April 1965), 94-97, 184, 186, 188, 190, 192-193.

5121 _____. "The Only Game in Town," Playboy, XIII (December 1966), 182-184, 266, 268-270.

5122 Kanter, Annette. "Garden of Verses," Statement, no. 24 (Spring 1968), 7-9.

5123 Kantor, Mackinlay. "So Pretty and So Green," Playboy, XIII (December 1966), 141, 288, 292, 294.

5124 Kanungsattam, Pira. "A Passing Wind," Landfall, no. 75 (September 1965), 234-236.

5125 Kapfer, Bonny. "The Clover Chain," UMD Humanist, XVI (Spring 1968), 35-43.

5126 Kaplan, Bernard. "One of the Seas Is Called Tranquility," Antioch Review, XXIX (Winter 1969-70), 461-471.

5127 Kaplan, Johanna. "Sickness," Commentary, XLVI (December 1968), 53-61.

5128 _____. "Sour or Suntanned, It Makes No Difference," Commentary, XLVII (May 1969), 67-74.

5129 Kar, Bimal. "The Tiger," Bhabani P. Ghose, trans., Bengali Literature, I (June/August 1966), 5-22.

5130 _____. "We Three Lovers and Bhubon," Marcia Terzo, trans., Bengali Literature, II (Autumn 1967), 86-100.

5131 Karanja, David. "Till It Rains Blood," Pan-African Journal, II (Summer 1969), 319-323.

5132 Karaslavov, Georgi. "St. Peter's Chapel," Zdravko Stankov, trans., Obzor, (Spring 1968), 15-36.

5133 Karchmer, Sylvan. "The Esurient Teacher," Northwest Review, VIII (Summer 1966), 7-18.

5134 _____. "A Golden Trio," University Review, XXXVI (Autumn 1969), 22-28.

5135 _____. "Immunity," Little Review of the Pacific Northwest, I (Fall 1965), 50-57.

5136 _____. "The Lists," Ball State University Forum, VI (Spring 1965), 49-53.

5137 _____. "Professor Miracle," South Dakota Review, IV (Autumn 1966), 68-77.

5138 _____. "Ten Minutes," West Coast Review, I (Spring 1966), 22-27.

5139 Karinthy, Ferenc. "Ante, Apud," Literary Review, IX (Spring 1966), 400-403.

5140 Karlen, Arno. "The Wise Nudnik of Vitebsk," Queen, CDXXXII (May 14-27, 1969), 106.

5141 Karp, Eleanor. "How to Write 'New Yorker' Stories," Harper's Magazine, CCXXXIII (July 1966), 69-74.

5142 Karp, Ivan C. "Doobie Doo," Cosmopolitan, CLX (March 1966), 108-113.

5143 Kaschnitz, Marie Luise. "I Love Herr X," Margaret D. Howie, trans., Scala International, (September 1969), 38-40.

5144 _____. "The Landslide," Scala International, (January 1967), 34-36.

5145 Kasdan, Sara. "'An Engagement Is a Happy Occasion No Matter What'," American Judaism, XIV (Summer 1965), 9.

5146 Kassák, Lajos. "Jacob the Monkey," New Hungarian Quarterly,

VIII (Winter 1967), 98.

5147 Kassam, Sadru. "The Child and the Water-Tap," Literary Review, XI (Summer 1968), 467-468.

5148 _____. "The Morning," Nexus, I (1966), 16-17.

5149 Kassan, Roberta. "Talk to Me," Seventeen, XXIV (September 1965), 112-113.

5150 Kassil, Lev. "Be Ready, Your Highness!" Eve Manning, trans., Soviet Literature, (no. 12 1965), 3-63.

5151 Kästner, Erich. "A Minor Incident," George Raymond Selden, trans., Scala International, (January 1966), 34-37.

5152 Kasumov, Imran. "The Summit Ahead," Vladimir Leonov, trans., Soviet Literature, (no. 12, 1969), 29-45.

5153 Katayev, Ivan. "Immortality," Soviet Literature, (no. 4, 1967), 125-129.

5154 Katayev, Valentin. "The Grass of Oblivion," Robert Daglish, trans., Soviet Literature, (no. 1, 1968), 88-142.

5155 _____. "The Grass of Oblivion/(Conclusion)," Robert Daglish, trans., Soviet Literature, (no. 2, 1968), 48-113.

5156 _____. "Our Father, Which Art in Heaven...," Soviet Literature, (no. 4, 1967), 85-92.

5157 Katema, Simon. "The Baby," New Writing from Zambia, no. 2 (1966), 8-9, 12-17.

5158 Katkov, Norman. "Give My Heart Ease," Good Housekeeping, CLXIV (May 1967), 86-87, 168, 170, 172-174.

5159 _____. "Love in San Francisco," Good Housekeeping, CLXIII (November 1966), 90-91, 208-209, 211-212, 214, 216.

5160 Katō Shūichi. "The Pavilion of Great Poets," Hilda Katō, trans. Japan Quarterly, XIII (October-December 1966), 476-488.

5161 Katona, Steve. "Fog," Ante, IV (Spring 1968), 69-74.

5162 Katz, Elia. "Reynold Stengrow's Short Story," New Directions 20, (1968), 143-157.

5163 Katz, Shlomo. "The Convention," Midstream, XV (November 1969), 46-53.

5164 _____. "My Redeemer Cometh," Midstream, XIII (May 1967), 37-55.

5165 ______. "My Servant Jacob," _Midstream_, XV (January 1969), 36-50.

5166 ______. "The Tide," _Midstream_, XIV (August/September 1968), 41-43.

5167 Katz, Steve. "Anti-Myths/Faust," _US_, no. 1 (June 1969), 117, 119-120.

5168 ______. "Anti-Myths/Goliath," _US_, no. 1 (June 1969), 120, 122-123.

5169 ______. "Anti-Myths/Nancy and Sluggo," _US_, no. 1 (June 1969), 109, 111-113.

5170 ______. "Anti-Myths/Poseidon," _US_, no. 1 (June 1969), 113-114, 116.

5171 ______. "The Lestriad," _Chicago Review_, XVII, no. 4 (1965), 5-46.

5172 ______. "Mythology: Diana," _Extensions_, no. 1 (1968), 27-28.

5173 ______. "Mythology: Hermes," _Extensions_, no. 3 (1969), 36-37.

5174 ______. "Some Exaggerations of Peter Prince," _Chicago Review_, XVIII, nos. 3 & 4 (1966), 111-141.

5175 ______. "The Sweet Salento, with Edmond Kulik, and Peter Stern among the Woptimists," _Paris Review_, XI (Winter-Spring 1968), 139-156.

5176 ______. "Three Satisfying Stories," _Epoch_, XVIII (Fall 1968), 3-19.

5177 Kauffman, George. "Divorce," _Dust_, I (Winter 1965), 84.

5178 Kaufman, Bob. "A Busy Shirt Died Last Night," _Umbra_, (1967-1968), 49.

5179 ______. "Notes from the Hot Gabardine Scene," _San Francisco Earthquake_, I (Winter 1968), 32-33.

5180 Kaufman, Lynne. "Before a Girl Marries," _Redbook_, CXXXIII (August 1969), 72, 150-153.

5181 ______. "Curfew," _Cosmopolitan_, CLIX (August 1965), 78-81.

5182 ______. "The Hills of the Bronx," _Ramparts_, III (January-February 1965), 42-47.

5183 _____. "Marcella Monique," Woman's Day, (October 1967), 66-67, 90, 92-93, 96.

5184 _____. "The Sulphur Baths," Cosmopolitan, CLXIV (June 1968), 130-135.

5185 _____. "The Sweet Yielding," Redbook, CXXXII (December 1968), 54-55, 142-143, 145-146.

5186 _____. "To Find My Heart Again," Good Housekeeping, CLXV (August 1967), 65-69.

5187 _____. " Wild Nights," Ladies' Home Journal, LXXXIV (October 1967), 148-153.

5188 Kaufman, Robert. "Please Don't Talk to Me--I'm in Training," Playboy, XIV (September 1967), 125, 214, 216-220, 222.

5189 Kaufman, Sue. "The First Day," Redbook, CXXIV (January 1965), 32-33, 75-76, 79.

5190 _____. "In the Woods of Truro," Southern Review, I (January 1965), 183-198.

5191 _____. "The Rescue," Southern Review, II (July 1966), 619-632.

5192 Kaufman, Wallace. "Promises of Spring," Red Clay Reader, no. 4 (1967), 84-95.

5193 _____. "Regard Me Well," Sewanee Review, LXXIII (July-September 1965), 362-376.

5194 _____. "A Road She Didn't Know," Shenandoah, XX (Autumn 1968), 32-46.

5295 _____. "The Road through Myton," Encounter, XXVII (September 1966), 3-8.

5196 _____. "A Second Good Bye," Carolina Quarterly, XIX (Spring 1967), 36-48.

5197 Kaufmann, F. "The Game," Prism International, VIII (Autumn 1968), 33-37.

5198 Kaupas, Julius. "The Organ of Kurkliškés," Peter Sears, adapt., Literary Review, VIII (Spring 1965), 341-353.

5199 Kavaler, Rebecca. "Compensation Claim," Nimrod, XII (Fall 1967), 34-41.

5200 Kavan, Anna. "Five More Days to Countdown," Encounter,

XXXI (July 1968), 45-49.

5201 _____. "High in the Mountains," London Magazine, VIII (July 1968), 54-59.

5202 _____. "Julia and the Bazooka," Encounter, XXXII (March 1969), 16-19.

5203 _____. "World of Heroes," Encounter, XXXIII (October 1969), 9-13.

5204 Kavanagh, H. J. "How Many Miles to London?" New Zealand Listener, LII (March 12, 1965), 8.

5205 _____. "A Place for Small Men," New Zealand Listener, LIII (August 27, 1965), 22-23.

5206 Kawabata, Yasunari. "The Moon on the Water," Imprint, IX (April 1969), 19-23.

5207 _____. "One Arm," Edward Seidensticker, trans., Japan Quarterly, XIV (January-March 1967), 60-70.

5208 _____. "The Sleeping Beauty," J. I. Ackroyd and Hiro Mukai, trans., Eastern Horizon, IV (March 1965), 53-64.

5209 Kawai, Haruo. "Waiting," Duel, no. 1 (Winter 1969), 70-75.

5210 Kawalec, Julian. "Home Coming," Edward Rothert, trans., Literary Review, X (Spring 1967), 353-360.

5211 Kawin, Bruce. "Deetjen's Inn," Columbia Review, XLVI, no. 1 (1965), 13-29.

5212 _____. "From a Novel," Columbia Review, XLVII, no. 2 (1967), 38-43.

5213 _____. "The Nature Man," Columbia Review, XLVI, no. 2 (1966), 10-19.

5214 Kay, Monte S. "Childe Abrams," Yale Literary Magazine, CXXXVI (March 1968), 9-13.

5215 Kay, Peter. "Not as the Rest of Men," Overland, no. 43 (Summer 1969-70), 23-26.

5216 Kayam, Umar. "My Wife, Madame Schlitz, and the Giant," Lenie Lumenta, trans., Solidarity, III (September 1968), 67-73.

5217 Kazakevich, Emmanuil. "A Father Visits His Son," Margaret Wettlin, trans., Soviet Literature, (no. 5, 1967), 3-26.

5218 Kazakov, Yuri. "Arcturus--the Hunting Dog," Soviet Literature, (no. 4, 1967), 185-200.

5219 _____. "Kabiasy--A Russian Ghost Story," Thomas P. Whitney, trans., Michigan Quarterly Review, IV (Winter 1965), 46-51.

5220 _____. "A Place to Spend the Night," Gabriella Azrael, trans., Tri-Quarterly, no. 3 (Spring 1965), 129-137.

5221 Kazan, Elia. "The Arrangement," Cosmopolitan, CLXII (June 1967), 140-144, 146-149.

5222 Kearins, John. "Dash Darnell, Writer in Residence," Long View Journal, I (Spring 1969), 135-145.

5223 _____. "Setting for a Raid," Long View Journal, I (Winter 1968), 103-108.

5224 Kearns, Lionel. "Enterprise," Prism International, VII (Summer 1967), 98-99.

5225 Keeble, G. R. G. "The Mission," The Cantuarian, (December 1965), 44.

5226 _____. "The Priest-King," The Cantuarian, (December 1966), 300-301.

5227 _____. "'To All Oxbridge Candidates: Don't Worry, That Was Not Your Last Interview'," The Cantuarian, (December 1967), 39.

5228 Keefauver, John. "The Man Who Said He Was Dead," Ante, III (Winter 1967), 55-56.

5229 Keefe, Frederick L. "The Woman Who Stayed Where She Was," New Yorker, XLI (November 6, 1965), 208, 211-216, 219.

5230 Keeley, Richard. "Once upon a Sidewalk," North American Mentor, IV (Winter 1966), 19.

5231 Keesing, Nancy. "Old and New," Southerly, XXVII, no. 3 (1967), 147-157.

5232 Keetch, Brent. "It's Autumn in the Country I Remember," Western Humanities Review, XXIII (Summer 1969), 209-214.

5233 Keillor, Garrison. "The Magic Telephone," Carleton Miscellany, X (Fall 1969), 80-89.

5234 Keister, Lorrie. "Breakfast Out," Red Cedar Review, VI (Winter 1968), 61-72.

5235 _____. "Friends," Four Quarters, XVIII (January 1969), 1-10.

5236 Keithley, George. "A Bus to Where You're Going," December, XI, nos. 1 & 2 (1969), 37-41.

5237 Kelleher, Victor M. K. "Only a Journey," Landfall, no. 82 (June 1967), 145-161.

5238 Kelley, William Melvin. "The Dentist's Wife," Playboy, XV (October 1968), 109, 140, 170-174, 176.

5239 _____. "Jest, Like Sam," Negro Digest, XVIII (October 1969), 61-64.

5240 Kellner, Esther. "Visitors from Town," McCall's, XCV (April 1968), 90-91, 150.

5241 Kelly, Bernard. "And in the Boxes, Treasure," South Dakota Review, V (Autumn 1967), 36-45.

5242 _____. "Game Called on Account of Darkness," Denver Quarterly, III (Spring 1968), 47-56.

5243 Kelly, David. "Rose Garrity," Four Quarters, XIV (March 1965), 31-39.

5244 Kelly, Eric. "The Conquered," Old Lady of Threadneedle Street, XLII (March 1966), 9-11.

5245 _____. "Offence in Elba," Old Lady of Threadneedle Street, XLIII (December 1967), 226.

5246 Kelly, Gwen. "Champagne and Chianti," Quadrant, XII (March-April 1968), 20-24.

5247 _____. "Water-Lilies," Quadrant, IX (July-August 1965), 14-19.

5248 Kelly, Robert. "An Alchemical Journal," Io Magazine, no. 4 (Summer 1967), 1-33.

5249 _____. "Self Inflicted Circuits," Io Magazine, no. 2 (February 1966), 39-47.

5250 Kelsey, Robin. "Kotzko Was a Writer Who Did Not Write," Quarry, XVII (Spring 1968), 32-33.

5251 Kemal, Yasar. "Water," Joseph S. Jacobson, trans., Literature East and West, XI (June 1967), 173-176.

5252 Kempton, James. "Coming to a Close," WIN, IV (August 1968), 6-7.

5253 Keneally, Thomas. "The Inquisitors," Meanjin Quarterly, XXVII (Autumn 1968), 42-51.

5254 Kennedy, Brownie. "Yonder Go," The Archive, LXXVIII (April 1966), 40-44.

5255 Kennedy, Raymond. "The Expulsion," Massachusetts Review, VII (Autumn 1966), 674-676.

5256 Kennon, Janie. "Three Stories/The Apprentice," Prism International, VIII (Spring 1969), 104-109.

5257 _____. "Three Stories/Don Quixote's Horse," Prism International, VIII (Spring 1969), 102-104.

5258 _____. "Three Stories/Story of a Poor Man," Prism International, VIII (Spring 1969), 100-101.

5259 Kent, Judy. "Spook Castle that Turned Into Castle of the Beautys, or The Watson Family, December, XI (1969), 43.

5260 Kent, Linda. "Late," December, XI (1969), 135.

5261 Kentfield, Calvin. "Near the Line," Texas Quarterly, IX (Summer 1966), 50-63.

5262 Kerbabayev, Berdy. "Born of a Miracle," Alice Ingman, trans., Soviet Literature, (no. 3, 1969), 3-82.

5263 _____. "The Land of Turkmenia," Anthony Wixley, trans., Soviet Literature, (no. 7, 1966), 3-8.

5264 _____. "The Shepherd," Anthony Wixley, trans., Soviet Literature, (no. 7, 1966), 48-55.

5265 Kernan, Michael. "Good Morning, Dear Elizabeth," Ladies' Home Journal, LXXXIV (November 1967), 100-101, 192-195.

5266 _____. "Will the Real Me Please Stand Up?" Ladies' Home Journal, LXXXVI (February 1969), 76-77, 107, 112, 114-116.

5267 Kerouac, Jack. "Good Blonde," Playboy, XII (January 1965), 137-140, 192-194.

5268 _____. "The Murder of Swinburne," Evergreen Review, XII (February 1968), 60-63, 110-118.

5269 _____. "Satori in Paris: 1," Evergreen Review, X (February 1966), 17-21, 74-79.

5270 _____. "Satori in Paris: 2," Evergreen Review, X (April 1966), 56-59, 78, 80, 82, 84, 86-88.

5271 _____. "Satori in Paris: 3," Evergreen Review, X (June 1966), 50-53, 80, 82, 84, 86, 88, 90.

5272 _____. "from Visions of Cody," The Once Series (Ice), I (1966-67), n.p. [13-15].

5273 Kersh, Gerald. "Crooked Bone," Saturday Evening Post, CCXLI (August 10, 1968), 64-65, 70-72, 73-76, 78.

5274 _____. "Somewhere Not Far from Here," Playboy, XII (March 1965), 120-121, 136-137, 178, 180-181.

5275 _____. "Trip Out on Red Lizzie," Saturday Evening Post, CCXLI (January 27, 1968), 50-52, 54-55.

5276 _____. "The Truth About Orlik," Playboy, XIII (December 1966), 165, 302-306.

5277 _____. "The Unbroken Heart," Courier, XLIV (June 1965), 50-59.

5278 Kesey, Ken. "Letters from Mexico," Ararat, VIII (Autumn 1967), 47-51.

5279 _____. "A Tape Stolen from Ken Kesey's Workhouse," Genesis West, III (Winter 1965), 38-39.

5280 Ketlinskaya, Vera. "Captain Borisov's Children," Tom Botting, trans., Soviet Literature, (no. 8, 1966), 109-114.

5281 _____. "Maturity," Michael Moor, trans., Soviet Literature, (no. 10, 1968), 79-91.

5282 _____. "Plateau above the Clouds," Tom Botting, trans., Soviet Literature, (no. 2, 1965), 2-43.

5283 Kettler, Robert. "The Sheltered," The Goodly Co., no. 2 (April 1965), 20-34.

5284 Kettlewell, Kathy. "Anna before the Forest," Readers & Writers, I (April-May 1967), 34-36.

5285 Kevelson, Roberta. "Deliverance From a Rainbarrel," Forum, V (Summer 1967), 49-54.

5286 Keyes, Daniel. "The Spellbinder," North American Review, IV (May 1967), 35-39.

5287 Keyes, John. "Notes on a Blemish," Edge, no. 4 (Spring 1965), 87-92.

5288 Kgositsile, Keorapetse. "The Ab/Original Mask," Negro Digest, XVIII (October 1969), 54-60.

5289 Kgositsile, Melba. "And They Will Be Astounded," Pan-African Journal, II (Spring 1969), 193-205.

5290 Khan, Mir Alim. "'Beauty or Beast'?" Pakistan Review, XVI (September 1968), 24-25.

5291 ______. "The Begum," Pakistan Review, XV (February 1967), 14-17.

5292 ______. "The Dream," Pakistan Review, XV (January 1967), 27-28.

5293 ______. "Ghosts," Pakistan Review, XV (December 1967), 33-34, 39, 43.

5294 ______. "Kismet," Pakistan Review, XV (August 1967), 22-24, 26.

5295 ______. "Kismet," Vision, XVII (November 1968), 8-10, 20.

5296 ______. "The Rescue," Pakistan Review, XV (November 1967), 16-18.

5297 ______. "Sooty," Pakistan Review, XV (May 1967), 27-29, 35.

5298 Khan, S. A. "Innocent Road," Pakistan Review, XIII (September 1965), 11-12, 14.

5299 Khanzadyan, Sero. "The Gorge Is Not What It Used to Be," Darya Efremova, trans., Soviet Literature, (no. 3, 1966), 97-107.

5300 Khodjer, Grigori. "The End of a Big House," Eve Manning, trans., Soviet Literature, (no. 4, 1966), 92-125.

5301 Khudainazarov, Berdynazar. "Sormovo--27," Anthony Wixley, trans., Soviet Literature, (no. 7, 1966), 94-112.

5302 Kibera, Leonard. "It's a Dog's Share in Our Kinshasa," Transition, VI, no. 29 (February-March 1967), 20-21.

5303 ______. "Letter to the Haunting Past," Nexus, I (1966), 24-25, 34.

5304 ______. "1954," Nexus, I (August 1967), 14-17, 19-20.

5305 ______. "The Spider's Web," Transition, VII, no. 33 (October/November 1967), 32-35.

5306 Kick, Joseph A. "A Step in Between," Ave Maria, CIII (February 5, 1966), 24-27.

5307 Kicknosway, Faye. "Jinni," Quartet, no. 20 (Fall 1967), 20-21.

5308 Kiely, Benedict. "A Ball of Malt and Madame Butterfly," Kenyon Review, XXXI (1969), 215-236.

5309 _____. "A Great God's Angel Standing," New Yorker, XLIV (August 24, 1968), 28-34.

5310 _____. "The House in Jail Square," Threshold, no. 21 (Summer 1967), 137-157.

5311 _____. "The Top of the Tower: Two Fragments from a Novel," Shenandoah, XVI (Summer 1965), 79-95.

5312 _____. "Wild Rover No More," Northwest Review, VIII (Spring 1967), 52-64.

5313 Killion, Jerry. "The Dark Cloud," Plaintiff, IV (Spring-Summer 1968), 16-17.

5314 Kim, Richard E. "The Martyred," Solidarity, II (January-February 1967), 97-151.

5315 _____. "The Martyred/(Conclusion)," Solidarity, II (January-February 1967), 111-154.

5316 Kimball, George. "Chartreuse, Black, and Ugly," Work, no. 5 (1968), 44.

5317 _____. "In My Life," The World, no. 13 (November 1968), n.p. [11].

5318 _____. "The Man of the House," Work, no. 4 (Summer/Fall/Winter 1966), 74-75.

5319 _____. "Murphy," Southern Review, V (January 1969), 170-183.

5320 Kimber, Robert B. "To Grandmother's House We Go," Carleton Miscellany, X (Spring 1969), 62-81.

5321 Kimbugwe, Henry. "An Old Bond," Transition, VI, no. 28 (1967), 40-41.

5322 Kimura, Joseph H. "Run-Down," Nexus, II (July 1968), 26-28.

5323 Kimzey, Ardis. "A Patch of Sun/(a read aloud story)," Long View, Journal, I (Spring 1969), 127-132.

5324 Kindlieber, Diego. "Hows Come Story #3," Overflow, I (Fall 1967), 33-34.

5325 King, Alexander. "Memoirs of a Mouse," McCall's, XCII (September 1965), 86-87, 147-148, 150-153, 156-159.

5326 King, Dorothy Willard. "The House of the Four Magnolias," Delta Review, VI (June 1969), 24-25, 63.

5327 King, Francis. "The Brighton Belle," Nova, (May 1966), 133, 136, 138, 141, 143, 145-146, 150.

5328 ______. "The Containers," London Magazine, VII (September 1967), 58-61.

5329 ______. "I Lived For You," Harper's Bazaar, C (March 1967), 238-239, 265, 271.

5330 ______. "I Lived For You," London Magazine, VI (September 1966), 47-59.

5331 ______. "Their Night," Harper's Bazaar, C (November 1967), 91, 93, 95, 97, 99.

5332 ______. "Their Night," Weekend Telegraph, no. 107 (October 14, 1966), 65-66, 69.

5333 King, Shannon. "The Old Man," Red Cedar Review, V (January 1967), 73-79.

5334 King, Woodie, Jr. "Listen to the Wind Blow," Negro Digest, XVII (June 1968), 90-98.

5335 Kingston, Jeremy. "God and the Tower and the Boy," Atlantic Monthly, CCXVI (October 1965), 80-87.

5336 Kiralyfalvi, Marthena. "Little Princess," New Leaven, XIX (1969), 55-64.

5337 Kirby, Chris. "Honeymoon," Good Housekeeping, CLXIII (September 1966), 94-95, 142-144.

5338 Kirby, David K. "Journey to Y," Delta, XX (1966), 44-45.

5339 ______. "Netter," Delta, XIX (1965), 17-20.

5340 Kirkpatrick, Dave. "On Commodities of Carried-over Puritanical Thought, the Defecation of which I Ordinarily Prefer to Keep to Myself," Mandala, no. 5 (1969), 35-36.

5341 Kirkpatrick, Smith. "Silence," Southern Review, IV (January 1968), 192-198.

5342 Kirkup, James. "The Man Who Ate Himself," Mundus Artium, I (Summer 1968), 6-8.

5343 _____. "The Part-Time Poetry Tutor," Mundus Artium, I (Spring 1968), 12-14.

5344 Kirmser, Jeune. "The Delinquent," Kansas Magazine, (1968), 87-93.

5345 Kirstein, Natalie. "Birdie's Hideaway," Midstream, XIV (October 1968), 37-46.

5346 _____. "The Policelady on the Corner," University Review, XXXIV (Summer 1968), 298-302.

5347 Kistner, Art. "Old Days," Nexus (San Francisco, Calif.), II (March-April 1965), 43-46.

5348 Kita Morio. "Birth," Clifton Royston, trans., Japan Quarterly, XVI (October-December 1969), 414-422.

5349 _____. "On the Rock Ridge," Clifton Royston, trans., Japan Quarterly, XVI (October-December 1969), 423-430.

5350 Kitaif, Theodore. "The Arch-Criminal," The Fiddlehead, no. 79 (March-April 1969), 70-82.

5351 _____. "The Escapee," Maguey, no. 2 (Autumn 1968), 56-57 [in English and Spanish on alternate pages].

5352 _____. "'Goodnight! Goodnight! See You Again Soon'," North American Review, IV (July 1967), 29-30.

5353 _____. "The Murderer Living Downstairs," Midwestern University Quarterly, II, no. 2 (1966), 63-71.

5354 _____. "Spectators," Arx, III (November 1969), 28-30.

5355 Kitchen, Paddy. "Linsey-Woolsey (an extract from a novel)," Transatlantic Review, no. 31 (Winter 1968-69), 71-79.

5356 Kittredge, William A. "Funny," Ante, IV (Summer-Fall 1968), 56-67.

5357 _____. "Hermitage," South Dakota Review, VI (Winter 1968-69), 18-26.

5358 _____. "Society of Eros," Northwest Review, VII (Fall-Winter 1965-66), 7-18.

5359 _____. "The Voice of Water," Minnesota Review, VII (1967), 272-280.

5360 _____. "The Waterfowl Tree," Northwest Review, VIII (Fall-Winter 1966-67), 7-20.

5361 Kizer, Carolyn. "A Slight Mechanical Failure," Quarterly Review of Literature, XV (1968), 343-354.

5362 Kjelgaard, Betty. "Aftermath of a Quarrel," Woman's Day, (September 1966), 42-43, 102-105.

5363 _____. "Out of Touch," Woman's Day, (August 1965), 34-35, 93-96.

5364 _____. "Poor Darling," Redbook, CXXXIII (August 1969), 79, 118-119.

5365 _____. "Too Bad, So Sad," Ladies' Home Journal, LXXXIV (September 1967), 88-89, 148-150.

5366 Klabund, A. H. "Three Stories/An Army Post Card and a Postage Stamp," E. M. Valk, trans., Stand, VIII, no. 1 (1966), 50-51.

5367 _____. "Three Stories/Bartholomew and the Young Man," E. M. Valk, trans., Stand, VIII, no. 1 (1966), 52-54.

5368 _____. "Three Stories/The Bear," E. M. Valk, trans., Stand, VIII, no. 1 (1966), 55-57.

5369 Klaich, Dolores. "The Driver," Transatlantic Review, no. 29 (Summer 1968), 80-90.

5370 Klaperman, Libby M. "Tale of a Kvittel," Jewish Life, XXXV (March-April 1968), 54-57.

5371 Klass, James B. "Ratkin," Carolina Quarterly, XX (Spring 1968), 5-22.

5372 Klaus, Bill. "A. J. Liggett and the Elephant," Human Voice Quarterly, III (Spring 1967), 4.

5373 _____. "The Passer," Human Voice Quarterly, III (Spring 1967), 4.

5374 _____. "The Return of A. J. Liggett," Human Voice Quarterly, III (Spring 1967), 4.

5375 _____. "Three Tales of Our Time," Trace, no. 61 (Summer 1966), 202-205.

5376 Kleiman, Edward. "from Mister Golden Boy/A New Novel," Alphabet, no. 16 (September 1969), 18-29.

5377 Klein, Daniel Martin. "Wolves in the Attic," Saturday Evening Post, CCXXXIX (June 18, 1966), 78-79.

5378 Klein, Marty. "Born on a Frosty Morning," Midwestern University Quarterly, I, no. 1 (1965), 49-56.

5379 Klein, Norma. "Accident," Nimrod, X (Autumn 1965), 1-5.

5380 _____. "The Accomplice," DeKalb Literary Arts Journal, II (Winter 1968), 15-37.

5381 _____. "The Boy in the Green Hat," Prairie Schooner, XLII (Summer 1968), 95-105.

5382 _____. "The End of the Holiday," University Review, XXXIV (Summer 1968), 291-294.

5383 _____. "The Garnet Necklace," Mademoiselle, LXII (April 1966), 184-185, 251-255.

5384 _____. "Going to China," Malahat Review, no. 8 (October 1968), 5-14.

5385 _____. "The Grey Buick," University Review, XXXV (Spring 1969), 178-186.

5386 _____. "In the Playground," Quartet, no. 23 (Summer 1968), 8-14.

5387 _____. "Independence Day," North American Review, III (November 1966), 30-35.

5388 _____. "Love, Schmuv," Prairie Schooner, XLIII (Summer 1969), 157-167.

5389 _____. "Magic," Mademoiselle, LXIV (April 1967), 180-181, 234-239.

5390 _____. "Mary," Canadian Forum, XLVII (July 1967), 114-116.

5391 _____. "Mastroianni at Grossingers," North American Review, IV (January 1967), 14-17.

5392 _____. "A Necessary Visit," Quartet, no. 19 (Summer 1967), 2-7.

5393 _____. "The Older Sister," Canadian Forum, XLV (January 1966), 231-233.

5394 _____. "A Portrait of Carrie Living in Sin," Midwestern University Quarterly, II, no. 4 (1967), 15-24.

5395 _____. "Side Effects," Quartet, no. 15 (Summer 1965), 8-13.

5396 _____. "Stop Bothering Me," Cosmopolitan, CLXVI (May

1969), 158-159.

5397 _____. "Teak," North American Review, VI (Spring 1969), 40-42.

5398 _____. "Three Stories/I: Sleeping Pills," Denver Quarterly, IV (Summer 1969), 46-82.

5399 _____. "Three Stories/II: A Past to Regret," Denver Quarterly, IV (Summer 1969), 46-82.

5400 _____. "Three Stories/III: Organs," Denver Quarterly, IV (Summer 1969), 46-82.

5401 _____. "A Toast for Sybil," North American Review, IV (November 1967), 19-22.

5402 _____. "A Train Ride to Paris," Plume & Sword, VII (Fall 1966), 34-37.

5403 _____. "The Web," University Review, XXXV (Summer 1969), 271-278.

5404 Kliewer, Warren. "Madeleine d'Evereaux, the Whole Earth Must Know I Love You So," Kansas Magazine, (1968), 33-38.

5405 Kline, Nancy E. "Games," Colorado Quarterly, XV (Summer 1966), 17-28.

5406 Kluge, Alexander. "An Experiment in Love," Esquire, LXVI (October 1966), 111.

5407 Knapp, Elizabeth. "The Flood on White Street," Four Quarters, XV (May 1966), 9-15.

5408 Knebel, Fletcher. "Trespass," Ladies' Home Journal, LXXXVI (November 1969), 157-164.

5409 _____. "Vanished," Cosmopolitan, CLXV (August 1968), 126-134, 136-140, 145-148, 150-154.

5410 Knemeyer, Jann. "The Foxx and the Mimi," Jeopardy, no. 1 (1966), 15-20.

5411 Knickerbocker, Conrad. "Diseases of the Heart," Kenyon Review, XXVIII (March 1966), 213-223.

5412 _____. "Not Wanted on the Voyage," Esquire, LXIII (June 1965), 104, 146-147.

5413 Knight, Damon. "Masks," Playboy, XV (July 1968), 124-126, 170-172.

5414 Knight, Elaine. "La Bruja," Ante, IV (Spring 1968), 57-58.

5415 _____. "The Cemetery," Ante, III (Winter 1967), 73-76.

5416 Knight, Etheridge. "By Reason of the Bondage," Negro Digest, XVII (February 1968), 54-63.

5417 _____. "My Father, My Bottom, My Fleas," Negro Digest, XV (August 1966), 64-71.

5418 _____. "On the Next Train South," Negro Digest, XVI (June 1967), 87-94.

5419 _____. "Reaching Is His Rule," Negro Digest, XV (December 1965), 61-63.

5420 Knight, William. "Richard P. Watson," Literary Review, XIII (Winter 1969-70), 215-221.

5421 Knoll, Harry Harrison. "A Bit of Iron Weed," PS, no. 8 (1965), 50-63.

5422 Knörr, Hilde. "Full Circle," Westerly, no. 4 (December 1968), 10-14.

5423 _____. "Pavan for a Pioneer," Westerly, no. 1 (1967), 5-10.

5424 Knowles, Alison. "Journal of the Identical Lunch," The Outsider, nos. 4 & 5 (1968-69), 182-184.

5425 Knowles, John. "Orphans of the Storm, Italian-style," Yale Literary Magazine, CXXXV (September 1966), 19-20.

5426 _____. "The Reading of the Will," Playboy, XV (April 1968), 80-82, 102, 187-191.

5427 Knowles, Joseph. "No Wine, No Bread," Pegasus, V (Winter 1967), 50-57.

5428 Knowles, Peter. "Two Commentaries," Prism International, VIII (Autumn 1968), 97-103.

5429 Knowlton, Robert A. "After All These Years," Good Housekeeping, CLX (March 1965), 90-91, 152, 154.

5430 _____. "The Country of the Heart," Good Housekeeping, CLXIV (January 1967), 58-59, 148, 150, 152-153.

5431 _____. "The Couple Across the Street," Good Housekeeping, CLXII (May 1966), 98-99, 144, 147.

5432 _____. "Evening Departure," Ladies' Home Journal, LXXXV

(June 1968), 64-65.

5433 _____. "A Game for Lovers," Good Housekeeping, CLXVII (September 1968), 88-89.

5434 _____. "A Handful of Daffodils," Woman's Day, (March 1967), 21, 62-63.

5435 _____. "Journey for Love," Good Housekeeping, CLXI (December 1965), 82-83, 236, 238-242.

5436 _____. "A Kiss for Diane," Good Housekeeping, CLXVI (April 1968), 120-121.

5437 _____. "The Lucky Bridegroom," Good Housekeeping, CLXII (June 1966), 80-82.

5438 _____. "Man in the Mirror," Ladies' Home Journal, LXXXIV (April 1967), 86-87, 145-147.

5439 _____. "The Man Who Learned to Listen," Good Housekeeping, CLXI (September 1965), 72-73, 130, 133, 135.

5440 _____. "North of Boston," McCall's, XCII (February 1965), 114-115, 182-183.

5441 _____. "Second Honeymoon," Good Housekeeping, CLXV (July 1967), 86-87.

5442 _____. "Second Nature," Good Housekeeping, CLX (January 1965), 56-57, 122, 124.

5443 _____. "Someone to Care," Good Housekeeping, CLXI (August 1965), 70-71, 148, 150-152.

5444 _____. "Sunday Is for Marriage," Good Housekeeping, CLXIII (July 1966), 80-81, 192-196.

5445 _____. "The True Believers," Good Housekeeping, CLXIII (November 1966), 94-95, 160-161.

5446 _____. "Two Wishes for Christmas," Good Housekeeping, CLXV (December 1967), 86-87.

5447 _____. "'Why, Mr. Mitchell!'," Ladies' Home Journal, LXXXV (October 1968), 86-87, 169-171.

5448 _____. "A Woman's Privilege," Good Housekeeping, CLXVI (May 1968), 84-85, 170, 172-173.

5449 _____. "The Wrong Way Home," Redbook, CXXIX (July 1967), 82-83, 114-115.

5450 Knox, Hilde. "Fire Won't Burn Stick," Quadrant, XII (November-December 1968), 60-66.

5451 Knox, Ray. "Autumn Leaves," New Zealand Listener, LVIII (May 10, 1968), 10.

5452 _____. "Friday Visit," New Zealand Listener, LVIII (October 25, 1968), 10.

5453 Knox-Mawer, Ronald. "Narle," Cornhill Magazine, no. 1043 (Spring 1965), 353-354.

5454 Kobe, William. "Just Once Now, Remember," UMD Humanist, XV (Spring 1967), 40-42.

5455 Kobler, Jay. "I Will Not Let You Go Until You Bless Me," Transatlantic Review, no. 31 (Winter 1968-69), 145-158.

5456 Koch, Claude. "Artist at Work," Four Quarters, XVIII (November 1968), 1-8.

5457 _____. "Look Up! Look Up!" Four Quarters, XVII (March 1968), 8-14.

5458 _____. "The Things of Spring," Four Quarters, XVII (May 1968), 1-4.

5459 _____. "You Taught Us Good," Four Quarters, XVIII (January 1969), 31-36.

5460 Koch, Kenneth. "from The Red Robins," Art and Literature, no. 5 (Summer 1965), 134-147.

5461 Koch, Michael. "Adagio," Four Quarters, XVI (January 1967), 1-6.

5462 Kochar, Rachia. "Naapet," Vladimir Talmy, trans., Soviet Literature, (no. 3, 1966), 75-96.

5463 Koenigsberg, Larry. "Tuesday Morning," Columbia Review, XLVI, no. 2 (1966), 30-33.

5464 Koerte, Helen. "The Story of Joe Canoe," Canadian Forum, XLVIII (February 1969), 252-253.

5465 Koertge, Ronald B. "Looking for a Place to Live," Wormwood Review, VIII, no. 1 (1968), 17.

5466 Koestler, Arthur. "The Chimeras," Playboy, XVI (May 1969), 145-148, 208.

5467 _____. "Episode," Encounter, XXXI (December 1968), 35-38.

5468 Koff, David. "Where the Auction Is," Transition, V, no. 24 (1966), 41-44.

5469 Kolar, Frank. "Felicia," Dare, III (March-April 1965), 40.

5470 Kolb, Ken. "Been Here and Gone Again," Ladies' Home Journal, LXXXIII (November 1966), 100-101, 162-164.

5471 Kolb, Peter. "Bimbley," Assay, XXII (Spring 1966), 57-62.

5472 Kolbeck, Lisa. "Justin Was Good," Seventeen, XXVIII (January 1969), 86-87, 111.

5473 Koller, Diane M. "An Ordinary Morning," Crucible, IV (Fall 1967), 11-12.

5474 _____. "What's To Do Now that Gernstein's Gone/(An Excerpt)," Crucible, V (Fall 1968), 31-32.

5475 Koller, James. "The Coming," Manhattan Review, no. 1 (1966), 11-16.

5476 Kolling, Wanda. "The Taste of Oranges," Carleton Miscellany, VII (Fall 1966), 46-55.

5477 Kolln, Martha. "The Changing Season," Southwest Review, LII (Spring 1967), 177-192.

5478 Kolozsvári-Grandpierre, Emil. "The Swing-Door," New Hungarian Quarterly, VII (Spring 1966), 205-214.

5479 Kolpacoff, Victor. "The Journey to Rutherford," Denver Quarterly, IV (Spring 1969), 33-44.

5480 _____. "The Room," New American Review, no. 1 (1969), 7-27.

5481 Kon, S. "Bedtime," Focus (Singapore), V, no. 1 (1967), 39-40.

5482 _____. "Inheritance," Focus (Singapore), V, no. 1 (1967), 5-7.

5483 _____. "The Martyrdom of Helena Rodrigues," Focus (Singapore), New Series, no. 1 (1967), 9-15.

5484 Konadu, S. A. "Chapter from a Novel/The Night-Watchers of Korle Bu," Okyeame, IV (December 1968), 36-40.

5485 Kondrya, Peter. "The Rebel Land," Literary Review, IX (Autumn 1965), 5-18.

5486 Konecky, Edith. "The Chastity of Magda Wickwire," Saturday

Evening Post, CCXXXVIII (July 31, 1965), 58-60, 62-65.

5487 Konetsky, Victor. "Salty Ice," George Yankovsky, trans., Soviet Literature, (no. 2, 1969), 3-55.

5488 Kononov, Alexander. "Stories about Lenin," Vladimir Leonov, trans., Soviet Literature, (no. 12, 1968), 45-50.

5489 Konstantinovsky, Ilya. "Term of Limitation," Eve Manning, trans., Soviet Literature, (no. 1, 1966), 58-133.

5490 Konwicki, Tadeusz. "A Modern Dreambook," Edward Rothert, trans., Literary Review, X (Spring 1967), 393-399.

5491 Koontz, Dean R. "Kittens," Readers & Writers, I (May-June 1966), 12-14.

5492 Koppi, Joseph. "The Hunter," Plaintiff, IV (Fall-Winter 1967-68), 36-39.

5493 Kops, Bernard. "Yes from No-Man's Land," American Judaism, XIV (Summer 1965), 10-11, 24, 26-27.

5494 Koptelov, Afanasi. "The Flame Will Flare/(Chapter from the Novel)," M. Efremova, trans., Soviet Literature, (no. 6, 1969), 141-179.

5495 Korab. "It Had Come to Pass," Midstream, XV (December 1969), 22-47.

5496 Korinets, Yuri. "Over There, Far Away, on the Other Side of the River/(Chapters from the Book)," Avril Pyman, trans., Soviet Literature, (no. 12, 1968), 85-101.

5497 Kosinski, Jerzy. "Steps," London Magazine, IX (April 1969), 5-16.

5498 Kostelanetz, Richard. "One Night Stood/A Narrative Fiction," Panache, no. 3 (1969), 39-43.

5499 Kosztolányi, Dezső. "Barkokhba," Thomas Kabdebo, trans., Commentary, XXXIX (April 1969), 56-60.

5500 Kotzwinkle, William. "Marie," New Orleans Review, I (Spring 1969), 251-252.

5501 Koumjian, Vaughn. "The Party," Ararat, VI (Winter 1965), 41-44.

5502 Kovach, Bill. "Doghole," Appalachian Review, II (Summer 1968), 34-37.

5503 Kovačič, Lojze. "Twilight is Falling on the Earth," Donald

Davenport, trans., Literary Review, XI (Winter 1967), 217-230.

5504 Kovacs, Herschel. "Eros Underground," The Smith, no. 4 (1965), 33-36.

5505 Kovalevska, Margarita. "The Vision from the Tower," Astrid Ivask, trans., Literary Review, VII (Spring 1965), 413-422.

5506 Koven, Stanley. "State of Grace," Dasein, nos. 4 & 5 (Winter/Spring 1965/66), 198-206.

5507 Kozol, Jonathan. "The Contest," Harvard Advocate, C (Fall 1966), 15-19.

5508 Kraf, Elaine. "Westward and Up a Mountain," Chelsea, nos. 22/23 (June 1968), 134-147.

5509 Kraft, Barbara. "The Descent of the Angel," Readers & Writers, I (January-February 1967), 26-28.

5510 Kramer, Max. "Mister Grundig Was a Very Fine Gentleman," Texas Quarterly, X (Spring 1967), 121-142.

5511 Kramer, Robert. [untitled], Silo, no. 10 (Fall 1966), 50-94.

5512 Kramm, Joseph. "December's Dialogue," Idea and Image, Charter Issue (1967), 26-29.

5513 Kranes, David. "The Interview," Western Humanities Review, XXIII (Spring 1969), 121-128.

5514 _____. "Snow," Lillabulero, II (Winter 1968), 12-15.

5515 _____. "The Wishbone," Transatlantic Review, no. 19 (Autumn 1965), 53-65.

5516 Krapivin, Vladislav. "Meeting My Brother," Vision, XV (December 1966), 29-39.

5517 _____. "Stars in the Rain," Anthony Wixley, trans., Soviet Literature, (no. 2, 1966), 78-108.

5518 Krasilovsky, Alexis. "With Excuses to Henry James," Grecourt Review, XI (May 1968), 70-73.

5519 Kraus, W. Keith. "The Machine," University Review, XXXIV (Spring 1968), 233-239.

5520 Krause, Ervin D. "Lament," University Review, XXXIII (December 1966), 101-106.

5521 _____. "The Shooters," Northwest Review, IX (Fall-Winter

1967-68), 4-25.

5522 _____. "The Witch," Northwest Review, VIII (Spring 1967), 31-47.

5523 Krebs, Katherine. "Think of Spring and Remember Summer," Cimarron Review, no. 6 (December 1968), 30-46.

5524 Kreda, William. "The World of Seymour Rottenberg," Prism International, IV (Winter 1965), 4-9.

5525 Kreisel, Henry. "The Broken Globe," Literary Review, VIII (Summer 1965), 484-495.

5526 Krickel, Edward. "Birds," Arlington Quarterly, I (Autumn 1967), 20-24.

5527 Kriegel, Leonard. "Another Birth," Ararat, VII (Summer 1966), 40-46.

5528 Krishnamoorthy, S. "The Nostalgia," S. Krishnamoorthy, trans., Triveni, XXXVII (January 1969), 30-36.

5529 Kristen, Marti. "At Arromanches," Canadian Forum, XLVIII (January 1969), 235-237.

5530 _____. "The Flowers of Glory," Approach, no. 58 (Winter 1966), 23-27.

5531 _____. "Grandma's Doll," North American Review, II (November 1965), 19-21.

5532 _____. "Los Hombres Terribles," Approach, no. 62 (Winter 1967), 10-15.

5533 _____. "Neighbor Heavenly," Phylon, XXVII (Summer 1966), 192-196.

5534 _____. "With the Guard," Trace, no. 60 (Spring 1966), 72-75.

5535 _____. "Xerxes Swill," Ante, IV (Summer-Fall 1968), 85-97.

5536 Kroetsch, Robert. "The Prophet," Sage, XI (Spring 1966), 19-30.

5537 _____. "The Ride," Tamarack Review, nos. 50-51 (1969), 88-102.

5538 Kroll, Jerri. "Beckett's Moran on Birds," Grecourt Review, X (April 1967), 6.

5539 Kron, Alexander. "The House and the Ship," Alice Ingman and V. Krivoshchekov, trans., Soviet Literature, (no. 6, 1966), 8-90.

5540 Krúdy, Gyula. "Sindbad's Autumn Journey," New Hungarian Quarterly, X (Summer 1969), 92-100.

5541 Kruger, Fania. "Eve of Atonement," Southwest Review, LII (Spring 1967), 144-151.

5542 Krumgold, Joseph. "Henry 3," Good Housekeeping, CLXV (July 1967), 67-69, 170-176, 180-186, 192-201, 206-208.

5543 Krumsiek, Howard. "Posted," Quartet, no. 23 (Summer 1968), 1-4.

5544 Krupat, Arnold. "Hilda/Part of a Book in Progress," The Quest, I (Fall-Winter 1966), 17-24.

5545 _____. "The Old Dogcatcher," The Quest, II (Spring 1967), 30-34.

5546 Kubicek, Tom. "The Sun in the Evening," Duel, no. 1 (Winter 1969), 81-89.

5547 Kubicki, Jan. "Occurrence at Snake Hill," Manuscript, XVIII (Spring 1965), 26-34.

5548 Kuch, T. D. C. "He/a fable," Aspects, no. 6 (January 1965), 7-8.

5549 _____. "Rebel," Dust, II (Fall 1965), 45-46.

5550 Kuehl, John. "Edge of the Desert," Forum, IV (Winter-Spring 1965), 43-46.

5551 Kuliyev, Klych. "In Astrabad/(An Excerpt from the Novel Grim Days)," Tom Botting, trans., Soviet Literature, (no. 7, 1966), 58-72.

5552 Kulkarni, G. A. "The Meeting," G. A. Kulkarni, trans., Triveni, XXXVIII (July 1969), 52-55.

5553 Kumin, Maxine. "Taming the Joplin Place," Southern Review, I (October 1965), 885-895.

5554 Kunasz, Paul. "All the Little Swingers," Redbook, CXXVII (September 1966), 60-61, 128-130.

5555 Kunert, Günter. "Four Prose Pieces/Forgetfulness," Christopher Middleton, trans., Stand, VII, no. 2 (1965), 60.

5556 _____. "Four Prose Pieces/The Polish Tree," Christopher

Middleton, trans., Stand, VII, no. 2 (1965), 60.

5557 ______. "Four Prose Pieces/Report," Christopher Middleton, trans., Stand, VII, no. 2 (1965), 61.

5558 ______. "Four Prose Pieces/The Shrieking of Bats," Christopher Middleton, trans., Stand, VII, no. 2 (1965), 61.

5559 ______. "Herr Robert, the Pursuer," Christopher Middleton, trans., Dimension, II, no. 2 (1969), 470-477 [in German and English on alternate pages].

5560 ______. "On the City Railway," Christopher Middleton, trans., Art and Literature, no. 10 (Autumn 1966), 177-180.

5561 Kunkwa, R. C. "Number Fourteen Kola," New Writing from Zambia, no. 1 (1969), 6-8, 11-15.

5562 Kuper, Adam. "One I Love," Cambridge Review, LXXXIX (May 17, 1968), 473-475.

5563 Kuper, Hilda. "Not Such a Bad Boy," Michigan Quarterly Review, V (Fall 1966), 279-281.

5564 Kuper, Jack. "Kubush," Tamarack Review, no. 42 (Winter 1967), 41-56.

5565 Kupperman, Mark. "from A Life in Progress," Red Cedar Review, V (April 1967), 5-12.

5566 ______. "Mother Goosed," Red Cedar Review, V (April 1967), 87-92.

5567 Kurinsky, Miriam. "The Saints of Canarsie," Literary Review, XII (Summer 1969), 435-444.

5568 Kurtz, Madalynne R. "Give My Heart Ease," Good Housekeeping, CLXVII (July 1968), 66-67, 137-140.

5569 ______. "The Night of the Full Moon," Saturday Evening Post, CCXL (July 1, 1967), 54-56, 58-59.

5570 ______. "Saxophones Sound Lonely," McCall's, XCV (July 1968), 82-83, 127-133.

5571 ______. "Waxing Wroth," Carleton Miscellany, VII (Summer 1966), 42-55.

5572 Kushner, Donn. "A Matter of Luck," The Fiddlehead, no. 68 (Spring 1966), 42-48.

5573 ______. "Two Europeans," Alphabet, no. 10 (July 1965), 32-39.

5574 _____. "The Witnesses," The Fiddlehead, no. 76 (Summer 1968), 4-19.

5575 Kuznetsov, Anatoli. "Old Mother Grunya's Deer," Soviet Literature, (no. 4, 1967), 201-206.

5576 _____. "The Walker-On," Robert Daglish, trans., Soviet Literature, (no. 3, 1969), 97-116.

5577 Kwolek, Constance. "Breugel Wedding," Ante, IV (Summer-Fall 1968), 78-81.

5578 Kyger, Joanne. [untitled], The World, no. 4 (June 1967), n.p. [3].

5579 _____. "A Novel," Caterpillar, nos. 8 & 9 (October 1969), 57-64.

5580 _____. "from Places to Go," Wild Dog, nos. 19 & 20 (December 8, 1965), 21-23.

5581 Kyrklund, Willy. "from the novel Mah the Master/(with a commentary by Yao and Li: the beginning)," George C. Schoolfield, trans., Literary Review, IX (Winter 1965-66), 285-289.

5582 La Barre, Harriet. "Love on a Perfect Day," Cosmopolitan, CLXIV (January 1968), 100-101.

5583 _____. "Natural Prey," Cosmopolitan, CLXVI (May 1969), 154-156.

5584 Lackner, Stephan. "Firman the Ferryman," Margaret D. Howie, trans., Scala International, (January 1968), 34-37.

5585 _____. "From Life," Margaret D. Howie, trans., Scala International, (July 1969), 35-37.

5586 _____. "The Islandman," George Raymond Selden, trans., Scala International, (April 1967), 34-36.

5587 Lacy, Ed. "The Plot Sickens," Courier, XLV (August 1965), 42-43.

5588 _____. "Strictly Would-be Poppa," Courier, XLIV (March 1965), 45-50.

5589 Lacy, Robert. "Win a Few, Loose a Few," Saturday Evening Post, CCXXXVIII (December 18, 1965), 70-75.

5590 Lagerkvist, Pär. "The Expectant Guest," R. A. Swanson, trans., Minnesota Review, VI (1966), 297-305.

5591 ______. "The Morning," R. A. Swanson, trans., Minnesota Review, VI (1966), 306-310.

5592 ______. "Two Stories/The Fragments," Roy Arthur Swanson, trans., Carolina Quarterly, XIX (Fall 1967), 5-13.

5593 ______. "Two Stories/Maurice Fleury," Roy Arthur Swanson, trans., Carolina Quarterly, XIX (Fall 1967), 14-25.

5594 Lagerlöf, Selma. "The City of Hatred," Jessie Bröchner, trans., Adam International Review, nos. 325-327 (1968), 195-197.

5595 Lagomarsino, E. "Good-bye Aristotle," Beyond Baroque 691, I (December 1968), 4-7.

5596 ______. "Goodbye, Aristotle," North American Review, VI (Spring 1969), 36-39.

5597 Laiche, Don. "Alone," Delta, XX (1966), 65-69.

5598 ______. "Before the First Trip," Delta, XXI (1967), 1-5.

5599 ______. "Waiting," Delta, XX (1966), 1-3.

5600 Laird, Bailey. "A Political Fiction," New Yorker, XLIII (September 16, 1967), 42-46.

5601 La Justica. "Don Felipe's Vision," New Campus Review, I (Winter 1967), 35-46.

5602 Lake, E. M. and James Hines. "Aftermath," Minnesota Review, V (October-December 1965), 274-280.

5603 Lakin, R. D. "Anyone Would Do the Same," Human Voice, V, nos. 1-4 (1969), 91-95.

5604 Lalić, Mihailo. "The Snow Is Melting," Biljana Šlijivić-Šmšić, trans., Literary Review, XI (Winter 1967), 193-205.

5605 Lally, Michael D. "Found a Groove," December, XI, nos. 1 & 2 (1969), 85-90.

5606 ______. "In the Backyard of My Mind," Gato Magazine, I (Autumn 1966), 21-24.

5607 ______. "Lovers Are Very Special People/(based on a 1964 news story)," Grande Ronde Review, II, no. 2 (1968), 27-28.

5608 Lambert, Spencer. "The Spider and the Fly," Evergreen Review, XII (May 1968), 33-35, 74-76, 78, 80.

5609 Lamott, Kenneth. "The Gamblers," Saturday Evening Post, CCXL (December 30, 1967), 54-58, 60-61.

5610 _____. "Gatsby and the Sea Gull," Harper's Magazine, CCXXXIII (October 1966), 113-117.

5611 _____. "The Kangaroo Lottery," Saturday Evening Post, CCXXXIX (March 26, 1966), 84-90, 92-93.

5612 Lampe, Friedo. "The Rape of Europa," Margaret D. Howie, trans., Scala International, (April 1968), 34-37.

5613 Lance, Kathryn. "Barbara Ann," Story: the Yearbook of Discovery, (1969), 38-50.

5614 Landau, Sidney. "Harold Was My Brother," Mad River Review, I (Fall-Winter 1965), 53-83.

5615 Lange, Horst. "Out of Such Stuff as Dreams...," George Raymond Selden, trans., Scala International, (March 1965), 32-35.

5616 _____. "The Sheat-fish," Margaret D. Howie, trans., Scala International, (March 1969), 34-36.

5617 Langford, Ernest. "The Potlatch," Tamarack Review, nos. 50-51 (1969), 20-35.

5618 Langford, Mitchell. "The Absurd Man Goes West," Nexus (San Francisco, Calif.), II (September-October 1965), 14-26.

5619 _____. "The Early-Late Show," December, IX (1967), 195-200.

5620 _____. "Won't You Be My Andrew Gyne?" Nexus (San Francisco, Calif.), III (January-February 1967), 12-14.

5621 Langner, Ilse. "The Poor Scrivener Pu," George Raymond Selden, trans., Scala International, (August 1966), 34-36.

5622 Lanning, George. "The Coast of Erie," Sewanee Review, LXXVI (January-March 1968), 49-75.

5623 Lao Khamhawm. "The Plank," Domnern Garden, trans., Solidarity, II (July-August 1967), 99-101.

5624 Lao She. "The Grand Opening," William A. Lyell, trans., East-West Review, III (Summer 1967), 170-182.

5625 Lapcheske, Christine. "Italian Bread, Italian Wine," New Leaven, XIX (1969), 18-20.

5626 Lape, Fred. "Her Eye on the Sparrows," Ave Maria, CI

(April 17, 1965), 22-25.

5627 Lardas, Konstantinos. "The Bird," Prairie Schooner, XLIII (Winter 1969/70), 385-392.

5628 _____. "The Usurpation," Literary Review, XIII (Winter 1969-70), 224-235.

5629 Lardner, Susan. "Family Portrait," Seventeen, XXVI (December 1967), 106-107, 157-158.

5630 _____. "Older Man," Seventeen, XXV (September 1966), 176-177, 218, 220, 222.

5631 Large, Thomas. "Mrs. Bluefoot's Radio," Intro, no. 1 (September 1968), 41-51.

5632 Larner, Jeremy. "Barbara Song," Cavalier, XV (April 1965), 20-21, 44-45.

5633 _____. "Oh, the Wonder!" Paris Review, no. 33 (1965), 15-36.

5634 _____. "They Are Taking My Letters," Harper's Magazine, CCXXXVII (October 1968), 45-57.

5635 Larroc, Pietra. "The Wagon Star," North American Mentor, IV (Spring 1966), 27-28, 30-33.

5636 Larsen, Carl. "The Big Baboon by the Light of the Moon Was Combing His Auburn Hair," Blackbird, I, no. 3 (1966), 51-53.

5637 _____. "Meet Miss Subways," Spero, I, no. 1 (1965), 52-54.

5638 _____. "The World Is Made of Snow/(from Chapter 8 of Walk East to the River)," Spero, I, no. 2 (1966), 3-7.

5639 Larsen, Eric E. "Skirmish," South Dakota Review, IV (Winter 1966), 70-82.

5640 Larsen, J. Joseph. "Astyanax," Dust, III (Winter-Spring 1967), 11-13.

5641 Larsen, Richard B. "Colored Alley," Arizona Quarterly, XXI (Autumn 1965), 212-220.

5642 _____. "Economic Man," DeKalb Literary Arts Journal, I (Fall 1966), 17-26.

5643 _____. "The Mourner," Southern Humanities Review, II (Fall 1968), 422-426.

5644 Larson, Charles R. "Up from Slavery," Kenyon Review, XXXI (1969), 507-528.

5645 Larson, Mary G. "How the West Was Won," Redbook, CXXXI (August 1968), 123-124.

5646 LaRue, Robert. "Mercy Killing," Sage, XI (Spring 1967), 181-200.

5647 Lash, Kenneth. "Annette: A Fable," New Directions 20, (1968), 134-139.

5648 Laster, Clara. "A Fair Trade," Human Voice, V, nos. 1-4 (1969), 110-115.

5649 Lastra, Bonifacio. "The Idiot Children," Donald A. Yates, trans., in "The 'Microtale': An Argentine Specialty," by Donald A. Yates, Texas Quarterly, XII (Summer 1969), 16.

5650 Latimer, Rebecca H. "A Turkish Bride Weeps," Literary Review, XII (Autumn 1968), 17-23.

5651 Latta, Richard. "A Child's World," Arx, III (November 1969), 12-13.

5652 _____. "His Looking-Glass Person," Arx, III (November 1969), 12.

5653 _____. "Looking Glass Puddles," Arx, III (November 1969), 13.

5654 Laub, Marshall. "A Matter of Logic," Edge, no. 8 (Fall 1968), 91.

5655 Lauer, Robert H. "The Quality of Mercy," Ave Maria, CIII (February 19, 1966), 24-25, 27.

5656 Laughridge, Mary. "Michael," Coraddi, (Winter 1969), 12-13.

5657 Laurence, Margaret. "Everything Is All Right," Adam International Review, nos. 313-315 (1967), 27-30.

5658 _____. "The Fire-Dwellers," Ladies' Home Journal, LXXXVI (March 1969), 127-134, 136, 137.

5659 Laurence, Michael. "The Legacy," Playboy, XV (November 1968), 135, 224-226, 228, 230, 232-240.

5660 Lauria, Frank. "Crazyface," US, no. 1 (June 1969), 49.

5661 Lauro, Mary V. "The Troublemaker," University Review, XXXII (December 1965), 83-90.

5662 Lavin, Mary. "Asigh," Dublin Magazine, VI (Summer 1967), 45-62.

5663 _____. "Fond Mother," Threshold, no. 22 (Summer 1969), 42-46.

5664 _____. "A Gentle Soul," Atlantic Monthly, CCXIX (May 1967), 80-87.

5665 _____. "A Glimpse of Katey," Georgia Review, XX (Winter 1966), 401-406.

5666 _____. "Happiness," New Yorker, XLIV (December 14, 1968), 60-67.

5667 _____. "The Lost Child," Southern Review, V (January 1969), 134-169.

5668 _____. "One Evening," Kenyon Review, XXIX (September 1967), 515-525.

5669 _____. "One Summer," New Yorker, XLI (September 11, 1965), 50-58, 60, 63-64, 66, 68, 70, 73-74, 76, 78, 80, 83, 85-86, 88, 90, 95-96, 98.

5670 _____. "The Patriot Son," Georgia Review, XX (Fall 1966), 301-317.

5671 _____. "A Pure Accident," Southern Review, V (July 1969), 790-818.

5672 Lavrenyov, Boris. "The Kshesinskaya Palace," Soviet Literature, (no. 4, 1967), 38-42.

5673 Law, Warner. "The Man Who Fooled the World," Saturday Evening Post, CCXLI (August 24, 1968), 38-51.

5674 _____. "The $1000 Cup of Crazy German Coffee," Playboy, XVI (May 1969), 90-92, 210-214, 216, 218.

5675 Lawal, Babatunde. "The Belly of the Night," Dust, II (Spring-Summer 1966), 11-21.

5676 Lawless, Ken. "Arena Grill," The World, no. 13 (November 1968), n.p. [31].

5677 Lawrance, J. N. [untitled], The Cantuarian, (December 1968), 31.

5678 _____. "Die Haare der Kleopatra," The Cantuarian, (August 1968), 198-199.

5679 Lawrence, D. H. "Mother and Daughter," Ararat, VI (Summer 1965), 5-17.

5680 Lawrence, Louisa. "The Full Extent of the Damage," McCall's, XCVI (September 1969), 76-77, 131-132, 134-136.

5681 Lawrence, Melody. "Eliah Sumatra the Third," Transatlantic Review, no. 21 (Summer 1966), 135-141.

5682 _____. "Ngorongoro Crater," Transatlantic Review, no. 27 (Winter 1967-68), 103-108.

5683 Lawrence, Vincent. "The White Walled Men," Transatlantic Review, no. 30 (Autumn 1968), 35-40.

5684 Lawrenson, Ian. "A Blue Rabbit," Art and Literature, no. 12 (Spring 1967), 178-183.

5685 Laws, Betty Ann. "Fantasy of the Faucets," Approach, no. 54 (Winter 1965), 15-23.

5686 Lawson, Jack B. "The Only God Whose Real Name We Know," Colorado Quarterly, XV (Winter 1967), 251-260.

5687 _____. "A Question of Taste," Massachusetts Review, VIII (Summer 1967), 457-467.

5688 Lawson, Todd S. J. "Herbie and I," Plaintiff, V (Fall 1968), 33-42.

5689 Lawson, William. "To the Editor," Plaintiff, V (Winter 1969), 21-22.

5690 Layne, Jeannette. "A Fistful of Rainbows," Bim, XII (January-June 1969), 249-253.

5691 _____. "Telephone Conversation," Bim, XII (July-December 1968), 151-155.

5692 Layne, Paul. "A Hot Day At the Fair," Bim, XII (January-June 1968), 127-133.

5693 _____. "Sunday Blues," Bim, XII (July-December 1968), 189-193.

5694 _____. "Sunny Barbados," Bim, XIII (July-December 1969), 46-51.

5695 Le Kim Kien. "Autumn, Love, and Rain," Hemisphere, XII (December 1968), 36-37.

5696 _____. "'Flood'--A Fable from Viet-Nam," Hemisphere, XI (July 1967), 34-36.

5697 _____. "Tu Uyen," Hemisphere, XII (April 1968), 34-36.

5698 Leach, Michael. "Evensong," Ave Maria, CV (April 1, 1967), 26-28.

5699 _____. "For Adults Only," Ave Maria, CIV (September 17, 1966), 24-27.

5700 Leahy, Jack Thomas. "The Bedroom Window," Prospero's Cell, I (April-June 1966), 13-22.

5701 _____. "Escargots à la Bordelaise via The Hanging Vineyards of the Golden Gate Bridge," Sou'wester, (Summer 1968), 20-22.

5702 _____. "The Gift," Prospero's Cell, I (April-June 1966), 23-27.

5703 _____. "Heaven Is behind the Moon," Northwest Review, VII (Spring-Summer 1965), 62-70.

5704 _____. "Like Snowflake. Like Ash." Jeopardy, no. 4 (Spring 1968), 48-49.

5705 _____. "Rails," Genesis West, III (Winter 1965), 67-68.

5706 _____. "The Sable Chain," Prospero's Cell, I, no. 3 (1966), 37-75.

5707 Leaman, Marion McCreedy. "Perverse Echo," California Review, no. 1 (Spring 1967), 37-50.

5708 Leamon, Warren. "Two Sections of Jason, A New Novel," Arlington Quarterly, I (Winter 1967-68), 143-172.

5709 Leasor, James. "Doctor Love Strikes Again," Vogue, CXLVI (November 1, 1965), 183, 218, 220-223.

5710 _____. "Dr. Jason Love and the Curious Equation," Vogue, CXLV (January 15, 1965), 70-71, 120, 122-123.

5711 _____. "Dr. Love, Hero, and Heroin," Vogue, CXLVII (February 15, 1966), 144, 146, 149, 153.

5712 Leaton, Anne. "From Indiana to the Dark via a Smile," Transatlantic Review, no. 30 (Autumn 1968), 52-59.

5713 Lebherz, Richard. " 'Say Goodbye to Miss Marianne MacCambridge Dear!'," Queen, CDXXVII (October 26, 1966), 72-74.

5714 Le Carré, John. "Bread on the Waters," Playboy, XII (December 1965), 194-195.

5715 _____. "Dare I Weep, Dare I Mourn?" Saturday Evening Post,

CCXL (January 28, 1967), 54-56, 60.

5716 ______. "The Looking-Glass War/Part I," Ladies' Home Journal, LXXXII (April 1965), 63-67, 102-104, 106-112, 114-120.

5717 ______. "The Looking-Glass War/Conclusion," Ladies' Home Journal, LXXXII (May 1965), 54-55, 98-99, 101, 103-105, 107-109, 111-114.

5718 ______. "Vienna," Weekend Telegraph, no. 91 (June 24, 1966), 25-26.

5719 ______. "What Ritual Is Being Observed Tonight?" Saturday Evening Post, CCXLI (November 2, 1968), 60-62, 64-65.

5720 Le Clézio, J. M. G. "The Flood," Peter Green, trans., Harper's Bazaar, CI (February 1968), 170-171, 213, 218.

5721 ______. "Heading for the Island," Daphne Woodward, trans., Encounter, XXV (November 1965), 17-23.

5722 ______. "It Seems to Me the Boat Is Heading for the Island," Richard Howard, trans., Vogue, CXLV (February 15, 1965), 102-103, 137-139, 141.

5723 Lederer, William J. "The Story of Pink Jade," McCall's, XCIV (December 1966), 100-101, 165-168.

5724 Ledoux, David. "See Wonder Cave," Red Clay Reader, no. 5 (1968), 96-103.

5725 Lee, Audrey. "I'm Going to Move out of This Emotional Ghetto," Negro Digest, XIX (December 1969), 63-68.

5726 ______. "Moma," Negro Digest, XVIII (February 1969), 53-65.

5727 Lee, Barbara. "Episode on a Toastrack," Delta (Cambridge, England), no. 45 (March 1969), 44-47.

5728 Lee, Lawrence. "An Alliance of Strangers," Sewanee Review, LXXVI (October-December 1968), 552-568.

5729 ______. "The Heroic Journey," Michigan Quarterly Review, V (Spring 1966), 125-130.

5730 ______. "The Marauding Crows," Georgia Review, XXII (Winter 1968), 489-500.

5731 Lee, Marjorie. "Alone At Last," Redbook, CXXVII (July 1966), 62-63, 100-102.

5732 ______. "Be Honest With Me," Redbook, CXXVIII (April 1967), 80-81.

5733 ______. "Did I Say It Was Funny?" Redbook, CXXVI (November 1965), 52-53, 117, 123.

5734 ______. "Just Among Friends," Redbook, CXXVII (June 1966), 82-83.

5735 Lee, Michael, F.S.C. "The Other War," Four Quarters, XVII (January 1968), 6-15.

5736 ______. "Sea Gulls," Four Quarters, XVII (March 1968), 15-19.

5737 Lee, Virginia. "Doubly Blessed," Good Housekeeping, CLXIX (December 1969), 78-79, 213-217.

5738 Leeb, M. "Quasi," Beyond Baroque 691, I (December 1968), 56.

5739 Leeds, Charlie. "I'm in Love with the Girl on the 3¢ Stamp/or/It's Her Irish Ass I'm After," Prism International, VIII (Spring 1969), 41-42.

5740 ______. "Kansas City Syndrome," Prism International, VIII (Spring 1969), 39-41.

5741 ______. "Rose O'Christ," Prism International, VIII (Spring 1969), 37.

5742 ______. "Sailboat in the Moonlight," Prism International, VIII (Spring 1969), 38-39.

5743 ______. "Two excerpts from To Hell with THIS Cock-Eyed World/The Man Who Loved Everything/Hello Sucker," Prism International, VIII (Spring 1969), 42-47.

5744 Leeds, Douglas B. "1941," Lance, V (Spring 1965), 1-2.

5745 Leeming, Owen. "Damage," Landfall, no. 90 (June 1969), 123-130.

5746 ______. "Road from Samarkand," Landfall, no. 74 (June 1965), 113-118.

5747 ______. "Wet Season," London Magazine, IX (June 1969), 48-56.

5748 Leffland, E. "The Forest," Epoch, XVIII (Winter 1969), 175-198.

5749 ______. "Two Stories/Inside," Quarterly Review of Literature,

XV (1968), 366-381.

5750 _____. "Two Stories/Vienna, City of My Dreams," Quarterly Review of Literature, XV (1968), 355-365.

5751 Leggett, John. "The Little Flames of Genius," Mademoiselle, LXV (June 1967), 138-139, 181, 183.

5752 _____. "Stalking the Muse on Publisher's Row," Harper's Magazine, CCXXX (January 1965), 64-66.

5753 _____. "You Take the Easy Road to Success in Writing," Harper's Magazine, CCXXXII (February 1966), 49-52.

5754 LeGuin, U. K. "Nine Lives," Playboy, XVI (November 1969), 128-129, 132, 220-222, 224, 226-228, 230.

5755 Lehane, Brendan. "Plum Tart," Queen, CDXXXIV (July 9, 1969), 72-74.

5756 Lehman, David C. "Poetry," Columbia Review, XLVII, no. 2 (1967), 52-54.

5757 Lehrman, Robert. "Mrs. Gardner's Orgy," Transatlantic Review, no. 29 (Summer 1968), 103-116.

5758 Leif, N. R. "Ship-Shape," Human Voice, V, nos. 1-4 (1969), 88-90.

5759 Leigh, James. "Yes It's Me and I'm Late Again," Playboy, XVI (March 1969), 105, 169-170, 172, 174-177.

5760 Leitch, Maurice. "From Work in Progress," Threshold, no. 20 (Winter 1966/67), 62-71.

5761 _____. "The Funeral," Threshold, no. 21 (Summer 1967), 54-63.

5762 Lelchuk, Alan. "Of Our Time," New American Review, no. 4 (August 1968), 215-264.

5763 _____. "Sundays," Transatlantic Review, no. 21 (Summer 1966), 141-153.

5764 _____. "Winter Image," Transatlantic Review, no. 32 (Summer 1969), 114-129.

5765 Lemke, Lillian. "Lancey Was Her Darling," Signature, I (June 1966), 29.

5766 Lemmon, Dallas M., Jr. "Dead Men Get No Tail," Arx, II (May 1968), 6-13.

5767 _____. "Glare," Arx, I (February 1968), 13-15.

5768 Lenart, Francis. "Buzzbug," New Zealand Listener, LVIII (April 26, 1968), 10.

5769 Lenero, Vincente. "The Perfect Adventure," Margaret S. Peden, trans., Tri-Quarterly, nos. 13/14 (Fall/Winter 1968-69), 367-374.

5770 Lengyel, József. "'Hohem' and 'Freier'," New Hungarian Quarterly, VI (Autumn 1965), 123-128.

5771 Lengyel, T. C. "Ursula," North American Mentor, V (Fall 1967), 5-7.

5772 Lenz, Hermann. "Water Sixty," George Raymond Selden, trans., Scala International, (June 1965), 34-37.

5773 Lenz, Siegfried. "The Blindfold," E. W. Gundel, trans., Dimension, II, no. 1 (1969), 16-25 [in German & English on alternate pages].

5774 _____. "A Coast Seen through Binoculars," Margaret D. Howie, trans., Scala International, (October 1969), 34-37.

5775 _____. "Danger for Santa Claus," Esquire, LXVIII (December 1967), 203, 110.

5776 _____. "A Humane Experiment/or The Pain Is Permissible," Geoffrey Brogan, trans., Mundus Artium, II (Winter 1968), 34-51 [in German and English on alternate pages].

5777 _____. "The Proof," George Raymond Selden, trans., Scala International, (May 1966), 28-32.

5778 _____. "The Sixth Birthday," Barbara Einhorn, E. W. Herd and Ian Fraser, trans., Landfall, no. 86 (June 1968), 157-164.

5779 Leon, J. A. "Some Notes on Three Mongoloid Configurations," Edge, no. 9 (Summer 1969), 119-123.

5780 Leonard, Constance Brink. "Some Things Just Feel Right," Redbook, CXXXII (December 1968), 66-67.

5781 Leonard, Marianne. "Carmen," Delta Review, V (August 1968), 50-53, 62.

5782 _____. "Memphis," Harper's Magazine, CCXXXIX (October 1969), 95-103.

5783 _____. "Sloths and Cockatoos," Delta Review, IV (May-June 1967), 48-49, 102-104.

5784 _____. "Stuffed Pussy Cats," Delta Review, VI (November-December 1969), 30-32, 96.

5785 Leone, Shirley. "The Thief," Western Review, III (Summer 1966), 51-54.

5786 Leonov, Leonid. "Skutarevsky," Avril Pyman, trans., Soviet Literature, (no. 5, 1969), 3-50.

5787 Leopold, Edward. "A Light Rain," Ante, II (Spring 1966), 61-70.

5788 Lerman, Louis. "Cheap Farber," Midstream, XIV (January 1968), 32-38.

5789 Lerner, Laurence. "My Aunt Alice," Contrast (Cape Town, South Africa), no. 16 (June 1967), 70-72, 77-93.

5790 Leslie, Eleanor. "Names and Faces," Cosmopolitan, CLXVI (June 1969), 138-141.

5791 _____. "Untitled Manuscript," Epoch, XVIII (Spring 1969), 271-279.

5792 Lessing, Doris. "Particularly Cats," Queen, CDXXVIII (March 15, 1967), 74-77.

5793 Lettau, Reinhard. "The Enemy," A. Leslie Willson, trans., Dimension, I, no. 1 (1968), 80-93 [in German and English on alternate pages].

5794 _____. "Two Tales/Mr. Paronne Tours the Provinces," Harper's Bazaar, XCVIII (March 1965), 206, 253.

5795 _____. "Two Tales/Potemkin's Carriage Passes through," Harper's Bazaar, XCVIII (March 1965), 205, 253.

5796 Letton, Jennette. "Allegra's Child," Redbook, CXXXII (February 1969), 165-187.

5797 Levertov, Denise. "In the Night," Chicago Review, XVIII, nos. 3 & 4 (1966), 22-25.

5798 Leviant, Curt. "Are You a Falasha?" North American Review, III (November 1966), 6-14.

5799 _____. "Mourning Call," Quarterly Review of Literature, XIII (1965), 357-374.

5800 _____. "Turnabout Is Fair Play," North American Review, IV (July 1967), 17-22.

5801 Levin, Beatrice. "The House across the Street," Ball State

University Forum, X (Autumn 1969), 71-79.

5802 _____. "A Little Death, a Little Dying," Arx, III (November 1969), 20-25.

5803 _____. "The Painting Machine," Arx, II (November 1968), 20-24.

5804 Levin, Ira. "Rosemary's Baby," Cosmopolitan, CLXIII (December 1967), 134-146, 148, 150-151, 154-157.

5805 Levin, Laurence M. "La Chamade," Prolog, VII (Winter 1969), 17-23.

5806 Levin, Nidra. "A Wedding Party in Piazza Navona," Perspective, XIV (Winter 1966), 67-83.

5807 Levin, Ruth. "The Cardinal Stays All Winter," Redbook, CXXXIV (December 1969), 102-103.

5808 Levine, Norman. "A Father," Adam International Review, nos. 313-315 (1967), 32-36.

5809 Levinge, Barbara. "Chimera," Cornhill Magazine, CLXXVI (Summer 1968), 426-432.

5810 Levinson, Deirdre. "Crouch," Commentary, XLI (May 1966), 60-64.

5811 _____. "The Homecoming of Joel Bialystock," Commentary, XXXIX (June 1965), 78-82.

5812 Levinson, Norma. "Mrs. Lark's Beautiful Coat," Redbook, CXXXII (December 1968), 80-81.

5813 _____. "Paradise on Tuesday," Redbook, CXXVII (August 1966), 64-65.

5814 Levinson, Rascha. "Description of a Situation," The Smith, no. 8 (March 1968), 89-99.

5815 Levoy, Myron. "Absurd, Absurd," Massachusetts Review, VIII (Spring 1967), 239-244.

5816 _____. "Vera," Western Humanities Review, XIX (Winter 1965), 37-41.

5817 Lewis, Barbara. "Two Dreams/The Bridge," For Now, no. 8 (c. 1966-68), 14.

5818 _____. "Two Dreams/A Killing," For Now, no. 8 (c. 1966-68), 14.

5819 [Lewis, C. Day] Nicholas Blake. "The Private Wound," Imprint, IX (April 1969), 65, 67, 69, 71, 73, 75, 77, 79, 81, 83, 85, 87, 89, 91, 93, 95, 97, 99, 101, 103, 105, 107, 109, 111, 113, 115.

5820 Lewis, Clayton W. "After the War," Story: the Yearbook of Discovery, (1969), 75-85.

5821 Lewis, Faye C. "A Summer of Youth and Age," Discourse, XI (Autumn 1968), 531-534.

5822 Lewis, Florence. "The Pink Girl," Trace, no. 67 (1968), 87-89.

5823 Lewis, Geraldine. "The Legacy," Woman's Day, (June 1965), 38-39, 104-105.

5824 Lewis, Janet. "The Breakable Cup," Saturday Evening Post, CCXXXVIII (February 27, 1965), 60-61, 63-66.

5825 Lewis, Joseph. "The Intellectual," William and Mary Review, VII (Winter 1969), 13-19.

5826 Lewis, Julie. "Dry Season," Westerly, (August 1966), 14-18.

5827 ______. "Flotsam," Westerly, no. 4 (1967), 21-23.

5828 Lewis, Lorna. "Love All My Faces," Redbook, CXXXIII (May 1969), 88-89, 166-167, 171-173.

5829 ______. "Merry Christmas, Mother! Merry Christmas, Barracliff!" Redbook, CXXXIV (December 1969), 96-97, 163, 165-168.

5830 Lewis, Lyle. "When the Boys Come Out to Play," Nexus, (San Francisco, Calif.), II (March-April 1965), 49-54.

5831 Lewis, Reba. "Hira Means a Diamond," Eastern Horizon, VII (November-December 1969), 58-62.

5832 ______. "Money Isn't Expensive," Eastern Horizon, IV (July 1965), 54-60.

5833 ______. "The Treasure," Eastern Horizon, VII (May-June 1968), 61-64.

5834 L'Hommedieu, D. F. "The Sleepy Sheep and the Wakeful Sheep," Literary Review, XIII (Winter 1969-70), 268-269.

5835 Liang, Lee Kok. "When the Saints Go Marching," Literature East and West, X (December 1966), 325-341.

5836 Liben, Meyer. "Ball of Fire," Commentary, XLIII (March 1967), 57-62.

5837 ______. "Change of Heart," Commentary, XXXIX (January 1965), 51-54.

5838 ______. "The Intermediary," Art and Literature, no. 4 (Spring 1965), 244-256.

5839 Liberman, M. M. "Letter from the Thirties," December, VII (1965), 9-14.

5840 Licht, Fred S. "Children of Spain," Sewanee Review, LXXIII (January-March 1965), 47-57.

5841 ______. "A Semblance of Authenticity," Carleton Miscellany, VI (Spring 1965), 54-72.

5842 ______. "Touch-for-Luck," Carleton Miscellany, VII (Fall 1966), 60-72.

5843 Lidin, Vladimir. "Three Stories/Earth Underneath the Wings," Margaret Wettlin, trans., Soviet Literature, (no. 5, 1966), 104-114.

5844 ______. "Three Stories/The Patter of Rain," Margaret Wettlin, trans., Soviet Literature, (no. 5, 1966), 114-123.

5845 ______. "Three Stories/Sagittarius," Margaret Wettlin, trans., Soviet Literature, (no. 5, 1966), 123-131.

5846 Lidman, Sara. "Missy," Carl Anderson, trans., Literary Review, IX (Winter 1965-66), 272-278.

5847 Lieb, Michael J. "Mirror, Mirror," William and Mary Review, VI (Winter 1968), 3-15.

5848 Lieber, Joel. "Eat a Sour Grape," Literary Review, X (Autumn 1966), 83-128.

5849 ______. "How Say You, Man," 25, I (October 1968), 38-39, 55.

5850 ______. "No Work for Abe Green," Epoch, XV (Spring 1966), 268-285.

5851 Lieber, Todd. "Whatever Happened to Art Calenti," The Archive, LXXVIII (April 1966), 4-11.

5852 Lieberman, Mark. "The Dog in the Chair," Ante, III (Summer 1967), 65.

5853 Lief, Ruth. "Child Care," Minnesota Review, VIII (1968), 42-43.

5854 _____. "Family Life," Minnesota Review, VIII (1968), 43-45.

5855 _____. "Untouched by Solemn Thought," Perspective, XV (Autumn 1967), 117-136.

5856 Lill, James. "Bastrop and the Beasts," Texas Quarterly, IX (Spring 1966), 159-163.

5857 Lilley, Merv. "Some Star of Courage," Overland, no. 32 (Spring 1965), 5-8.

5858 Linblad, Lois. "Soup," Prospero's Cell, II (Spring 1967), 21-31.

5859 Lind, Jakov. "Landscape in Concrete," Ramparts, V (June 1966), 32-50.

5860 _____. "Soul of Wood," Ramparts, III (March 1965), 25-55.

5861 Lindall, Edward. "The Turning Point," Woman's Day, (February 1965), 44-45, 116-120.

5862 Linde, Jed. "The Last Aztec Mystic," Mexico Quarterly Review, II (July 1965), 147-151.

5863 _____. "A Sudden Transfusion," Dust, IV (Summer 1969), 16-18.

5864 Lindholm, Charles. "From a Novel," Columbia Review, XLVIII, no. 1 (1967), 44-51.

5865 _____. "Gunsill!" Columbia Review, XLVIII, no. 2 (1968), 41-47.

5866 Lindner, Robert A. "Where Are You Going Baby Bye?" Delta Review, V (March 1968), 16-18, 21-25, 58.

5867 Lindsay, Elena. "The Mediator," New Zealand Listener, (February 10, 1967), 6.

5868 Lindsay, LeRoy R. "Michael's Hand," Twigs, no. 2 (1966), 28-31.

5869 Lindsley, T. R. "A Time to Stand," Delta, XIX (1965), 1-3.

5870 Liner, Amon. "Cannibals and Cartwheels/Scenes and Visions XXXIII," Grande Ronde Review, no. 6 (1966), n.p. [25-26].

5871 Link, Curtis. "The Turquoise Beads," South Dakota Review, VII (Summer 1969), 126-129.

5872 Link, Robert. "Disfigurement," Georgia Review, XXII

(Winter 1968), 509-514.

5873 Linneman, William R. "Here Is No Water," Sage, XI (Fall 1966), 103-115.

5874 _____. "They Endured," Ball State University Forum, VII (Winter 1966), 53-59.

5875 Linney, Romulus. "From The Captivity of Pixie Shedman," Red Clay Reader, no. 2 (1965), 79-83.

5876 Lins, Hermann. "Attempt to Move," Ulf Zimmerman, trans., Dimension, II, no. 3 (1969), 646-671 [in German and English on alternate pages].

5877 Lintula, John. "It's Cold Outside," UMD Humanist, XIV (Spring 1966), 17.

5878 LinYatta. "Fitting," Evergreen Review, XIII (May 1969), 22-24.

5879 Lipatov, Vil. "A Village Detective," Avril Pyman, trans., Soviet Literature, (no. 4, 1968), 7-74.

5880 Lipnick, W. "Tonight I'm Going to Die in the Electric Chair," Nexus (San Francisco, Calif.), II (March-April 1965), 49-52.

5881 Littke, Lael J. "The Day We Lost Max," Ladies' Home Journal, LXXXVI (October 1969), 84-85.

5882 Litvinov, Ivy. "Babuska," New Yorker, XLIV (July 20, 1968), 30-34.

5883 _____. "Call It Love," New Yorker, XLV (November 29, 1969), 54-60, 62, 64, 67-70, 73-74, 76, 78-80.

5884 _____. "Farewell to the Dacha," New Yorker, XLIII (September 16, 1967), 47-54.

5885 _____. "She Knew She Was Right," New Yorker, XLIV (September 28, 1968), 42-49.

5886 _____. "Sowing Asphodel," New Yorker, XLII (April 23, 1966), 50-56.

5887 _____. "Wet Spring," New Yorker, XLV (May 10, 1969), 38-41.

5888 Litwak, Leo. "The Oath," Commentary, XLVIII (August 1969), 33-37.

5889 Liu Ching. "Kai-hsia and Sheng-pao," Sidney Shapiro, trans.,

Eastern Horizon, V (January 1966), 54-62.

5890 Livingston, Dinah. "Grow Old Along with Me," Mademoiselle, LXIII (August 1966), 292-293, 384-387.

5891 Livingston, Peter. "Red Men in Melanesia," Overland, no. 39 (Spring 1968), 34-35.

5892 _____. "Variations in Black Magic," Australian Letters, VIII (January 1968), 30-34.

5893 Livingston, Thomas. "The Arbitrator," Playboy, XVI (May 1969), 157, 160, 194-196, 199.

5894 Liyong, Taban lo. "Two Stories/He and Him," Transition, VII, no. 36 (1968), 60-61.

5895 _____. "Two Stories/Tombe 'Gworong's Own Story," Transition, VII, no. 36 (1968), 60.

5896 Llewellyn, Alun. "The Severed Self," Anglo-Welsh Review, XV (Summer 1965), 30-41.

5897 Llewellyn, Richard. "The End of the Rug," Cosmopolitan, CLXVI (January 1969), 114-118, 122-131, 134-137, 140-143.

5898 _____. "O, Feast of Happy Mari," McCall's, XCIV (December 1966), 70-71, 156-159.

5899 Lobban, Joyce A. "The Shadow of Hemi," New Zealand Listener, LX (March 7, 1969), 12, 19.

5900 LoCicero, T. V. "The Jungle Plant," University Review, XXXIII (December 1966), 83-92.

5901 Lock, Ezzard. "The Investigation," Daily Telegraph Magazine, no. 264 (October 31, 1969), 67-68, 72.

5902 Locklin, Gerald. "The Bummer," New Orleans Review, I (Winter 1969), 169-171.

5903 _____. "Mogen," New Orleans Review, I (Spring 1969), 277-278.

5904 _____. "The Monopoly Story," TransPacific, no. 1 (Summer 1969), 41-45.

5905 Lockridge, Richard. "Murder in False Face," Redbook, CXXX (April 1968), 161, 163-185.

5906 _____. "Troubled Journey," Good Housekeeping, CLXIX (August 1969), 62-65, 172-176, 186-201.

5907 Lockridge, Ross. "The Procrastinators," Pegasus, IV, no. 2 (1966), 11-12.

5908 Lodge, David. "The Man Who Couldn't Get Up," Weekend Telegraph, no. 84 (May 6, 1966), 57, 59-60.

5909 Loeser, Katinka. "Brothers and Sisters Have I None," New Yorker, XLI (May 1, 1965), 44-50.

5910 _____. "College in the Rain," New Yorker, XLIV (April 13, 1968), 38-39.

5911 _____. "Don't Give My Body to Science, the Dying Mother Said," New Yorker, XLI (October 30, 1965), 57-62.

5912 _____. "How I Spent My Summer Vacation," Redbook, CXXVII (September 1966), 64-65, 132-134.

5913 _____. "January Nuptials for Miss Fairweather," New Yorker, XLI (January 29, 1966), 27-31.

5914 _____. "The Life and Death of Little Children," New Yorker, XLII (August 27, 1966), 26-27.

5915 _____. "Marmee," New Yorker, XLII (June 25, 1966), 28-32.

5916 _____. "Messy and Windy," Redbook, CXXXII (February 1969), 90-91.

5917 _____. "To All a Good Night," Redbook, CXXVIII (December 1966), 58-59.

5918 _____. "Where Early Falls the Dew," McCall's, XCIII (March 1966), 98-99, 155-158, 162-163.

5919 Loewinsohn, Ron. "L'Autre," Wild Dog, no. 15 (March 1965), 9.

5920 _____. "The Lifeboat," Occident, I (Spring/Summer 1967), 67-75.

5921 Lofts, Norah. "The Lost Queen/(Part I)," Good Housekeeping, CLXVIII (January 1969), 63-65, 179-194.

5922 _____. "The Lost Queen/(Conclusion)," Good Housekeeping, CLXVIII (February 1969), 76-77, 180, 182, 186, 188, 190, 192, 194-204, 217-218.

5923 _____. "Something Young About the House," Ladies' Home

Journal, LXXXV (October 1968), 92-93, 161-165.

5924 _____. "The Touchstone," Cosmopolitan, CLXI (August 1966), 96-100.

5925 Loftus, Peter. "Jago and the Deep Night," Westerly, no. 2 (July 1969), 25-37.

5926 _____. "Under the Lid," Australian Letters, VIII (January 1968), 81-87.

5927 Logan, Drayton. "The Story of Magnus," Sundial, I (Spring 1966), 29-36.

5928 Logan, John. "The Cigars," Minnesota Review, V (January-April 1965), 35-38.

5929 Logan, Louis Dell. "Alligator's Hopes in a Tadpole Town," New Mexico Quarterly, XXXVII (Summer 1967), 112-128.

5930 _____. "The Bill Collector," Story: the Yearbook of Discovery, (1968), 38-52.

5931 Loginov, Victor. "The Colour of Scalded Milk," Avril Pyman, trans., Soviet Literature, (no. 7, 1968), 123-133.

5932 Logue, Trinita. "After Work," Ave Maria, CV (February 4, 1967), 26-28.

5933 _____. "The End of the World," Ave Maria, CII (August 7, 1965), 24-26.

5934 Loloji, James Chipatela. "Storm," New Writing from Zambia, no. 1 (1968), 5-7.

5935 Lomax, Almena. "In the Faraway Country of Montgomery, Alabama," Harper's Magazine, CCXXXVII (September 1968), 51-52, 57-63.

5936 Lonergan, Ann. "The Malibu Story," Ante, I (Fall 1965), 3-15.

5937 Long, Robert E. "Farewell to Joey," University Review, XXXV (Spring 1969), 306-310.

5938 Longee, Lynda. "If You Can't Lick 'Em," Seventeen, XXIV (January 1965), 86, 116-117.

5939 Longley, John Lewis, Jr. "The Rites of Spring," Southern Review, II (July 1966), 641-656.

5940 Longrigg, Roger. "Love," Cosmopolitan, CLXVII (August 1969), 120-121.

5941 Longsio, Carol. "Just because It's Christmas," UMD Humanist, XIII (Spring 1965), 16-18.

5942 Longstreet, Nancy Jo. "Titled Day," Sequoia, X (Winter 1965), 47-56.

5943 Longstreet, Stephen. "Dinner at Pedlock House," American Judaism, XV (Winter 1965-66), 22-23, 53-56.

5944 Lonidier, Lynn. "The Birds of Permanent Residence," Ball State University Forum, VII (Winter 1966), 46-52.

5945 _____. "Continuo," Genesis West, III (Winter 1965), 69-78.

5946 Lönn, Öystein. "Accident," Timothy Schiff, trans., Literary Review, XII (Winter 1968-69), 233-236.

5947 Loomis, Edward. "Three Love Stories/Hunger," New Mexico Quarterly, XXXVII (Summer 1967), 183-187.

5948 _____. "Three Love Stories/Peyote," New Mexico Quarterly, XXXVII (Summer 1967), 187-191.

5949 _____. "Three Love Stories/The Wolf," New Mexico Quarterly, XXXVII (Summer 1967), 177-182.

5950 Loomis, Susan. "The Fire Is Dying," Twigs, no. 5 (Fall 1969), 191-200.

5951 Lopate, Phillip. "Basic Facts Leading Toward an Analysis," Columbia Review, XLIX, no. 2 (1969), 12-13.

5952 Lopez, Barry. "The Gift," Ave Maria, CIII (March 19, 1966), 22-23.

5953 Lord, Peter. "Friday Night at the Project and Tenuous Relationships Reaching to Long Island," Duel, no. 1 (Winter 1969), 5-9.

5954 Lord, Ruth K. "Oh Lord, Remember Me," Ladies' Home Journal, LXXXIII (April 1966), 88-89, 129-131.

5955 Lorden, Peter. "An Island for One," Discourse, X (Spring 1967), 183-189.

5956 Lorimer, Elizabeth. "Chameleon," Scottish International, no. 6 (April 1969), 53-54.

5957 Lovell, Dorothy. "Father Bear," Bim, XIII (July-December 1969), 25-30.

5958 _____. "Grannie's Birthday," Bim, XII (July-December 1968), 167-174.

5959 ______. "The Shoe," Bim, XII (January-June 1969), 239-243.

5960 Lowenfels, Walter. "How It Started," El Corno Emplumado, no. 17 (January 1966), 58.

5961 ______. "How It Started," Human Voice, I (August 1965), 83.

5962 ______. "Nazim Hikmet/1902-1963," Intrepid, no. 6 (1966), n.p. [18-19].

5963 Lowry, David. "Just a Good Story," Plaintiff, V (Fall 1968), 6.

5964 ______. "Just a Good Story. Part II," Plaintiff, V (Winter 1969), 8-10.

5965 Lowry, John. "The Crooked Tree," Four Quarters, XVI (March 1967), 26-32.

5966 ______. "The Great Dog," Georgia Review, XXI (Spring 1967), 101-106.

5967 ______. "The Mother, the Cat, and the Girl," Plume & Sword, VII (Fall 1966), 3-7.

5968 ______. "A Mystery," Works, I (Summer 1968), 24-25.

5969 ______. "Roy," Red Clay Reader, no. 6 (1969), 102-105.

5970 Lowry, Malcolm. "Bulls of the Resurrection," Prism International, V (Summer 1965), 4-11.

5971 Lowry, Robert. "The Colosseum," Human Voice Quarterly, II (May 1966), 61.

5972 ______. "The Flat," Mt. Adams Review, II (Winter 1967-68), 22-23.

5973 ______. "The Kiss," Carleton Miscellany, VI (Fall 1965), 58-60.

5974 ______. "The Little Outhouse That Burned Down," Human Voice Quarterly, II (February 1966), 3, 24-25.

5975 ______. "A Lively Museum of Youth and Desire," Carleton Miscellany, VIII (Spring 1967), 40-72.

5976 ______. "A Lively Museum of Youth and Desire: Book II," Red Clay Reader, no. 4 (1967), 45-53.

5977 ______. "A Lively Museum of Youth and Desire (excerpts from Book III)," Trace, no. 68 (1968), 313-319.

5978 _____. "Revolt in the Desert," Mt. Adams Review, II (Winter 1967-68), 24-25.

5979 _____. "Silent Night," Human Voice Quarterly, II (May 1966), 61.

5980 _____. "White Birthday," The Goodly Co., no. 3 (August 1965), 18-23.

5981 Lowther, Pat. "The Perfect Game," Prism International, V (Winter-Spring 1966), 52-61.

5982 Luard, Nicholas. "The Warm and Golden War," Mademoiselle, LXV (July 1967), 93-125.

5983 Lubis, Mochtar. "Contract Coolies," A. H. Johns, trans., Hemisphere, X (December 1966), 23-25.

5984 _____. "Love Comes Later," Solidarity, III (October 1968), 68-72.

5985 _____. "The Murderer," Solidarity, IV (August 1969), 39-42.

5986 _____. "The Sacred Grave," Solidarity, II (July-August 1967), 47-53.

5987 _____. "The Teak House," Quadrant, X (May-June 1966), 7-11.

5988 _____. "Two Stories/The Spice of Life," Solidarity, I (July-September 1966), 44-47.

5989 _____. "Two Stories/The Teak House," Solidarity, I (July-September 1966), 41-44.

5990 Lubka, Nancy. "The Summer People," Queen's Quarterly, LXXV (Winter 1968), 720-730.

5991 Luckmann, Wayne. "The Buried Life," Discourse, XI (Summer 1968), 374-379.

5992 Ludwig, Jack. "A Death of One's Own," Tamarack Review, no. 46 (Winter 1968), 79-84.

5993 _____. "Einstein and this Admirer," London Magazine, V (September 1965), 65-74.

5994 _____. "Shirley," Tamarack Review, nos. 50-51 (1969), 52-68.

5995 _____. "Two Parables/Dedalus and Icarus," Soundings, II (Spring 1965), 147.

5996 _____. "Two Parables/Parable of a Bookworm," Soundings, II (Spring 1965), 145-146.

5997 Ludwig, Myles Eric. "A Game of Squash," Carolina Quarterly, XIX (Spring 1967), 71-79.

5998 _____. "Rabbit," Trace, no. 61 (Summer 1966), 194-201.

5999 _____. "Snowy Egrets Meet in Summer," Carolina Quarterly, XVIII (Fall 1966), 28-35.

6000 Lumpkin, Ramona. "Tabula Rosa," Alta, no. 5 (Spring 1968), 299.

6001 Lunario, Filomena. "Eight Dollars To Spend on Sunday," Seventeen, XXVII (January 1968), 100.

6002 Lund, Jeffrey. "Tomorrow Was Graduation," William and Mary Review, VII (Winter 1969), 28-35.

6003 Lund, Mary Graham. "My Second Home," Kansas Magazine, (1967), 88-93.

6004 Lundahl, Gene. "The Judas Goat," Denver Quarterly, I (Summer 1966), 85-95.

6005 Lunde, David and James Sallis. "Weatherman," New Worlds, no. 181 (April 1968), 28-30.

6006 Lundkvist, Artur. "Tiny Woman, Many Children," Marie Skramstad, trans., Literary Review, IX (Winter 1965-66), 191-201.

6007 Lungu, Raisa. "Tokens of Luck," Vladimir Talmy, trans., Soviet Literature, (no. 11, 1965), 4-47.

6008 Lupan, Ana. "A Good Turn," Eve Manning, trans., Soviet Literature, (no. 11, 1965), 54-61.

6009 Luria, Jack. "The Hugger and the Hugged," Harper's Magazine, CCXXXIV (March 1967), 62-64.

6010 Lurie, Morris. "Fenner," Nova, (October 1967), 150-154.

6011 _____. "Happy Times," Daily Telegraph Magazine, no. 218 (December 6, 1968), 50-51, 53, 55.

6012 _____. "Home Is," Transatlantic Review, no. 30 (Autumn 1968), 132-141.

6013 _____. "The Larder," Weekend Telegraph, no. 113 (November 25, 1966), 57-58.

6014 _____. "A Scholar of Ancient Battlements," Nova, (October 1967), 154, 156, 158, 161.

6015 Lutz, John. "Big Game," Signature, II (August 1967), 34-35, 54, 56-57, 59, 64-65.

6016 _____. "The Wounded Tiger," Signature, II (November 1967), 44-45, 98, 101-102, 104, 106, 108-110, 112, 114.

6017 Luz, Helen. [untitled], Grande Ronde Review, no. 3 (Summer 1965), n.p. [35-36].

6018 Lyall, Larry. "Dust," Midwestern University Quarterly, I, no. 2 (1965), 1-4.

6019 Lyles, Peggy Willis. "Camera Obscura," Prairie Schooner, XLII (Spring 1968), 62-77.

6020 Lynch, John A. "Everything Will Be All Right," Perspective, XV (Spring-Summer 1967), 17-25.

6021 _____. "Marriage," Discourse, XII (Spring 1969), 220-224.

6022 _____. "A Small Passion," Virginia Quarterly Review, XLV (Autumn 1969), 650-663.

6023 Lynds, Dennis. "The Animal that Howls Unheard," Northwest Review, VII (Spring 1966), 66-80.

6024 _____. "Squares with Thin Red," Minnesota Review, VII (1967), 187-193.

6025 _____. "Why Girls Ride Sidesaddle," Minnesota Review, V (May-July 1965), 123-131.

6026 Lyngar, Mona. "Variation on a Theme," Virginia Willard, trans., Literary Review, XII (Winter 1968-69), 245-250.

6027 Lyon, Harris Merton. "Scarlet and White/A Posthumous Story," Arlington Quarterly, I (Spring 1968), 83-105.

6028 Lyon, Roy M. "The Train Doesn't Stop Here Anymore," Texas Quarterly, IX (Spring 1966), 22-33.

6029 Lyons, Augusta Wallace. "All the Lovely Possibilities," Redbook, CXXX (December 1967), 143-169.

6030 _____. "Date with an Arab," New Renaissance, I (Spring 1969), 46-51.

6031 _____. "The Fight against Hope," New Renaissance, I (Winter 1969), 44-51.

6032 Lyons, Edward. "The Deserted," New Renaissance, I (December 1969), 20-26.

6033 Lyons, Richard. "Bi-Poligopoly," Wisconsin Review, IV (Fall 1968), 13-15.

6034 _____. "Faithfully Served," DeKalb Literary Arts Journal, III (Summer 1969), 1-22.

6035 _____. "Herbie," Discourse, XII (Summer 1969), 329-343.

6036 _____. "Little Matter," Discourse, XI (Spring 1968), 269-275.

6037 Lyons, Ruth. "In Spain There Is a Saying," Redbook, CXXX (January 1968), 56-57, 96, 98-100.

6038 _____. "The Lost Days," McCall's, XCII (May 1965), 102-103, 197-202.

6039 _____. "Something Nice," Seventeen, XXIV (November 1965), 138-139, 230, 232, 234-235.

6040 Lytle, Andrew. "A Wake for the Living," Sewanee Review, LXXV (October-December 1967), 585-627.

6041 J. F. M. "A Character in Search of an Author," New Zealand Listener, LIII (December 10, 1965), 4.

6042 Ma Hao-lin and Tao Chia-shan. "The Soldiers Chairman Mao Has Sent Us," Tai Chin-wan, trans., Eastern Horizon, VI (June 1967), 60-62.

6043 MacAlpine, Roderick. "Slow Ice," London Magazine, IV (February 1965), 56-62.

6044 Macauley, Robie. "Dressed in Shade," Shenandoah, XVII (Autumn 1965), 3-24.

6045 _____. "For Want of a Nail," Cosmopolitan, CLXIII (October 1967), 152-157.

6046 _____. "That Day," Playboy, XIV (November 1967), 113, 213-214.

6047 Macdonald, Fiona. "Isadora's Afternoon," Queen, CDXXIX (August 2, 1967), 54.

6048 MacDonald, John D. "The Annex," Playboy, XV (May 1968), 84-86, 88, 220-221.

6049 _____. "Bright Orange Shroud," Cosmopolitan, CLVIII (April 1965), 98-111, 115-119, 123-133.

6050 _____. "Darker Than Amber," Cosmopolitan, CLX (April 1966), 118-137, 141-146, 148-151.

6051 _____. "Funny Man," Saturday Evening Post, CCXXXIX (May 21, 1966), 64-66, 68.

6052 _____. "One Fearful Yellow Eye," Cosmopolitan, CLXI (November 1966), 140-146, 148, 150, 152, 154-163, 170-177.

6053 _____. "Quarrel," Playboy, XIV (May 1967), 95, 167-168.

6054 MacDonald, Ross. "The Demon Lover," Cosmopolitan, CLIX (December 1965), 110-118, 120-133, 136-139.

6055 MacDonald, W. J. "Chapter Twenty-Seven: Auguste Pamphile/ from a novel--A Cage for Every Bird," Alphabet, no. 17 (December 1969), 30-34.

6056 MacDougall, Ruth Doan. "The Man to Marry," Redbook, CXXV (September 1965), 161, 163-185.

6057 MacEachron, Grace. "An Open House," Readers & Writers, I (May-June 1966), 15-18.

6058 Macefield, E. Wilson. "Somewhere in Another Town," Ave Maria, CII (August 14, 1965), 24-26.

6059 MacEwen, Gwendolyn. "Animal Syllables," Alphabet, no. 15 (December 1968), 16-20.

6060 _____. "Fragments from a Childhood," Alphabet, no. 15 (December 1968), 10-15.

6061 MacInnes, Helen. "The Salzburg Connection," Imprint, VIII (February 1969), 48-77, 79, 81, 83, 85, 87, 89, 91, 93, 95, 97, 99, 101, 103, 105, 107, 109, 111-114.

6062 _____. "The Salzburg Connection," Redbook, CXXXI (September 1968), 73-80, 115-118, 120-123.

6063 _____. "The Salzburg Connection/(Part 2)," Redbook, CXXXI (October 1968), 80-81, 134, 136, 138, 140-142, 144-145.

6064 _____. "The Salzburg Connection/(Conclusion)," Redbook, CXXXII (November 1968), 84-85, 138, 140, 142, 144, 146, 148-150, 153, 157-158, 160.

6065 Mack, Ed. "A Play about a Clown, a Flower, and a Boy," Mandala, no. 5 (1969), 11-24.

6066 MacKellar, John D. "Sleepytime Down South," Northwest Review, VIII (Summer 1966), 43-59.

6067 MacKenzie, Nancy K. "The Wrong Silence," Prairie Schooner, XLI (Winter 1967), 361-378.

6068 Mackenzie, Seaforth. "I Have Three People," Westerly, (December 1966), 40-42.

6069 ______. "Maiden's Hill," Westerly, (December 1966), 72-84.

6070 ______. "The Model," Westerly, (December 1966), 46-71.

6071 ______. "The Old Adam," Westerly, (December 1966), 43-45.

6072 Mackey, Ernan. "First Farewell," Redbook, CXXV (September 1965), 58-59, 114, 116.

6073 ______. "The Lady and the Lifeguard," Redbook, CXXIX (August 1967), 42.

6074 ______. "Oh, My Darling Daughter," Redbook, CXXVII (October 1966), 66-67, 112, 114-115.

6075 MacKinnon, Lilian Vaux. "Cape Breton Picnic," Queen's Quarterly, LXXIV (Summer 1967), 248-254.

6076 MacLean, Frazer. "Friday Afternoon," Epoch, XV (Fall 1965), 41-58.

6077 MacLennan, Don. "The Wonderful Life and Resurrection of a Guru," Contrast (Cape Town, South Africa), no. 13 (December 1965), 30-42.

6078 MacLeod, Alistair. "The Boat," Massachusetts Review, IX (Spring 1968), 247-266.

6079 MacLeod, Charlotte. "Mine to Love," Good Housekeeping, CLXIV (February 1967), 86-87.

6080 MacLeod, James L. "The Jesus Flag," Georgia Review, XXI (Summer 1967), 198-209.

6081 Macklin, F. A. "Act of Blood," North American Review, V (September-October 1968), 37-40.

6082 Maclow, Jackson. [untitled], Damascus Road, no. 3 (1967), 28-38.

6083 MacMillan, Ian T. "Ashes," Massachusetts Review, X (Autumn 1969), 765-770.

6084 ______. "In the Ring," Midwestern University Quarterly, II, no. 3 (1967), 15-35.

6085 ______. "John Ballard," Arizona Quarterly, XXV (Spring 1969), 18-35.

6086 ______. "Light and Power," Georgia Review, XXII (Spring 1968), 58-73.

6087 ______. "Vernal Equinox," December, VII (1965), 56-66.

6088 MacNeal, Martha. "Anomaly's Eyes," Harper's Magazine, CCXXX (February 1965), 91-94.

6089 MacNeil, Janie J. "Attending Guest," Grok, I (February-May 1967), 11-13.

6090 MacNish, Linda. "We Learn By Loving," Good Housekeeping, CLXIX (November 1969), 104-105.

6091 Macourek, Miloš. "Five Animal Sketches," Jiři Theiner, trans., Literary Review, XIII (Fall 1969), 64-67.

6092 Madden, David. "The Builder," Wormwood Review, VIII, no. 1 (1968), 2-3.

6093 ______. "Cassandra Singing," Lillabulero, I (Winter 1967), 18-23.

6094 ______. "Chapter from Cassandra Singing," Ann Arbor Review, no. 1 (Fall 1967), 10-17.

6095 ______. "Cassandra Singing--excerpt from a novel," Cimarron Review, I (September 1967), 22-31.

6096 ______. "from Cassandra Singing," South Dakota Review, V (Winter 1967-68), 68-79.

6097 ______. "Children of a Cold Sun," North American Review, IV (July 1967), 24-28.

6098 ______. "The Day the Flowers Came," Playboy, XV (September 1968), 137, 142, 254-256.

6099 ______. "Lone Riding," Southwest Review, LI (Summer 1966), 221-236.

6100 ______. "Love Makes Nothing Happen," Southwest Review, LIII (Summer 1968), 266-275.

6101 ______. "Nothing Dies but Something Mourns," Carleton Miscellany, IX (Fall 1968), 24-88.

6102 ______. "On Target," December, XI (1969), 29-37.

6103 ______. "The Pale Horse of Fear," Twigs, no. 5 (Fall 1969), 82-98.

6104 ______. "The Singer," Kenyon Review, XXVIII (January 1966), 79-107.

6105 _____. "Traven," Southern Review, IV (April 1968), 346-391.

6106 Maddow, Ben. "The Circumcision of James Buttonwood," Playboy, XV (December 1968), 187, 301-302, 304-308, 310.

6107 _____. "Stamp Out Illiteracy, but Slowly," Genesis West, III (Winter 1965), 79-82.

6108 _____. "The Wind Machine," Harper's Magazine, CCXXXIII (August 1966), 55-60.

6109 _____. "You, Johann Sebastian Bach," Hudson Review, XX (Autumn 1967), 389-416.

6110 Maddox, Bruce. "Title: Fiction," Wild Dog, no. 21 (March 1966), 27-28.

6111 Maddux, Robert. "A Walk in the Spring Rain," McCall's, XCVI (September 1969), 110-118.

6112 Madocs, Rita. "The Absence of Valdemar," North American Review, II (Spring 1965), 32-40.

6113 _____. "Best Regards to Mr. Cary Grant," McCall's, XCIV (August 1967), 62-63.

6114 _____. "The Chagall Bride," Ladies' Home Journal, LXXXIII (August 1966), 58-59, 113-115.

6115 _____. "Fandango," Ladies' Home Journal, LXXXIII (January 1966), 66-67, 112-114.

6116 _____. "Girl Watcher," McCall's, XCIV (April 1967), 68-69, 126, 128.

6117 _____. "He Could Have Loved Me," Ladies' Home Journal, LXXXVI (April 1969), 100-101, 153-154.

6118 _____. "I Never Thought of You as Henry," Redbook, CXXVIII (February 1967), 74-75, 126, 128, 130-131.

6119 _____. "The Saturday People," McCall's, XCIV (October 1966), 118-119, 166, 169-170, 172.

6120 _____. "The Stargazer," McCall's, XCIV (January 1967), 46-47, 100-103.

6121 _____. "The Trouble with Marriage," McCall's, XCIV (September 1967), 94-95, 152-153, 156.

6122 Madrid-Malo, Néstor. "The Last Tree," Américas, XVII (September 1965), 35-37.

6123 Magilligan, Sue. "Lost: One Kaleidoscope," *Seventeen*, XXVI (January 1967), 79, 114.

6124 Magnuson, Jim. "Has Anybody Found Me Yet?" *Niobe*, no. 2 (1966), 39-55.

6125 ______. "Welcome Home, George," *Niobe*, no. 1 (1965), 74-85.

6126 Magowan, Robin. "Mary Book," *Chicago Review*, XXI (December 1969), 46-64, 67-79.

6127 ______. "from *Z*," *Chicago Review*, XX & XXI (May 1969), 216-247.

6128 Mahfouz, Naguib. "An Alarming Voice," A. F. Cassis, trans., *Literature East and West*, XIII (December 1969), 386-394.

6129 ______. "A Poet in His Own Way," *Vision*, XV (December 1966), 25-27, 50.

6130 Maier, William. "Kate Herself," *Good Housekeeping*, CLXIX (October 1969), 104-105, 180, 182, 184, 186-188.

6131 ______. "The Young Biddy," *McCall's*, XCIV (March 1967), 84-85, 146-151, 153.

6132 Mailer, Norman. "The Greatest Thing in the World," *Story*, I (May 1967), 23-27, 94-95.

6133 ______. "The Last Night," *Nova*, (January 1967), 84-89.

6134 ______. "The Taming of Denise Gondelman," *Avant Garde*, no. 3 (May 1968), 40-45.

6135 Maimane, Arthur. "The Day After," *Transition*, V, no. 27 (1966), 8-12.

6136 Main, J. M. "Lillian," *Perspective*, XV (Autumn 1968), 213-224.

6137 Mainwaring, Geoffrey. "My Visit with Simon's Mother," *Stand*, X, no. 3 (1969), 40-42.

6138 Major, Andre. "Hiverner?" W. D. Godfrey, trans., *Prism International*, VI (Autumn 1966), 16-20.

6139 Major, Clarence. "Church Girl," *Human Voice*, III (Summer-Fall 1967), 39-40.

6140 ______. "Excerpts from a Novel in Progress," *Trace*, no. 68 (1968), 296-304.

6141 Major, J. W., Jr. "The Driver's Test," Georgia Review, XIX (Fall 1965), 288-298.

6142 _____. "Friedman," Epoch, XIV (Winter 1965), 152-165.

6143 _____. "Kranzler and Urban Transition," Prairie Schooner, XLII (Spring 1968), 1-17.

6144 _____. "Like the Siberian Snows," Minnesota Review, VI (1966), 3-14.

6145 _____. "The Rebellion," Prairie Schooner, XXXIX (Fall 1965), 191-201.

6146 _____. "Saints and Sinners and All Sorts of Lunatics," Western Humanities Review, XXI (Spring 1967), 129-138.

6147 _____. "Those Eager and Willing Young Ladies," Perspective, XVI (Autumn 1969), 113-125.

6148 Makanin, Vladimir. "The Straight Line," Robert Daglish, trans., Soviet Literature, (no. 2, 1967), 2-51.

6149 _____. "The Straight Line/(Conclusion)," Robert Daglish, trans., Soviet Literature, (no. 3, 1967), 34-135.

6150 Makaza, Webster. "The Slave," The Classic, II, no. 3 (1967), 26-33.

6151 Malamud, Bernard. "An Exorcism," Harper's Magazine, CCXXXVII (December 1968), 76-80, 85-89.

6152 _____. "Man in the Drawer," Atlantic Monthly, CCXXI (April 1968), 70-78, 83-93.

6153 _____. "Man in the Drawer," Bennington Review, III (Winter 1969), 53-64, 69-83.

6154 _____. "Man in the Drawer," London Magazine, VIII (September 1968), 30-72.

6155 _____. "My Son the Murderer," Esquire, LXX (November 1968), 102-104, 152.

6156 _____. "Pictures of Fidelman," Atlantic Monthly, CCXXII (December 1968), 63-68, 69-70.

6157 _____. "A Pimp's Revenge," Playboy, XV (February 1968), 68-70, 126, 156-164, 166.

6158 Malamud, Paul. "A Portrait of Birdsman," Yale Literary Magazine, CXXXVII (September 1968), 8-14.

6159 Malaparte, Curzio. "Mamma Marcia," Rex Benedict, trans., Evergreen Review, X (August 1966), 46-49.

6160 Malaret, Niso. "Instant Idiot," Américas, XVII (February 1965), 34-37.

6161 Malcolm, Patricia. "Shake the Tambourine and I Will Dance for You," Jeopardy, no. 1 (1966), 43-48.

6162 Malcomson, Rodney. "By the Skin of Her Teeth," New Writing from Zambia, no. 1 (1967), 9-11.

6163 Malec, Alexander B. "Elmo," Colorado Quarterly, XVI (Winter 1968), 255-266.

6164 _____. "Matayama," Colorado Quarterly, XV (Summer 1966), 63-67.

6165 _____. "Project Inhumane," Colorado Quarterly, XIII (Spring 1965), 356-364.

6166 Malik, Tariq Yazdani. "The Cantina," Pakistan Review, XVII (May 1969), 39-42.

6167 Malkas, Mark. "A Plea for the Domestication of the Unicorn," Tri-Quarterly, no. 10 (Fall 1967), 20-36.

6168 Malkoff, Karl. "Adrien or Not," Ararat, VIII (Autumn 1967), 2-7.

6169 Mallet-Joris, Françoise. "Breaking It Off," Peter Green, trans., Mademoiselle, LXI (June 1965), 108-109, 135-136.

6170 _____. "Marie," Peter Green, trans., Harper's Bazaar, XCVIII (May 1965), 162-163, 185, 200.

6171 Malley, Charles. "The Fullback," Columbia, XLIX (January 1969), 24-27.

6172 Maloff, Saul. "The Limits of Sound," Northwest Review, VIII (Fall-Winter 1966-67), 32-45.

6173 _____. "Masquerade," Saturday Evening Post, CCXXXIX (February 12, 1966), 44-47, 49.

6174 Malone, John. "Ground Glass," New American Review, no. 3 (1968), 214-225.

6175 Maloney, Ralph. "The Best Man," Atlantic Monthly, CCXVII (May 1966), 51-56.

6176 _____. "Gallantry," Atlantic Monthly, CCXVI (November 1965), 73-77.

6177 _____. "Harry W. A. Davis, Jr." Atlantic Monthly, CCXV (June 1965), 58-62.

6178 _____. "Last Stop before the Carbarn," Atlantic Monthly, CCXVIII (July 1966), 63-68, 73-75.

6179 _____. "What I Need Don't Come in Suitcases," Atlantic Monthly, CCXX (October 1967), 113-115.

6180 Malpass, Eric. "All's Right With the World," Redbook, CXXVI (January 1966), 119-145.

6181 _____. "By the Light of the Moon," Redbook, CXXIX (September 1967), 143, 145-171.

6182 _____. "Speed the Parting Guest," Redbook, CXXX (January 1968), 52-53, 87-90.

6183 _____. "You Can't Win With Gaylord," Redbook, CXXVIII (March 1967), 72-73, 161-164.

6184 Maltz, Albert. "The Prisoner's Dog," Saturday Evening Post, CCXLI (July 13, 1968), 48-53.

6185 _____. "The Spoils of War," Saturday Evening Post, CCXLI (October 5, 1968), 64-66, 70-72.

6186 Manalli, F. S. "Paradise, It's a Nice Place," Perspective, XVI (Winter-Spring 1969), 29-39.

6187 _____. "Strategic Withdrawal," Literary Review, XII (Summer 1969), 485-504.

6188 Mandala, T. L. "The Baboon and the Tortoise," Expression, no. 1 (1968), 9-10.

6189 Mandel, George. "The Day the Time Changed," Saturday Evening Post, CCXXXVIII (November 6, 1965), 56-61, 65.

6190 Mándy, Iván. "Girl from the Swimming Pool," New Hungarian Quarterly, X (Winter 1969), 90-95.

6191 _____. "An Ordinary Member," Literary Review, IX (Spring 1966), 413-420.

6192 _____. "Private Lives," New Hungarian Quarterly, VIII (Summer 1967), 140-155.

6193 Maner, William. "The Honeymoon Bush," Cosmopolitan, CLIX (December 1965), 98-100, 102-103.

6194 _____. "More Than Memory," Good Housekeeping, CLXIV (April 1967), 96-97, 277-281.

6195 ______. "Something Personal," Woman's Day, (July 1968), 34-35, 89.

6196 ______. "You Be Mrs. Gallagher," Woman's Day, (February 1968), 80, 115-116.

6197 Manfred, Frederick. "Boys Will Be Boys," Minnesota Review, V (January-April 1965), 25-35.

6198 ______. "Good-Hearted Man," Minnesota Review, VI (1966), 103-120.

6199 Mankowitz, Wolf. "An Expensive Love Story," Cosmopolitan, CLXII (May 1967), 132-134, 136.

6200 Mann, Heinrich. "Scene," Margaret D. Howie, trans., Scala International, (July 1968), 32-34.

6201 Mann, Iki. "Simon Rad/(extract from a longer story)," Nexus, I (August 1967), 26-27.

6202 Mann, Monika. "Savonarola, Little Herr Friedemann, and the Visit of a Yankee," Anneliese and Ruth Braun, trans., Adam International Review, nos. 322-324 (1967), 49-53.

6203 Mann, Peggy. "The Summer Lady," Redbook, CXXIX (September 1967), 68-69, 118-121.

6204 Manne, Victor. "Joshua's Day," Transatlantic Review, no. 20 (Spring 1966), 41-50.

6205 ______. "Messenger of Chaos," Transatlantic Review, no. 18 (Spring 1965), 96-103.

6206 Manning, Harvey. "Asleep Not In the Deep," Prospero's Cell, I (April-June 1966), 29-67.

6207 Manning, Olivia. "An Elegy for Eebou," Adam International Review, no. 300 (1963-65), 134-136.

6208 ______. "Innocent Pleasures," Encounter, XXVII (July 1966), 9-15.

6209 Manning, Rosemary. "The Garland of Friendship," Mademoiselle, LXI (October 1965), 140-141, 187-192.

6210 Manoogian, Kathryn. "Sweet Red Onions," Ararat, VI (Winter 1965), 22-24.

6211 Mansfield, Katherine. "In a Cafe," Readers & Writers, I (October-November 1966), 12-13.

6212 Mansoor, Zafar. "His Own Blood," Pakistan Review, XVII

(October 1969), 33-36.

6213 Manto, Saadat Hasan. "The Eyes," Nusrat Ali, trans., Pakistan Review, XIV (November 1966), 21-22.

6214 _____. "Surma," Qaisar Afzal, trans., Vision, XV (August 1965), 12.

6215 Manville, W. H. "Let's Not Talk about Getting Married," Cosmopolitan, CLXVI (April 1969), 158-159.

6216 Marbo, Botticelli. "Herbert," Mt. Adams Review, II (Fall 1965), 18-19.

6217 Marcello, P. "Strange Dreams," Expression, no. 2 (n.d.), 5-15.

6218 Marcus, Allan. "From the novel Miracles/A Cinematic Romance," Genesis West, III (Winter 1965), 83-93.

6219 Marek, Margot. "Squirrels," University Review, XXXII (December 1965), 112-121.

6220 Margalith, S. H. "'Believe in God: You Have Teeth!'," Avant Garde, no. 1 (January 1968), 46-49.

6221 Margeson, John. "Spider Road," Queen's Quarterly, LXXIV (Autumn 1967), 429-436.

6222 Margolis, William J. "Five Chapters from Mendota/The Journal of Doubting Thomas," Nexus (San Francisco, Calif.), III (January-February 1967), 2-6.

6223 Margoshes, David. "Well, Well, Well: Three Very Deep Subjects," Consumption, I (Winter 1968), 22-29.

6224 Marinbach, Gershen. "The 'Tzillender'," Jewish Life, XXXIII (September-October 1965), 39-42.

6225 Marinetti, F. T. "Let's Kill the Moonlight," Paolo Lionni, trans., San Francisco Earthquake, I (Summer/Fall 1968), 50-51.

6226 Marinković, Ranko. "A Man With a Dead Soul," Maria Malby, trans., Literary Review, XI (Winter 1967), 175-184.

6227 Marion, James. "'Little Lamb, Who Made Thee?'," New Zealand Listener, LIII (October 29, 1965), 4.

6228 Markandaya, Kamala. "The Captain's Cabin," Lugano Review, I, no. 2 (1965), 10-16.

6229 Markevičius, A. "The Death of Padaiga," Clark Mills, trans.,

Literary Review, VIII (Spring 1965), 354-362.

6230 Markov, Georgi. "Father and Son/Book I," Vladimir Talmy, trans., Soviet Literature, (no. 8, 1966), 3-96.

6231 _____. "Father and Son/Book Two," Vladimir Talmy, trans., Soviet Literature, (no. 9, 1966), 1-89.

6232 Marks, George A., Jr. "Cold Heart," Redbook, CXXVIII (January 1967), 56-57, 105-107.

6233 _____. "Good-bye, Kitten," Redbook, CXXVI (February 1966), 50-51, 108-110.

6234 Marks, Jay Glenn, Jr. "Walk in the Sun," Sequoia, XII (Autumn 1966), 4-9.

6235 Marks, Mitchell. "Snobol in July," Yale Literary Magazine, CXXXVIII (Winter 1969), 28-35.

6236 Marks, Peter. "The Human Zero," Signature, I (September 1966), 40. 72, 74, 76.

6237 Marlott, Margaret. "The Life of a Little Windling," Canadian Forum, XLVI (July 1966), 87-88.

6238 Marlowe, Dan. "A Casual Crime," Signature, I (November 1966), 32.

6239 Marlowe, Derek. "The Assassin (Part I)," Saturday Evening Post, CCXXXIX (September 10, 1966), 50-52, 54, 56-57, 59-65.

6240 _____. "The Assassin (Part II)," Saturday Evening Post, CCXXXIX (September 24, 1966), 44-54, 56-58.

6241 _____. "The Assassin (Conclusion)," Saturday Evening Post, CCXXXIX (October 8, 1966), 60-62, 68-70, 74-76.

6242 Marmorstein, Robert. "A Name on the Wall," University Review, XXXI (June 1965), 293-300.

6243 Maropis, Petro S. "Saturday Night," Esquire, LXVI (November 1966), 132, 134, 164, 167-168.

6244 Marotta, Giuseppe. "A Sicilian Wedding," Frances Frenaye, trans., The Quest, I (Fall-Winter 1966), 6-10.

6245 Maroun, Edouard. "Badolos," Dorothy Blair, trans., The Classic, II, no. 2 (1966), 22-32.

6246 Marple, Jean and Gerald Jonas. "The Stand-in," Paris Review, XII (Summer 1969), 98-104.

6247 Marqués, René. "The Blue Kite," Eloïse Roach, trans., Américas, XVII (May 1965), 30-33.

6248 _____. "Three Men by the River," Kal Wagenheim, trans., Caribbean Review, I (Winter 1969), 7.

6249 Marriott, Alice. "That Woman," Southwest Review, LII (Summer 1967), 250-261.

6250 Marriott, Anne. "A Day Like Spring," The Fiddlehead, no. 82 (August-October 1969), 48-51.

6251 Marriott, Jack. "Story," Ambit, no. 24 (1965), 5-7.

6252 _____. "Striped in the Dark," Ambit, no. 28 (1966), 8-13.

6253 Marsden, Catherine G. "A Gift for the Christ Child," Américas, XXI (November-December 1969), 28.

6254 Marsh, Van. "The Lie," Greensboro Review, IV (Spring 1969), 37-52.

6255 Marsh, Willard. "Blood Harvest," Denver Quarterly, I (Spring 1966), 130-151.

6256 _____. "Contraband," South Dakota Review, VI (Autumn 1968), 123-126.

6257 _____. "Love's Not Time's Fool," Denver Quarterly, IV (Spring 1969), 17-32.

6258 _____. "Lucky Louie," Transatlantic Review, no. 32 (Summer 1969), 71-75.

6259 _____. "Mending Wall," Southern Review, V (October 1969), 1192-1204.

6260 Marshall, Alan. "Four Sunday Suits," Meanjin Quarterly, XXV (March 1966), 5-20.

6261 _____. "The Three-legged Bitch," Meanjin Quarterly, XXVII (Autumn 1968), 16-29.

6262 _____. "Wild Red Horses," Meanjin Quarterly, XXVIII (Summer 1969), 446-460.

6263 Marshall, Howard. "Ahavoh Kletzhy's Conversion," Nexus (San Francisco, Calif.), II (September-October 1965), 45-48.

6264 _____. "Dedication," Manhattan Review, no. 3 (1967), 15-20 [issue is double bound in opposite directions and doubly paginated].

6265 _____. "Maitland Walters," West Coast Review, I (Spring 1966), 36-39.

6266 _____. "Wieniewska's Discovery," Midwestern University Quarterly, II, no. 2 (1966), 49-54.

6267 Marshall, Jack. "Janowski the Leg Man," Cavalier, XV (September 1965), 52-53, 62, 85-88.

6268 Marshall, Leonore. "A Matter of Taste," Prairie Schooner, XLIII (Fall 1969), 305-311.

6269 _____. "The Meteor Boy," Sewanee Review, LXXVI (January-March 1968), 117-133.

6270 Martin, Carilee. "A Conversation with Fat Harry One Breeze of a Day," Coraddi, (Arts Festival 1969), 17.

6271 Martin, Claire. "Paris-Montreal," Robert Gibbs, trans., Literary Review, VIII (Summer 1965), 496-502.

6272 _____. "Three Points in My Life," Philip Stratford, trans., Tamarack Review, no. 43 (Spring 1967), 5-18.

6273 Martin, Frances. "The Dare," Southerly, (1969), 285-287.

6274 Martin, Richard. "The Rabbit," Washington and Jefferson Literary Journal, III, no. 1 (1969), 47.

6275 Martin, Terry. "The Wishing Stone," Redbook, CXXX (March 1968), 167, 169-191.

6276 Martinez, Al. "Horris Is the Name of the Game," El Grito, I (Summer 1968), 36-37.

6277 Martinez Moreno, Carlos. "The Siren," John Cameron Murchison, trans., Tri Quarterly, nos. 13/14 (Fall/Winter 1968-69), 452-479.

6278 Martínez Viademonte, Hugo. "The Pampa," Américas, XX (November-December 1968), 36-37.

6279 Martins, Hildegarde J. "Prince Street Is Different," Ball State University Forum, X (Autumn 1969), 64-68.

6280 Maryamov, Alexander. "Polar August," Tom Botting, trans., Soviet Literature, (no. 6, 1965), 85-118.

6281 Mashkin, Gennadi. "Sparkling Blue Ocean, Ship Gleaming White," Eve Manning, trans., Soviet Literature, (no. 5, 1966), 3-103.

6282 Masiye, Ndereya S. "His Own Medicine," New Writing from

Zambia, no. 1 (1967), 3-7.

6283 Maslen, Elizabeth. "Mr. Jenkins Has an Experience," Focus (Singapore), New Series, no. 1 (1967), 19-27.

6284 Mason, Michael. "A Good Education: Spontaneous Demonstration I," Evergreen Review, XII (October 1968), 52-54, 59.

6285 _____. "The Man in the Fake Chanel Suit," Evergreen Review, XI (June 1967), 69, 103-104.

6286 Massey, Jane. "Je Te Plumerai," Statement, no. 21 (Spring 1965), 7-13.

6287 Massey, M. "Bar-o-Logue," Overflow, II, no. 3 (1969), 64-66.

6288 Masters, Hilary. "The Game in Season," Quarterly Review of Literature, XIV (1967), 381-388.

6289 Masterson, R. M. "The Amazon Gift," Courier, XLV (August 1965), 38-39.

6290 Masuda, Jeffrey Norman. "The Welcome Hearth," Washington Square Review, I (Spring 1965), 23-26.

6291 Matevosyan, Grant. "We and Our Mountains," Vladimir Talmy, trans., Soviet Literature, (no. 10, 1968), 3-78.

6292 Mather, Berkely. "The Diamond Watch," Saturday Evening Post, CCXL (April 8, 1967), 64-70.

6293 Mathers, Peter. "Report on the Recent Activities of Thomas Scurgeon," Overland, no. 43 (Summer 1969-70), 5-9.

6294 Mathes, William. "Swan Feast," New American Review, no. 1 (1967), 109-121.

6295 Matheson, Richard. "A Drink of Water," Signature, II (April 1967), 44-47.

6296 _____. "Prey," Playboy, XVI (April 1969), 165, 198-200, 202.

6297 Mathews, Bob. "Where's Clarence Tonight?" Delta, XIX (1965), 24-28.

6298 Mathews, Harry. "The Escape from Jacksongrad," Art and Literature, no. 7 (Winter 1965), 9-32.

6299 _____. "Jacksongrad," Paris Review, IX (Spring-Summer 1965), 116-156.

6300 _____. "The Scenario," Mother, no. 5 (Summer 1965), 41-57.

6301 _____. "Tradition and the Individual Talent: the 'Bartislava Spiccato'," Paris Review, XII (Fall 1969), 103-105.

6302 Mathews, R. D. "The Biggest Bridge in the World," Tamarack Review, no. 43 (Spring 1967), 41-54.

6303 _____. "Climber," LXXIII (Summer 1966), Queen's Quarterly, 235-243.

6304 _____. "Paris: April," Canadian Forum, XLIV (March 1965), 277-278.

6305 Mathews, Robin. "Anniversary," Canadian Forum, XLVII (July 1967), 81-84.

6306 Mathewson, Joseph. "The Hole over Mrs. McDeeley," Yale Literary Magazine, CXXXV (September 1966), 43-45.

6307 Matiani, Shailesh. "No Attachment," Prashant K. Sinha, trans., Avenues, II (April 1969), 20-24, 42.

6308 Matthews, Jack. "Another Story," Sewanee Review, LXXVII (July-September 1969), 426-439.

6309 _____. "The Betrayal," Malahat Review, no. 10 (April 1969), 20-28.

6310 _____. "A Cat May Look," Southwest Review, L (Autumn 1965), 398-403.

6311 _____. "The Cycle," Ante, II (Summer 1966), 68-69.

6312 _____. "The Ending of Meg Vickers," Malahat Review, no. 5 (January 1968), 105-113.

6313 _____. "The Fish Pond," Southern Humanities Review, I (Spring 1967), 68-75.

6314 _____. "The Ghost of First Crow," Niobe, no. 2 (1966), 5-15.

6315 _____. "Gluck, the Silent Oracle," Ante, III (Winter 1967), 7-18.

6316 _____. "The Hotel," Massachusetts Review, VIII (Autumn 1967), 621-628.

6317 _____. "The Immortal Dog," Jeopardy, no. 5 (Spring 1969), 193-200.

6318 ______. "In the Neighborhood of Dark," North American Review, IV (September 1967), 19-25.

6319 ______. "Inviolate on Shawnee St.," North American Review, III (July 1966), 32-36.

6320 ______. "The Knife," Yale Review, LVIII (Winter 1969), 249-262.

6321 ______. "Love Song for Doris Ballinger," Carleton Miscellany, IX (Fall 1968), 94-100.

6322 ______. "My Son," Prairie Schooner, XL (Spring 1966), 71-76.

6323 ______. "The Names of My Brothers," Georgia Review, XX (Spring 1966), 51-63.

6324 ______. "The Neighbor," Carleton Miscellany, X (Summer 1969), 86-92.

6325 ______. "Night, and a Fire on the Hill," North American Review, III (May 1966), 10-15.

6326 ______. "The Pilgrimage," Prism International, VII (Summer 1967), 58-66.

6327 ______. "Schlachner, the Hero," December, IX (1967), 9-17.

6328 ______. "A Slightly Different World," North American Review, IV (March 1967), 26-31.

6329 ______. "A Story Not About Richardson," Ante, III (Fall 1967), 45-54.

6330 ______. "The Strong One," University Review, XXXIII (October 1966), 11-18.

6331 ______. "Thobqueh's Tale," Prism International, VII (Autumn 1967), 18-26.

6332 ______. "'When the Shark, Babe...'," North American Review, III (January 1966), 16-20.

6333 ______. "Writer's Tale," Ante, II (Winter 1966), 49-57.

6334 ______. "The Yard Man," Prism International, VIII (Summer 1968), 24-30.

6335 Matthias, John E. "By Way of the Ruins: a Love Poem," Sequoia, XI (Autumn 1965), 14-28, 34-53.

6336 Mattox, Austin. "Blackballed," Signature, I (July 1966), 22.

6337 Matushkin, Vasili. "Lyubasha," Anthony Wixley, trans., Soviet Literature, (no. 5, 1967), 27-110.

6338 Mauermann, Mary Ann. "The Best Things in Life," Redbook, CXXXII (February 1969), 80-81, 152-155, 159.

6339 Maxwell, Peter. "A Bullet/To Whom It May Concern," Tropix, I, no. 4 (1966), 44-48.

6340 Maxwell, William. "Further Tales about Men and Women," New Yorker, XLI (August 7, 1965), 22-27.

6341 _____. "Further Tales about Men and Women," New Yorker, XLI (October 16, 1965), 50-54.

6342 _____. "Further Tales about Men and Women," New Yorker, XLI (November 13, 1965), 51-56.

6343 _____. "Further Tales about Men and Women," New Yorker, XLI (December 11, 1965), 54-60.

6344 _____. "Further Tales about Men and Women," New Yorker, XLI (December 25, 1965), 26-33.

6345 _____. "The Gardens of Mont-Saint-Michel," New Yorker, XLV (August 9, 1969), 30-39.

6346 May, James Boyar. "The Reprobate," Manhattan Review, no. 1 (1966), 47-52.

6347 May, Naomi. "Hush Hush," Nova, (February 1969), 82-87.

6348 Mayer, Bernadette. [untitled], 0 to 9, no. 5 (January 1969), 20-24.

6349 _____. [untitled], 0 to 9, no. 5 (January 1969), 47-49.

6350 _____. "Half a Chair," The World, no. 12 (June 1968), n.p. [71].

6351 _____. "One Thing," 0 to 9, no. 4 (June 1968), 44-48.

6352 _____. "Story," 0 to 9, (1968) [published separately].

6353 Mayer, Tom. "A Cold Wind," New Mexico Quarterly, XXXVI (Summer 1966), 101-104.

6354 _____. "Dead Dog," New Mexico Quarterly, XXXVII (Winter 1968), 357-362.

6355 _____. "The Eastern Sprints," Playboy, XIII (May 1966), 108-109, 120, 176, 179-181.

6356 _____. "A Green-Broke Stud," Atlantic Monthly, CCXVIII (October 1966), 76-78.

6357 _____. "My Father and the Fighter," Saturday Evening Post, CCXXXIX (October 22, 1966), 78-80, 83.

6358 _____. "Old Acquaintance," Weekend Telegraph, no. 106 (October 7, 1966), 57-58, 61.

6359 Mayewski, Pawel. "The Assassin," Lotus, no. 1 (1968), 26-30.

6360 Mayfield, Carl. "A Familiar Tale," University Review, XXXV (Spring 1969), 224-228.

6361 Mayfield, Lydia. "Our Nell," Kansas Magazine, (1967), 84-86.

6362 Mayhall, Jane. "The Popegano Bit," Michigan Quarterly Review, VI (Winter 1967), 29-36.

6363 Maynard, Barbara Ann. "The Visit," New Mexico Quarterly, XXXV (Summer 1965), 169-177.

6364 Maynard, Fredelle Bruser. "The Red Dress," Saturday Evening Post, CCXL (June 17, 1967), 58-62.

6365 Maynard, Rona. "Paper Flowers," Ladies' Home Journal, LXXXII (October 1965), 74-76, 166.

6366 Mayne, Richard. "Maigret and the Happening," Encounter, XXXI (September 1968), 33-35, 38-39.

6367 Mayson, Kathleen. "At the Strip," New Zealand Listener, LII (February 19, 1965), 12.

6368 _____. "It Goes by Tens," New Zealand Listener, (June 2, 1967), 8, 18.

6369 _____. "The Kill," New Zealand Listener, (November 17, 1967), 6, 32.

6370 _____. "Sea-Change," New Zealand Listener, (April 7, 1967), 6, 22.

6371 _____. "The Traitor," New Zealand Listener, LVIII (September 13, 1968), 10.

6372 Mazor, Julian. "The Boy Who Used Foul Language," New Yorker, XLIV (March 30, 1968), 30-42.

6373 _____. "Mary Jane," Shenandoah, XVIII (Spring 1967), 13-47.

6374 _____. "Rock Creek," New Yorker, XLII (December 17, 1966), 53-57.

6375 Mazzaro, Jerome. "The Living and the Dead," Mad River Review, II (Summer 1966), 3-15.

6376 Mbui, Bernard and Samuel Kahiga. "Cops and Robbers," Nexus, I (August 1967), 9-11.

6377 _____ and Samuel Kahiga. "The Oat," Nexus, I (1966), 5-7.

6378 McAfee, Thomas. "Lady of the World," Epoch, XVI (Spring 1967), 195-203.

6379 _____. "The Last of Ben Bo," Midwestern University Quarterly, II no. 3 (1967), 1-5.

6380 _____. "This Is His Living Room," Midwestern University Quarterly, I, no. 3 (1966), 1-8.

6381 McBain, Ed. "Fuzz," Saturday Evening Post, CCXLI (September 21, 1968), 51-62, 78.

6382 McBaine, Lynn. "The Mathematician," Sou'wester, (Spring 1969), 67-71.

6383 McCabe, Thomas J. "Well-Oiled Fighting Machine," Four Quarters, XVII (November 1967), 11-13.

6384 McCall, John. "The Causes of III," Ante, IV (Spring 1968), 15-26.

6385 _____. "Perfectly Candid," Vagabond, no. 5 (Summer 1967), 36-45.

6386 McCants, Billie Lee. "Underneath the Garden," Nimrod, XII (Spring 1968), 5-14.

6387 McCarthy, Cormac. "Bounty," Yale Review, LIV (Spring 1965), 368-374.

6388 _____. "The Dark Waters," Sewanee Review, LXXIII (April-June 1965), 210-216.

6389 McCarthy, Mary. "Birds of America," Southern Review, I (July 1965), 644-683.

6390 McCarthy, Nan. "Semper Fidelis," Grok, I (February-May 1967), 19-22.

6391 McCarthy, Tim. "Grandmother Meave and the Watering of Her Own Private Priest," Ante, IV (Spring 1968), 29-45.

6392 McCartin, James T. "Dreams of a Young Girl," Good Housekeeping, CLXIX (July 1969), 60-61, 118-119, 121, 123-125.

6393 McCauley, Carole Spearin. "File #437: Kerstin Muller," Pyramid, no. 5 (1969), 32-39.

6394 McCawley, A. W. "... But in Batallions," Delta, XIX (1965), 33-40.

6395 McCawley, Allen Mills. "Pammy," Delta, XX (1966), 51-58.

6396 McClanahan, Ed. "Generations Yet Unborn: a fragment," Sequoia, XIII (Autumn 1968), 1-2.

6397 _____. "Gurney at the Beach," Per/Se, I (Summer 1966), 13-25.

6398 McCleary, Oren. "End of a Year," Massachusetts Review, VIII (Autumn 1967), 653-664.

6399 McClellan, Woody. "Homecoming," Overflow, II, no. 3 (1969), 18-31.

6400 McClintock, Michael W. "Faintly Falling," Carleton Miscellany, X (Spring 1969), 4-18.

6401 McCord, Howard. "The Brigadier and the Nephew," Goodly Co., no. 12 (July 1968), 11-16.

6402 _____. "The Layman's Guide to Castration," Goodly Co., no. 4 (December 1965), 30-39.

6403 _____. "The Life of Battleship Billy," Western Humanities Review, XIX (Autumn 1965), 327-333.

6404 McCord, Jean. "Every Day Is Yesterday," Seventeen, XXIV (May 1965), 142-143, 223-224.

6405 _____. "Images of Loss," Seventeen, XXIV (August 1965), 246-247, 381-382, 384-387.

6406 McCorkle, Susanna. "Cornelia," Mademoiselle, LXIX (August 1969), 304-305, 372-375.

6407 McCormack, Jean. "The Party," New Zealand Listener, LIII (November 12, 1965), 4.

6408 _____. "The Purple Rose," New Zealand Listener, LIV (April 29, 1966), 6.

6409 McCormick, Eliza. "The Bright Side," Epoch, XVI (Fall 1966), 83-93.

6410 McCormick, James. "Claudine," Ave Maria, CVI (July 22, 1967), 26-28.

6411 ______. "Commander Spider and Captive Fly," Epoch, XIV (Spring 1965), 221-239.

6412 ______. "Father's Keeper," Ave Maria, CIV (December 10, 1966), 26-29.

6413 ______. "Father's Keeper," Transatlantic Review, no. 22 (Autumn 1966), 39-46.

6414 ______. "Mr. Twohands among the Rune Stones," New American Review, no. 2 (January 1968), 206-215.

6415 ______. "Sad Accumulations of the Past," Quarterly Review of Literature, XV (1968), 382-392.

6416 McCotter, John. "Bergeron/A Fable," Delta Review, IV (March-April 1967), 64-69.

6417 McCourt, Edward. "The Medicine Woman," Queen's Quarterly, LXXIII (Spring 1966), 75-84.

6418 McCoy, Helen. "Mr. Splitfoot," Cosmopolitan, CLXV (September 1968), 154-158, 160, 162, 164-165, 170, 172-185.

6419 McCoy, Jane. "My Grandfather Ate Green Grapes," Cimarron Review, no. 5 (September 1968), 70-80.

6420 McCray, Frank. "Parade of Packers," UMD Humanist, XV (Spring 1967), 33-39.

6421 McCullers, Carson. "The March," Redbook, CXXVIII (March 1967), 64-65, 114, 116, 118-120, 122-123.

6422 McCully, Helen and Dorothy Crayder. "The Christmas Pony," Woman's Day, (December 1966), 34-37, 78-80, 85-87.

6423 McCutcheon, R. W. "Fact of the Matter," Overflow, I (Fall 1967), 17-23.

6424 McDonald, Angus. "Within These Confines," Wisconsin Review, III (Spring 1968), 2-4.

6425 McDonald, J. D. "After Twenty-five Years," New Zealand Listener, LIII (December 24, 1965), 4.

6426 ______. "Big Fair," New Zealand Listener, (July 28, 1967), 6, 23.

6427 ______. "The Happiest Day," New Zealand Listener, LII (May 21, 1965), 5.

6428 ______. "Lonely Island," New Zealand Listener, LIII (September 17, 1965), 4.

6429 ______. "One Rainy Afternoon," New Zealand Listener, LII (April 15, 1965), 12-13.

6430 ______. "Pacific Landfall," New Zealand Listener, LIV (February 18, 1966), 6.

6431 ______. "The Palolo Rising," New Zealand Listener, LII (January 8, 1965), 5, 16.

6432 ______. "Ship Mates," New Zealand Listener, LIII (July 23, 1965), 4.

6433 ______. "Urgency," New Zealand Listener, (October 27, 1967), 6, 19.

6434 ______. "The White Nights," New Zealand Listener, LII (April 30, 1965), 21.

6435 ______. "Wonderful Man," New Zealand Listener, LIV (May 6, 1966), 6.

6436 McDonald, Walt. "Three Sisters," New Campus Review, II (Spring 1969), 17-23.

6437 McDougall, John. "Boss-Hater," New Zealand Listener, LIV (April 15, 1966), 4.

6438 McEldowney, Dennis. "Own Your Own," New Zealand Listener, LVII (May 3, 1968), 10.

6439 McElroy, Joseph. "The Accident," New American Review, no. 2 (January 1968), 172-191.

6440 McFadden, David. "from The Great Canadian Sonnet," Ant's Forefoot, no. 3 (Winter 1969), 27-29.

6441 McFadden, Michael Greer. "Aunt Cap's Dying Day," William and Mary Review, VI (Spring 1968), 41-52.

6442 McGahern, John. "The Four-Letter Word," Queen, CDXXIII (March 24, 1965), 78-79.

6443 ______. "Korea," Atlantic Monthly, CCXXIV (October 1969), 94-96.

6444 McGarty, Patric. "Snowbirds," Manuscript, XVIII (Spring 1965), 37-47.

6445 McGerr, Patricia. "The Face in My Mirror," Good Housekeeping, CLXVII (July 1968), 82-83.

6446 _____. "Johnny Lingo and the Eight-Cow Wife," Woman's Day, (November 1965), 44-45, 120B, 120F, 136.

6447 McGiffin, Lee. "The Carefree Years," Redbook, CXXIV (April 1965), 161-186, 188.

6448 McGinnis, Lila Sprague. "Secrets of a Clock Watcher," Good Housekeeping, CLXIV (March 1967), 94-95.

6449 _____. "This House, Our Home," Good Housekeeping, CLXIX (October 1969), 114-115, 189-190.

6450 McGivern, John. "Lie Down, I Want to Talk to You," Cosmopolitan, CLXIV (February 1968), 130-134, 136-146, 148-151, 154-155, 160-165.

6451 McGivern, Patrick. "Master of the Ball Hawks," Playboy, XVI (April 1969), 127, 138, 183.

6452 McGivern, William P. "Caper of the Golden Bulls," Cosmopolitan, CLX (February 1966), 112-129, 133-135, 137-143.

6453 McGrath, Charles. "Armageddon," Yale Literary Magazine, CXXXVI (March 1968), 15-16.

6454 McGrath, Eamonn. "Honour Thy Father/(from a novel in progress)," Dublin Magazine, VII (Autumn/Winter 1968), 27-35.

6455 McGrath, James. "The Angel Girl," American, III (Fall 1967), 18-27.

6456 _____. "The Fort Lee Story," American, IV (Spring 1968), 32-38, 54.

6457 McGrath, Margaret. "Father Gabriel and the Old Folks," Columbia, XLV (April 1965), 21-23, 42.

6458 McGregor, Matthew W. "Porkchops with Whiskey and Ice Cream," Virginia Quarterly Review, XLIV (Spring 1968), 265-284.

6459 MacGrian, Michael. "Farewell to a Kid," Threshold, no. 21 (Summer 1967), 66-73.

6460 McGuire, Marion. "I Surely Will Recall of You," Perspective, XIV (Spring 1965), 53-64.

6461 McHaney, Tom. "Last of the Civil War Orphans," Per/Se, II (Summer 1967), 3-9.

6462 McInerny, Ralph. "Addressee Unknown," Redbook, CXXVIII (March 1967), 76-77.

6463 _____. "And Nor Your Yellow Hair," Redbook, CXXXI (October 1968), 82-83, 159-161.

6464 _____. "The Beginning of Tomorrow," Good Housekeeping, CLXVII (August 1968), 78-79.

6465 _____. "Breaking Free," Redbook, CXXIX (September 1967), 76-77, 108-109.

6466 _____. "An Evening for Julie," Good Housekeeping, CLXVI (February 1968), 88-89.

6467 _____. "I Don't Want to Be Like You," Redbook, CXXXIII (June 1969), 72-73, 118-120.

6468 _____. "Make Me Chased, Lord," Redbook, CXXVIII (April 1967), 62-63, 113-115.

6469 _____. "The Pain of Possession," Redbook, CXXVIII (December 1966), 46-47, 119, 121-122.

6470 _____. "Past, Present and Always," Good Housekeeping, CLXVIII (February 1969), 90-91.

6471 _____. "A Season of Endings," Redbook, CXXIX (August 1967), 157, 159-174.

6472 _____. "There Comes a Day," Good Housekeeping, CLXIX (July 1969), 74-75, 164-165.

6473 _____. "Two Hearts, Vulnerable," Redbook, CXXX (November 1967), 76-77, 135-138.

6474 _____. "When a Girl Is Twenty-Five," Good Housekeeping, CLXV (October 1967), 96-97.

6475 McInnes, Gay. "A Shock for Mr. Peters," New Zealand Listener, LVIII (April 19, 1968), 6, 22.

6476 McIntosh, Charles D. "A Hatchet for Rent," Signature, II (February 1967), 42-43, 80, 82.

6477 McKay, Mort. "They Also Serve," Canadian Forum, XLVI (October 1966), 158-161.

6478 McKee, Mel. "Gentler Than," DeKalb Literary Arts Journal, II (Spring 1968), 1-8, 10-21.

6479 _____. "The Sileni Boxes," DeKalb Literary Arts Journal, I (Winter 1967), 15-27.

6480 McKellar, Sonora. "Out of My Window," Antioch Review, XXVII (Fall 1967), 346-361.

6481 McKelway, St. Clair. "The Presbyterian Captives," New Yorker, XLV (April 12, 1969), 45-52.

6482 McKenna, Richard. "The Sons of Martha," Harper's Magazine, CCXXXIV (February 1967), 64-72.

6483 McKenney, Kenneth. "Four for Katinka," New Zealand Listener, LII (April 2, 1965), 5, 13.

6484 _____. "In Time for Dinner," New Zealand Listener, LIV (March 11, 1966), 4.

6485 _____. "The Time of the Stork," New Zealand Listener, LII (February 12, 1965), 5.

6486 McKenzie, M. E. "The Lavender Dress," Southern Review, II (July 1966), 633-640.

6487 McKimmey, James. "The Abiding Heart," Good Housekeeping, CLXIX (November 1969), 94-95, 268, 275-277, 279-280, 283-284.

6488 _____. "Hope Is Forever," Good Housekeeping, CLXVIII (May 1969), 106-107.

6489 _____. "Trick or Treat," Signature, II (October 1967), 27.

6490 McKinley, Georgia. "The Fragile Heaven," Redbook, CXXV (August 1965), 58-59, 104-106

6491 McKinney, Irene. "The Long Green Moment," North American Mentor, VI (Fall 1968), 9-14.

6492 McKnight, Donald. "Juan Morillo and Mama," The Smith, no. 10 (December 1968), 140-143.

6493 McLaren, John. "End of the Lesson," Westerly, no. 1 (April 1969), 20-24.

6494 McLaughlin, Ann L. "The Smiling Buddha," American, I (Spring 1965), 48-49, 72.

6495 _____. "The Visiting Hour," American, I (Fall 1965), 24-25, 58-60.

6496 McLaverty, Michael. "The Circus Ring," Threshold, no. 21 (Summer 1967), 1-12.

6497 McLeod, E. Vessie. "The Difference," Queen's Quarterly, LXXII (Autumn 1965), 542-548.

6498 McMahon, Bryan. "Green Reflections," Occident, II (Spring/Summer 1968), 57-64.

6499 McMahon, Janet. "Helping Gout," William and Mary Review, VII (Winter 1969), 76-77.

6500 _____. "The Newlyweds," William and Mary Review, VII (Spring 1969), 63-66.

6501 McMahon, Jeremiah. "Mr. Swift and His Remarkable Thing," Playboy, XV (October 1968), 103-104, 186.

6502 McMartin, Sean. "The God in the Middle," South Dakota Review, VI (Autumn 1968), 47-63.

6503 _____. "Music for One Hand Only," Phylon, XXX (Summer 1969), 197-202.

6504 McMasters, Terry. "The Phantom," Foxfire, II (June 1968), 41-43.

6505 McMichael, K. D. "The Real Thing," New Zealand Listener, (February 23, 1968), 6, 26.

6506 McMorries, Maurice. "Tarzan at the Funeral Feast," California Review, no. 1 (Spring 1967), 65-69.

6507 McMorrow, Fred. "... And Be a Good Boy," Good Housekeeping, CLXIV (February 1967), 82-83, 180, 182, 184, 186.

6508 _____. "Confession," Saturday Evening Post, CCXL (October 21, 1967), 72-74, 78-79.

6509 McNair, Kate. "The Year That Christmas Came Early," Woman's Day, (December 1969), 30, 32-33, 80, 83-84, 86.

6510 McNair, Thomas W. "Deliverance," Arlington Quarterly, II (Autumn 1969), 132-144.

6511 McNamara, Eugene. "A Change of Scene," University of Windsor Review, IV (Spring 1969), 54-58.

6512 _____. "The Ethics of Survival," Denver Quarterly, IV (Spring 1969), 66-73.

6513 _____. "Made in Canada," Queen's Quarterly, LXXV (Winter 1968), 597-612.

6514 _____. "A Note on the Academic Life," Texas Quarterly, IX (Spring 1966), 168-170.

6515 _____. "On One Side of Silence," Quartet, no. 24 (Fall 1968), 13-15.

6516 _____. "The Terrible Trap," Ave Maria, CIII (April 23, 1966), 26-29.

6517 _____. "To Burn," Canadian Forum, XLVII (January 1968), 230-231.

6518 _____. "A Walk to the Paradise Garden," Evidence, no. 10 (1967), 161-167.

6519 _____. "The Way to Concord," Quartet, no. 19 (Summer 1967), 9-14.

6520 _____. "What More Will the Bones Allow," Edge, no. 8 (Fall 1968), 99-106.

6521 McNamara, Tom. "The Goordian Angel Speakin' Easy," Wormwood Review, VI, no. 3 (1966), 9.

6522 _____. "Hymn to Vazec Hall," Dust, III (Fall 1966), 8.

6523 McNamara, Winston. "Another Week," Westerly, (August 1966), 39-45.

6524 McNear, Robert. "Death's Door," Playboy, XVI (March 1969), 124-126, 200-202, 204-206.

6525 _____. "Menu," Cosmopolitan, CLXI (July 1966), 104-106.

6526 McNeill, Louise. "The Woodsrunners," Appalachian Review, II (Spring 1968), 33-36.

6527 McNeill, R. A. "The Trip," Bim, XI (January-June 1966), 74-77.

6528 McNeirn, Michael. "Getting to Know Julie," New Yorker, XLIII (November 11, 1967), 59-66.

6529 McNiece, James. "Action for Longshot," Colorado Quarterly, XIV (Autumn 1965), 161-176.

6530 _____. "Dreamlight," Tri-Quarterly, no. 16 (Fall 1969), 137-148.

6531 _____. "Plump Little Pink Ones," Tri-Quarterly, no. 6 (Spring 1966), 133-143.

6532 McPhee, John. "Ruth, the Sun Is Shining," Playboy, XV (April 1968), 114-116, 126, 186.

6533 McPherson, James Alan. "Gold Coast," Atlantic Monthly, CCXXII (November 1968), 74-81.

6534 _____. "A Matter of Vocabulary," Atlantic Monthly, CCXXIII (February 1969), 55-60, 61-63.

6535 _____. "Of Cabbages and Kings," Atlantic Monthly, CCXXIII

(April 1969), 57-63.

6536 McPherson, Shirley. "My Friends in Argentina," The Quest, II (Fall 1967), 205-218.

6537 McRobbie, Peter. "The Great Jaunt," Nimrod, XIII (Spring 1969), 7-12.

6538 McShane, Ed. "Effigies," Ave Maria, CIII (February 12, 1966), 22-24.

6539 McShane, Mark. "The Crimson Madness of Little Doom," Cosmopolitan, CLX (March 1966), 126-141, 143-149.

6540 McTague, Edward J. "The Bishop Tees Off," Four Quarters, XV (November 1965), 1-6.

6541 _____. "The Girl from Denmark," Four Quarters, XV (March 1966), 22-28.

6542 McWhirter, George. "The Entertainment," Ann Arbor Review, no. 7 (1969), 11-13.

6543 _____. "The Extinction of 'H'," Prism International, VIII (Spring 1969), 83-93.

6544 McWhirter, Millie. "Good-bye to Maribeth," Cosmopolitan, CLIX (August 1965), 100-105.

6545 McWhirter, William A. "When (and if) Better Presidents Are Made, Billy Birch Will Make Them...," Harper's Bazaar, CII (January 1969), 148-149, 80.

6546 Meacock, Norma. "In Marriage," Transatlantic Review, no. 23 (Winter 1966-67), 16-22.

6547 _____. "What Are They Saying?" Transatlantic Review, no. 26 (Autumn 1967), 48-50.

6548 Meade, Walter. "American Primitive," Texas Quarterly, IX (Summer 1966), 74-85.

6549 _____. "The Deeds of Men," Seventeen, XXIV (September 1965), 146-147, 253-255.

6550 _____. "An Error of Judgment," Saturday Evening Post, CCXXXVIII (January 30, 1965), 48-50, 54-55.

6551 _____. "Girl in the Motel," Cosmopolitan, CLVIII (April 1965), 84-88.

6552 _____. "A Person Apart," Redbook, CXXIV (January 1965), 50-51.

6553 ______. "Someplace Wonderful," Cosmopolitan, CLIX (September 1965), 100-102, 104-105.

6554 ______. "The Swordsmen," Readers & Writers, I (May-June 1966), 8-11.

6555 Meader, Duncan Y. "And Magnolia," New Yorker, XLIII (April 8, 1967), 40-47.

6556 Meakin, Colin. "Scramble Net," Daily Telegraph Magazine, no. 259 (September 26, 1969), 61-62, 66-67.

6557 Mechem, James. "Dear Paulina...Tenting Tonight," Américas, XIX (August 1967), 33-37.

6558 ______. "Ouled Nail, She Waits for Me," Sumac, I (Spring 1969), 60-62.

6559 ______. "from Recovery," Art and Literature, no. 7 (Winter 1965), 197-209.

6560 ______. "Renata: It's Really You," Red Clay Reader, no. 6 (1969), 48-51.

6561 Meckel, Christoph. "The Crow," A. P. Schroeder, trans., Prism International, VIII (Autumn 1968), 63-68.

6562 ______. "An Unpleasant Story," Christopher Middleton, trans., Dimension, I, no. 2 (1968), 294-297 [in German and English on alternate pages].

6563 Medelman, John. "The Gear and Flaps Man," Esquire, LXIII (May 1965), 94, 96-97.

6564 Mednick, Murray. "Carlos," Transatlantic Review, no. 28 (Spring 1968), 127-130.

6565 Medoff, Mark. "Something Worth Something," Arx, II (March 1969), 21-26.

6566 Meeker, Hubert M. "Will We Ever Get There?" Mad River Review, I (Spring-Summer 1965), 63-80.

6567 Meeter, Glen. "Don't You Remember Me?" South Dakota Review, VI (Spring 1968), 13-28.

6568 ______. "A Harvest," Epoch, XVIII (Fall 1968), 50-60.

6569 ______. "Waiting for Daddy," Redbook, CXXXIV (November 1969), 76-77, 128, 130, 132.

6570 Meghani, Jhaverchand. "A Lamp of Humanity," Vinod Meghani, trans., Indian Literature, IX (July-Sept. 1966), 56-70.

6571 _____. "A Lamp of Humanity," Vinod Meghani, trans., Indian Literature, X (April-June 1967), 32-65.

6572 Mehta, Dina. "The Fastidious Housewife," Cosmopolitan, CLXI (July 1966), 98-102.

6573 _____. "Kamala's Story," Imprint, VIII (March 1969), 51-56.

6574 Mehta, Ved. "All Found in London," New Yorker, XLV (September 18, 1965), 144, 147-148, 150, 152, 154, 157-158, 160, 163-164.

6575 _____. "The Companion of St. Michael and St. George," New Yorker, XLI (December 11, 1965), 205-208, 210, 213-214, 216.

6576 _____. "The Music Master," New Yorker, XLI (April 24, 1965), 42-50.

6577 _____. "Ram, Ram, Ram," New Yorker, XLI (January 29, 1966), 34-38, 40, 43-44, 46, 49-50, 52, 57-58, 60, 63-64, 66, 69-70, 72-74, 76, 78, 80, 82, 84-87.

6578 Meier, D. V. "The Gun," Crucible, VI (Fall 1969), 32, 34.

6579 Meilen, Bill. "Homage Call," Anglo-Welsh Review, XVII (Winter 1969), 141-145.

6580 Meinert, Anneliese. "All Gamblers Tell Lies," Margaret D. Howie, trans., Scala International, (November 1968), 34-36.

6581 Meiring, Jane. "In Memoriam," Contrast (Cape Town, South Africa), no. 14 (November 1966), 13-18.

6582 Melbourn, Richard N. "Blue Time for Carla," Cosmopolitan, CLXVI (April 1969), 152-157.

6583 Melen, Terrance. "Far Thunder," Canadian Forum, XLVI (December 1966), 209-211.

6584 _____. "Friday Night and Saturday Morning," Canadian Forum, XLVI (June 1966), 63-65.

6585 Melnick, Norman. "The Creature in the 1921 Studebaker," Per/Se, I (Winter 1966), 14-17.

6586 Méndez-M., Miguel. "From the Collected Narratives (Unpublished)/'Tragedies of the Northwest'/Tata Casehua," Octavio I. Romano-V., trans., El Grito, II (Winter 1969), 17-31.

6587 Mendoza, Durango. "Summer Water and Shirley," Prairie Schooner, XL (Fall 1966), 219-228.

6588 Mercer, David. "Huggy Bear," Nova, (November 1967), 162-163, 165, 167.

6589 _____. "The Long Crawl through Time," New Writers, no. 3 (1965), 119-131.

6590 Merchant, Paul. "The Grasshopper," Alta, no. 7 (Winter 1968-69), 23.

6591 Meredith, Rita. "Hideous," Nexus (San Francisco, Calif.), II (September-October 1965), 49-50.

6592 _____. "The Life & Death of Fernando," Quartet, no. 15 (Summer 1965), 18-21.

6593 _____. "A Tangy Sort of Cheese: Irrationale for Mouse-Fanciers," Quartet, no. 9 (Winter 1965), 19-21.

6594 Meriwether, Louise M. "Daddy Was a Number Runner," Antioch Review, XXVII (Fall 1967), 325-337.

6595 _____. "A Happening in Barbados," Antioch Review, XXVIII (Spring 1968), 43-52.

6596 _____. "The Large End of the Strop," Negro Digest, XVIII (November 1968), 55-62.

6597 Merkel, Fred H. "Sex and the Single Dog," Statement, no. 23 (Spring 1967), 12-16.

6598 Merrick, Joan. "The Coster Cup," Old Lady of Threadneedle Street, XLV (June 1969), 82-83.

6599 Merrill, Anne. "The Private Life of Ifor Tombo," Harper's Bazaar, CII (May 1969), 193, 238, 246.

6600 Merrill, J. M. "The Commonest Thing," The Quest, I (Winter 1965-66), 38-43.

6601 Merwin, W. S. "The Remembering Machines of Tomorrow," New Yorker, XLV (November 29, 1969), 52-53.

6602 _____. "Three Stories/The Academy," Quarterly Review of Literature, XVI, nos. 3-4 (1969), 390-402.

6603 _____. "Three Stories/Campbell," Quarterly Review of Literature, XVI, nos. 3-4 (1969), 402-413.

6604 _____. "Three Stories/The Flyover," Quarterly Review of Literature, XVI, nos. 3-4 (1969), 413-422.

6605 Mészöly, Miklós. "Report on Five Mice," New Hungarian Quarterly, IX (Autumn 1968), 131-137.

6606 Metcalf, John. "The Children Green and Golden," Wascana Review, III, no. 1 (1968), 25-38.

6607 _____. "The Estuary," West Coast Review, III (Spring 1968), 13-21.

6608 _____. "I've Got It Made," Canadian Forum, XLV (April 1965), 12-13.

6609 _____. "Keys and Watercress," Tamarack Review, no. 45 (Autumn 1967), 10-20.

6610 _____. "One for Cupid," Edge, no. 6 (Spring 1967), 19-24.

6611 _____. "Robert, Standing," The Fiddlehead, no. 82 (November-December 1969), 29-36.

6612 Metcalfe, Philip. "The Road to Madras," Paris Review, XII (Spring 1969), 43-51.

6613 Metcalfe, William. "Loon Lake," Edge, no. 9 (Summer 1969), 39-40.

6614 Metz, Robin. "Doughboy," Epoch, XVIII (Winter 1969), 123-141.

6615 _____. "Winter Range," Paris Review, XII (Spring 1969), 94-129.

6616 Metzger, Deena Posy. "A Metaphor," Ante, III (Fall 1967), 5-17.

6617 _____. "What Rough Beast," Voyages, II (Fall 1968), 86-91.

6618 _____. "from What Rough Beast/a novel," Beyond Baroque 692, I (July 1969), 33.

6619 Meyer, David. "First Dreams," North American Review, IV (March 1967), 11-13.

6620 Meyer, Gordon. "Anglophilia," London Magazine, V (April 1965), 21-27.

6621 _____. "Collision," London Magazine, VIII (June 1968), 20-32.

6622 _____. "Tenancy at Sufferance," London Magazine, VI (October 1966), 5-23.

6623 Meyer, John H. "A Hero's Welcome," Solstice, no. 7 (1968), 34-39.

6624 Meyer, June. "A Elegy of Place," American Dialog, II (October-November 1965), 37.

6625 Meyer, Thomas. "The Grindstone (a narrative)," Caterpillar, no. 7 (April 1969), 147.

6626 Meyers, Howard. "The End of Uroborus," Chicago Review, XIX (June 1967), 96-105.

6627 Meyers, Juno. "Redemption Centers," Esquire, LXV (January 1966), 73, 124, 126-128.

6628 Meyers, Robert, Jr. "Puppy Love Is Mainly Flowers," Redbook, CXXXII (April 1969), 102-103.

6629 Meyers, William. "Sequatchie," Esquire, LXVIII (July 1967), 67-71, 102-106, 108, 110.

6630 Mhango, M. K. Bazuka. "An Endless Struggle," Expression, no. 1 (1968), 19-23.

6631 Mian, M. Ashiq. "The Search," Pakistan Review, XIII (September 1965), 47-48, 50.

6632 Michael, J. C. "In Which an Agrarian Reformer Hears a Prophecy, of the Day the World Turns off," Westerly, no. 2 (July 1968), 21-26.

6633 Michaels, Leonard. "City Boy," Paris Review, X (Fall 1966), 40-50.

6634 _____. "Crossbones," New American Review, no. 3 (1968), 141-143.

6635 _____. "The Deal," Massachusetts Review, VII (Winter 1966), 61-70.

6636 _____. "Fingers and Toes," Paris Review, XI (Winter-Spring 1968), 12-24.

6637 _____. "Going Places," Transatlantic Review, no. 23 (Winter 1966-67), 109-114.

6638 _____. "A Green Thought," Evergreen Review, XIII (April 1969), 33-35.

6639 _____. "Making Changes," Transatlantic Review, no. 26 (Autumn 1967), 84-91.

6640 _____. "Manikin," Massachusetts Review, IX (Winter 1968), 33-38.

6641 Michaelson, John. "A Modern Fable," Literary Review, XII (Autumn 1968), 24-26.

6642 Michaelson, L. W. "The Concert-Goer," North American Review, IV (March 1967), 5-9.

6643 _____. "The Rabbit that Lost Its Nose," North American Review, II (July 1965), 21-27.

6644 Micheline, Jack. "Praise to the Original Mind Who Breathes Fresh Air," VDRSVPVDRSVPVDRSVP, (1969), n.p. [back page].

6645 Michener, Richard L. "Spring Will Be a Little Late This Year," Discourse, XII (Autumn 1969), 540-547.

6646 Michiels, Ivo. "The Sentry," Elisabeth Eybers, trans., Delta (Amsterdam), XI (Autumn 1968), 47-57.

6647 Mickelberry, William. "Outside the City," Florida Quarterly, II (January 1969), 20-26.

6648 _____. "A Walk in the Park," Florida Quarterly, II (January 1969), 52-57.

6649 Micklo, Anne Marie. "One More Place," Manuscript, XVIII (Spring 1965), 17-22.

6650 Micus, Maureen. "Man from Lima," Plaintiff, V (Fall 1968), 21.

6651 Middleton, Edwin. "Some Can't Wait Till Church Lets Out," Greensboro Review, no. 7 (Summer-Fall 1969), 74-83.

6652 Middleton, Elizabeth H. "A Sense of Duty," University Review, XXXIV (Autumn 1967), 24-30.

6653 Middleton, O. E. "The Crows," Landfall, no. 81 (1967), 59-73.

6654 Midwood, Barton. "Automotive Immortality," Esquire, LXVIII (October 1967), 110, 172.

6655 _____. "The Burglars," Paris Review, XII (Summer 1969), 88-97.

6656 _____. "On the Face of It," Queen, CDXXVII (December 21, 1966), 36-37.

6657 _____. "One's Ship," Paris Review, IX (Winter 1966), 147-151.

6658 _____. "The Sheriff," Esquire, LXVIII (November 1967), 149.

6659 _____. "Ticktacktoe," Esquire, LXX (July 1968), 77.

6660 _____. "Under the Mount of Saturn," Esquire, LXVI (August 1966), 124, 126, 128.

6661 _____. "What of It?" Transatlantic Review, no. 22 (Autumn 1966), 32-37.

6662 Mielke, Warren. "Catch Me a Wave," UMD Humanist, XVI (Spring 1968), 4.

6663 _____. "The Prize," UMD Humanist, XV (Winter 1967), 11-13.

6664 Mieželaitis, Eduardas. "Lyrical Studies," Anthony Wixley, trans., Soviet Literature, (no. 4, 1966), 3-37.

6665 Mihaly, M. Ball. "About Life and Rabbits Don't Steal," Appalachian Review, III (Fall 1968), 34-38.

6666 Mikkelsen, John. "Where the Action Is," Signature, II (April 1967), 22.

6667 Milch, David. "Judy Is Dead," Yale Literary Magazine, CXXXIV (May 1966), 4-8.

6668 Mill, G. A. "The Afternoon Your Old Man Dies," The Pluralist, no. 6 (August 1966), 43-44.

6669 Miller, Arthur. "Please Don't Kill Anything," Avant Garde, no. 4 (September 1968), 50-51.

6670 _____. "The Recognitions," Esquire, LXVI (July 1966), 76, 118.

6671 _____. "Search for a Future," Saturday Evening Post, CCXXXIX (August 13, 1966), 64-68, 70.

6672 Miller, Barbara. "Mama," Western Review, IV (Winter 1967), 23-26.

6673 _____. "May Wine," Grande Ronde Review, II, no. 2 (1968), 13-17.

6674 Miller, Brown. "Darkurz," Dust, III (Winter-Spring 1967), 9-11.

6675 Miller, Cecilia Parsons. "To Leave Them Snug," Human Voice, IV, nos. 1 & 2 (1968), 82-85.

6676 Miller, Clive T. "Where They Burn the Dead," Ararat, VIII (Autumn 1967), 14-24.

6677 Miller, Clyde. "Ride Out in Companies," Denver Quarterly, IV (Autumn 1969), 37-100.

6678 Miller, Connie. "The Stars Are Always There," Westerly, no. 4 (December 1969), 38-41.

6679 Miller, Frances. "Two Haitian Folk Tales/Donkey Works for Horse's Pleasure," Unicorn Journal, no. 2 (1968), 8-9.

6680 _____. "Two Haitian Folk Tales/The Green Fish," Unicorn Journal, no. 2 (1968), 7-8.

6681 Miller, Frank. "The Crossroad," Washington and Jefferson Literary Journal, I, no. 1 (1966), 37-38.

6682 _____. "David," Washington and Jefferson Literary Journal, I, no. 2 (1967), 47-48.

6683 Miller, H. C. "Wigglesworth," Westerly, no. 4 (1967), 57-61.

6684 Miller, Heather Ross. "Chel," Red Clay Reader, no. 2 (1965), 50-52.

6685 _____. "Delphi," Salmagundi, no. 9 (Spring 1969), 31-37.

6686 _____. "Maria Is Hurt," Red Clay Reader, no. 5 (1968), 13-18.

6687 _____. "A Spiritual Divorce," Greensboro Review, IV (Winter 1968), 25-31.

6688 _____. "War Games," Carolina Quarterly, XXI (Winter 1969), 6-15.

6689 Miller, J. L. "The Two Men Who Found a Treasure," Freelance (St. Louis, Mo.), n.p. [39].

6690 Miller, Jim Wayne. "A Card to Ruthie," Appalachian Review, I (Winter 1967), 32-36.

6691 _____. "The Disrespectful Savages," Midwestern University Quarterly, II, no. 4 (1967), 91-101.

6692 _____. "The Man Who Feared A Lot," Midwestern University Quarterly, II, no. 2 (1966), 33-41.

6693 Miller, John. "Charlie," Prospero's Cell, II (Summer 1967), 9-36.

6694 Miller, Merrill. "The End of Eternity," Texas Quarterly, IX (Autumn 1966), 72-79.

6695 Miller, Ruth. "Fingers," Contrast (Cape Town, South Africa), no. 12 (July 1965), 82-84.

6696 _____. "Perspectives," Contrast (Cape Town, South Africa), no. 19 (November 1968), 41-48, 57-65.

6697 Miller, Vassar. "Tea Party," Midwestern University Quarterly, I, no. 4 (1966), 45-53.

6698 Miller, Warren. "An Invitation to the Voyage," Saturday Evening Post, CCXXXVIII (April 24, 1965), 54-56, 58, 60, 62-63.

6699 _____. "The Spanish Suit," Saturday Evening Post, CCXXXIX (November 19, 1966), 64-68, 70, 73-74.

6700 Millett, Anthony. "He Lived Vicariously," Limbo, I (January 1965), 22-27.

6701 Mills, A. R. "The Girl in the White Dress," Confrontation, no. 2 (Spring 1969), 32-36.

6702 Mills, H. B. "Out of a Storm," Redbook, CXXIV (March 1965), 62-63, 96, 98, 100-102.

6703 Mills, John. "Joust in Eight Rounds/A Rigmarole," Evidence, no. 9 (1965), 72-97.

6704 _____. "The Road Runner/A Rigmarole," Evidence, no. 10 (1967), 17-44.

6705 Mills, William. "Mr. Bo," New Orleans Review, I (Spring 1969), 230-233.

6706 Millward, Pamela. "To the Bridge," Out of Sight, I, no. 1 (1966), 32-33.

6707 Milton, John R. "La Bruja Who Missed," Ball State University Forum, X (Autumn 1969), 11-18.

6708 _____. "A Small Betrayal," Western Review, V (Winter 1968), 22-35.

6709 Mims, Harley. "Memoirs of a Shoeshine Boy: A Section of a Novel," Antioch Review, XXVII (Fall 1967), 315-320.

6710 Minasian, Archie. "Out from Under," Ararat, VII (Spring 1966), 12-15.

6711 _____. "The Painter and Biff's Father," Armenian Review, XIX (Spring 1966), 29-32.

6712 _____. "Professor Persone and the Music Lovers," Ararat, VII (Winter 1966), 30-33.

6713 Mincher, Philip. "Artist's Life," New Zealand Listener,

(December 15, 1967), 6, 19.

6714 ______. "The Bowman," New Zealand Listener, (May 26, 1967), 6, 24.

6715 ______. "The Fight," New Zealand Listener, (February 24, 1967), 6, 19.

6716 ______. "A Kind of Faith," New Zealand Listener, LXI (July 4, 1969), 8.

6717 ______. "A Kind of Madness," New Zealand Listener, LXI (May 23, 1969), 12.

6718 ______. "The Long Road Home," New Zealand Listener, (September 30, 1966), 6, 25.

6719 ______. "The Mace," Landfall, no. 85 (March 1968), 69-80.

6720 ______. "My Ship Is So Small," New Zealand Listener, LIV (February 11, 1966), 4.

6721 ______. "One Day on the Pukeko," New Zealand Listener, LVIII (August 30, 1968), 10, 14.

6722 ______. "A Piece of Steel," New Zealand Listener, LIII (July 9, 1965), 5.

6723 ______. "A Question of Values," New Zealand Listener, (August 19, 1966), 6, 22.

6724 ______. "The Spartans," New Zealand Listener, LIII (November 5, 1965), 4.

6725 ______. "The Sporting Life," New Zealand Listener, LVIII (May 17, 1968), 10, 25.

6726 ______. "Upstream," New Zealand Listener, LIV (June 3, 1966), 6, 22.

6727 ______. "The Veterans of Marathon," New Zealand Listener, (December 16, 1966), 6, 27.

6728 Minor, William. "The Anniversary," Colorado Quarterly, XVII (Summer 1968), 19-32.

6729 ______. "The Drive-in," Per/Se, I (Spring 1966), 37-43.

6730 Minot, Stephen. "Crossings," Redbook, CXXVIII (February 1967), 70-71, 113-114.

6731 ______. "Freddie and the Cat Woman," Carleton Miscellany, VIII (Spring 1967), 2-16.

6732 _____. "I Remember the Day God Died Like It Was Yesterday," Carleton Miscellany, VII (Summer 1966), 2-13.

6733 _____. "Journey to Ocean Grove," Carleton Miscellany, X (Summer 1969), 19-38.

6734 _____. "The Prodigal's Father," Carleton Miscellany, IX (Spring 1968), 2-18.

6735 _____. "Small Point Bridge," Virginia Quarterly Review, XLV (Winter 1969), 68-78.

6736 Minot, Steven. "Teddy, Where Are You?" Ladies' Home Journal, LXXXV (September 1968), 98-99, 122-125.

6737 Minton, M. Cronan. "Gulls over Memphis, or The Glorious Demise of Mrs. Laramore," Virginia Quarterly Review, XLIII (Summer 1967), 435-455.

6738 Minus, Edward. "The Greyhound Minstrel," Red Clay Reader, no. 6 (1969), 42-47.

6739 Miranda, LaVerne. "The Ugly Story," Ante, II (Winter 1966), 62-65.

6740 Mirsky, Mark. "Simcha," Ararat, VIII (Autumn 1967), 62-64.

6741 Mishell, Donald. "Pithecanthropus Erectus," Trace, nos. 62 & 63 (Fall-Winter 1966-67), 345-352.

6742 Mishev, Georgi. "Fermentation," Svetoslaw Piperov, trans., Obzor (Spring 1969), 54-57.

6743 Mishima, Yukio. "Patriotism," Geoffrey W. Sargent, trans., Esquire, LXV (April 1966), 106-107, 109, 166, 168-170, 173-174, 175.

6744 _____. "Swaddling Clothes," Ivan Morris, trans., Cosmopolitan, CLX (April 1966), 102-105.

6745 Mitcham, Carl. "The Wonders of Modern Science," Arx, I (November 1967), 12-19, 42-45.

6746 Mitchell, Adrian. "Nostalgia--Now Threepence Off," Poetmeat, no. 8 (1965), 65-66.

6747 Mitchell, David. "The Voices of Spring," Redbook, CXXVII (September 1966), 68-69.

6748 Mitchell, Don. "Alcohol Tripping," Harper's Magazine, CCXXXIX (September 1969), 84-91.

6749 Mitchell, Giles. "Come to Dust," Goodly Co., no. 12 (July 1968), 19-26.

6750 Mitchell, John H., Jr. "The Sheep Killers," Yale Literary Magazine, CXXXIII (May 1965), 23-33.

6751 Mitchell, Julian. "The Grocer's Assistant," Evergreen Review, XIII (November 1969), 48-52, 65-69.

6752 Mitchell, Kathryn J. "A Dangerous Thing," Negro Digest, XIV (October 1965), 72-78.

6753 Mitchell, Ken. "Everybody Gets Something Here," Wascana Review, I, no. 1 (1966), 46-51.

6754 Mitchell, M. R. "Two Houses," Human Voice, IV, no. 3 (1968), 10-15.

6755 Mitchell, William R. "The Way, the Truth, and the Life," Beyond Baroque 691, I (December 1968), 12-16, 55.

6756 Mitcho, Patricia R. "To Understand a Need," UMD Humanist, XIV (Spring 1966), 18-21.

6757 Mitra, Bamacharan. "Sweetmeat," J. M. Joardar, trans., Bhubaneswar Review, no. 3 (Summer 1969), 20-28.

6758 Mitra, Bimal. "The Episode before Suicide," Anjali Sircar, trans., Bengali Literature, I (May 1966), 19-40.

6759 Mitra, Narendranath. "The Dreamers," Enakshi Chatterjee, trans., Bengali Literature, II (Autumn 1967), 64-71.

6760 _____. "In Quest of Beauty," Enakshi Chatterjee, trans., Arizona Quarterly, XXIII (Winter 1967), 327-334.

6761 Mitura, Rita. "The Struggle," Ave Maria, CVII (April 20, 1968), 26-28.

6762 Miyazawa, Kenji. "The Bears of Mt. Nametoko," Masako Ohnuki, trans., Chicago Review, XX (June 1968), 24-31.

6763 _____. "Northguard General Son Ba Yu and the Three Doctor Brothers," Masako Ohnuki, trans., Chicago Review, XX (June 1968), 42-53.

6764 _____. "Oppel and the Elephant," Masako Ohnuki, trans., Chicago Review, XX & XXI (May 1969), 77-82.

6765 _____. "The Origin of the Deer Dance," Masako Ohnuki, trans., Chicago Review, XX (November 1968), 33-39.

6766 _____. "The Restaurant of Large Orders," Masako Ohnuki, trans., Chicago Review, XXI (December 1969), 96-100.

6767 _____. "Wild Pear," Burton Watson, trans., East-West Review, II (Spring-Summer 1965), 62-66.

6768 _____. "The Wildcat and the Acorns," Masako Ohnuki, trans., Chicago Review, XXI (December 1969), 88-93.

6769 Moat, John. "Rachel," Panache, no. 3 (1969), 44-55.

6770 _____. "Sam," Panache, no. 2 (1968), 13-26.

6771 Moberg, David. "Gooseflowers Gay/A Novel of Passion," Mother, no. 5 (Summer 1965), 34-37.

6772 Moe, Rusty C. "Except Adrienne Carpenter," Green River Review, II (May 1969), 43-47.

6773 Moffett, David. "The Night the Store Burned Down," The Archive, LXXIX (September 1966), 16-17.

6774 Mohamed, F. I. "An Unfulfilled Date," Nexus, I (August 1967), 23-24.

6775 Mohanty, Gopinath. "House," Dhirendra Kumar Samantray, trans., Bhubaneswar Review, no. 1 (Summer 1968), 56-65.

6776 Mohanty, Surendra. "Krushnachuda," Debidas Mohapatra and Sitakanta Mohapatra, trans., Bhubaneswar Review, no. 1 (Summer 1968), 66-70.

6777 Mohapatra, Godavarish. "Only a Spoon," J. M. Joardar, trans., Bhubaneswar Review, no. 2 (Winter 1968-69), 70-73.

6778 Mohme, John. "There's No Smile Like a Mother's Smile," Trace, no. 61 (Summer 1966), 206-208.

6779 Moldova, György. "The Invincible Eleven," New Hungarian Quarterly, VII (Winter 1966), 50-69.

6780 Molina, Antonio Fernández. "The Man," Jack Garlington, trans., Western Humanities Review, XXI (Winter 1967), 31-34.

6781 Molinaro, Ursule. "Candied Desire," Lotus, no. 1 (1968), 20-23.

6782 _____. "Desire Game," Evergreen Review, X (April 1966), 46-49.

6783 _____. "Early Morning Mother," Extensions, no. 1 (1968), 58-65.

6784 _____. "Hatred Needs a Friend," Edge, no. 4 (Spring 1965), 38-44.

6785 Molitor, K. P. "The Confrontation," Plaintiff, V (Spring-Summer 1969), 4-6.

6786 Molla, Mobarak A. "The Face Is Unknown," Pakistan Review, XIV (December 1966), 34.

6787 _____. "My Young Man," Pakistan Review, XIV (July 1966), 24-25.

6788 _____. "The Sentence," Pakistan Review, XIV (May 1966), 42-43.

6789 Molloy, F. Michael. "The Dropout," Southerly, (1969), 305-308.

6790 Molnar, Anne. "All That Long Summer," Quarry, XV (March 1966), 15-19.

6791 Molusi, Maurmo. "My Glorious Lost Fate," Contrast (Cape Town, South Africa), no. 22 (December 1969), 21-29.

6792 Molyneux, Thomas W. "Before, Once," Sewanee Review, LXXV (July-September 1967), 462-481.

6793 _____. "Jimmy Outlaw," Shenandoah, XIX (Summer 1968), 19-46.

6794 _____. "Kick," Shenandoah, XX (Winter 1969), 29-46.

6795 _____. "Moderately and Fairly Regularly," Quarterly Review of Literature, XVI, nos. 3-4 (1969), 423-433.

6796 _____. "A Part of It," Greensboro Review, II (December 1966), 21-29.

6797 _____. "The Wrath Bearing Tree," Greensboro Review, I (May 1966), 40-56.

6798 Momaday, N. Scott. "Three Sketches from House Made of Dawn," Southern Review, II (October 1966), 933-945.

6799 _____. "Two Sketches from House Made of Dawn," New Mexico Quarterly, XXXVII (Summer 1967), 101-111.

6800 _____. "Two Tales from The Journey of Tai-Me/The Arrow," Little Square Review, nos. 5 & 6 (Spring & Summer 1968), 31.

6801 _____. "Two Tales from The Journey of Tai-Me/The Beginning," Little Square Review, nos. 5 & 6 (Spring & Summer 1968), 30.

6802 Monaghan, Eileen. "Mother Goose Continued/or/The Further Adventures of the Bear Family," UMD Humanist, XV (Winter 1967), 43, 45.

6803 Monk, Elizabeth Graham. "The Enemy: Love," Seventeen, XXIV (February 1965), 118-119, 204-205.

6804 Montagu, Elizabeth. "Incubus," Transatlantic Review, no. 19 (Autumn 1965), 92-104.

6805 Montale, Eugenio. "Butterfly of Dinard," William Weaver, trans., Art and Literature, no. 9 (Summer 1966), 50-51.

6806 _____. "The Director," Origin (Kyoto, Japan), no. 11 (October 1968), 18-20.

6807 _____. "English Gentleman," William Weaver, trans., Art and Literature, no. 9 (Summer 1966), 57-59.

6808 _____. "An English Gentleman," G. Singh, trans., London Magazine, VIII (February 1969), 29-31.

6809 _____. "The Flight of the Hawk," William Weaver, trans., Art and Literature, no. 9 (Summer 1966), 60-62.

6810 _____. "The House with Two Palm-Trees," William Weaver, trans., Art and Literature, no. 9 (Summer 1966), 52-56.

6811 _____. "The Man in Pyjamas," G. Singh, trans., London Magazine, VIII (February 1969), 28-29.

6812 _____. "The Paintings in the Cellar," G. Singh, trans., London Magazine, VIII (November 1968), 60-63.

6813 _____. "The Snow Statue," William Weaver, trans., Art and Literature, no. 9 (Summer 1966), 63-64.

6814 _____. "Tale of an Unknown," Origin (Kyoto, Japan), no. 11 (October 1968), 13-17.

6815 Montana, Antonio. "The Cursed Fog," Américas, XIX (July 1967), 26-28.

6816 Montgomery, Marion. "Kingdom by the Sea," New Mexico Quarterly, XXXV (Summer 1965), 145-162.

6817 _____. "A Mess of Pardiges," Georgia Review, XX (Winter 1966), 444-453.

6818 _____. "The Return," Arlington Quarterly, I (Winter 1967-68), 189-200.

6819 _____. "Vacation," Southwest Review, LIV (Summer 1969), 301-313.

6820 _____. "A Visitation," University Review, XXXII (October 1965), 38-42.

6821 Moody, Minnie Hite. "The Man Who Shot General Zollicoffer," Georgia Review, XIX (Fall 1965), 299-308.

6822 Moody, R. Bruce. "Water," New Yorker, XLI (June 26, 1965), 24-31.

6823 Mooney, Michael. "The Colossus of North Hackett," Perspective, XVI (Winter-Spring 1969), 67-79.

6824 Mooraj, Anwer. "The Story of Helen or The Trojan Whore," Ambit, no. 24 (1965), 22-23.

6825 Moorcock, Michael. "A Cure for Cancer," New Worlds, no. 188 (March 1969), 4-20.

6826 _____. "The Delhi Division," New Worlds, no. 185 (December 1968), 23-27.

6827 Moore, Brian. "The Apartment Hunter/An Excerpt from the Novel A Woman of No Identity," Tamarack Review, no. 41 (Autumn 1966), 53-64.

6828 _____. "A Vocation," Threshold, no. 21 (Summer 1967), 49-53.

6829 Moore, Harold. "An American Dilemma," Colorado Quarterly, XV (Autumn 1966), 165-177.

6830 _____. "Incident at Billy Springs," Esquire, LXVII (May 1967), 124-125, 166, 168.

6831 _____. "The Wild West," Colorado Quarterly, XIII (Winter 1965), 227-238.

6832 Moore, Jack B. "Don't Die, Jeff Chandler," Esquire, LXV (April 1966), 134-137, 152, 154, 158, 160-162, 164, 166.

6833 Moore, John. "Among the Quiet Folks," Saturday Evening Post, CCXL (January 14, 1967), 52-54, 56-59.

6834 _____. "Mr. Catesby Brings It Off," Ladies' Home Journal, LXXXIV (February 1967), 82-83, 138-141.

6835 _____. "Sword Cactus," Saturday Evening Post, CCXL (July 29, 1967), 50-55.

6836 Moore, Keith. "The Girl Who Gave the Stellar Report," Western Humanities Review, XX (Autumn 1966), 333-348.

6837 Moore, Lina Espina. "Heart of the Lotus/(First Half),"

Solidarity, III (June 1968), 57-90.

6838 _____. "Heart of the Lotus/(Second Installment)," Solidarity, III (July 1968), 59-76.

6839 _____. "Heart of the Lotus/(Conclusion)," Solidarity, III (August 1968), 43-61.

6840 _____. "Reunion," Solidarity, I (October-December 1966), 86-90.

6841 Moore, Sharon. "Sleep," New Yorker, XLIV (June 1, 1968), 30-37.

6842 Moore, William. "The Getaway," Literary Review, XII (Summer 1969), 512-515.

6843 _____. "Voyeur," Literary Review, XII (Autumn 1968), 27-34.

6844 Moorhouse, Frank. "The American Poet's Visit," Southerly, XXVIII (1968), 275-285.

6845 _____. "The Dirty Girl," Stand, VIII, no. 4 (1967), 4-11.

6846 _____. "Her Mother's Visit," Westerly, no. 3 (1967), 10-15.

6847 _____. "Nish," The Pluralist, no. 4 (May 1965), 18-19.

6848 Moorse, George. "A Goodbye for Charlotte," Harper's Bazaar, XCVIII (April 1965), 101, 103, 105, 107, 109, 111.

6849 Moravia, Alberto. "The Chase," Angus Davidson, trans., Redbook, CXXXIII (September 1969), 76, 155, 157.

6850 _____. "The Escape," Angus Davidson, trans., Atlantic Monthly, CCXV (January 1965), 87-89.

6851 _____. "Insomnia Together," Cavalier, XV (April 1965), 38-39, 40.

6852 _____. "A Jealousy Trilogy/Jealousy Plays Tricks," Cosmopolitan, CLIX (September 1965), 109-111.

6853 _____. "A Jealousy Trilogy/The Man Who Watched," Cosmopolitan, CLIX (September 1965), 107-109.

6854 _____. "A Jealousy Trilogy/Mere Objects," Cosmopolitan, CLIX (September 1965), 106-107.

6855 _____. "Reconciliation," Angus Davidson, trans., Redbook, CXXXIII (September 1969), 77, 157-158.

6856 ______. "Roman Quartet/Celestina," Playboy, XV (December 1968), 190, 224.

6857 ______. "Roman Quartet/A Man of Power," Playboy, XV (December 1968), 194, 208.

6858 ______. "Roman Quartet/A Midding Type," Playboy, XV (December 1968), 193, 236-237.

6859 ______. "Roman Quartet/Wake Up!" Playboy, XV (December 1968), 189, 244.

6860 Moray, Ann. "Tom Tinker Ellis," Mademoiselle, LXVI (December 1967), 100-101, 154-159.

6861 Morefield, John. "Irises," Florida Quarterly, II (April 1969), 1-16.

6862 Moreland, Charles, Jr. "The Top Hat Motel," Negro Digest, XVIII (June 1969), 72-82.

6863 Morgan, Berry. "Andrew," New Yorker, XLII (July 2, 1966), 25-28.

6864 ______. "Barrand's Landing," New Yorker, XLIII (March 11, 1967), 54-56.

6865 ______. "The Flower Gully," New Yorker, XLIV (August 24, 1968), 35-37.

6866 ______. "Miss Idella, the Travelling Hoe Lady," New Yorker, XLII (December 10, 1966), 53-55.

6867 ______. "Mr. Collier," New Yorker, XLV (October 18, 1969), 58-60.

6868 ______. "Mr. Dock," New Yorker, XLIV (January 11, 1969), 34-36.

6869 ______. "The Organ Piece," New Yorker, XLII (August 13, 1966), 24-26.

6870 ______. "The Pepper Trick," New Yorker, XLIII (April 22, 1967), 53-55.

6871 ______. "Robert," New Yorker, XLV (July 19, 1969), 22-25.

6872 ______. "Seven Whiteface," New Yorker, XLII (July 23, 1966), 32-33.

6873 Morgan, Gabriela. "The Prodigal Daughter," Jeopardy, no. 5 (Spring 1969), 72-73.

6874 Morgan, Robert. "The Exile," Panache, no. 3 (1969), 56-61.

6875 _____. "Sunday Afternoon," Greensboro Review, no. 7 (Summer-Fall 1969), 34-43.

6876 Móricz, Zsigmond. "Jóska Samu Kis," New Hungarian Quarterly, VIII (Winter 1967), 3-8.

6877 Morli, Anthony. "Miss Sakura or the Lady in Question," Solidarity, IV (November 1969), 51-69.

6878 Morner, Stanley. "Blood Brothers and Goodbye, Etc.," December, IX, nos. 2/3 (1967), 78-82.

6879 _____. "A Season on the American Prairie," Kansas Magazine, (1967), 41-51.

6880 Morphett, Tony. "A Dull Night for TV," Overland, no. 41 (Winter 1969), 28-29.

6881 _____. "Objector," Overland, no. 34 (Autumn 1966), 17-18.

6882 Morreale, Ben. "Brook Farm II: A Memoir," Antioch Review, XXV (Winter 1965-66), 577-590.

6883 Morressy, John. "The Man at the Wall," New Orleans Review, I (Summer 1969), 313-315.

6884 Morris, Edita. "A Goldfish in Detroit," Eastern Horizon, VII (January-February 1968), 57-60.

6885 _____. "Guerrillero with a Flower Between His Lips," Eastern Horizon, VII (March-April 1968), 58-62.

6886 _____. "The Sorrow of Ape-in-Pants," American Dialog, IV (Spring 1967), 13-14.

6887 Morris, Herbert. "Everything Fortunate and Deep with Love," Trace, nos. 62 & 63 (Fall-Winter 1966-67), 433-448.

6888 Morris, J. Riviere. "As a Man Soweth," Southerly, XXVIII (1968), 172-181.

6889 _____. "The Day a Man Died," Southerly, XXVII, no. 3 (1967), 174-178.

6890 _____. "One Weekend," Australian Letters, VIII (January 1968), 25-29.

6891 _____. "'Onward Christian Soldiers'," Southerly, (1969), 140-151.

6892 _____. "The Run," Southerly, XXVI, no. 3 (1966), 175-178.

6893 _____. "Who'll Take a Glove?" Westerly, no. 2 (July 1968), 19-20.

6894 Morris, Mary. "Mom-Mom," Soundings, IV (Spring 1967), 55-61.

6895 Morris, Myra. "The Swan," Overland, no. 31 (Autumn 1965), 11-13.

6896 Morris, Patricia Ann. "Kwa Wenderling," Riverside Quarterly, II (June 1966), 105-119.

6897 Morris, Rebecca. "The Good Humor Man," New Yorker, XLIII (June 17, 1967), 29-36.

6898 Morris, Sara. "(from a tin cup of dreams)," Aldebaran Review, no. 2 (1968), 37-38.

6899 Morris, Taylor. "Retreat from the Sea," New Yorker, XLI (May 22, 1965), 45-53.

6900 Morris, Tina. "from 'Journeys/Cages'," Poetmeat, no. 13 (Spring 1967), 25-29.

6901 Morris, Wright. "Drrdla," Esquire, LXXII (August 1969), 87-90.

6902 _____. "Green Grass, Blue Sky, White House," New Yorker, XLV (October 25, 1969), 56-62.

6903 _____. "Lover, Is that You?" Esquire, LXV (March 1966), 70, 132-134, 136-137.

6904 _____. "Since When Do They Charge Admission," Harper's Magazine, CCXXXVIII (May 1969), 65-70.

6905 Morrison, Arthur. "Behind the Shade," Nova, (October 1969), 56, 60, 62.

6906 Morrison, Dorothy. "The Last Supper," Coraddi, (Fall 1967), 20.

6907 Morrison, H. R. W. "Questions," Queen's Quarterly, LXXVI (Summer 1969), 319-335.

6908 Morrison, John. "The Blind Man's Story," Overland, no. 34 (Autumn 1966), 5-11.

6909 _____. "Murder on the One-Thirty," Meanjin Quarterly, XXV (September 1966), 279-289.

6910 _____. "Tinkle, Tinkle, Little Bell," Meanjin Quarterly, XXIV (March 1965), 89-99.

6911 _____. "The Trinket Box," Meanjin Quarterly, XXVI (Summer 1967), 412-422.

6912 Morrison, Richard. "Dutch Funeral," Kansas Magazine, (1967), 54-57.

6913 _____. "The Wake," Kansas Magazine, (1965), 32-36.

6914 Morrow, Patrick. "A Primrose for Mrs. Powdie," DeKalb Literary Arts Journal, I (Summer 1967), 36-44.

6915 Morrow, Susan. "Dancing with a Tiger/(Part I)," Good Housekeeping, CLXVII (July 1968), 59-61, 168-175, 180-187.

6916 _____. "Dancing with a Tiger/(Conclusion)," Good Housekeeping, CLXVII (August 1968), 72-73, 166-172, 174-176, 180-184, 189-191.

6917 _____. "The Insiders/(Part I)," Good Housekeeping, CLXIV (February 1967), 70-73, 196-204, 206-208, 211-218, 220, 222, 224, 231-235.

6918 _____. "The Insiders/(Conclusion)," Good Housekeeping, CLXIV (March 1967), 98-99, 216-222, 224-226, 228-232, 234-240, 242-246, 253.

6919 _____. "The Promise," Good Housekeeping, CLX (May 1965), 94-95, 188-192, 194.

6920 _____. "Trouble in Mind," Good Housekeeping, CLXIII (July 1966), 76-77, 177-180.

6921 Morse, Kate. "Wars and Storms Are Good to Be Rid Of," Arx, I (March 1967), 15-24.

6922 Mortimer, Penelope. "My Friend Says It's Bullet-Proof," Nova, (August 1967), between pages 64-65 [i-xvi].

6923 _____. "My Friend Says It's Bullet-Proof/Part II," Nova, (September 1967), after page 120 [i-viii].

6924 Morton, Frederic. "Abby in Andalusia," Cavalier, XV (December 1965), 22-23, 60-61, 86-88.

6925 _____. "Etta at Night," Playboy, XII (November 1965), 86-88, 180-182, 184.

6926 _____. "The Guest," Transatlantic Review, no. 19 (Autumn 1965), 83-90.

6927 Morton, Richard M. "Peake's Pond," Georgia Review, XIX (Summer 1965), 211-218.

6928 ______. "Waiting at the Old Home," Georgia Review, XXI (Spring 1967), 81-86.

6929 Mosallem, Norman. "Bicycles," Chicago Review, XX (November 1968), 19-25.

6930 ______. "The Breakfast Room at the Hotel Salaam-Salaam," Carolina Quarterly, XIX (Fall 1967), 50-56.

6931 ______. "Cameras," Chicago Review, XX, no. 1 (1968), 54-57.

6932 ______. "Goldfish," Carolina Quarterly, XVIII (Winter 1966), 4-8.

6933 ______. "A Man Who Loved Gounod," Chicago Review, XVIII no. 1 (1965), 45-54.

6934 ______. "The Prince of Aquitaine," Carolina Quarterly, XX (Spring 1968), 35-43.

6935 ______. "Then You Recall Kunigunde?" Chicago Review, XVIII no. 1 (1965), 67-70.

6936 ______. "To the Girls at Their Wedding Suppers," Carolina Quarterly, XX (Winter 1968), 55-64.

6937 ______. "To the Girls Who Cross Lake Geneva," Chicago Review, XX, no. 1 (1968), 75-84.

6938 ______. "The Tosca Meditations," Chicago Review, XVIII, no. 1 (1965), 5-10.

6939 Moscoso, Jose G., Jr. "Erasmo," Lance, V (Winter 1965), 14-16.

6940 Moscoso-Gongora, Peter. "Manolo," Chelsea, no. 26 (May 1969), 121-127.

6941 ______. "Story No. 3," Transatlantic Review, no. 19 (Autumn 1965), 5-23.

6942 Moscrip, Carol. "Children at Play," Spectrum, VIII (Winter 1965), 74-75.

6943 Moseley, William. "Old Solitaire," Epoch, XIX (Fall 1969), 69-82.

6944 ______. "The Preacher and Margery Scott," Virginia Quarterly Review, XLIII (Summer 1967), 409-420.

6945 ______. "Strong Is Your Hold O Mortal Flesh," Virginia Quarterly Review, XLV (Autumn 1969), 637-649.

6946 _____. "Voices," Readers & Writers, I (January-February 1967), 8-11.

6947 Mosley, Nicholas. "A Morning in the Life of Intelligent People," Esquire, LXX (September 1968), 106-109, 150, 152.

6948 Moss, Maryan. "School Gala," New Zealand Listener, LVIII (June 7, 1968), 10, 24.

6949 Mostert, Noel. "The Buffalo," Saturday Evening Post, CCXXXVIII (January 30, 1965), 40-42, 46-47.

6950 Motley, Willard. "The Grammar School Dance Lesson," December, XI, nos. 1 & 2 (1969), 90-92.

6951 Motsisi, Casey. "Boy-Boy," The Classic, II, no. 4 (1968), 58-60.

6952 Mott, Wilma. "No Choice," UMD Humanist, XIV (Winter 1966), 27-28.

6953 Moulton, Elizabeth. "In the Fun House," Redbook, CXXVI (February 1966), 64-65.

6954 Mountzoures, H. L. "The Beating," New Yorker, XLII (August 20, 1966), 30-32.

6955 _____. "Bits of Glass," New Yorker, XLIV (August 17, 1968), 26-31.

6956 _____. "A Day in the Country," New Yorker, XLIII (February 10, 1968), 29-35.

6957 _____. "The Empire of Things," New Yorker, XLIII (September 23, 1967), 46-49.

6958 _____. "Epithalamion," New Yorker, XLII (March 26, 1966), 46.

6959 _____. "An Examination," New Yorker, XLIII (January 20, 1968), 28-34.

6960 _____. "The Executor," New Yorker, XLV (September 20, 1969), 44-47.

6961 _____. "Fathers," New Yorker, XLII (January 21, 1967), 24-26.

6962 _____. "Hill No. 641," Antioch Review, XXIX (Winter 1969-70), 517-524.

6963 _____. "In Transit," New Yorker, XLIII (December 16, 1967), 50-52.

6964 _____. "A Lecture," New Yorker, XLII (April 23, 1966), 170, 173-176.

6965 _____. "The Medium," Redbook, CXXXIV (November 1969), 72-73, 153, 155, 157-158.

6966 _____. "The Music of the Tree," New Yorker, XLI (January 8, 1966), 24-26.

6967 _____. "The 1930 Olympics," New Yorker, XLV (April 5, 1969), 127-130.

6968 _____. "The Pigeon," New Yorker, XLII (July 16, 1966), 32-34.

6969 _____. "Putting Things in Order," Redbook, CXXXI (July 1968), 68-69, 123-125.

6970 _____. "A Reunion," New Yorker, XLII (Feb. 11, 1967), 42-44.

6971 _____. "Twigs," New Yorker, XLIV (May 4, 1968), 48-51.

6972 Mowat, John. "Slaughter of the Goldfish," Ikon (Leeds, Eng.), I (Spring 1965), 13-17.

6973 Moyo, Steven Phaniso. "Nothing Odd," Transatlantic Review, no. 31 (Winter 1968-69), 130-140.

6974 Moyse, Arthur. "Chapter Two/May God Forgive You Tuli Kupferberg/or a Chapter in Search of a Novel," Poetmeat, nos. 9 & 10 (Summer 1965), 38-44.

6975 Mpofu, Stephen. "The Hotel Samaritan," New Writing from Zambia, no. 2 (1966), 18-20.

6976 Mrabet, Mohammed. "The Spring," Paul Bowles, trans., Transatlantic Review, no. 21 (Summer 1966), 53-57.

6977 Mrozek, Slawomir. "Ad Astra," Encounter, XXX (March 1968), 26-35.

6978 _____. "Manuscript Found in a Forest," Adam Czerniawski, trans., Stand, VII, no. 2 (1965), 52-53.

6979 _____. "Two Short Stories by Slawomir Mrozek/The Faithful Guardian," Konrad Syrop, trans., Mademoiselle, LXVIII (January 1969), 112, 130-131.

6980 _____. "Two Short Stories by Slawomir Mrozek/Hope," Konrad Syrop, trans., Mademoiselle, LXVIII (Jan. 1969), 113, 131-132, 138.

6981 MsColl, Isobel. "The Oddity," Threshold, no. 21 (Summer 1967), 94-104.

6982 Mtonga, H. "The Exact Man," New Writing from Zambia, no. 1 (1969), 29-34.

6983 Mudrick, Marvin. "Cleopatra," Hudson Review, XIX (Spring 1966), 81-91.

6984 Muehl, Carol Callaway. "Robert Butterfly," Ave Maria, CVI (July 29, 1967), 26-28.

6985 _____. "You Are Dark and Eight," Ave Maria, CV (June 24, 1967), 28-30.

6986 Mukhammadiev, Fazliddin. "The House on the Outskirts," Eve Manning, trans., Soviet Literature, (no. 9, 1967), 63-103.

6987 Mukherjee, Bharati. "Debate on a Rainy Afternoon," Massachusetts Review, VII (Spring 1966), 257-270.

6988 Mukhtar, Askad. "Sisters," Alice Ingman, trans., Soviet Literature, (no. 12, 1967), 38-47.

6989 Mulder, Tiny. "Seventh Summer," Elizabeth Willems-Treeman, trans., Delta (Amsterdam), VIII (Winter 1965-66), 51-6.

6990 Mulisch, Harry. "Four Anecdotes on Death," Ina Rike, trans., Delta (Amsterdam), XI (Winter 1968-69), 5-17.

6991 _____. "Spit and Image," R. B. Powell, trans., Transatlantic Review, no. 28 (Spring 1968), 39-45.

6992 Muller, David G., Jr. "The Traitor," Lance, V (Spring 1965), 35-41.

6993 Muller, Rita. "The Door," West Coast Review, III (Winter 1969), 42-44.

6994 Mulligan, Gerard. "Busrides," Epoch, XIX (Fall 1969), 3-13.

6995 Mundis, J. J. "The Luger Is a 9mm Automatic Handgun with a Parabellum Action," New Worlds, no. 188 (March 1969), 36-39.

6996 Munro, Alice. "Postcard," Tamarack Review, no. 47 (Spring 1968), 23-31, 33-39.

Munro, H. H. See Saki.

6997 Munro, James. "Die Rich Die Happy," Cosmopolitan, CLX (June 1966), 128-148, 153-156, 158-161.

6998 Munson, Genevieve. "Good-Bye, Sweet Summer, Good-Bye," Seventeen, XXVI (August 1967), 296-297, 409-410, 412-415, 417-419, 421-422.

6999 _____. "Old Raccoon," Seventeen, XXVIII (August 1969), 438-442, 444-445, 450.

7000 _____. "That's Why I Loved Chauncey Meadors," Seventeen, XXVI (June 1967), 108-109, 176, 178-181.

7001 Munteanu, Francisc. "A Slice of Bread," Literary Review, X (Summer 1967), 501-512.

7002 _____. "A Slice of Bread," Meanjin Quarterly, XXV (September 1966), 297-305.

7003 Murdoch, Iris. "The Time of the Angels," Cosmopolitan, CLXII (January 1967), 102-106.

7004 Muro, Amando. "Hungry Men," Arizona Quarterly, XXIII (Spring 1967), 34-38.

7005 _____. "Mala Torres," Arizona Quarterly, XXIV (Summer 1968), 163-168.

7006 _____. "María Tepache," Arizona Quarterly, XXV (Winter 1969), 343-347.

7007 _____. "More Hobo Sketches," Arizona Quarterly, XXI (Autumn 1965), 255-260.

7008 _____. "Night Train to Fort Worth," Arizona Quarterly, XXIII (Autumn 1967), 250-254.

7009 _____. "Road Buddy," Arizona Quarterly, XXII (Autumn 1966), 269-273.

7010 _____. "Something about Two Hoboes," Arizona Quarterly, XXV (Summer 1969), 120-124.

7011 _____. "Something about Two Mexicans," New Mexico Quarterly, XXXVI (Autumn 1966), 258-266.

7012 _____. "Sunday in Little Chihuahua," New Mexico Quarterly, XXXV (Autumn 1965), 223-230.

7013 Murphy, Alberta. "The Annunciation," Antioch Review, XXVIII (Winter 1968-69), 493-504.

7014 Murphy, John J. "The Unharvested," Four Quarters, XV (November 1965), 7-12.

7015 Murphy, Michael J. "The Weakness," Threshold, no. 21 (Summer 1967), 19-30.

7016 Murphy, Phil. "Prophet Still, If Bird or Devil," Saturday Night, LXXXII (December 1967), 25-30.

7017 Murray, Albert. "Stonewall Jackson's Waterloo," Harper's Magazine, CCXXXVIII (February 1969), 59-64.

7018 Murray, Bettie Jane. "Two Separate People," Redbook, CXXXIV (November 1969), 80-81, 193-194, 196, 202, 205.

7019 Murray, Chalmers S. "Simon and the Sea Sarpent," South Carolina Review, II (November 1969), 16-21.

7020 Murray, Francis. "The Alligator Didn't Like Her Roll-On Deodorant," Human Voice Quarterly, II (May 1966), 59-60.

7021 ______. "Around the World in 17 Days," Cimarron Review, no. 4 (June 1968), 32-36.

7022 ______. "Humphrey Bogart and the Campbell Soup Cans," Nexus (San Francisco, Calif.), II (September-October 1965), 35-37.

7023 ______. "A Nice Day to Fly," Nexus (San Francisco, Calif.), II (March-April 1965), 18-21.

7024 ______. "The Nun Who Came in from the Cold," North American Review, III (September 1966), 6-7.

7025 ______. "Please Pass the Instant Poi," North American Review, II (November 1965), 25-27.

7026 ______. "Professor, What Are Those Infernal Goats Doing in the Classroom?" Nexus (San Francisco), II (May-June 1965), 22-23.

7027 ______. "Talcum X and the Seven Giants," Nexus (San Francisco, Calif.), II (November-December 1965), 16-19.

7028 ______. "The Water Buffalo Failed to Signal a U-Turn," Pyramid, no. 4 (1969), 24-25.

7029 Murray, Neil. "An Old Man," Soundings, II (Spring 1965), 140-144.

7030 Murthy, U. R. Anantha. "Initiation," U. R. Anantha Murthy and V. K. Natraj, trans., final version by Gary Willis, Transatlantic Review, no. 22 (Autumn 1966), 98-107.

7031 Murti, K. V. Suryanarayana. "The Floods," Triveni, XXXVI (October 1967), 19-27.

7032 Mushanga, Musa. "Folk Tales from Ankole," Transition, V, no. 22 (1965), 26-30.

7033 Musil, Robert. "The Flypaper," Michael Roloff, trans., Harper's Bazaar, CII (June 1969), 68.

7034 _____. "The Lady from Portugal," Eithne Wilkins & Ernst Kaiser, trans., Encounter, XXIV (April 1965), 34-36.

7035 _____. "The Lady from Portugal," Eithne Wilkins & Ernst Kaiser, trans., Harper's Bazaar, XCVIII (October 1965), 226-227, 293, 295-298, 300-301.

7036 Mvalo, W. Rex. "Hyena Takes a Wife," Expression, no. 1 (1968), 4-7.

7037 Myers, Juno. "Green Wind," Cosmopolitan, CLIX (November 1965), 101-107.

7038 Myers, Lou. "East 180th Street," Niobe, no. 2 (1966), 21-30.

7039 _____. "The Landlord," Evergreen Review, X (December 1966), 56-60.

7040 _____. "Leatheroid Sofa," Niobe, no. 2 (1966), 33-34.

7041 _____. "Tomorrow's Cousin Milton," Niobe, no. 2 (1966), 37.

7042 Myers, Walter. "How Long Is Forever?" Negro Digest, XVIII (June 1969), 52-57.

7043 Myrer, Anton. "The Intruder," Cosmopolitan, CLVIII (February 1965), 112-133, 138-140.

7044 Myrick, David Lee. "Dark Morning," Foxfire, II (March 1968), 53-58.

7045 Nabokov, Vladimir. "Ada," Playboy, XVI (April 1969), 94-98, 100, 104, 245-246, 248, 250, 252, 254, 256.

7046 _____. "An Affair of Honor," Dmitri Nabokov, trans., New Yorker, XLII (September 3, 1966), 37-42, 44, 47-48, 50, 55-56, 58, 63-66.

7047 _____. "Despair," Playboy, XII (December 1965), 106-108, 202, 287-290, 292, 294-296, 298.

7048 _____. "Despair/Part II," Playboy, XIII (January 1966), 126-127, 156, 158, 194-195, 197-198.

7049 _____. "Despair/Part III," Playboy, XIII (February 1966), 90-92, 102, 145-149.

7050 _____. "Despair/Part IV," Playboy, XIII (March 1966), 102-104, 156-158, 160-168, 170-172.

7051 _____. "Despair/Conclusion," Playboy, XIII (April 1966),

150-152, 178-188, 190, 192-193.

7052 ______. "The Eye," Playboy, XII (January 1965), 80-82, 84, 92, 218-220.

7053 ______. "The Eye/Part II," Playboy, XII (February 1965), 72-74, 106, 156, 158, 161.

7054 ______. "The Eye/Part III," Playboy, XII (March 1965), 82-83, 142-146, 148-149.

7055 Nadkarni, Shirish. "Shanti," Avenues, II (May 1969), 22-26.

7056 Nafus, Charles F. "Dr. Spuck's Baby Show," Arx, II (October 1968), 26-27.

7057 ______. "Island Fortress," Arx, II (February 1969), 50-58.

7058 ______. "Saturday Afternoon Bullfight," Arx, III (September 1969), 2-4.

7059 Nagibin, Yuri. "The Ringleader/(From Stories of My Childhood)," Margaret Wettlin, trans., Soviet Literature, (no. 6, 1968), 117-126.

7060 ______. "Winter Oak," Soviet Literature, (no. 4, 1967), 174-181.

7061 Nagthe, Subhan. "Rahim," Literary Half-Yearly, IX (January 1968), 76-81.

7062 Nagy, Lajos. "May 1919," New Hungarian Quarterly, X (Spring 1969), 18-45.

7063 Nahikian, Marie. "Animal Crackers," Coraddi, (Arts Festival 1969), 32-34.

7064 Nahm, Milton C. "Morning in Taos: A Pride of Children," Texas Quarterly, XI (Spring 1968), 80-87.

7065 Naipaul, V. S. "The Heart," Weekend Telegraph, no. 136 (May 12, 1967), 43-44, 46.

7066 Nair, S. "Mrs. Kimble," Literary Review, XI (Summer 1968), 472-474.

7067 Nairn, John. "Paddy," Westerly, no. 3 (October 1968), 36-40.

7068 Najovits, Simson R. "The Wailing Western Wall," West Coast Review, IV (Spring 1969), 1-7.

7069 Nakashian, Yeghia. "The Pumpkin with a Scorpion Within,"

Armenian Review, XVIII (Spring 1965), 34-37.

7070 Nałkowska, Zofia. "Beside the Railroad Track," Edmund Ordon, trans., Literary Review, X (Spring 1967), 261-265.

7071 Naqvi, S. A. H. "How Very Sincere Indeed!" Pakistan Review, XVII (October 1969), 38-40.

7072 Narasimhachar, K. T. "The Wedding," Triveni, XXXV (July 1966), 64-72.

7073 Narayan, Badri. "The Princess with Three Breasts," Transatlantic Review, no. 23 (Winter 1966-67), 53-55 [retold from The Panchatantra].

7074 _____. "The Silver Plate," Transatlantic Review, no. 22 (Autumn 1966), 108-113.

7075 Narayan, R. K. "A Breath of Lucifer," Playboy, XVI (July 1969), 129-130, 155-156.

7076 _____. "A Horse and Two Goats," New Yorker, XL (January 23, 1965), 30-32.

7077 _____. "Seventh House," New Yorker, XLIV (August 3, 1968), 30-33.

7078 _____. "Uncle," New Yorker, XLV (December 13, 1969), 54-60.

7079 Nash, H. C. "Catching Up," Minnesota Review, IX (1969), 253-256.

7080 Nash, Michael. "The Overflowing Vacuum," Soundings, II (Spring 1965), 98-99.

7081 Natale-Regina, J. "Pea Green," Transatlantic Review, no. 28 (Spring 1968), 136-138.

7082 Nathan, Norman. "Diary of an Immigrant," University Review, XXXII (June 1966), 283-286.

7083 _____. "Happiness," Forum, VI (Summer 1968), 32-34.

7084 _____. "The Promise," University Review, XXXVI (Autumn 1969), 116-122.

7085 _____. "A Time Out of Time," University Review, XXXIV (Autumn 1967), 61-64.

7086 Natusch, Sheila. "The Chimney," New Zealand Listener, LIII (December 24, 1965), 23.

7087 _____. "Mind the Weka!" New Zealand Listener, (March 15, 1968), 6.

7088 _____. "Panic Department," New Zealand Listener, (August 12, 1966), 11.

7089 _____. "Speed Bonny Boat," New Zealand Listener, (August 4, 1967), 6.

7090 Naughton, Bill. "A Bit of Bread and Jam," Contrast, I (1968), 61-68.

7091 _____. "Cockney Mum," Contrast, I (1968), 27-33.

7092 _____. "Gift of the Gab," Contrast, I (1968), 75-80.

7093 _____. "Maggie's First Reader," Contrast, I (1968), 69-74.

7094 _____. "A Real Good Smile," Contrast, I (1968), 43-50.

7095 _____. "Seventeen Oranges," Contrast, I (1968), 12-15.

7096 _____. "A Skilled Man," Contrast, I (1968), 51-60.

7097 _____. "Spit Nolan," Contrast, I (1968), 3-11.

7098 _____. "Timothy," Contrast, I (1968), 16-26.

7099 _____. "Tom's Sister," Contrast, I (1968), 34-42.

7100 Naumoff, Lawrence. "A Case of Devotion," Carolina Quarterly, XIX (Winter 1967), 5-8.

7101 Naz. "First Love," Pakistan Review, XV (May 1967), 16-24, 32.

7102 _____. "Forestalled," Pakistan Review, XVI (January 1968), 12-14.

7103 _____. "Hired Husband," Pakistan Review, XVI (October 1968), 14-19, 21.

7104 _____. "The Lamp-Lighter," Pakistan Review, XVI (August 1968), 26-31.

7105 _____. "My Phupho," Pakistan Review, XVI (May 1968), 20-24.

7106 Neall, Hilary. "Changes," Quarterly Review of Literature, XVI, nos. 3-4 (1969), 434-464.

7107 Nedreass, Torborg. "Music from a Blue Well," Elizabeth Rokkan, trans., Literary Review, XII (Winter 1968-69), 188-196.

7108 Nedwed, Nancy. "Duet," Assay, XXI (Spring 1965), 15-22.

7109 Neely, E. J. "The Big Road," University Review, XXXII (March 1966), 219-223.

7110 ______. "The Song of Ruby Ella," New Mexico Quarterly, XXXV (Autumn 1965), 245-256.

7111 Neilson, Alice W. "The Bells of El Amialco," Texas Quarterly, XI (Autumn 1968), 117-129.

7112 ______. "The Bus to the Bay of Banderas," Texas Quarterly, IX (Winter 1966), 26-51.

7113 Neish, Alex. "Before the Undertaker Comes," New Writers, no. 5 (1966), 65-152.

7114 Nekrasov, Victor. "Private Lyutikov," Soviet Literature, (no. 4, 1967), 151-161.

7115 ______. "Sudak," Valentina Scott, trans., Soviet Literature, (no. 9, 1965), 102-132.

7116 ______. "That Damn Number Seven," Robert Daglish, trans., Soviet Literature, (no. 8, 1968), 72-89.

7117 Nelson, Anne W. "Another Time," Crucible, IV (Spring 1968), 45.

7118 ______. "Bridesday," Crucible, III (Fall 1966), 17-18.

7119 ______. "Bus Station," Crucible, II (Fall 1965), 30-31.

7120 ______. "The King James Version," Crucible, V (Fall 1968), 21-22, 24-26.

7121 ______. "The Statue of Liberty," Crucible, VI (Fall 1969), 36-38.

7122 ______. "Warm Colors: Take the Poets," Crucible, IV (Spring 1968), 44.

7123 ______. "Winter Night," Crucible, IV (Spring 1968), 45.

7124 ______. "With Fields II," Crucible, IV (Spring 1968), 44.

7125 Nelson, C. E. "Henry," Epoch, XIV (Winter 1965), 114-123.

7126 Nelson, D. E. "Measuring," Kansas Magazine, (1968), 83-85.

7127 Nelson, Donawyne. "The Sorcerer," Mademoiselle, LX (January 1965), 42-43, 124.

7128 Nelson, William. "Jody," Yale Literary Magazine, CXXXIV (September 1965), 6-12.

7129 Nemec, David. "On the Produce Dock," Transatlantic Review, no. 26 (Autumn 1967), 5-29.

7130 Nemerov, Howard. "The Nature of the Task," Virginia Quarterly Review, XLII (Spring 1966), 234-243.

7131 Nemes, György. "One Brief Moment/(excerpts from a novel)," New Hungarian Quarterly, VII (Autumn 1966), 78-88.

7132 Nesbit, Stephen R. "A Party," Cavalier, XV (June 1965), 56-58, 60, 90.

7133 Nesin, Aziz. "Long Live Science," Literary Review, XI (Spring 1968), 325-332.

7134 Nesovich, Peter. "from Escape Artist with Trick Knee," Carolina Quarterly, XX (Fall 1968), 71-79.

7135 _____. "The Russian General Prepares for Dawn," Carolina Quarterly, XXI (Spring 1969), 38-41.

7136 Nesser, Dennis W. "Birth of Water," Delta, XX (1966), 33-36.

7137 Neugeboren, Jay. "The Child," Minnesota Review, V (August-October 1965), 200-204.

7138 _____. "Connorsville, Virginia," Transatlantic Review, no. 31 (Winter 1968-69), 11-23.

7139 _____. "Corky's Brother," Transatlantic Review, no. 25 (Summer 1967), 5-37.

7140 _____. "Ebbets Field," Transatlantic Review, no. 24 (Spring 1967), 64-76.

7141 _____. "Elijah," Works, II (Spring 1969), 4-23.

7142 _____. "A Family Trip," Transatlantic Review, no. 32 (Summer 1969), 25-30.

7143 _____. "Finkel," Esquire, LXXII (October 1969), 128, 209-213.

7144 _____. "Luther," Commentary, XLI (January 1966), 42-48.

7145 _____. "The Pass," Mademoiselle, LXIX (October 1969), 164-165, 208-212.

7146 _____. "Something Is Rotten in the Borough of Brooklyn,"

Ararat, VIII (Autumn 1967), 27-34.

7147 ______. "The Zodiacs," Transatlantic Review, no. 20 (Spring 1966), 84-95.

7148 Neville, Helen. "The Kitchen Maid," Aphra, I (Fall 1969), 6-25.

7149 Newa, Henry M. "It's a Sin," Expression, no. 2 (n.d.), 25-32.

7150 Newby, Anthony. "Cry from the Heart of a Demigod," Week-end Telegraph, no. 79 (April 1, 1966), 59, 61, 65.

7151 Newhouse, Edward. "Hungarians," New Yorker, XLI (November 27, 1965), 57-64.

7152 Newlin, Louisa. "Our Last Day in Venice," Atlantic Monthly, CCXVI (October 1965), 121-124.

7153 ______. "Our Last Day in Venice," Cornhill Magazine, no. 1047 (Spring 1966), 198-204.

7154 Newlove, Donald. "The Dead Man's Float of the Moon," Evergreen Review, XII (April 1968), 33-35, 72.

7155 ______. "Trumpet," Evergreen Review, XIII (November 1969), 20-23, 56-62.

7156 Newman, Bill. "O Lamentable Brother," DeKalb Literary Arts Journal, I (Summer 1967), 1-13.

7157 Newman, C. J. "An Arab Up North," Tamarack Review, no. 47 (Spring 1968), 45-53, 55-65, 67-70.

7158 ______. "My Brother Solomon, the Bible, and the Bicycle," Tamarack Review, no. 43 (Spring 1967), 22-35.

7159 Newman, David. "The Dirigible," New Mexico Quarterly, XXXV (Winter 1965-66), 324-329.

7160 Newman, Harry. "A Man Like Me," Transatlantic Review, no. 30 (Autumn 1968), 41-51.

7161 ______. "The Teacher's Pet School," San Francisco Earthquake, I (Fall 1967), 56-63.

7162 Newrick, Olive. "The Frog Prince," Stand, VII, no. 4 (1965), 61-68.

7163 Newton, Peter J. F. "Talking to Shadows," The Pluralist, no. 3 (Summer 1965), 40-43.

7164 Newton, Suzanne. "His Own Sweet Wife," Long View Journal, I (Winter 1968), 9-22.

7165 _____. "A Matter of Trust," Long View Journal, I (Spring 1969), 177-192.

7166 Ngugi, James. "Uhuru," Meanjin Quarterly, XXV (December 1966), 420-430.

7167 Nhat Hanh. "The Return Path of Thoughts," Vo-Dinh, trans., Unicorn Journal, no. 3 (1969), 17-36.

7168 Nichols, Olivia M. "Imogene," DeKalb Literary Arts Journal, III (Spring 1969), 21-25.

7169 [Nicholson], Nicole. "Conversation between Two Gentlemen Who Meet Face to Face on a Narrow Log Crossing over a Deep Ravine," Ante, III (Summer 1967), 30-31.

7170 _____. "How Hagen, a Specialized Craftsman, Became a Bum and (in Consecutive Order) a Pigeon-Killer, a Pacifist, a Communist and a Lifer," Ante, III (Summer 1967), 5-10.

7171 _____. "Sharon Nathanson," Analecta, II (Winter 1968), 63-64.

7172 _____. "The Wedding Dress," Ante, II (Summer 1966), 49-55.

Nicole. See Nicholson.

7173 Nicoloff, Philip. "The Wildest Ride," Saturday Evening Post, CCXXXVIII (July 17, 1965), 48-54, 58.

7174 Nieh, Hua-Ling. "The Several Blessings of Ta-Nien Wang," Atlantic Monthly, CCXVIII (December 1966), 91-94.

7175 Nierenberg, Edwin. "Pax in Bello," North American Review, VI (Winter 1969), 48-60.

7176 _____. "Sashay on Man," Sage, XI (Fall 1966), 87-99.

7177 Nigg, J. E. "Errantry," New Campus Review, II (Fall 1968), 17-23.

7178 _____. "Where Freedom Lies," New Campus Review, II (Spring 1969), 27-30.

7179 Nikitin, Sergei. "A Falling Star," Tom Botting, trans., Soviet Literature, (no. 5, 1965), 3-42.

7180 _____. "The Water of Life," Alice Ingman and Tom Botting, trans., Soviet Literature, (no. 12, 1966), 64-91.

7181 Nikolayeva, Galina. "Alvik," Alice Ingman, trans., Soviet Literature, (no. 10, 1968), 97-122.

7182 Nilsson, Usha S. "Paper Flowers," Arizona Quarterly, XXI (Autumn 1965), 261-273.

7183 Nissenson, Hugh. "The American," American Judaism, XIV (Winter 1964-65), 13, 52-53.

7184 _____. "The Crazy Old Man," Esquire, LXX (August 1968), 96-97, 110.

7185 _____. "In the Reign of Peace," Harper's Magazine, CCXXXIX (July 1969), 63-65.

7186 _____. "On Jaffa Road," Midstream, XV (May 1969), 23-25.

7187 _____. "A Woman for Titus," Playboy, XIII (October 1966), 93, 102, 197.

7188 Nivens, Don. "Adios, Bracero," Ante, III (Fall 1967), 19-26.

7189 Niyazi, Fatekh. "The Third Daughter," Alice Ingman, trans., Soviet Literature, (no. 9, 1967), 44-62.

7190 Nizar-Jan, Esmail. "The Land Freedom Fighter," Nexus, I (January 1968), 5-10.

7191 Nkhata, Kenneth. "The Monster and His Son," New Writing from Zambia, no. 2 (1968), 3-6.

7192 Nkunika, Billy. "Shamo's Down Fall," New Writing from Zambia, no. 1 (1966), 7-13.

7193 Noell, Tonia. "The Egg," Silo, no. 7 (Spring 1965), 2-6.

7194 Noice, Tony. "Farewell Performance," Signature, II (July 1967), 40-41, 52.

7195 Nolan, William F. "Papa's Planet," Playboy, XV (April 1968), 131, 182-183.

7196 _____. "The Party," Playboy, XIV (April 1967), 133, 156-158, 161.

7197 _____. "The Pop-Op Caper," Playboy, XIV (October 1967), 76-78, 80, 86, 185-188.

7198 Nolledo, Willi. "Cadena de Amor," Quarterly Review of Literature, XVI, nos. 3-4 (1969), 465-487.

7199 Nonveiller, Heinz. "The Birth," Quadrant, XIII (May-June 1969), 60-65.

7200 _____. "That Part of the World," Meanjin Quarterly, XXVI (Winter 1967), 165-175.

7201 Noreen, Eddie. "He'll Be Back," Plaintiff, IV (Spring-Summer 1968), 46-50.

7202 _____. "What Happened to Peltier?" Plaintiff, V (Spring-Summer 1969), 44-47.

7203 Norman, Bruce. "Ices for My Love," Transatlantic Review, no. 18 (Spring 1965), 90-95.

7204 Norman, Guy. "Before the Dance Begins," Good Housekeeping, CLXVI (February 1968), 78-79, 156-160.

7205 _____. "Take My Hand," Good Housekeeping, CLXI (November 1965), 88-89, 243-246.

7206 Norris, Hoke. "The Final Distance," Redbook, CXXIX (June 1967), 66-67, 137-140.

7207 _____. "Ghost," Playboy, XV (June 1968), 91, 102, 190, 192, 194.

7208 _____. "Grandma Was a Flapper," University Review, XXXVI (Autumn 1969), 3-12.

7209 _____. "It's Not Far, but I Don't Know the Way," Playboy, XIV (June 1967), 93, 191-194.

7210 _____. "Look Away," Playboy, XII (July 1965), 58-60, 130-136.

7211 _____. "Prometheus and the First Born," Carolina Quarterly, XXI (Winter 1969), 52-68.

7212 _____. "Speak to Me of Love," University Review, XXXII (March 1966), 207-218.

7213 _____. "Twist," Prairie Schooner, XL (Spring 1966), 1-16.

7214 _____. "Voo Doo," Georgia Review, XXII (Summer 1968), 222-235.

7215 Norse, Harold. "A Chocolate Rose," VDRSVPVDRSVPVDRSVP, (1969), n. p. [back page].

7216 Nosov, Nikolai. "Dunno on the Moon," Margaret Wettlin, trans., Soviet Literature, (no. 12, 1968), 5-38.

7217 Nossack, Hans Erich. "The Penknife," Marc Tangner, trans., Dimension, I, no. 3 (1968), 568-581 [in German & English on alternate pages].

7218 _____. "The Signpost," Margaret D. Howie, trans., Scala International, (May 1968), 34-37.

7219 Nour, Nazli. "Which Land Is Mine," New Writers, no. 5 (1966), 153-190.

7220 Novak, Helga. "Two Stories/The Bookmark," A. Leslie Willson, trans., Dimension, II, no. 1 (1969), 224-225 [in German and English on alternate pages].

7221 _____. "Two Stories/Main Post Office," A. Leslie Willson, trans., Dimension, II, no. 1 (1969), 219-223 [in German and English on alternate pages].

7222 Novak, Slobodan. "Little Lukre Does Not Know What To Do with Money," Vasa D. Mihailovich, trans., Literary Review, XI (Winter 1967), 258-262.

7223 Novalis. "from Heinrich von Ofterdingen," Vito Acconci and Bernadette Mayer, trans., 0 to 9, no. 1 (April 1967), 29-55.

7224 Nowlan, Alden. "The Guide," Canadian Forum, XLV (April 1965), 11-12.

7225 _____. "His Native Place," The Fiddlehead, no. 81 (August-October 1969), 28-40.

7226 _____. "Humbly, for Fyodor," Prism International, VII (Autumn 1967), 88-91.

7227 _____. "The Innermost One," Edge, no. 8 (Fall 1968), 92-94.

7228 _____. "Miracle at Indian River," The Fiddlehead, no. 75 (Spring 1968), 5-13.

7229 _____. "Notes toward a Plot for an Unwritten Short Story," Canadian Forum, XLVI (February 1967), 254-255.

7230 _____. "Rumours of War," West Coast Review, IV (Fall 1969), 1-9.

7231 _____. "There Was An Old Woman From Wexford," Prism International, IX (Autumn 1969), 30-39.

7232 _____. "The Thin Red Line," The Fiddlehead, no. 78 (January-February 1969), 87-91.

7233 _____. "The Unnatural Son," Canadian Forum, XLVIII (April 1968), 16-17.

7234 _____. "Who Was the Greatest Writer Who Ever Lived?"

Adam International Review, nos. 313-315 (1967), 57-64.

7235 Noyes, Dennis A. "La Danza Primordial," Red Cedar Review, V (January 1967), 35-41.

7236 Noyse, Steve. "Just Before the Snow," Arx, II (February 1969), 22-25.

7237 Nugent, Tom. "The Princess of Hamburger Heaven," Twigs, no. 5 (Fall 1969), 185-190.

7238 Nulle, S. H. "The Convert," The Fiddlehead, no. 70 (Winter 1967), 30-37.

7239 Nutt, Mary E. "All My Yesterdays," Good Housekeeping, CLX (April 1965), 86-87, 208, 210, 212, 214, 216, 218-219.

7240 Nuttall, Jeff. "from Work in Progress," Ambit, no. 26 (1965/66), 30-33.

7241 Nybakken, David. "No Ordinary Indian," The Fiddlehead, no. 76 (Summer 1968), 40-49.

7242 Nye, Robert. "The Amber Witch," Art and Literature, no. 10 (Autumn 1966), 191-216.

7243 _____. "from Doubtfire," Michigan Quarterly Review, VII (Spring 1968), 99-102.

7244 Oakley, Barry. "Callaghan's Day," Quadrant, IX (March-April 1965), 26-31.

7245 _____. "Crimson Jumper, White Stripes," Meanjin Quarterly, XXVII (Winter 1968), 162-166.

7246 _____. "Father Carroll," Southerly, XXV, no. 2 (1965), 91-97.

7247 _____. "The Tallest Poet in the World," Meanjin Quarterly, XXVIII (Spring 1969), 359-364.

7248 _____. "A Wild Ass of a Man," Meanjin Quarterly, XXVI (Autumn 1967), 56-66.

7249 Oates, Joyce Carol. "Accomplished Desires," Esquire, LXIX (May 1968), 102-103, 178-180, 182, 184, 186, 188.

7250 _____. "All the Beautiful Women," Saturday Evening Post, CCXLI (June 29, 1968), 50-52, 54, 56.

7251 _____. "Archways," Cosmopolitan, CLVIII (March 1965), 76-81.

7252 _____. "The Assailant," Prairie Schooner, XXXIX (Winter 1965/66), 330-336.

7253 _____. "At the Seminary," Kenyon Review, XXVII (Summer 1965), 483-502.

7254 _____. "Boy & Girl," Prism International, VIII (Spring 1969), 4-17.

7255 _____. "By the River," December, X (1968), 72-80.

7256 _____. "Childhood," Epoch, XVI (Spring 1967), 204-222.

7257 _____. "The Children," Transatlantic Review, no. 32 (Summer 1969), 48-63.

7258 _____. "Convalescing," Virginia Quarterly Review, XLV (Summer 1969), 430-450.

7259 _____. "Dreams," Prairie Schooner, XLIII (Winter 1969-70), 331-351.

7260 _____. "Dying," Transatlantic Review, no. 20 (Spring 1966), 64-79.

7261 _____. "The Dying Child," Antioch Review, XXVI (Summer 1966), 247-263.

7262 _____. "The Four Seasons," Virginia Quarterly Review, XLII (Winter 1966), 95-107.

7263 _____. "Four Summers," Yale Review, LVI (Spring 1967), 406-425.

7264 _____. "A Garden of Earthly Delights," Shenandoah, XVII (Winter 1966), 21-43.

7265 _____. "Gifts," Kenyon Review, XXVIII (September 1966), 499-520.

7266 _____. "The Girl with the Beautiful Face," University Review, XXXIII (March 1967), 180-188.

7267 _____. "A Girl Worth Two Million," Cosmopolitan, CLXVI (February 1969), 120-127.

7268 _____. "The Heavy Sorrow of the Body," Northwest Review, X (Summer 1968), 4-26.

7269 _____. "How I Contemplated the World from the Detroit House of Correction and Began My Life Over Again," Tri-Quarterly, no. 15 (Spring 1969), 5-21.

7270 ______. "How We Fall in Love," New Orleans Review, I (Summer 1969), 326-330.

7271 ______. "In the Region of Ice," Atlantic Monthly, CCXVIII (August 1966), 78-85.

7272 ______. "In the Warehouse," Transatlantic Review, no. 25 (Summer 1967), 96-102.

7273 ______. "An Interior Monologue," Esquire, LXXI (February 1969), 84-85, 92-93.

7274 ______. "'Joy, Let Us Praise Thee'," Southwest Review, LI (Autumn 1966), 377-389.

7275 ______. "A Lecture upon the Shadow," Southern Humanities Review, II (Winter 1968), 53-69.

7276 ______. "A Love Story," Cosmopolitan, CLXIII (July 1967), 116-122.

7277 ______. "The Molesters," Quarterly Review of Literature, XV (1968), 393-409.

7278 ______. "Norman and the Killer," Southwest Review, L (Spring 1965), 121-140.

7279 ______. "Out of Place," Virginia Quarterly Review, XLIV (Summer 1968), 428-440.

7280 ______. "Private Life," Yale Review, LIX (Autumn 1969), 79-96.

7281 ______. "Prose and Poetry," Carleton Miscellany, IX (Spring 1968), 36-54.

7282 ______. "Shame," Atlantic Monthly, CCXXI (June 1968), 80-88.

7283 ______. "The Silent Child," Epoch, XV (Spring 1966), 195-214.

7284 ______. "The Spiral," Shenandoah, XX (Winter 1969), 3-21.

7285 ______. "Splendid Architecture," Antioch Review, XXVIII (Fall 1968), 305-324.

7286 ______. "The Stone House," Quarterly Review of Literature, XIII (1965), 381-411.

7287 ______. "A Story of an Ordinary Girl," Texas Quarterly, XI (Summer 1968), 217-230.

7288 _____. "Sunday Dinner," Tri-Quarterly, no. 10 (Fall 1967), 63-101.

7289 _____. "The Sweet Enemy," Southern Review, III (July 1967), 653-720.

7290 _____. "The Thief," North American Review, III (September 1966), 10-17.

7291 _____. "Two Poets," Northwest Review, VIII (Spring 1967), 7-26.

7292 _____. "Unmailed, Unwritten Letters," Hudson Review, XXII (Spring 1969), 19-39.

7293 _____. "The Voyage to Rosewood," Shenandoah, XVIII (Summer 1967), 3-22.

7294 _____. "Waiting," Epoch, XVII (Spring 1968), 250-269.

7295 _____. "The Way Back in from out There," Southwest Review, LII (Spring 1967), 209-223.

7296 _____. "What Death with Love Should Have to Do," Literary Review, IX (Autumn 1965), 19-36.

7297 _____. "The Wheel of Love," Esquire, LXVIII (October 1967), 134-137, 158, 160, 162.

7298 _____. "Where Are You Going, Where Have You Been?" Epoch, XVI (Fall 1966), 59-76.

7299 _____. "The Woman Who Disappeared," University Review, XXXIV (Summer 1968), 243-257.

7300 Oatman, Eric. "A Shortage of Rainbows," Analecta, II (Winter 1968), 11-20.

7301 O'Brien, Bill T. "The Escape Artist," Prism International, VIII (Autumn 1968), 13-18.

7302 _____. "from Summer of the Black Sun," Prism International, IX (Autumn 1969), 4-24.

7303 O'Brien, Edna. "August Is a Wicked Month," Cosmopolitan, CLIX (August 1965), 90-99.

7304 _____. "Brothers and Sisters," Transatlantic Review, no. 30 (Autumn 1968), 13-14.

7305 _____. "Let the Rest of the World Go By," Ladies' Home Journal, LXXXII (July 1965), 48-49, 104.

7306 _____. "The Love Object," New Yorker, XLIII (May 13, 1967), 42-52.

7307 _____. "My First Love," Ladies' Home Journal, LXXXII (June 1965), 60-61.

7308 _____. "An Outing," Nova, (May 1968), 120-121, 123, 128, 130.

7309 _____. "Paradise," Cosmopolitan, CLXVII (August 1969), 110-119.

7310 _____. "A Woman at the Seaside," Mademoiselle, LX (March 1965), 168-169, 231-237.

7311 O'Brien, Flann. "from The Third Policeman," Transatlantic Review, no. 25 (Summer 1967), 78-83.

7312 O'Brien, Janice. "Sentiments of a Standby in Terminal Tremens," Ave Maria, CV (January 7, 1966), 24-26.

7313 O'Brien, Katherine. "The Glass Box," New Zealand Listener, (July 21, 1967), 6.

7314 _____. "Such Beautiful Scenery," New Zealand Listener, LX (May 2, 1969), 12, 19.

7315 O'Brien, Roma. "When the Bough Breaks," Overland, no. 32 (Spring 1965), 11-15.

7316 Obudo, Nathaniel. "They Stole Our Cattle," Literary Review, XI (Summer 1968), 475-478.

7317 O'Connell, Charles C. "Mountain Man," Columbia, XLV (May 1965), 24-26, 43-44.

7318 O'Connell, Jean S. "The Monday Child," McCall's, XCIV (April 1967), 92-93, 130-134.

7319 O'Connor, Flannery. "Parker's Back," Esquire, LXIII (April 1965), 76-78, 151-152, 154-155.

7320 O'Connor, Frank. "An Act of Charity," New Yorker, XLIII (May 6, 1967), 48-51.

7321 _____. "The Cheat," Saturday Evening Post, CCXXXVIII (May 8, 1965), 78-80, 82, 84-85.

7322 _____. "The Corkerys," New Yorker, XLII (April 30, 1966), 45-51.

7323 _____. "A Life of Your Own," Saturday Evening Post, CCXXX-VIII (February 13, 1965), 40-41, 43, 44-45.

7324 _____. "A Mother's Warning," Saturday Evening Post, CCXL (October 7, 1967), 54-57.

7325 _____. "The School for Wives," New Yorker, XLII (November 5, 1966), 59-66.

7326 O'Connor, John. "Neilly and the Fir Tree," Threshold, no. 21 (Summer 1967), 129-134.

7327 O'Connor, Nancy Harrison. "Prisoners," The Circle, no. 3 (1968), 1-9.

7328 O'Connor, Rev. Norman, C.S.P. "Vatican II," Ave Maria, CI (January 23, 1965), 20-23.

7329 O'Connor, Philip F. "Abner's Blues," December, X (1968), 121-125.

7330 _____. "Gerald's Song," Western Humanities Review, XXIII (Autumn 1969), 291-294.

7331 _____. "Gino," Four Quarters, XV (March 1966), 1-9.

7332 _____. "Lady Bug, Lady Bug," Transatlantic Review, no. 24 (Spring 1967), 101-104.

7333 _____. "The Man on the Bed," Ball State University Forum, VIII (Autumn 1967), 7-9.

7334 _____. "Matter of Ages," The Smith, no. 10 (December 1968), 134-139.

7335 _____. "Pagan!" Four Quarters, XIV (January 1965), 5-10.

7336 O'Dea, Michael. "With a Buglar and Rifle Volley," Plaintiff, V (Spring-Summer 1969), 34-35.

7337 O'Dell, David. "In This Quiet Place," Chelsea, no. 16 (March 1965), 3-19.

7338 _____. "A Trio of Seasons," Nexus (San Francisco, Calif.), II (July-August 1965), 55-66.

7339 _____. "A Trio of Seasons [part two]," Nexus (San Francisco, Calif.), II (September-October 1965), 51-63.

7340 _____. "A Trio of Seasons [conclusion]," Nexus (San Francisco, Calif.), II (November-December 1965), 39-50.

7341 Oderman, Stuart. "Steps without End," Dust, III (Winter-Spring 1967), 29-38.

7342 Odio, Eunice. "There Once Was a Man...," Américas, XX

(February 1968), 33-38.

7343 O'Donnell, G. M. "The Place," Cornhill Magazine, no. 1050 (Winter 1966/67), 409-413.

7344 O'Donnell, Mary Kathleen. "Mirage," Atlantic Monthly, CCXX (October 1967), 87-90, 95-96.

7345 O'Donnell, Peter. "Modesty Blaise," Cosmopolitan, CLIX (November 1965), 118-124, 126-129, 135-142, 144-147.

7346 _____. "Sabre-Tooth," Cosmopolitan, CLXI (July 1966), 108-125, 128-130, 132-135.

7347 Ōe Kenzaburō. "Aghwee the Sky Monster," John Nathan, trans., Evergreen Review, XII (May 1968), 44-48, 62-72.

7348 _____. "The Catch," John Bester, trans., Evergreen Review, XI (February 1967), 53-72.

7349 _____. "Lavish Are the Dead," John Nathan, trans., Evergreen Review, IX (November 1965), 17-21, 77-85.

7350 _____. "Lavish Are the Dead," John Nathan, trans., Japan Quarterly, XII (April-June 1965), 193-211.

7351 Oehler, Mike. "Dinner at Goyo's," Southwest Review, LIV (Autumn 1969), 400-412.

7352 Oerton, R. T. "Guilty, My Lord," Twentieth Century, CLXXV (Third Quarter, 1967), 60-64.

7353 O'Faolain, Julia. "Afternoon in Elba," London Magazine, VI (September 1966), 31-39.

7354 _____. "Death Duties," Kenyon Review, XXVII (Spring 1965), 321-335.

7355 _____. "First Conjugation," London Magazine, VI (March 1967), 5-16.

7356 _____. "It's a Long Way to Tipperary," London Magazine, VIII (January 1969), 5-21.

7357 _____. "Lots of Ghastlies," Mademoiselle, LXVIII (April 1969), 245, 308-310, 320.

7358 _____. "The Man Who Lost His Image," London Magazine, VII (August 1967), 5-18.

7359 _____. "Melancholy Baby," Cornhill Magazine, no. 1054 (Winter 1967/68), 292-309.

7360 _____. "A Political Animal," Saturday Evening Post, CCXLI (September 7, 1968), 60-65.

7361 _____. "Pray for Grace, Poor Little Sinner," Saturday Evening Post, CCXL (February 25, 1967), 79-80, 82, 84.

7362 _____. "That Bastard Berto," London Magazine, VII (March 1968), 11-22.

7363 O'Faolain, Sean. "Charlie's Greek," Cornhill Magazine, no. 1048 (Summer 1966), 258-271.

7364 _____. "Dividends," McCall's, XCIII (September 1966), 114-115, 168-172, 174-176.

7365 _____. "Don Juan in Dublin," Saturday Evening Post, CCXXXVIII (June 19, 1965), 48-51, 54, 56.

7366 _____. "A Fool of a Man," Saturday Evening Post, CCXLI (March 23, 1968), 58-62, 66.

7367 _____. "The Heat of the Sun," Atlantic Monthly, CCXVIII (September 1966), 70-75.

7368 _____. "The Jungle of Love," Saturday Evening Post, CCXXXIX (August 13, 1966), 54-60, 62-63.

7369 _____. "The Kitchen," Atlantic Monthly, CCXXIII (June 1969), 42-45.

7370 _____. "Operation Rosebud," Redbook, CXXVII (August 1966), 58-60, 105-111.

7371 _____. "The Planets of the Years," Ladies' Home Journal, LXXXVI (September 1969), 102-103, 161-163.

7372 _____. "The Talking Trees," Playboy, XVI (January 1969), 95-96, 104, 136, 240.

7373 _____. "Three Shapes of Love," Atlantic Monthly, CCXV (March 1965), 124-128.

7374 _____. "What a Stunning Night!" Saturday Evening Post, CCXLII (December 28, 1968-January 11, 1969), 46-47, 51-52.

7375 O'Flaherty, Liam. "The Conger Eel," Contrast, I (1968), 125-128.

7376 _____. "His First Flight," Contrast, I (1968), 112-115.

7377 _____. "A Pot of Gold," Contrast, I (1968), 104-111.

7378 _____. "The Reaping Race," Contrast, I (1968), 83-90.

7379 _____. "A Red Petticoat," Contrast, I (1968), 129-138.

7380 _____. "A Shilling," Contrast, I (1968), 91-94.

7381 _____. "Three Lambs," Contrast, I (1968), 99-103.

7382 _____. "Trapped," Contrast, I (1968), 116-124.

7383 _____. "The Wild Goat's Kid," Contrast, I (1968), 139-146.

7384 _____. "The Wren's Nest," Contrast, I (1968), 95-98.

7385 Ogburn, Charlton, Jr. "The Yard," Harper's Magazine, CCXXXV (July 1967), 55-59.

7386 Ogilvie, Elisabeth. "Bellwood," Good Housekeeping, CLXVI (June 1968), 74-75, 182, 184, 186, 188, 190, 192, 194, 196-200, 208-214, 219-224.

7387 _____. "Island of Shadows," Good Housekeeping, CLXIX (November 1969), 83-85, 222, 224, 227-228, 230, 233-234, 236, 238, 240, 242, 244, 246, 248, 250, 252, 254-262, 264.

7388 _____. "With a Change of Season," Good Housekeeping, CLXVII (October 1968), 102-103, 176, 178, 180-182.

7389 Ogot, Grace. "The Hero," Nexus, I (August 1967), 5-8.

7390 O'Hagan, D. J. "Between Floors," New Zealand Listener, LIII (November 26, 1965), 4.

7391 O'Haire, Frank. "Losers Can Be Champs," Columbia, XLIX (July 1969), 24-28.

7392 O'Hanlon, Redmond. "The Brothers," Threshold, no. 22 (Summer 1969), 32-39.

7393 O'Hara, J. D. "The Bridge," Carleton Miscellany, VII (Fall 1966), 73-76.

7394 _____. "Once More into the Breach, Dear," Western Humanities Review, XX (Autumn 1966), 309-316.

7395 _____. "Puzzle Pieces," Quartet, no. 12 (Fall 1965), 16-18.

7396 _____. "Shadows of a Shadow (Nervous reaction to a synergistic overdose of Borges on top of Nabokov)," Texas Quarterly, IX (Spring 1966), 18-21.

7397 _____. "Street Scene," Western Humanities Review, XXI

(Summer 1967), 225-226.

7398 _____. "Swat," Western Humanities Review, XXII (Winter 1968), 11-16.

7399 O'Hara, John. "Afternoon Waltz," Saturday Evening Post, CCXXXIX (April 23, 1966), 56-60, 62, 64, 66, 69-72, 74.

7400 _____. "The Assistant," New Yorker, XLI (July 3, 1965), 22-28.

7401 _____. "Barred," Saturday Evening Post, CCXL (October 7, 1967), 60-62.

7402 _____. "Fatimas and Kisses," New Yorker, XLII (May 21, 1966), 44-53.

7403 _____. "The Gambler," New Yorker, XLI (May 1, 1965), 40-42.

7404 _____. "The Gangster," Saturday Evening Post, CCXL (November 18, 1967), 56-58, 60-62, 64-66.

7405 _____. "A Good Location," New Yorker, XLI (September 4, 1965), 29-31.

7406 _____. "Good Samaritan," Saturday Evening Post, CCXLI (November 30, 1968), 62-64, 66, 68-70.

7407 _____. "The Gunboat and Madge," Saturday Evening Post, CCXL (February 25, 1967), 64-66, 68, 70, 72, 74-77.

7408 _____. "How Old, How Young," New Yorker, XLIII (July 1, 1967), 28-32.

7409 _____. "The Jama," Saturday Evening Post, CCXXXIX (October 22, 1966), 58-60, 65-66, 68.

7410 _____. "Leonard," New Yorker, XLII (February 26, 1966), 33-37.

7411 _____. "The Neighborhood," New Yorker, XLI (May 15, 1965), 49-53.

7412 _____. "The Private People," Saturday Evening Post, CCXXXIX (December 17, 1966), 56-58, 61, 62, 64, 66-70, 72.

7413 _____. "The Sunroom," Saturday Evening Post, CCXLII (February 8, 1969), 40-42, 44, 46-48.

7414 _____. "Yostie," Saturday Evening Post, CCXXXIX (June 4, 1966), 46-48, 52-58, 60, 62.

7415 O'Hara, Kenneth. "The Bird-Cage," Cosmopolitan, CLXVI (February 1969), 128-136, 138-145, 148-151, 154-157.

7416 Ohel, Milla. "The Immolation of Ya-Wa," Literary Review, XI (Spring 1968), 269-297.

7417 Ohle, Louis D. "Sunday in Symbolville," Delta, XXI (1967), 55-67.

7418 Okpaku, Joseph O. O. "Under the Iroko Tree," Literary Review, XI (Summer 1968), 481-554.

7419 Okudshava, Bulat. "Stomoxys," Wolfgang Hirschberg, trans., Ararat, X (Spring 1969), 14-23.

7420 O'Laughlin, Sean. "A Dime for Christmas," Columbia, XLVII (December 1967), 24-28.

7421 Olesha, Yuri. "Human Material," Soviet Literature, (no. 4, 1967), 114-117.

7422 Oliphant, Robert. "Schulespiel," Western Humanities Review, XX (Autumn 1966), 291-299.

7423 Olive, Jeannie. "Dinner of Herbs," Prairie Schooner, XXXIX (Summer 1965), 95-107.

7424 Oliver, Charles. "The Pacific Spring," Southwest Review, LI (Autumn 1966), 326-338.

7425 _____. "The Perishing," Southwest Review, LIII (Summer 1968), 299-308.

7426 _____. "Sole Rider," Southwest Review, LIV (Winter 1969), 49-57.

7427 _____. "Those Who Bid Me Play," Nimrod, X (Spring 1966), 1-7.

7428 Oliver, Diane A. "Health Service," Negro Digest, XV (November 1965), 72-79.

7429 _____. "Key to the City," Red Clay Reader, no. 2 (1965), 17-21.

7430 _____. "Mint Juleps Not Served Here," Negro Digest, XVI (March 1967), 58-66.

7431 _____. "Neighbors," Sewanee Review, LXXIV (April-June 1966), 470-488.

7432 _____. "Traffic Jam," Negro Digest, XV (July 1966), 69-78.

7433 Oliver, Kitty. "Mama," Florida Quarterly, II (January 1969), 4-16.

7434 Oliver, Robert T. "How Shakespeare Came to Lame Bear Gulch," Ball State University Forum, VII (Winter 1966), 33-36.

7435 Olsen, Hank. "As Fair Flowers Fade," Prism International, VI (Autumn 1966), 50-57.

7436 _____. "The Bride Sat in Sad Satin," Ave Maria, CI (January 9, 1965), 18-22.

7437 _____. "Starscape," Prism International, VI (Autumn 1966), 96-107.

7438 Olsen, Paul. "The Exception and the Rule," Southern Review, I (January 1965), 167-182.

7439 _____. "The Flag Is Down," Southern Review, V (April 1969), 549-562.

7440 Olson, Charles. "Stocking Cap," Harper's Bazaar, C (July 1967), 100-101.

7441 Olson, Gregory. "Electric Cowboy," Assay, XXIII (Spring 1967), 53-61.

7442 Olson, Roy Victor. "Hard Way to Allakaket," Columbia, XLVII (May 1967), 24-29.

7443 Olson, Ted. "Petroglyph Joanez," Sage, XI (Spring 1967), 167-175.

7444 Olson, Toby. "The Girl with the Profile of a Shark," Minnesota Review, IX (1969), 221-222.

7445 _____. "The Sixth Column, the Fourth Entry," Minnesota Review, IX (1969), 223-225.

7446 Olson, Yvonne. "Parasite," UMD Humanist, XIV (Spring 1966), 37-43.

7447 Olumba, Rufus. "The Bank of the Niger on a Summer Morning," Nigerian Students Voice, II (January 1965), 6-7.

7448 O'Malley, Jane. "Three's a Crowd," Good Housekeeping, CLXIX (August 1969), 80-81.

7449 Omre, Arthur. "In the Spirit of Christmas," Carolyn Gelland, trans., American Scandinavian Review, LIII (December 1965), 403-410.

7450 Ong Soo Chuat. "Checkmate," Focus (Singapore), III, no. 3, 17-20.

7451 _____. "The Glass Cage," Focus (Singapore), IV, no. 1, 3-10.

7452 Onn, Patrick Ng Kah. "The Interview," Literature East and West, X (December 1966), 348-356.

7453 O'Nolan, Brian. "After Hours," Threshold, no. 21 (Summer 1967), 15-18.

7454 Oppenheimer, Joan L. "Has Anybody Here Seen Barbie?" Seventeen, XXIV (July 1965), 104-105, 124-126, 128.

7455 Oppenheimer, Joel. "A Quiet Sunday at Home," Evergreen Review, XIII (December 1969), 18-20.

7456 Oppenheimer, Monroe. "The Car Pool," Redbook, CXXXIII (May 1969), 100-101.

7457 _____. "A Day of Magic," Redbook, CXXIX (August 1967), 38-39.

7458 O'Reilly, Patrick. "Channel of Violence," Canadian Forum, XLVII (January 1968), 231-232.

7459 Örkény, István. "The Hundred and Thirty-Seventh Psalm," New Hungarian Quarterly, VIII (Summer 1967), 131-139.

7460 _____. "One-Minute Stories/Art and the Illuminating Experience," New Hungarian Quarterly, X (Autumn 1969), 64-65.

7461 _____. "One-Minute Stories/The Death of the Spectator," New Hungarian Quarterly, X (Autumn 1969), 73-74.

7462 _____. "One-Minute Stories/Dial 170-100," New Hungarian Quarterly, X (Autumn 1969), 71-73.

7463 _____. "One-Minute Stories/Introspection," New Hungarian Quarterly, X (Autumn 1969), 67-68.

7464 _____. "One-Minute Stories/On My Health," New Hungarian Quarterly, X (Autumn 1969), 66-67.

7465 _____. "One-Minute Stories/Self-Fulfilment," New Hungarian Quarterly, X (Autumn 1969), 65-66.

7466 _____. "One-Minute Stories/Thoughts in a Cellar," New Hungarian Quarterly, X (Autumn 1969), 64.

7467 _____. "One-Minute Stories/To the Salt Cellar," New Hungarian Quarterly, X (Autumn 1969), 68-70.

7468 _____. "There Is No Pardon," Literary Review, IX (Spring 1966), 439-441.

7469 Orlovsky, Peter. "Bombay 1962," Intrepid, no. 6 (1966), n.p. [11-12].

7470 Orpaz, Itzhak. "The Hunting of the Doe," Now, no. 1 (1969), 61-75.

7471 _____. "The Hunting of the Doe," Tirzah Sandbank, trans., Stand, VIII, no. 4 (1967), 15-23.

7472 Orpheus, J. "Last Letter Home," The Archive, LXXX (December 1967), 12-13.

7473 Orrell, Patrick M. "The Enthusiastic Supporter," Lance, V (Winter 1965), 46-49.

7474 Ortego, Philip D. "Chicago Blues," Arx, II (April 1969), 5-6.

7475 _____. "The Coming of Zamora, a Story," El Grito, I (Spring 1968), 12-17.

7476 Ortiz, Simon J. "Woman Singing," South Dakota Review, VII (Summer 1969), 34-44.

7477 Osborn, Carolyn. "The Apex Man," Red Clay Reader, no. 3 (1966), 6-12.

7478 _____. "The Vulture Descending Each Day," Texas Quarterly, XI (Winter 1968), 127-138.

7479 Osborne, Helena. "The Intruders," Cornhill Magazine, no. 1054 (Winter 1967/68), 248-258.

7480 _____. "The Yellow Gold of Tiryns," Cosmopolitan, CLXVII (October 1969), 166-172, 174-182, 186-187, 191-193, 196-197.

7481 O'Shannon, Nóirín. "The Black Widdow," Dublin Magazine, VI (Autumn/Winter 1967), 15-26.

7482 Osier, John. "Dry Leaves," Georgia Review, XXI (Winter 1967), 470-475.

7483 _____. "The Ritual," Georgia Review, XXII (Winter 1968), 446-453.

7484 _____. "Showman," Nimrod, XI (Spring 1967), 1-11.

7485 Osmond, Andrew and Douglas Hurd. "The Smile on the Face of the Tiger," Imprint, IX (May 1969), 21-29, 31, 33, 35, 37, 39, 41, 43, 45, 47, 49, 51, 53, 55, 59, 61, 63, 65, 67, 69, 71, 73, 75, 77, 79, 81, 83, 85, 87, 89, 91, 93-116.

7486 Ostrow, Joanna. "Celtic Twilight," New Yorker, XLIII (April 29, 1967), 41-49.

7487 _____. "Used in the Highlands Since Time Immemorial," New Yorker, XLIV (November 30, 1968), 59-67.

7488 Ostrow, William. "Two Professions," William and Mary Review, VI (Spring 1968), 104-112.

7489 O'Sullivan, A. Don. "Griffith's Gift," Mademoiselle, LXII (February 1966), 139, 183-184.

7490 _____. "Pity the Poor Coots," Mademoiselle, LX (March 1965), 151-153, 242-243.

7491 O'Sullivan, Joe. "Only a Few of Us Left," Ave Maria, CV (March 18, 1967), 24-26.

7492 O'Sullivan, Vincent. "The Abroad," Landfall, no. 76 (December 1975), 322-335.

7493 Oszart, Victor. "A Damn Juan," Panache, I, no. 1 (1965), 46-60.

7494 Otero y Herrera, Alfredo. "The Bending of a Twig," Arizona Quarterly, XXV (Spring 1969), 68-76.

7495 Ottlik, Géza. "Love," Literary Review, IX (Spring 1966), 432-438.

7496 Overton, Ronald. "Charity," Soundings, III (Spring 1966), 44-45.

7497 _____. "Sick Benny Rose," Soundings, II (Spring 1965), 1-8.

7498 Overy, G. Martin. "Bull Price," Weekend Telegraph, no. 57 (October 22, 1965), 39-40, 42, 44.

7499 Owen, Guy. "The Conversion of Doodle," Foxfire, II (Fall-Winter 1968), 33, 111-114.

7500 Owens, Peter. "Moved," North American Review, VI (Fall 1969), 61-64.

7501 Owens, R. A. "The Intruder," New Zealand Listener, (July 29, 1966), 6.

7502 Owens, Rochelle. "The Queen of Greece," Some/thing, I (Winter 1965), 8-16.

7503 Owens, William A. "'We Had Us Some Christmas!'," Ladies' Home Journal, LXXXIII (December 1966), 100-101, 131-133.

7504 Owoyele, David. "The Beggars' Tree," Transatlantic Review, no. 22 (Autumn 1966), 114-118.

7505 Ozaki, Kazuo. "The Day of the Wedding," Hiro Mukai, trans., Hemisphere, XI (January 1967), 7-12.

7506 Ozick, Cynthia. "Envy; or, Yiddish in America," Commentary, XLVIII (November 1969), 33-53.

7507 ______. "The Paggan Rabbi," Hudson Review, XIX (Autumn 1966), 425-454.

7508 R. G. P. "What a Memory," New Zealand Listener, LII (April 2, 1965), 20.

7509 Pace, Elizabeth. "The Bird," Ave Maria, CV (January 21, 1967), 22-24.

7510 ______. "Cradle," Idea and Image, I, no. 2 (1968), 24-25.

7511 Pacis, Donel B. "And in the Dark, the Lovers," Solidarity, IV (February 1969), 51-57.

7512 Packard, George V. "It's No Good Knowing a Girl Named Judy," Redbook, CXXXI (August 1968), 118-119.

7513 Packer, Barbara. "The Blue Eagle," Mademoiselle, LXV (August 1967), 276-277, 333-338.

7514 Packer, Nancy. "Ars Gratia," Per/Se, I (Fall 1966), 32-37.

7515 ______. "Early Morning, Lonely Ride," Southwest Review, LII (Autumn 1967), 380-392.

7516 ______. "End of a Game," Ararat, VIII (Autumn 1967), 52-61.

7517 ______. "Front Man in Line," Yale Review, LV (Autumn 1965), 107-117.

7518 Packer, Vin. "Jimmy from Another World," Cosmopolitan, CLXV (August 1968), 100-105.

7519 ______. "New York Will Break Your Heart, Baby," Redbook, CXXX (February 1968), 78-79.

7520 ______. "Nothing Personal," Redbook, CXXXII (March 1969), 84-85.

7521 _____. "What Do You Want to Say to Me?" Cosmopolitan, CLXII (March 1967), 136-141.

7522 Padgett, Ron and Ted Berrigan. "Big Travel Dialogues," Kulcher, no. 20 (Winter 1965-66), 2-29.

7523 _____. "Bill," Kulcher, no. 19 (Autumn 1965), 3-6.

7524 _____. "Dog," Mother, no. 8 (May Days, 1967), 54-57.

7525 _____ and Tom Veitch. "Ernest Hemingway's Hangnail," Columbia Review, XLVIII, no. 3 (1969), 43-45.

7526 _____. "An Idea that Clara Related to Wallace," Lines, no. 4 (March 1965), 23-24.

7527 _____ and Ted Berrigan. "Inner Landscapes," 0 to 9, no. 3 (January 1968), 79-81.

7528 [_____ and Ted Berrigan] Ronald and Edmund Beaumont. "A Pink Valentine," Mother, no. 5 (Summer 1965), 71-78.

7529 _____. "Portrait of Alex," The World, no. 12 (June 1968), n.p. [35].

7530 _____ and Tom Veitch. "From Star * Gut," Columbia Review, XLIX, no. 2 (1969), 20-23.

7531 _____ and Tom Veitch. "Star-Gut," San Francisco Earthquake, I (Spring 1968), 23-32.

7532 _____ and Ted Berrigan. "Tristan Unsalted," The World, no. 2 (March 1967), n.p. [5-9].

7533 Paff, Barbara. "The Baal Fertility Rite," Pegasus, V (Winter 1967), 5-7.

7534 Paige, Harry W. "The Summer of the Sweet Return," South Dakota Review, VII (Autumn 1969), 74-84.

7535 Painter, Charlotte. "At Tepeyac: 1532 A.D.," Western Review, V (Summer 1968), 14-18.

7536 _____. "'Bye, Lena'," Massachusetts Review, VIII (Spring 1967), 269-274.

7537 _____. "Sandbox," Massachusetts Review, IX (Autumn 1968), 653-659.

7538 Painter-Downes, Mollie. "The Empty Place," New Yorker, XLI (March 27, 1965), 42-49.

7539 Palazuelos, Juan-Augustin. "The Social Worker/A Novel,"

Susana Heringman, Sydney B. Smith, and Juan-Augustin Palazuelos, trans., Ambit, no. 40 (1969), 20-23.

7540 Paley, Grace. "Distance," Atlantic Monthly, CCXX (December 1967), 111-115.

7541 _____. "Faith: In a Tree," New American Review, no. 1 (1967), 51-67.

7542 _____. "Gloomy Tune," Genesis West, III (Winter 1965), 13-15.

7543 _____. "Living," Genesis West, III (Winter 1965), 11-12.

7544 _____. "North-East Playground," Ararat, VIII (Autumn 1967), 25-26.

7545 _____. "Politics," WIN, IV (August 1968), 32-33.

7546 _____. "The Sad Story about the Six Boys about To Be Drafted in Brooklyn," Ikon, I (July 4, 1967), 22.

7547 _____. "The Sad Story about the Six Boys about To be Drafted in Brooklyn," WIN, III (December 1967), 18.

7548 _____. "Two Stories from Five Buroughs," Esquire, LXIX (March 1968), 88-89, 151-152.

7549 Paliani, Richard Howard. "Dilemma," Expression, no. 1 (1968), 25-32.

7550 Pallister, Jan. "Death Is a Jewish Dancer," Beyond Baroque 692, I (July 1969), 38-40.

7551 Palmer, Candida. "When the Fires Burn Low," Green River Review, I (May 1969), 15-21.

7552 Palmer, William. "Prologue and Chapter Six/Coyhaique," Genesis West, III (Winter 1965), 18-37.

7553 Panayotopoulos, I. M. "Flower of Horror," Mary P. Gianos, trans., Athene, XXVII (Autumn 1966), 3-8, 34-37.

7554 _____. "Island in the Distance," Mary P. Gianos, trans., Athene, XXVIII (Spring-Summer 1967), 3-6, 21.

7555 Panella, Vincent. "The Essence of a Common Ordinary Night," Nexus (San Francisco, Calif.), II (July-August 1965), 24-29.

7556 Pang Khye Guan. "The Bitter Times," Focus (Singapore), IV, no. 1, 18-19.

7557 Panigrahi, Bhagabati. "The Game," Sadhana Acharya, trans.,

Bhubaneswar Review, no. 2 (Winter 1968-69), 66-69.

7558 Panova, Vera. "Notes for a Novel," Robert Daglish, trans., Soviet Literature, no. 1 (1966), 21-56.

7559 Pansing, Nancy Pelletier. "The Visitation," Intro, no. 1 (September 1968), 104-124.

7560 Paolozzi, Eduardo. "Moonstrips--General Dynamic F.U.N.," Ambit, no. 33 (1967), 7-25.

7561 _____. "Things/A Novel," Ambit, no. 41 (1969), 25-32.

7562 _____. "Why We Are in Vietnam/A Novel," Ambit, no. 40 (1969), 27-34.

7563 Pap, Károly. "Blood," New Hungarian Quarterly, X (Winter 1969), 30-41.

7564 Papadiamantis, Alexandros. "A Dream on the Wave," G. N. Vlahavas, trans., Athene, XXVII (Spring 1966), 3-7, 37.

7565 _____. "The Exorcist," G. N. Vlahavas, trans., Athene, XXVI (Winter 1966), 9-11, 15.

7566 _____. "Love in the Snow," N. D. Diamantides, trans., Athene, XXVII (Autumn 1966), 11-12.

7567 Papastamatiu, Basilia. "The Shared Thoughts; Free Prose, of Basilia Papastamatiu," Ronald Christ, trans., Tri-Quarterly, nos. 13/14 (Fall/Winter 1968-69), 255-277.

7568 Paris, Elizabeth. "A Summer of Fans," Georgia Review, XXI (Spring 1967), 14-24.

7569 Paris, Matthew. "Low Mass," December, X (1968), 119-120.

7570 Parise, Goffredo. "The Good Life," Caroline Moorehead, trans., London Magazine, VII (November 1967), 32-35.

7571 _____. "Wife in the Saddle," Melton Davis, trans., Evergreen Review, XII (July 1968), 28-31, 70-71.

7572 Park, Edevain. "Essential Services," Cosmopolitan, CLXI (September 1966), 98-104.

7573 Park, Maeva. "Call to a Stranger," Redbook, CXXIX (August 1967), 175-188.

7574 Parker, Dorothy. "Arrangement in Black and White," Contrast, II (1969), 132-136.

7575 _____. "Clothe the Naked," Contrast, II (1969), 79-88.

7576 _____. "Here We Are," Contrast," II (1969), 65-74.

7577 _____. "Horsie," Contrast, II (1969), 20-36.

7578 _____. "The Standard of Living," Contrast, II (1969), 99-105.

7579 _____. "Too Bad," Contrast, II (1969), 43-54.

7580 _____. "You Were Perfectly Fine," Contrast, II (1969), 116-119.

7581 _____. "The Waltz," Contrast, II (1969), 1-5.

7582 Parker, L. "A Fable," The Cantuarian, (April 1968), 108-109.

7583 Parker, Thomas. "Troop Withdrawal--The Initial Step," Harper's Magazine, CCXXIX (August 1969), 61-68.

7584 Parley, Kay. "Kleckner," Prism International, V (Autumn 1965), 20-29.

7585 Parr, J. L. "A Golden Land of Summer Enchantment," The Fiddlehead, no. 74 (Winter 1968), 42-74.

7586 Parr, Jack. "Ah Youth, Ah Joy!" Alphabet, no. 10 (July 1965), 17-31.

7587 Parr, Wallace. "Later," Salmagundi, II (Fall 1968), 96-108.

7588 Parra-Figueredo, A. "The Lake at Hamilton's Bluff," Kansas Quarterly, I (Winter 1968), 19-23.

7589 _____. "Sanchez Escobar at the Circus," Quartet, no. 20 (Fall 1967), 23-27.

7590 Pascoe, Jean. "How Mother Tamed the Wilderness," Woman's Day, (July 1967), 66-67, 103.

7591 Pasolini, Pier Paolo. "Extracts from Teorema," Antonia Scott, trans., Scottish International, no. 7 (August 1969), 8-12.

7592 Pasqual, Mary. "Bells," Ave Maria, CVII (January 20, 1968), 26-28.

7593 _____. "The Dream," Ave Maria, CVI (October 14, 1967), 24-27.

7594 Passuth, László. "The Meeting/(From the novel Lagoons)," Paul Tabori, trans., Literary Review, XI (Autumn 1967), 83-94.

7595 Patalinjug, Ricardo I. "The Violet Hour," Literature East and West, XIII (December 1969), 246-261.

7596 Patch, Stephen. "The Girl Who Sang with the Beatles," New Yorker, XLIV (January 11, 1969), 26-33.

7597 Patnaik, Anant. "Retract," K. M. Acharya, trans., Bhubaneswar Review, no. 3 (Summer 1969), 13-19.

7598 Paton, Alan. "The Quarry," Contrast (Cape Town, South Africa), no. 19 (November 1968), 9-17.

7599 Patrick, Jean. "Saturday Afternoon," New Zealand Listener, LIII (October 1, 1965), 4.

7600 Patten, Brian. "Extract from Atomic Adam," Solstice, no. 5 (1966), 28-30.

7601 Pattison, Jane. "The Italian Violinist," Seventeen, XXVI (March 1967), 142-143, 224-229.

7602 Pauker, John. "Berlin," Carleton Miscellany, VIII (Winter 1967), 2-42.

7603 _____. "Budapest '48," Voyages, I (Autumn 1967), 32-41.

7604 _____. "Miss Matulah," Quartet, no. 10 (Spring 1965), 8-11.

7605 _____. "The Real Literary Figure of 1939," Quartet, no. 13 (Winter 1966), 21-26.

7606 Paulding, James E. "The Red Coal," The Smith, no. 8 (March 1968), 128-132.

7607 Paulk, William. "The Humble and the Damned," Green River Review, I (November 1968), 31-41.

7608 Paulson, John. "The Politician," Illuminations, no. 3 (Summer 1967), 14.

7609 Paustovsky, Konstantin. "Book of Wanderings," Margaret Wettlin, trans., Soviet Literature, (no. 6, 1965), 3-43.

7610 _____. "Grocery Labels," Peter Henry, trans., Stand, IX, no. 2 (1967), 16-28.

7611 _____. "Someone Else's Manuscript," Avril Pyman, trans., Soviet Literature, (no. 3, 1969), 83-96.

7612 _____. "The Telegram," Soviet Literature, (no. 4, 1967), 53-63.

7613 Pavese, Cesare. "Summer Storm," Encounter, XXVII (August 1966), 19-28.

7614 _____. "Summer Storm," Harper's Bazaar, C (May 1967), 120-121, 100-102, 104-105, 107-108.

7615 Pavis, Jesse A. "The School," The Gauntlet, I (Fall 1967), 43-50.

7616 Pavlenko, Pyotr. "The Voice that Calls," Soviet Literature, (no. 4, 1967), 118-124.

7617 Paxton, Norma. "Gold," Solstice, no. 4 (1966), 7.

7618 _____. "Reminiscence," Solstice, no. 4 (1966), 6.

7619 _____. "Whistler," Solstice, no. 4 (1966), 8.

7620 Payne, Basil. "Pennies," Dublin Magazine, VII (Autumn/Winter 1968), 66-72.

7621 Payne, I. W. "A Cycle of Rain," Westerly, no. 3 (October 1968), 16-17.

7622 Payne, Millicent. "A Christmas of Long Ago," Bim, XI (January-June 1967), 253-259.

7623 Paz y Mino, Julio. "Cigars," Ave Maria, CI (May 8, 1965), 22-25.

7624 Pearlman, Edith. "The Liniments of Love," Seventeen, XXVIII (September 1969), 160-161, 214.

7625 _____. "Ring Out the New," Seventeen, XXVIII (December 1969), 96-97, 163-164, 166.

7626 _____. "Which Eleanor Am I?" Seventeen, XXVIII (May 1969), 148-149, 232-236.

7627 Pearson, William. "The Muses of Ruin," Playboy, XII (September 1965), 147-148, 179-180.

7628 Peattie, Elia W. "A Childless Madonna," Prairie Schooner, XLI (Summer 1967), 143-151.

7629 Peden, William. "The Pilgrims," New Mexico Quarterly, XXXVI (Spring 1966), 5-25.

7630 _____. "Requiem," Denver Quarterly, II (Autumn 1967), 53-70.

7631 Pelieu, Claude. "from Cut-Ups & Cut Ins: Interactioninteractioninteractioninter," Mary Beach, trans., San Francisco Earthquake, I (Winter 1968), 22-29.

7632 _____. "from Cut Ups: Parody of Night (2nd version),"

San Francisco Earthquake, I (Fall 1967), 17-24.

7633 ______. "Medleys & Abraca-caha," New Directions 19, (1966), 165-168.

7634 Pelin, Elin. "All Souls' Day," Obzor, (no. 4, 1968), 5-10.

7635 ______. "The Eyes of Saint Spiridon," Obzor, (no. 4, 1968), 17-20.

7636 ______. "The Windmill," Obzor, (no. 4, 1968), 10-17.

7637 Pelle, Alex. "Moonlight Becomes You," Cosmopolitan, CLXV (August 1968), 108-110, 145.

7638 Pendelton, Elsa. "The Mathematician: By His Wife," Analecta, II (Winter 1968), 46-48.

7639 Pène du Bois, William. "The Alligator Case," Ladies' Home Journal, LXXXII (August 1965), 62-63, 106-108.

7640 Pennanen, Eila. "Two Together," Juhani Jaskari, trans., American Scandinavian Review, LIV (June 1966), 178-181.

7641 Penner, Jonathan. "Monkey Business," Tri-Quarterly, no. 10 (Fall 1967), 128-148.

7642 ______. "The West-Chop Season (chapter from a novel in progress)," Tri-Quarterly, no. 5 (Winter 1966), 41-53.

7643 Penniman, Marjorie. "The Faithful Departed," Quartet, no. 17 (Winter 1967), 3-12.

7644 Pentecost, Hugh. "Dead Woman of the Year," Cosmopolitan, CLXIV (January 1968), 102-121, 124-126, 128-129, 131-133.

7645 ______. "The Evil that Men Do," Cosmopolitan, CLX (May 1966), 128-132, 134-136, 138-147, 151-153, 156-161.

7646 ______. "The Golden Trap," Cosmopolitan, CLXII (January 1967), 112-118, 120-125, 129-134, 136-141.

7647 Penzoldt, Ernst. "With a Child's Eyes," Margaret D. Howie, trans., Scala International, (December 1967), 34-37.

7648 Percival, Harold. "Mind over Body," Contrast (Cape Town, South Africa), no. 21 (August 1969), 75-82.

7649 Percy, H. R. "Mankipoo," Queen's Quarterly, LXXVI (Autumn 1969), 454-465.

7650 Percy, Walker. "The Last Gentleman/Two Excerpts from the Forthcoming Novel," Harper's Magazine, CCXXXII (May 1966), 54-56, 59-61.

7651 Perelman, S. J. "Afternoon with a Pint-Sized Faun," New Yorker, XLI (December 4, 1965), 55-57.

7652 ______. "And, In the Center Ring, that Stupendous Death-Defying Daredevil...," New Yorker, XLIV (May 11, 1968), 38-40.

7653 ______. "Anna Trivia Pluralized," New Yorker, XLII (November 26, 1966), 53-55.

7654 ______. "Are You Decent, Mem-Sahib?" New Yorker, XLI (August 28, 1965), 28-31.

7655 ______. "Be a Cat's-Paw! Lose Big Money!" New Yorker, XLV (July 26, 1969), 31-33.

7656 ______. "Call Me Monty, and Grovel Freely," New Yorker, XLIV (November 23, 1968), 56-58.

7657 ______. "Calling All Moths: Candle Dead Ahead," New Yorker, XLV (May 3, 1969), 33-35.

7658 ______. "Caution--Beware of Excess Prophets," New Yorker, XLI (October 23, 1965), 53-55.

7659 ______. "Caveat Emptor, Fortissimo et Philadelphia," New Yorker, XLI (June 19, 1965), 28-30.

7660 ______. "Come, Costly Fido, for I Am Sick with Love," New Yorker, XLIV (December 7, 1968), 56-59.

7661 ______. "Dear Sir or Madam," New Yorker, XLIII (June 3, 1967), 31-33.

7662 ______. "Five Little Biceps and How They Flew," New Yorker, XLIV (October 19, 1968), 53-54.

7663 ______. "Hark! Whence Came Those Pear-Shaped Drones," New Yorker, XLV (November 1, 1969), 46-48.

7664 ______. "The Hermit Crab," New Yorker, XLIII (July 15, 1967), 26-27.

7665 ______. "Hey, What's Wriggling Around that Caduceus?" New Yorker, XLII (June 18, 1966), 32-35.

7666 ______. "In Spite of All Temptations/To Belong to Other Nations," New Yorker, XLIII (March 25, 1967), 44-47.

7667 ______. "Let a Snarl Be Your Umbrella," New Yorker, XLII (January 14, 1967), 26-27.

7668 ______. "Lock Lips--Monkey Shines in the Bridgework,"

New Yorker, XLIII (October 7, 1967), 47-49.

7669 _____. "Moonstruck at Sunset," New Yorker, XLV (August 16, 1969), 28-31.

7670 _____. "Murder on the Roof," New Yorker, XLI (February 19, 1966), 32-34.

7671 _____. "Naked in Piccadilly, W. 1," New Yorker, XLIII (January 27, 1968), 29-30.

7672 _____. "No Autographs Please--I'm Invisible," New Yorker, XLI (September 18, 1965), 46-49.

7673 _____. "Out of This Nettle, Danger," New Yorker, XLV (November 29, 1969), 49-51.

7674 _____. "Paint Me a Pinion Immortal, Limner Dear," New Yorker, XLIII (May 6, 1967), 41-43.

7675 _____. "The Rape of the Drape," New Yorker, XLII (September 24, 1966), 56-58.

7676 _____. "Sex and the Single Boy," New Yorker, XLI (May 8, 1965), 40-43.

7677 _____. "She Walks in Beauty--Single File, Eyes Front, and No Hanky-Panky," New Yorker, XLV (February 22, 1969), 32-34.

7678 _____. "Six Daggers East," New Yorker, XLI (February 27, 1965), 28-31.

7679 _____. "10:30, and All Quiet on West Forty-fifth Street," New Yorker, XLIII (December 23, 1967), 24-26.

7680 _____. "Three Loves Had I, in Assorted Flavors," New Yorker, XLV (March 22, 1969), 34-37.

7681 _____. "Thunder under the Kalahari/or, Aliquid Novi Ex Botswana," New Yorker, XLIV (December 21, 1968), 29-32.

7682 _____. "To Err Is Human, To Forgive Supine," New Yorker, XLV (October 4, 1969), 36-38.

7683 _____. "Too Many Undies Spoil the Crix," New Yorker, XLII (October 22, 1966), 53-55.

7684 Perera, Padma. "Mauna," New Yorker, XLII (October 29, 1966), 205-210, 213-216, 219-222, 225-228, 231.

7685 _____. "Three Is Company," New Yorker, XLV (March 29, 1969), 34-44.

7686 Perera, Victor. "The Conversion," Commentary, XLVI (August 1968), 44-52.

7687 Perkins, Warren. "A Celebration," Harvard Advocate, CIII (December 1969), 8-17.

7688 Perret, Christopher. "The Phoney," Trace, nos. 62 & 63 (Fall-Winter 1966-67), 429-432.

7689 Perri-Figueredo, Armando. "This Side of Bahia Honda," Four Quarters, XVIII (January 1969), 11-19.

7690 Perrin, Ursula. "Promises to Keep," Ladies' Home Journal, LXXXIV (March 1967), 151-158, 175-178.

7691 Perry, Grace. "Passing Through," Cimarron Review, no. 8 (June 1969), 100-102.

7692 _____. "Passing Through," Westerly, no. 2 (July 1969), 22-24.

7693 _____. "What's To Become of You, Louisa?" Westerly, no. 3 (October 1968), 30-32.

7694 Perry, Margaret. "Gaston," Ball State University Forum, VIII (Autumn 1967), 11-15.

7695 _____. "Lions, Kings and Dragons," Panache, no. 3 (1969), 20-30.

7696 Perry, Ralph. "Call Me Uncas," Quarto, (Fall 1965), 11-13.

7697 Perry, Ronald. "Three Laotian Tales," Hudson Review, XXI (Summer 1968), 263-282.

7698 Perry, W. D. "The Flight of the Red Calliope," Trace, no. 65 (Summer 1967), 252-259.

7699 Perry, William. "The Kansas City Horn," Arizona Quarterly, XXV (Autumn 1969), 252-262.

7700 Perutz, Kathrin. "An American Success," Washington Square Review, II (Winter 1966), 15-22.

7701 Pervomaisky, Leonid. "Katerina's New House," Eve Manning, trans., Soviet Literature, (no. 9, 1968), 24-65.

7702 _____. "Melnikov Street," Eve Manning, trans., Soviet Literature, (no. 6, 1968), 93-103.

7703 _____. "Wild Honey," Vladimir Talmy, trans., Soviet Literature, (no. 5, 1965), 43-80.

7704 Pesta, John. "Friday Night," Ave Maria, CIV (July 2, 1966), 26-28.

7705 ______. "Silver Flowers," Four Quarters, XVI (January 1967), 19-23.

7706 ______. "Snowdrift," Prairie Schooner, XLII (Fall 1968), 212-224.

7707 ______. "Sundaydream," Ave Maria, CII (July 10, 1965), 22-24.

7708 ______. "What're You Going To Do?" Ave Maria, CIII (January 22, 1966), 22-24.

7709 Peterson, Anita. "Granny Floats," UMD Humanist, XVII (Winter 1969), 13-16.

7710 Peterson, Dale. "My Uncle's Red Pepper Farm," Sequoia, XIII (Autumn 1968), 8-11.

7711 Peterson, Norman C. "Before the Sun Goes Down," Arx, II (October 1968), 16-20.

7712 ______. "The Famous Adventure of the Ghost Wolves," Arx, I (April 1967), 16-19.

7713 ______. "The Ghost in the Road," Arx, I (July-August 1967), 14-22.

7714 ______. "Oberland," Arx, I (June 1967), 14-21.

7715 ______. "Rape and Reaction," Arx, I (November 1967), 30-36, 46-54.

7716 ______. "Rotten Rope," Arx, I (October 1967), 11-15, 27-31.

7717 ______. "The Tumblebug," Arx, I (September 1967), 7-10, 28-32.

7718 Peterson, Owen. "The Special," Seventeen, XXIV (January 1965), 81, 122.

7719 Petesch, Natalie. "Minerva at the Peace Corps," New Mexico Quarterly, XXXV (Winter 1965-66), 344-358.

7720 ______. "The Truth," University Review, XXXI (June 1965), 243-256.

7721 ______. "Zhenia and the Wicked One," New Orleans Review, I (Winter 1969), 156-159.

7722 Petlewski, Paul. "Summer Sketch," Cavalier, XV (July 1965), 60, 83-87.

7723 Petrakis, Harry Mark. "Dark Eye," Playboy, XV (December 1968), 123, 296, 298.

7724 _____. "The Gold of Troy," Playboy, XIII (September 1966), 127, 224, 226.

7725 _____. "Homecoming," U.S. Catholic and Jubilee, XXIV (June 1969), 30-36.

7726 _____. "Rosemary," Mademoiselle, LXVI (February 1968), 134-135, 171-175.

7727 _____. "The Sweet Life," Confrontation, no. 1 (Spring 1968), 3-13.

7728 _____. "When Greek Meets Greek/from A Dream of Kings," Ladies' Home Journal, LXXXIV (February 1967), 99-100, 135.

7729 _____. "The Witness," Playboy, XIV (March 1967), 79, 160-162, 164.

7730 Petrides, George. "Pax Africana," Red Cedar Review, III (Spring 1965), 5-12.

7731 Petroff, J. A. "Old Man," New Campus Review, I (Winter/Spring 1968), 27-31.

7732 Petronius. "The Satyricon of Petronius: A New Take," Edgar A. Bunning, trans. [colloquial translation of excerpts], Avant Garde, no. 7 (January 1969), 36-41.

7733 Petrov, Evgeni and Ilya Ilf. "A Man of Many Parts," Soviet Literature, (no. 4, 1967), 93-96.

7734 Petrovic, Veljko. "Janos and Macko," Svetozar Koljevic, trans., Malahat Review, no. 4 (October 1967), 5-19.

7735 Petry, Ann. "The Migraine Workers," Redbook, CXXIX (May 1967), 66-67, 125-127.

7736 _____. "The New Mirror," New Yorker, XLI (May 29, 1965), 28-36, 38, 40, 43-44, 46, 49-50, 52, 55.

7737 Pettit, Marilyn. "No Fit Place for a Child to Play," Red Cedar Review, IV (Spring 1966), 47-52.

7738 Pettus, Clyde. "You Know What I Mean?" Georgia Review, XXIII (Summer 1969), 183-195.

7739 Pfeiffer, Nancy. "Heart's Gift," Columbia, XLVI (December 1966), 24-28.

7740 Pfister, Robert C. "Lazlo and Regina," Discourse, XI (Spring 1968), 230-239.

7741 Pfundstein, Roy. "Soon," Ball State University Forum, X (Autumn 1969), 29-32.

7742 Phelan, Michael. "Afterthought," Ave Maria, CII (July 3, 1965), 18-22.

7743 _____. "The Lonely Furrow," Ave Maria, CIV (August 20, 1966), 24-26.

7744 _____. "The Lonely Furrow/Part II," Ave Maria, CIV (August 27, 1966), 24-26.

7745 _____. "The Lonely Furrow/Conclusion," Ave Maria, CIV (September 3, 1966), 24-27.

7746 _____. "Prospects of Sadness," Ave Maria, CII (December 4, 1965), 24-29.

7747 Phelps, Donald. "Excerpt from a Novel: Wheel Night," For Now, no. 8 (c. 1966-68), 114-117.

7748 Phelps, Everett Dean. "You Know What They Say," Virginia Quarterly Review, XLIV (Summer 1968), 441-457.

7749 Philbrook, Rose. "Can You Blame Her, If She's Blind?" Four Quarters, XVII (November 1967), 1-10.

7750 Philips, Judson. "Just for Laughs," Cosmopolitan, CLVIII (June 1965), 106-125, 128-135, 138-139.

7751 Philipson, Morris. "Decision-Making," Southern Review, I (April 1965), 352-360.

7752 _____. "The Loathsome Emotion," Epoch, XV (Winter 1966), 155-161.

7753 Phillips, John. "Bleat Blodgette," Paris Review, XI (Summer-Fall 1967), 12-46.

7754 _____. "The Lunchblower," December, XI (1969), 136-138.

7755 Phillips, John Randolph. "Family Matter," Redbook, CXXV (July 1965), 52-53, 86-90.

7756 Phillips, Michael. "The Class D League," North American Review, V (May-June 1968), 13-18.

7757 _____. "How to Play the Game," Nimrod, XI (Spring 1967), 18-30.

7758 _____. "Initiation," Forum, VI (Fall-Winter 1968), 35-41.

7759 _____. "Ottie," Nimrod, X (Winter 1966), 28-33.

7760 Phillips, Robert. "In a Country of Strangers," Carleton Miscellany, X (Winter 1969), 60-72.

7761 _____. "The Land of Lost Content," Carleton Miscellany, VIII (Fall 1967), 78-88.

7762 _____. "Mealy Marshall and the Whore of Babylon," Southern Humanities Review, II (Spring 1968), 173-184.

7763 _____. "The Quality of Feeling," Carleton Miscellany, X (Spring 1969), 46-55.

7764 Phiri, Naphy Monty. "Vumbo," New Writing from Zambia, no. 1 (1968), 12-13, 16-22.

7765 Phoenice, J. "The Seismic Sea," Limbo, II (November 1966), 3-12.

7766 Pickering, Michael. "The Day Teddington Sank," Old Lady of Threadneedle Street, XLII (December 1966), 209-211.

7767 _____. "Typically English," Old Lady of Threadneedle Street, XLI (December 1965), 209-213.

7768 Pickett, T. H. "The Last Rites," Georgia Review, XX (Winter 1966), 463-466.

7769 Picouli, Katy. "The Letter," Athene, XXVII (Winter 1967), 7-8.

7770 Piedmonte, M. A. "Sermon in South Philadelphia," Nexus (San Francisco, Calif.), II (May-June 1965), 54-57.

7771 Piercy, Marge. "Going over Jordan," Transatlantic Review, no. 22 (Autumn 1966), 148-157.

7772 _____. "Love Me Tonight, God," Paris Review, XI (Winter 1968), 185-200.

7773 Pierog, P. "A Story," Win Magazine, (July 1969), 24.

7774 Pieyre de Mandiargues, André. "The Tide," Richard Howard, trans., Evergreen Review, XI (April 1967), 32-33, 98-99.

7775 Pilnyak, Boris. "A Tale of the Unextingushed Moon," Brian Pearce, trans., Stand, VIII, no. 1 (1966), 25-43.

7776 Pincus, Oscar. "Goodbye to Europe," Midstream, XIII (June/July 1967), 46-56.

7777 Pinelli, Joseph. "Excerpts from Book I," Lines, no. 6 (November 1965), 35-41.

7778 _____. "from Striations," Work, no. 5 (1968), 13-14.

7779 Pinget, Robert. "Between Fantoine and Agapa," Raymond Federman, trans., Contemporary Literature in Translation, no. 5 (Spring 1969), 18-19.

7780 _____. "The Cucumbers," Raymond Federman, trans., Contemporary Literature in Translation, no. 5 (Spring 1969), 19.

7781 Pinon, Nelida. "Brief Flower," Gregory Rabassa, trans., TriQuarterly, nos. 13/14 (Fall/Winter 1968-69), 341-348.

7782 Pinter, Harold. "The Black & White," Transatlantic Review, no. 21 (Summer 1966), 51-52.

7783 _____. "Tea Party," Playboy, XII (January 1965), 124-125, 218.

7784 Pinto, Peter L. "Hills of Rome," Carolina Quarterly, XVIII (Winter 1966), 9-15.

7785 Piontek, Heinz. "The Gate to the World," Margaret D. Howie, trans., Scala International, (April 1969), 34-36.

7786 _____. "Passage toward the Horizon," Andreas Schroeder, trans., Contemporary Literature in Translation, no. 1 (1968), 5-6.

7787 _____. "The Sadness in a Bear's Breast," George Raymond Selden, trans., Scala International, (August 1965), 34-37.

7788 _____. "Time and the Woman," Elaine Robson-Scott, trans., Malahat Review, no. 1 (January 1967), 41-44.

7789 Pis'mennyi, Aleksandr. "Vaska and Vasilii Vasil'yevich," Jan Solecki, trans., Prism International, VI (Autumn 1966), 58-81.

7790 Pizzuto, Antonio. "Outside the Station," William Weaver, trans., London Magazine, VII (March 1968), 56-59.

7791 Plá, Josefina. "Roasted Peanuts," Américas, XX (August 1968), 32-35.

7792 Plagemann, Bentz. "Beautiful to Behold," Good Housekeeping, CLXI (July 1965), 70-71, 124, 126-128.

7793 _____. "I Know My Love," Good Housekeeping, CLX (February 1965), 76-77, 176, 178, 180-182.

7794 Plante, David. "The Buried City," Transatlantic Review, no. 24 (Spring 1967), 78-85.

7795 Plastino, Jane Hammers. "The Dissenter," Ave Maria, CII (September 25, 1965), 21-25.

7796 Plath, Sylvia. "Johnny Panic and the Bible of Dreams," Atlantic Monthly, CCXXII (September 1968), 54-60.

7797 Platonov, Andrei. "The Engine Driver," Imprint, VIII (December 1968), 45-50.

7798 _____. "Fro," Katharine Lampert, trans., London Magazine, VII (June 1967), 12-35.

7799 _____. "In the Beautiful and Violent World," Soviet Literature, (no. 4, 1967), 102-113.

7800 _____. "The Third Son," Joseph Barnes, trans., Harper's Magazine, CCXXXIX (November 1969), 87-89.

7801 Platt, Charles. "ID," New Worlds, no. 188 (March 1969), 44-46.

7802 Playfair, Rhoda E. "The Time of the Singing of Birds," Queen's Quarterly, LXXV (Spring 1968), 147-154.

7803 du Plessix Gray, Francine. "For the Love of Joan Riley," Mademoiselle, LXVIII (March 1969), 200-201, 235-236, 244, 246-250.

7804 _____. "The Governess," New Yorker, XLII (January 14, 1967), 28-38, 40, 42, 45.

7805 _____. "Lucien, Octave, Victoire, Emile," New Yorker, XLIII (July 29, 1967), 26-34.

7806 Pleynet, Marcelin. "Flagellation," Bernard Frechtman, trans., Lugano Review, I, no. 1 (1965), 46-51.

7807 Plimpton, Sarah. "The Old Woman," Paris Review, XII (Summer 1969), 32-38.

7808 Pogodin, Radi. "What a Debt Means," Eve Manning, trans., Soviet Literature, (no. 12, 1968), 59-82.

7809 Pohl, Frederik. "Lovemaking," Playboy, XIII (December 1966), 221, 278.

7810 _____. "The Schematic Man," Playboy, XVI (January 1969), 195-196, 237.

7811 _____. "Speed Trap," Playboy, XIV (November 1967), 159, 200-201, 203-204.

7812 Poindexter, Gloria. "If You Throw a Silver Dollar Down on the Ground," Prospero's Cell, II (Spring 1967), 33-40.

7813 Polevoy, Boris. "A Bedtime Story," Soviet Literature, (no. 4, 1967), 144-150.

7814 Polikoff, Barbara. "All in Good Time," McCall's, XCIV (January 1967), 50-51, 122-123.

7815 ______. "Hammerhead," Literary Review, XII (Spring 1969), 367-380.

7816 ______. "Think of Them," Redbook, CXXV (May 1965), 60-61.

7817 Polillo, Pasquale Louis. "Surprise," Phylon, XXX (Winter 1969), 86-93.

7818 Polk, Dora. "Success Story," Anglo-Welsh Review, XVIII, no. 41 (Summer 1969), 91-96.

7819 Polk, Duvan. "A Promise of Oranges," Good Housekeeping, CLXVIII (February 1969), 80-81, 140-142, 144, 146.

7820 ______. "This Time Forever," Good Housekeeping, CLXVI (April 1968), 100-101, 216, 218, 220-224.

7821 Pollack, Barbara. "Why?" UMD Humanist, XIV (Spring 1966), 22-24.

7822 Pollman, Olaf. "Rooms," Edge, no. 7 (Winter 1967/68), 39-42.

7823 Pollock, Rollene. "A Field of Tall Corn," Carolina Quarterly, XVII (Spring 1965), 17-22.

7824 Ponge, Francis. "Appendix to The Notebook of the Pine Woods/I Extra Pages," Origin (Kyoto, Japan), no. 9 (April 1968), 30-32.

7825 ______. "Fauna and Flora," Frederick Brown, trans., Contemporary Literature in Translation, no. 4 (Spring 1969), 32-34.

7826 ______. "Fauna and Flora/from Siding with Things," Paul Watsky, trans., Stony Brook, nos. 3-4 (1969), 238-240.

7827 ______. "9 Pieces/The Boat," Origin, Series 3, no. 15 (1969), 10.

7828 ______. "9 Pieces/The Frog," Origin, Series 3, no. 15 (1969), 11.

7829 _____. "9 Pieces/The Insignificant," Origin, Series 3, no. 15 (1969), 7.

7830 _____. "9 Pieces/The Last Simplicity," Origin, Series 3, no. 15 (1969), 9.

7831 _____. "9 Pieces/The Metamorphosis," Origin, Series 3, no. 15 (1969), 14.

7832 _____. "9 Pieces/The Radio," Origin, Series 3, no. 15 (1969), 15.

7833 _____. "9 Pieces/The Stones," Origin, Series 3, no. 15 (1969), 13.

7834 _____. "9 Pieces/The Telephone," Origin, Series 3, no. 15 (1969), 12.

7835 _____. "9 Pieces/Young Girl," Origin, Series 3, no. 15 (1969), 8.

7836 _____. "The Notebook of the Pine Woods," Origin (Kyoto, Japan), no. 9 (April 1968), 1-11.

7837 _____. "Of Water," Daphne Buckle, trans., Contemporary Literature in Translation, no. 1 (1968), 20-21.

7838 _____. "The Orange," Rosmarie Waldrop, trans., Contemporary Literature in Translation, no. 6 (Winter 1969), 30.

7839 _____. "The Potato, Nuptial Habits of Dogs," Merloyd Lawrence, trans., Transatlantic Review, no. 21 (Summer 1966), 95-98.

7840 _____. "Prose Sketches," Art and Literature, no. 12 (Spring 1967), 225-252.

7841 _____. "Rain," Daphne Buckle, trans., Contemporary Literature in Translation, no. 3 (Winter 1968), 30.

7842 _____. "Seashores," Frederick Brown, trans., Contemporary Literature in Translation, no. 3 (Winter 1968), 30-31.

7843 _____. "from The Seine (II)," Lane Dunlop, trans., Western Humanities Review, XXII (Autumn 1968), 341-357.

7844 _____. "Snails," Frederick Brown, trans., Contemporary Literature in Translation, no. 1 (1968), 18-20.

7845 _____. "Taking Sides with Things/The Candle," Frederick Brown, trans., Harper's Bazaar, CII (September 1969), 263.

7846 _____. "Taking Sides with Things/Door Delights," Frederick

Brown, trans., Harper's Bazaar, CII (September 1969), 263.

7847 ______. "Taking Sides with Things/Fire," Frederick Brown, trans., Harper's Bazaar, CII (September 1969), 262.

7848 ______. "Taking Sides with Things/The Oyster," Frederick Brown, trans., Harper's Bazaar, CII (September 1969), 263.

7849 ______. "Taking Sides with Things/Rain," Frederick Brown, trans., Harper's Bazaar, CII (September 1969), 262.

7850 ______. "Two Texts from The Parti Pris of Things," Lane Dunlop, trans., Transatlantic Review, no. 27 (Winter 1967-68), 11-13.

7851 Ponicsan, Darryl. "The Juggler and His Daughter," Illuminations, no. 3 (Summer 1967), 28-29.

7852 Ponnech, Ben. "Sociology 482 (Lab Course)," Statement, no. 21 (Spring 1965), 14-17.

7853 Pons, Maurice. "Rosa," Keith Botsford, trans., Delos, no. 3 (1969), 5-40.

7854 Popescu, Dumitru Radu. "The Hanged Doll," Literary Review, X (Summer 1967), 553-560.

7855 Popovici, Titus. "The Thirst," Literary Review, X (Summer 1967), 527-536.

7856 Popovsky, Norman. "On a Hot Summer Afternoon," Sou'wester, (Spring 1968), 46-48.

7857 Popp, Hans A. "The Modern Generation," Georgia Review, XXII (Fall 1968), 392-399.

7858 Porges, Arthur. "Bank Night," Signature, I (January 1966), 41-43, 52, 56.

7859 ______. "Invasion of Privacy," Signature, I (March 1966), 42-44.

7860 Porter, Caryl. "Summer Landscape," Wisconsin Review, III (Spring 1968), 28.

7861 ______. "Three Legends Out of Nowhere," Illuminations, no. 1 (Summer 1965), 9.

7862 Porter, Donald. "Senehem's Pyramid," Beyond Baroque 692, I (July 1969), 50-58.

7863 Porter, Hal. "My Pal Rembrandt," Meanjin Quarterly, XXVIII

(Autumn 1969), 5-18.

7864 _____. "Seeing, Not Seeing," Meanjin Quarterly, XXVIII (Autumn 1969), 29-44.

7865 Porter, Joe Ashby. "Annie Gill," Occident, III (Spring/Summer 1969), 13-50.

7866 _____. "Destruction of Gods," Occident, II (Spring/Summer 1968), 73-86.

7867 Porter, John. "The Age of Descent," Playboy, XV (March 1968), 102-103, 142-143.

7868 _____. "Checkmate," Mademoiselle, LXIX (June 1969), 128-129, 151-154.

7869 _____. "The Cruel Kiss," Cosmopolitan, CLXIII (August 1967), 118-121.

7870 _____. "The Red Nun," Cosmopolitan, CLXVII (September 1969), 160-162.

7871 Porter, Katherine Anne. "Martyr," Cosmopolitan, CLVIII (April 1965), 92-93.

7872 Porterfield, Nolan. "Home from a War," Sewanee Review, LXXIII (January-March 1965), 74-93.

7873 Portis, Charles. "Traveling Light (Part I)," Saturday Evening Post, CCXXXIX (June 18, 1966), 54-55, 58, 60, 62, 64-68, 70, 73, 75-77.

7874 _____. "Traveling Light (Conclusion)," Saturday Evening Post, CCXXXIX (July 2, 1966), 48-50, 63-64, 66, 68, 70, 72, 74-75.

7875 _____. "True Grit (Part I)," Saturday Evening Post, CCXLI (May 18, 1968), 68-75, 77-78, 80-82, 84-85.

7876 _____. "True Grit (Part II)," Saturday Evening Post, CCXLI (June 1, 1968), 46-50, 52-53, 56-61.

7877 _____. "True Grit (Conclusion)," Saturday Evening Post, CCXLI (June 15, 1968), 44-46, 50-57.

7878 Poston, Patricia. "The Image of the Dream," Good Housekeeping, CLXVIII (June 1969), 96-97.

7879 Potok, Chaim. "The Cats of 37 Alfasi Street," American Judaism, XVI (Fall 1966), 12-13, 25-26, 28-29.

7880 _____. "The Chosen," Ladies' Home Journal, LXXXIV

(May 1967), 149-156, 158, 160-162.

7881 Potter, Daniel. "Midnight Watch," McCall's, XCIV (June 1967), 80-81, 102-105.

7882 _____. "Tell Me about the Wind," Redbook, CXXXII (January 1969), 64-65, 130-133.

7883 Potter, Jeffrey. "Lower Case 'n'," Evergreen Review, IX (June 1965), 62-63.

7884 Potter, Nancy A. J. "Divorcing the Dead Husband," Kenyon Review, XXIX (January 1967), 69-85.

7885 _____. "The Happiest You've Ever Been," Massachusetts Review, VII (Summer 1966), 479-491.

7886 _____. "In Union Sweet," Prairie Schooner, XLI (Fall 1967), 288-299.

7887 _____. "Just Tell Me All Your Troubles," Shenandoah, XVIII (Summer 1967), 27-47.

7888 _____. "The Old Wife," Malahat Review, no. 10 (April 1969), 96-103.

7889 _____. "The Summer of the Spaniards," Arizona Quarterly, XXIII (Autumn 1967), 207-219.

7890 _____. "There Won't Be Any Scars At All," McCall's, XCVI (March 1969), 94-95, 157-161.

7891 _____. "We Have Seen the Best of Our Times," Kenyon Review, XXVII (Winter 1965), 113-130.

7892 Potts, Jean. "The Only Good Secretary," Cosmopolitan, CLIX (July 1965), 100-115, 118-123, 125-127.

7893 Pound, Louise. "By Homeopathic Treatment," Prairie Schooner, XLI (Summer 1967), 204-212.

7894 Poverman, Charles. "Eighteen," Yale Literary Magazine, CXXXIV (October 1965), 22-32.

7895 Powell, Anthony. "A Reference for Lady Chatterly's Lover," Vogue, CXLVIII (December 1966), 126-127, 130-131, 136.

7896 Powell, Clarence Alva. "Abner's Ascension," Canadian Forum, XLVIII (February 1969), 252-253.

7897 _____. "Bed-Fellows," Mandala, no. 3 (1968), 11-14.

7898 _____. "Four Knights In a Barroom," Human Voice Quarterly,

II (Winter 1966), 173-180.

7899 _____. "The Grasshopper," Illuminations, no. 3 (Summer 1967), 14.

7900 _____. "The Hogs/(As related to the author by Loal Arnold)," Genesis: Grasp, I, no. 2 (1969), 7-9.

7901 _____. "The Hold-up: A Dialogue," Mandala, no. 5 (1969), 64-65.

7902 _____. "Legends," Illuminations, no. 3 (Summer 1967), 14.

7903 _____. "The Lethal Beast," Nexus (San Francisco, Calif.), II (November-December 1965), 30-31.

7904 Powell, Mark. "The Birthday Treat," Transatlantic Review, no. 29 (Summer 1968), 41-44.

7905 Power, Mark. "excerpt from Cash or Pity," The Circle, no. 3 (1968), 12-17, 19-30.

7906 Power, Michael. "A New Face," Cornhill Magazine, no. 1045 (Autumn 1965), 62-67.

7907 Powers, Bolling. "The Night of the Possum," Twigs, no. 5 (Fall 1969), 99-118.

7908 _____. "Years of the Locusts," Shenandoah, XX (Autumn 1968), 49-64.

7909 Powers, J. F. "Bill," New Yorker, XLV (May 17, 1969), 34-40.

7910 _____. "Priestly Fellowship," New Yorker, XLV (September 27, 1969), 36-46.

7911 Powers, William. "I'm from Olin," Cimarron Review, no. 9 (September 1969), 37-44.

7912 Powys, T. F. "The Kingfisher," Kenyon Review, XXIX (March 1967), 197-206.

7913 _____. "The Red Petticoat," Kenyon Review, XXIX (March 1967), 217-222.

7914 _____. "The Wine-Fed Tree," Kenyon Review, XXIX (March 1967), 207-216.

7915 Poyk, Gerson. "The Swinging Mirror," Musafir Hidayat, trans., Quadrant, XIII (September-October 1969), 49-51.

7916 _____. "The Swinging Mirror," Musafir Hidayat, trans.,

Solidarity, III (September 1968), 64-66.

7917 Prahl, Earl Jean. "Muldoon the Wanderer," Little Review of the Pacific Northwest, I (Fall 1965), 2-29.

7918 Pramudya Ananta Tur. "Caged," Soh Liantji, trans., Westerly, (October 1966), 69-75.

7919 _____. "Darkness," Theresa Yo, trans., Westerly, (October 1966), 76-91.

7920 _____. "Letter to a Friend from the Country," Harry Aveling, trans., Quadrant, XIII (September-October 1969), 59-64.

7921 _____. "The Reward of Marriage," Ann Kumar, trans., Westerly, (October 1966), 43-68.

7922 Prashker, Ivan. "Peter," Redbook, CXXXI (May 1968), 78-79.

7923 Prasniewski, Margaret. "Come Back, Peter ... Come Back, Paul," Redbook, CXXV (July 1965), 46-47, 97-99.

7924 Pratt, Jonathan. "Girl on a Dark Road," Saturday Evening Post, CCXXXIX (December 3, 1966), 66-68, 70, 72.

7925 Pratt, Richard L. "The Crescent Moon," Lance, V (Spring 1965), 24-26.

7926 _____. "Two for a Nickel," Lance, V (Winter 1965), 1-3.

7927 Pravdin, Lev. "Mallows in Bloom," Asya Shoyett, trans., Soviet Literature, (no. 2, 1965), 92-126.

7928 Preda, Marin. "Encounter in the Fields," Literary Review, X (Summer 1967), 489-500.

7929 Prentiss, Karl. "You May Well Wonder, Marty," Playboy, XIV (May 1967), 135-136, 138, 140.

7930 Press, Howard. "Embrace," Landfall, no. 89 (March 1969), 7-9.

7931 Preston, Betty Brown. "Summer Spooks," Seventeen, XXVIII (July 1969), 92-93, 142, 144-145.

7932 Prewitt, James. "Mrs. Mellioni," Southern Review, IV (April 1968), 437-446.

7933 Price, Jonathan. "Test Case," Transatlantic Review, no. 28 (Spring 1968), 90-94.

7934 Price, K. Arnold. "The Lark in the Clear Air," Dublin Magazine, VIII (Spring/Summer 1969), 51-62.

7935 Price, Nancy. "The Invisible Ones," Virginia Quarterly Review, XLIV (Winter 1968), 98-107.

7936 _____. "White Mouse," Virginia Quarterly Review, XLV (Winter 1969), 79-87.

7937 Price, Reynolds. "A Dog's Death," Southern Review, IV (April 1968), 392-395.

7938 _____. "The Happiness of Others," Southern Review, V (October 1969), 1176-1182.

7939 _____. "Invitation," Shenandoah, XIX (Autumn 1967), 37-39.

7940 _____. "The Knowledge of My Mother's Coming Death," Southern Review, IV (July 1968), 720-724.

7941 _____. "Scars," Esquire, LXX (December 1968), 184-185, 272-273, 275-276, 278-280.

7942 _____. "Truth and Lies," Southern Review, I (April 1965), 292-306.

7943 Price, William N., Jr. "A-104," DeKalb Literary Arts Journal, I (Fall 1966), 5-10.

7944 Principato, Tina M. "Peter Comes Home," Ave Maria, CVI (December 16, 1967), 26-29.

7945 Pringle, Peggy. "Distances," The Archive, LXXVIII (April 1966), 22-27, 30-32.

7946 Prishvin, Mikhail. "The Old Mushroom," Soviet Literature, (no. 4, 1967), 21-25.

7947 Pritam, Amrita. "Empty Canvas," M. S. Batra, trans., Avenues, II (January 1968), 24-27.

7948 _____. "A House Unbuilt," Mahendra Kulasrestha, trans., Eastern Horizon, IV (January 1965), 59-63.

7949 _____. "Stench of Kerosene," Khushmant Singh, trans., Eastern Horizon, VI (February 1967), 57-60.

7950 _____. "The Weed," Raj Gill, trans., Eastern Horizon, V (May 1966), 59-62.

7951 Pritchett, V. S. "The Cage Birds," Queen, CDXXXII (December 18, 1968), n.p. [between pages 32 & 33].

7952 _____. "The Captain's Daughter," New Yorker, XLV (December 27, 1969), 28-32.

7953 _____. "Chatty," New Yorker, XLIV (April 13, 1968), 42-50.

7954 _____. "Creative Writing," New American Review, no. 6 (April 1969), 165-175.

7955 _____. "Debt of Honor," New Yorker, XLIII (December 30, 1967), 27-34.

7956 _____. "The Honeymoon," Harper's Magazine, CCXXXIII (February 1966), 59-65.

7957 _____. "The Nest Builder," New Yorker, XLI (December 11, 1965), 61-65.

7958 _____. "The Nest Builder," Nova, (July 1966), 88-90.

7959 _____. "Our Oldest Friend," Encounter, XXXIII (July 1969), 17-23.

7960 _____. "The Skeleton," New Yorker, XLIII (March 5, 1966), 44-50, 52, 54, 57, 58, 60, 65-66, 68, 71-72, 74, 76-78.

7961 Proctor, Roy. "Confessions of a Happily Married Man," Approach, no. 63 (Spring 1967), 23-34.

7962 _____. "Duodenum," DeKalb Literary Arts Journal, II (Summer 1968), 30-37.

7963 _____. "Sunday Morning," Midwestern University Quarterly, II, no. 4 (1967), 57-86.

7964 Proskurin, Pyotr. "The Sixth Night," Margaret Wettlin, trans., Soviet Literature, (no. 11, 1969), 3-52.

7965 Proulx, E. A. "Thief," Seventeen, XXV (October 1966), 128-129, 200-203.

7966 Pryce, D. J. "Katherine," New Zealand Listener, (January 20, 1967), 6.

7967 Pryce-Jones, David. "On the Way to St. Catherine's," Cornhill Magazine, CLXXVII (Summer 1969), 313-322.

7968 Przezdziecki, Jerzy. "Moving Stones/Against the Sun," Roger Tait, trans., Scottish International, no. 8 (October 1969), 7.

7969 _____. "Moving Stones/From the Old Arabian Legend," Roger Tait, trans., Scottish International, no. 8 (October 1969), 6.

7970 ______. "Moving Stones/The Great Performance," Roger Tait, trans., Scottish International, no. 8 (October 1969), 11.

7971 ______. "Moving Stones/The Hands," Roger Tait, trans., Scottish International, no. 8 (October 1969), 10.

7972 ______. "Moving Stones/The Roof," Roger Tait, trans., Scottish International, no. 8 (October 1969), 8-9.

7973 Publow, Richard. "A Patron of the Marks," Pegasus, IV, no. 1 (1966), 5-12.

7974 Pucay, Alfred C. "The Silence of an Afternoon," Solidarity, I (January-March 1966), 81-87.

7975 ______. "Tomorrow: A Simple Heartache," Diliman Review, XIV (January 1966), 43-58.

7976 Pudumaipithan. "Cavern of Enlightenment," V. S. Maniam, trans., Indian Literature, XII (June 1969), 27-32.

7977 Puechner, Ray. "The Junk Man," Dare, VI (January-February 1968), 40-43.

7978 Pulaski, Jack. "A Midget Epic," Goddard Journal, II (Winter 1968), 36-39.

7979 Purdy, Andrew James. "Master of the Courts," The Smith, no. 10 (December 1968), 8-53.

7980 Purdy, James. "Mr. Cough Syrup and the Phantom Sex," December, VIII (1966), 175-177.

7981 ______. "Mr. Evening," Harper's Bazaar, CI (September 1968), 268-271, 178, 180, 184, 186, 192, 194.

7982 ______. "Mr. Evening," New Directions 21, (1969), 30-49.

7983 ______. "Scrap of Paper," Evergreen Review, XI (August 1967), 22-25, 81-82.

7984 ______. "Scrap of Paper," New Directions 20, (1968), 35-44.

7985 Purdy, Ken W. [untitled], Playboy, XIII (October 1966), 109, 202-203.

7986 ______. "The Antine Bay Magenta," Playboy, XV (August 1968), 95.

7987 ______. "Big Daddy Says Yes, Big Daddy Says No," Playboy, XV (December 1968), 141.

7988 _____. "Chronicle of an Event," Playboy, XIII (April 1966), 84-86, 88, 220, 222-223.

7989 _____. "The Dannold Cheque," Playboy, XVI (September 1969), 162-164, 264-265.

7990 _____. "Friendship," Playboy, XII (August 1965), 109.

7991 _____. "Hello, Charlie, Goodbye," Playboy, XIII (August 1966), 62-64, 72.

7992 _____. "Long Way Up, Short Way Down," Playboy, XIV (November 1967), 107, 112, 234-236.

7993 _____. "Shall We Go Under the Ice Together?" Playboy, XV (October 1968), 124-126, 148, 176-178.

7994 _____. "Testimony Concerning Edward Darwin Caparell," Playboy, XIV (September 1967), 121, 160, 236-238.

7995 _____. "This Time, Tomorrow," Playboy, XII (February 1965), 62-64, 172-174.

7996 Purpi, Jo Ann. "Of Bubble Gum and Salt Tears," Quarterly, LXIV (Fall 1967), 11-14.

7997 Putrament, Jerzy. "Holy Bullet," Jerzy Hummel, trans., Literary Review, X (Spring 1967), 299-314.

7998 Puzo, Mario. "First Sundays," Redbook, CXXX (February 1968), 90-91, 139-140, 142-143.

7999 _____. "The Godfather," Cosmopolitan, CLXVII (August 1969), 122-131.

8000 Pynchon, Thomas. "The Shrink Flips," Cavalier, XVI (March 1966), 32-33, 88-92.

8001 _____. "The World (This One), the Flesh (Mrs. Oedipa Maas), and the Testament of Pierce Inverarity," Esquire, LXIV (December 1965), 170-173, 296, 298-303.

8002 Pyros, J. "September 21st," The Fair, II (Winter 1967), 15-17.

8003 Quammen, David. "The Sucker-Puncher," Yale Literary Magazine, CXXXV (January 1967), 12-19.

8004 Quartesan, Sergio. "The Apartment House," Frances Frenaye, trans., Chelsea, nos. 18/19 (June 1966), 89-108.

8005 Queen, Ellery. "The House of Brass," Redbook, CXXX (January 1968), 127-153.

8006 _____. "The Little Spy," Cavalier, XV (January 1965), 54-56.

8007 Queneau, Raymond. "from The Bark Tree," Barbara Wright, trans., Transatlantic Review, no. 29 (Summer 1968), 11-13.

8008 _____. "from Exercises in Style," Barbara Wright, trans., 0 to 9, no. 2 (August 1967), 37-48.

8009 _____. "A Multiple Choice Story," Dale McConathy, trans., Harper's Bazaar, CII (November 1968), 210-211.

8010 Quertermous, Max. "Night Train to Memphis," University Review, XXXV (Winter 1968), 106-112.

8011 Quick, Robb. "Present," Pegasus, III (Spring 1965), 32-37.

8012 Quin, Ann. "Every Cripple Has His Own Way of Walking," Nova, (December 1966), 125, 127, 129, 133, 135.

8013 _____ and Robert Sward. "Living in the Present," Ambit, no. 34 (1968), 20-21.

8014 _____. "Motherlogue," Transatlantic Review, no. 32 (Summer 1969), 101-105.

8015 _____. "Tripticks," Ambit, no. 35 (1968), 9-16.

8016 Quindsland, Ann Cecilia. "Memories," William and Mary Review, VII (Spring 1969), 84-86.

8017 Quinn, Dennis. "Oktoberfest," Nexus (San Francisco, Calif.), II (September-October 1965), 38-39.

8018 Quinn, James K. "A Kind of Christmas," Jeopardy, no. 5 (Spring 1969), 201-204.

8019 Quinn, Kevin. "O'Keel and the Substitute Devil," Ave Maria, CIII (March 12, 1966), 24-28.

8020 Quirk, John. "The Rookie," Saturday Evening Post, CCXXXVIII (November 20, 1965), 64-65, 68, 70-72, 74-76, 78, 80-82.

8021 _____. "The Rookie (Conclusion)," Saturday Evening Post, CCXXXVIII (December 4, 1965), 56-60, 64-70, 72-73.

8022 Rabeei, M. "The Deaf-Mute," Maliha Ansari, trans., Vision, XV (December 1966), 20-22, 52.

8023 Rabkin, Eric S. "Last Wednesday and Then Sunday," Epoch, XVII (Fall 1967), 57-61.

8024 Radcliff, Donald. "Song of the Simidor," Literary Review, X (Winter 1966-1967), 204-230.

8025 Rader, Dotsun. "Chapter 69/from a forthcoming novel," Bones, no. 1 (Fall 1967), 14-17.

8026 _____. "David Cartwright," Evergreen Review, XIII (May 1969), 30-32, 78-82.

8027 _____. "Government-Inspected Meat," Evergreen Review, XIII (November 1969), 28-30, 32-33, 63-65.

8028 _____. "White Death," Bones, no. 2 (Winter 1968-69), 42-43.

8029 Radichkov, Yordan. "High Noon," Obzor, (no. 4, 1968), 32-47, 49-54.

8030 Radin, N. M. S. "An Academic Mirror," The Cantuarian, (August 1967), 451-452.

8031 _____. "Lament of a Large City," The Cantuarian, (December 1967), 27-28.

8032 _____. "Such Beautiful Artificial Hands," The Cantuarian, (April 1968), 104.

8033 Rådström, Pär. "The Story of Jock," Walter Foote, trans., Literary Review, IX (Winter 1965-66), 290-295.

8034 Radványi, Ervin. "From Bed to Bed to Bed," New Hungarian Quarterly, IX (Autumn 1968), 138-142.

8035 Rae, George William. "The Glass Man," Approach, no. 55 (Spring 1965), 4-14.

8036 Raes, Hugo. "Boom in Benelux," Christopher Levenson, trans., Delta (Amsterdam), XI (Winter 1968-69), 26-33.

8037 Raffel, Burton. "The Lady of the Lake," Texas Quarterly, XI (Spring 1968), 171-183.

8038 Raffel, Mia. "Snailsfeet," New Directions 21, (1969), 116-127.

8039 Rafferty, Michael. "The Voice of a Young Woman," University Review, XXXV (Spring 1969), 197-202.

8040 Rahanujan, Shouri. "from The Yellow Fish," Chicago Review, XX (November 1968), 50-80.

8041 Raiguel, Philip. "Journal of the Killer Crows," Jeopardy, no. 5 (Spring 1969), 74-79.

8042 Rainov, Bogomil. "And the Blue Flowers," Obzor, (Winter 1967), 20-30.

8043 Rajani, Karl. "Why Lord Ganesh Has an Elephant's Head," Expression, no. 1 (1968), 16-17.

8044 Rajaram, Madhurantakam. "Life Donor," B. Syamala Rao, trans., Triveni, XXXIV (April 1965), 33-46.

8045 Rajaratnam, S. "The Tiger," Literature East and West, X (December 1966), 368-373.

8046 Rakhim, Ibraghim. "Destiny/(Chapters from the Novel)," Alice Ingman, trans., Soviet Literature, (no. 12, 1967), 48-81.

8047 Rákosy, Gergely. "The Cobweb," New Hungarian Quarterly, VI (Summer 1965), 104-121.

8048 Ramkumar. "The Sounds," R. S. Yadav, trans., Indian Literature, VIII, no. 2 (1965), 28-37.

8049 Ramon-Fortune, B. "Voice of an Oyster," Bim, XII (July-December 1968), 146-150.

8050 Ramsden, J. D. "Slave October," Plaintiff, IV (Fall-Winter 1967-68), 42-44.

8051 Ramsey, Robert. "In the Corncrib," Red Clay Reader, no. 3 (1966), 15-17.

8052 _____. "A Sadness of the Head," Man About Town, I (June/July 1967), 16-20.

8053 Ranck, Helen. "A Winter Morning," Michigan Quarterly Review, VIII (Winter 1969), 45-48.

8054 Randal, Narena. "And So I Sing," Landfall, no. 82 (June 1967), 171-189.

8055 _____. "Chaplinesque," Landfall, no. 76 (December 1975), 339-341.

8056 _____. "The Garage," Landfall, no. 86 (June 1968), 181-198.

8057 Randall, Dudley. "Incident on a Bus," Negro Digest, XIV (August 1965), 70-71.

8058 _____. "Victoria," Negro Digest, XV (May 1966), 64-72.

8059 Randall, Florence Engel. "First Chill," Redbook, CXXIX (October 1967), 76-77.

8060 ______. "Happy Birthday to You," Ladies' Home Journal, LXXXVI (April 1969), 88-89, 147-149.

8061 ______. "No One Kicks Cans Any More," Redbook, CXXIV (April 1965), 74-75.

8062 ______. "The Place of Sapphires," Cosmopolitan, CLXV (November 1968), 160-166, 168, 170-172, 174, 176-177, 183-190.

8063 ______. "So Near to Me," Good Housekeeping, CLX (January 1965), 64-65, 146, 148.

8064 ______. "Wait for My Call," Cosmopolitan, CLVIII (February 1969), 108, 110-111.

8065 ______. "The Watchers," Harper's Magazine, CCXXX (March 1965), 96-98, 100-101, 104.

8066 Randall, Margaret. "Another Look at the Tarot," El Corno Emplumado, no. 15 (July 1965), 137-138.

8067 ______. "Birth," West Coast Review, III (Fall 1968), 25-29.

8068 ______. "Birth I," Vincent the Mad Brother of Theo, no. 1 (1966), 1-3.

8069 ______. "The Black, Market," Minnesota Review, VIII (1968), 126-130.

8070 ______. "Shoe Shine Boy," Negro Digest, XV (September 1966), 53-55.

8071 ______. "Unside," El Corno Emplumado, no. 15 (July 1965), 135-137.

8072 Randall, Virginia Powell. "The Centurion," Columbia, XLIX (April 1969), 24-27.

8073 Randolph, William. "from One Moving Part," Consumption, II (Spring 1969), 15-17.

8074 Ranieri, Nick. [untitled], Arx, I (February 1968), 7-10.

8075 ______. "Riddles, Rhythm and Cat," Latitudes, II (Spring 1968), 22-26.

8076 ______. "Still Life," Arx, II (July 1968), 8-12.

8077 Rao, Dhanikonda Hanumanta. "Acid Test," D. Venkata Rao, trans., Treveni, XXXVIII (April 1969), 42-47.

8078 Raper, Jack. "Winter Wrappings," South Carolina Review,

II (November 1969), 38-48.

8079 Rascoe, Judith. "The Mother of Good Fortune," Atlantic Monthly, CCXXIII (June 1969), 84-88, 90.

8080 Rascovich, Mark. "The Eagles," Saturday Evening Post, CCXXXIX (January 29, 1966), 54-56, 58-65, 68.

8081 ______. "The Haunted Battleground," Saturday Evening Post, CCXXXIX (February 12, 1966), 50-52, 56-58, 61-64, 66-67.

8082 ______. "The Russians Who Came for Christmas," Mademoiselle, LXVIII (December 1968), 102-105, 144-147, 149-154.

8083 Rasmussen, Jorgen G. "The Jury in the Ball-Room," Wisconsin Review, III (Spring 1968), 30-32.

8084 Rasputin, Valentin. "Money for Maria," Margaret Wettlin, trans., Soviet Literature, (no. 4, 1969), 42-127.

8085 Rath, Roger. "Swanee Sings It When He Flies," Midwestern University Quarterly, II, no. 2 (1966), 1-17.

8086 Rauf, Abdur. "Dilbar Khan's Exploits," Pakistan Review, XIV (November 1966), 34-36.

8087 ______. "Mother," Pakistan Review, XV (March 1967), 19-20.

8088 ______. "Not All Lavender," Pakistan Review, XIII (September 1965), 36-38.

8089 Raushenbush, Burns. "A Day in March," West Coast Review, II (Spring 1967), 5-9.

8090 Ravel, Aviva. "About Face," Canadian Forum, XLVII (October 1967), 151-154.

8091 Ravignant, Patrick. "An Edge on Darkness," Queen, CDXXV (August 11, 1965), 54-56.

8092 Ravitch, Mark M. "Letter to a Colleague," Esquire, LXVII (June 1967), 106-107, 184-186, 188.

8093 Rawak, Pate S. "Adults Only," Lance, V (Spring 1965), 9-12.

8094 Rawlings, Marjorie Kinnan. "Fish Fry and Fireworks," Florida Quarterly, I (Summer 1967), 1-18.

8095 Raworth, Tom. "The Relationship," Solstice, no. 1 (1966), 28.

8096 _____. "from A Serial Biography," Solstice, no. 3 (1966), 40-41.

8097 _____. "A Serial Biography," Wivenhoe Park Review, no. 1 (Winter 1965), 2-12.

8098 Rawson, Nick. "Texts," New Writers, no. 3 (1965), 63-98.

8099 Ray, David. "The Brawl & Two Burgers," Epoch, XVII (Winter 1968), 157-162.

8100 _____. "The Thirty-Eight Page Letter F. Kafka Once Wrote," Epoch, XIV (Spring 1965), 208-216.

8108 Rayfield, Fred. "The President's Golden Zipper/A Fable," Avant Garde, no. 6 (January 1969), 38-41.

8102 Raynor, Owen. "The Playmate," Readers & Writers, I (April-May 1967), 24-29.

8103 Raza, Hassan. "The Gentleman," Pakistan Review, XVI (July 1968), 33.

8104 Reacher, M. H. "Aunt Matilda's Cat," The Cantuarian, (April 1968), 106.

8105 Reams, Christine. "The Game," Negro Digest, XVII (March 1968), 54-63.

8106 Reaves, Verne. "Winter Notes from a Summer Soldier," December, VII (1965), 39-50.

8107 Rebreanu, Vasile. "The Colt," Literary Review, X (Summer 1967), 561-562.

8108 Rebsamen, Frederick. "The True Story of Billy Buckles," Malahat Review, no. 2 (April 1967), 11-15.

8109 Rechy, John. "By the Motel Pool," Evergreen Review, XI (December 1967), 30-32, 91-92.

8110 _____. "Returning to Los Angeles," London Magazine, VIII (June 1968), 36-56.

8111 Redfield, Malissa. "A Sense of Happiness," Ladies' Home Journal, LXXXIII (July 1966), 63-70.

8112 Reed, Jack. "Once Time Again," Harvard Advocate, CII (Fall 1968), 6-8.

8113 Reed, John R. "Love Story," Ante, IV (Summer-Fall 1968), 37-40.

8114 Reed, Kit. "As Things Were," Cosmopolitan, CLIX (September 1965), 91-92, 94.

8115 _____. "At Central," Seventeen, XXVII (June 1968), 110-111, 146, 150, 152.

8116 _____. "Cynosure," Nova, (February 1967), 80-81, 83, 85-86.

8117 _____. "Sully's Men," Cosmopolitan, CLVIII (February 1965), 103, 105-107.

8118 _____. "The Weddings," Ladies' Home Journal, LXXXVI (November 1969), 100-101, 152-155.

8119 Reese, Joe. "The Day We Sold the Farm," Southwest Review, LII (Winter 1967), 45-51.

8120 Reese, John. "Double Exposure," Playboy, XII (February 1965), 116, 120, 142-143.

8121 Reeves, Campbell. "A Criss-Cross of Cousins," Long View Journal, I (Winter 1968), 59-69.

8122 Reeves, Doug. "A Shonuff Real Man," DeKalb Literary Arts Journal, III (Spring 1969), 1-11.

8123 Rege, P. S. "Savitri," Kumad Mehta, trans., Indian Literature, XI (January-March 1968), 77-91.

8124 _____. "Savitri," Kumad Mehta, trans., Indian Literature, XI (April-July 1968), 77-99.

8125 Regnier, Nita. "The Near End," Redbook, CXXXII (April 1969), 96-97, 134-135.

8126 _____. "An Opening of Doors," Redbook, CXXXIV (November 1969), 159-181.

8127 _____. "A Small, Completing Step," Redbook, CXXXI (August 1968), 68-69, 135-137.

8128 _____. "Someone Special," Redbook, CXXXIII (May 1969), 78-79, 129, 131.

8129 Rehder, Jesse. "The Surgeon," Lillabulero, I (Winter 1967), 1-15.

8130 Rehn, Jens. "A Sweet Tooth," George Raymond Selden, trans. Scala International, (November 1966), 34-36.

8131 Reid, Alastair. "My Friend Wainscott," Playboy, XII (February 1965), 107.

8132 Reid, Joyce. "Neville's Fire Brigade," New Zealand Listener, LII (May 14, 1965), 5, 16.

8133 ______. "The Wedding Guest," New Zealand Listener, (March 3, 1967), 6, 14.

8134 Reifler, Samuel. "Lululu," Chelsea, no. 17 (August 1965), 45-57.

8135 ______. "Nocturnes and Reveilles for My Son," Harper's Bazaar, CI (March 1968), 166-167, 104, 106, 108, 110-111, 113, 114.

8136 Reinbold, James. "Recollections of Rolf Lederer and Ramon Cabinas," Greensboro Review, no. 7 (Summer-Fall 1969), 22-30.

8137 Reinhardt, Diane Drew. "The Downcome," Yale Literary Magazine, CXXXV (May 1967), 12-16.

8138 Reinhardt, James M. "The Stranger," Prairie Schooner, XLIII (Fall 1969), 298-299.

8139 Remmerde, Joe. "A Time of Returning," Things, no. 3 (Spring 1966), 24-37.

8140 Remsbury, J. A. "John Pim's Crooked Eye," Focus (Singapore), New Series, no. 1 (1967), 28-34.

8141 Renard, Jules. "The Jewel," Elizabeth Roget, trans., Harper's Bazaar, XCIX (May 1966), 140.

8142 Renek, Morris. "Siam Miami," Cosmopolitan, CLXVII (July 1969), 108-111, 122-123.

8143 Rennie, Peter. "I Could Kill Someone," New Zealand Listener, (December 22, 1967), 6.

8144 Renno, Peter. "A Rose Is More than a Rose," Cimarron Review, no. 2 (December 1967), 4-15.

8145 Reno, Raymond H. "In Manila Once," Ave Maria, CI (January 2, 1965), 20-23.

8146 ______. "The Users," Ave Maria, CI (June 19, 1965), 20-24.

8147 ______. "The Winter," Ave Maria, CII (July 31, 1965), 22-26.

8148 Rense, Paige. "Ciao, Sherry!" Cosmopolitan, CLXIII (November 1967), 144-149.

8149 Resnik, Henry. "Another Sex Triangle," Vogue, CL (September 1, 1967), 345, 351, 353.

8150 Ressner, Lydia. "The Silver Teapot Is at the Bottom of the Sea," Quarterly Review of Literature, XV (1968), 410-422.

8151 Revelli, George. "Commander Amanda Nightingale," Evergreen Review, XIII (January 1969), 24-29, 62-67.

8152 Rexroad, Gregory. Itzã," North American Review, IV (January 1967), 29-33.

8153 Reyburn, Wallace. "The Illiterate Angels," Queen, CDXXV (Christmas Issue, 1965), 124.

8154 Reynolds, David. "Intermezzo," Quarry, XVIII (Spring 1969), 23-28.

8155 _____. "Out of the Morning Shade," Quarry, XVII (Summer 1968), 18-31.

8156 Reynolds, Lawrence Judson. "Jacob and the Faith Healer," Greensboro Review, III (Winter 1967), 24-36.

8157 _____. "Love," Greensboro Review, I (May 1966), 62-75.

8158 _____. "One Dominique'r Hen," Greensboro Review, II (December 1966), 30-38.

8159 _____. "Secrets," New Orleans Review, I (Spring 1969), 259-261.

8160 _____. "The Stick Matchman," Carolina Quarterly, XIX (Winter 1967), 53-57.

8161 _____. "That Grand Canyon," Intro, no. 1 (September 1968), 87-103.

8162 _____. "To Sleep in Such a Bed," Greensboro Review, IV (Spring 1969), 57-70.

8163 Reynolds, Louise. "Neighbors in the Gutter," New Renaissance, I (Fall 1968), 44-49.

8164 Rhamon, C. A. "October Child," Roanoke Review, III (Fall 1969), 39-49.

8165 Rheyns, Randolph. "After the Ball," Harvard Advocate, CI (December 1967), 13-17.

8166 Rhoades, Virginia N. "Mauds' Ming," Sewanee Review, LXXVI (January-March 1968), 90-105.

8167 Rhode, R. Hamilton. "The Editor's Girl," UMD Humanist,

XIII (Spring 1965), 29-35.

8168 Rhodin, Eric. "Ugly Man," Seventeen, XXV (October 1966), 114-115, 187-189.

8169 Rhys, Jean. "I Spy a Stranger," Art and Literature, no. 8 (Spring 1966), 41-53.

8170 _____. "The Lotus," Art and Literature, no. 11 (Winter 1967), 165-174.

8171 _____. "The Sound of the River," Art and Literature, no. 9 (Summer 1966), 192-197.

8172 _____. "Temps perdi," Art and Literature, no. 12 (Spring 1967), 121-138.

8173 Rich, Barbara. "The Gift," Redbook, CXXVIII (January 1967), 52-53.

8174 Richard, Adrienne. "One Christmas in Montana," Harper's Magazine, CCXXXI (December 1965), 102-106.

8175 Richards, Caroline. "Telegram from Mr. Smooth," Seventeen, XXV (August 1966), 278-279, 420-423.

8176 Richards, Virginia Rotan. "Saturday Matinee," Grecourt Review, XI (May 1968), 54-65.

8177 Richardson, Dorothy. "March Moonlight," Harper's Bazaar, C (November 1967), 182, 154, 160, 162, 164, 166, 174, 176.

8178 Richardson, William. "Dream on the Mountain," California Review, no. 1 (Spring 1967), 19-27.

8179 _____. "The Wound/Excerpt from a Novel in Progress," California Review, no. 2 (Spring 1968), 14-22.

8180 Richie, Donald. "Bodo, the Priest," Evergreen Review, XI (April 1967), 67, 105-106.

8181 Richie, Mary. "Hunt and Destroy," New American Review, no. 6 (April 1969), 64-68.

8182 Richler, Mordecai. "Dinner with Ormsby-Fletcher," New American Review, no. 1 (1967), 70-80.

8183 _____. "A Liberal Education," Paris Review, XI (Winter-Spring 1968), 55-65.

8184 _____. "St. Urbain's Horseman," Tamarack Review, no. 41 (Autumn 1966), 137-142, 145-150, 153-156, 159-160.

8185 _____. "This Year at the Arabian Night's Hotel," Tamarack Review, no. 47 (Spring 1968), 9-18.

8186 Richmond, Jane. "Slides," New Yorker, XLII (November 26, 1966), 188-190.

8187 Richter, Tellmond. "The Million Dollar Salesman," University Review, XXXIII (Summer 1967), 243-251.

8188 Ridenour, Ron. "Affluency's Answer," Ball State University Forum, X (Autumn 1969), 21-26.

8189 Riding, Laura. "A Last Lesson in Geography," Art and Literature, no. 6 (Autumn 1965), 28-43.

8190 Rieger, Catherine. "Survival Test," Redbook, CXXX (November 1967), 157, 159-185.

8191 Rieth, Marian. "Acts of Corporal Charity," Seventeen, XXV (July 1966), 90-91, 146-147.

8192 _____. "The Lake-Lover," Seventeen, XXIV (September 1965), 138-139, 241-243.

8193 _____. "No Boy. I'm a Girl!" Seventeen, XXVI (March 1967), 132-133, 180, 182, 184, 186.

8194 _____. "Pitch, Pass and Dribble," Seventeen, XXIV (March 1965), 154, 222-227.

8195 Rifa'yah, Yaseen. "Paralysis," Maliha Ansari, trans., Vision, XVI (October 1967), 25, 30.

8196 Rigby, Peter and Gideon Senyagwa. "The Tale of the Ungrateful Grandfather," Transition, VI, no. 28 (1967), 34-36.

8197 Riley, Brett. "Sidney and the Dogs," Atlantic Monthly, CCXX (December 1967), 70-74.

8198 Rilke, Rainer Maria. "The Eleventh Dream," Miguel Gonzalez-Gerth, trans., Trace, no. 57 (Summer 1965), 133-134.

8199 Rima. "Bari Haveli," Pakistan Review, XIV (April 1966), 34-38.

8200 _____. "'The Dirge of the Stones'," Pakistan Review, XIV (January 1966), 38-41.

8201 _____. "The Mask," Pakistan Review, XIV (March 1966), 27, 32.

8202 _____. "Youth," Pakistan Review, XIV (October 1966), 21, 38.

8203 Rindfleisch, Norval. "A Cliff of Fall," Epoch, XVIII (Fall 1968), 87-107.

8204 _____. "The Summer of His Discontent," Literary Review, XI (Autumn 1967), 13-26.

8205 Ringer, Vivian. "A Simple No," Redbook, CXXV (May 1965), 52-53, 108, 110, 112.

8206 Ristikivi, Karl. "The Seventh Witness," Literary Review, VIII (Spring 1965), 383-392.

8207 Ritchie, Bill. "The Great Game," Limbo, I (February 1965), 2-13.

8208 Ritchie, Elisavietta. "The Eel," Ann Arbor Review, nos. 5 & 6 (1969), 63-66.

8209 Ritchie, Jack. "Gemini 74," Signature, I (February 1966), 28.

8210 _____. "Hot Air Pilot," Signature, II (June 1967), 34-36, 76, 84, 86.

8211 _____. "Put Your Head upon My Knee," Signature, II (August 1967), 16.

8212 _____. "Six-Second Hero," Signature, II (May 1967), 20.

8213 Ritchie, Malcolm. "Saliva from the Stage of the New Live Deathshow/And/or Stained Notices to the Harmschool's Inductionboard/And/or All the World's a Cage," Transatlantic Review, no. 30 (Autumn 1968), 90-95.

8214 Riter, Faye. "The Rim of Reality," Epoch, XVII (Winter 1968), 99-108.

8215 Ritter Aislán, Eduardo. "Carmela's Marriage," Américas, XXI (July 1969), 32-34.

8216 Rive, Richard. "Middle Passage," Contrast (Cape Town, South Africa), no. 21 (August 1969), 37-44.

8217 Rivers, Conrad Kent. "Chinese Food," Negro Digest, XV (October 1966), 53-56.

8218 Robbe-Grillet, Alain. "L'Immortelle," Lane Dunlop, trans., Harper's Bazaar, XCIX (March 1966), 206, 255-256, 263.

8219 _____. "From: La Maison de Rendez-vous," Richard Howard, trans., Evergreen Review, X (October 1966), 50-53, 92.

8220 Robbins, Jhan. "Runaway Husband," Woman's Day, (July 1967), 64-65, 80, 82, 85-86.

8221 Robbins, Maggie. "Three Exemplary Adventures and Addenda," Silo, no. 7 (Spring 1965), 40-49.

8222 Robbins, Margaret. "The Collection," New Zealand Listener, LXI (August 8, 1969), 12.

8223 Roberts, John. "The Purse," Nexus, I (August 1967), 21-22.

8224 Roberts, Neil. "Diane," Delta (Cambridge, England), no. 44 (October 1968), 40-42.

8225 Roberts, Phyllis. "The Way to the Lions," Ante, II (Winter 1966), 5-17.

8226 Roberts, Randall. "Angels and God," Nimrod, IX (Winter 1965), 24-27.

8227 Roberts, Sheila. "Next Time," Contrast (Cape Town, South Africa), no. 20 (March 1969), 11-16.

8228 _____. "A Small Change," Contrast (Cape Town, South Africa), no. 22 (December 1969), 58-62.

8229 _____. "The Touch of Your Hand," Contrast (Cape Town, South Africa), no. 19 (November 1968), 67-73.

8230 Robin, Ralph. "In Woods and Fastnesses," Encounter, XXXI (August 1968), 17-21.

8231 _____. "Lamina 96," Encounter, XXVII (October 1966), 46-50.

8232 _____. "The Night Visitors," Massachusetts Review, VIII (Summer 1967), 421-429.

8233 _____. "Oh, I Had to Call Bayard," Carleton Miscellany, X (Winter 1969), 2-12.

8234 _____. "When Everything Falls Apart Be Polite," Encounter, XXIX (November 1967), 28-33.

8235 Robins, Corinne. "The Bar/(Novel Excerpt)," For Now, no. 5 (c. 1966-68), 57-65.

8236 _____. "The View from St. Luke's," El Corno Emplumado, no. 18 (April 1966), 130-138.

8237 _____. "The View from St. Luke's," For Now, no. 4 (c. 1966-68), 44-52.

8238 Robins, Edmund. "Nice Knowing You," Mexico Quarterly Review, III, no. 1 (1968), 48-53.

8239 _____. "A Primitive," Mexico Quarterly Review, III, no. 2 (1968), 61-69.

8240 Robinson, Barbara. "Almost Any Friday," McCall's, XCVI (June 1969), 72-73, 130-131.

8241 _____. "The Bed," McCall's, XCIII (October 1965), 134-135, 172, 174, 176.

8242 _____. "Big White Naked Bird," McCall's, XCV (November 1967), 104-105, 139, 141-142.

8243 _____. "The Christmas Pageant," McCall's, XCV (December 1967), 112-113, 175-176, 178.

8244 _____. "The Fainter," McCall's, XCIII (September 1966), 76-77, 177-179.

8245 _____. "For Everything a Season," McCall's, XCII (September 1965), 104-105, 136, 138.

8246 _____. "Happy Birthdays," McCall's, XCVII (October 1969), 104-105, 141-142.

8247 _____. "The Last Time Home," McCall's, XCIV (November 1966), 120-121, 188-190, 192.

8248 _____. "Louisa May and the Facts of Life," Redbook, CXXXII (April 1969), 92-93, 154, 156-157, 159.

8249 _____. "'Mrs. Carroway, My Name Is Peabody, and I Represent...'," McCall's, XCIII (July 1966), 78-79, 128-129.

8250 _____. "Pie in the Morning," McCall's, XCIII (August 1966), 62-65, 137-149.

8251 _____. "Really? At Your Age?" McCall's, XCVI (February 1969), 96-97, 127-128.

8252 _____. "Someone to Love," McCall's, XCIII (March 1966), 88-89, 164-168.

8253 _____. "Surprise Package," McCall's, XCIII (December 1965), 112-113, 170, 172-175.

8254 _____. "The Trouble with Parents," McCall's, XCV (May 1968), 94-95, 131-135.

8255 _____. "That Day When I Was Lost," Good Housekeeping,

CLXI (October 1965), 84-85, 256-262.

8256 _____. "A Thousand Miles Across the Street," Good Housekeeping, CLX (June 1965), 82-83, 197-199, 204, 206-207.

8257 Robinson, Bill. "Herbert Haynes," Coraddi, (Fall 1968), 19.

8258 Robinson, Donald. "Dragons!" Approach, no. 60 (Summer 1966), 42-44.

8259 Robinson, Frank M. "A Life in the Day Of," Playboy, XVI (June 1969), 153-154, 212-213.

8260 _____. "The Wreck of the Ship John B.," Playboy, XIV (June 1967), 80-84, 92, 208, 210, 212-216, 218-220.

8261 Robinson, Fred. "Chimera," Assay, XXIV (Spring 1968), 38-44.

8262 _____. "Chimera," Minnesota Review, VIII (1968), 312-316.

8263 _____. "Ernie," Assay, XXII (Spring 1966), 5-6.

8264 _____. "Jim," Assay, XXV (Spring 1969), 29-33.

8265 _____. "Oyster," Consumption, I (Fall 1967), 11-15.

8266 Robinson, Louie. "Jacob's Dilemma," Negro Digest, XIV (April 1965), 84-88.

8267 Robinson, Sondra Till. "Aunt Izzy's Teeth," Redbook, CXXXI (August 1968), 121-123.

8268 Robitaille, Gerald. "The Last and Final Revelation," El Corno Emplumado, no. 17 (January 1966), 26.

8269 Roces, Alejandro R. "Of Cocks and Choreographers," Solidarity, I (October-December 1966), 105-124.

8270 Rochberg, Paul. "The Silver Talons of Piero Kostrov," Chelsea, no. 17 (August 1965), 6-24.

8271 Roche, Maurice. "Crossing," Harry Matthews, trans., Paris Review, XI (Fall 1968), 129-142.

8272 Rock, E. S. "Home," North American Review, III (May 1966), 30-33.

8273 _____. "Storm," Western Humanities Review, XX (Summer 1966), 213-218.

8274 _____. "Tramontane," The Smith, no. 8 (March 1968), 47-75.

8275 _____. "Tramontane (Part II)," The Smith, no. 10 (December 1968), 100-120.

8276 Rodgers, Carolyn M. "Blackbird in a Cage," Negro Digest, XVI (August 1967), 66-71.

8277 _____. "A Statistic, Trying to Make It Home," Negro Digest, XVIII (June 1969), 68-71.

8278 Rodgers, Mary Augusta. "The Affectionate Divorce," Redbook, CXXIX (July 1967), 70-71, 112-113.

8279 _____. "Bless This House," Good Housekeeping, CLXV (August 1967), 69-71, 184, 186, 188, 190, 193-196, 198-200, 206-210, 216-220.

8280 _____. "One Moment to Cherish," Good Housekeeping, CLXII (February 1966), 78-79, 168, 170-172, 174.

8281 _____. "Success Story," Ladies' Home Journal, LXXXVI (October 1969), 86-87, 152-154.

8282 _____. "This Time Last Year," Redbook, CXXVIII (January 1967), 48-49, 84-87.

8283 Rodgers, Nancy. "The Cruise," Grecourt Review, VIII (April 1965), 21-23.

8284 Roditi, Edouard. "The Boulissa's Pilgrimage," Literary Review, XI (Autumn 1967), 39-45.

8285 Rodriguez, William V. "The Naked Man," Minnesota Review, IX (1969), 206-212.

8286 [No entry.]

8287 Roecker, William A. "Answer for Another Question," Wisconsin Review, III (Spring 1968), 20-23.

8288 _____. "Big Iron," Per/Se, III (Summer 1968), 22-26.

8289 _____. "Float Fever," Intro, no. 1 (September 1968), 125-33.

8290 _____. "Wet Track," Northwest Review, VIII (Sum. 1966), 70-7.

8291 Rogen, Peter. "The Other Harry," Yale Literary Magazine, CXXXV (November 1966), 10-16.

8292 Rogers, Patrick W. "The Only Way," Foxfire, I (Spring 1967), 62-69.

8293 Rogers, Ronald. "The Angry Truck," South Dakota Review,

VII (Summer 1969), 114-118.

8294 Rogin, Gilbert. "Cheering Up Charley," New Yorker, XLIII (January 27, 1968), 32-37.

8295 _____. "How It Turns Out," New Yorker, XLV (November 15, 1969), 59-61.

8296 _____. "The Indoor Bird Watcher," New Yorker, XLII (April 2, 1966), 40-44.

8297 _____. "Lesser Married," New Yorker, XLI (February 27, 1965), 32-40.

8298 _____. "The Players," New Yorker, XLII (April 30, 1966), 40-43.

8299 _____. "A Short Novel," New Yorker, XLI (January 1, 1966), 28-34.

8300 _____. "Solving the World's Problems," New Yorker, XLIV (July 27, 1968), 29-30.

8301 _____. "The Something of the World," New Yorker, XLIV (March 2, 1968), 34-38.

8302 _____. "Time and Effort," New Yorker, XLV (April 19, 1969), 36-37.

8303 _____. "Them Apples," Weekend Telegraph, no. 111 (November 11, 1966), 61.

8304 _____. "To the Fjord Country," New Yorker, XLV (September 20, 1969), 39-41.

8305 _____. "Two Men of Affairs," New Yorker, XLIV (May 25, 1968), 33-35.

8306 _____. "An Uncompleted Investigation," New Yorker, XLII (July 9, 1966), 22-24.

8307 _____. "An Uncompleted Investigation, Furthered and Annotated," New Yorker, XLIII (March 4, 1967), 37-39.

8308 _____. "You Say What I Feel," New Yorker, XLV (July 12, 1969), 29-33.

8309 _____. "What We See Before Us," New Yorker, XLIV (July 6, 1968), 28-29.

8310 Rohde, Barbara. "A Frog Called Mystery," Redbook, CXXIV (February 1965), 64-65.

8311 _____. "Katrin's Crusade," Redbook, CXXVI (November 1965), 64-65, 140-143.

8312 _____. "Rise Up and Hear the Bells," McCall's, XCIV (July 1967), 76-77, 128-130.

8313 Rojas, Carlos. "In Defense of Judas," H. E. Francis, trans., DeKalb Literary Arts Journal, I (Winter 1967), 1-10.

8314 Rolfe, Patricia. "The Eyes of the Church," Quadrant, XIII (May-June 1969), 51-59.

8315 Rolfs, Mary Jane. "The Enrichment of Artie Brown," Forum, VII (Summer 1969), 30-35.

8316 _____. "The Lonely Ones," Prairie Schooner, XLI (Fall 1967), 306-316.

8317 _____. "The Man Who Knew Everything," Redbook, CXXXIV (December 1969), 78-79, 158-160.

8318 _____. "The Star In the Cactus Garden," Forum, VII (Summer 1969), 36-42.

8319 _____. "This Day of Blessings," Good Housekeeping, CLXVII (November 1968), 92-93, 181-184, 186, 188, 190.

8320 _____. "To Meet My Beloved," Good Housekeeping, CLXIII (August 1966), 76-77, 184, 186-192.

8321 Rollow, David. "Dean and Frieda," Intro, no. 2 (September 1969), 9-43.

8322 Rolnikaite, Marija. "I Must Tell You," Avril Pyman, trans., Soviet Literature, (no. 12, 1965), 64-135.

8323 Roman, Howard. "How Was Everything in Cleveland?" Redbook, CXXX (February 1968), 92-93, 108-112.

8324 Rome, Florence. "Melanie's People," Cosmopolitan, CLVIII (January 1965), 85-88.

8325 Romuld, Conrad. "Me and Charlie and the Concen-trated Ground," Wascana Review, I, no. 2 (1966), 16-25.

8326 Ronai, Peter. "Mercenaries We," Nexus (San Francisco, Calif.), II (July-August 1965), 43-45.

8327 _____. "Wretches, Utter Wretches!" Dust, III (Fall 1967), 21-25.

8328 Ronayne, Maurice. "Be It Ever So Jumbled," Ave Maria, CIII (May 14, 1966), 27-28.

8329 Ronck, Ronn. "Shelby's Hill," Nimrod, X (Spring 1966), 12-14.

8330 Rooke, Leon. "Ancistrodon Priscivorus: Albion Gunther Jones and the Water Viper/Number Five in a Series of River Stories," Carolina Quarterly, XXI (Spring 1969), 4-16.

8331 _____. "Field Service Four Hundred Forty-Nine from the Five Hundred Field Songs of the Daughters of the Vieux Carré," Lillabulero, I (Fall 1967), 15-29.

8332 _____. "Further Adventures of a Cross Country Man," Carolina Quarterly, XIX (Spring 1967), 105-114.

8333 _____. "The Hatted Mannequins of 54th Street," Carolina Quarterly, XXI (Spring 1969), 65-82.

8334 _____. "The Ice House Gang," Carolina Quarterly, XVIII (Fall 1966), 5-9.

8335 _____. "Load Every Rift with One," Carolina Quarterly, XX (Fall 1968), 7-47.

8336 _____. "Sing Me No Love Songs, I'll Say You No Prayers," Epoch, XV (Winter 1966), 111-131.

8337 Rooney, Annie and Sinclair Beiles. "Alice in Progress," San Francisco Earthquake, I (Summer/Fall 1968), 60.

8338 _____ and Sinclair Beiles. "Bones," San Francisco Earthquake, I (Summer/Fall 1968), 60-61.

8339 _____ and S. Beiles. "Collectors Corner," VDRSVPVDRSVP-VDRSVPVDRSVP, (1969), n.p. [front page].

8340 _____ and Sinclair Beiles. "Extract from a Speech on the Cuban Problem," San Francisco Earthquake, I (Summer/Fall 1968), 63-64.

8341 _____ and Sinclair Beiles. "From 'Breakout'--A Study of One Year Olds in the Paris Literary World," San Francisco Earthquake, I (Summer/Fall 1968), 61-63.

8342 _____ and Sinclair Beiles. "Radio Cairo Reporting," San Francisco Earthquake, I (Summer/Fall 1968), 64-65.

8343 _____ and Sinclair Beiles. "Where to Find Alice in Progress," San Francisco Earthquake, I (Summer/Fall 1968), 65-66.

8344 Root, Judith. "The Good Wife," The Fiddlehead, no. 65 (Summer 1965), 35-44.

8345 Root, William Pitt. "Orpheo's Room," Assay, XXI (Spring 1965), 27-33.

8346 _____. "Orpheo's Room," Greensboro Review, I (May 1966), 76-82.

8347 _____. "That Poor Man," Intro, no. 2 (September 1969), 133-140.

8348 Roperos, Godofredo M. "The Father," Literature East and West, XIII (December 1969), 300-308.

8349 Roripaugh, Robert A. "The Last Longhorn," Sage, XI (Spring 1966), 49-58.

8350 Rorvik, Honor. "The Magistrate and the Mole," Courier, XLV (September 1965), 64-65.

8351 Rose, Charles. "The Bandage," Delta Review, V (April 1968), 64-67, 73-76.

8351a Rose, Kenn Sherwood. "A White World Not of Our Time," Alaska Review (Contemporary Alaskan Literature issue), IV, no. 4 (1969), 80-85.

8352 Rose, Lawrence F. "The Hell Fruit," Imprint, VIII (December 1968), 53-61, 63, 65, 67, 69, 71, 73, 75, 77, 79, 81, 83-84, 87, 89, 91, 93, 95, 97, 99, 101-102, 105, 107, 109, 111, 113, 115, 117, 119, 121, 123, 125, 127-128.

8353 Rosen, H. R. "The Shotgun," New Campus Review, II (Spring 1969), 3-5.

8354 Rosen, Norma. "Sheltering a Life," Redbook, CXXV (October 1965), 88-89, 152-154.

8355 Rosenak, Michael. "A Key in Manhattan," Midstream, XI (September 1965), 40-52.

8356 _____. "Pictures and Frames," Midstream, XIII (October 1967), 44-57.

8357 _____. "Stories and Games," Epoch, XVI (Fall 1966), 35-51.

8358 _____. "Treason," Jewish Frontier, XXXIII (November 1966), 25-8.

8359 Rosenbach, Willa. "The Visits on Sunday," Soundings, III (Spring 1966), 82-87.

8360 Rosenbaum, Veryl. "Needles and Pins," Arx, III (June 1969), 25-7.

8361 Rosenberg, Elsa. "Abraham Muscovitch's Michael," Saturday Night, LXXXI (March 1966), 32-36.

8362 Rosenberg, Michael. "I Had the Bread in My Hand, and the Cheese," Maguey, no. 2 (Autumn 1968), 32-37 [in English and Spanish on alternate pages].

8363 Rosenman, Adina. "A Few Grains," Occident, I (Spring/Summer 1967), 55-59.

8364 Rosenthal, Irving. "The Mouse King," Floating Bear, no. 33 (1967), n.p. [21-22].

8365 _____. "Four Sections from Sheeper," Evergreen Review, XI (April 1967), 49, 100-103.

8366 Rosenthal, Marshall. [untitled story], Work, no. 3 (Winter 1965-1966), 94-96.

8367 Rosenthal, William. "Cold Wind of Autumn," Arizona Quarterly, XXIV (Summer 1968), 117-132.

8368 Roshchin, Mikhail. "Twenty Minutes or So," Anthony Wixley, trans., Soviet Literature, (no. 8, 1966), 97-108.

8369 Roslyakov, Vasili. "One of Us," Vladimir Talmy, trans., Soviet Literature, (no. 11, 1969), 53-80.

8370 Rosmer, Lynn. "The Furnished Room," The Phoenix (Second Semester 1965-66), 8-25.

8371 Ross, David. "Toussaint," Art and Literature, no. 11 (Winter 1967), 175-179.

8372 Ross, Donald H. "The Black Bull," Sage, XI (Fall 1967), 315-324.

8373 Ross, Irwin. "Joe and Ella's Place," Ball State University Forum, VII (Autumn 1966), 67-70.

8374 Ross, Kevin. "A Few Notes about the Arabian Onyx," Seventeen, XXV (June 1966), 98-99, 170-175.

8375 Ross, Linnea. "The Price of Sophistication," UMD Humanist, XIII (Spring 1965), 42-44.

8376 Ross, Maggie. "The Girl from the Golden City," Nova, (November 1968), 116, 120, 123, 128, 131, 133, 136.

8377 Ross, Rex B., III. "The Dark Chance; A Novel in Three Parts," North American Review, II (September 1965), 32-60.

8378 Rossner, Judith. "Please Think of Me As a Friend," Ararat, VIII (Winter 1967), 12-15.

8379 _____. "Voyage of the Earth Maiden," Cosmopolitan, CLXIV (May 1968), 160-164, 166.

8380 Roth, Henry. "Final Dwarf," Atlantic Monthly, CCXXIV (July 1969), 57-61.

8381 ______. "The Surveyor," New Yorker, XLII (August 6, 1966), 22-30.

8382 Roth, Henry H. "Cantos," Minnesota Review, IX (1969), 22-27.

8383 ______. "The Children from Avenue C," Silo, no. 7 (Spring 1965), 29-40.

8384 ______. "The Cinderella Kid," New American Review, no. 7 (August 1969), 204-215.

8385 ______. "Come, Please Come," Abyss, (January-February 1967), n.p. [30-36].

8386 ______. "Confrontations," South Dakota Review, VI (Autumn 1968), 104-114.

8387 ______. "The Couriers," Ann Arbor Review, no. 7 (1969), 13-16.

8388 ______. "Dance!" Prism International, VIII (Summer 1968), 54-64.

8389 ______. "Dear Sister Jane," December, IX, nos. 2/3 (1967), 18-20.

8390 ______. "Dialogue for a Sunday," Midwestern University Quarterly, I, no. 3 (1966), 37-41.

8391 ______. "Dining Out," Minnesota Review, VIII (1968), 121-122.

8392 ______. "Don't You Weep, Don't You Moan and Don't You Wave The New York Review of Books at Me!" Arx, I (March 1968), 21-24.

8393 ______. "Edgar and Olivia," Midwestern University Quarterly, II, no. 1 (1966), 23-30.

8394 ______. "Esther and the Wise Man," Four Quarters, XIV (January 1965), 17-25.

8395 ______. "Family Jacobs," Transatlantic Review, no. 27 (Winter 1967-68), 75-81.

8396 ______. "First of April," Abyss, II (January-February 1968), 53-54.

8397 ______, trans. & ed. of Kenjiro Sashi. "From Image to Expression," Minnesota Review, IX (1969), 83-87.

8398 ______. "Growing Up/Section from a novel: Love Zap,"

<u>Beyond Baroque 692</u>, I (July 1969), 22-25.

8399 _____. "Hot House Rose," <u>The Fiddlehead</u>, no. 80 (May-July 1969), 84-90.

8400 _____. "Journeyman," <u>Ann Arbor Review</u>, nos. 5 & 6 (1969), 12-15.

8401 _____. "Letters," <u>Beyond Baroque 691</u>, I (December 1968), 44-45.

8402 _____. "Love Zap," <u>Lillabulero</u>, II (Winter 1968), 24-27.

8403 _____. "Man, Look at Them Bases," <u>Voyages</u>, II (Spring 1969), 56-60.

8404 _____. "Michael/(A Tale in Two Parts)," <u>Arx</u>, II (July 1968), 13-50.

8405 _____. "Michael/(Conclusion)," <u>Arx</u>, II (August 1968), 14-30.

8406 _____. "A Mother in Four Portraits," <u>Arx</u>, I (April 1968), 13-16.

8407 _____. "O'Brian," <u>Aspects</u>, no. 9 (March 1967), 2-4.

8408 _____. "Of Frail Pigeons and Red Roses," <u>The Quest</u>, II (Fall 1967), 187-195.

8409 _____. "Point Your Ass Home," <u>Manhattan Review</u>, no. 1 (1966), 36-40.

8410 _____. "Remember Macao," <u>Arx</u>, II (February 1969), 40-45.

8411 _____. "Ryan," <u>Jeopardy</u>, no. 5 (Spring 1969), 205-217.

8412 _____. "Sam's Land," <u>December</u>, VII (1965), 36-38.

8413 _____. "Scenes/Fable," <u>Genesis: Grasp</u>, I, no. 3 (1969), 35-36.

8414 _____. "Scenes/On Frustration," <u>Genesis: Grasp</u>, I, no. 3 (1969), 37-42.

8415 _____. "Scenes/On the Same Exact Lay," <u>Genesis: Grasp</u>, I, no. 3 (1969), 42-45.

8416 _____. "Shomer's Ride," <u>Analecta</u>, no. 1 (Fall 1967), 23-25.

8417 _____. "Sour Muse," <u>Abyss</u>, (January-February 1967), n.p. [36-40].

8418 _____. "Sour Muse," The Fiddlehead, no. 76 (Summer 1968), 29-37.

8419 _____. "Suburban Miscellany," The Quest, III (Winter-Spring 1969), 105-115.

8420 _____. "Suits of Paper," Ann Arbor Review, no. 4 (Summer 1968), 27-31.

8421 _____. "Der Tag," Red Clay Reader, no. 2 (1965), 53-62.

8422 _____. "The Way Things Are," December, XI, nos. 1 & 2 (1969), 71-74.

8423 _____. "When Day and Nights Are Done," Lillabulero, no. 7 (Summer/Fall 1969), 14-19.

8424 _____. "Who Speaks? My Faith/My Vanity," Minnesota Review, IX (1969), 231-238.

8425 Roth, Mary. "When the Rocks Melt with the Sun," Limbo, II (November 1966), 31-36.

8426 Roth, Philip. "Civilization and Its Discontents," New American Review, no. 3 (1968), 7-81.

8427 _____. "In Trouble--Excerpt from a new novel," Atlantic Monthly, CCXVIII (November 1966), 72-79.

8428 _____. "The Jewish Blues," New American Review, no. 1 (1967), 136-164.

8429 _____. "A Jewish Patient Begins His Analysis," Esquire, LXVII (April 1967), 104, 107, 191-193.

8430 _____. "Nature Boy (excerpt from When She Was Good)," Cosmopolitan, CLXIII (September 1967), 130-134.

8431 _____. "A New Man," Saturday Evening Post, CCXL (February 11, 1967), 50-52, 54, 56, 59.

8432 _____. "O Beautiful for Spacious Skies," Harper's Magazine, CCXXXIII (November 1966), 66-78.

8433 Rothberg, Abraham. "The Dürer Hands," Transatlantic Review, no. 18 (Spring 1965), 130-141.

8434 _____. "Pluto Is the Furthest Planet," Yale Review, LIV (Winter 1965), 219-233.

8435 _____. "The Sand Dunes," Southwest Review, LIII (Spring 1968), 153-166.

8436 _____. "The Thousand Doors/(Conclusion)," Ladies' Home Journal, LXXXIII (January 1965), 50-51, 80-87.

8437 Rothgeb, Dix. "Boots," Cosmopolitan, CLXII (March 1967), 128-130, 132-135.

8438 Rottenberg, Annette T. "Waiting," Florida Quarterly, I (Winter 1968), 13-24.

8439 Roueché, Berton. "The Gun," Evergreen Review, X (August 1966), 63-65.

8440 _____. "The Lug Wrench," New Yorker, XLV (June 7, 1969), 32-34.

8441 _____. "Phone Call," New Yorker, XLI (August 28, 1965), 38-39.

8442 _____. "The Raspberry Patch," Evergreen Review, XII (September 1968), 58-61.

8443 Roussel, Raymond. "Among the Blacks," Ron Padgett, trans., Bones, no. 2 (Winter 1968-69), 65-71.

8444 _____. "The Greenish Skin," Rayner Heppenstall, trans., Harper's Bazaar, C (November 1967), 111, 172.

8445 _____. "The Skate's Scales," Rayner Heppenstall, trans., Harper's Bazaar, CII (March 1969), 200, 124.

8446 _____. "Two Stories/The Old Gentleman's White Curls," Rayner Heppenstall, trans., London Magazine, VIII (August 1968), 78-81.

8447 _____. "Two Stories/The Skate's Scales," Rayner Heppenstall, trans., London Magazine, VIII (August 1968), 81-84.

8448 Rowe, Winthrop. "The Valley of the Blind," Red Cedar Review, V (April 1967), 19-32.

8449 Roy, Gregor. "The Monster, the Eagle and the Irish God," Columbia, XLV (March 1965), 24-27, 45-46.

8450 Roy, Raja Tridiv. "Child of the Mountain Stream," Pakistan Review, XVI (July 1968), 30-32.

8451 _____. "I See Thine Image through My Tears," Pakistan Review, XVII (March 1969), 26-29, 47.

8452 _____. "'To Err Is Human, to Forgive Divine'," Pakistan Review, XVI (November 1968), 41-43.

8453 Roy, Ram Bachan. "Nonsense," P. K. S., trans., Avenues,

II (January 1969), 22-23.

8454 Roy, Sachi Rout. "All Over a Paisa," Manoranjan Hota, trans., Bhubaneswar Review, no. 3 (Summer 1969), 29-33.

8455 Rozewicz, Tadeusz. "The Interrupted Exam," Edward Rothert, trans., Literary Review, XIII (Winter 1969-70), 243-255.

8456 Ruark, Robert. "Accidentally Good," Playboy, XIII (December 1966), 138-140, 146, 315.

8457 _____. "Afternoon in Andalusia," Playboy, XII (September 1965), 158-160, 228-230, 232-233.

8458 _____. "Barbara," Playboy, XII (August 1965), 80, 108, 138-140.

8459 _____. "Sheila," Playboy, XII (June 1965), 90-92, 94, 202, 205-208, 210.

8460 Rubens, Robert. "'Kressmann's'," Art and Literature, no. 8 (Spring 1966), 192-205.

8461 Rubin, David. "Lamprey," Transatlantic Review, no. 32 (Summer 1969), 92-101.

8462 _____. "Longing for America," Virginia Quarterly Review, XLII (Summer 1966), 410-433.

8463 Rubin, Edith. "The End of the Wedding," Mademoiselle, LXVI (April 1968), 244-245, 281-287.

8464 Rubin, Michael. "Bread, Wine and Thou," Redbook, CXXX (March 1968), 66-67, 134, 136, 138.

8465 _____. "Service," Kenyon Review, XXX (1968), 85-93.

8466 Rubin, Rick. "Jepson's Last Motto," Cavalier, XV (May 1965), 18-19, 22, 80-83.

8467 _____. "The Ungreat Inscape of Jimmy the Straight," Nexus (San Francisco, Calif.), II (January-February 1965), 5-8.

8468 _____. "Weekends Are the Happy Time," Cavalier, XV (March 1965), 20-21, 88-93.

8469 Rubin, Ronald S. "The Banks of Mississippi," Transatlantic Review, no. 18 (Spring 1965), 127-129.

8470 Rudnicki, Adolf. "Yom Kippur," Reuben Ainsztein, trans., Literary Review, X (Spring 1967), 318-331.

8471 Rudo, R. M. "Old Irreplaceable Me," Redbook, CXXV (August 1965), 46-47.

8472 Rudolph, William. "A Friend up the Road," Consumption, I (Spring 1968), 15-19, 22-26, 28-30.

8473 Rufus, Sidney Herbert. "The Last Will and Testament of Sidney Herbert Rufus," Wormwood Review, V, no. 4 (1965), 23-24.

8474 Rugel, Miriam. "Paper Poppy," Kenyon Review, XXX (1968), 493-507.

8475 _____. "The Sapphire Door," New Renaissance, I (Winter 1969), 16-22.

8476 Ruggero, Henri. "The Banana Man," Long View Journal, I (Spring 1969), 25-33.

8477 _____. "What Part of the Cow Is the Veal?" Crucible, V (Spring 1969), 41-43.

8478 Rugyendo, Hanny. "Kemitare," Nexus, II (July 1968), 29-32.

8479 Rukeyser, Muriel. "Little," Ladies' Home Journal, LXXXII (February 1965), 82-85, 87, 89.

8480 Rule, Jane. "Anyone Will Do," Redbook, CXXXIII (October 1969), 108-109.

8481 _____. "Moving On," Redbook, CXXXI (June 1968), 86-87.

8482 _____. "Not an Ordinary Wife," Redbook, CXXXIII (August 1969), 70-71, 136-137.

8483 Rulfo, Juan. "Luvina," Peter Glusker, trans., Stand, IX, no. 2 (1967), 31-35.

8484 _____. "Matilde Arcangel," Margaret Shedd, trans., Kenyon Review, XXVIII (March 1966), 187-193.

8485 _____. "Tell Them Not to Kill Me," John Brushwood, trans., El Corno Emplumado, no. 14 (April 1965), 107-111.

8486 _____. "They Gave Us the Land," Jean Franco, trans., Encounter, XXV (September 1965), 15-17.

8487 Rumaker, Michael. "Gringos," Evergreen Review, IX (November 1965), 54-57, 70-76.

8488 _____. "The Truck," Evergreen Review, XI (April 1967), 58-63.

8489 Ruoro, Peter. "End of Month," Literary Review, XI (Summer 1968), 423-429.

8490 ______. "Two Women," Transition, V, no. 20 (1965), 43-45.

8491 Rushing, Jane Gilmore. "The Albright Women," Redbook, CXXXI (May 1968), 155-177.

8492 Rushing, Marie Morris. "The Fix-It-Man," Vagabond, I, no. 3 (1966), 38-42.

8493 Rushmore, Robert. "Open Water," London Magazine, VI (December 1966), 46-57.

8494 ______. "The Winning Game," London Magazine, V (February 1966), 8-17.

8495 Rusinek, Michal. "Tanks in the Valley of Starvation," David I. Welsh, trans., Literary Review, X (Spring 1967), 275-283.

8496 Russ, Joanna. "Life in a Furniture Store," Epoch, XV (Fall 1965), 71-82.

8497 ______. "My Mother's House," Epoch, XVI (Winter 1967), 137-141.

8498 ______. "Scenes from Domestic Life," Consumption, II (Fall 1968), 22-33.

8499 ______. "This Afternoon," Cimarron Review, no. 6 (December 1968), 60-66.

8500 ______. "This Night, at My Fire," Epoch, XV (Winter 1966), 99-102.

8501 ______. "The Throwaways," Consumption, II (Spring 1969), 26-31.

8502 ______. "Visiting," Manhattan Review, no. 3 (1967), 15-18 [issue is double bound in opposite directions and doubly paginated].

8503 Russell, Franklin. "A Madness of Nature," New American Review, no. 2 (January 1968), 134-141.

8504 Russell, Randee. "The Greenleaf Graft," Mademoiselle, LXVII (August 1968), 328-329, 378-380.

8505 Russell, Ray. "The Better Man," Playboy, XIII (July 1966), 67, 163.

8506 ______. "Chariot of Fire," Playboy, XII (September 1965), 102-104, 110, 216-220, 222-225.

8507 ______. "Comet Wine," Playboy, XIV (March 1967), 66-68,

128-129, 134, 137-138.

8508 ______. "Gemini," Playboy, XVI (June 1969), 143-144, 200-201.

8509 ______. "Here Comes John Henry," Playboy, XV (September 1968), 115, 118, 209, 212-213.

8510 ______. "A Most Miraculous Organ," Playboy, XIII (November 1966), 103, 197-200.

8511 ______. "Ripples," Playboy, XIV (October 1967), 87.

8512 ______. "Turn Left at Mata Hari," Playboy, XV (April 1968), 128-130, 192, 194, 196.

8513 Rutsala, Vern. "Night Driving," Southwest Review, LI (Winter 1966), 29-35.

8514 Ryan, James. "'Become as Little Children'," Montparnasse Review, no. 2 (1966), 41-50.

8515 ______. "Heat," Nexus (San Francisco, Calif.), II (July-August 1965), 46-51.

8516 ______. "A Nice Goodbye," Montparnasse Review, no. 1 (1965), 25-34.

8517 Ryan, John Fergus. "A Decent Interval," Kulcher, no. 17 (Spring 1965), 57-71.

8518 ______. "Linden Street," Delta Review, VI (June 1969), 46-49, 64.

8519 ______. "The Nuthouse Pikings," Evergreen Review, XII (February 1968), 30-32, 71-74.

8520 Ryan, William F. "No Buttons, No Springs," American, II (Spring 1966), 11-12, 34, 57-59.

8521 ______. "Nothing Like a Holocaust," American, I (Spring 1965), 10-11, 61-64.

8522 ______. "The Pile," American, I (Fall 1965), 12-13, 42-45, 47-48, 66.

8523 ______. "Reindeer Games," American, IV (Spring 1968), 7-11, 55.

8524 ______. "Song on Side Two," American, II (Fall 1966), 52-63.

8525 ______. "Wait for the Wagon," American, III (Spring 1967), 32-36.

8526 Rylenkov, Nikolai. "Recollections," Margaret Wettlin, trans., *Soviet Literature*, (no. 2, 1969), 56-74.

8527 Ryther, Marta. "What Can You Do about a Dead Child?" *Readers & Writers*, I (October-November 1966), 28-30, 32.

8528 Saalbach, Ann. "Four-Eyes and Me," *The Archive*, LXXIX (May 1967), 18-22.

8529 ______. "Now a Very Long Time Ago," *The Archive*, LXXX (September 1967), 23-26.

8530 Saba, Umberto. "Quickies," *Origin* (Kyoto, Japan), no. 3 (October 1966), 14-15.

8531 Sabato, Ernesto. "Report on the Blind/Part III from *Sobre heroes y tumbas*," Stuart M. Gross, trans., *Tri-Quarterly*, nos. 13/14 (Fall/Winter 1968/69), 95-105.

8532 Sabel, Charles. "A Story, a Dialogue, a Speech," *Harvard Advocate*, CI (December 1967), 2-3.

8533 Sachs, Ed. "All the People and All the Places and All the Things," *University Review*, XXXII (March 1966), 168-178.

8534 Sack, John R. "The Abbot and Otis Strong," *Ave Maria*, CI (February 20, 1965), 20-24.

8535 ______. "The Blues *molto Allegro*," *Ave Maria*, CII (October 23, 1965), 22-23.

8536 ______. "The Twelfth Degree," *Ave Maria*, CI (June 12, 1965), 22-25.

8537 Sack, Joy. "The Soft Fine Rain," *Contrast* (Cape Town, South Africa), no. 12 (July 1965), 31-38.

8538 Sadenwater, Gerald W. "Another Day," *Ave Maria*, CIV (October 29, 1966), 26-30.

8539 ______. "The Manipulators," *Four Quarters*, XVII (May 1968), 19-28.

8540 Sadka, Donna. "The Hermaphrodite," *Westerly*, (May 1966), 46-49.

8541 Sadoveanu, Mihail. "A Letter from the Ancress Olimbiada," *Literary Review*, X (Summer 1967), 441-452.

8542 Saeed, Ahmad. "A Billion Eyes, One Picture," *Pakistan Review*, XVII (August 1969), 25-28.

8543 ______. "A Set of Gold Bangles," *Pakistan Review*, XVII

(December 1969), 33-34.

8544 Saenz, Dalmiro A. "Far South," Michael G. Gafner, trans., Texas Quarterly, IX (Winter 1966), 134-138.

8545 Sagan, Françoise. "La Chamade: Part I," Cosmopolitan, CLXI (November 1966), 123-130.

8546 _____. "La Chamade: Part II," Cosmopolitan, CLXI (December 1966), 124-132.

8547 _____. "The Heart-Keeper," Cosmopolitan, CLXV (December 1968), 154-165, 168-169, 171-177.

8548 _____. "Help! ... Or Something," Adrienne Folk, trans., Vogue, CL (July 1967), 76-77.

8549 _____. "Lola's Visit," Daily Telegraph Magazine, no. 210 (October 11, 1968), 63, 66, 70.

8550 Sahgal, Nayantara. "The Trials of Siru," Triveni, XXXV (January 1967), 17-27.

8551 Said, Yunus. "The Devil's Choice," Vision, XVIII (December 1969), 15-22.

8552 _____. "Insomnia," Vision, XVII (December 1968), 24-28, 61.

8553 Saidi, William. "The Very Smartly Dressed Man," New Writing from Zambia, no. 1 (1966), 13-19.

8554 Saint, Nicholas. "Deep in the Heart of Texas," Esquire, LXVII (March 1967), 86-87, 89, 147-152.

8555 Sainte-Soline, Claire. "The Tree," Katherine Campbell, trans., Chelsea, no. 17 (August 1965), 28-33.

8556 Sainz, Gustavo. "Selfportrait with Friends," John Cameron Murchison, trans., Tri-Quarterly, nos. 13/14 (Fall/Winter 1968/69), 117-134.

8557 Sáiz, Víctor. "Multiple Guilt," Américas, XVIII (June 1966), 34-37.

8558 Saki. "The Chaplet," Contrast, II (1969), 137-141.

8559 _____. "Dusk," Contrast, II (1969), 94-98.

8560 _____. "The Lumber Room," Contrast, II (1969), 125-131.

8561 _____. "The Mappined Life," Contrast, II (1969), 55-59.

8562 ______. "Morlvera," Contrast, II (1969), 106-110.

8563 ______. "The Mouse," Contrast, II (1969), 89-93.

8564 ______. "Mrs. Packletide's Tiger," Contrast, II (1969), 15-19.

8565 ______. "The Philanthropist and The Happy Cat," Contrast, II (1969), 60-64.

8566 ______. "The Reticence of Lady Anne," Contrast, II (1969), 75-78.

8567 ______. "The Romancers," Contrast, II (1969), 111-115.

8568 ______. "The Sheep," Contrast, II (1969), 37-42.

8569 ______. "Sredni Vashtar," Contrast, II (1969), 120-124.

8570 ______. "Tobermory," Contrast, II (1969), 6-14.

8571 ______. "The Wolves of Cernogratz," Contrast, II (1969), 142-146.

8572 Sakol, Jeannie. "Shirley, the Kisses of Her Buttered Mouth," Cosmopolitan, CLXV (August 1968), 106-107.

8573 Sakren, Paul. "Loose: On the Loose: By the Loose: From the Loose," Beyond Baroque 692, I (July 1969), 14-15.

8574 Saks, Katia. "The Doll," Américas, XVIII (September 1966), 28-30.

8575 Salahuddin, Mobashir. "Ravings of a Man Dying," Pakistan Review, XVI (June 1968), 42, 44.

8576 Salas, Floyd. "The King's X," Evergreen Review, XI (August 1967), 42-45, 98-99.

8577 Sale, R. T. "At the Dark Edge, How Great the Darkness Is," Carolina Quarterly, XVII (Winter 1965), 41-71.

8578 Salih, Tayeb. "A Handful of Dates," Denys Johnson-Davies, trans., Encounter, XXVI (January 1966), 22-24.

8579 Salinas, Louis Omar. "Once I Was a Cowboy and Once I Was Hamlet," Statement, no. 22 (Fall 1966), 58-60.

8580 Salinger, J. D. "Hapworth 16, 1924," New Yorker, XLI (June 19, 1965), 32-40, 42, 44, 49-50, 52, 55-56, 58, 60-62, 67-68, 70, 72-74, 77-78, 80, 85-86, 88, 90, 92-96, 98, 100, 102-108, 111-113.

8581 Sallar, William. "The Mozart Express," University Review, XXXVI (Autumn 1969), 97-100.

8582 Sallis, James. "Bubbles," New Worlds, no. 183 (October 1968), 15-18.

8583 _____. "Kazoo," New Worlds, no. 174 (1967), 36, 45.

8584 _____ and David Lunde. "Weatherman," New Worlds, no. 181 (April 1968), 28-30.

8585 Salmon, R. S. "The Cotswolds in August," Old Lady of Threadneedle Street, XLV (June 1969), 87-89.

8586 _____. "My Pink Elephant," Old Lady of Threadneedle Street, XLI (December 1965), 218-221.

8587 Salomon, Frank. "Tree St.," Things, no. 2 (Summer 1965), 27-29.

8588 Salter, James. "Am Strande von Tanger," Paris Review, XI (Fall 1968), 12-24.

8589 _____. "Sundays," Paris Review, X (Summer 1966), 140-148.

8590 Saltonstall, Stephen. "Icarus/Excerpts from a novel," Harvard Advocate, C (November 1965), 6-12.

8591 Saltzman, Nolan. "The Chronicle of the Holies," The Quest, I (Fall-Winter 1966), 46-57.

8592 Samberg, Paul. "Dreams," Epoch, XV (Spring 1966), 239-248.

8593 Samuel, Edwin. "The Thirty-three Cardinals," Jewish Frontier, XXXII (May 1965), 20-24.

8594 Sanchez, Tony Richard. "Waiting," Stanford Chaparral, LXIX (Election 1968), 22-24.

8595 Sanchez Ferlosio, Rafael. "Teeth, Gunpowder, February," Arena, no. 23 (April 1965), 40-45.

8596 Sandberg, Peter L. "On the Iowa," Literary Review, XII (Spring 1969), 381-393.

8597 _____. "The Rhyme of Lancelot," South Dakota Review, VI (Autumn 1968), 69-75.

8598 Sandberg-Diment, Erik. "Below the Grate," Nimrod, XII (Fall 1967), 4-8.

8599 ______. "For Want of a Match," University Review, XXV (Winter 1968), 124-128.

8600 ______. "The Golden Mirrors of Yesterday," South Dakota Review, V (Winter 1967-68), 36-47.

8601 ______. "Olaf's Visit," The Quest, I (Summer 1966), 71-77.

8602 ______. "The Princess of Fog," The Quest, II (Spring 1967), 40-48.

8603 Sandemose, Aksel. "The Story of Gulnare," Gustaf Lannestock, trans., Literary Review, XII (Winter 1968-69), 155-169.

8604 Sander, Joseph. "The Family: A Tale of Long Ago," North American Review, VI (Summer 1969), 68-72.

8605 Sanders, Ed. "The Meeting between Elizabeth Barrett and Robert Browning," Mother, no. 7 (Mother's Day 1966), 15-17.

8606 Sanders, Lucy Ann. "Three Doors Down," Soundings, III (Spring 1966), 1-7.

8607 ______. "Two Stories/The Little Brown Pad," Soundings, II (Spring 1965), 118-122.

8608 ______. "Two Stories/The Scrapbook," Soundings, II (Spring 1965), 123-127.

8609 Sanders, Ronald. "The Burglar," Mainstream, XI (September 1965), 65-74.

8610 Sanders, Scott. "Bus South," Stand, X, no. 3 (1969), 44-49.

8611 ______. "The Operation," Cambridge Review, LXXXIX (February 16, 1968), 289-290.

8612 Sandison, A. C. "Digging for Victory," Old Lady of Threadneedle Street, XLIII (December 1967), 210-215.

8613 Sanford, James. "The Mouse and the Bear," Washington Square Review, I (Winter 1965), 56-61.

8614 Sansom, William. "Banjulele Days," Cornhill Magazine, CLXXVI (Spring 1968), 323-330.

8615 ______. "Cops and Robber," Encounter, XXIV (May 1965), 5-11.

8616 ______. "Day Out," Daily Telegraph Magazine, no. 195 (June 28, 1968), 29, 31-32.

8617 _____. "Goodbye," Nova, (October 1966), 192-193, 196, 201.

8618 _____. "Lighthouse and Lion," London Magazine, IV (March 1965), 3-12.

8619 _____. "Love at First Sight," Encounter, XXXI (October 1968), 19-21.

8620 _____. "October Song," McCall's, XCIV (September 1967), 72-73, 118, 120, 122, 123, 124.

8621 _____. "Time and True Love," Adam International Review, nos. 301-303 (1966), 19-20.

8622 _____. "The Ulcerated Milkman," London Magazine, V (November 1965), 7-20.

8623 Sánta, Ferenc. "Twenty Hours/Chapter from a novel," New Hungarian Quarterly, VI (Spring 1965), 5-74.

8624 Santas, Constantine. "Dreams and Reality," The Fair, II (Spring 1968), 2-7.

8625 _____. "A Hour of Mourning," The Fair, I (January 1966), 19-34.

8626 Santos, Bienvenido V. "Without Heir," Literature East and West, IX (March 1965), 75-78.

8627 Santucci, Carol Hope. "Jewels," Washington Square Review, II (Winter 1966), 35-38.

8628 Sapozhnikov, Vladimir. "Two Stories/First Cock-Crow," Dorian Rottenberg, trans., Soviet Literature, (no. 7, 1965), 108-124.

8629 _____. "Two Stories/Lake Karakhol," Dorian Rottenberg, trans., Soviet Literature, (no. 7, 1965), 95-108.

8630 Sargent, Betsy. "The Gold Piano," The Archive, LXXX (December 1967), 5-9.

8631 Sargeson, Frank. "Charity Begins at Home," Landfall, no. 79 (September 1966), 221-226.

8632 _____. "City and Suburban," Landfall, no. 73 (March 1965), 4-9.

8633 _____. "Conversation in a Train/or What Happened to Michael's Boots?" Landfall, no. 84 (December 1967), 352-361.

8634 _____. "A Final Cure," Landfall, no. 82 (June 1967), 130-138.

8635 _____. "An Imaginary Conversation/William Yate and Samuel Butler," Landfall, no. 80 (December 1966), 349-357.

8636 _____. "An International Occasion," Landfall, no. 92 (December 1969), 315-332.

8637 _____. "A Man and His Wife," Queen, CDXXIV (April 7, 1965), 82-84.

8638 Sarkadi, Imre. "Three Short Stories/Intimation," New Hungarian Quarterly, VII (Summer 1966), 144-146.

8639 _____. "Three Short Stories/Oedipus Blinded," New Hungarian Quarterly, VII (Summer 1966), 132-144.

8640 _____. "Three Short Stories/The Wolf," New Hungarian Quarterly, VII (Summer 1966), 147-151.

8641 Sarnoff, Irving. "Hindsight," Minnesota Review, VI (1966), 182-184.

8642 Saroyan, William. "Accident at the County Fair," Cavalier, XV (April 1965), 24-25, 63.

8643 _____. "Alive," Weekend Telegraph, no. 81 (April 15, 1966), 41, 43, 45-46.

8644 _____. "Being Refined," Playboy, XII (May 1965), 113, 187-189.

8645 _____. "The Biggest Watermelon Lady Anybody Ever Saw," Saturday Evening Post, CCXXXVIII (September 11, 1965), 56-59.

8646 _____. "The Crying Man of Paris," Status, I (December 1965), 56-57, 81-82.

8647 _____. "Don't Laugh Unless It's Funny," Playboy, XIII (July 1966), 93-94, 151-152.

8648 _____. Goodby Dolly," Status, I (November 1965), 48-51, 94, 96.

8649 _____. "Help, the Newsboy Hollered," McCall's, XCIV (May 1967), 88-89.

8650 _____. "Madness in the Family," Saturday Evening Post, CCXL (June 17, 1967), 56-57.

8651 _____. "Pointy Shoes," Saturday Evening Post, CCXXXVIII (May 22, 1965), 44-46, 48, 52-56, 58, 60-64.

8652 _____. "The Swimmers," Playboy, XIII (November 1966), 117, 201-204.

8653 _____. "Three Tales/Feasting," Saturday Evening Post, CCXL (October 7, 1967), 69-70.

8654 _____. "Three Tales/Mystic Games," Saturday Evening Post, CCXL (October 7, 1967), 68-69.

8655 _____. "Three Tales/The Trial of the Kaiser," Saturday Evening Post, CCXL (October 7, 1967), 68.

8656 _____. "A Valentine," Playboy, XIII (February 1966), 77, 188.

8657 Sarraute, Nathalie. "She," Maria Jolas, trans., Harper's Bazaar, XCIX (July 1966), 61.

8658 _____. "She [second selection]," Maria Jolas, trans., Harper's Bazaar, C (May 1967), 84.

8659 _____. "Tropisms," Harper's Bazaar, XCIX (October 1966), 188-189, 273-274.

8660 Sarudzai. "The Picture," Negro Digest, XVIII (May 1969), 54-56.

8661 Sashi, Kenjiro. "From Image to Expression," Henry H. Roth, trans. and ed., Minnesota Review, IX (1969), 83-87.

8662 Sasso, Laurence J., Jr. "In the Midst of Life," Plume & Sword, VII (Fall 1966), 8-10.

8663 Sassoon, R. L. "The Diagram," Chicago Review, XVII, no. 4 (1965), 110-137.

8664 Sastri, D. V. Krishna. "A Temple Tank/(A Sketch)," D. Anjaneyulu, trans., Triveni, XXXIII (January 1965), 73-77.

8665 Sata, Ineko. "Cry Alone," John J. Roberts, trans., Meanjin Quarterly, XXVI (Spring 1967), 295-299.

8666 Satterfield, John. "But You See Very Little from a Turret," Southern Humanities Review, II (Summer 1968), 344-348.

8667 _____. "A Hunger Yet to Be Fulfilled," Red Clay Reader, no. 3 (1966), 33-43.

8668 _____. "The Man Who Wrestled Alligators for Tarzan," Red Clay Reader, no. 6 (1969), 18-31.

8669 _____. "A Time for Hyperbole," Epoch, XV (Spring 1966), 252-264.

8670 _____. "Where Were You When Peace Came?" Florida Quarterly, I (Winter 1968), 1-8.

8671 Saunders, R. A. "The Corner," Jewish Frontier, XXXIII (January 1966), 18-22.

8672 Savage, Bill. "Rope," Jeopardy, no. 5 (Spring 1969), 79-80.

8673 Savage, John. "The Getaway," Saturday Evening Post, CCXXXIX (May 7, 1966), 76-77.

8674 _____. "The Girl with 15 Speeds," Ladies' Home Journal, LXXXIV (March 1967), 94-95, 173.

8675 _____. "The Girls across the Water," Redbook, CXXVIII (February 1967), 86-87.

8676 _____. "The Greenest Girl in Ireland," Redbook, CXXX (April 1968), 80-81.

8677 _____. "Love the Whole Girl," Redbook, CXXXIII (July 1969), 96-97.

8678 Savory, Teo. "A Dried Mermaid," Approach, no. 58 (Winter 1966), 32-37.

8679 Sawyer, Philip L. "The Fire House," Georgia Review, XXI (Winter 1967), 457-461.

8680 _____. "In Memory of a Friend," Wormwood Review, VII, no. 2 (1967), 3-5.

8681 Sawyer, William. "from Neurasthenic Hero," Ambit, no. 31 (1966/67), 20-22.

8682 _____. "Wandsworth Prison and Military Detention--1916," Ambit, no. 25 (1965), 6-11.

8683 Sayre, Nora. "The Failures of Adultery," Cosmopolitan, CLXV (September 1968), 140-144.

8684 _____. "The Summer Husbands," London Magazine, VIII (February 1969), 33-43.

8685 Sayres, William. "Are You a Strawberry Man, Mr. Brinton?" North American Review, IV (September 1967), 11-15.

8686 _____. "A Countryman's Hand," North American Review, III (July 1966), 28-31.

8687 _____. "The Cult of Tranquillity," Southwest Review, LII (Spring 1967), 115-131.

8688 _____. "Fury," Ante, III (Spring 1967), 5-13.

8689 _____. "The Greatest Story Ever Written--in Baxter, Wis.,"

Kansas Magazine, (1968), 100-103.

8690 _____. "Values, Values, Who's Got the Values?" Ante, II (Spring 1966), 23-41.

8691 Scannell, E. J. "Brown," Arlington Quarterly, II (Autumn 1969), 118-130.

8692 Scarth, Lynda. "The Funeral," Landfall, no. 87 (September 1968), 258-267.

8693 Šćepanović, Branimir. "The Death of Mr. Goluža," Donald Davenport, trans., Literary Review, XI (Winter 1967), 243-250.

8694 Schaeling, Marianne. "The Last Jack-o'-Lantern," Seventeen, XXIV (October 1965), 138-139, 152, 155.

8695 _____. "We Have Something in Common," Seventeen, XXIV (June 1965), 82-83, 136, 138, 140, 143.

8696 Schell, Bonnie Henderson. "The Bob," DeKalb Literary Arts Journal, I (Winter 1967), 48-63.

8697 Schemmerling, Carl. "Long Live Porfirio Montez," Trace, no. 60 (Spring 1966), 33-45.

8698 _____. "Passenger Pigeons," Trace, no. 56 (Spring 1965), 65-84.

8699 Schickele, René. "Angelica," Margaret D. Howie, trans., Scala International, (November 1967), 34-37.

8700 Schiff, Hilda. "The Evil that Men Do," Anglo-Welsh Review, XV (Summer 1965), 81-85.

8701 _____. "The Olympians," Anglo-Welsh Review, XVII (Winter 1969), 86-92.

8702 Schiller, Marvin. "In the Bosom of the Family," Carleton Miscellany, IX (Summer 1968), 81-95.

8703 Schiller, Rose Leiman. "Victory," Analecta, no. 1 (Fall 1967), 27-29.

8704 Schimenz, Roberta M. "One More Time," Aspects, no. 8 (October 1966), 8-10.

8705 Schindler, Edythe. "Jolly Season," American Judaism, XVI (Winter 1966-67), 14-15, 38-39.

8706 _____. "The Original Circle," Ave Maria, CI (February 6, 1965), 20-23.

8707 _____. "Peril Point," North American Review, II (July 1965), 44-47.

8708 Schirmbeck, Heinrich. "Othello," Margaret D. Howie, trans., Scala International, (August 1968), 34-36.

8709 _____. "The Singing of the Spiders," George Raymond Selden, trans., Scala International, (July 1966), 30-33.

8710 Schnabel, Ernst. "One Hundred Hours from Bangkok," George Raymond Selden, trans., Scala International, (October 1966), 34-37.

8711 Schneid, Otto. "The Clay War," DeKalb Literary Arts Journal, II (Winter 1968), 73-79.

8712 Schneider, Daniel J. "A Martyr of the Modern World," Discourse, XII (Summer 1969), 308-321.

8713 _____. "The Muskie," University Review, XXXIV (Winter 1967), 83-94.

8714 _____. "Sketching Swans in Watchland," Ball State University Forum, IX (Winter 1968), 69-78.

8715 _____. "A Very Nice Young Man," Minnesota Review, V (May-July 1965), 99-112.

8716 Schnell, Dorothy J. "Stories to Grow on," DeKalb Literary Arts Journal, II (Spring 1968), 48-50.

8717 Schoen, Barbara. "Identity Crisis," Seventeen, XXV (February 1966), 134-135, 232-234.

8718 _____. "'Tis Better To Have Loved...," Seventeen, XXIV (May 1965), 150-151, 230-233.

8719 Schoettler, James. "I Am Five. My Turtle Died," El Corno Emplumado, no. 13 (January 1965), 17-18.

8720 Schohl, William. "Smiling Bones," Ave Maria, CIV (December 24, 1966), 23-26.

8721 Schram, Irene. "Dance-Thing," Minnesota Review, IX (1969), 120-124.

8722 _____. "Mother," Carolina Quarterly, XXI (Fall 1969), 30-33.

8723 Schreiber, John J. "Hot Summer's Sweet Sweat," Columbia, XLVI (July 1966), 24-27.

8724 Schulberg, Budd. "A Latin from Killarney," Playboy, XV

(January 1968), 115, 204-205.

8725 ______. "Say Good Night to Owl," Redbook, CXXV (August 1965), 62-63, 127-131.

8726 ______. "Señor Discretion Himself," Playboy, XIII (January 1966), 140-142, 240-244, 246.

8727 Schulman, Joel. "There Will Be a Singing," Ante, II (Spring 1966), 47-53.

8728 Schultheis, Robert. "Climbing," North American Review, IV (November 1967), 27-30.

8729 ______. "The Fall," South Dakota Review, VI (Spring 1968), 56-63.

8730 Schultz, John. "Daley Goes Home," Evergreen Review, XII (December 1968), 38-45, 72-79.

8731 ______. "Jesse Had a Wife," Evergreen Review, XII (March 1968), 79-82.

8732 ______. "Morgan," Evergreen Review, XIII (June 1969), 56-66.

8733 ______. "The Offending Party," Evergreen Review, XII (June 1968), 41-44, 76-81.

8734 ______. "from Way," Chicago Review, XIX (June 1967), 46-50.

8735 ______. "Two Excerpts from Way: The Stories of Creation," Chicago Review, XVIII, nos. 3 & 4 (1966), 156-167.

8736 Schupan, Charlotte. "The Slap," Story: the Yearbook of Discovery, (1968), 79-84.

8737 Schütt, Bertil. "The Child that Screamed," Harley Sachs, trans., Literary Review, IX (Winter 1965-66), 279-283.

8738 Schuyler, James and John Ashbery. "At Mrs. Kelso's," Art and Literature, no. 12 (Spring 1967), 73-85.

8739 ______ and John Ashbery. "Further Adventures," Paris Review, XI (Summer 1968), 32-54.

8740 Schwabe Prather, George. "Heavenly Storm Over Acumal," Mexico Quarterly Review, II (Fall 1967), 34-43.

8741 Schwartz, Elkanah. "A Fish in a Whirlpool," Jewish Life, XXXVI (January 1969), 33-40.

8742 Schwartz, Eugene. "The Interpretation of Dreams/or Superboy at Sarah Lawrence," Columbia Review, XLVI, no. 2 (1966), 67-91.

8743 _____. "US," Columbia Review, XLVII, no. 1 (1966), 43-59.

8744 Schwartz, Joe. "Just Who Was It Invited You to the Party?" Transatlantic Review, no. 29 (Summer 1968), 126-130.

8745 Schwartz, Jonathan. "A Fine Silk Thread," Redbook, CXXVII (September 1966), 70-71, 134-137.

8746 _____. "The Gypsy Student," Seventeen, XXVI (April 1967), 154-155, 237, 239-241.

8747 _____. "The Project," Carleton Miscellany, IX (Winter 1968), 39-52.

8748 _____. "A Singular Honor," Redbook, CXXVIII (November 1966), 68-69, 154-156, 158-160.

8749 _____. "The Voices of the Wind," Redbook, CXXX (March 1968), 74-75, 116, 119.

8750 _____. "Waiting," Carleton Miscellany, VIII (Spring 1967), 99-105.

8751 Schwartz, Judith. "The Family," Prism International, VI (Spring 1967), 13-24.

8752 Schweitzer, Gertrude. "The Intruder," Good Housekeeping, CLXVII (September 1968), 82-83, 138, 140, 142-143, 145-146.

8753 _____. "Miss Elizabeth Landon, M.D.," Good Housekeeping, CLXVIII (May 1969), 84-87, 214-224, 226, 228, 230, 233-234, 236, 245-246, 248, 250, 256.

8754 _____. "My Child Is Missing," Good Housekeeping, CLXIV (January 1967), 62-63, 128-130, 132.

8755 _____. "The Promise of a Quiet Girl," Good Housekeeping, CLXIII (October 1966), 92-93, 165-168, 170, 172.

8756 _____. "This Time Tomorrow," Good Housekeeping, CLXV (September 1967), 79-81, 192, 194, 196, 198, 200, 202, 208-212, 214-220, 222, 224-226, 228-229, 236, 241-242.

8757 Scott, John. "By the Waters of Lethe," Queen, CDXXVII (November 9, 1966), 66-68.

8758 _____. "Something for Everybody," Queen, CDXXVII (Christmas Issue, 1966), 98-100.

8759 Scott, Natalie. "Lantana," Westerly, no. 1 (April 1969), 13-16 [mistakenly attributed to Daphne Hillman, but corrected in following issue].

8760 Scott, Terrence D. "The Cat," Westerly, (Summer 1966), 34-35.

8761 Scott, Virgil. "Home Is Where the Heart Is," Red Cedar Review, VI (Winter 1968), 5-12.

8762 Scott, Sir Walter. "Richard and Saladin," Adam International Review, nos. 325-327 (1968), 162-163.

8763 Scovel, Carl. "Joy to the Whole Wide World," McCall's, XCIII (December 1965), 108-109, 162-164.

8764 Scruggs, Susan. "Last Night," William and Mary Review, VI (Spring 1968), 29-39.

8765 Seaburg, Alan. "The Pregnant Fish," Discourse, XII (Spring 1969), 261-265.

8766 _____. "The Train," Discourse, XII (Summer 1969), 396-400.

8767 _____. "The Wait," Discourse, XI (Autumn 1968), 464-467.

8768 Seager, Allan. "Colorless in Limestone Caverns," Playboy, XV (November 1968), 109, 114, 190.

8769 _____. "The Good Doctor," Playboy, XIII (March 1966), 99, 154-155.

8770 _____. "The Good Doctor," Weekend Telegraph, no. 114 (December 2, 1966), 47-48.

8771 _____. "No More Roses," Saturday Evening Post, CCXXXVII (March 27, 1965), 52-58, 60.

8772 _____. "The Rope," Atlantic Monthly, CCXV (January 1965), 79-82.

8773 Seager, Laura. "Mother, Mother!" Mademoiselle, LXII (January 1966), 84-85.

8774 Seal, Graham. "Eyes," Canadian Forum, XLVI (June 1966), 55-57.

8775 _____. "Good Morning Mr. Spink," Canadian Forum, XLVI (February 1967), 256-257.

8776 _____. "The Lark's on the Wing," Transatlantic Review, no. 18 (Spring 1965), 103-106.

8777 Seale, George. "Dilemma, Mi Amigo," Texas Quarterly, IX (Spring 1966), 111-124.

8778 Seale, J. David. "The Return," Delta, XIX (1965), 8-11.

8779 Searcy, David. "Flash Gordon Whom I Loathe," Southwest Review, LIV (Winter 1969), 27-35.

8780 Searles, Vera. "Slippers for David," Prairie Schooner, XLI (Spring 1967), 52-56.

8781 Searls, Hank. "A Pebble and a Diamond," Woman's Day, (January 1967), 26-27, 77-80.

8782 Sears, Dennis Patrick. "The Bullying Ones," Ave Maria, CIII (March 26, 1966), 18-19.

8783 Sebastian, Paul. "Jumping to Conclusions," Mademoiselle, LXVII (October 1968), 169, 194-197.

8784 Sedgwick, H. "A Cat Named Frankenstein," Greensboro Review, IV (Winter 1968), 36-48.

8785 _____. "Never Enough People," Greensboro Review, no. 7 (Summer-Fall 1969), 54-56.

8786 See, Frank M. "The Dog," University Review, XXXVI (Winter 1969), 83-88.

8787 Segal, Lore. "Donald's Hilda," Quarterly Review of Literature, XIV (1967), 389-411.

8788 Segers, Charles. "Do You Want Me to Help You?" Redbook, CXXXII (February 1969), 72-73, 160, 162-164.

8789 Seghers, Anna. "The Outing of the Dead Schoolgirls," Witold Tulasiewicz and Caroline Walmsley, trans., Kenyon Review, XXXI (1969), 613-642.

8790 Sei Shōnagon. "The Pillow Book of Sei Shōnagon," Ivan Morris, trans., Harper's Bazaar, CI (December 1967), 164-165, 178-179.

8791 Seib, Kathleen Hurst. "A Bit Much," Seventeen, XXV (March 1966), 142-143, 220, 223-224, 226.

8792 Seibert, Robert Earl. "Sitting in the Park One Day in the Very Merry Month of May," Midwestern University Quarterly, II, no. 3 (1967), 55-57.

8793 Seidel, Ina. "The Orange," George Raymond Selden, trans., Scala International, (July 1965), 34-37.

8794 Seiden, Melvin. "Feeny," Epoch, XVIII (Spring 1969), 314-342.

8795 ______. "On Stromboli," Epoch, XVI (Winter 1967), 105-127.

8796 Seitakov, Beki. "The Boy from the Kara-kum Desert," Anthony Wixley, trans., Soviet Literature, (no. 7, 1966), 75-80.

8797 Seitter, Jean. "The Seascape," Mademoiselle, LXIII (August 1966), 294-295, 380-383.

8798 Selby, Hubert, Jr. "Fat Phil's Day/A Vignette," Evergreen Review, XI (August 1967), 52-53.

8799 ______. "Happy Birthday," Evergreen Review, XIII (August 1969), 34-37, 74.

8800 Seldin, Scott. "See the Lovely Young Lady with the Rubber Tree Branch," American, II (Fall 1966), 32-34.

8801 Seldon, Maurice. "Prelude," Weekend Telegraph, no. 55 (October 8, 1965), 53, 55, 57.

8802 Selgirts, Albert Kenneth. "Pebblemen on Wire," Sequoia, XI (Spring 1966), 15-21.

8803 Sellars, Killian. "The Emissary," Ave Maria, CIII (June 4, 1966), 26-29.

8804 Sellars, Mary. "Exit Smiling," Seventeen, XXV (November 1966), 150-151, 216, 218.

8805 Semin, Vitalii. "Asa Alexandrovna," Anatole Forostenko, trans., Tri-Quarterly, no. 15 (Spring 1969), 158-170.

8806 Semmler, Clement. "Penitence," Meanjin Quarterly, XXV (December 1966), 393-404.

8807 Semrick, Skip. "For Future Perfect," DeKalb Literary Arts Journal, II (Summer 1968), 11-17.

8808 Semyonov, Georgi. "Forty-four Nights," Hilda Perham, trans., Soviet Literature, (no. 2, 1965), 64-91.

8809 Semyonov, Yulian. "Dunechka and Nikita," Margaret Wettlin, trans., Soviet Literature, (no. 12, 1966), 3-63.

8810 Sen, Kalyan. "The Sea," Manuj Chatterji, trans., Indian Literature, XII (September 1969), 59-72.

8811 Senapati, Fakir Moham. "Ananta, the Widow's Son," Jayanta Mohapatra, trans., Bhubaneswar Review, no. 1 (Summer 1968), 38-55.

8812 _____. "Father and Son," Padmalaya Das, trans., Indian Literature, VIII, no. 1 (1965), 36-43.

8813 _____. "Patent Medicine," Jayanta Mohapatra, trans., Bhubaneswar Review, no. 3 (Summer 1969), 1-12.

8814 Senchak, Aurelia D. "The Mill Worker," The Smith, no. 8 (March 1968), 28-34.

8815 Senesi, Mauro. "The Breach," Elaine Maclachlan, trans., Queen, CDXXV (July 28, 1965), 66-67.

8816 _____. "A Dog for Rock," Atlantic Monthly, CCXVIII (November 1966), 125-127.

8817 _____. "Latin Boy," Elaine Maclachlan, trans., Texas Quarterly, X (Spring 1967), 44-53.

8818 _____. "The Nonconformists," Modern Age, X (Fall 1966), 399-403.

8819 _____. "White and Yellow," Stand, XI, no. 1 (1969-70), 51-56.

8820 Seneviratne, Maureen. "The Opal," Hemisphere, X (August 1966), 33-35.

8821 _____. "The Seer," Hemisphere, XIII (October 1969), 34-36.

8822 Seng, Goh Pok. "The Temple Bells," Literature East and West, X (December 1966), 341-347.

8823 Sentman, Georgia. "Sinner," Cosmopolitan, CLXV (December 1968), 150-152.

8824 _____. "Softer after Midnight," Cosmopolitan, CLXIV (January 1968), 94-98.

8825 Senyagwa, Gideon and Peter Rigby. "The Tale of the Ungrateful Grandfather," Transition, VI, no. 28 (1967), 34-36.

8826 Seow Geok-Hua. "Birthday Presents," Focus (Singapore), IV, no. 1, n.d., 23-24.

8827 _____. "Thoughts at Sixty-nine," Focus (Singapore), V, no. 1 (1967), 20-21.

8828 Sepulveda, James. "The Gallery," Assay, XXIII (Spring 1967), 42-46.

8829 Serafimovich, Alexander. "Two Deaths," Soviet Literature, (no. 4, 1967), 16-20.

8830 Serling, Robert J. "The President's Plane Is Missing," Imprint, VIII (June 1968), 24-42, 45-54.

8831 Sernaker, Richard. "The Incendiaries," Occident, II (Spring/Summer 1968), 11-29.

8832 Seth, Satish C. "The Compensation," Avenues, I (July 1968), 19-22.

8833 Setterlund, Carol. "Remnant," Four Quarters, XV (January 1966), 27-32.

8834 Severdija, Nada. "Some Deep and Meaningful Relationships," Readers & Writers, II (Summer 1968), 16-21.

8835 Seward, Gwyn. "The Invisible Worm," The Quest, I (Summer 1966), 37-52.

8836 Shaara, Michael. "Groomsday," McCall's, XCV (March 1968), 106-107, 147-148.

8837 Shaeling, Marianne. "The Happening," Seventeen, XXV (May 1966), 168-169, 261-263.

8838 Shafer, Elizabeth. "And Pride and Stubbornness Remain," Four Quarters, XVII (January 1968), 22-33.

8839 Shaginian, Marietta. "The Dog that Did Not Recognize Its Master," Vera Von-Wiren Garczynski, trans., Ararat, IX (Summer 1968), 9-11.

8840 ______. "Vakho," Vera Von-Wiren Garczynski, trans., Ararat, X (Summer 1969), 20-27.

8841 Shah, Syed Sami Saeed. "A Shiny Gold Medal," Pakistan Review, XIV (June 1966), 39-40.

8842 ______. "A Speck of Sand," Pakistan Review, XIII (December 1965).

8843 Shahab, Qudratullah. "Maa Ji," Alauddin Masood, trans., Review, I (October 1968), 47-59.

8844 Shahab, Syed Alwi. "Experiment," Focus (Singapore), V, no. 1 (1967), 26-31.

8845 ______. [Al-Shahab]. "Kleptomania," Focus (Singapore), New Series, no. 1 (1967), 16-18.

8846 Shahnazarian, Sempad. "Revolt Against Heaven," Armenian

Review, XXI (Winter 1968), 61-69.

8847 Shainberg, Lawrence. "Some Wallace Stevens," Esquire, LXXII (October 1969), 116, 223-225.

8848 Shami, Janset Berkok. "An Orphan of History," Cornhill Magazine, no. 1047 (Spring 1966), 211-215.

8849 ______. "The Scream of Growing Up," Cornhill Magazine, CLXXVII (Winter 1969-70), 452-456.

8850 Shamyakin, Ivan. "A Naked Heart," Eve Manning, trans., Soviet Literature, (no. 4, 1965), 11-90.

8851 Shanahan, William. "Free Ride," Ave Maria, CI (May 1, 1965), 22-25.

8852 Shannon, Charlotte. "Immigrant Family," Prairie Schooner, XLI (Summer 1967), 104-117.

8853 Shannon, Jean. "A Man of Action," The Quest, III (Winter-Spring 1969), 132-147.

8854 Shapiro, David. "Four Stories/1. The Children of Scotland," Mother, no. 5 (Summer 1965), 23.

8855 ______. "Four Stories/2. Walking," Mother, no. 5 (Summer 1965), 23.

8856 ______. "Four Stories/3. Water Collects," Mother, no. 5 (Summer 1965), 23.

8857 ______. "Four Stories/4. Girl in Her Teens," Mother, no. 5 (Summer 1965), 23.

8858 Shapiro, Herman. "For All These," Jewish Frontier, XXXII (September 1965), 18-21.

8859 Shapiro, Teri. "Nothing but the Truth," University Review, XXXV (Summer 1969), 311-314.

8860 Sharif, M. Raihan. "The Green Echo," Review, II (December 1968), 41-62.

8861 ______. "The Touchstone," Review, I (August 1968), 72-83.

8862 Sharma, Vera. "Ranjini," Triveni, XXXVI (April 1967), 62-69.

8863 ______. "Repentence," Triveni, XXXIV (July 1965), 35-39.

8864 Sharp, Frederick. "Reuben," Caught, I (1969), 20-21.

8865 Sharp, Margery. "The Anniversary Gift," Ladies' Home Journal, LXXXIII (February 1966), 60-61, 113-116.

8866 ______. "The Girl Who Won an Island," McCall's, XCVI (May 1969), 80-81, 147-149.

8867 ______. "In Pious Memory," Ladies' Home Journal, LXXXIV (April 1967), 101-108, 148-150, 152-153.

8868 ______. "With This Ring," Ladies' Home Journal, LXXXV (September 1968), 88-89, 148-149, 152.

8869 Shastri, Sri Lalit Kumar. "An Encounter with Jesus," S. Krishnan, trans., Triveni, XXXVII (October 1968), 27-31.

8870 ______. "Just for a Day," Triveni, XXXVI (July 1967), 43-47.

8871 Shatraw, Harriet B. "The Aeroplane and the Comet," University Review, XXXIII (December 1966), 136-141.

8872 ______. "Higher Ground," University Review, XXXI (June 1965), 277-282.

8873 ______. "Overtones," University Review, XXXV (Autumn 1969), 43-48.

8874 ______. "Parade," University Review, XXXIV (Spring 1968), 193-198.

8875 Shaw, Helen. "The Coat," Landfall, no. 91 (September 1969), 245-258.

8876 ______. "The Countess," Limbo, II (October 1965), 21-29.

8877 Shaw, Irwin. "God Was Here But He Left Early," Esquire, LXX (July 1968), 94-95, 119, 122, 124-126.

8878 ______. "The Man Who Married a French Wife," Nova, I (March 1965), 165-166, 169, 171, 173, 176, 178.

8879 ______. "The Mannichon Solution," Playboy, XIV (December 1967), 110-114, 116, 122, 282-284, 286, 288.

8880 ______. "Where All Things Wise and Fair Descend," Playboy, XIV (February 1967), 70-72, 74, 171-173.

8881 ______. "Whispers in Bedlam," Playboy, XVI (February 1969), 75-78, 80, 86, 206-210, 212-216, 218-221.

8882 Shaw, Patrick W. "The Loneliest Tiger," Cimarron Review, no. 7 (March 1969), 15-29.

8883 Shaw, Stuart. "Montreal Receives Solly Krakowitz," Alphabet, no. 11 (December 1965-March 1966), 8-16 [issue number mistakenly printed as no. 8].

8884 Sheardy, R. Thomas. "The Stargazers," Red Cedar Review, IV (Spring 1966), 58-63.

8885 Sheck, Henry. "My Machine SHE," Beyond Baroque 692, (July 1969), 46.

8886 Sheckley, Robert. "Can You Feel Anything When I Do This?" Playboy, XVI (August 1969), 105, 148-151.

8887 _____. "Cordle to Onion to Carrot," Playboy, XVI (December 1969), 159, 162, 308, 310-312.

8888 Shedd, Harry Graves. "The Nerve of Corny Johnson," Prairie Schooner, XLIII (Spring 1969), 67-73.

8889 Shedd, Margaret. "... According to His Folly," Cornhill Magazine, no. 1045 (Autumn 1965), 41-56.

8890 Sheehan, William. "University of London: Summer," Yale Literary Magazine, CXXXIV (May 1966), 10-12.

8891 Sheehy, Gail. "Love-Sounds of a Wife," Cosmopolitan, CLXII (April 1967), 145-152, 175.

8892 Sheffield, April. "What Do You Think of Giacometti?" Cosmopolitan, CLXVII (October 1969), 164-165.

8893 Shefner, Evelyn. "The American Uncle," Southern Review, II (July 1966), 675-688.

8894 _____. "In 7," North American Review, IV (July 1967), 31-33.

8895 _____. "The Invitations," Colorado Quarterly, XVI (Autumn 1967), 143-158.

8896 _____. "Mary Johnson, I Know You," Denver Quarterly, III (Summer 1968), 61-68.

8897 _____. "Notes on a Water Crisis," Cimarron Review, no. 7 (March 1969), 41-44.

8898 Shefner, Vadim. "The Modest Genius/A Fairy-Tale for Grown-Ups," Eve Manning, trans., Soviet Literature, (no. 5, 1968), 120-133.

8899 Sheil, Graham. "Immortality," Southerly, (1969), 114-129.

8900 _____. "Robbo's Boy," Quadrant, XII (March-April 1968), 52-58.

8901 Shein, Brian. "The Obelisk," Prism International, VIII (Summer 1968), 100-102.

8902 _____. "Will You Go Hunt, My Lord?" Prism International, VII (Autumn 1967), 72-80.

8903 Shelnutt, Eve. "Affectionately, Harold," Mademoiselle, LXV (August 1967), 278-279, 344.

8904 Shen, James C. Y. "The Ashes of Mt. Asama," Minnesota Review, VI (1966), 199-207.

8905 _____. "Mr. Chang," Antioch Review, XXV (Summer 1965), 271-282.

8906 Shen Tsung-Wen. "After Rain," David Kidd, trans., East-West Review, III (Summer 1967), 183-189.

8907 Shepherd, Don. "The Hatcher Theory," Negro Digest, XV (January 1966), 74-76.

8908 Sheraton, Ray. "A Faint Taste of Triumph," New Zealand Listener, LIV (February 25, 1966), 8.

8909 _____. "Go Polish Your Horn," New Zealand Listener, LIII (July 30, 1965), 4.

8910 _____. "A Long, Long Way from Town," New Zealand Listener, (July 1, 1966), 6, 19.

8911 Sherman, Sandy. "Suspended Paralysis of Three Corners of a House," The Fair, I (March 1966), 2-4.

8912 Sherris, Rona. "The Incomparable Chapeau," Ladies' Home Journal, LXXXIII (January 1966), 64-65, 100-102.

8913 _____. "The Last of the Suffragettes," Ladies' Home Journal, LXXXIII (May 1966), 82-83, 145-148.

8914 Shestinsky, Oleg. "Short Stories/Happiness," Louis Zelikoff, trans., Soviet Literature, (no. 3, 1965), 105-106.

8915 _____. "Short Stories/The Most Important Thing...," Lily Zelikova, trans., Soviet Literature, (no. 3, 1965), 109-111.

8916 _____. "Short Stories/An Undying Echo of War," Lily Zelikova, trans., Soviet Literature, (no. 3, 1965), 107-109.

8917 Shields, Yvonne. "Hobgoblin," UMD Humanist, XIV (Spring 1966), 7-8.

8918 _____. "Lost Sheep," UMD Humanist, XVI (Spring 1968), 8-11.

8919 Shilling, Dana. "Mrs. Wright," Seventeen, XXVII (January 1968), 85.

8920 Shim, Eduard. "The Boy in the Forest," Avril Pyman, trans., Soviet Literature, (no. 1, 1968), 3-87.

8921 Shipley, Margaret. "The Tea Bowl of Ninsei Nomura," Denver Quarterly, III (Summer 1968), 38-48.

8922 Shireman, Alvin. "No Heart for Hunting," Assay, XXIV (Spring 1968), 5-14.

8923 Shirley, Sylvia. "Sundays Are for Relatives," New Renaissance, I (Spring 1969), 25-37.

8924 Shiver, J. Arthur. "Exit to Nowhere," Arx, III (May 1969), 5-7.

8925 Shockley, Ann Allen. "Ain't No Use in Crying," Negro Digest, XVII (December 1967), 69-78.

8926 _____. "The Funeral," Phylon, XXVIII (Spring 1967), 95-101.

8927 _____. "To Be a Man," Negro Digest, XVIII (July 1969), 54-65.

8928 Sholokhov, Mikhail. "And Quiet Flows the Don/(An Excerpt)," Stephen Garry and Robert Daglish, trans., Soviet Literature, (no. 1, 1966), 8-20.

8929 _____. "The Foal," Soviet Literature, (no. 4, 1967), 130-136.

8930 _____. "They Fought for Their Country," Robert Daglish, trans., Soviet Literature, (no. 10, 1969), 3-39.

8931 Shore, Wilma. "Ever Devoted, Ever True," Antioch Review, XXVI (Spring 1966), 33-41.

8932 _____. "Lully, Lullay, Thou Little Tiny Child," Antioch Review, XXVIII (Winter 1968-69), 451-459.

8933 _____. "Sixteen, Sweet and Sour," Woman's Day, (April 1967), 34-35, 80-82.

8934 Shratter, Alan. "from Who Greased the Spit Valve?/II. Scherzo," Red Cedar Review, VI (September 1968), 41-47.

8935 Shrewsbury, Tom. "Psychedelic Church," Columbia, XLVIII (June 1968), 24-27.

8936 Shriver, Margaret. "On the Other Side of the Door," Southwest Review, L (Winter 1965), 50-67.

8937 Shrubb, Peter. "Life Abroad," Transatlantic Review, no. 28 (Spring 1968), 108-119.

8938 _____. "The Swagman," Transatlantic Review, no. 22 (Autumn 1966), 130-138.

8939 Shuffler, Jack C. "The Itchy Tooth," Evergreen Review, XII (April 1968), 61-63.

8940 _____. "Parts, Shared," Evergreen Review, XII (August 1968), 18-21, 69.

8941 Shugayev, Vyacheslav. "I Flee and Return," Vladimir Talmy, trans., Soviet Literature, (no. 10, 1966), 3-47.

8942 Shukshin, Vasili. "Inner Content," Avril Pyman, trans., Soviet Literature, (no. 6, 1968), 138-145.

8943 Shulman, Jason. [untitled], Riverrun, no. 2 (1968), 46-49.

8944 Shulman, Milton. "Kill Three/(Part 1)," Saturday Evening Post, CCXL (October 21, 1967), 50-53, 56, 58, 62-63, 66, 68-71.

8945 _____. "Kill Three/(Conclusion)," Saturday Evening Post, CCXL (November 4, 1967), 62-66, 68-70, 72-74, 76-77.

8946 Shultz, Paul K. "Back from Thermopylae," William and Mary Review, V (Winter 1967), 5-11.

8947 _____. "The Wind Is Many-Colored," William and Mary Review, IV (Winter 1966), 15-18.

8948 Shuttle, Penelope. "An Excusable Vengeance," New Writers, no. 6 (1967), 99-168.

8949 Shyer, Marlene Fanta. "Big Evening," Redbook, CXXVII (May 1966), 56-57.

8950 _____. "Decision by Firelight," Good Housekeeping, CLXI (June 1965), 74-75, 128, 130, 132.

8951 _____. "Far from My Loving Arms," Good Housekeeping, CLXVIII (April 1969), 90-91, 162, 164-165.

8952 _____. "The Favorite," Good Housekeeping, CLXI (October 1965), 90-91, 160, 162-163.

8953 _____. "The Feud," Good Housekeeping, CLXV (October 1967), 100-101, 151-153.

8954 _____. "Gray House, Black Trim," Redbook, CXXV (August 1965), 66-67, 115-116, 119.

8955 _____. "A Great Day for the Home Team," Good Housekeeping, CLXVII (November 1968), 96-97, 268-269, 271-272.

8956 _____. "He Loves Me, He Loves Me Not," Good Housekeeping, CLXVII (July 1968), 70-71, 190-192.

8957 _____. "Just a Simple Bride," Good Housekeeping, CLXIV (May 1967), 90-91, 175-179.

8958 _____. "Just the Man for You," McCall's, XCIII (November 1965), 112-113, 183-184.

8959 _____. "Just What the Doctor Ordered," Good Housekeeping, CLXVII (October 1968), 96-97, 271-273.

8960 _____. "Life and Love Upstairs," Good Housekeeping, CLX (May 1965), 112-113.

8961 _____. "The Man from Philadelphia," Good Housekeeping, CLXVI (February 1968), 74-75, 188, 190-191.

8962 _____. "My Husband, Her Son," Good Housekeeping, CLXVI (June 1968), 86-87, 158, 160-161.

8963 _____. "Not Like the Others," Redbook, CXXVII (August 1966), 68.

8964 _____. "One Out of Seven," Redbook, CXXVIII (November 1966), 60-61, 136, 138, 140.

8965 _____. "The Pantry Kiss," Redbook, CXXVI (January 1966), 46-47.

8966 _____. "Rainy Sunday," Redbook, CXXIX (June 1967), 82-83.

8967 _____. "Rx: One Mended Heart," Good Housekeeping, CLXI (November 1965), 92-93, 152, 154, 158, 160, 162.

8968 _____. "Second Impressions," Redbook, CXXIV (February 1965), 50-51, 106-108, 110.

8969 _____. "The Semiperfect Man," Redbook, CXXVII (July 1966), 50-51, 110-113.

8970 _____. "A Sure Thing," Redbook, CXXXIII (June 1969), 90-91.

8971 _____. "The Trouble with Anchovies," McCall's, XCIV (February 1967), 128-129, 185-187.

8972 Sibolski, Francis J. "No One Waved Back," Nexus (San Francisco, Calif.), II (September-October 1965), 40-43.

8973 Sica, Alan. "Peter Smith Meets the Man," William and Mary Review, VI (Spring 1968), 69-73.

8974 Siddiqui, Shaukat. "Tantiyah," Abul Khair and Janet M. Powers, trans., Arizona Quarterly, XXII (Spring 1966), 41-52.

8975 Sidlosky, Carolyn. "Six Blocks from Velco's," Seventeen, XXVIII (January 1969), 84-85, 110.

8976 Sieburg, Friedrich. "Good Days with Monsieur Derain," Margaret D. Howie, trans., Scala International, (September 1968), 34-36.

8977 Siegel, Benjamin. "A Free Man," Redbook, CXXIV (March 1965), 155-178.

8978 _____. "In the Beginning," Redbook, CXXVIII (December 1966), 147, 149-171.

8979 Siegel, Jules. "In the Land of Morning Calm, Déjà Vu," Esquire, LXXII (November 1969), 142-143, 198-200, 202, 204, 206, 208, 212, 216, 218.

8980 _____. "The Man Who Believed in Christmas Trees," New American Review, no. 5 (January 1969), 61-78.

8981 Siewart, Wayne F. "The Dream of Father Martin On a September Morning," Mexico Quarterly Review, III, no. 2 (1968), 35-37.

8982 _____. "The Schnickelfritz Kids," Mexico Quarterly Review, III, no. 3 (1969), 44-56.

8983 Sikat, Rogelio R. "The Prisoner," Literature East and West, XIII (December 1969), 291-299.

8984 Šikula, Vincent. "Evenings with Rosarka," Literary Review, XIII (Fall 1969), 112-117.

8985 Silberman, Glyn. "And an 8 Oz. Can of Conscience, Please," Purple Renoster, no. 9 (Spring 1969), 33-34.

8986 Sillitoe, Alan. "Cuthbert," Southern Review, V (July 1969), 819-830.

8987 _____. "Mimic," Encounter, XXXII (January 1969), 3-14.

8988 _____. "The Road," Transatlantic Review, no. 29 (Summer 1968), 30-40.

8989 Silone, Ignazio. "Return to Fontamara," Quadrant, IX (May-June 1965), 7-12.

8990 Silver, James. "Eight Months on a Chinese Junk," San Francisco Earthquake, I (Summer/Fall 1968), 68-73.

8991 ______. "Incredible Happening 534," VDRSVPVDRSVPVDRSVP-VDRSVP, (1969), n.p. [back page].

8992 Silver, Margery. "Against the Dying of the Light," Massachusetts Review, VI (Spring-Summer 1965), 543-555.

8993 Silverman, Rosemary. "The Blue Veils of the Tuaregs," Midstream, XIV (May 1968), 32-36.

8994 ______. "Friday," Texas Quarterly, X (Summer 1967), 20-35.

8995 ______. "The Greatest Place on Earth," Colorado Quarterly, XVII (Autumn 1968), 163-176.

8996 ______. "The Happy Family," Midstream, XIV (November 1968), 27-32.

8997 ______. "Heroes and Lovers," Redbook, CXXVIII (January 1967), 44-45, 107-108, 110-112.

8998 ______. "Joy," Colorado Quarterly, XVI (Summer 1967), 65-69.

8999 ______. "Lights," University Review, XXXIV (Summer 1968), 307-311.

9000 ______. "Thy People Shall Be My People," Midstream, XV (November 1969), 26-33.

9001 ______. "What Comes After the Happily Ever After?" Redbook, CXXXII (December 1968), 60-65, 105-107.

9002 Silverton, Doris. "Lord God, King of the Universe and President of the Motion Picture Academy," Saturday Evening Post, CCXLI (April 6, 1968), 56-60.

9003 Simckes, L. S. "Shmatte, or Father Abraham," Massachusetts Review, X (Summer 1969), 437-455.

9004 Simion, Pap. "The Triangle," Literary Review, X (Summer 1967), 517-526.

9005 Simmons, Andrew. "Sorrow in the Morning," University Review, XXXI (March 1965), 227-230.

9006 ______. "The Unusual and Successful Death of Melon Williams,"

Midwestern University Quarterly, II, no. 1 (1966), 110-124.

9007 Simmons, B. Charles. "James Washburn," Negro Digest, XIV (June 1965), 73-79.

9008 Simmons, Roger. "The Wooden Lady," New Campus Writing, (1966), 70-103.

9009 Simon, Barney. "The Fourth Day of Christmas," The Classic, II, no. 3 (1967), 39-46.

9010 _____. "The 4th Day of Christmas," Transition, VI, no. 30 (April/May 1967), 16-19.

9011 Simon, Eugene F. "The Fourth Dimension Black," Readers & Writers, II (Summer 1968), 31-34.

9012 Simon, Mina Lewiton. "The Bracelet," New Yorker, XLIV (February 8, 1969), 32-38.

9013 _____. "Fugue in Three Voices," New Yorker, XLII (October 1, 1966), 133-134, 136, 138, 140, 145-146, 148.

9014 Simon, William. "Opportunity," North American Review, V (January 1968), 23-32.

9015 Simonov, Konstantin. "A Name that Did Not Die," Soviet Literature, (no. 4, 1967), 162-165.

9016 Simons, Kosti. "The Legend of the Yellow Truck," Southerly, XXVI, no. 4 (1966), 249-258.

9017 Simpamba, S. J. "A Predicament," New Writing from Zambia, no. 2 (1968), 19-22.

9018 Simpson, James Wesley. "An Old Man's Illusion," Arx, I (March 1967), 2-5.

9019 Sims, Andy. "Gum--A Story for Children," Alta, no. 7 (Winter 1968-69), 58-59.

9020 Sims, Dean. "And All Things that Creep," Cimarron Review, no. 2 (December 1967), 76-78.

9021 Sinclair, Andrew. "The Atomic Band," Transatlantic Review, no. 21 (Summer 1966), 40-46.

9022 Sinclair, Bennie Lee. "Sisters," South Carolina Review, I (May 1969), 30-38.

9023 Sinclair, M. P. "The Piper's Song," Northwest Review, VII (Spring 1966), 54-56.

9024 Sinclair, Marianne. "Bosie and Oscar," Aylesford Review, VIII (Autumn 1966), 104-110.

9025 _____. "Bosie at the Zoo [second extract]," Aylesford Review, VIII (Summer 1966), 42-45.

9026 _____. "Bosie in London," Aylesford Review, VII (Winter 1965/Spring 1966), 253-257.

9027 Sinclair, Thomas. "Champion Red Archer," Yale Review, LV (Winter 1966), 227-249.

9028 Singe, Miles. "Night of Flower Power," New Zealand Listener, (February 2, 1968), 6.

9029 Singer, Isaac Bashevis. "The Boudoir," Isaac B. Singer and Elizabeth Shub, trans., Vogue, CXLVII (April 1, 1966), 148-149, 214.

9030 _____. "The Brooch," Alma Singer and Elizabeth Pollet, trans., Chicago Review, XVIII, nos. 3 & 4 (1966), 7-17.

9031 _____. "The Cafeteria," Isaac B. Singer and Dorothea Straus, trans., New Yorker, XLIV (December 28, 1968), 27-33.

9032 _____. "The Colony," Evelyn Torton Beck, trans., Commentary, XLVI (November 1968), 57-61.

9033 _____. "The Courtship," Playboy, XIV (September 1967), 145, 200-202, 204, 206-207.

9034 _____. "The Dead Fiddler," New Yorker, XLIV (May 25, 1968), 42-46, 48, 51-52, 54, 57-58, 60, 63, 66-68, 71-72.

9035 _____. "A Friend of Kafka," Isaac B. Singer and Elizabeth Shub, trans., New Yorker, XLIV (November 23, 1968), 59-63.

9036 _____. "Henne Fire," Playboy, XV (May 1968), 92-94, 204-205.

9037 _____. "The Key," Evelyn Torton Beck, trans., New Yorker, XLV (December 6, 1969), 65-68.

9038 _____. "The Lecture," Playboy, XIV (December 1967), 184, 294-296, 298, 300.

9039 _____. "The Letter Writer," Alizah Shevrin and Elizabeth Shub, trans., New Yorker, XLIII (January 13, 1968), 26-36, 38, 41-42, 44, 47-49, 52, 54.

9040 _____. "A Match for a Princess," Isaac B. Singer and Elizabeth Shub, trans., Redbook, CXXIX (August 1967), 68-

69, 149-151, 154-155.

9041 _____. "'My Adventures as an Idealist'," Aliza Shevrin and Elizabeth Shub, trans., Saturday Evening Post, CCXL (November 18, 1967), 68-73.

9042 _____. "The Needle," Isaac B. Singer and Elizabeth Shub, trans., Cosmopolitan, CLXI (August 1966), 113-115.

9043 _____. "On the Way to the Poorhouse," Playboy, XVI (October 1969), 117-118, 269-271.

9044 _____. "One Day of Happiness," Isaac B. Singer and Elizabeth Pollet, trans., Cavalier, XV (September 1965), 18-19, 78-84.

9045 _____. "The Parrot," Ruth Whitman, trans., Harper's Magazine, CCXXXII (June 1966), 59-66.

9046 _____. "A Passage to America," Herman Eichenthal and Elaine Gottlieb, trans., Lotus, no. 1 (1968), 5-12.

9047 _____. "Pigeons," Esquire, LXVIII (August 1967), 76-79.

9048 _____. "Powers," Isaac B. Singer and Dorothea Straus, trans., Harper's Magazine, CCXXXV (October 1967), 76-78, 83-87.

9049 _____. "The Prodigal Fool," Isaac B. Singer and Elizabeth Shub, trans., Saturday Evening Post, CCXXXIX (February 26, 1966), 64-66, 68-69.

9050 _____. "The Riddle," Chana Faerstein and Elizabeth Pollet, trans., Playboy, XIV (January 1967), 164-166, 253-254.

9051 _____. "The Séance," Encounter, XXV (July 1965), 14-19.

9052 _____. "The Secret," Chana Kleinerman, trans., Commentary, XL (October 1965), 72, 74.

9053 _____. "The Slaughterer," Mirra Ginsburg, trans., New Yorker, XLIII (November 25, 1967), 60-65.

9054 _____. "The Strong," American Judaism, XV (Winter 1965-66), 20-21.

9055 _____. "Three Stories for Children/The First Shlemiel," Elizabeth Shub, trans., Commentary, XLII (July 1966), 45-48.

9056 _____. "Three Stories for Children/The Mixed-Up Feet and the Silly Bridegroom," Elizabeth Shub, trans., Commentary, XLII (July 1966), 43-45.

9057 _____. "Three Stories for Children/The Snow in Chelm," Elizabeth Shub, trans., Commentary, XLII (July 1966), 41, 43.

9058 _____. "Two Corpses Go Dancing," Joseph Singer and Elizabeth Pollet, trans., Commentary, XL (August 1965), 45-49.

9059 _____. "Two Stories/Shrewd Todie and Lyzer the Miser," Isaac B. Singer and Elizabeth Shub, trans., Audience, Pilot Issue (Spring 1968), 104-107.

9060 _____. "Two Stories/When Shlemiel Went to Warsaw," Isaac B. Singer and Elizabeth Shub, trans., Audience, Pilot Issue (Spring 1968), 108-112.

9061 _____. "The Warehouse," Cavalier, XVI (January 1966), 40, 88-90.

9062 _____. "Yanda," Isaac B. Singer and Dorothea Straus, trans., Harper's Magazine, CCXXXVI (May 1968), 43-47.

9063 _____. "Yash the Chimney Sweep," Mirra Ginsburg, trans., Saturday Evening Post, CCXLI (May 4, 1968), 66-69.

9064 _____. "Zeitl and Rickel," Mirra Ginsburg, trans., Hudson Review, XXI (Spring 1968), 127-137.

9065 Singer, Patty. "Noon Walk in an Asylum II," Nimrod, XIII (Winter 1969), 37-42.

9066 Singh, Khushwant. "Black Jasmine," Evergreen Review, IX (September 1965), 54-58.

9067 _____. "The Convert," Wascana Review, II, no. 2 (1967), 54-63.

9068 _____. "Journey through Golden Rain," Imprint, VIII (April 1968), 13-14.

9069 Singh, Shiva Prasad. "Arundhati," Shri Ram Sevak Singh, trans., Triveni, XXXIV (January 1966), 29-42.

9070 _____. "Karmanasha's Defeat," Jai Ratan, trans., Imprint, IX (July 1969), 53-58.

9071 Sionil Jose, F. "The God Stealer," Literature East and West, IX (March 1965), 44-63.

9072 Sire, Glen and Jane. "The Girl in the Green Hat," McCall's, XCIV (November 1966), 106-107, 150-154.

9073 _____. "Somewhere There Have To Be Daffodils," Good Housekeeping, CLXVI (April 1968), 104-105, 224-227.

9074 Sisskind, Mitchell. "The Dawn of a New Day," Columbia Review, XLV (Spring 1965), 2-4.

9075 _____. "A Day I'll Never Forget," Columbia Review, XLVIII, no. 3 (1969), 5-8.

9076 _____. "A Day I'll Never Forget," Paris Review, XII (Summer 1969), 17-22.

9077 _____. "A Manual of Arms," Columbia Review, XLVI, no. 2 (1966), 44-52.

9078 _____. "A Mean Teacher," Columbia Review, XLVIII, no. 2 (1968), 4-10.

9079 _____. "Thoughts of a Fireman," Tri-Quarterly, no. 10 (Fall 1967), 116-117.

9080 Sisson, C. H. "A Self-Induced Retirement," Queen, CDXXIV (May 5, 1965), 82-84.

9081 Sitati, Paul. "'The Sheep Eat the Men'," Nexus, I (1966), 18-20.

9082 Sizonenko, Alexander. "The Seelow Heights," Vladimir Leonov, trans., Soviet Literature, (no. 9, 1968), 96-103.

9083 Sjögren, Peder. "Tears in Your Sleep," Literary Review, IX (Winter 1965-66), 237-241.

9084 Sjogren, Theodore. "Everybody Else in Free," Red Cedar Review, V (April 1967), 53-81.

9085 _____. "A Legacy of Silence," Red Cedar Review, V (January 1967), 49-65.

9086 _____. "The Storm," Red Cedar Review, VI (January 1968), n.p. [61-91].

9087 Skarmeta, Antonio. "First Comes the Sea," Ceclia Boisier, trans., Arizona Quarterly, XXIII (Summer 1967), 184-191.

9088 Skeete, Monica. "The Emigrant," Bim, XII (July-December 1968), 196-201.

9089 _____. "The Road," Bim, XIII (July-December 1969), 2-8.

9090 _____. "Spanish Figurine," Bim, XII (January-June 1968), 70-74.

9091 Skelton, Barbara. "Born Losers," London Magazine, V (May 1965), 7-18.

9092 _____. "Gloomsville," London Magazine, IV (January 1965), 21-30.

9093 _____. "We Remember You from the Last Time, Sir," London Magazine, VIII (April 1968), 10-20.

9094 Skelton, Billy. "Fix Fog Nozzles!" Delta Review, V (July 1968), 64-68, 70-72.

9095 Skillings, R. D. "An Atrocity," Trace, no. 65 (Summer 1967), 241-248.

9096 _____. "Before the Funeral," Trace, no. 70 (1969), 117-125.

9097 _____. "Deadwatch," Prairie Schooner, XLIII (Winter 1969/70), 373-381.

9098 _____. "Eels," Arizona Quarterly, XXIV (Autumn 1968), 209-222.

9099 _____. "The Gardens of the Sea," Transatlantic Review, no. 30 (Autumn 1968), 117-125.

9100 _____. "Indians," Lugano Review, I, no. 2 (1965), 24-35.

9101 _____. "A Length of Rope," Arizona Quarterly, XXI (Summer 1965), 109-114.

9102 _____. "Native Son," South Dakota Review, VI (Summer 1968), 29-44.

9103 _____. "Silly Buffalo and His Friends," Carleton Miscellany, IX (Summer 1968), 64-76.

9104 Skinner, Knute. "A Room for Sixty Francs," Quartet, no. 12 (Fall 1965), 1-11.

9105 Skir, Leo. "Angelina-in-the-Wilderness/or, The Last Freedom," Evergreen Review, XII (October 1968), 58-61.

9106 _____. "The Boys of Jerusalem," Evergreen Review, XII (December 1968), 46-49, 80-84.

9107 _____. "A Nocturnal Emission in the House of George Orenstein," Evergreen Review, XII (April 1968), 45-46, 78-79.

9108 _____. "Other Chanukahs," Commentary, XXXIX (March 1965), 56-61.

9109 _____. "This Is a Picture," Evergreen Review, XIII (October 1969), 22-25, 27, 56-62.

9110 Sklar, Dusty. "Ramon Navarro, My Own True Love," Virginia Quarterly Review, XLI (Autumn 1965), 571-579.

9111 ______. "Sisyphus at the Breakfast Table," Human Voice, IV, no. 3 (1968), 5-9.

9112 Skow, John. "'I Want to Smoke Pot'," Saturday Evening Post, CCXLI (January 27, 1968), 42-45.

9113 Škvorecky, Josef. "from The Cowards," Jeanne Nemcová, trans., Stand, X, no. 2 (1969), 32-34.

9114 ______. "Eine kleine Jazzmusik," Alice Denesová, trans., Literary Review, XIII (Fall 1969), 47-61.

9115 ______. "Pink Champagne," Peter Kussi, trans., Evergreen Review, XIII (March 1969), 56-59, 71-74.

9116 Slaatten, Evelyn. "Say One for Me," Cornhill Magazine, CLXXVII (Summer 1969), 342-351.

9117 Sladden, J. M. "I Hear the Train's Left," Westerly, no. 3 (October 1969), 12-18.

9118 Slade, Leon. "Catharsis," Southerly, (1969), 93-95.

9119 ______. "Stronger than Friction," Westerly, no. 3 (October 1969), 10-11.

9120 Sladek, John and Thomas M. Disch. "Danny's New Friends from Deneb," Mademoiselle, LXVII (September 1968), 58, 76, 100.

9121 ______. "The Design," Ambit, no. 35 (1968), 31-32.

9122 ______. "The Man from Not-Yet," Playboy, XV (June 1968), 103, 185-186, 188-189.

9123 Slate, Lane. "The Simplest Things," Stanford Chaparral, LXVIII (Winter 1968), 44-61.

9124 Slaymaker, Brian. "The Departure," Red Cedar Review, V (April 1967), 37-42.

9125 Sledge, G. Allen. "Winsome, Lose Some," Seventeen, XXIV (August 1965), 96, 105, 108, 114.

9126 Sleet, C. P. "Vestibules of Glory," Westerly, no. 2 (July 1968), 27-30.

9127 Slesar, Henry. "The Assassin from MVX-TV," Signature, II (July 1967), 18.

9128 _____. "The Game As It Is Played," Signature, I (June 1966), 51-52, 54, 60.

9129 _____. "I Do Not Like Thee, Dr. Feldman," Playboy, XVI (June 1969), 127, 216, 218.

9130 _____. "Melodramine," Playboy, XII (August 1965), 68-70, 150-152.

9131 _____. "The Prisoner," Playboy, XIV (July 1967), 83, 142-143.

9132 _____. "Speak," Signature, I (January 1966), 20.

9133 Sloan, Robert J. "Frenchy," Dare, III (January 1965), 22.

9134 Sloane, Donald Laurent. "Through Leanness and Desire," Negro Digest, XVII (December 1967), 79-84.

9135 Sloman, Joel. "First Little Green," The World, no. 13 (November 1968), n.p. [25].

9136 Slote, Alfred. "Falling Leaves," Saturday Evening Post, CCXXXVIII (November 6, 1965), 48-50, 52-53.

9137 Sluckis, Mikolas. "The Road Swings Round to Us," Eve Manning, trans., Soviet Literature, (no. 9, 1965), 2-66.

9138 Smart, Mae. "An Old Woman's Story," New Yorker, XLV (December 13, 1969), 50-51.

9139 Smart, Peter. "All Good Things, the Best of Friends," Intro, no. 1 (September 1968), 155-169.

9140 Smelsar, Frances. "The Television Woman," Prairie Schooner, XLI (Spring 1967), 39-47.

9141 Smirnov, Vasili. "On the Eve," Eve Manning, trans., Soviet Literature, (no. 1, 1965), 65-115.

9142 _____. "The Spring of 'Seventeen/(Chapters from The Discovery of the World)," Eve Manning, trans., Soviet Literature, (no. 10, 1967), 19-97.

9143 Smith, Andrew. "The Ring," Atlantic Monthly, CCXV (April 1965), 125-127.

9144 Smith, Barry. "The Trap," New Mexico Quarterly, XXXVI (Spring 1966), 80-89.

9145 Smith, Bruce. "Alan," Nimrod, XIII (Spring 1969), 19-23.

9146 Smith, Charlie. "To Be Cold a Long Time," The Archive,

LXXX (December 1967), 27-29.

9147 ______. "Life in the Bag," The Archive, LXXIX (December 1966), 5-8.

9148 ______. "A Wayfall Stranger," The Archive, LXXIX (April 1967), 10-12.

9149 Smith, Constance. "George and the Dragon," Ave Maria, CII (July 17, 1965), 22-24.

9150 Smith, D. L. W. "Absolution," Delta Review, VI (November-December 1969), 74-77.

9151 Smith, D. V. "What Didn't Happen," Human Voice Quarterly, II (February 1966), 3, 25.

9152 Smith, Dinitia E. R. [untitled story], Grecourt Review, IX (February 1966), 17-23.

9153 Smith, Don N. "A Box of Three," Trace, no. 67 (1968), 106-109.

9154 Smith, Elizabeth. "When Shall We Love," Redbook, CXXXIII (May 1969), 175-197.

9155 Smith, Frank. "The Snow Leopard Trots," Work, no. 4 (Summer/Fall/Winter 1966), 87-89.

9156 Smith, Graeme Kinross. "The Man Figure," Westerly, no. 3 (1967), 38-46.

9157 Smith, Iain Crichton. "Sweets to the Sweet," Stand, XI, no. 1 (1969-70), 24-28.

9158 Smith, J. Holland. "Tape Transcribed," Weekend Telegraph, no. 60 (November 12, 1965), 55-56, 58.

9159 Smith, Jean. "Frankie Mae," Negro Digest, XVII (June 1968), 84-89, 42-48.

9160 ______. "The Machine," Negro Digest, XVII (November 1967), 60-74.

9161 ______. "That She Would Dance No More," Negro Digest, XVI (January 1967), 59-68.

9162 Smith, Jeanette. "Flower o' the Snow," UMD Humanist, XV (Winter 1967), 5-7.

9163 Smith, Judy. "Aftermath of a Party," UMD Humanist, XIII (Spring 1965), 27-28.

9164 Smith, Lee. "Still Life," Ladies' Home Journal, LXXXVI (August 1969), 62-63, 89.

9165 Smith, Lucian. "Saturday Night at the Movies," Plaintiff, IV (Fall-Winter 1967-68), 17-18.

9166 Smith, Marcus. "No Nonsense," Quartet, no. 24 (Fall 1968), 1-4.

9167 Smith, Martin. "Felix," Ararat, VIII (Autumn 1967), 82-87.

9168 Smith, Mason. "The Glowing of Such Fire," Texas Quarterly, XI (Spring 1968), 88-93.

9169 Smith, Melvin. "Sketches and Poem/One Hundred and Two Games," The Phoenix, (First Semester 1965-66), 15.

9170 ______. "Sketches and Poem/The Professional," The Phoenix, (First Semester 1965-66), 14-15.

9171 ______. "Sketches and Poem/The Protest," The Phoenix, (First Semester 1965-66), 14.

9172 Smith, Michael Jm. "A Cock Crows over a Hung-Up Dirty Old Locomotive," Literary Magazine of Tufts University, II, no. 1 (1967), 109.

9173 ______. "The Deluge," Literary Magazine of Tufts University, I, no. 2 (1966), 38.

9174 ______. "The Eighth Day Reality of Adam's Thaw," Literary Magazine of Tufts University, I, no. 2 (1966), 13-14.

9175 Smith, O. T. "Boss," New Zealand Listener, LVIII (July 12, 1968), 10.

9176 Smith, Patrick D. "The Checker Board," Delta Review, III (Spring 1966), 44-45, 83-92.

9177 Smith, Peggy. "No Movement...," Evidence, no. 9 (1965), 50-59.

9178 Smith, Ralph. "From The Night of the German Man," Red Clay Reader, no. 2 (1965), 83-85.

9179 ______. "Watch Out for Snipers, Horatio," Red Clay Reader, no. 5 (1968), 26-30.

9180 Smith, Ray. "Cape Breton Is the Thought-Control Center of Canada," Tamarack Review, no. 45 (Autumn 1967), 39-53.

9181 ______. "Colours," Prism International, VIII (Autumn 1968), 43-57.

9182 Smith, Richard. "Rendezvous," Free Lance, IX, no. 2 (1965), 8-10.

9183 Smith, Ron. "A Quiet Evening Away from Home," Westerly, (August 1966), 34-38.

9184 Smith, Rosslyn. "A Fashion in Porcelain," Westerly, no. 3 (October 1968), 18-19.

9185 _____. "Miniature," Westerly, no. 1 (April 1969), 10-12.

9186 _____. "Nautilus," Westerly, no. 2 (1967), 12-15.

9187 Smith, Stephen E. "The Owl," Crucible, VI (Fall 1969), 5-8.

9188 Smith, W. P. J. "The Goose in the Bottle," University Review, XXXII (October 1965), 3-9.

9189 Smolich, Yuri. "Patron of Arts Knyaz Kovsky," Vladimir Leonov, trans., Soviet Literature, (no. 9, 1968), 5-17.

9190 Smoot, William R., II. "Resignation," Aesop's Feast, I (January 1969), 23-30.

9191 Smuul, Juhan. "Monologues," Hilda Perham, trans., Soviet Literature, (no. 9, 1969), 3-42.

9192 Smyth, George W. "The Brave Fool," Four Quarters, XVII (January 1968), 1-5.

9193 _____. "The Burden," Southwest Review, LIII (Spring 1968), 186-193.

9194 _____. "Feast of Images," Works, II (Spring 1969), 36-40, 42-50.

9195 _____. "Inside the Memory Bank," North American Review, V (May-June 1968), 26-28.

9196 _____. "Into the Water," University Review, XXXV (Winter 1968), 119-123.

9197 _____. "The Sleepwalker," Discourse, X (Autumn 1967), 456-462.

9198 _____. "Timepiece," Arlington Quarterly, II (Autumn 1969), 18-25.

9199 Snegiryov, Evgeni. "Bear Me Three Sons," Eve Manning, trans., Soviet Literature, (no. 7, 1968), 110-122.

9200 Snegiryov, Gennadi. "Three Stories/The Aral Sea," Margaret

Wettlin, trans., Soviet Literature, (no. 6, 1968), 146-148.

9201 ______. "Three Stories/Julka," Margaret Wettlin, trans., Soviet Literature, (no. 6, 1968), 149.

9202 ______. "Three Stories/Wild Beast," Margaret Wettlin, trans., Soviet Literature, (no. 6, 1968), 148.

9203 Snider, James G. "Down To a Sunless Sea," Edge, no. 6 (Spring 1967), 85-96.

9204 Snow, Karen. "Fortune Cookies," Michigan Quarterly Review, V (Summer 1966), 159-161.

9205 ______. "Pipe-Smoke and Perfume," Michigan Quarterly Review, VII (Fall 1968), 259-261.

9206 Snyder, John. "Banana Peels," Gato Magazine, II (Spring-Summer 1967), 14-17.

9207 ______. "Dirty Dishes," New Mexico Quarterly, XXXV (Spring 1965), 58-62.

9208 ______. "Misty," Dust, II (Spring-Summer 1966), 29-31.

9209 ______. "Uncle Web," Gato Magazine, I (Autumn 1966), 18-20.

9210 Snyder, Lynn J. "An Unfamiliar Brand," Midwestern University Quarterly, II, no. 3 (1967), 73-79.

9211 Snyder, Richard. "Death and the Detroit Lions," The Quest, I (Spring 1966), 44-54.

9212 ______. "A Late Decorum for De Koven Street," The Fiddlehead, no. 75 (Spring 1968), 49-57.

9213 Snyder, Robert F. "The Zebra Fingerprint," Mt. Adams Review, II (Winter 1967-68), 14-15.

9214 Sobolev, Leonid. "The Lore of Omens," Eve Manning, trans., Soviet Literature, (no. 7, 1968), 97-109.

9215 ______. "Tatian, the Scout," Soviet Literature, (no. 4, 1967), 97-101.

9216 Sobral, Geraldo. "The Yellow Umbrella," Barry Munn, trans., Prism International, VII (Autumn 1967), 102-107.

9217 Soebbing, Denise. "Birthday Vigil," Quarterly, LXIII, no. 1 (1966), 29-33.

9218 Soenharjo, Bibsy. "The Butterfly and the Sun," Literary Review, XI (Autumn 1967), 76-80.

9219 Sohar, Paul. "Beloved," Writer's Forum, I (Fall 1965), 17-19, 50-52.

9220 Sohmer, Stephen T. "Nine-Five," Southern Review, II (July 1966), 657-674.

9221 Sokolova, Natalia. "Short Stories/The Eleventh Step," Asya Shoyett, trans., Soviet Literature, (no. 4, 1965), 92-95.

9222 _____. "Short Stories/The Flow of Factory Life," Asya Shoyett, trans., Soviet Literature, (no. 4, 1965), 95.

9223 _____. "Short Stories/A Gypsy Tells My Fortune," Asya Shoyett, trans., Soviet Literature, (no. 4, 1965), 95-97.

9224 _____. "Short Stories/Hands," Asya Shoyett, trans., Soviet Literature, (no. 4, 1965), 91.

9225 _____. "Short Stories/Peter Vischer, Sr.," Asya Shoyett, trans., Soviet Literature, (no. 4, 1965), 100-101.

9226 _____. "Short Stories/The Soldier's Death," Asya Shoyett, trans., Soviet Literature, (no. 4, 1965), 97-98.

9227 _____. "Short Stories/We Have Moved," Asya Shoyett, trans., Soviet Literature, (no. 4, 1965), 98-100.

9228 Sokolov-Mikitov, Ivan. "The Voices of Earth," Eve Manning, trans., Soviet Literature, (no. 8, 1968), 125-137.

9229 Soldati, Mario. "The Man in Black," Michael Bullock, trans., Malahat Review, no. 8 (October 1968), 73-76.

9230 Soleta, Justin. "A Murder on the Town," Ave Maria, CIII (April 30, 1966), 6.

9231 Solomita, Stephen. "At Home a Wednesday Evening," Niobe, no. 1 (1965), 40-46.

9232 Solomon, Carl. "The Adventures of Zig-Zag," VDRSVP-VDRSVPVDRSVP, (1969), n.p. [front page].

9233 _____. "from the files of Carl Solomon--1962," Intrepid, no. 6 (1966), n.p. [13-14].

9234 _____. "The Young Man Who Went Away," Intrepid, no. 5 (March 1965), n.p. [37].

9235 Solomon, Olivia Pienezza. "Fire," Ball State University Forum, X (Autumn 1969), 53-59.

9236 Solow, Martin. "Nobody Asks Ronald Coleman to Kiss Them--Not Even Selma Wolinsky," Signature, I (May 1966), 66-68.

9237 _____. "'Roses You Want? I'll Give You Roses!'," Signature, II (May 1967), 46-50, 52, 54, 58.

9238 Solzhenitsyn, Alexander. "Breathing," Harry Willetts, trans., Encounter, XXIV (March 1965), 3-9.

9239 _____. "Liars," Thomas P. Whitney, trans., Saturday Evening Post, CCXLI (September 21, 1968), 32-34, 80-84, 86-90, 92.

9240 _____. "The Right Hand," Atlantic Monthly, CCXXIII (May 1969), 45-49.

9241 Soman, Florence Jane. "The Girl with Love in Her Eyes," Good Housekeeping, CLXV (July 1967), 76-77, 129-131.

9242 _____. "My Secret, Your Secret," Good Housekeeping, CLXIX (December 1969), 92-93.

9243 _____. "One More Promise," Good Housekeeping, CLXII (June 1966), 82-84.

9244 _____. "One Unhappy Bachelor," Good Housekeeping, CLXV (November 1967), 90-91, 172, 174-178.

9245 _____. "Picture of Success," Good Housekeeping, CLXII (February 1966), 71-73, 194, 196-198, 200, 202, 204, 206, 208, 210-216, 223-231.

9246 _____. "Something Wonderful," Good Housekeeping, CLXIX (September 1969), 84-85, 158-159, 161-162.

9247 Somayajulu, Chaganti. "Leaves of the Soap-Nut Tree," R. Appalaswamy, trans., Literary Half-Yearly, VI (July 1965), 55-60.

9248 Somerlott, Robert. "The Inquisitor's House," Mademoiselle, LXVII (July 1968), 91-124.

9249 Somerville, Lee. "To Kill a King," Columbia, XLIX (November 1969), 24-28.

9250 Sommers, F. J. "Close by My Side," Good Housekeeping, CLXII (June 1966), 84-86.

9251 Song Pyong-Su. "Shorty Kim," Yu E. Song, trans., Malahat Review, no. 6 (April 1968), 5-21.

9252 Sonnino, Lee. "A Day in the Holiday of Dr. Carver," Alta, no. 7 (Winter 1968-69), 55-57.

9253 Sorensen, Jerold G. "A Game Called Death," December, VIII (1966), 33-36.

9254 Sørensen, Villy. "The Two Inventors," Encounter, XXIV (June 1965), 17-19.

9255 Sorenson, Gene. "An Act of Desperation," Arx, II (August 1968), 2-8.

9256 ______. "Divorces and Other Minor Disturbances," Arx, I (June 1967), 4-13.

9257 ______. "Lordsville," Arx, I (March 1967), 6-14.

9258 ______. "One Thousand Eight Hundred Thirty Six Days," Arx, I (October 1967), 20-22.

9259 ______. "Tell It Slant," Arx, I (July-August 1967), 6-12.

9260 Sorrells, Robert T. "Drowning," Western Humanities Review, XXII (Winter 1968), 47-57.

9261 ______. "Speech after Long Silence," Southern Humanities Review, III (Winter 1969), 43-57.

9262 Sorzano, M. Griffin. "The Perfect House," Kansas Magazine, (1965), 98-102.

9263 Sōseki, Natsume. "Ten Nights of Dream," Itō Aiko and Graeme Wilson, trans., Japan Quarterly, XVI (July-September 1969), 314-327.

9264 Soto, Pedro Juan. "The Sniper," Kal Wagenheim, trans., Caribbean Review, I (Fall 1969), 3-5.

9265 Sourian, Peter. "The Gate," Ararat, VI (Autumn 1965), 18-24.

9266 Southerly, George. "The Mole and Mrs. Kimber," Daily Telegraph Magazine, no. 250 (July 25, 1969), 34-36, 38.

9267 Southern, Terry. "The Blood of a Wig," Evergreen Review, XI (October 1967), 22-24, 87-90.

9268 Spacks, Barry. "The Beard," Carleton Miscellany, IX (Summer 1968), 12-23.

9269 ______. "I Will Listen," Quarterly Review of Literature, XV (1968), 423-429.

9270 Spade, Stephen G. "The Box," The Phoenix, (Second Semester 1965-66), 28-30.

9271 Spark, Muriel. "Alice Long's Dachshunds," New Yorker, XLIII (April 1, 1967), 36-40.

9272 _____. "Exotic Departures," New Yorker, XLII (January 28, 1967), 31-32.

9273 _____. "The House of the Famous Poet," New Yorker, XLII (April 2, 1966), 46-50.

9274 _____. "Ladies and Gentlemen," Harper's Magazine, CCXXXI (July 1965), 60-64.

9275 _____. "The Mandelbaum Gate/Abdul's Orange Groves," New Yorker, XLI (August 7, 1965), 28-34, 36, 39-40, 44, 46, 51-52, 54, 56-58, 61-65.

9276 _____. "The Mandelbaum Gate/Barbara Vaughan's Identity," New Yorker, XLI (July 10, 1965), 25-32, 34, 37-38, 40, 45-46, 48, 51-52.

9277 _____. "The Mandelbaum Gate/A Delightful English Atmosphere," New Yorker, XLI (July 24, 1965), 26-34, 36, 39-40, 42, 47-48, 53-54.

9278 _____. "The Mandelbaum Gate/Freddy's Work," New Yorker, XLI (May 15, 1965), 54-59.

9279 _____. "The Public Image (Part I)," Cosmopolitan, CLXV (August 1968), 117-124.

9280 _____. "The Public Image (Part II)," Cosmopolitan, CLXV (September 1968), 146-153.

9281 _____. "The Public Image (Part III)," Cosmopolitan, CLXV (October 1968), 154-160.

9282 _____. "The Public Image (Conclusion)," Cosmopolitan, CLXV (November 1968), 152-156, 158.

9283 _____. "The Public Image," Nova, (June 1968), 104-105, 107.

9284 Sparrow, Giordian. "Babes in the Cottonwood," Antioch Review, XXVI (Winter 1966-67), 514-527.

9285 Spears, Drew. "A Diamond Ring," The Archive, LXXIX (September 1966), 7-10.

9286 _____. "Shaping Mounds on the Wall," The Archive, LXXIX (April 1967), 30-33.

9287 Speas, Jan Cox. "Happy Anniversary, Darling," Good Housekeeping, CLX (June 1965), 92-93, 156, 158, 160.

9288 _____. "There's One in Every Family," Woman's Day, (June 1966), 38-39, 88, 92, 94-96.

9289 Speer, Laurel. "A Knife Incident," The Smith, no. 5 (1965), 22-37.

9290 Speicher, John. "Ashgraves Loves a Mystery," Cavalier, XV (August 1965), 56-62, 82-84.

9291 _____. "Blind Man and the Rusty Bird," Story, I (May 1967), 74-88.

9292 _____. "Looking for Baby Paradise," Cavalier, XVI (February 1966), 40-43, 64, 66-72.

9293 Spence, Alan. "Silver in the Lamplight," Scottish International, no. 8 (October 1969), 27-32.

9294 Spencer, Colin. "The Room," Transatlantic Review, no. 21 (Summer 1966), 111-114.

9295 Spencer, Elizabeth. "The Absence," New Yorker, XLII (September 10, 1966), 53-54.

9296 _____. "The Adult Holiday," New Yorker, XLI (June 12, 1965), 35-36.

9297 _____. "A Bad Cold," New Yorker, XLIII (May 27, 1967), 38-39.

9298 _____. "Knights and Dragons," Redbook, CXXV (July 1965), 127, 129-151.

9299 _____. "On the Gulf," Delta Review, V (February 1968), 44-46.

9300 _____. "The Pincian Gate," New Yorker, XLII (April 16, 1966), 50-52.

9301 _____. "Those Bufords," McCall's, XCIV (January 1967), 76-77, 124, 126.

9302 Spencer, Sharon D. "The Last Constant Lover," Forum, IV (Fall-Winter 1965), 32-38.

9303 _____. "When the Twisters Come...," Ball State University Forum, VII (Autumn 1966), 56-63.

9304 Spettigue, Doug. "Edge of Christmas," The Fiddlehead, no. 80 (May-July 1969), 13-23.

9305 Spicehandler, Daniel. "Black Barbecue," Transatlantic Review, no. 22 (Autumn 1966), 17-30.

9306 ______. "The Race of Scorpions," Transatlantic Review, no. 28 (Spring 1968), 32-38.

9307 Spicer, Jack. "The Scroll-work on the Casket," Whe're, no. 1 (Summer 1966), 28.

9308 Spiegel, Joy. "Don't Hang Up," The Fiddlehead, no. 63 (Winter 1965), 43-46.

9309 ______. "Job's Laughter," Ball State University Forum, VI (Spring 1965), 28-30.

9310 Spielberg, Peter. "In Adam's Room," West Coast Review, III (Fall 1968), 15-22.

9311 ______. "Palimpsest," Abyss, I (March-April 1967), n.p. [5-8].

9312 ______. "Palimpsest," Wascana Review, III, no. 1 (1968), 60-62.

9313 ______. "Radix Malorum," Southern Humanities Review, III (Fall 1969), 372-381.

9314 ______. "The Room," Florida Quarterly, I (October 1968), 5-11.

9315 ______. "The Unicorn Tamed," Mad River Review, II (Summer 1966), 57-60.

9316 Spigle, Naomi Halperin. "For Everything, a Season," Ave Maria, CVI (October 21, 1967), 26-27.

9317 Spike, Paul. "A. B. Dick," Columbia Review, XLIX, no. 2 (1969), 6-11.

9318 ______. "Abraham's Tent," Columbia Review, XLVIII, no. 1 (1967), 20-22.

9319 ______. "Excerpts from The Diary of Noel Wells," Columbia Review, XLIX, no. 1 (1969), 15-21.

9320 ______. "Multi," Paris Review, XII (Summer 1969), 44-58.

9321 Spinard, Norman. "Bug Jack Barron/Part 4," New Worlds, no. 181 (April 1968), 12-22, 44-59.

9322 ______. "Bug Jack Barron/Part 6," New Worlds, no. 183 (October 1968), 45-59.

9323 ______. "Deathwatch," Playboy, XII (November 1965), 121, 192-193.

9324 Spinetti, Victor. "The Revolutionary," Queen, CDXXIX (August 2, 1967), 43.

9325 Spingarn, Lawrence P. "The Ambassador," Southern Humanities Review, I (Spring 1967), 12-20.

9326 ______. "An Autumn Journey," Denver Quarterly, III (Autumn 1968), 73-84.

9327 ______. "Houses in the Sand," Florida Quarterly, II (January 1969), 84-90.

9328 ______. "Journey in New Clothes," University Review, XXXV (Spring 1969), 296-300.

9329 ______. "The Lady with the Shears," University Review, XXXIII (Summer 1967), 279-285.

9330 ______. "The Medicine Man," Southern Humanities Review, I (Fall 1967), 254-270.

9331 ______. "Memory and Desire," Quarterly Review of Literature, XV (1968), 430-442.

9332 ______. "Regatta," Dalhousie Review, XLVI (Winter 1966-67), 466-474.

9333 ______. "The Ritual Bath," Wascana Review, IV, no. 1 (1969), 53-59.

9334 ______. "The Ruins," Queen's Quarterly, LXXIV (Summer 1967), 294-301.

9335 ______. "The Statues," University Review, XXXIV (Spring 1968), 214-222.

9336 Spracklen, Myrtle. "The Most Unobtainable Bride," New Frontiers, X, no. 2 (1965), 60-68.

9337 Spratling, William. "El Loro," Mexico Quarterly Review, II (July 1965), 167-168.

9338 ______. "Tata Luis," Mexico Quarterly Review, II (July 1965), 169-170.

9339 Spyropulos, Diana. "The Flute," Readers & Writers, II (Summer 1968), 22-24.

9340 Squier, Jerrie. "Down," Prairie Schooner," XLII (Fall 1968), 251-262.

9341 Squires, Flora. "Aunt Suzie's Rooster," Bim, XII (July-December 1967), 11-14.

9342 Ssemuwanga, J. "Ten Long Years," Dialogue (Nairobi, Kenya), no. 2 (October-December 1965), 14-15.

9343 Stace, Jeanette. "The Hole," New Zealand Listener, (July 8, 1966), 6.

9344 Stack, R. L. "R.I.P.," Ave Maria, CII (August 28, 1965), 22-24.

9345 Stack, Vivian. "The Day She Saw Things as They Are," Panache, I, no. 1 (1965), 1, 13-26.

9346 _____. "Evelyn," Panache, I, no. 1 (1965), 27-41.

9347 _____. "Their Eyes Don't Open For Two Weeks," Panache, no. 3 (1969), 32-37.

9348 Stacton, David. "Little Brother Nun," Virginia Quarterly Review, XLIII (Spring 1967), 264-280.

9349 _____. "Notes Written in the Self of a Man with a Singular Distaste for Writing Anything Down," Transatlantic Review, no. 28 (Spring 1968), 7-21.

9350 _____. "An Old Man Crosses the Border," Southwest Review, LI (Winter 1966), 46-62.

9351 _____. "A Visit to the Master," Virginia Quarterly Review, XLI (Summer 1965), 403-421.

9352 Stadelhofen, Marcie Miller. "The Apollonian Way," Massachusetts Review, X (Winter 1969), 50-54.

9353 Stafford, Jean. "The Philosophy Lesson," New Yorker, XLIV (November 16, 1968), 59-63.

9354 Stager, Carol. "C'est la Guerre," Trace, no. 59 (Winter 1966), 384-392.

9355 _____. "A Matter of Forward," Ante, IV (Spring 1968), 59-63.

9356 _____. "The Rockettes from Behind," Ante, III (Winter 1967), 3-5.

9357 Stahl, Hermann. "Escape into Space," George Raymond Selden, trans., Scala International, (September 1965), 34-36.

9358 Stallman, Leanne. "The Patient," Story: the Yearbook of Discovery, (1969), 86-98.

9359 Stallman, Robert L. "The Hunters," South Dakota Review, VI (Winter 1968-69), 85-100.

9360 Stamatov, Georgi P. "The Narzanovs," Petko Drenkov, trans., Obzor, (Summer 1968), 60-70.

9361 ______. "Villa at the Seaside," Petko Drenkov, trans., Obzor, (Summer 1968), 57-60.

9362 Stanbury, C. M., II. "A Secret History of the Earth," December, IX, nos. 2/3 (1967), 89-94.

9363 Stancu, Zaharia. "A Gamble with Death/(Fragment)," Literary Review, X (Summer 1967), 467-472.

9364 Standen, Michael. "The Oldest Soldier," Stand, VIII, no. 3 (1966), 7-11.

9365 Standish, Robert. "All Strictly Legal," Courier, XLV (November 1965), 45-50.

9366 ______. "Cold Justice," Courier, XLIV (April 1965), 37-44.

9367 ______. "Cold Storage," Courier, XLV (December 1965), 46-52.

9368 ______. "The Lady of the Emeralds," Courier, XLV (September 1965), 57-63.

9369 ______. "The Marriage Counsellor," Courier, XLIV (February 1965), 45-52.

9370 ______. "The Miraculous Formula," Courier, XLIV (January 1965), 53-60.

9371 ______. "My Aunt Maggie," Courier, XLIV (June 1965), 37-44.

9372 ______. "The Philosopher," Courier, XLV (August 1965), 29-36.

9373 ______. "The Praying Lady," Courier, XLV (October 1965), 41-49.

9374 ______. "Treasure Trove," Courier, XLV (July 1965), 45-52.

9375 Stanev, Emilian. "The Death of a Bird," Marguerite Alexieva, trans., Obzor, (Fall 1968), 11-14.

9376 ______. "The Walk," Marguerite Alexieva, trans., Obzor, (Fall 1968), 15-22.

9377 ______. "Wolves' Nights," Marguerite Alexieva, trans., Obzor, (Fall 1968), 3-10.

9378 Stanfill, Dorothy. "Goodbye, Ocie May," Lit (Lambda Iota Tau), no. 6 (Spring 1965), 4-13.

9379 Stanford, Don. "Little Miss Tiger," Redbook, CXXXI (June 1968), 141-164.

9380 Stang, C. Gerald. "I Like Hogs Because...," December, IX nos. 2/3 (1967), 200.

9381 Stanton, Johnny. "The Dharma Bums," Columbia Review, XLVIII, no. 3 (1969), 30-37.

9382 ______. "The First Inauguration," The World, no. 10 (February 1968), n.p. [11].

9383 ______. "from Helping the Guy with the Prostitutes/an autobiographical story," Columbia Review, XLVIII, no. 2 (1968), 56-70.

9384 ______. "From Here to Eternity," Columbia Review, XLIX, no. 2 (1969), 47-55.

9385 ______. "Hi!" Columbia Review, XLVI, no. 2 (1966), 34-38.

9386 ______. "from Mangled Hands," Bones, no. 1 (Fall 1967), 50-56.

9387 ______. "Two Chapters from/Mangled Hands," Columbia Review, XLVII, no. 1 (1966), 11-16.

9388 ______. "Two Chapters from/Mangled Hands," Columbia Review, XLVII, no. 2 (1967), 55-63.

9389 ______. "The Most Unforgetable Character I Ever Met," Yale Literary Magazine, CXXXVIII (May 1969), 6-7.

9390 ______. "Paper," Mother, no. 8 (May Day, 1967), 80-83.

9391 ______. "Chapter Five/Thought," Angel Hair, no. 4 (Winter 1967-68), n.p. [32-34].

9392 ______ and David Anderson. "Time Is On Our Side," Columbia Review, XLIX, no. 2 (1969), 65-89.

9393 ______. "Three Stories/The Rathole," Columbia Review, XLVIII, no. 1 (1967), 31-32.

9394 ______. "Three Stories/The Whole Thing," Columbia Review, XLVIII, no. 1 (1967), 28-31.

9395 ______. "Three Stories/Ye Old Sketch," Columbia Review, XLVIII, no. 1 (1967), 33-35.

9396 Stanton, Will. "Beyond Recall," Woman's Day, (November

1968), 38-39, 76, 78, 80, 82.

9397 _____. "Butterfinger," Redbook, CXXVI (April 1966), 78-79, 141-143.

9398 _____. "The Cookie Rebellion," Redbook, CXXVIII (February 1967), 66-67, 107-109, 113.

9399 _____. "Did Anybody Miss Me?" Redbook, CXXIX (September 1967), 64-65, 130, 132-135.

9400 _____. "A Few Words of Advice," Redbook, CXXIV (April 1965), 60-61, 131-134.

9401 _____. "The Four-Way Pool," Woman's Day, (March 1969), 52-53, 101-104.

9402 _____. "The Golden Evenings," McCall's, XCII (January 1965), 54-55, 124, 126.

9403 _____. "A Good Time to Be Alive," Redbook, CXXIX (May 1967), 52-53, 120-122.

9404 _____. "I'm Having All Kinds of Fun," Redbook, CXXVII (June 1966), 60-61, 131, 136-137, 140-143.

9405 _____. "The Keeper of the Trash," Redbook, CXXXI (September 1968), 82-83, 126, 128-129, 131, 133, 135.

9406 _____. "A Little Potato Salad Goes a Long Way," Redbook, CXXXI (August 1968), 64-65, 131-134.

9407 _____. "Only the Lucky Ones," Redbook, CXXVI (February 1966), 58-59, 122-124, 126-127.

9408 _____. "The Riotous Life," Redbook, CXXVII (August 1966), 48-49, 90, 92, 94.

9409 _____. "A Small Favor," McCall's, XCIII (November 1965), 122-123, 214-217.

9410 _____. "The Summer of the Car," Ladies' Home Journal, LXXXV (April 1968), 108-109, 141-145.

9411 _____. "What Mistletoe?" Ladies' Home Journal, LXXXIV (December 1967), 64-65, 119-123.

9412 Stark, Ellen. "Judgements," Mademoiselle, LXVII (August 1968), 330-331, 380-384.

9413 _____. "Judgements," Silo, no. 11 (Spring 1967), 1-18.

9414 _____. "On the Way," Silo, no. 8 (Fall 1965), 52-60.

9415 _____. "The Waste Sad Time," Silo, no. 13 (Spring 1968), 33-59.

9416 Stark, Sharon. "Help Me with the Deo Gratias," Ave Maria, CIV (August 13, 1966), 20-23.

9417 Starr, B. J. "Before the Wet," Four Quarters, XVIII (November 1968), 27-34.

9418 _____. "Coming of Age in Korea," The Smith, no. 10 (December 1968), 69-84.

9419 Staten, Patricia S. "Thanatopsis," Four Quarters, XVIII (May 1969), 7-14.

9420 Stead, C. K. "A Fitting Tribute," Kenyon Review, XXVII (Spring 1965), 279-301.

9421 Stead, Christina. "The Dianas," Nova, (January 1968), 89-96.

9422 _____. "George," Paris Review, X (Winter-Spring 1967), 12-48.

9423 _____. "The Huntress," Saturday Evening Post, CCXXXVIII (October 23, 1965), 76-78, 80-83, 85-88.

9424 _____. "The Puzzleheaded Girl," Kenyon Review, XXVII (Summer 1965), 399-456.

9425 _____. "The Woman in the Bed," Meanjin Quarterly, XXVII (Summer 1968), 430-452.

9426 Steadman, Mark. "Annie's Love Child," Red Clay Reader, no. 6 (1969), 107-116.

9427 Steeds, Lucy. "The Betrayal," Prism International, VII (Autumn 1967), 54-58.

9428 Steegmuller, Francis. "Soirée à la chandelle," Harper's Bazaar, XCVIII (September 1965), 304, 321, 323.

9429 Steel, Anthony. "On the Sands," Anglo-Welsh Review, XVIII, no. 41 (Summer 1969), 29-43.

9430 Steele, Leighton. "Trips," Spectrum, VIII (Spring 1965), 2-11.

9431 Steele, Max. "A Caracole in Paris," New Mexico Quarterly, XXXVII (Summer 1967), 157-176.

9432 _____. "Color the Daydream Yellow," Quarterly Review of Literature, XV (1968), 443-457.

9433 _____. "Fiction, Fact, and Dream," Carolina Quarterly, XVIII (Fall 1966), 42-57.

9434 _____. "From the French Quarter," Esquire, LXIV (November 1965), 109-110.

9435 _____. "Long Vacation," Cosmopolitan, CLXVII (November 1969), 160-162, 164-166, 168.

9436 _____. "The Most Unbelievable Character I'll Ever Forget," Lillabulero, I (Winter 1967), 31-33.

9437 _____. "The Ragged Halo," South Carolina Review, I (November 1968), 23-37.

9438 _____. "Rock Like a Fool," Red Clay Reader, no. 4 (1967), 25-29.

9439 Steely, Mike. "The Great Truth--Explanation of An Elegy/ 397123 (Mike Steely)," Red Cedar Review, III (Spring 1965), 35-36.

9440 Steen, John Warren. "Pa and Tomcat," Long View Journal, I (Spring 1969), 85-89.

9441 Steensma, Robert C. "Spring Burial," North Dakota Quarterly, XXXIV (Summer 1966), 67-72.

9442 Steers, Nina A. "Ariabella," Américas, XIX (December 1967), 31-36.

9443 Stefánsson, Halldór. "Cruelty," Hallberg Hallmundsson, trans., American Scandinavian Review, LVII (September 1969), 293-295.

9444 Stegner, Page. "Hawks and Harriers," Mademoiselle, LXVII (September 1968), 176-177, 188-189, 191-192.

9445 _____. "The Man Who Came to Stay," McCall's, XCVII (October 1969), 82-83, 130, 132, 134-138, 140.

9446 Steigman, Benjamin M. "Fact-Finding," Discourse, VIII (Autumn 1965), 362-369.

9447 Stein, Agnes. "Twelve Tones to Whatever," Colorado Quarterly, XVII (Winter 1969), 265-279.

9448 Stein, David Lewis. "The Night of the Little Brown Men," Saturday Night, LXXXII (March 1967), 29-31.

9449 Stein, Gerald. "All Creatures Great and Small," Redbook, CXXIV (January 1965), 36-37, 88-91.

9450 _____. "Have Another Cupcake, Jack," Redbook, CXXVII (May 1966), 79, 104-107.

9451 _____. "Milk Is Good for Skinny Kids," Redbook, CXXVI (December 1965), 62-63, 130-132.

9452 Steinberg, Barry. "The Nazi Machine," Story: the Yearbook of Discovery, (1969), 15-37.

9453 Steinberg, Rafael. "Day of Good Fortune," Playboy, XIV (May 1967), 74-76, 82, 165-166.

9454 Stelmakh, Mikhail. "The Return of the Wild Swans," Margaret Wettlin, trans., Soviet Literature, (no. 3, 1965), 2-104.

9455 Stephens, M. G. "Pig," The World, no. 6 (August 1965), n.p. [31-33].

9456 Stephens, Prescot. "An Object of Pity," Old Lady of Threadneedle Street, XLIII (September 1967), 146-149.

9457 Stephens, Rosemary. "Cousin Meggy," Seventeen, XXVII (March 1968), 150-151, 230, 232-233.

9458 Sterling, Thomas. "Bedlam's Rent," Paris Review, XI (Winter-Spring 1968), 177-188.

9459 Stern, Daniel. "My Life: or The Death of Isaac Mendez," University of Windsor Review, V (Fall 1969), 38-43.

9460 Stern, Richard Martin. "A Beginning," McCall's, XCIII (June 1966), 68-69, 164-166.

9461 _____. "Milius and Melanie," Hudson Review, XXI (Autumn 1968), 487-504.

9462 _____. "The Turning Point," Redbook, CXXV (June 1965), 131-153.

9463 Sterner, Margaret Condron. "A Change of Heart," Columbia, XLIX (February 1969), 24-27.

9464 _____. "The Father and the Sun," Columbia, XLIX (September 1969), 23-26.

9465 _____. "The Good Fight," Columbia, XLVIII (November 1968), 24-28.

9466 _____. "Language of the Heart," Columbia, XLVII (October 1967), 24-27.

9467 _____. "Small World," Columbia, XLVII (February 1967), 24-27.

9468 _____. "Willful Will," Columbia, XLVI (February 1966), 24-27.

9469 Sterry, Rich. "Brooks Too Broad for Leaping," Red Cedar Review, V (January 1967), 23-29.

9470 _____. "The Real Us," Redbook, CXXXII (January 1969), 50-51, 125-127.

9471 _____. "Troubadour," Redbook, CXXXIII (June 1969), 68-69, 121, 123, 125.

9472 Stetson, Nancy. "After the Night," Good Housekeeping, CLXIX (September 1969), 92-93.

9473 _____. "Something To Grow On," Good Housekeeping, CLXVIII (April 1969), 118-119.

9474 Stevens, Errol. "The Bearded One," Pegasus, IV, no. 1 (1966), 49-61.

9475 Stevens, Franklin. "Bad Dreams," Manhattan Review, no. 1 (1966), 23-29.

9476 _____. "Daydreams," Beyond Baroque 692, I (July 1969), 17.

9477 Stevens, Lauren P. "The Cave," Ball State University Forum, VII (Autumn 1966), 71-80.

9478 Stevens, Walter W. "Tomorrow's Nobody," Discourse, XI (Winter 1968), 62-64.

9479 Stevenson, James. "Notes from a Bottle," New Yorker, XLIV (February 8, 1969), 31.

9480 _____. "Speed Clean," New Yorker, XLIV (October 19, 1968), 165-166, 168, 170.

9481 Stevenson, Kay L. "My Brother Who Is Dearly Loved," Good Housekeeping, CLXVIII (June 1969), 82-83, 134, 136-138, 141.

9482 Stevenson, Paul. "The Pop Bottle Man's Music Box Birthday," Nimrod, XIII (Spring 1969), 33-36.

9483 Stevenson, William. "The Turtle Watcher," Harper's Bazaar, XCIX (May 1966), 128-129, 204-205, 210-211.

9484 Stewart, Dolores. "Goldilocks," Pyramid, no. 4 (1969), 40-42.

9485 Stewart, Donald C. "An Afternoon on Heron Creek," Four Quarters, XVI (March 1967), 21-25.

9486 _____. "The Ferry to Vermont," New Yorker, XL (January 30, 1965), 26-27.

9487 _____. "Gustave Berger," Kansas Magazine, (1967), 20-23.

9488 Stewart, Edward. "The Barefoot Soprano," Esquire, LXV (March 1966), 112-115, 123-124, 126, 128-130.

9489 _____. "Never Let a Cat Go Hungry," Ladies' Home Journal, LXXXII (September 1965), 58-59, 109-112.

9490 Stewart, Fred Mustard. "The Mephisto Waltz," Cosmopolitan, CLXVI (March 1969), 152-162, 164, 166, 168-174, 176-179.

9491 Stewart, J. Clayton. "To Fight Fire--Burn," Discourse, XI (Spring 1968), 183-190.

9492 Stewart, J. I. M. "A Venation of Centaurs," Malahat Review, no. 11 (July 1969), 97-112.

9493 Stewart, John D. "A Tanner a Time," Threshold, no. 21 (Summer 1967), 41-46.

9494 Stewart, Mary. "Airs above the Ground/(Part 1)," Good Housekeeping, CLXI (August 1965), 59-63, 192-214.

9495 _____. "Airs above the Ground/(Conclusion)," Good Housekeeping, CLXI (September 1965), 76-77, 184-188, 190, 192, 194, 196, 198, 200-202, 210-218, 220-224, 229-236.

9496 _____. "The Wind Off the Small Isles," Good Housekeeping, CLXVII (October 1968), 91-93, 210, 212, 214, 216, 218, 220, 222, 243-244, 246, 248, 250-252, 254, 259, 261-267.

9497 Stewart, Mary Dale. "In a Pillar of a Cloud," New Campus Writing, (1966), 104-111.

9498 Stewart, Natacha. "By a Lake in the Bois," New Yorker, XLIII (October 14, 1967), 52-55.

9499 _____. "In the Middle of Nowhere," New Yorker, XL (January 9, 1965), 29-36.

9500 _____. "A Mack Sennett Comedy," New Yorker, XLI (October 2, 1965), 46-48.

9501 _____. "Portraits in a Village," New Yorker, XLII (February 4, 1967), 32-38.

9502 Stewart, Ora Pate. "The Tramp," Texas Quarterly, XI (Summer 1968), 248-254.

9503 Stewart, T. K. "The Cogitator," Ante, III (Winter 1967), 52-54.

9504 Stigen, Terje. "Aunt Felicia's Cat," Amanda Langemo, trans., American Scandinavian Review, LVI (June 1968), 176-180.

9505 ______. "Easter Morning," Amanda Langemo, trans., American Scandinavian Review, LV (March 1967), 56-60.

9506 ______. "The Gardener," Amanda Langemo, trans., American Scandinavian Review, LIV (June 1966), 174-177.

9507 ______. "The Professor," Amanda Langemo, trans., American Scandinavian Review, LVI (December 1968), 397-401.

9508 Stiles, George. "Lines from the Quick," New American Review, no. 4 (August 1968), 178-181.

9509 ______. "The Reprieve," Literary Half-Yearly, VIII (January & July 1967), 91-112.

9510 Stiles, Martha Bennett. "The Samovar," Georgia Review, XXI (Summer 1967), 260-267.

9511 ______. "Sylvia's Mother," Seventeen, XXIV (October 1965), 142-143, 160, 162, 164.

9512 Stillwell, Mary Kathryn. "Angel on a Curtain Rod," New Leaven, no. 16 (1966), 31-35.

9513 Stinnett, Loni. "My Love Is Like a Red, Red Rose," McCall's, XCV (October 1967), 108-109.

9514 Stirling, Monica. "The Summer of a Dormouse," McCall's, XCIV (June 1967), 70-73, 106, 108-114, 116-118, 120-128.

9515 Stivens, Dal. "The Big-Hearted Racehorse," Hemisphere, X (February 1966), 23-26.

9516 ______. "The Blue Wren," Quadrant, X (May-June 1966), 64-66.

9517 ______. "The Lecturer in English," Meanjin Quarterly, XXV (June 1966), 144-153.

9518 ______. "Metamorphosis," Hemisphere, XI (February 1967), 22-24.

9519 ______. "The Pepper-Tree," Hemisphere, IX (February 1965), 33-35.

9520 ______. "The Remarkable Cockerel," Eastern Horizon, IV (April 1965), 50-55.

9521 ______. "The Ring-In," Southerly, XXVI, no. 3 (1966), 147-151.

9522 _____. "Sanctuary," Northern American Review, II (September 1965), 8-9.

9523 _____. "The Talkative Turtle," Eastern Horizon, IV (September 1965), 58-60.

9524 _____. "Wild Dog," Texas Quarterly, X (Spring 1967), 156-163.

9525 Stokes, Harry. "Eat at Maxy's," The Archive, LXXX (December 1967), 21-24.

9526 Stokes, Terry. "The Dummy," December, XI, nos. 1 & 2 (1969), 66-67.

9527 _____. "The Market Place in the Hungry Times," Sou'wester, (Winter 1969), 70-82.

9528 Stoll, Harry. "The Decider," Dust, IV (Summer 1969), 7-15.

9529 Stolz, Mary. "I Love You--Truly," Good Housekeeping, CLXII (January 1966), 68-69.

9530 _____. "Ici, on Parle What?" Seventeen, XXIV (April 1965), 148-149, 195, 197, 200, 202, 205, 207.

9531 _____. "The Rage to Wed," Woman's Day, (October 1966), 46-47, 116-120.

9532 _____. "Rue for Remembrance," Woman's Day, (July 1966), 36-37, 93-95.

9533 Stone, Alma. "Clap for Our Boys," Antioch Review, XXVI (Spring 1966), 107-118.

9534 _____. "The Street Corner Coordinator," Antioch Review, XXIX (Summer 1969), 200-211.

9535 Stone, Ed. "Not a Worry in the World," The Smith, no. 8 (March 1968), 103-113.

9536 Stone, Philip Alston. "The Dead," Southern Review, IV (October 1968), 1041-1072.

9537 _____. "Private Forsyth & the Interpreter," Per/Se, II (Summer 1967), 45-47.

9538 Stone, Robert. "Farley the Sailor," Saturday Evening Post, CCXL (January 14, 1967), 42-44, 46, 48-51.

9539 _____. "Porque No Tiene, Porque Le Falta," New American Review, no. 6 (April 1969), 198-226.

9540 ______. "Thunderbolts in Red, White, and Blue," Saturday Evening Post, CCXL (January 28, 1967), 62-64, 66-71.

9541 Stoppard, Tom. "The Story," Evergreen Review, XII (July 1968), 52-55.

9542 Storti, Frank. "Boxes," Nexus (San Francisco, Calif.), III (March-April 1967), 13-17.

9543 Stout, Robert Joe. "Ah! Middletown!" Prospero's Cell, I (Winter 1967), 47-50.

9544 ______. "Ah! Paris!" Ante, III (Summer 1967), 51-59.

9545 ______. "The Almond Trees," Arx, I (April 1968), 17-20.

9546 ______. "Big Daddy," North American Review, V (January 1968), 36.

9547 ______. "The Black Cong," Arx, II (December 1966), 32-41.

9548 ______. "The Cage," Goodly Co., no. 9 (June 1967), 20-27.

9549 ______. "The Choice," Arx, II (August 1968), 9-13.

9550 ______. "Christmas at Aunt Sarah's," The Quest, II (Fall 1967), 219-239.

9551 ______. "A God for Thelma," Four Quarters, XVII (May 1968), 29-38.

9552 ______. "The Goddess," Arx, II (November 1968), 2-6.

9553 ______. "Hawaiian Teak," Arx, II (January 1969), 21-32.

9554 ______. "The Heirs (Part I)," Arx, III (July 1969), 16-26.

9555 ______. "The Heirs (Part II--Conclusion)," Arx, III (August 1969), 26-36.

9556 ______. "The King of the Yippies," Arx, III (May 1969), 12-15.

9557 ______. "A Letter to Orlando," Arx, III (September 1969), 9-14.

9558 ______. "Love that Spring Kills," Arx, I (October 1967), 4-9, 39-52.

9559 ______. "Mote in the Pond's Eye," Georgia Review, XXI (Summer 1967), 238-243.

9560 ______. "The Mythmakers," Arx, II (May 1968), 14-31.

9561 _____. "Nice Young Man," Kansas Magazine, (1967), 31-37.

9562 _____. "A Place of Need," Four Quarters, XIV (May 1965), 7-17.

9563 _____. "Run, Run, Run," Arx, II (April 1969), 20-23.

9564 _____. "The Storm," Arx, II (February 1969), 4-11.

9565 _____. "A Stroll by the Sea," Arx, II (June 1968), 23-34.

9566 _____. "The Surrender," Arx, II (October 1968), 30-35.

9567 _____. "Susan," Arx, I (December 1967), 31-42.

9568 _____. "The Truce," Goodly Co., no. 13 (November 1968), 31-35.

9569 _____. "Why Not Say You Loved Her?" Four Quarters, XVIII (May 1969), 1-6.

9570 _____. "The Wolf," Arx, II (March 1969), 5-11.

9571 Strachey, Isobel. "The Cruise," London Magazine, VII (September 1967), 8-16.

9572 Strachey, Lytton. "Ermyntrude and Esmeralda," Playboy, XVI (January 1969), 179, 184, 202, 224-230.

9573 Strahan, Lynne. "The Five Years after Letter," Meanjin Quarterly, XXIV (March 1965), 103-110.

9574 Straker, Warren. "Faded Jeans and Banners Bright," Overland, no. 42 (Spring 1969), 5-7.

9575 Strandjev, Kosta. "Cramps," Svetoslaw Piperov, trans., Obzor, (Spring 1969), 58-64.

9576 Stranger, Joyce. "Breed of Giants," Saturday Evening Post, CCXL (June 3, 1967), 44-47, 50, 52, 54-56, 58, 60, 62-64, 66-67.

9577 _____. "The Running Foxes," Saturday Evening Post, CCXXXIX (May 7, 1966), 50-54, 58, 60-67, 70-74.

9578 Strauss, Theodore. "A Place for Jimmy," Good Housekeeping, CLX (January 1965), 54-55, 160, 162-175, 181, 184-188.

9579 Streeter, Edward. "Keep Moving, Please," McCall's, XCIII (December 1966), 56-57, 128-131.

9580 Strehlow, Loretta. "Anyone Can Buy an Easter Lily," Redbook, CXXV (June 1965), 64-65, 90-91.

9581 Strelke, Barbara. "A Matter of Choice," Cimarron Review, no. 9 (September 1969), 85-86.

9582 Strickler, Patrick. "Another Afternoon," Ave Maria, CV (April 8, 1967), 26-27, 29.

9583 _____. "Pokagon," Ave Maria, CVI (September 2, 1967), 26-29.

9584 _____. "A Pride of Lions," Ave Maria, CVII (February 3, 1968), 26-28.

9585 Strindberg, August. "In the Midsummertime," Erik Sandberg-Diment, trans., The Quest, II (Spring 1968), 283-292.

9586 _____. "The Sound Sleeper," Erik Sandberg-Diment, trans., The Quest, II (Fall 1967), 163-168.

9587 _____. "Vestman's Sealing Adventure," Arvid Paulson, trans., American Scandinavian Review, LIV (March 1966), 55-59.

9588 Strohmier, David. "Old Billy," Pegasus, III (Winter 1965), 5-12.

9589 Stromberg, Scott. "The Falling Out," Quartet, no. 28 (Fall 1969), 24-27.

9590 Strong, Jonathan. "Patients," Atlantic Monthly, CCXXIII (March 1969), 42-45.

9591 _____. "Tike's Days," Tri-Quarterly, no. 10 (Fall 1967), 176-181.

9592 _____. "Walks," Shenandoah, XXI (Autumn 1969), 33-39.

9593 Strugatsky, Arkadi and Boris. "An Emergency Case," Vision, XV (April 1969), 11-20.

9594 _____. "Six Matches," Leonard Stoklitsky, trans., Soviet Literature, (no. 5, 1968), 74-90.

9595 _____. "Wanderers and Travellers," Vision, XV (September 1966), 10-13.

9596 Strunk, Orlo. "Yes, Sir," Cimarron Review, no. 3 (March 1968), 71-79.

9597 Struther, Jan. "The Kiss in Colin's Eyes," Ararat, VIII (Summer 1967), 8-13.

9598 Stuart, Dabney. "Katherine," William and Mary Review, III (Spring 1965), 69-73.

9599 Stuart, Donald R. "The Blue Horse," Meanjin Quarterly, XXIV (March 1965), 55-61.

9600 Stuart, Jesse. "The Accident," Saturday Evening Post, CCXXXIX (November 19, 1966), 54-56, 60, 62.

9601 _____. "Beside the Still Waters," Ball State University Forum, VI (Spring 1965), 3-8.

9602 _____. "Can You Win by Losing?" University Review, XXXIII (October 1966), 25-32.

9603 _____. "Coal Miner's Son," Arizona Quarterly, XXV (Autumn 1969), 209-216.

9604 _____. "Come Live a Century with Me," University Review, XXXIX (Autumn 1967), 50-56.

9605 _____. "Does the Army Always Get Its Man?" Kansas Quarterly, I (Winter 1968), 31-37.

9606 _____. "Earth Men," Arizona Quarterly, XXI (Spring 1965), 41-52.

9607 _____. "Fiddlesticks and Firebugs," Prairie Schooner, XLI (Spring 1967), 1-10.

9608 _____. "Freedom within Freedom's Wall," Literature East and West, IX (June 1965), 114-119.

9609 _____. "Good Old State Bus but Who Cares," Literature East and West, XI (March 1967), 52-54.

9610 _____. "Holiday with the Larkses," Southwest Review, LIV (Summer 1969), 274-287.

9611 _____. "Home for the Bed," Georgia Review, XIX (Summer 1965), 169-175.

9612 _____. "Hot Trumpeter of Love," Green River Review, I (November 1968), 5-13.

9613 _____. "The House that James Built," Ball State Teachers College Forum, VI (Winter 1965), 13-23.

9614 _____. "How Educational Progress Came to Greenwood Country," Arizona Quarterly, XXIII (Spring 1967), 64-77.

9615 _____. "How to Thread a Needle," Ohio University Review, IX (1967), 16-30.

9616 _____. "In Memory Of," Ball State University Forum, IX (Summer 1968), 24-29.

9617 ______. "Judge Ripper's Day," New Mexico Quarterly, XXXV (Spring 1965), 82-94.

9618 ______. "The Latest Thing in America," Kansas Magazine, (1966), 38-44.

9619 ______. "The Lawyer and the Chicken Thief," Arlington Quarterly, II (Summer 1969), 32-48.

9620 ______. "A Little Piece of Striped Candy-Colored String," Southwest Review, LIII (Spring 1968), 131-138.

9621 ______. "Little Wooden Boy," Arizona Quarterly, XXIV (Winter 1968), 309-324.

9622 ______. "Love Is a Quadratic Equation," Ball State University Forum, IX (Summer 1968), 57-61.

9623 ______. "Love Is Where You Have Found It," Minnesota Review, V (May-July 1965), 113-120.

9624 ______. "Maria McDowell," North Dakota Quarterly, XXXVI (Autumn 1968), 19-25.

9625 ______. "Maybelle's First-Born," Prairie Schooner, XLII (Fall 1968), 189-200.

9626 ______. "Mission Incomplete," Green River Review, II (Fall 1969), 3-12.

9627 ______. "Neighbors in the Hills," Kansas Magazine, (1965), 47-51.

9628 ______. "On the Map," Ball State University Forum, VII (Spring 1966), 6-13.

9629 ______. "Our Sammie," Esquire, LXX (October 1968), 204-205, 290-293.

9630 ______. "Our Tom-the-Hammer," Green River Review, I (November 1968), 14-21.

9631 ______. "Ragmop," Four Quarters, XV (March 1966), 29-36.

9632 ______. "Still the Champion," Four Quarters, XV (January 1966), 1-6.

9633 ______. "Sweet Meadows," Ball State University Forum, IX (Summer 1968), 47-55.

9634 ______. "There! She's Done It! Done It Again!" Appalachian Review, I (Summer 1966), 24-28.

9635 _____. "A Thousand Years Is a Long Time," Arizona Quarterly, XXIII (Autumn 1967), 227-242.

9636 _____. "Two Worlds," Georgia Review, XXI (Winter 1967), 449-456.

9637 _____. "Uncle Felix and the Party Emblem," Georgia Review, XX (Summer 1966), 136-144.

9638 _____. "Uncle Tom and the Navy," Southwest Review, LIII (Autumn 1968), 374-380.

9639 _____. "W-Hollow Man," Arizona Quarterly, XXIV (Summer 1968), 147-162.

9640 _____. "Who Has the Luck Anyway," Statement, no. 25 (Spring 1969), 1-8.

9641 _____. "Who's the Future?" Four Quarters, XVI (March 1967), 10-15.

9642 Stuart, Neal Gilkyson. "The Journey," Redbook, CXXIV (January 1965), 40-41, 91-95.

9643 Sturgeon, Theodore. "The Nail and the Oracle," Playboy, XII (October 1965), 101-102, 152, 154, 156, 158-159.

9644 Sturges, A. E. "A Change," Meanjin Quarterly, XXIX (September 1965), 308-316.

9645 Sturm, Carol. "The Aardvark in the Elephant House," Phylon, XXVI (Fall 1965), 277-281.

9646 _____. "Fly, Fly Away," Prairie Schooner, XXXIX (Spring 1965), 61-71.

9647 _____. "The Kid Who Fractioned," Prairie Schooner, XL (Fall 1966), 191-202.

9648 _____. "The Twigs," Minnesota Review, V (January-April 1965), 8-15.

9649 Styron, William. "The Confessions of Nat Turner," Harper's Magazine, CCXXXV (September 1967), 51-102.

9650 _____. "Virginia: 1831," Paris Review, IX (Winter 1966), 13-45.

9651 Suarez Galban, Eugenio. "Fame," Ave Maria (April 9, 1966), 24-26.

9652 Suhl, Yuri. "A Fish for the Consul," Prairie Schooner, XXXIX (Fall 1965), 234-242.

9653 _____. "Table 26," Texas Quarterly, IX (Summer 1966), 24-32.

9654 Sukenick, Ronald. "The Kite," New American Review, no. 1 (1967), 200-211.

9655 _____. "What's Your Story," Paris Review, XI (Fall 1968), 33-51.

9656 Sulkin, Sidney. "Old Man," Cimarron Review, no. 9 (September 1969), 6-20.

9657 Sullivan, D. H. "The Grid," Evidence, no. 10 (1967), 81-88.

9658 _____. "The Separator," Canadian Forum, XLVI (March 1967), 275-277.

9659 Sullivan, Eugene. "The Golden Needle," Redbook, CXXX (December 1967), 56-57.

9660 Sullivan, Pamela Wylie. "The Coming-out Party," Seventeen, XXVI (May 1967), 150-151, 250.

9661 _____. "Miriam," Seventeen, XXVI (November 1967), 150-151, 232, 234, 236, 238-239.

9662 _____. "The Survivors," Seventeen, XXV (May 1966), 164-165, 258-260.

9663 Sullivan, Roll. "It Rained This Morning," William and Mary Review, III (Winter 1965), 21.

9664 Sullivan, Tom. "Amanda Jones," Ave Maria, CVI (July 15, 1967), 26-28.

9665 _____. "Comrade Christmas: Being the Authentic and True History of Ebenezer Scrooge, Capitalist and Enemy of the Workers," Ave Maria, CVIII (December 21, 1968), 20-25.

9666 _____. "The Trial and Death of Wherley Wilson," Ave Maria, CV (April 29, 1967), 26-29.

9667 Summers, Hollis. "The Penitent," Red Clay Reader, no. 5 (1968), 81-91.

9668 _____. "The Third Ocean," Hudson Review, XXII (Summer 1969), 232-252.

9669 Summers, John. "You'd Be Far Better Off in a Home," New Zealand Listener, LII (April 9, 1965), 5, 15.

9670 Summy, Irene M. "Anders," Westerly, no. 3 (1967), 5-7.

9671 ______. "The Birth of Peggy Grey," Westerly, no. 2 (July 1969), 5-21.

9672 ______. "Descendants of Tigers," Southerly, (1969), 193-197.

9673 ______. "A Different World," Westerly, (May 1966), 13-15.

9674 ______. "A Girl Named Chris," Westerly, no. 1 (March 1968), 28-29.

9675 ______. "Journey Through Yesterday," Westerly, (Summer 1966), 20-23.

9676 ______. "Mormor," Overland, no. 39 (Spring 1968), 24-26.

9677 ______. "The Secret," Southerly, XXVIII (1968), 295-299.

9678 Sundman, Per Olof. "The Dishwasher," Mary Anderson Seeger, trans., Literary Review, IX (Winter 1965-66), 327-333.

9679 ______. "The Man Who Washed His Dishes," Gerd Bloxham, trans., American Scandinavian Review, LVII (June 1969), 176-180.

9680 ______. "The Seekers," Arvid Paulson, trans., American Scandinavian Review, LII (June 1965), 183-187.

9681 Sunwall, James. "The Frost Giant," North American Review, III (July 1966), 19-23.

9682 ______. "Mirror of Night," Western Humanities Review, XIX (Summer 1965), 243-248.

9683 Surmelian, Leon. "Tale of the Lad with Golden Locks," Ararat, X (Winter 1969), 34-40.

9684 Susann, Jacqueline. "The Love Machine," Imprint, IX (September 1969), 19-34, 37-50.

9685 ______. "The Love Machine/Part I," Ladies' Home Journal, LXXXVI (May 1969), 153-160.

9686 ______. "The Love Machine/Conclusion," Ladies' Home Journal, LXXXVI (June 1969), 121-128.

9687 ______. "Valley of the Dolls," Cosmopolitan, CLX (June 1966), 115-120.

9688 Sussman, Roy. "The Sea Gulls," Yale Literary Magazine, CXXXIII (May 1965), 3-8.

9689 Sutton, Llewellyn. "I Believe in Fairies," Old Lady of Threadneedle Street, XLIII (June 1967), 92-95.

9690 ______. "Not Like Us," Old Lady of Threadneedle Street, XLV (June 1969), 93-95.

9691 ______. "Steroid 1073, 4th Galaxy," Old Lady of Threadneedle Street, XVIV (December 1968), 210-211.

9692 ______. "The Veteran," Old Lady of Threadneedle Street, XLII (March 1966), 12-13.

9693 Sutton, William. "The Deacon's Dilemma," Roanoke Review, III (Fall 1969), 21-29.

9694 Swados, Harvey. "The Tree of Life," McCall's, XCII (June 1965), 84-85, 168, 170.

9695 Swails, Laurell. "Descent," Prism International, IV (Spring 1965), 4-14.

9696 Swain, Jessica. "A Section of Silence," Work, no. 1 (Summer 1965), 46-51.

9697 Swan, Jon. "The Field," Michigan Quarterly Review, V (Winter 1966), 44-50.

9698 Swanson, Donald C. "Aphonios," Minnesota Review, VI (1966), 37-43.

9699 Sward, Robert. "Helpful Bird, Helpful Dog: Sections from a Novel," Denver Quarterly, III (Winter 1969), 60-66.

9700 ______. "Hotel Rivello," Tri-Quarterly, no. 16 (Fall 1969), 149-157.

9701 ______. "The Jurassic Shales/Novel in Progress," Extensions, no. 3 (1969), 14-34.

9702 ______. "From The Jurassic Shales, a Novel," Transatlantic Review, no. 29 (Summer 1968), 14-16.

9703 ______ and Ann Quin. "Living in the Present," Ambit, no. 34 (1968), 20-21.

9704 Swarthout, Glendon. "Going to See George," Esquire, LXIV (July 1965), 72, 74, 111.

9705 Sweet, Elizabeth. "Walker in the Dust," Negro Digest, XIV (February 1965), 54-60.

9706 Sweet, Robert Burdette. "A Chapter from the Novel Dame America," Western Humanities Review, XXIII (Winter 1969), 9-21.

9707 ______. "Enemies' Camp," Chelsea, no. 16 (March 1965), 123-130.

9708 ______. "Run, Turnip!" Occident, III (Spring/Summer 1969), 121-136.

9709 Swenson, Alan. "Eclipse," The Fiddlehead, no. 77 (Fall 1968), 9-29.

9710 ______. "The Reunion," Discourse, XII (Summer 1969), 401-408.

9711 ______. "The Way Things Are," Abyss, II, no. 2 (1969), 70-75.

9712 ______. "The Yogi of Westchester County," Forum, VII (Fall-Winter 1969), 44-51.

9713 Swidler, Gertrude. "Young Love," American, I (Spring 1965), 38-40.

9714 Swift, Graham. "A Break," Solstice, no. 9 (1969), 27-28, 30-32.

9715 Swingle, Larry. "Take the World Lid Off. I Know the Birthday of Everything. It Is Time to Flower," Mother, no. 6 (Thanksgiving, 1965), 10-13.

9716 Swink, Charles. "Those Who Care," Good Housekeeping, CLXII (February 1966), 82-83, 186-188.

9717 Sykes, Jon. "So Many Foxes This Year," Coraddi, (Arts Festival 1969), 9-12.

9718 Symons, Julian. "Bonzo," London Magazine, VII (August 1967), 20-30.

9719 Sypher, Jim. "Barstow," Spectrum, VIII (Summer 1966), 144-146.

9720 Szabó, István. "The Glory of Pál Fekete," New Hungarian Quarterly, VI (Summer 1965), 90-95.

9721 ______. "God's Creatures," New Hungarian Quarterly, X (Autumn 1969), 112-127.

9722 Szabó, László Cs. "King Solomon," Literary Review, IX (Spring 1966), 443-454.

9723 Szántó, Erika. "The Flat Is Empty," New Hungarian Quarterly, X (Spring 1969), 66-75.

9724 Szanto, George H. "The Celebrated Case of Brother Sebastian," Four Quarters, XVIII (March 1969), 26-36.

9725 ______. "For the Record," Alta, no. 7 (Winter 1968-69), 37-38.

9726 _____. "Mom," Alta, no. 7 (Winter 1968-69), 35-37.

9727 Szerb, Antal. "Love in a Bottle," New Hungarian Quarterly, X (Winter 1969), 45-54.

9728 Szlyk, John J. "Holy Thursday," Lance, V (Winter 1965), 43-45.

9729 Szohner, Gabriel. "From Jokers and Wild Flowers," Alphabet, no. 17 (December 1969), 38-46.

9730 Szukalski, Stanislav. "The Mute Singer," Cornhill Magazine, no. 1043 (Spring 1965), 355-367.

9731 Tabak, May Natalie. "Small Change," Kenyon Review, XXX (1968), 627-651.

9732 Taber, Gladys. "Whisper Farewell," Good Housekeeping, CLXVI (May 1968), 90-91, 190, 192.

9733 Taccad-Cammayo, Ines. "People of Consequence," Solidarity, IV (December 1969), 26-30.

9734 Tagore, Rabindranath. "Rashmoni's Son," Mary Lago, Tarum Gupta and Amiya Chakravarty, trans., Chicago Review, XIX, no. 1 (1966), 5-32.

9735 Tahir, Judy. "Here We Go Again," New Leaven, no. 16 (1966), 8-17.

9736 Taikeff, Stanley. "The Face," Abyss, (January-February 1967), n.p. [41-42].

9737 _____. "The New Suit," Abyss, I (May-June 1967), n.p. [26-32].

9738 _____. "The Nosebleed," Abyss, I (May-June 1967), n.p. [32-44].

9739 Taiko, Hirabayashi. "The Black Age," Edward Seidensticker, trans., Solidarity, III (March 1968), 11-19.

9740 Takahashi, Hiromi. "The Duel at Yamazaki-Daira," Greensboro Review, III (Winter 1967), 65-82.

9741 Takeda Taijun. "The Eatingest Girl," John Nathan, trans., Japan Quarterly, XII (October-December 1965), 483-489.

9742 Taktsis, Costas. "A Diplomatic Episode," Iain Watson, trans., London Magazine, VIII (December 1968), 74-84.

9743 _____. "A Few Pennies for the Salvation Army," London Magazine, VIII (May 1968), 12-18.

9744 ______. "A Visit," David Plante and Costas Taktsis, trans., London Magazine, VII (July 1967), 58-62.

9745 Taleon, Jorshinelle L. "Step, Step!" Diliman Review, XIV (April 1966), 101-108.

9746 Talese, Gay. "Getting Even," Mademoiselle, LXV (May 1967), 158-159, 204-207.

9747 Tamási, Aron. "The Golden Mouse," Literary Review, IX (Spring 1966), 473-480.

9748 ______. "The Messenger," New Hungarian Quarterly, VII (Winter 1966), 76-81.

9749 Tampieri de Estrella, Susana. "The Universal Face," H. E. Francis, Transatlantic Review, no. 23 (Winter 1966-67), 114-118.

9750 Tan, Henry. "The Pastor," UMD Humanist, XV (Spring 1967), 3-5.

9751 Tan Chek Hin. "An Outcast," Focus (Singapore), V, no. 1 (1967), 34-36.

9752 Taner, Haldun. "Konchinas," Larry Fisher and Allan Gall, trans., Literature East and West, XI (June 1967), 169-172.

9753 Tanino, Aki. "Bride of a Samuri," Aki Tanino, trans. and adapt., Evergreen Review, X (October 1966), 24-28, 82, 84, 86, 88.

9754 ______. "The Million-Dollar Collateral," Aki Tanino, trans., Meanjin Quarterly, XXVI (Spring 1967), 300-312.

9755 ______. "The One Thousand Ryo Pledge," Aki Tanino, trans. and adapt., Evergreen Review, XIII (March 1969), 24-27, 63-65.

9756 ______. "The Tattooed Wife," Aki Tanino, trans., and adapt., Evergreen Review, XII (July 1968), 14-17, 69-70.

9757 Tannenbaum, Sheldon. "The Huge Dull Night under the Stars," Epoch, XIV (Winter 1965), 178-184.

9758 Tao Chia-shan and Ma Hao-lin. "The Soldiers Chairman Mao Has Sent Us," Tai Chin-wan, trans., Eastern Horizon, VI (June 1967), 60-62.

9759 Targan, Barry. "And Their Fathers Who Begat Them," Esquire, LXIX (January 1968), 108-109, 111, 127-128, 130.

9760 ______. "Harry Belten and the Mendelssohn Violin Concerto,"

Esquire, LXVI (July 1966), 95-97, 118-122.

9761 _____. "Tickets," Prairie Schooner, XXXIX (Winter 1965/66), 285-298.

9762 Tarnoff, Lorna. "'The Devil's Trill'," Manuscript, LVIII (Spring 1965).

9763 Tasca, Jules E. "A Matter of Survival," Ave Maria, CI (May 15, 1965), 22-25.

9764 Tassone, G. L. "Room 312," Playboy, XIV (August 1967), 105-106, 142-145.

9765 Tatad, Francisco S. "The Unhappiest Man," Solidarity, I (October-December 1966), 91-98.

9766 Tatarka, Dominik. "Two Stories/The Apostle of Morning Thought," Jeanne Némcová, trans., Literary Review, XIII (Fall 1969), 83-86.

9767 _____. "Two Stories/The Green Blanket," Jeanne Némcová, Literary Review, XIII (Fall 1969), 86-89.

9768 Tate, Joan. "Sam & Me," Seventeen, XXVIII (March 1969), 156-159, 215, 218, 220, 223, 226.

9769 Tate, Sister Judith, O. S. B. "Train Ride," Nimrod, IX (Spring 1965), 13-19.

9770 Tate, Laurence. "The Search," Red Cedar Review, III (Spring 1965), 17-24, 27-30.

9771 Tate, Peter. "Mars Pastorale/or, I'm Fertile, Said Felix," New Worlds, no. 174 (1967), 38-45.

9772 Taub, Peggy. "God's Beard," Aspects, no. 10 (August 1967), 11-15.

9773 Taube, Myron. "Bach Is for the Loving Kind," University Review, XXXIII (March 1967), 169-174.

9774 _____. "The Confession," University Review, XXXIV (Spring 1968), 204-210.

9775 _____. "The Explosion," Seventeen, XXIV (March 1965), 130-131, 208-210.

9776 _____. "The Gift," University Review, XXXV (Winter 1968), 88-94.

9777 _____. "Heshy," Discourse, VIII (Summer 1965), 259-265.

9778 _____. "Him," University Review, XXXVI (Autumn 1969), 29-34.

9779 _____. "The House Divided," University Review, XXXV (Summer 1969), 250-256.

9780 _____. "The Kaddish," Discourse, XI (Spring 1968), 160-169.

9781 _____. "The King of Honor," Carolina Quarterly, XVII (Spring 1965), 3-15.

9782 _____. "The Kiss," Seventeen, XXV (September 1966), 164-165, 228, 230, 233.

9783 _____. "The Lesson," Discourse, XI (Winter 1968), 42-52.

9784 _____. "The Magician," Quartet, no. 24 (Fall 1968), 19-23.

9785 _____. "Margaret," Discourse, IX (Winter 1966), 93-100.

9786 _____. "Margo," Discourse, IX (Spring 1966), 185-192.

9787 _____. "The Perfect Lover," University Review, XXXVI (Winter 1969), 123-134.

9788 _____. "The Professional," Minnesota Review, V (January-April 1965), 3-7.

9789 _____. "Saul," University Review, XXXV (Spring 1969), 219-223.

9790 _____. "Shelley," University Review, XXXI (March 1965), 204-208.

9791 _____. "The Smell of Heather," University Review, XXXV (Autumn 1968), 3-10.

9792 _____. "The Student," University Review, XXXIV (Summer 1968), 276-282.

9793 _____. "The Tree," Discourse, X (Summer 1967), 312-319.

9794 Taubes, Susan. "The Patient," Transatlantic Review, no. 23 (Winter 1966-67), 101-108.

9795 _____. "The Sharks," Virginia Quarterly Review, XLI (Winter 1965), 102-107.

9796 Tavel, Ronald. "Two Excerpts from Street of Stairs," Chicago Review, XVIII, no. 2 (1965), 74-81.

9797 Taves, Ernest. "The Fire Fighters," Playboy, XVI (August 1969), 94-96, 155-156, 158.

9798 Taylor, Chet. "The Last of the Renaissance Men," Prism International, VIII (Summer 1968), 104-117.

9799 ______. "The Man Who Would Not Speak to His Wife," Northwest Review, IX (Fall-Winter 1967-68), 43-47.

9800 ______. "The Pin-Point Passer," Corral 1965, 76-82.

9801 Taylor, Clarence. "Golden Nightmare," Delta Review, IV (September 1967), 35-37, 67.

9802 Taylor, Coley. "Uncle Jake's Send-Off," Mexico Quarterly Review, III, no. 3 (1969), 62-67.

9803 Taylor, David. "Jason," Works, I (Autumn 1967), 14-24.

9804 ______. "Let's Play Old Men," Works, I (Summer 1968), 13-18.

9805 ______. "Panda," The Outsider, nos. 4 & 5 (1968-69), 3-18.

9806 Taylor, Don. "A Sign from the Gods," Courier, XLV (July 1965), 56-61.

9807 Taylor, Eleanor Ross. "Jujitsu," Sewanee Review, LXXVII (October-December 1969), 654-659.

9808 Taylor, Elizabeth. "The Devastating Boys," McCall's, XCIII (May 1966), 102-103, 172-174, 176.

9809 ______. "Hôtel du Commerce," Cornhill Magazine, no. 1046 (Winter 1965/66), 86-95.

9810 ______. "The Fly-Paper," Cornhill Magazine, CLXXVII (Spring 1969), 235-241.

9811 ______. "In and Out the Houses," Saturday Evening Post, CCXLI (December 14, 1968), 44-46, 48-50.

9812 ______. "Sisters," New Yorker, XLV (June 21, 1969), 38-41.

9813 ______. "Tall Boy," New Yorker, XLII (December 31, 1966), 30-34.

9814 ______. "Vron and Willie," New Yorker, XL (January 16, 1965), 34-39.

9815 ______. "'Well, Here We Are'," McCall's, XCVII (November 1969), 74-75, 168-171.

9816 Taylor, F. H. Griffin. "House of Gold," New Orleans Review, I (Fall 1968), 70-77.

9817 Taylor, G. A. "The Last Game," Columbia, XLVI (September 1966), 24-28.

9818 Taylor, George. "The Eyes of Sonny Hoover," Carolina Quarterly, XX (Fall 1968), 53-61.

9819 Taylor, Grace A. "The Last Hours," Redbook, CXXXII (January 1969), 66-67.

9820 ______. "When the Fog Lifts," Columbia, XLVIII (August 1968), 24-29.

9821 Taylor, Harry H. "The Cage," South Dakota Review, VI (Spring 1968), 64-72.

9822 ______. "Clothes," Kansas Magazine, (1968), 95-98.

9823 ______. "The Diary of a Short Visit," The Quest, I (Fall-Winter 1966), 29-40.

9824 ______. "The Guards," South Dakota Review, IV (Winter 1966), 63-69.

9825 ______. "Locking Up," Ball State University Forum, VII (Winter 1966), 42-45.

9826 ______. "Night Trip," Red Clay Reader, no. 3 (1966), 98-102.

9827 ______. "O Careless Love," Free Lance, X (Second Half, 1966), 16-27.

9828 ______. "Tristan," Prism International, IX (Summer 1969), 4-13.

9829 ______. "Up at the Fort," South Dakota Review, IV (Autumn 1966), 57-64.

9830 ______. "Will the Walls Come Down," Kansas Magazine, (1967), 1-5.

9831 ______. "The Woman in the Tree," Quartet, no. 18 (Spring 1967), 2-8.

9832 Taylor, Jeanne A. "A House Divided," Antioch Review, XXVII (Fall 1967), 298-305.

9833 ______. "Only Clowns Passing Through," Antioch Review, XXVII (Fall 1967), 307-314.

9834 Taylor, Jill. "Merry Christmas, Billy Penn!" Columbia, XLVIII (December 1968), 24-27.

9835 _____. "The Mutt and Jeff," Columbia, XLVIII (May 1968), 27-32.

9836 Taylor, John A. "Our Home Is on the Rocks," Mandala, no. 1 (1968), 26-30, 32-34.

9837 Taylor, Laurie. "Brown Blankets," Discourse, XII (Spring 1969), 202-207.

9838 _____. "Competence and Competence," Discourse, XI (Autumn 1968), 526-530.

9839 Taylor, Mary Ann. "Trespass," Sewanee Review, LXXV (January-March 1967), 1-24.

9840 Taylor, Peter. "A Cheerful Disposition," Sewanee Review, LXXV (April-June 1967), 243-265.

9841 _____. "Daphne's Lover," Sewanee Review, LXXVII (April-June 1969), 225-250.

9842 _____. "Dean of Men," Virginia Quarterly Review, XLV (Spring 1969), 258-293.

9843 _____. "The Elect," McCall's, XCV (April 1968), 106-107, 168-169, 172.

9844 _____. "The End of Play," Virginia Quarterly Review, XLI (Spring 1965), 248-265.

9845 _____. "First Heat," Shenandoah, XIX (Winter 1968), 28-36.

9846 _____. "Mrs. Billingsby's Wine," New Yorker, XLIII (October 14, 1967), 56-60.

9847 _____. "Tom, Tell Him," Sewanee Review, LXXVI (April-June 1968), 159-186.

9848 Taylor, Reg. "Hip," Australian Letters, VIII (January 1968), 22-24.

9849 Taylor, Theodore. "The Girl Who Took Risks," Saturday Evening Post, CCXL (July 15, 1967), 50-55.

9850 Taylor, Walter. "A Way of Dying," North American Review, IV (May 1967), 21-24.

9851 Taylor, Will. "Reverend Nelms and My Salvation," DeKalb Literary Arts Journal, III (Winter 1969), 26-28.

9852 Ťažký, Ladislav. "Amenmária," Karel Kornel, trans., Literary Review, XIII (Fall 1969), 99-110.

9853 Tchakmakian, Pascal. "Those Human Needs," Armenian Review, XXII (Spring 1969), 64-70.

9854 Teall, Kaye Moulton. "Sea Change," McCall's, XCIII (May 1966), 74-75, 142-145.

9855 _____. "To Live Happily Ever After," Good Housekeeping, CLXVII (August 1968), 68-69, 130-133, 135.

9856 Tedford, Ingrid. "Amelio's," Canadian Forum, XLVIII (June 1968), 62-64.

9857 Tejani, Bahadur. "The Writer," Avenues, I (October-November 1968), 32-36, 41-42.

9858 Tekeyan, Charles. "Have You Ever Heard a Swan Cry?" Trace, nos. 62 & 63 (Fall-Winter 1966-67), 329-335.

9859 _____. "The Waiter Without Teeth/And the Lady Whose Coat Was Too Big," The Smith, no. 4 (1965), 18-23.

9860 Telpaz, Gideon. "Resurrection," Massachusetts Review, VI (Winter-Spring 1965), 321-335.

9861 Telpugov, Victor. "Short Stories/Ice from Mozhaisk," Vladimir Talmy, trans., Soviet Literature, (no. 5, 1967), 118-119.

9862 _____. "Short Stories/Matveyich," Vladimir Talmy, trans., Soviet Literature, (no. 5, 1967), 117-118.

9863 _____. "Short Stories/Night Lights," Vladimir Talmy, trans., Soviet Literature, (no. 5, 1967), 115-116.

9864 _____. "Short Stories/The Toy Boat," Vladimir Talmy, trans., Soviet Literature, (no. 5, 1967), 113-115.

9865 Tembo, Albert L. "Witchcraft," New Writing from Zambia, no. 1 (1968), 3-4.

9866 Templar, Andrea. "Lila," Manuscript, XVIII (Spring 1965), 58-61.

9867 Temple, Willard. "Local Girl Makes Good," Good Housekeeping, CLX (June 1965), 88-89, 180, 182, 184.

9868 _____. "That Old College Try," Good Housekeeping, CLXIV (January 1967), 52-53, 163-175, 181-189.

9869 Templeton, Edith. "The Darts of Cupid," New Yorker, XLIV (November 2, 1968), 60-66, 68, 71-72, 74, 77-78, 80, 83-84, 88, 91-92, 94, 97-100, 105-106, 108, 111-112, 114, 117-118, 120-122.

9870 _____. "The Dress Rehearsal," New Yorker, XLV (April 5, 1969), 34-44.

9871 _____. "Equality Cake," New Yorker, XLII (November 12, 1966), 56-67.

9872 _____. "Talking of Count Sternborn," New Yorker, XLII (October 15, 1966), 54-63.

9873 Tendryakov, Vladimir. "A Century's Journey," Eve Manning and Tom Botting, trans., Soviet Literature, (no. 10, 1965), 64-137.

9874 Tenhoff, Pandora. "Splish and Splash," Plaintiff, V (Winter 1969), 13-16.

9875 Terrell, Robert L. "Tea Party," Evergreen Review, XII (December 1968), 34-37, 72.

9876 Terrill, Kathryn. "A New Country," Assay, XXIII (Spring 1967), 25-34.

9877 Terry, Marshall. "Grass," Southwest Review, LIV (Summer 1969), 248-254.

9878 _____. "Snow and Poetry," Southwest Review, L (Spring 1965), 179-183.

9879 Terry, Walter S. "The Bottomless Well," Georgia Review, XIX (Fall 1965), 337-349.

9880 Tertz, Abram. "The Makepeace Experiment," Manya Harari, trans., Harper's Magazine, CCXXX (June 1965), 51-58.

9881 _____. "Pkhentz," Encounter, XXVI (April 1966), 3-13.

9882 Teter, George. "Intimacy," Harvard Advocate, XCIX (April 1965), 28-29.

9883 Thacker, Eric and Anthony Earnshaw. "Musrum," Evergreen Review, XIII (February 1969), 46-49, 69-74.

9884 Thaler, Susan. "The Eight O'Clock of Morning." Woman's Day, (April 1968), 56-57, 110-111, 115.

9885 _____. "The Rose Dress," Redbook, CXXXIII (May 1969), 98-99, 138, 140.

9886 _____. "Saturday Matinee," Woman's Day, (March 1968), 48-49, 100, 102.

9887 Thanvi, Shaukat. "Who Should Provide the Grass," Pakistan Review, XVII (December 1969), 39-42.

9888 Thawley, William J. "Janus," Four Quarters, XIX (November 1969), 14-18.

9889 Thayer, Douglas H. "The Rabbit Hunt," Brigham Young University Studies, IX (Winter 1969), 198-208.

9890 _____. "The Rooster," Colorado Quarterly, XVI (Autumn 1967), 194-206.

9891 Thelwell, Mike. "Bright an' Mownin' Star," Massachusetts Review, VII (Autumn 1966), 655-670.

9892 _____. "The Organizer," Story: the Yearbook of Discovery, (1968), 15-37.

9893 Themerson, Stefan. "Chapter 11 from Bayamus a novel," 0 to 9, no. 2 (August 1967), 65-72.

9894 Theron, Etienne. "School for Cats and Dogs," Contrast (Cape Town, South Africa), no. 20 (March 1969), 81-91.

9895 Theroux, Alexander. "Mrs. Proby Gets Hers," London Magazine, IX (September 1969), 5-36.

9896 Theroux, Paul. "Fragments from a Central African Journal," Malahat Review, no. 2 (April 1967), 5-10.

9897 _____. "The Man Who Read Graham Greene," North American Review, VI (Summer 1969), 62-65.

9898 _____. "A Real Russian Ikon," Commentary, XLVIII (December 1969), 69+.

9899 _____. "Two in the Bush," Atlantic Monthly, CCXXII (July 1968), 74-79, 84.

9900 Thiess, Frank. "The Wife of Signor Calabresi," Margaret D. Howie, trans., Scala International, (November 1969), 34-37.

9901 Thom, Robert. "The Day It All Happened, Baby," Esquire, LXVI (December 1966), 220-224, 130, 134, 137-138, 140, 142, 146, 148, 150, 154, 156, 158, 160.

9902 Thomajan, P. K. "Buzzo, the Fumble Bee," Armenian Review, XIX (Spring 1966), 33-34.

9903 Thomas, Audrey Callahan. "If One Green Bottle...," Atlantic Monthly, CCXV (June 1965), 83-87.

9904 Thomas, Dorothy. "The Holy Stove," Redbook, CXXX (January 1968), 48-49, 121-122, 124-126.

9905 _____. "Joy Cometh in the Morning," Redbook, CXXVIII (December 1966), 50-51, 134-140.

9906 _____. "Violets Are Brief," Redbook, CXXVIII (April 1967), 78-79, 119-121.

9907 Thomas, Frances. "Blue Beads," Columbia, XLVII (November 1967), 24-28.

9908 Thomas, Mack. "Green Grapes," Cosmopolitan, CLVIII (January 1965), 81-83.

9909 Thomas, P. "Batman!" Dare, IV (March 1966), 40.

9910 Thomas, Peter. "Believing Where We Cannot Prove," Anglo-Welsh Review, XVIII, no. 41 (Summer 1969), 83-86.

9911 Thomas, Shirley. "A Girl Didn't Stand a Chance," Westerly, (August 1966), 30-31.

9912 Thomas, Virgil. "Where's Your Feathers?" Seventeen, XXVII (February 1968), 146-147, 198-199.

9913 Thompson, Bill. "A Vignette," Arx, III (May 1969), 19.

9914 Thompson, Claude. "Spring Planting," Negro Digest, XVI (December 1966), 59-67.

9915 Thompson, Colin. "Full Employment," Queen, CDXXXIV (August 6-19, 1969), 67, 84.

9916 Thompson, David. "O Danny Boy," New Zealand Listener, (March 17, 1967), 6, 15.

9917 Thompson, Eric. "Adam, Adam, Shave Your Face," Paris Review, XI (Summer 1968), 140-160.

9918 Thompson, Frank H., Jr. "Billy in Wonderland," Prairie Schooner, XL (Spring 1966), 60-65.

9919 Thompson, Gale. "New Landing/Two Excerpts," Silo, no. 12 (Fall 1967), 11-18, 22-24.

9920 Thompson, James W. "See What Tomorrow Brings," Trans-atlantic Review, no. 29 (Summer 1968), 44-50.

9921 Thompson, John. "A Condition of Servitude," Commentary, XLVII (March 1969), 45-50.

9922 _____. "Jack Frost," Harper's Magazine, CCXXXVII (November 1968), 140-144.

9923 Thompson, Joy. "The Last Rose," University Review, XXXII

(October 1965), 67-72.

9924 Thompson, Kent. "Because I Am Drunk," Quarry, XVIII (Spring 1969), 37-47.

9925 _____. "The Death of Comedy," Tamarack Review, no. 49 (1969), 33-41.

9926 _____. "Mad Indian at the Hockey Game," West Coast Review, IV (Fall 1969), 25-28.

9927 _____. "The Man Who Cried Faith," New Campus Review, I (May 1966), 2-8.

9928 Thompson, Mary McCollough. "A Knot in the String," Niobe, no. 1 (1965), 59-64.

9929 Thompson, Paul. "The Last Laugh," Transatlantic Review, no. 20 (Spring 1966), 50-54.

9930 Thompson, Robert. "Day and Night," Intro, no. 2 (September 1969), 87-96.

9931 Thompson, Sheila S. "Nightmare," The Quest, II (Spring 1966), 311-326.

9932 Thomsen, Keith. "One Pair of Pants, Size 32W-32L," UMD Humanist, XIV (Winter 1966), 14-18.

9933 Thomson, A. M. "The Visitors," New Zealand Listener, (July 22, 1966), 6.

9934 Thomson, Margaret. "Children in Their Masks," Redbook, CXXV (October 1965), 72-73, 155, 169, 171-172.

9935 Thordarson, Agnar. "The Thief," Paul Schach, trans., American Scandinavian Review, LVII (December 1969), 400-404.

9936 Thorne, Lynn. "The Prisoner," Prism International, VII (Autumn 1968), 123-126.

9937 Thornton, Bob. "Excerpt From a Novel in Progress," Assay, XXII (Spring 1966), 28-40.

9938 Thorp, Ella. "David," Mademoiselle, LXIX (May 1969), 178-179, 217, 230-232.

9939 Thorp, Roderick. "The Detective," Cosmopolitan, CLXI (October 1966), 119-127.

9940 Thorsteinsson, I. G. "The Bronze Maidens from Bellevue," Hallberg Hallmundsson, trans., Vagabond, I, no. 3 (1966), 29-34.

9941 _______. "An Old Story," D. E. Askey, trans., American Scandinavian Review, LVII (March 1969), 62-65.

9942 Thuo, James. "The Begotten Son," Nexus, II (July 1968), 13-17.

9943 Thurber, James. "The White Rabbit Caper," P. S. (August 1966), 16-18.

9944 Thu-Van. "The Medium," Lewis Galantiere, trans., Solidarity, I (October-December 1966), 99-104.

9945 Tibber, Robert. "The Food of Love," Ladies' Home Journal, LXXXIV (June 1967), 80-81, 105.

9946 _____. "Madame Gonzalez," Cosmopolitan, CLVIII (March 1965), 82-83.

9947 _____. "Sleeping Beauty," McCall's, XCV (September 1968), 86-87, 129-130.

9948 Tibbs, Ben. "Census," Goodly Co., no. 12 (July 1968), 29-35.

9949 _____. "Play," Goodly Co., no. 7 (November 1966), 22-23.

9950 Tiempo, Edilberto K. "The Election," Solidarity, IV (January 1969), 49-64.

9951 _____. "Kulisising Hari," Solidarity, III (May 1968), 25-30.

9952 _____. "The Sunbird," Solidarity, IV (August 1969), 30-36.

9953 Tiempo, Edith. "Un Bel Di," Solidarity, IV (May 1969), 1-24.

9954 Tien, Garnet K. "'As in Thy Faith'," Columbia, XLVIII (April 1968), 24-27.

9955 _____. "That Ruth Might Walk," Columbia, XLVII (March 1967), 23-26.

9956 Tierney, Jean. "Lebreton Flats," Canadian Forum, XLV (April 1965), 13-14.

9957 Tikhonov, Nikolai. "The Apple Tree," Soviet Literature, (no. 4, 1967), 82-84.

9958 Timmons, Wayne. [untitled], Sou'wester, (Spring 1969), 63-66.

9959 _____. "The King of the Mountain," Sou'wester, (Spring 1968), 24-26.

9960 Tingom, Elizabeth. "The Spirit of the Road," New Yorker, XLV (August 16, 1969), 32-39.

9961 Tipton, James. "The Arms of Venus," New Orleans Review, I (Spring 1969), 264-265.

9962 Titov, Vladislav. "All Death Despite," Alice Ingman and Tom Botting, trans., Soviet Literature, (no. 7, 1967), 3-79.

9963 Titze, Kurt. "The Foreigner," Westerly, (August 1965), 36-41.

9964 Tobey, Fred S. "Four Cups to a Quart," Signature, I (April 1966), 52, 54.

9965 ______. "Never Hit a Lady," Signature, II (September 1967), 24.

9966 Tobias, Tobi. "Candy," Canadian Forum, XLVIII (December 1968), 214.

9967 Tobino, Mario. "The Biassoli Family," William Weaver, trans., Transatlantic Review, no. 18 (Spring 1965), 32-46.

9968 Todd, Jean. "A Matter of Faith," Kansas Magazine, (1968), 53-58.

9969 Toddie, Jean. "The Lady with the Lute," Seventeen, XXVI (September 1967), 160-161, 214, 218.

9970 Toft, Joseph. "Pumpkin," Alphabet, no. 13 (June 1967), 18-29.

9971 Tokareva, Viktoria. "Nothing Comes Easy at First," Vytas Dukas, trans., Mundus Artium, II (Spring 1969), 12-16.

9972 Toland, Stuart. "Haunted Heart," Cosmopolitan, CLIX (December 1965), 104-109.

9973 Toler, Sister Colette, S.C. "Alley-Oop," Ave Maria, CI (March 13, 1965), 22-24, 30.

9974 ______. "A Matter of Optics," Ave Maria, CII (September 4, 1965), 22-24.

9975 Tolkien, J. R. R. "Smith of Wootton Major," Redbook, CXXX (December 1967), 58-61, 101, 103-107.

9976 Tolley, Natalie. "The Sportsman," New Zealand Listener, (January 6, 1967), 6.

9977 Tolnay, Thomas. "Gertrude's Easter," Four Quarters, XVII (March 1968), 31-35.

9978 Tolstoy, Alexei. "The Russian Character," Soviet Literature, (no. 4, 1967), 31-37.

9979 Tomelty, Joseph. "Lucinda and the Birds," Threshold, no. 21 (Summer 1967), 84-89.

9980 Tomey, Michael. "Briefly Georgianne," Wisconsin Review, II (May 1967), 16-17.

9981 Tomkins, Calvin. "Virginia," Playboy, XIV (March 1967), 103, 139-141.

9982 Tooby, B. C. "Day After Yesterday," The Cantuarian, (August 1965), 423-425.

9983 ______. "The Galleon," The Cantuarian, (April 1966), 111-114.

9984 Toperoff, Sam. "A Spoonful of Nothing," Atlantic Monthly, CCXVIII (August 1966), 50-55.

9985 Topor, Roland. "A Father's Sacrifice," Margaret Crosland, trans., London Magazine, VIII (October 1968), 47-53.

9986 ______. "The Favorite," Nova, (September 1968), 96, 98-99.

9987 ______. "The Sphinx," Nova, (September 1968), 101, 103.

9988 Torre-Nilsson, Leopold. "He Who Howls," Agnes Moncy, trans., Tri-Quarterly, nos. 13/14 (Fall/Winter 1968-69), 489-502.

9989 Tottenham, John. "'Go on, Johnny, Go on!'," Intro, no. 2 (September 1969), 77-86.

9990 Toumanian, Hovannes. "Gikor," Mischa Kudian, trans., Ararat, IX (Spring 1968), 12-18.

9991 Towers, Robert. "The Engagement," Cosmopolitan, CLIX (October 1965), 104-109.

9992 Towle, Tony. "The Filter," Mother, no. 7 (Mother's Day 1966), 34.

9993 ______. "I Quit Staring," Mother, no. 5 (Summer 1965), 62.

9994 ______. "The Most Thrilling Adventure of My Career," Mother, no. 5 (Summer 1965), 62.

9995 ______. "The Review," Mother, no. 7 (Mother's Day, 1966), 33.

9996 ______. "Thank You," Mother, no. 7 (Mother's Day, 1966), 32.

9997 Townley, Rod. "Time Pieces," North American Review, IV (March 1967), 34-35.

9998 Trachtenberg, Inge. "The Calm," Arizona Quarterly, XXV (Spring 1969), 44-52.

9999 _____. "On a Dark Tuesday," Four Quarters, XVIII (March 1969), 23-25.

10000 Tranum, Joel. "At the Railroad Station (from Kapa the Blind, a novel in progress)," New Campus Writing, (1966), 112-133.

10001 Traven, B. "A Saint in Pain," Michigan Quarterly Review, IV (Fall 1965), 266-273.

10002 Travers-Deacon, John. "Fellow Travellers-I," Old Lady of Threadneedle Street, XLIII (September 1967), 165-166.

10003 Treacy, M. F. "The Other Side of the Moon," Western Review, IV (Summer 1967), 75-77.

10004 Treit, Dal. "Crow in the High Woods," Malahat Review, no. 10 (April 1969), 73-85.

10005 Trevisan, Dalton. "Two Stories/The Elephant's Graveyard," Gregory Rabassa, trans., Tri-Quarterly, nos. 13/14 (Fall/Winter 1968-69), 295-296.

10006 _____. "Two Stories/Good Evening, Sir," Gregory Rabassa, trans., Tri-Quarterly, nos. 13/14 (Fall/Winter 1968-69), 292-294.

10007 _____. "The Vampire of Curitiba," Mark Strand and Alair Gomes, trans., Quarterly Review of Literature, XV (1968), 458-462.

10008 Trevor, William. "An Evening with John Joe Dempsey," London Magazine, IX (November 1969), 19-41.

10009 _____. "A Happy Family," Antioch Review, XXVII (Spring 1967), 89-102.

10010 _____. "A Happy Family," London Magazine, VI (November 1966), 33-46.

10011 _____. "The Hotel of the Idle Moon," Transatlantic Review, no. 23 (Winter 1966-67), 5-16.

10012 _____. "The Last Lunch of the Season," Transatlantic Review, no. 19 (Autumn 1965), 23-35.

10013 _____. "Memories of Youghal," Transatlantic Review, no.

32 (Summer 1969), 15-25.

10014 ______. "Miss Smith," Transatlantic Review, no. 25 (Summer 1967), 70-78.

10015 ______. "The Penthouse Apartment," London Magazine, VII (May 1967), 24-50.

10016 ______. "Raymond Bamber and Mrs. Fitch," Queen, CDXXVIII (June 7, 1967), 33-37.

10017 ______. "The Table," Antioch Review, XXVII (Summer 1967), 195-210.

10018 Trickett, Rachel. "The Schoolmasters," Cornhill Magazine, no. 1044 (Summer 1965), 392-438.

10019 Trillin, Calvin. "Barnett Frummer Accepts with Pleasure," New Yorker, XLI (December 18, 1965), 47-49.

10020 ______. "Barnett Frummer and Rosalie Mondle Meet Superman: A Love Story," New Yorker, XLI (April 17, 1965), 40-43.

10021 ______. "Barnett Frummer Hears a Familiar Ring," New Yorker, XLII (July 2, 1966), 22-24.

10022 ______. "Barnett Frummer in Urban Crisis," Esquire, LXXII (November 1969), 169, 258-259.

10023 ______. "Barnett Frummer Is an Unbloomed Flower," New Yorker, XLI (February 5, 1966), 34-36.

10024 ______. "Barnett Frummer Learns to Distinguish Packaged Paprika from the Real Article," New Yorker, XLIII (April 8, 1967), 36-38.

10025 ______. "For Worse Is Better and Sickness Is in Health," New Yorker, XLV (November 22, 1969), 53-56.

10026 ______. "Roland Magruder, Freelance Writer," New Yorker, LXI (August 14, 1965), 26-27.

10027 Trimmer, Daniel. "A Warm Place on the Asylum Floor," North American Review, III (January 1966), 25-28.

10028 Triplett, Samuel. "Helped Himself Himself," Nexus (San Francisco, Calif.), III (March-April 1967), 2-6.

10029 Trist, Margaret. "Old Summer," Overland, no. 39 (Spring 1968), 27-31.

10030 Trivelpiece, Laurel. "No Boundaries At All," Red Clay

Reader, no. 6 (1969), 52-56.

10031 _____. "Standing Still in the Air," Four Quarters, XVIII (May 1969), 15-21.

10032 Trocchi, Alexander. "Four Stories/A Being of Distances," New Writers, no. 3 (1965), 9-21.

10033 _____. "Four Stories/The Holy Man," New Writers, no. 3 (1965), 22-31.

10034 _____. "Four Stories/A Meeting," New Writers, no. 3 (1965), 47-60.

10035 _____. "Four Stories/Peter Pierce," New Writers, no. 3 (1965), 32-46.

10036 Trott, Susan. "Francis: The City, the Saint, the Statue, the Boy," Mademoiselle, LXII (December 1965), 104-105, 160.

10037 _____. "Suzanne," Mademoiselle, LXV (May 1967), 34, 36, 44.

10038 Trotter, Magret G. "The Birthday," Georgia Review, XXIII (Spring 1969), 74-79.

10039 Trotter, William. "The Beach/from a novel in progress," Red Clay Reader, no. 3 (1966), 107-112.

10040 Trotzig, Birgitta. "Chapters from The Exposed," Roland Hindmarsh, trans., Transition, VII, no. 36 (1968), 16-21.

10041 Trudell, Dennis. "The Greenbaum Principle," Human Voice, IV, no. 4 (1968), 27-36.

10042 _____. "Himalaya," Approach, no. 61 (Fall 1966), 8-17.

10043 _____. "Penance," Prism International, VI (Autumn 1966), 82-93.

10044 _____. "Sojourn in a Bare Place," Lillabulero, I (Summer 1967), 26-33.

10045 _____. "Starkle, Starkle," Western Humanities Review, XXIII (Spring 1969), 101-106.

10046 Trueblood, Harriett Pratt. "A Fork in the Road," Redbook, CXXVIII (February 1967), 155, 157-179.

10047 Truter, Christina. "A Book at Bedtime," Contrast (Cape Town, South Africa), no. 11 (March 1965), 78-83.

10048 ______. "In a Garden," Contrast (Cape Town, South Africa), no. 17 (November 1967), 11-17.

10049 ______. "A Night Out," Contrast (Cape Town, South Africa), no. 13 (December 1965), 69-76.

10050 Tucci, Niccolo. "The Worst," Esquire, LXIV (August 1965), 79-80, 82, 120.

10051 Tucholsky, Kurt. "Bread and Tears," Harry Zohn, trans., Scala International, (January 1965), 34.

10052 ______. "The Fifth Season," Harry Zohn, trans., Scala International, (January 1965), 34-35.

10053 ______. "Where Do the Holes in the Cheese Come From?" Harry Zohn, trans., Scala International, (January 1965), 32-34.

10054 Tucker, Eva. "When She Comes Back," London Magazine, VII (January 1968), 73-79.

10055 Tucker, Helen. "Such a Quiet Thing," Ladies' Home Journal, LXXXIV (November 1967), 98-99, 149-153.

10056 Tucker, James. "Two Dollars," Sou'wester, II (Fall 1968), 73-77.

10057 Tucker, Kay. "Lady Lavender," William and Mary Review, VII (Spring 1969), 27-30.

10058 Tuohy, Frank. "A Floral Tribute," New Yorker, XLI (April 10, 1965), 40-44.

10059 ______. "A Learner's Licence," London Magazine, V (August 1965), 5-15.

10060 ______. "The Palladian Bridge," London Magazine, V (April 1965), 6-11.

10061 ______. "Ructions or An Historical Footnote on the Cold War," Cornhill Magazine, CLXXVII (Autumn 1969), 415-428.

10062 ______. "A Short Story," Queen, CDXXXI (August 28, 1968), 53-55.

10063 ______. "A Special Relationship," Encounter, XXV (August 1965), 26-31.

10064 ______. "Thunderbolt," Nova, (May/June 1969), 152, 155, 157.

10065 _____. "The Trap," Encounter, XXIV (January 1965), 40-43.

10066 Turco, Lewis. "The Catalogue Idea," The Quest, III (Summer-Fall 1968), 40-47.

10067 _____. "The Hillsdale Epistles," Carleton Miscellany, VII (Summer 1966), 17-32.

10068 _____. "The Invention," Quartet, no. 26 (Spring 1969), 15, 24-25.

10069 _____. "One Sunday Morning," Carleton Miscellany, X (Summer 1969), 96-99.

10070 _____. "Pleasant Dell," Carleton Miscellany, VI (Spring 1965), 72-79.

10071 _____. "The Prison," Quartet, no. 24 (Fall 1968), 10-11.

10072 _____. "Salt," Quartet, no. 21 (Winter 1968), 10-12.

10073 Turley, Eleni Michalis. "Tomorrow I Am John," Texas Quarterly, X (Summer 1967), 184-185.

10074 Turnage, Martha. "'Nothing Comes Out of a Sack but What You Put in It'," William and Mary Review, VI (Spring 1968), 57-63.

10075 Turner, C. "The Beginning of Tomorrow," Good Housekeeping, CLXIV (June 1967), 100-101.

10076 _____. "Early One Morning," Good Housekeeping, CLXIII (October 1966), 108-109.

10077 _____. "Lady in Blue," Good Housekeeping, CLXI (September 1965), 80-81, 240, 242.

10078 _____. "Long Live Love!" Good Housekeeping, CLXVI (May 1968), 110-111.

10079 _____. "One of the Family," Good Housekeeping, CLXV (September 1967), 94-95.

10080 _____. "A Valentine for Janie," Good Housekeeping, CLXII (February 1966), 90-91.

10081 Turner, Steven. "A Nail in the Heel," Arlington Quarterly, I (Winter 1967-68), 226-237.

10082 Turner, Thomas C. "The Vundula," Antioch Review, XXVIII (Fall 1968), 367-375.

10083 Turner, Tom Oliphant. "Sore-Tail Cats," Georgia Review, XXIII (Fall 1969), 375-385.

10084 Turner, Virginia Casey. "A Grave Must Have a Stone," Twigs, no. 2 (1966), 1-11.

10085 Tushnet, Leonard. "Balaam," Nimrod, XII (Winter 1968), 5-13.

10086 ______. "Bandiera Rossa," Four Quarters, XIX (November 1969), 1-8.

10087 ______. "Bobby Bobby," Ball State University Forum, X (Autumn 1969), 46-50.

10088 ______. "The Culture Vulture," Jewish Frontier, XXXIII (October 1966), 21-24.

10089 ______. "The Discount Store," Per/Se, II (Spring 1967), 21-24.

10090 ______. "A Goodly Apple," Ball State Teachers College Forum, VI (Winter 1965), 31-35.

10091 ______. "I'm Not a Snob," University Review, XXXIII (March 1967), 226-228.

10092 ______. "A Little Fatherly Advice," Forum, IV (Winter-Spring 1967), 43-46.

10093 ______. "Mother of the Gracchi," University Review, XXXII (October 1965), 26-30.

10094 ______. "The Nearest Field," Four Quarters, XV (May 1966), 28-36.

10095 ______. "New York Is Full of Lonely People," Modern Age, XIII (Fall 1969), 403-406.

10096 ______. "Obituary," Four Quarters, XVIII (November 1968), 35-40.

10097 ______. "Poire Hélène," DeKalb Literary Arts Journal, II (Winter 1968), 46-61.

10098 ______. "Raisins in the Cabbage," Prairie Schooner, XLII (Summer 1968), 162-169.

10099 ______. "The Rod of Aesculapius," Forum, VII (Spring 1969), 16-20.

10100 ______. "Short Flight into the Invisible," University Review, XXXV (Autumn 1968), 68-72.

10101 [no entry]

10102 ______. "Summer Job," Midwestern University Quarterly, II, no. 3 (1967), 37-46.

10103 ______. "Thanks," Discourse, XII (Winter 1969), 88-94.

10104 ______. "A Week with Lilith," Prairie Schooner, XLI (Spring 1967), 64-71.

10105 Tutt, Ralph. "Family Plots," Sewanee Review, LXXIV (July-September 1966), 597-648.

10106 Tuttle, Anthony. "The Out-of-Towner," Redbook, CXXIV (April 1965), 64-65, 104, 121-125.

10107 Tyler, Anne. "As the Earth Gets Old," New Yorker, XLII (October 29, 1966), 60-64.

10108 ______. "The Common Courtesies," McCall's, XCV (June 1968), 62-63, 115-116.

10109 ______. "Dry Waters," Southern Review, I (April 1965), 259-291.

10110 ______. "The Feather Behind the Rock," New Yorker, XLIII (August 12, 1967), 26-30.

10111 ______. "The Genuine Fur Eyelashes," Mademoiselle, LXIX (January 1967), 102-103, 136-138.

10112 ______. "I'm Not Going to Ask You Again," Harper's Magazine, CCXXXI (September 1965), 88-98.

10113 ______. "The Saints in Caesar's Household," The Archive, LXXIX (September 1966), 18-21.

10114 ______. "The Tea-Machine," Southern Review, III (January 1967), 171-179.

10115 ______. "Two People and a Clock on the Wall," New Yorker, XLII (November 19, 1966), 207-208, 210, 212, 214, 217.

10116 ______. "Who Would Want a Little Boy?" Ladies' Home Journal, LXXXV (May 1968), 132-133, 156-158.

10117 Tyner, Paul. "How You Play the Game," New Yorker, XLII (January 28, 1967), 34-42, 44.

10118 ______. "Vittorio and the Llamas," Turk's Head Review, (Summer 1969), 8-10.

10119 Tyre, Nedra. "Typed for Murder," Signature, II (January

1967), 38-41, 64, 66.

10120 Tyutyunnik, Grigor. "Sieve, Oh Sieve!" Eve Manning, trans., Soviet Literature, (no. 9, 1968), 124-129.

10121 Uda, Lowell. "Crabs," North American Review, V (November-December 1968), 33-37.

10122 _____. "Ulu," TransPacific, no. 1 (Summer 1969), 32-35.

10123 _____. "Vanity Realized in Childhood," Readers & Writers, I (January-February 1967), 12-15.

10124 Udell, I. L. In the Dust of the Valley, South Dakota Review, VII (Spring 1969), 9-105.

10125 Ueda, Akinari. "The Ghoul-Priest," Donald Richie and Yuji Konno, trans., Evergreen Review, XII (November 1968), 58-60, 62.

10126 Ugolnik, Anthony. "Andrei," Ave Maria, CIV (August 6, 1966), 26-29.

10127 _____. "Benny," Ave Maria, CIV (July 16, 1966), 24-27.

10128 _____. "Cass," Ave Maria, CIV (July 23, 1966), 22-25.

10129 _____. "Yadvyga," Ave Maria, CIV (July 30, 1966), 16-19.

10130 Uhlman, Fred. "Fable IV," Aylesford Review, VII (Autumn 1965), 172-183.

10131 _____. "Fable V," Aylesford Review, VII (Winter 1965/ Spring 1966), 245-252.

10132 _____. "Three Fables: III," Aylesford Review, VII (Summer 1965), 110-114.

10133 Ulansky, Gene. "An Exciting Night in Enugu," Phylon, XXX (Fall 1969), 303-305.

10134 Ullian, Robert. "Too Soon for Cherries," Grecourt Review, IX (May 1966), 6-7.

10135 Ullman, James Michael. "The Dinner Party," Signature, I (July 1966), 34-35.

10136 Ulsh, Wayne. "Why Is Joe Fleet Running Tonight?" Ave Maria, CI (April 3, 1965), 20-23.

10137 Umezaki Haruo. "The Birthmark on S's Back," Clifton Royston, trans., Japan Quarterly, XVI (January-March 1969), 78.

10138 ______. "A Found in Three Parts," Clifton Royston, trans., Japan Quarterly, XV (October-December 1968), 481-488.

10139 Umoja, Hekima. "Bolombo's Uprising," Stanford Chaparral, LXIX (Election 1969), 8-14.

10140 Unger, Rustine. "The Blind Date," Era, II (Spring 1965), 40-49.

10141 Updike, John. "Amor Vincit Omnia Ad Nauseam," New Yorker, XLV (April 5, 1969), 33.

10142 ______. "Avec la Bébé-Sitter," New Yorker, XLI (January 1, 1966), 24-27.

10143 ______. "Bech in Rumania," New Yorker, XLII (October 8, 1966), 54-63.

10144 ______. "Bech Takes Pot Luck," New Yorker, XLIV (September 7, 1968), 28-36.

10145 ______. "The Bulgarian Poetess," New Yorker, XLI (March 13, 1965), 44-51.

10146 ______. "Cemeteries," Transatlantic Review, no. 32 (Summer 1969), 5-10.

10147 ______. "The Corner," New Yorker, XLV (May 24, 1969), 38-41.

10148 ______. "Couples," Nova, (August 1968), 82-83, 85, 87.

10149 ______. "The Day of the Dying Rabbit," New Yorker, XLV (August 30, 1969), 22-26.

10150 ______. "Deus Dixit," Esquire, LXIV (September 1965), 100-102.

10151 ______. "During the Jurassic," Transatlantic Review, no. 21 (Summer 1966), 47-50.

10152 ______. "Eros Rampart," Harper's Magazine, CCXXXVI (June 1968), 59-64.

10153 ______. "The Family Meadow," New Yorker, XLI (July 24, 1965), 24-25.

10154 ______. "Four Sides of One Story," New Yorker, XLI (October 9, 1965), 48-52.

10155 ______. "Harv Is Plowing Now," New Yorker, XLII (April 23, 1966), 46-48.

10156 _____. "Henry Bech Takes Pot Luck," Nova, (June/July 1969), 108, 110, 112, 115, 117, 119-120.

10157 _____. "The Hermit," New Yorker, XLI (February 20, 1965), 38-46.

10158 _____. "The Hillies," New Yorker, XLV (December 20, 1969), 33-35.

10159 _____. "I Am Dying, Egypt, Dying," Playboy, XVI (September 1969), 118-120, 250, 254-260.

10160 _____. "I Will Not Let Thee Go, Except Thou Bless Me," New Yorker, XLV (October 11, 1969), 50-53.

10161 _____. "Man and Daughter in the Cold," New Yorker, XLIV (March 9, 1968), 34-36.

10162 _____. "Marching Through Boston," New Yorker, XLI (January 22, 1966), 34-38.

10163 _____. "Museums and Women," New Yorker, XLIII (November 18, 1967), 57-61.

10164 _____. "My Lover Has Dirty Fingernails," New Yorker, XLI (July 17, 1965), 28-31.

10165 _____. "One of My Generation," New Yorker, XLV (November 15, 1969), 57-58.

10166 _____. "The Pro," New Yorker, XLII (September 17, 1966), 53-54.

10167 _____. "The Rescue," New Yorker, XL (January 2, 1965), 28-31.

10168 _____. "The Slump," Esquire, LXX (July 1968), 104-105.

10169 _____. "The Store," New Yorker, XLI (April 3, 1965), 41-43.

10170 _____. "The Taste of Metal," New Yorker, XLIII (March 11, 1967), 49-51.

10171 _____. "Under the Microscope," Transatlantic Review, no. 28 (Spring 1968), 5-7.

10172 _____. "The Wait," New Yorker, XLIII (February 17, 1968), 34-40, 42, 45-46, 48, 51-52, 54, 57-58, 60, 65-66, 68, 70, 72, 77-78, 80, 83-84, 86, 89-90, 92, 95-96.

10173 _____. "The Witnesses," New Yorker, XLII (August 13, 1966), 27-29.

10174 _____. "Your Lover Just Called," Harper's Magazine, CCXXXIV (January 1967), 48-51.

10175 Upton, John. "Enter Hamlet, Amid Sad Drums," Australian Letters, VIII (January 1968), 16-21.

10176 Upton, Robert J. "Young Lambs Bound," Nexus (San Francisco, Calif.), II (March-April 1965), 55-67.

10177 Upward, Edward. "The Rotten Elements," London Magazine, IX (June 1969), 12-27.

10178 Urdang, Constance. "Natural History," Carleton Miscellany, VIII (Summer 1967), 16-83.

10179 Ure, Joan. "It's My Day for Leaving Home," Scottish International, no. 6 (April 1969), 11-12.

10180 Urmuz. "After the Storm," Miron and Carola Grindea, trans., Adam International Review, nos. 322-324 (1967), 44-46.

10181 _____. "Algazy & Grummer," Miron and Carola Grindea, trans., Adam International Review, nos. 322-324 (1967), 25-27.

10182 _____. "A Bit of Metaphysics and Astronomy/An Unfinished Essay," Miron and Carola Grindea, trans., Adam International Review, nos. 322-324 (1967), 46-47.

10183 _____. "Cotadi and Dragomir," Miron and Carola Grindea, trans., Adam International Review, nos. 322-324 (1967), 41-44.

10184 _____. "The Fuchsiad/An Heroic-Erotic (and Musical) Prose Poem," Miron and Carola Gindea, trans., Adam International Review, nos. 322-324 (1967), 30-37.

10185 _____. "The Funnel and Stamate/A Novel in Four Parts," Miron and Carola Grindea, trans., Adam International Review, nos. 322-324 (1967), 21-24.

10186 _____. "Gayk," Miron and Carola Grindea, trans., Adam International Review, nos. 322-324 (1967), 39-40.

10187 _____. "Going Abroad," Miron and Carola Grindea, trans., Adam International Review, nos. 322-324 (1967), 38-39.

10188 _____. "Ismail and Turnavitu," Miron and Carola Grindea, trans., Adam International Review, nos. 322-324 (1967), 28-29.

10189 Urn, Althaea. "The Animal Room," Texas Quarterly, XI (Winter 1968), 99-107.

10190 Urquhart, Fred. "Weep No More, My Lady," Queen, CDXXVII (August 4, 1966), 36-39.

10191 Ustinov, Peter. "The Frontiers of the Sea," Cornhill Magazine, no. 1048 (Summer 1966), 221-239.

10192 _____. "The Swiss Watch," Atlantic Monthly, CCXVIII (October 1966), 84, 87-94.

10193 Uwechia, Kiki. "Brass," London Magazine, VIII (March 1969), 5-20.

10194 Uzzell, Douglas. "Chapter 20," Arx, II (January 1969), 4-6.

10195 Vaca, Nick C. "Martín," El Grito, I (Fall 1967), 25-31.

10196 Vachon, Jingo Viitala. "The Catalogs of Long Ago," Human Voice, III (Summer-Fall 1967), 55-56.

10197 _____. "The Old Lumberjacks," Human Voice, III (Summer-Fall 1967), 56-57.

10198 Vachon, John. "You Can Make a Million," Panache, no. 2 (1968), 56-64.

10199 Vaid, Krishna Baldev. "We Indians," Western Humanities Review, XXIII (Autumn 1969), 305-310.

10200 Vajay, Szabolcs. "The Pot," Literary Review, IX (Spring 1966), 481-486.

10201 Valaoritis, Nanos. "Impressions of Attica," VDRSVPVDRSVP-VDRSVP, (1969), n.p. [back page].

10202 _____. "The Story of Scroloboulopoulos," VDRSVPVDRSVP-VDRSVP, (1969), n.p. [front and back pages].

10203 Valgardson, W. D. "The Call," Alphabet, no. 12 (August 1966), 18-21.

10204 _____. "The Edge of the Garden," The Fiddlehead, no. 70 (Fall 1966), 52-57.

10205 Valjee, Rafiq. "The Artist Who Loved Me," Pakistan Review, XV (October 1967), 24-27.

10206 _____. "The Riddle," Pakistan Review, XVII (January 1969), 23-26.

10207 _____. "A Shattered Image," Pakistan Review, XV (June 1967), 36-37, 44.

10208 Van Buskirk, Alden. [untitled], El Corno Emplumado, no.

15 (July 1965), 133-134.

10209 Vance, Eleanor Graham. "Jeremy's Christmas," Ladies' Home Journal, LXXXV (December 1968), 90-91, 132.

10210 Vance, Joel M. "The Last of the Red Hot Heroes," Modern Age, XIII (Spring 1969), 179-185.

10211 Vancil, Gary. "Parody on The Use of Force by William Carlos Williams," Assay, XXII (Spring 1966), 46-48.

10212 Vandenhoff, Anne. "A Man Like Us," Ave Maria, CV (May 6, 1967), 26-28, 30.

10213 Van De Velde, Roger. "How Long Do Ten Months Last?" Delta (Amsterdam), X (Autumn 1967), 123-133.

10214 Van Duyne, May C. "Peacock Eggs," Literary Review, X (Winter 1966-1967), 246-256.

10215 Van Lare, B. Canary. "The Land Sublime," North American Review, III (January 1966), 20-21.

10216 _____. "Who Will Save the Evergreens?" North American Review, III (July 1966), 14-15.

10217 Van Lenten, H. H. "The Muezzin's Son," Literary Review, XII (Spring 1969), 291-307.

10218 Van Ostaijen, Paul. "Ika Loch's Brothel," E. M. Beekman, trans., New Directions 21, (1969), 94-105.

10219 _____. "Obsequies," E. M. Beekman, trans., Mundus Artium, II (Spring 1969), 58-61 [in Dutch and English on alternate pages].

10220 Van Zeller, Hubert. "Bed and Breakfast," Cornhill Magazine, CLXXVII (Autumn-Winter 1968-69), 105-123.

10221 _____. "Isn't This Where We Came In?" Cornhill Magazine, no. 1045 (Autumn 1965), 12-25.

10222 _____. "Local Time," Cornhill Magazine, no. 1049 (Autumn 1966), 335-359.

10223 van Zyl, Tania. "The Pool," Contrast (Cape Town, South Africa), no. 21 (August 1969), 49-59.

10224 Vargas Llosa, Mario. "Chapter One from/The Green House," Gregory Rabassa, trans., Tri-Quarterly, nos. 13/14 (Fall/Winter 1968-69), 152-165.

10225 Varkey, Ponkunnam. "Veeran," K. M. George, trans., Indian Literature, IX (July-September 1966), 77-85.

10226 Varnado, S. L. "On a Field Gules," Delta Review, V (May 1968), 42-45, 73-74, 77, 80.

10227 Varshavsky, Ilya. "A Raid Takes Place at Midnight," Vladimir Talmy, trans., Soviet Literature, (no. 5, 1968), 112-119.

10228 Vasta, Edward. "The Little Hidden Apple," Minnesota Review, V (October-December 1965), 292-306.

10229 Veder, Bob. "Black Betty," Literary Review, XI (Spring 1968), 341-351.

10230 _____. "One for All Almost None," Prairie Schooner, XLII (Summer 1968), 144-154.

10231 Veitch, Pat. "The Cloak Also...," Southerly, (1969), 45-55.

10232 _____. "The Dance and Mr. Emery," Southerly, XXVII, no. 4 (1967), 288-292.

10233 _____. "The Word Made Flesh," Southerly, (1969), 176-183.

10234 Veitch, Tom. "Beads of Brains/from 'The Luis Armed Story'," Columbia Review, XLIX, no. 2 (1969), 60-63.

10235 _____ and Ron Padgett. "Ernest Hemingway's Hangnail," Columbia Review, XLVIII, no. 3 (1969), 43-45.

10236 _____. "The Foundation of Our Empire/from The Luis Armed Story," Angel Hair, no. 6 (Spring 1969), n.p. [15-19].

10237 _____. "He Thought of the Women He Had Known. It Was Like Saying the Rosary/from: Mr. Flint, a novel," Mother, no. 4 (February-March 1965), 9-11.

10238 _____. "The Luis Armed Story," Art and Literature, (Winter 1967), 182-195.

10239 _____. "The Moon Device," Lines, no. 4 (March 1965), 14-17.

10240 _____. "A Negress in China," Paris Review, XI (Winter 1968), 80-83.

10241 _____. "Something Awful," The World, no. 9 (December 1967), n.p. [61].

10242 _____ and Ron Padgett. "From Star * Gut," Columbia

Review, XLIX, no. 2 (1969), 20-23.

10243 ______ and Ron Padgett. "Star-Gut," San Francisco Earthquake, I (Spring 1968), 23-32.

10244 ______ and Dick Gallup. "Strawberries/from The Planetary Route," Yale Literary Magazine, CXXXVIII (May 1969), 29-32.

10245 ______. "Yoga Exercises," Kulcher, no. 19 (Autumn 1965), 18-21.

10246 ______. "You Got a Point There, Pop," The Once Series (Spice), I (1966-67), n.p. [20-21].

10247 Velde, Paul. "Bird of Paradise," Abyss, (January-February 1967), n.p. [47-51].

10248 ______. "The Man Who Didn't Like Flowers," Abyss, (January-February 1967), n.p. [43-46].

10249 Velembovskaya, Irina. "Larion and Varvara," Avril Pyman, trans., Soviet Literature, (no. 8, 1967), 79-131.

10250 Venkataramani, K. "Mother," R. Nalina, trans., Triveni, XXXVII (April 1968), 54-61.

10251 Venuto, Mike. "100 Yards from Highway 15," American, II (Fall 1966), 38-43.

10252 ______. "The Snatchman Cometh," American, III (Spring 1967), 40-43.

10253 Ver Duft, Lee. "A Florentine Difference," North American Mentor, IV (Winter 1966), 17-18, 20.

10254 Veres, Péter. "Two Stories/Genesis," New Hungarian Quarterly, VIII (Summer 1967), 116-125.

10255 ______. "Two Stories/A Long Day," New Hungarian Quarterly, VIII (Summer 1967), 125-130.

10256 Verma, Nirmal. "The Burning Bush," Susan Neild, trans., Literature East and West, XII (December 1968), 163-173.

10257 Vermandel, Janet. "Murder at Expo 67," Cosmopolitan, CLXIII (October 1967), 158-162, 164, 166-172, 174-175, 180-182, 184-187.

10258 ______. "Scratch a Lover," Redbook, CXXXII (April 1969), 185-207.

10259 Vernon, Lorraine. "The Paper Jesus," Alphabet, no. 13

(June 1967), 30-33.

10260 Vesaas, Tarjei. "The Horse from Hogget," James Wesley Brown, trans., Stand, IX, no. 3 (1968), 2-6.

10261 _____. "The Ice Palace," Elizabeth Rokkan, trans., Cornhill Magazine, no. 1046 (Winter 1965-66), 113-128.

10262 _____. "In the Fish's Golden Youth," Tim Schiff, trans., American Scandinavian Review, LVI (September 1968), 287-290.

10263 _____. "Snow," Kenneth Chapman, trans., Literary Review, XII (Winter 1968-69), 170-175.

10264 _____. "Three Quiet Men," Kenneth Chapman, trans., Literary Review, XII (Summer 1969), 516-518.

10265 Vian, Boris. "The Voyage to Khonostrov," Richard Seaver, trans., Evergreen Review, XI (October 1967), 58-61, 86.

10266 Viator, James E., Jr. "A Noncommunicable Disease," Delta, XXI (1967), 21-23.

10267 Vickers, F. B. "The Early Years," Westerly, no. 4 (1967), 51-55.

10268 _____. "The Pilot Plant," Eastern Horizon, V (February 1966), 56-62.

10269 Victor, Charles B. "Haircut," Midwestern University Quarterly, I, no. 4 (1966), 88-94.

10270 _____. "Number 781," Trace, no. 68 (1968), 292-295.

10271 Vidal, Gore. "Myra Breckinridge," Cosmopolitan, CLXV (August 1968), 111-115.

10272 _____. "Washington, D.C. (excerpt)," Cosmopolitan, CLXIII (August 1967), 106-112.

10273 Vilhotti, Jerry. "The Jinx Gods," Literary Review, IX (Summer 1966), 575-580.

10274 _____. "Lights that Dangled," Literary Review, XII (Spring 1969), 324-329.

10275 Villavivencio, Silvio. "'It Is Here,' Says Felipe," Octavio I. Romano-V., trans., El Grito, II (Fall 1968), 33-39.

10276 _____. "The Mirror," Octavio I. Romano-V., trans., El Grito, II (Winter 1969), 54-60.

10277 Vimal, G. P. "The Eucalyptus," Western Humanities Review, XXII (Summer 1968), 215-219.

10278 Vincent, M. G. "The Vineyard," Meanjin Quarterly, XXVI (Spring 1967), 322-327.

10279 Vincent, Rosemary. "The Father," New Zealand Listener, LIV (April 7, 1966), 8, 25.

10280 ______. "Love Story," New Zealand Listener, LIV (January 14, 1966), 5.

10281 ______. "The Music Lesson," New Zealand Listener, LIV (June 10, 1966), 6.

10282 ______. "The School Reunion," New Zealand Listener, (July 15, 1966), 6, 18.

10283 Vincent-Barwood, Aileen. "The Awakening," Redbook, CXXVI (February 1966), 62-63, 143-146.

10284 ______. "Beyond the Papaw Tree," Cosmopolitan, CLVIII (May 1965), 115-116, 118-119.

10285 Viray, Manuel A. "The Beleaguered," Solidarity, II (November-December 1967), 63-67.

10286 ______. "Broken Glass," Solidarity, II (September-October 1967), 57-61.

10287 ______. "Dark Eyes," Solidarity, II (September-October 1967), 62-66.

10288 ______. "First in Haldama," Solidarity, III (April 1968), 78-81.

10289 ______. "Formation," Solidarity, II (November-December 1967), 68-74.

10290 ______. "Lapse," Solidarity, II (November-December 1967), 44-53.

10291 ______. "One Man's Death...," Solidarity, II (November-December 1967), 54-57.

10292 ______. "Portrait of a Great Man," Solidarity, II (September-October 1967), 67-71.

10293 ______. "Shawl from Kashmir," Solidarity, II (September-October 1967), 52-56.

10294 ______. "To Prepare a Face," Solidarity, II (November-December 1967), 58-62.

10295 ______. "Verdict," Solidarity, II (November-December 1967), 39-43.

10296 Vise, Barbara. "A Flat Spin," Queen, CDXXX (May 8, 1968), 44, 47.

10297 Vishnya, Ostap. "Sniping," Vladimir Leonov, trans., Soviet Literature, (no. 9, 1968), 130-134.

10298 Vithalkar, D. S. "The Birth of a Baby," D. S. Vithalkar, trans., Triveni, XXXVII (July 1968), 32-40.

10299 ______. "The Fly," D. S. Vithalkar, trans., Triveni, XXXVI (July 1967), 60-64.

10300 Vivante, Arturo. "Adria," New Yorker, XLV (March 8, 1969), 31-32.

10301 ______. "Angels in the Air," New Yorker, XLII (June 25, 1966), 24-27.

10302 ______. "A Gift of Joy," New Yorker, XLIV (June 1, 1968), 118.

10303 ______. "The Holborn," New Yorker, XLIV (September 14, 1968), 57.

10304 ______. "Last Rites," New Yorker, XLI (May 22, 1965), 42-43.

10305 ______. "Lesson in the Dark," Southern Review, II (October 1966), 946-951.

10306 ______. "The Lighthouse," New Yorker, XLIII (January 20, 1968), 26-27.

10307 ______. "The Little Ark," New Yorker, XLII (November 19, 1966), 61-63.

10308 ______. "Mr. Harty," New Yorker, XLI (January 22, 1966), 81-87.

10309 ______. "A Moment," New Yorker, XLIV (November 9, 1968), 195-196.

10310 ______. "The Orchard," New Yorker, XLIV (June 15, 1968), 24-27.

10311 ______. "The Room," New Yorker, XLII (July 30, 1966), 24-25.

10312 ______. "The Secret," New Yorker, XLII (May 7, 1966), 47-51.

10313 _____. "The Visit," New Yorker, XLI (July 3, 1965), 29-31.

10314 _____. "The Waiting Room," New Yorker, XLI (March 20, 1965), 40-45.

10315 Vizinczey, Stephen. "Crime and Sentiment," Weekend Telegraph, no. 131 (April 7, 1967), 34-36, 38.

10316 _____. "From 'In Praise of Older Women'," Tamarack Review, no. 36 (Summer 1965), 20-34.

10317 _____. "On Mothers of Little Children," Prism International, IV (Spring 1965), 52-64.

10318 Vladimirov, Leonid. "Forty Years to Pension Time," Avril Pyman, trans., Soviet Literature, (no. 10, 1965), 3-63.

10319 Vlastaru, Boris. "The Little Poplar," Eve Manning, trans., Soviet Literature, (no. 11, 1965), 62-65.

10320 Voelcker, Hunce. "The Slime/The Old White House/The Yellow Rose::Link III," The World, no. 4 (June 1967), n.p. [22-26].

10321 Vogel, Albert W. "Bennie," Quartet, no. 13 (Winter 1966), 11-16.

10322 _____. "The Horse and the Butterfly," Ball State University Forum, VI (Spring 1965), 35-48.

10323 _____. "The Point of Decision," North American Review, III (September 1966), 24-26.

10324 Vogel, Amos. "Philosophy in the Surf," Evergreen Review, X (June 1966), 41.

10325 Völckers, Otto. "The Blacksmith of the Gods," George Raymond Selden, trans., Scala International, (October 1965), 34-37.

10326 von Dassow, Richard. "The Shiny Dream," Prospero's Cell, I, no. 3 (1966), 9-23.

10327 Von der Vring, Georg. "The Flute in the Harbour," George Raymond Selden, trans., Scala International, (August 1967), 35-37.

10328 Vondra, Vladimir. "A Legend of Saintly Folly," Marian Wilbraham, trans., Literary Review, XIII (Fall 1969), 15-27.

10329 Vonnegut, Kurt, Jr. "Fortitude," Playboy, XV (September 1968), 98-100, 102, 106, 217-218.

10330 ______. "Welcome to the Monkey House," Playboy, XV (January 1968), 95, 156, 196, 198, 200-201.

10331 Von Rezzori, Gregor. "Memoirs of an Anti-Semite," New Yorker, XLV (April 26, 1969), 42-52, 54, 57-58, 60, 63-64, 66, 69-70, 72, 77-78, 80, 83.

10332 von Scholz, Wilhelm. "The Astronaut," George Raymond Selden, trans., Scala International, (February 1966), 36-37.

10333 Voss, T. "A Royal Visit," Tri-Quarterly, no. 10 (Fall 1967), 195-201.

10334 Votaw, Galja Barish. "The Journey," Approach, no. 56 (Summer 1965), 8-21.

10335 Vroom, Barbara. "The Hole," New Yorker, XLII (August 6, 1966), 96-97.

10336 ______. "Weekend Confrontation with the Soc. Rels.," New Yorker, XLIII (December 2, 1967), 199-200, 202, 204, 206, 210, 212.

10337 Vyskočil, Ivan. "Jacob's Well," Rosemary Kavanová, trans., Literary Review, XIII (Fall 1969), 72-76.

10338 ______. "Jacob's Well," Rosemary Kavanová, trans., Stand, X, no. 2 (1969), 54-56.

10339 Wade, John Stevens. "Mr. Four Letters," Wormwood Review, V, no. 2 (1965), 14.

10340 ______. "Mr. Lavender," New Frontiers, XI, no. 1 (1966), 12-13.

10341 ______. "Mr. Lavender," Wormwood Review, VII, no. 2 (1967), 5-7.

10342 Wade, Seth. "Roots," December, VII (1965), 19.

10343 Wadham, Kay. "Living with Dandy," New Zealand Listener, (August 5, 1966), 6, 14.

19344 Waggaman, William H. "The Batting Eye," Columbia, XLIX (May 1969), 24-29.

10345 Wagner, Linda W. "Bucky," Ave Maria, CIV (July 9, 1966), 24-27.

10346 Wagnon, Drew. "Alto," Wild Dog, no. 16 (April 1965), 33-34.

10347 ______ and Fielding Dawson. "Test," Wild Dog, no. 21

(March 1966), 1-4.

10348 Wagoner, David. "The Escape Artist," Harper's Magazine, CCXXX (May 1965), 102-104, 110-114, 116, 119-120.

10349 Wahab, M. Arif. "'The Wall'," Pakistan Review, XIII (August 1965), 9-11.

10350 Waheed, Farzana. "The Beggar Women," Pakistan Review, XVII (December 1969), 36-38.

10351 Wain, John. "Darkness," Harper's Bazaar, XCVIII (August 1965), 78-79, 144, 150.

10352 _____. "Darkness," Weekend Telegraph, no. 115 (December 9, 1966), 59, 61, 64, 68-69.

10353 _____. "The Life Guard," Esquire, LXXI (February 1969), 70-73, 108, 142-144.

10354 _____. "Manhood," Ladies' Home Journal, LXXXII (January 1965), 92d, 92f, 92h, 92j.

10355 _____. "While the Sun Shines," Playboy, XIV (April 1967), 78-80, 82, 195-196.

10356 Wajiragnana, Polpitimukalane, Rev. "Two Stories/The Mystery of Esala Perahera," Prism International, VIII (Autumn 1968), 4-6.

10357 _____. "Two Stories/Prediction," Prism International, VIII (Autumn 1968), 6-7.

10358 Wakefield, Dan. "Autumn Full of Apples," Redbook, CXXV (September 1965), 74-75.

10359 _____. "The Rich Girl," Playboy, XIII (June 1966), 84-85, 94, 176-178, 180-181.

10360 _____. "A Visit from Granny," Denver Quarterly, I (Winter 1967), 69-73.

10361 Walbert, Claude. "The Dream Denied," Free Lance (Cleveland, Ohio), X (First Half, 1966), 33-36.

10362 _____. "The New Conception," Four Quarters, XV (November 1965), 18-22.

10363 Waldman, Anne. "Love's Tombstone," The World, no. 5 (July 1967), n.p. [45].

10364 Waldo, Ives. "From a Novel in Progress," Solstice, no. 2 (1966), 18-21.

10365 Waldvogle, Jerold. "Fever Note," New Campus Review, I (May 1966), 19.

10366 Walen, Philip. "Bleakness, Farewell/7-10:V:64, Revised 26:I:65," Coyote's Journal, no. 8 (1967), 98-104.

10367 Walford, Roy L. "An Expedition in Search of Little Fish," Evergreen Review, XIII (April 1969), 16-19, 64-70.

10368 _____. "Three Versions of the Oriental Squat: A Triptych," Evergreen Review, XII (February 1968), 64-70.

10369 Walker, Alice. "The Child Who Favored Daughter," Denver Quarterly, II (Summer 1967), 99-108.

10370 _____. "Strong Horse Tea," Negro Digest, XVII (June 1968), 53-60.

10371 Walker, Charlotte. "Monserrate," Story: the Yearbook of Discovery, (1968), 53-58.

10372 Walker, Don. "Beyond a Far Country," Western Humanities Review, XXI (Summer 1967), 201-208.

10373 _____. "Sound of Strangers," Western Humanities Review, XIX (Summer 1965), 217-222.

10374 Walker, Marjorie. "The Grey and Silent Places," Epoch, XVI (Fall 1966), 23-34.

10375 Walker, Susan. "Five O'Clock," The Archive, LXXX (April 1968), 23-24, 31.

10376 Walker, T. Mike. "The Search," Writer's Forum, I (May 1965), 25-28.

10377 Walker, Ted. "The Bow," New Yorker, XLIII (September 2, 1967), 34-37.

10378 _____. "The Cremation," New Yorker, XLV (March 1, 1969), 33-37.

10379 _____. "Donovan's Boots," New Yorker, XLV (November 8, 1969), 51-53.

10380 _____. "The Haircut," New Yorker, XLIII (September 23, 1967), 50-54.

10381 _____. "The Peaches," New Yorker, XLIV (October 12, 1968), 56-59.

10382 _____. "The Satellite," New Yorker, XLIV (February 24, 1968), 38-42.

10383 _____. "Something of a Miracle," New Yorker, XLIV (May 18, 1968), 36-40.

10384 _____. "The Spikers," New Yorker, XLIV (November 16, 1968), 56-58.

10385 Walker, William O. "Somewhere I Have Never Traveled," New Campus Writing, (1966), 134-143.

10386 Wallace, Irving. "The Plot (excerpt, Part I)," Cosmopolitan, CLXIII (August 1967), 122-129.

10387 _____. "The Plot (excerpt, Part II)," Cosmopolitan, CLXIII (September 1967), 136-143, 165.

10388 Wallace, Jerry D. "Mr. Emerson's Umbrella," Ave Maria, CIV (October 22, 1966), 24-26.

10389 Wallace, Mary. "Brendan," McCall's, XCIII (February 1966), 74-77, 135-146, 148-153.

10390 _____. "Brendan's Birthday Party," Woman's Day, (March 1965), 62-63, 100, 102-104.

10391 _____. "The Island," McCall's, XCIII (August 1966), 88-89, 150-153.

10392 _____. "The Man on the Corner," Redbook, CXXX (November 1967), 78-79, 140, 142-144, 146-148.

10393 _____. "Reason for Gladness," McCall's, XCII (August 1965), 72-75, 155-156, 158-161, 163-164, 166-168, 170-173.

10394 Wallace-Crabbe, Chris. "Going to Cythera," Yale Literary Magazine, CXXXIV (May 1966), 20-21.

10395 Walmsley, J. K. "Hapless Harold v. Two Faced Ted," The Cantuarian, (August 1966), 206-207.

10396 _____. "To Err Is Human," The Cantuarian, (April 1967), 367-369.

10397 Walser, Martin. "After Siegfried's Death," Christopher Middleton, trans., Stand, VII, no. 4 (1965), 22-27.

10398 _____. "Four Stories/The Angel," Judy Barnebey, trans., The Fair, II (Summer 1968), 4.

10399 _____. "Four Stories/Ibsen's Nora or The Chips," Judy Barnebey, trans., The Fair, II (Summer 1968), 3-4.

10400 _____. "Four Stories/Servant Girl's Tale," Judy Barnebey, trans., The Fair, II (Summer 1968), 2-3.

10401 _____. "Four Stories/The Walk," Judy Barnebey, trans., The Fair, II (Summer 1968), 5-6.

10402 _____. "Kleist in Thun," Robert Scott, trans., 0 to 9, no. 2 (August 1967), 1-12.

10403 _____. "The Little Berliner," Harriett Watts, trans., Delos, no. 1 (1968), 135-141.

10404 Walsh, Stewart. "A Summer's Day Gone Sour," Wisconsin Review, III (Fall 1967), 4-7.

10405 Walter, Eugene. "The Charmer," Transatlantic Review, no. 21 (Summer 1966), 124-133.

10406 Walter, Nina. "The Dishes," Modern Age, XIII (Summer 1969), 297-303.

10407 Walter, Robert. "Monday, Tuesday, Wednesday, and the Rest of Life," Man About Town, II (July 1968), 28-29.

10408 Walters, Sherwyn. "Path of Despair," Bim, XIII (July-December 1969), 40-44.

10409 Walters, Thomas N. "August Gypsy Grandfather," Crucible, V (Spring 1969), 36-37.

10410 Waltham, Clae. "Not for Every Eye," Redbook, CXXV (August 1965), 147-159.

10411 Walton, David. "The Charm," Quartet, no. 25 (Winter 1969), 1-5.

10412 _____. "The Final Phone Call," North American Review, V (March-April 1968), 27-29.

10413 _____. "In the Wake," Western Humanities Review, XXIII (Autumn 1969), 321-327.

10414 _____. "Joshua Calchus," Appalachian Review, II (Fall 1967), 35-38.

10415 _____. "Madelaine," Story: the Yearbook of Discovery, (1968), 85-91.

10416 _____. "Three Deaths," Quartet, no. 22 (Spring 1968), 6-11.

10417 Walton, Sam. "Dog Is God Spelled Backwards," Georgia Review, XXIII (Winter 1969), 518-526.

10418 Waluconis, Carl. "The Poison Animal Crackers," Dust, IV (Summer 1969), 37-43.

10419 _____. "The Poison Animal Crackers," Jeopardy, no. 5 (Spring 1969), 81-86.

10420 Wampler, Martin. "Saturday, Riding Down," Consumption, I (Summer 1968), 26-29.

10421 Wanner, Irene. "The Indian," Twigs, no. 5 (Fall 1969), 175-184.

10422 Wantling, William. "A Doctor Had Explained It Once," Nexus (San Francisco, Calif.), II (January-February 1967), 35-36.

10423 _____. "A Silent Afternoon," Prism International, IV (Spring 1965), 44-46.

10424 Ward, Dick. "Tiger in the Bedroom," Spectrum, VIII (Winter 1965), 97-100.

10425 Ward, John. "The Ruin," Anglo-Welsh Review, XVII, no. 39 (Summer 1968), 78-92.

10426 Ward, Philip. "In the House of Rumelitz," West Coast Review, IV (Fall 1969), 21-22.

10427 _____. "The Life and Library of Johann Ziegler," The Quest, II (Fall 1967), 196-199.

10428 _____. "Stones," Transatlantic Review, no. 31 (Winter 1968-69), 80-82.

10429 _____. "Vicente in Lurinha," Transatlantic Review, no. 23 (Winter 1966-67), 118-119.

10430 Ward, Robert. "from The Town of Thatched Rooves/...In Which the Narrator Becomes a Mountain Man and Harvests the Grapes of Wrath...," Carolina Quarterly, XXI (Fall 1969), 7-14.

10431 _____. "from The Town of Thatched Rooves/...In Which the Narrator Meets the Phantom of Cleveland and Learns that There Is No Business Like Show Business...," Carolina Quarterly, XXI (Fall 1969), 15-20.

10432 Ward, Tony. "Jenny's First Class Journey," The Park, no. 1 (1968), 10-30.

10433 Wardell, George. "Fistula/An American Folk Tale," The Fair, I (January 1966), 2-16.

10434 Ware, Leon. "Golden Saturday," Woman's Day, (March 1966), 48-49, 97-100.

10435 _____. "Lord, Keep Me Safe," Good Housekeeping, CLXIII (September 1966), 86-87, 193-194, 196, 198, 200.

10436 Ware, Ron. "Mai," Wascana Review, IV, no. 2 (1969), 53-58.

10437 Warhol, Andy. "Ondine's Mare," Evergreen Review, XII (September 1968), 26-31, 77-78.

10438 Waring, M. W. "The Witnesses," Ladies' Home Journal, LXXXIV (October 1967), 155-166.

10439 Warlick, Joan W. "Pink Poufs from a Funeral Spray," Long View Journal, I (Spring 1969), 37-42.

10440 Warner, Sylvia Townsend. "A Brief Ownership," New Yorker, XLIII (October 7, 1967), 140, 142, 144, 146.

10441 _____. "The Candles," New Yorker, XLI (February 5, 1966), 38-41.

10442 _____. "The Cheese," New Yorker, XLV (June 14, 1969), 43.

10443 _____. "Item, One Empty House," New Yorker, XLII (March 26, 1966), 131-132, 134, 136, 138.

10444 _____. "Johnnie Brewer," New Yorker, XLI (April 10, 1965), 45-50.

10445 _____. "Oxenhope," New Yorker, XLII (July 9, 1966), 25-29.

10446 _____. "A Pair of Duelling Pistols," New Yorker, XLIII (February 17, 1968), 29-31.

10447 _____. "A Saint (Unknown) with Two Donors," New Yorker, XL (January 2, 1965), 33-38.

10448 _____. "Sopwith Hall," New Yorker, XLV (November 22, 1969), 57-60.

10449 _____. "Truth in the Cup," New Yorker, XLIV (December 7, 1968), 62-64.

10450 _____. "A Visionary Gleam," New Yorker, XLIII (June 3, 1967), 36-41.

10451 _____. "A Winding Stair, a Fox Hunt, a Fulfilling Situation, Some Sycamores, and the Church at Henning," New Yorker,

XLII (February 26, 1966), 38-41.

10452 Warren, Kelly. "The Sixth Day of Rest," Plaintiff, V (Spring-Summer 1969), 38-40.

10453 Warsh, Lewis. "Alone in Rome," The World, no. 13 (November 1968), n.p. [35].

10454 ______. "Memoirs," The World, no. 7 (October 1967), n.p. [3].

10455 Wartofsky, Victor. "Thomas," Quartet, no. 14 (Spring 1966), 6-10.

10456 Washburne, Rick. "To the Breakers," Man About Town, I (June 1968), 43-45.

10457 Wasser, Lawrence. "Plot of Gold," Signature, I (April 1966), 28.

10458 Wasserman, Reuven. "The Bus to Kinneret," Hirshel Silverman, trans., Damascus Road, no. 2 (1965), 34-35.

10459 Waterhouse, Mary. "The Blue Gown," UMD Humanist, XIV (Winter 1966), 29-33.

10460 Wathen, Richard. "Louisville--1930," Green River Review, I (May 1969), 31-39.

10461 Watkins, Griffith. "Call Me By My Proper Name," Westerly, (August 1966), 21-26.

10462 ______. 'Know the Deep River," Westerly, (May 1966), 40-44.

10463 ______. "Madame Halina," Meanjin Quarterly, XXV (September 1966), 334-339.

10464 Watkins, Roy. "Christine," Art and Literature, no. 10 (Autumn 1966), 55-70.

10465 ______. "The Criminal," Intro, no. 1 (September 1968), 20-33.

10466 Watkinson, Valerie. "Ghost of a Dead Dream," Woman's Day, (May 1965), 44-45, 106, 108-108D.

10467 ______. "The Mangrove Crab," Woman's Day, (May 1966), 46-47, 107-111.

10468 ______. "The Wondering Day," Woman's Day, (November 1967), 42-43, 86-88, 109.

10469 Watson, Cynthia. "Daddy's Coming Home," Lit (Lambda Iota Tau), IX (Autumn 1968), 44-48.

10470 Watson, Lyall. "How I Caught a Whale in the Thames," Daily Telegraph Magazine, no. 243 (June 6, 1969), 43-44, 46.

10471 Watson, Wilfrid. "Collage," Literary Review, VIII (Summer 1965), 503-510.

10472 Waugh, Harriet. "The New Life," Cornhill Magazine, CLXXVII (Spring 1969), 215-222.

10473 _____. "A Terrible Beauty," Queen, CDXXXIII (May 28-June 10, 1969), 76-77, 98.

10474 Wavell, Derek. "Belinda File," Solstice, no. 6 (1967), 15-21.

10475 Weales, Gerald. "Friends and Strangers," Antioch Review, XXVII (Winter 1967-68), 508-514.

10476 Weathers, Tom, Jr. "The Mill," Red Clay Reader, no. 2 (1965), 63-64.

10477 Weathers, Winston. "The Games That We Played," Georgia Review, XXI (Spring 1967), 39-45.

10478 _____. "Metaphysical Music," North American Review, III (January 1966), 11-13.

10479 _____. "Monday Nights at Mrs. Gasperi's," New Mexico Quarterly, XXXV (Summer 1965), 128-136.

10480 _____. "Red River," Arlington Quarterly, II (Summer 1969), 72-75.

10481 _____. "St. Stephen's Green," Literary Review, XIII (Winter 1969-70), 208-214.

10482 Weaver, Gordon A. "The Day I Lost My Distance," Minnesota Review, VI (1966), 25-35.

10483 _____. "The Entombed Man of Thule," Prism International, VII (Autumn 1967), 34-39.

10484 _____. "Gold Moments and Victory Beer," December, IX, nos. 2 & 3 (1967), 47-55.

10485 _____. "Haskell Hooked on the Northern Cheyenne," North American Review, III (November 1966), 24-29.

10486 _____. "Low Blue Man," North American Review, II (Spring 1965), 14-19.

10487 _____. "Oskar Hansen Jr. Speaks To His Son," Denver Quarterly, III (Winter 1969), 39-59.

10488 _____. "Reasons I Insist You Call Me By My Right Name," Latitudes, II (Spring 1968), 2-8.

10489 _____. "Suds' Sunday," Perspective, XIV (Spring 1965), 21-26.

10490 Weaver, Ken. "Adios Lecture," San Francisco Earthquake, I (Winter 1968), 15-16.

10491 Weaver, Lloyd. "The Tax Return of John Doe," Signature, II (March 1967), 20.

10492 Webb, Bernice Larson. "Lost and Found," Kansas Magazine, (1968), 1-4.

10493 Webb, Charles. "Love, Roger," Cosmopolitan, CLXVII (September 1969), 164-170, 172-183, 186-187, 190-193.

10494 Webb, Ethel. "Welcome Home," Westerly, no. 1 (1967), 11-16.

10495 Webb, Frances. "The Great & Wonderful Death," New Renaissance, I (December 1969), 43-49.

10496 Webb, Leland. "The Ballad of Tremble Dove," Redbook, CXXVII (October 1966), 62-63, 119, 121-122.

10497 Webb, Sharon. "Out of Mind," Man About Town, I (June/July 1967), 8-10.

10498 Weber, Helen. "Rusty," University Review, XXXIV (Winter 1967), 127-132.

10499 Weber, Nancy. "End of a Friendship," Cosmopolitan, CLXIV (March 1968), 158-160.

10500 Wedde, Ian. "The Classic Line," Landfall, no. 91 (September 1969), 224-226.

10501 Weeden, Val. "By the Poplars," Woman's Day, (July 1965), 36-37, 96-100.

10502 Weeks, Jack. "A Big Bloody Cockbird," Saturday Evening Post, CCXL (March 11, 1967), 70-73, 75, 77.

10503 Weeks, Mary Lyle. "Sing Me a Song of Left Tackle," Seventeen, XXIV (October 1965), 130-131, 208, 210, 212, 214, 216, 218.

10504 Weesner, Theodore. "Andrew His Son," New Yorker, XLIII

(November 4, 1967), 54-63.

10505 _____. "The Survivors," Saturday Evening Post, CCXXXVIII (June 5, 1965), 62-64, 66-73.

10506 Wegner, Robert. "How Lightning Shot Out of the Rat's Ass," Readers & Writers, I (October-November 1966), 14-20, 27.

10507 _____. "The Woman with Concave Breasts," Esquire, LXIII (February 1965), 83, 85, 124-125.

10508 Weidman, Jerome. "The Absolute Darlings," McCall's, XCII (July 1965), 62-63, 144-148.

10509 _____. "The Friends of Mary Fowler," Redbook, CXXV (July 1965), 58-59, 110, 119-121, 124-125.

10510 _____. "Good Man, Bad Man," Saturday Evening Post, CCXL (July 1, 1967), 48-53.

10511 _____. "Mrs. Gregory Is in Industrial Diamonds," Cavalier, XV (August 1965), 18-19, 38, 78-80.

10512 _____. "Second Breakfast," Playboy, XIV (February 1967), 83, 108, 150-151.

10513 _____. "The Wife of the Man Who Suddenly Loved Women," Ladies' Home Journal, LXXXIII (June 1966), 72-73, 122, 124, 126-127.

10514 Weiler, P. Garrett. "Cut-Hand," South Dakota Review, VI (Summer 1968), 14-24.

10515 Weinberger, Florence. "In the Summer of Margo," Nimrod, (Spring 1968), 16-20.

10516 Weingarten, Violet. "Fertility Rite," Saturday Evening Post, CCXL (August 12, 1967), 54-57.

10517 _____. "The Man Who Saw through Heaven," Atlantic Monthly, CCXVIII (September 1966), 103-106.

10518 _____. "Mrs. Beneker," Nova, (February 1968), 80, 82-83, 85.

10519 Weinstein, Rocio Aitana. "The Subway Car," Wascana Review, II, no. 1 (1967), 54-60.

10520 Weinstock, E. B. "Cardinal Piccolomini," New Campus Writing, (1966), 144-156.

10521 Weintraub, Ruth Claire. "A Twig from Judas," Prism International, VI (Autumn 1966), 114-129.

10522 Weinzweig, Helen. "Surprise!" Canadian Forum, XLVII (March 1968), 276-279.

10523 Weisbrod, Rosine. "The Ninth Cold Day," Virginia Quarterly Review, XLV (Summer 1969), 451-463.

10524 Weisman, Edward H. "Nice Boy," DeKalb Literary Arts Journal, II (Spring 1968), 38-43.

10525 Weismann, Donald L. "If You Live Long Enough," New Mexico Quarterly, XXXVII (Spring 1967), 54-58.

10526 Weiss, Alexander. "Selections from The Human Actions of a Zookeeper/(a work in progress)," Nexus (San Francisco, Calif.), III (March-April 1967), 40-41.

10527 Weiss, Ernst. "Mending a Ruptured Heart," Margaret D. Howie, trans., Scala International, (February 1968), 34-37.

10528 Weiss, Miriam S. "Arrivals and Departures," McCall's, XCII (July 1965), 58-59, 109-111.

10529 _____. "Days of Hope and Glamour," Redbook, CXXVIII (March 1967), 68-69, 150-153.

10530 _____. "The Game," Colorado Quarterly, XVII (Autumn 1968), 197-205.

10531 _____. "39," Ladies' Home Journal, LXXXII (November 1965), 90-91, 156-158.

10532 Weiss, Peter. "My Place," Christopher Middleton, trans., Encounter, XXV (December 1965), 3-7.

10533 Weissenborn, Theodor. "Herr Gasenzer's Voice," Margaret D. Howie, trans., Scala International, (December 1968), 34-37.

10534 _____. "The Rapids," George Raymond Selden, trans., Scala International, (April 1965), 34-36.

10535 _____. "The Strange Life of Cousin Liborius," George Raymond Selden, trans., Scala International, (March 1967), 35-37.

10536 Weissner, Carl. "Death TV," VDRSVPVDRSVPVDRSVP, (1969), n.p. [front and back pages].

10537 _____. "Muschar Blee Rosch," San Francisco Earthquake, I (Summer/Fall 1968), 75-80.

10538 _____. "The Orion Dream Stuff/(fragment)," San Francisco Earthquake, I (Winter 1968), 9-10.

10539 _____. "Say Unsay/Say Unsay," San Francisco Earthquake, I (Winter 1968), 11-14.

10540 _____. "Stasis Inc.," VDRSVPVDRSVPVDRSVP, (1969), n.p. [front page].

10541 _____. "The Subcutaneous Kid," Vincent the Mad Brother of Theo, no. 2 (1968), n.p. [55-57].

10542 _____. "that old PANlite Prism con," San Francisco Earthquake, I (Winter 1968), 8-9.

10543 _____. "We Got Off," VDRSVPVDRSVPVDRSVP, (1969), n.p. [back page].

10544 Welch, Julie. "Under a Loose Heading," Daily Telegraph Magazine, no. 241 (May 23, 1969), 26-27.

10545 Weller, Howard L. "The Aliens," University Review, XXXIV (Spring 1968), 223-226.

10546 _____. "The Fall," Dare, III (September-October 1965), 16.

10547 _____. "It's a Long Journey Home," Literary Review, IX (Summer 1966), 581-591.

10548 Wellershoff, Dieter. "The Edge of Darkness," Jean Hollander, trans., Dimension, II, no. 1 (1969), 182-193 [in German and English on alternate pages].

10549 Welles, Patricia. "Babyhip," Ladies' Home Journal, LXXXIV (September 1967), 135-146.

10550 Wells, Dick. "The Mysterious Fate of an Orlong," Prospero's Cell, I (Winter 1967), 51-64.

10551 Welsh, D. "Tale," Work, no. 3 (Winter 1965-1966), 87-89.

10552 Welsh, Elizabeth. "A Horse for Brother Jamieson," Texas Quarterly, XI (Summer 1968), 168-179.

10553 Welty, Eudora. "The Demonstraters," New Yorker, XLII (November 26, 1966), 56-63.

10554 _____. "The Optimist's Daughter," New Yorker, XLV (March 15, 1969), 37-46, 48, 50, 53-54, 56, 61-62, 64, 67-68, 70, 75-76, 78, 81-82, 84, 86, 88, 93-95, 98, 100, 103-106, 111-114, 117-120, 125-128.

10555 Wentz, Richard V. "The Flats," William and Mary Review, III (Spring 1965), 43-51.

10556 _____. "Seldom We Find," William and Mary Review,

III (Winter 1965), 35-41.

10557 Wercenski, Patricia. "Afterthoughts," UMD Humanist, XVII (Winter 1969), 5-6.

10558 Wertheim, Bill. "Burial," Columbia Review, XLV (Spring 1965), 50-56.

10559 West, Anthony. "Katie Crawford," Vogue, CLIV (September 1, 1969), 448-449, 456, 458, 460-466.

10560 _____. "Miss Millard," New Yorker, XLIII (November 11, 1967), 132, 134, 137-138, 140, 142, 144, 149-150, 152, 154, 156, 159-160, 162, 165-166, 168, 171-174, 177-179.

10561 _____. "Mr. Keogh," New Yorker, XLIII (July 8, 1967), 29-38, 40, 42-44, 46-48, 50-51.

10562 _____. "Mrs. Barker," New Yorker, XLII (May 14, 1966), 52-56, 58, 61-62, 64, 67-68, 70, 73-74, 76, 78, 80, 83-84, 86, 89-90, 92, 95-96, 98, 100, 105-106, 108, 110, 113.

10563 West, Jessamyn. "The Birthday Suit," Saturday Evening Post, CCXLI (October 5, 1968), 74-75, 78-80.

10564 _____. "Good-bye, Bossy," Ladies' Home Journal, LXXXII (June 1965), 82-83, 107-110.

10565 _____. "A Matter of Time/Part I," Redbook, CXXVII (September 1966), 163, 165-191.

10566 _____. "A Matter of Time/Part II," Redbook, CXXVII (October 1966), 165, 167-193.

10567 _____. "Mother of Three," Redbook, CXXX (April 1968), 68-69, 120-121, 123-124.

10568 _____. "Underground," Good Housekeeping, CLXVI (January 1968), 73-75, 174-182, 192, 196-206.

10569 West, Morris. "The Tower of Babel," Imprint, VIII (August 1968), 57-77, 79-95, 97, 99, 101, 103, 105, 107, 109, 111-127, 129-137, 139, 141, 143, 145.

10570 _____. "The Tower of Babel/Part I," McCall's, XCV (May 1968), 43-54.

10571 _____. "The Tower of Babel/Part Two," McCall's, XCV (June 1968), 41-48.

10572 _____. "The Tower of Babel/Part Three," McCall's, XCV (July 1968), 57-70.

10573 West, Thomas A., Jr. "In the Midst of Victory," Arx, III (May 1969), 29-32.

10574 ______. "Interruption in August," Four Quarters, XVII (May 1968), 11-18.

10575 ______. "Johnny Boy," University of Portland Review, XX (Spring 1969), 37-48.

10576 ______. "Kay Bealby's Pain," Arx, III (September 1969), 21-25.

10577 ______. "The Most Fabulous Gift," Pyramid, no. 1 (1968), 28-30.

10578 ______. "No More the Voice Like Death," Arx, III (November 1969), 6-7.

10579 ______. "The Power," Arx, II (July 1968), 2-6.

10580 ______. "The Sincerity of Coby Sedgwick," Four Quarters, XVIII (May 1969), 31-36.

10581 ______. "Stand Up to Die," Cimarron Review, no. 5 (September 1968), 14-21.

10582 ______. "The Travels of Alfred Nolan, Esq.," Arx, III (June 1969), 3-7.

10583 ______. "The Volunteer," Four Quarters, XVII (November 1967), 25-31.

10584 Westburg, John Edward. "Bacchus and Tutankaton Conspire to Restore Ammon to the Temples of Thebes/A Fragment from The Middle Book of Aristaeus," North American Mentor, V (Fall 1967), 15-22.

10585 ______. "A Fragment from The Book of Yareb," North American Mentor, IV (Fall 1966), 17-19.

10586 ______. "A Fragment from the First Book of Teiresias/Excerpt from The Madness of Bacchus," North American Mentor, VI (Fall 1968), 3-8.

10587 ______. "Second Part of The Book of Melampus the Minyan/An Excerpt from The Madness of Bacchus," North American Mentor, V (Spring 1967), 25, 27-33.

10588 Westlake, Donald E. "Devilishly," Signature, I (August 1966), 34-35.

10589 ______. "God Save the Mark," Cosmopolitan, CLXII (May 1967), 138-142, 144, 146-148, 150-151, 154-156, 161-162, 164-171.

10590 _____. "It," Playboy, XV (September 1968), 165-166.

10591 _____. "Somebody Owes Me Money," Playboy, XVI (July 1969), 104-105, 142, 166-167, 169-173, 175-181.

10592 _____. "Somebody Owes Me Money/Conclusion," Playboy, XVI (August 1969), 116-117, 130, 205-208, 210-212, 214, 216-220.

10593 _____. "Who Stole Sassi Manoon?" Cosmopolitan, CLXV (October 1968), 164-168, 170-172, 174-176, 178-182, 188-191, 194-199.

10594 Weston, Christine. "The First Frost," Redbook, CXXVI (December 1965), 66-67, 120-121, 125-126.

10595 Weston, John. "The Waiting Time," Texas Quarterly, XI (Spring 1968), 199-208.

10596 Weyer, Susan. "Hang-Up," McCall's, XCV (January 1968), 54-55, 99-100.

10597 _____. "This Day for Thanks," Good Housekeeping, CLXI (November 1965), 82-83, 264, 266, 272, 277-278.

10598 Weyne, Mark. "The Perfect Type," Moonlight Review, I (Winter 1967-68), 46-57.

10599 Weyrauch, Wolfgang. "Something's Happening," Earl N. Lewis, trans., Dimension, II, no. 1 (1969), 75-89 [in German and English on alternate pages].

10600 Wham, David. "Brandy/A Novella," The Fair, I (March 1966), 5-42.

10601 _____. "Brandy/A Novella/Conclusion," The Fair, I (May 1966), 7-66.

10602 _____. "Doctor Plugus," The Fair, II (Spring 1968), 11-23.

10603 Wheatcroft, John. "Daffodils," Four Quarters, XV (May 1966), 23-27.

10604 _____. "Honeysuckle," Nimrod, X (Winter 1966), 1-14.

10605 _____. "I Love You, Joe Gish," Sage, XI (Fall 1967), 305-311.

10606 _____. "Image of Departure," Georgia Review, XX (Fall 1966), 328-336.

10607 Whedon, Julia. "It's Magic Time," Ladies' Home Journal,

LXXXIV (January 1967), 58-59, 105.

10608 _____. "Rubbings," Harper's Magazine, CCXXXVIII (April 1969), 58-61.

10609 Wheeler, Kristi. "Harters, Portage Corner," Minnesota Review, VIII (1968), 326-331.

10610 _____. "The Painter," Minnesota Review, VII (1967), 129-131.

10611 Wheelis, Allen. "Sea-Girls," Yale Review, LV (Summer 1966), 570-584.

10612 _____. "The Signal," Ramparts, V (July 1966), 28-36.

10613 Whelan, Gloria. "The Other Shore," University Review, XXXIV (Autumn 1967), 57-60.

10614 _____. "Teach Me, Only Teach, Love!" Michigan Quarterly Review, VI (Spring 1967), 109-114.

10615 Whelan, Sandra. "The Miracle in the Stone," Columbia, XLVII (June 1967), 24-28.

10616 _____. "Save Me the Days," Columbia, XLVI (May 1966), 24-27.

10617 Wheway, John. "Bald," Stand, XI, no. 1 (1969-70), 32-33.

10618 Whipple, William. "Gilly," Midwestern University Quarterly, I, no. 3 (1966), 10-16.

10619 White, Antonia. "Surprise Visit," Art and Literature, no. 6 (Autumn 1965), 196-204.

10620 White, Bradford G. "Dreams in the Sky," Literary Review, XIII (Winter 1969-70), 189-202.

10621 White, Dori. "The First Year," Redbook, CXXXIII (August 1969), 76, 143.

10622 _____. "To Be a Girl," Good Housekeeping, CLXVII (September 1968), 78-79, 162, 164, 166.

10623 _____. "Under Sentence of Death," Redbook, CXXIX (September 1967), 82-83.

10624 _____. "Woman's Work," Redbook, CXXVII (August 1966), 66-67.

10625 White, Edgar J. "Killing Tim's God," Yale Literary Magazine, CXXXIV (January 1966), 13-23.

10626 _____. "The Speeder," Yale Literary Magazine, CXXXV (January 1967), 24-28.

10627 _____. "The Style of Going," Yale Literary Magazine, CXXXV (May 1967), 23-27.

10628 White, Ellington. "The Hant Watchers," Southern Review, II (October 1966), 919-932.

10629 White, Gail Brockett. "The Great Byron Forgery," Quartet, no. 28 (Fall 1969), 19-23.

10630 White, Herbert D. "The Elephant," Ohio University Review, XI (1969), 38-46.

10631 White, James P. "Hidden," North American Mentor, V (Winter 1967), 3, 6-7, 9-10.

10632 _____. "I'll Fetch Thee Brooks from Spotted Nooks," Kansas Quarterly, I (Winter 1968), 61-66.

10633 _____. "Tommy," Ball State University Forum, VIII (Spring 1967), 47-55.

10634 White, M. E. "A Summer Evening's Wake," Paris Review, X (Winter-Spring 1967), 168-175.

10635 White, Patrick. "Five-Twenty," Southerly, XXVIII (1968), 3-25.

10636 _____. "A Social Occasion," Meanjin Quarterly, XXIV (March 1965), 18-24.

10637 White, Richard. "An Adult's Garden of Verses," Ave Maria, CIII (April 2, 1966), 20-21.

10638 _____. "Remember Pearl Harbor? She Was a Lovely Girl," Ave Maria, CII (November 20, 1965), 22-24.

10639 _____. "'Shazam!' and All That," Ave Maria, CI (January 16, 1965), 20-22.

10640 White, Robin. "The Fault-Finding Committee," University Review, XXXII (March 1966), 187-193.

10641 _____. "Walker's Peak," Saturday Evening Post, CCXXXVIII (January 16, 1965), 48-54, 58-59.

10642 White, Vera Randal. "Let's Be Friends," Seventeen, XXV (April 1966), 162-163, 254-259.

10643 _____. "Natural Immunity," McCall's, XCIV (October 1966), 122-123, 177-181.

10644 ______. "A Night for Celebration," Saturday Evening Post, CCXXXVIII (December 4, 1965), 50-54.

10645 ______. "You Can't Buy People," Saturday Evening Post, CCXL (May 6, 1967), 78-80, 82-83.

10646 White, Victor. "The Chief Disciple," Arlington Quarterly, I (Summer 1968), 104-109.

10647 ______. "The Hotel," Southwest Review, L (Winter 1965), 20-36.

10648 ______. "In the Glass House," South Dakota Review, III (Autumn 1965), 10-20.

10649 ______. "Neighbor in the Room," Southwest Review, LIV (Spring 1969), 147-166.

10650 White, Wallace. "Against a Backdrop," Atlantic Monthly, CCXIX (March 1967), 75-80, 85.

10651 ______. "Three Crises in the Lives of Dope Friends," Esquire, LXXI (March 1969), 122-124.

10652 ______. "Wood," Atlantic Monthly, CCXV (May 1965), 76-81.

10653 White, William M. "A Man's Day in Court," Ball State University Forum, VIII (Autumn 1967), 44-50.

10654 Whitehall, Joseph. "Bobby," Atlantic Monthly, CCXIX (May 1967), 57-62.

10655 Whitehall, Richard. "Another Paleface Bit the Dust," Texas Quarterly, X (Spring 1967), 178-186.

10656 Whitehill, Joseph. "Living on the Edge," Hudson Review, XX (Summer 1967), 225-254.

10657 ______. "One Night for Several Samurai," Hudson Review, XVIII (Summer 1965), 193-229.

10658 ______. "The Round Brass Elevator," Hudson Review, XIX (Spring 1966), 57-80.

10659 Whitelock, Derek. "Rainbow Trout," Southerly, XXVI, no. 2 (1966), 107-114.

10660 Whiteson, Leon. "Mrs. Kalyannis," Transatlantic Review, no. 19 (Autumn 1965), 121-132.

10661 Whiting, G. D. "Run into Dark," Dust, I (Winter 1965), 73-76.

10662 Whitman, William. "The Fat Man," Chicago Review, XX (November 1968), 5-8.

10663 Whitmore, George. "Clemma," Silo, no. 12 (Fall 1967), 37-48.

10664 Whitney, Phyllis. "Columbella," Cosmopolitan, CLXI (August 1966), 116-127, 132-143.

10665 _____. "Hunter's Green," Cosmopolitan, CLXIV (May 1968), 168-174, 176-186, 188, 190, 192-198.

10666 Whitus, Jerry D. "An Early Winter," Corral 1965, 56-63.

10667 Wibberley, Jane. "Colour Girl," Solstice, no. 2 (1966), 35-37.

10668 Wickham, John. "Meeting In Milkmarket," Bim, XII (July-December 1967), 3-8.

10669 Wicks, Graeme. "Little Jessie," Meanjin Quarterly, XXV (December 1966), 444-452.

10670 Wiebe, Dallas E. "Skyblue on the Dump," Paris Review, X (Fall 1966), 139-151.

10671 Wiebe, Ruby H. "Millstone for the Sun's Day," Tamarack Review, no. 44 (Summer 1967), 56-64.

10672 Wieners, John. "Letters," Intrepid, no. 6 (1966), n.p. [8-10].

10673 Wiesel, Elie. "The Madmen of Sighet," Neal Kozodoy, trans., Commentary, XLV (May 1968), 38-41.

10674 Wiggins, Barbara. "Who Weeps for Ma?" DeKalb Literary Arts Journal, II (Fall 1967), 38-45.

10675 Wilde, Oscar. "The Happy Prince," Ladies' Home Journal, LXXXIV (December 1967), 62-63, 125-128.

10676 _____. "The Selfish Giant," Parallel, I (November-December 1966), 25-30.

10677 Wilding, Michael. "Canal Run," Overland, no. 37 (Spring 1967), 4-9.

10678 _____. "Joe's Absence," Southerly, XXVIII (1968), 37-53.

10679 _____. "Like Rat Turds to Me," Alta, no. 7 (Winter 1968-69), 46-51.

10680 _____. "A Month in the Country," Alta, no. 5 (Spring

1968), 297-298.

10681 _____. "Thank You, Miss," London Magazine, VI (September 1966), 88-95.

10682 _____. "Yes, We Unzip Bananas," Westerly, no. 2 (July 1968), 5-7.

10683 Wildman, Eugene. "from The Subway Singer," Chicago Review, XIX (June 1967), 26-36.

10684 Wildman, John Hazard. "The Queen's Picture," Southern Review, I (April 1965), 406-420.

10685 _____. "The Sword," Southern Review, IV (April 1968), 415-422.

10686 Wilkinson, Martin. "The Drinker," Transatlantic Review, no. 24 (Spring 1967), 87-92.

10687 Wilkinson, Sylvia. "Jimson," Red Clay Reader, no. 3 (1966), 102-106.

10688 _____. "Jimson," William and Mary Review, V (Spring 1967), 13-21.

10689 _____. "A Maypop from Merton," Red Clay Reader, no. 6 (1969), 79-84.

10690 _____. "Patch in the Dutch Boy's Britches," Tri-Quarterly, no. 10 (Fall 1967), 183-189.

10691 Willard, N. "Graffito," Prospero's Cell, II (Summer 1967), 5-8.

10692 _____. "The Hucklebone of a Saint," Perspective, XIV (Winter 1967), 195-212.

10693 Willard, Nancy. "The Beautiful Sunday," Michigan Quarterly Review, VII (Fall 1968), 243-248.

10694 _____. "The Boy Who Ran with the Dogs," Epoch, XVII (Spring 1968), 218-227.

10695 _____. "Judgement City and Lonely Town," Chicago Review, XXI (December 1969), 20-35.

10696 _____. "The Lively Anatomy of God," Chicago Review, XX (June 1968), 5-18.

10697 _____. "Saints," University Review, XXXIII (Summer 1967), 252-260.

10698 _____. "Theo's Girl," Massachusetts Review, X (Winter 1969), 59-76.

10699 Willeford, Charles. "Nowhere for a Gone Cat," Man About Town, I (June/July 1967), 22-23.

10700 Willey, Mary Louise. "The Imprisonment," Hudson Review, XIX (Summer 1966), 215-252.

10701 Williams, Charles. "The Wrong Venus," Cosmopolitan, CLXI (September 1966), 112-117.

10702 Williams, D. "Dr. Sensations' Conversion," Plaintiff, IV (Fall-Winter 1967-68), 34.

10703 Williams, Denis. "Sperm of God," Transition, VI, no. 28 (1967), 9-13.

10704 Williams, Dennis. "The Coloring Book," For Now, no. 7 (c. 1966-68), 78-87.

10705 _____. "The Coloring Book: Part Two," For Now, no. 8 (c. 1966-68), 100-113.

10706 Williams, Doris B. "A Case for Gallantry," Nimrod, XII (Fall 1967), 10-16.

10707 Williams, Gene. "The Deterrent," New Yorker, XLI (February 20, 1965), 141-143, 147-149.

10708 _____. "Les Enfants du Thalia," New Yorker, XL (February 6, 1965), 28-29.

10709 _____. "May You Live in Interesting Times," New Yorker, XLV (August 2, 1969), 27-29.

10710 _____. "Paper Tiger, Burning Bright," New Yorker, XLI (October 30, 1965), 52-54.

10711 _____. "Sticky My Fingers, Fleet My Feet," New Yorker, XLI (September 11, 1965), 46-48.

10712 _____. "The Yellow Brick Road," New Yorker, LXII (June 4, 1966), 32-34.

10713 Williams, Hugo. "Allah Giveth and Allah Taketh Away," London Magazine, V (April 1965), 28-33.

10714 _____. "A Road to the Isles," London Magazine, VI (November 1966), 51-56.

10715 Williams, Jan. "Pig Money," Bim, XI (July-December 1966), 205-213.

10716 ______. "The Weaker Sex," Bim, XI (January-June 1966), 93-98.

10717 Williams, Joan. "Jesse," Esquire, LXXII (November 1969), 164-165, 249-250, 253, 255-257.

10718 ______. "The Passenger from Roebourne," Westerly, no. 4 (December 1969), 44-48.

10719 ______. "Pariah," McCall's, XCIV (August 1967), 80-81, 123-124, 126.

10720 ______. "Spring Is Now," Virginia Quarterly Review, XLIV (Autumn 1968), 626-640.

10721 Williams, John A. "The Man Who Cried I Am," Ramparts, VI (November 1967), 34-82.

10722 ______. "The Party," Lotus, no. 1 (1968), 15-16.

10723 Williams, Joy. "Another Season," Prairie Schooner, XL (Summer 1966), 123-130.

10724 ______. "Baby, Tonight I Rolled Pinto Lee," Colorado Quarterly, XVI (Summer 1967), 21-36.

10725 ______. "Dimmer," Paris Review, XII (Fall 1969), 121-151.

10726 ______. "Dr. Caligari Loves," Virginia Quarterly Review, XLV (Summer 1969), 464-480.

10727 ______. "In Search of Boston," New Campus Writing, (1966), 157-169.

10728 ______. "Jefferson's Beauty," Paris Review, XI (Winter 1968), 23-34.

10729 ______. "The Retreat," Paris Review, XI (Fall 1968), 88-101.

10730 ______. "The Roomer," Carolina Quarterly, XVII (Winter 1965), 29-37.

10731 ______. "'2'," Transatlantic Review, no. 30 (Autumn 1968), 84-90.

10732 Williams, Laura. "Wonderful Couple--Great Team!" Redbook, CXXXIII (July 1969), 92-93, 136-138, 140.

10733 Williams, Lawrence. "The Girl with the Hometown Look," Good Housekeeping, CLXV (September 1967), 90-91, 148, 150, 152.

10734 ______. "A Matter of Living," Redbook, CXXXIX (July 1967), 64-65, 104-106.

10735 ______. "Pride of My Heart," Good Housekeeping, CLXIV (May 1967), 92-93.

10736 ______. "Proud Moment," Good Housekeeping, CLXVI (June 1968), 82-83, 140-144, 146-148.

10737 ______. "The Swingers," Good Housekeeping, CLXIII (November 1966), 98-99, 236-238, 240, 242-244, 246.

10738 ______. "The Treasure," Good Housekeeping, CLXIV (March 1967), 92-93, 162, 164-165, 167-169.

10739 Williams, Lucille C. "The Cornish Cup," Four Quarters, XIV (January 1965), 1-4.

10740 Williams, Malcolm. "Early Fall," Anglo-Welsh Review, XVII (Winter 1969), 176-183.

10741 Williams, Miller. "One Saturday Afternoon," Prairie Schooner, XL (Summer 1966), 151-165.

10742 ______. "There Aren't Any Foxes in that Cave," Red Clay Reader, no. 3 (1966), 83-90.

10743 ______. "The Wall," Shenandoah, XVI (Spring 1965), 71-80.

10744 Williams, Mona. "The Marriage Makers," Cosmopolitan, CLXIV (February 1968), 124-128.

10745 Williams, Pieter. "In the Shadow," North American Mentor, VI (Fall 1968), 15, 17-20.

10746 Williams, Richard. "The Yellow Teapot," Ave Maria, CIII (March 19, 1966), 24-25.

10747 Williams, Ronald. "Grandma's Game," Negro Digest, XV (May 1966), 76-83.

10748 Williams, S. A. "Tell Martha Not to Moan," Massachusetts Review, IX (Summer 1968), 443-458.

10749 Williams, Tennessee. "Grand," Daily Telegraph Magazine, no. 215 (November 15, 1968), 51, 54, 58, 62.

10750 ______. "Mama's Old Stucco House," Esquire, LXIII (January 1965), 86-88, 90.

10751 ______. "Mama's Old Stucco House," Weekend Telegraph, no. 33 (May 7, 1965), 49-52, 54.

10752 Williams, Thomas. "All Trades, Their Tackle and Trim," Esquire, LXIV (November 1965), 102-103.

10753 ______. "Dark Hill Farm," Saturday Evening Post, CCXLII (January 25, 1969), 46-48, 50-52.

10754 ______. "The Snows of Minnesota," New Yorker, XLI (February 12, 1966), 32-40.

10755 ______. "The Survivors," New Yorker, XLI (August 21, 1965), 32-40.

10756 Williams, Travis. "Niggers Don't Cry," Negro Digest, XV (September 1966), 56-59.

10757 Williamson, David. "From a Novel in Progress," Alphabet, no. 12 (August 1966), 26-37.

10758 Willingham, Calder. "A Clowny Night in the Red-Eyed World," Playboy, XII (March 1965), 66-68, 70, 74, 128, 131-132, 134-135.

10759 ______. "What Star So Humble," New Yorker, XL (January 16, 1965), 30-31.

10760 Willis, Meredith Sue. "The Baby Sitter," Mademoiselle, LXIX (August 1969), 302-303, 357-360.

10761 ______. "Rosenoire," Focus, (1968), 14-19.

10762 Wilmore, Stephen R. "The Committee," Negro Digest, XIX (December 1969), 54-61.

10763 Wilner, Herbert. "The Baby Sitter of Burgenland," Redbook, CXXVI (April 1966), 82-83, 112-114, 116.

10764 ______. "Dovisch among the Savages," Saturday Evening Post, CCXXXVIII (June 19, 1965), 58-60, 62-68, 70, 72.

10765 ______. "Dovisch in Hippyland," Esquire, LXIX (March 1968), 110, 112-113, 122-124, 132, 134, 136.

10766 ______. "A Gift Every Morning," Esquire, LXVI (August 1966), 106-108, 129.

10767 ______. "No Medal for Sonny," Saturday Evening Post, CCXXXIX (November 5, 1966), 58-60, 62.

10768 Wilson, Colin. "Margin of Darkness," Minnesota Review, VI (1966), 268-295.

10769 Wilson, Edmund. "The Death of a Soldier," New Yorker, XLIII (May 13, 1967), 62, 64, 67-68, 70, 73-76, 78, 80, 85.

10770 _____. "Lieutenant Franklin," New Yorker, XLIII (May 13, 1967), 121-122, 125-128, 131-136, 138, 140-147.

10771 Wilson, Eileen. "The Wait," Ave Maria, CV (January 14, 1967), 26-27, 31.

10772 Wilson, Fredde M. "Black Daedalus Dreaming," Negro Digest, XIX (November 1969), 64-69.

10773 _____. "The Willie Bob Letters," Negro Digest, XVIII (January 1969), 63-69.

10774 Wilson, Gahan. "The Manuscript of Doctor Arness," Playboy, XIII (August 1966), 73, 157-158.

10775 _____. "The Sea Was Wet as Wet Could Be," Playboy, XIV (May 1967), 83, 124, 142, 144.

10776 Wilson, Gail. "All the Little Owls," Grecourt Review, XI (February 1968), 13-17.

10777 Wilson, H. H. "The Peacock Days," Meanjin Quarterly, XXV (March 1966), 34-42.

10778 Wilson, Jack Lowther. "Roast Beef's the Thing to Eat," Queen's Quarterly, LXXII (Winter 1966), 651-656.

10779 _____. "Singing," Tamarack Review, no. 37 (Autumn 1965), 47-53.

10780 _____. "The Sunday Man," Canadian Forum, XLVI (May 1966), 29-32.

10781 Wilson, John Grant. "Country Cop," New Zealand Listener, (May 19, 1967), 6, 14.

10782 _____. "Cross Purposes," New Zealand Listener, (September 2, 1966), 6, 15.

10783 _____. "A Lesson for Miss Sims," New Zealand Listener, (March 10, 1967), 6, 18.

10784 _____. "One Good Turn Makes a Circle," New Zealand Listener, (December 2, 1966), 6, 26.

10785 _____. "Wasted Talent," New Zealand Listener, LII (June 4, 1965), 4.

10786 _____. "You Can't Be Cruel to an Elephant," New Zealand Listener, LIV (June 24, 1966), 6.

10787 Wilson, Joseph. "Of Ben and the Bomb," Ave Maria, CIV (October 8, 1966), 6.

10788 Wilson, Martha. "The Plain Brown Bird," Redbook, CXXVII (August 1966), 62-63.

10789 Wilson, Martin. "Mr. Lim," New Zealand Listener, (April 5, 1968), 6.

10790 Wilson, Robert. "The World Outside Illinois," December, VIII (1966), 46-53.

10791 Wilson, Robley, Jr. "The Apple," Carleton Miscellany, IX (Winter 1968), 24-34.

10792 _____. "Others," Carleton Miscellany, VI (Fall 1965), 4-29.

10793 _____. "A Stay at the Ocean," Carleton Miscellany, X (Summer 1969), 39-54.

10794 Wilson, Rosalind. "The Famous Rutland Pearls," Ladies' Home Journal, LXXXII (May 1965), 68-69, 122, 124-125.

10795 Wilson, Shirley M. "Mama's Girl," DeKalb Literary Arts Journal, II (Summer 1968), 51-56.

10796 Wilt, Jean. "The Chocolate Minute," Ave Maria, CVII (February 17, 1968), 26-28.

10797 Wimberly, Lowry C. "Tall and Straight," Prairie Schooner, XL (Winter 1966), 292-302.

10798 Winchester, Otis. "The Devil under Kansas," Kansas Magazine, (1965), 23-27.

10799 _____. "An Egg Illumined," Nimrod," XIV (Fall 1969), n.p. [10-11].

10800 Winkfield, Trevor. "Nature Study," Yale Literary Magazine, CXXXVIII (May 1969), 10-11.

10801 _____. "Travelogues," Paris Review, XL (Winter 1968), 132-135.

10802 Winn, Janet Bruce. "Dried Rose Petals in a Silver Bowl," Evidence, no. 10 (1967), 4-11.

10803 _____. "Sprung Rhythm," Prairie Schooner, XXXIX (Spring 1965), 1-10.

10804 Winnick, Harriet. "Bring Your Heart Next Thursday," University Review, XXXII (October 1965), 59-63.

10805 Winnicki, Henrietta. "Clockwise," Ave Maria, CVII (April 27, 1968), 26-29.

10806 Winslow, Joyce Madelon. "Benjamin Burning," Intro, no. 1 (September 1968), 62-79.

10807 Winslow, Pete. "The Anarchist," Aldebaran Review, no. 3 (1968), 21.

10808 Wiseman, William J., Jr. "A River's Loss," adapted from Karl Gunnarson's "Som Dräng in Finland," A. Hjalmar Haglund, trans., Nimrod, XII (Winter 1968), 17-32.

10809 Wiser, William. "The History of Solitude," Carleton Miscellany, X (Spring 1969), 24-41.

10810 _____. "Hitchhike Ride to Miracleville," Cosmopolitan, CLVIII (June 1965), 93-97.

10811 _____. "House of Blues," Kenyon Review, XXVIII (March 1966), 231-250.

10812 _____. "The Man Who Wrote Letters to Presidents," Playboy, XIV (August 1967), 77, 80, 116.

10813 _____. "Nobody Knows Why the Big Wind Blows," Carleton Miscellany, IX (Summer 1968), 46-59.

10814 _____. "Predators," Cosmopolitan, CLIX (November 1965), 108-113.

10815 Witkiewicz, Stanislaw Ignancy. "Insatiability/Two Scenes from a Novel," Louis Iribarne, trans., Delos, no. 1 (1968), 7-23.

10816 Witt, Harold. "The Absinthe Drinkers," University Review, XXXII (October 1965), 10-16.

10817 Wittenberg, Corinne. "In the Talmudic Tradition," American Judaism, XV (Spring 1966), 16-17, 57-58.

10818 Witting, Amy. "The Early Settler," New Yorker, XLIV (May 18, 1968), 42-44.

10819 _____. "Goodbye, Ady, Goodbye, Joe," New Yorker, XLI (November 6, 1965), 51-58.

10820 Witty, S. K. "Homecoming," Yale Literary Magazine, CXXXIV (November 1965), 46-63.

10821 Wodehouse, P. G. "The Battle of Squashy Hollow," Saturday Evening Post, CCXXXVIII (June 5, 1965), 50-51, 54, 58-60.

10822 _____. "Bingo Bans the Bomb," Playboy, XII (January 1965), 93, 206-208, 212.

10823 ______. "First Aid for Freddie," Playboy, XIII (October 1966), 143, 148, 198, 201-202.

10824 ______. "George and Alfred," Playboy, XIV (January 1967), 109, 182, 200, 202-203.

10825 ______. "A Good Cigar Is a Smoke," Playboy, XIV (December 1967), 123-124, 138, 272-275.

10826 ______. "Jeeves and the Greasy Bird," Playboy, XII (December 1965), 127, 134, 238, 240-242.

10827 ______. "Stylish Stout," Playboy, XII (April 1965), 77, 152-153.

10828 ______. "Ukridge Starts a Bank Account," Playboy, XIV (July 1967), 79, 136-141.

10829 Woiwode, L. "Beyond the Bedroom Wall," New Yorker, XLII (March 5, 1966), 38-41.

10830 ______. "The Boy," New Yorker, XLIV (August 31, 1968), 32-38, 42, 44-53.

10831 ______. "The Brothers," New Yorker, XLII (May 21, 1966), 43.

10832 ______. "The Contest," New Yorker, XLV (November 1, 1969), 50-56.

10833 ______. "The Deathless Lovers," New Yorker, XLI (July 10, 1965), 20-21.

10834 ______. "Don't You Wish You Were Dead," New American Review, no. 7 (August 1969), 90-109.

10835 ______. "The History Lesson," New Yorker, XLIII (September 30, 1967), 47-50, 52, 54, 57-58, 60, 63-64, 66, 69-70, 72, 77-80, 83.

10836 ______. "The Horses," New Yorker, XLIV (December 28, 1968), 24-26.

10837 ______. "The Long Trip," New Yorker, XLIV (July 13, 1968), 26-34.

10838 ______. "Near the Straits of Mackinac," New Yorker, XLII (April 9, 1966), 40-44.

10839 ______. "An Old Man," New Yorker, XLIV (April 20, 1968), 44-45.

10840 ______. "On This Day," New Yorker, XLIII (September 9,

1967), 44-49.

10841 _____. "Pheasants," New Yorker, XLIII (November 18, 1967), 62-66.

10842 _____. "The Visitation," New Yorker, XLII (September 10, 1966), 56-61.

10843 _____. "What Can Blow the Wind Away?" Mademoiselle, LXVIII (February 1969), 162-163, 188-189, 192-193, 195.

10844 Wolf, H. R. "To the Fair," Negro Digest, XIV (July 1965), 58-59.

10845 Wolf, Leonard. "Willie," Sewanee Review, LXXV (July-September 1967), 421-435.

10846 Wolf, Sam. "The Job," Transatlantic Review, no. 18 (Spring 1965), 85-89.

10847 Wolfe, Bernard. "The Hot Sauces of Magda," Playboy, XV (February 1968), 88-90, 188-192.

10848 _____. "How Simon Got His Bureau," Playboy, XIII (February 1966), 68-70, 78, 150-154.

10849 _____. "The Roach Powder in the Maple Walnut," Playboy, XIII (May 1966), 86-88, 90, 216-222, 224.

10850 Wolfe, Gene. "The Green Wall Said," New Worlds, no. 174 (1967), 26-27.

10851 Wolfe, Karl Michael. "Indian Mound," Delta Review, V (June 1968), 50-56, 58-64.

10852 Wolfe, Tom. "The Voices of Village Square," Queen, CDXXV (Christmas Issue, 1965), 149-150.

10853 Wolitzer, Hilma. "In the Flesh," New American Review, no. 5 (January 1969), 165-169.

10854 _____. "Today, a Woman Went Mad in the Supermarket," Saturday Evening Post, CCXXXIX (March 12, 1966), 50-52, 54.

10855 Wolkers, Jan. "Candy Floss," Transatlantic Review, no. 18 (Spring 1965), 18-23.

10856 _____. "Wax Fruit," R. R. Symonds, trans., London Magazine, IX (July/August 1969), 9-37.

10857 Wolper, Roy S. "A Vacation," Wascana Review, I, no. 1 (1966), 62-73.

10858 _____. "When Money Talked to Me," Texas Quarterly, IX (Autumn 1966), 24-30.

10859 Wood, Clair G. "Cape Cod Incident," Human Voice, V, nos. 1-4 (1969), 40-45.

10860 Wood, Elizabeth Scull. "Charleswater," Silo, no. 11 (Spring 1967), 18-30.

10861 Wood, James Playsted. "Harry and I," Georgia Review, XIX (Spring 1965), 68-71.

10862 _____. "The Whale in the Attic," Georgia Review, XIX (Winter 1965), 459-464.

10863 Wood, John. "Description," Compass, (Summer 1965), 45-46.

10864 Wood, Kerry. "The Poacher's Game," Ave Maria, CV (May 20, 1967), 24-27.

10865 Wood, Malcolm. "The Appraiser," Saturday Evening Post, CCXXXVIII (April 10, 1965), 54-56, 58-61, 63-64.

10866 _____. "The Get-Together," Colorado Quarterly, XIV (Spring 1966), 329-344.

10867 _____. "Home Fires Burning," Saturday Evening Post, CCXXXVIII (July 3, 1965), 52-53, 55-56, 58-59.

10868 Wood, Margery. "The Bride," Carleton Miscellany, VIII (Fall 1967), 42-58.

10869 Wood, Nancy. "The Last Five Dollar Baby," Denver Quarterly, IV (Spring 1969), 45-65.

10870 Wood, P. S. "O Tannenbaum," New Yorker, XLV (December 20, 1969), 75-76, 78, 80, 82, 84-85.

10871 Wood, Russell. "A Georgia Peach," Georgia Review, XXII (Spring 1968), 3-11.

10872 Wood, Ted. "The Fish," Tamarack Review, no. 49 (1969), 48-59.

10873 Wood, William. "A Sailing Tan," Carolina Quarterly, XVII (Spring 1965), 26-37.

10874 Woodbury, Benjamin L., III. "No Defense," Lance, V (Spring 1965), 32-34.

10875 _____. "Tom Collins," Lance, V (Winter 1965), 17-18.

10876 Woodcock, P. R. "When I'm Cleanin' Windows," Westerly, no. 3 (October 1969), 19-20.

10877 Woodford, Bruce and B. G. Gasper. "The Rope, a Fugue from Hell," Aesop's Feast, I (January 1969), 9-19.

10878 Woodley, Inez. "My Son, the Shepherd," Redbook, CXXX (December 1967), 52-53, 96, 98, 100.

10879 _____. "A Summer's Tale," Redbook, CXXXIII (July 1969), 90-91, 131-132.

10880 Woodman, Marion. "Christo Mente Maria," Alphabet, no. 11 (December 1965-March 1966), 45-52 [issue number mistakenly printed as no. 8].

10881 Woods, William Crawford. "He that Died of Wednesday," Esquire, LXXI (June 1969), 115, 213-217.

10882 _____. "A Mirror of the Waves," Intro, no. 2 (September 1969), 53-76.

10883 _____. "The Viping Hour," New American Review, no. 7 (August 1969), 114-125.

10884 Woolf, Douglas. "The Ice Cream Man," El Corno Emplumado, no. 15 (July 1965), 16-20.

10885 _____. "John-Juan," Origin (Kyoto, Japan), no. 5 (April 1967), 32-64.

10886 _____. "John-Juan [continued]," Origin (Kyoto, Japan), no. 6 (July 1967), 1-57.

10887 _____. "The Love Letter," New Directions 19, (1966), 232-243.

10888 _____. "Notes for an Autobituary," Coyote's Journal, no. 2 (1965), 44-50.

10889 _____. "Ya!/An Extract from a New Novel," Delta (Cambridge, England), no. 46 (Winter 1969), 48-51.

10890 Woos, Joachim Heinrich. "Unlucky Stroke," Signature, I (September 1966), 24.

10891 Wooten, Anna. "The Barn," Coraddi, (Winter 1969), 5-8.

10892 _____. "Sea Level," Coraddi, (Arts Festival 1969), 39-43.

10893 Wooton, Carl. "Final Arrangements," Ball State University Forum, VIII (Autumn 1967), 17-22.

10894 _____. "That Summer Day," Literary Review, IX (Autumn 1965), 65-76.

10895 _____. "Under Silent Stars," Georgia Review, XXI (Summer 1967), 218-225.

10896 Worth, Ellis. "The Detour," Kansas Magazine, (1967), 61-63.

10897 _____. "Etiquette and the Cattleman," Latitudes, II (Spring 1968), 44-47.

10898 _____. "The Inspector General," Ikon (Leeds, Eng.), I (January 1966), 9-11.

10899 _____. "The Lost Nephew," Kansas Magazine, (1965), 54-58.

10900 _____. "The Path," North American Mentor, VI (Spring 1968), 17-20, 22.

10901 Worthen, Holly. "A Possible Misunderstanding of an Exchange of Some Pink and Gold Pearls," Kenyon Review, XXVIII (November 1966), 612-639.

10902 Wosk, G. M. "A Way of Life in the Climate of Death," Twigs, no. 5 (Fall 1969), 201-217.

10903 Wosk, Goldie. "Hear Me, Carla," December, VII (1965), 186-189.

10904 Wouk, Herman. "Don't Stop the Carnival," Ladies' Home Journal, LXXXII (November 1965), 139-146.

10905 Wright, Austin. "Camden," Paris Review, XI (Winter 1968), 49-71.

10906 Wright, Charles. "Notebook from Ischia & Three Snapshots from Ponza," North American Review, II (May 1965), 32-34.

10907 _____. "Sonny and the Sailor," Negro Digest, XVII (August 1968), 63-67.

10908 Wright, Dan. "Looking for Fludd," Yale Literary Magazine, CXXXIV (October 1965), 16-20.

10909 Wright, J. S. N. "'Story'," Stand, XI, no. 1 (1969-70), 44-47.

10910 _____. "Various Properties," Stand, XI, no. 1 (1969-70), 41-43.

10911 Wright, Peter R. "My Life Is a Dream," Lance, V (Winter 1965), 29.

10912 Wright, Richard. "Bright and Morning Star," Negro Digest, XVIII (December 1968), 53-77.

10913 Wrobel, Sylvia. "Postcards from Roland," Red Cedar Review, VI (Winter 1968), 23-27.

10914 Wuori, G. K. "Turtles," Minnesota Review, IX (1969), 163-173.

10915 Wurlitzer, Rudolph. "The Boiler Room," Atlantic Monthly, CCXVII (March 1966), 127-132, 134-136, 138-139.

10916 _____. "The Octopus," Paris Review, X (Summer 1966), 113-126.

10917 Wyatt, Ken. "These Last Strands," Delta, XX (1966), 5-9.

10918 Wyatt, Lawrence. "The Chair," Arizona Quarterly, XXI (Spring 1965), 64-73.

10919 _____. "Color Hungry," Discourse, XI (Autumn 1968), 477-485.

10920 _____. "Jesus Under the Pear Tree," Western Humanities Review, XXIII (Autumn 1969), 329-332.

10921 Wyatt, R. V. "Trap," The Cantuarian, (August 1965), 430.

10922 Wynd, Oswald. "A Long Walk from the Gate," Woman's Day, (January 1965), 38-39, 86, 89, 90.

10923 Wyndham, John. "Wise Child," Playboy, XIV (May 1967), 125, 175-180.

10924 Wynne, Carolyn. "The Bus Trip," University Review, XXXII (December 1965), 143-150.

10925 _____. "Little Boy Blue," Arizona Quarterly, XXI (Autumn 1965), 234-242.

10926 _____. "The Old Camping Grounds," Carolina Quarterly, XVII (Winter 1965), 72-77.

10927 Yadav, Kim. "Against the Rising Sun," Imprint, IX (December 1969), 55-61, 63, 65, 67, 69-70, 73, 75, 77, 79, 81, 83, 85, 87, 89, 91, 93, 95, 97, 99, 101, 103, 105, 107, 109, 111, 113, 115, 117, 119, 121, 123, 125.

10928 Yakovlev, Yuri. "The Persecution of Red-Heads," Vladimir Talmy, trans., Soviet Literature, (no. 12, 1968), 107-147.

10929 Yakubov, Adyl. "Daughter of the Mountains," Peggy Brown, trans., Soviet Literature, (no. 12, 1967), 82-91.

10930 Yaney, George L. "The Good Mayor," Georgia Review, XXII (Winter 1968), 464-472.

10931 Yáñez, Agustín. "The Lean Lands," Ethel Brinton, trans., Caribbean Review, I (Summer 1969), 8-9.

10932 Yankovich, Sister Emmanuel. "The Good News," Ave Maria, CII (December 18, 1965), 23-24.

10933 Yanovsky, V. S. "The Atlantic Charter," The Quest, II (Spring 1967), 64-66.

10934 _____. "The Dardanelles," The Quest, II (Spring 1966), 253-255.

10935 _____. "Double Nelson," The Quest, I (Winter 1965-66), 5-20.

10936 _____. "Ninety-Six in the Shade," The Quest, I (Summer 1966), 5-13.

10937 _____. "Task and Realization," The Quest, I (Spring 1966), 5-13.

10938 Yanovsky, Yuri. "The Heir to the Dynasty," Alice Ingman, trans., Soviet Literature, (no. 9, 1968), 18-23.

10939 Yap, Arthur. "A Silly Little Story," Focus (Singapore), IV, no. 1, 15-16.

10940 Yashin, Alexander. "A Feast of Rowanberries," Avril Sokolova, trans., Soviet Literature, (no. 6, 1966), 92-101.

10941 Yashpal. "Slime of Sin," Prabhakar Machwe, trans., Indian Literature, XI (April-June 1968), 68-81.

10942 Yates, J. Michael. "Concerning A Temple," Wascana Review, I, no. 2 (1966), 6-10.

10943 _____. "The Hunter Who Loses His Human Scent," Beyond Baroque 691, I (December 1968), 57-61.

10944 _____. "I, Quixote, Librarian," Jeopardy, no. 4 (Spring 1968), 55.

10945 _____. "I, Quixote, Librarian," The Quest, II (Spring 1967), 55-56.

10946 _____. "Man in the Glass Octopus," Wascana Review, I, no. 2 (1966), 5-6.

10947 _____. "The Man of Qualification," Quartet, no. 14 (Spring 1966), 24.

10948 _____. "The Passage of Sono Nis," Jeopardy, no. 4 (Spring 1968), 50-54.

10949 _____. "The Passage of Sono Nis," Tamarack Review, no. 46 (Winter 1968), 40-47.

10950 _____. "Whiteford O. McGuff's Change," The Quest, I (Summer 1966), 58-62.

10951 Yates, Richard. "The Good and Gallant Woman," Saturday Evening Post, CCXXXVIII (September 11, 1965), 48-55.

10952 _____. "To Be a Hero," Saturday Evening Post, CCXXXVIII (September 25, 1965), 52-58, 60-69.

10953 Yeo, Dale. "The Waiting Room," UMD Humanist, XIII (Spring 1965), 38-39.

10954 Yeroukhan. "The Story of Little Shep," Mischa Kudian, trans., Ararat, IX (Winter 1968), 14-18.

10955 Yevtushenko, Yevgeni. "The Chicken-God," David Mann, trans., Harper's Magazine, CCXXXI (August 1965), 64-68, 73-75.

10956 _____. "The Good Citizen," David Mann, trans., Redbook, CXXX (February 1968), 74-75, 113-114, 116-118.

10957 Yglesias, Jose. "The Goodbye Land/The News from Columbus," New Yorker, XLIII (March 25, 1967), 48-56, 59-60, 62, 65-66, 68, 71-72, 74, 79-80, 82, 85-86, 88, 91-92, 94, 99-100, 102, 105-106, 108, 111-112, 114.

10958 _____. "The Goodbye Land/The Way There," New Yorker (March 18, 1967), 51-60, 62, 65-66, 68, 73-74, 76, 79, 82, 87-88, 90, 93-94, 96, 101-102, 104, 107, 110, 115-116, 118.

10959 Yokomitsu Riichi. "The Fly," John Nathan, trans., Japan Quarterly, XII (January-March 1965), 72-75.

10960 _____. "Spring, in a Surrey," John Nathan, trans., Japan Quarterly, XII (January-March 1965), 65-71.

10961 York, Andrew. "The Co-ordinator," Cosmopolitan, CLXII (February 1967), 124-130, 132-139, 143-147, 150, 152-155.

10962 _____. "The Eliminator," Cosmopolitan, CLXI (October 1966), 132-136, 138, 140-141, 143-147, 149-151, 155-161.

10963 Young, Al. "Chicken Hawk's Dream," Spero, I, no. 2 (1966), 19-21.

10964 _____. "Moon Watching by Lake Chapala," Aldebaran Review, no. 3 (1968), 33-34.

10965 _____. "My Old Buddy Shakes, Alas, and Grandmama Claude," Nexus (San Francisco, Calif.), II (May-June 1965), 44-49.

10966 _____. "The Question Man & Why I Dropped Out," Nexus (San Francisco, Calif.), II (November-December 1965), 32-36.

10967 Young, Charles. "Harold Lynch Makes Bid for Notoriety," Carolina Quarterly, XIX (Spring 1967), 85-92.

10968 Young, Dalene. "Bianca," Ante, I (Spring 1965), 4-16.

10969 _____. "Feather Joey's My Friend," Ante, IV (Spring 1968), 3-12.

10970 Young, Dave. "While the Band Played On," The Archive, LXXX (May 1968), 16-21.

10971 Young, Gilbert. "The Unfinished Work," Epoch, XVI (Winter 1967), 99-104.

10972 Young, Judy. "The Holidays/or/Yes Virginia, There Is a Maryjane," The Phoenix (Fall 1968), 38-41.

10973 Young, Kim. "An Evening at Home with Betsy and Ed," Mexico Quarterly Review, III, no. 4 (1969), 74-77.

10974 Young, Marguerite. "Mr. Spitzer's Cocoon Psychology," Harper's Bazaar, XCVIII (July 1965), 78-79, 114, 118-119.

10975 _____. "The Quest for the Heart/An Excerpt from Miss MacIntosh My Darling," Mademoiselle, LXI (September 1965), 195, 215-218, 231.

10976 Young, Noel. "Dillon, " California Review, no. 1 (Spring 1967), 54-62.

10977 Young, Patrick. "The Snowfield," Prairie Schooner, XL (Fall 1966), 211-218.

10978 Young, Tracy. "A Beginning," Seventeen, XXIV (January 1965), 65, 99.

10979 Younglove, Gary D. "Snowflakes in His Wake," Four Quarters, XVIII (May 1969), 37-44.

10980 Youngpeter, Helen. "Lincoln Bridge Is Falling Down," Ave

Maria, CVI (September 9, 1967), 26-29.

10981 _____. "The Time for Love Is Short," Ave Maria, CVII (January 6, 1968), 26-30.

10982 Youree, Gary. "The Honorable Discharge of Private Sam," Avant Garde, no. 5 (November 1968), 40-43.

10983 _____. "Peace Movement," Avant Garde, no. 2 (March 1968), 50-53.

10984 Yovkov, Yordan. "The Postal Watermill," Peter Tempest, trans., Obzor, (Winter 1967), 46-54.

10985 _____. "The Sin of Ivan Belin," Peter Tempest, trans., Obzor, (Winter 1967), 54-61.

10986 _____. "The White Swallow," Peter Tempest, trans., Obzor, (Winter 1967), 43-46.

10987 Yudkin, Vivian. "One Dark Delinquent Night," Vagabond, I, no. 2 (1966), 14-22.

10988 Yu-Hwa, Lee. "An Afternoon of Surmises," Southwest Review, LII (Autumn 1967), 344-351.

10989 _____. "The Bomb-Proof Inn," Literary Review, XI (Spring 1968), 306-318.

10990 _____. "The Monument," Arizona Quarterly, XXIII (Spring 1967), 45-60.

10991 _____. "The Scholar's Woman," Massachusetts Review, VI (Autumn 1965), 785-800.

10992 Yurick, Sol. "...And a Friend to Sit By Your Side," Bennington Review, III (Winter 1969), 3-12.

10993 _____. "'And Not in Utter Nakedness...'," Transatlantic Review, no. 23 (Winter 1966-67), 72-86.

10994 _____. "The Before and After of Hymie Farbotnik, or, The Sticking Point," Quarterly Review of Literature, XVI, nos. 3-4 (1969), 496-508.

10995 _____. "The Bird-Whistle Man," Transatlantic Review, no. 31 (Winter 1968-69), 29-33.

10996 _____. "Do They Talk about Genet in Larchmont," Confrontation, no. 2 (Spring 1969), 18-30.

10997 _____. "Not with a Whimper, but...," Transatlantic Review, no. 25 (Summer 1967), 38-65.

10998 _____. "Tarantella," Transatlantic Review, no. 31 (Winter 1968-69), 23-28.

10999 Zabor, Joel. "Rudd: S & Co.," Riverrun, (May 1967), 16-22.

11000 Zachary, Hugh. "Big Fishes and Little Fishes," Four Quarters, XV (May 1966), 1-8.

11001 _____. Matter of Honor, The Smith, Special Issue no. 2 (1969), 1-10.

11002 Zachry, Rose. "Carnival," Delta Review, VI (April 1969), 22-23.

11003 Zack, David. "Long Pig," Beyond Baroque 692, I (July 1969), 11-12.

11004 _____. "No Appointment--No Disappointment," Dust, IV (Summer 1969), 24-28.

11005 _____. "Woofy Tale #5/One Day's Diamond," Beyond Baroque 691, I (December 1968), 9.

11006 _____. "Woofy Tale #6/An Artichoke Lion and a Maned Camel Fern," Beyond Baroque 691, I (December 1968), 11.

11007 _____. "Woofy Tale #9/The Furry Serpent and His Buttercup," Beyond Baroque 692, I (July 1969), 27.

11008 Zagoren, Ruby. "The Flood that Thawed," Columbia, XLV (December 1965), 8-9.

11009 Zagrebelny, Pavel. "Companions on the Road," Eve Manning, trans., Soviet Literature, (no. 9, 1968), 104-110.

11010 Zakaras, Paul. "The Boarder," Consumption, I (Winter 1968), 11-15.

11011 _____. "The Fighter," Discourse, XI (Autumn 1968), 515-517.

11012 _____. "The Indian," Discourse, XI (Autumn 1968), 518-519.

11013 Zaka-ur-Rahman. "'The Lonely Moment of a Lonely Night'," Pakistan Review, XVI (November 1968), 28.

11014 _____. "Red Roses of Memories," Pakistan Review, XVI (January 1968), 37-40.

11015 _____. "'River Is a Strong Brown God'," Pakistan Review, XVI (December 1968), 13-15, 20.

11016 ______. "The Voice of the Knife," Pakistan Review, XVI (March 1968), 42-46.

11017 Zalygin, Sergei. "By the Irtysh/From the Chronicles of Krutiye Luki Village," Eve Manning, trans., Soviet Literature, (no. 7, 1965), 3-94.

11018 ______. "Salt Valley," Alice Ingman, trans., Soviet Literature, (no. 5, 1969), 51-124.

11019 Zamyatin, Yevgeny. "The Lion," Mirra Ginsburg, trans., Saturday Evening Post, CCXXXIX (October 22, 1966), 72-74.

11020 ______. "The Miracle of Ash Wednesday," Mirra Ginsburg, trans., Kenyon Review, XXVIII (November 1966), 640-649.

11021 Zander, William. "A Lack of Grace," December, X (1968), 15-21.

11022 Zanders, John. "Fugue for an Island," New Campus Writing, (1966), 170-178.

11023 Zar, Rubin. "Jews in Lithuania Before the 20th Century [short sketches]," Arx, III (August 1969), 13-23.

11024 ______. "My Early Youth in Lithuania," Arx, II (April 1969), 24-25.

11025 ______. "That Man Hewitt," Arx, II (December 1968), 26-27.

11026 Zavada, Mary. "The Appointed House," Ave Maria, CII (July 24, 1965), 24-27.

11027 Zavatsky, William. "You, the Dissembled," New Frontiers, X, no. 1 (1965), 20-24.

11028 Zbanatsky, Yuri. "Full Buckets," Michael Moor, trans., Soviet Literature, (no. 9, 1968), 66-72.

11029 Zeigerman, Gerald. "Where the Ivy Fails to Grow," Mademoiselle, LXIV (February 1967), 127, 187, 191-193.

11030 Zeiss, Tod Rolf. "The Fable of Molly d'Fleur," Readers & Writers, I (April 1968), 12-16, 23-25.

11031 ______. "Mr. Acton's Final Role," Four Quarters, XVII (January 1968), 35-48.

11032 Zekowski, Arlene. "Seasons of the Mind," South Dakota Review, IV (Winter 1966), 48-58.

11033 Zeldis, Chayyim. "Mud," Jewish Frontier, XXXIII (June 1966), 23-25.

11034 _____. "The Platoon Commander," Jewish Frontier, XXXII (October 1965), 43, 45-49, 51-53, 55.

11035 Zelent, Maria. "Kannitverstan," New Leaven, no. 16 (1966), 5-7.

11036 Zetterling, Mai. "Boat-Train to Finland," London Magazine, VII (May 1967), 53-58.

11037 Zeugner, John F. "The Correspondent," December, XI (1969), 119-130.

11038 _____. "The Tennis Player," Perspective, XV (Winter-Spring 1968), 139-165.

11039 _____. "The Rescue," Southern Humanities Review, III (Fall 1969), 322-337.

11040 Zhukov, Yuri. "Men of the Thirties/A Documentary Story," Rose Prokofieva, trans., Soviet Literature, (no. 8, 1967), 50-78.

11041 Zidar, Pavle. "May God Grant Us Happiness," Donald Davenport, trans., Literary Review, XI (Winter 1967), 251-257.

11042 Zielinski, Stanislaw. "Uncle From Heaven," Edward Rothert, trans., Literary Review, XI (Autumn 1967), 95-110.

11043 Zietlow, E. R. "Winter Wheat," South Dakota Review, V (Autumn 1967), 56-60.

11044 Zigan, Nancy. "Run, Paddy, Run," Man About Town, I (April 1967), 10-11.

11045 Zilber, Jacob. "Rumination," Ante, IV (Summer-Fall 1968), 74-77.

11046 Zimmerman, Eleanor B. "Homage to Gertrude," Wormwood Review, IX, no. 3 (1969), 8-9.

11047 Zimmerman, Joanne. "Everybody Loves Saturday Night," December, IX, nos. 2 & 3 (1967), 113-134.

11048 _____. "Parisian Episode," University Review, XXXIV (Winter 1967), 149-152.

11049 _____. "Smitty's Haven," Western Humanities Review, XXIII (Summer 1969), 235-248.

11050 _____. "Some of My Best Friends," University Review,

XXXV (Autumn 1968), 40-50.

11051 _____. "Tropical Fish," Kansas Quarterly, I (Winter 1968), 73-79.

11052 _____. "Yours Very Truly," Kansas Magazine, (1967), 96-100.

11053 Zimmerman, Roger. "Nobody Understands," Sou'wester, (Summer 1967), 14-21.

11054 Zimmerman, Toni. "Christina's Diary," Minnesota Review, IX (1969), 181-187.

11055 Zimmermann, Barbara. "Merrilee Rodick and the Cat," Intro, no. 2 (September 1969), 123-312.

11056 Zimpel, Lloyd. "Burying Blackie," Carleton Miscellany, IX (Summer 1968), 2-7.

11057 _____. "Ovenmen," Massachusetts Review, IX (Autumn 1968), 677-691.

11058 _____. "Over North Mountain," Cimarron Review, no. 4 (June 1968), 12-31.

11059 _____. "They Lay There Bleeding," December, X (1968), 33-36.

11060 _____. "What's So Funny?" Quartet, no. 18 (Spring 1967), 12-17.

11061 Zobarskas, Stepas. "A Woman's Laugh," Literary Review, XII (Autumn 1968), 94-101.

11062 Zobel, Joseph. "The Gramophone," P. Gering and J. Nicholas, trans., The Classic, II, no. 2 (1966), 34-43.

11063 Zorin, Leo. "The Apocalypse Machine," New Worlds, no. 185 (December 1968), 10-13.

11064 _____. "The Man Who Was Dostoevsky," New Worlds, no. 181 (April 1968), 31-32.

11065 _____. "Plekhanov Screams," New Worlds, no. 188 (March 1969), 40-41, 43.

11066 Zorn, George A. "Mr. and Mrs. McGill," Perspective, XIV (Spring 1965), 3-20.

11067 Zoryan, Stefan. "The Orchard," Alice Ingman, trans., Soviet Literature, (no. 3, 1966), 25-29.

11068 Zoshchenko, Mikhail. "The Aristocrat," Soviet Literature, (no. 4, 1967), 79-81.

11069 Zoss, Joel. "The New Agent," New Worlds, no. 185 (December 1968), 32-39.

11070 _____. "The Valve Transcript," New Worlds, no. 181 (April 1968), 42-43.

11071 Zubavin, Boris. "The Postman and the King," Margaret Wettlin, trans., Soviet Literature, (no. 6, 1968), 104-116.

11072 Zuckmayer, Carl. "As If It Were Part of Me," George Raymond Selden, trans., Scala International, (December 1966), 34-36.

11073 Zuidema, Nancy. "The Club," Diliman Review, XIV (April 1966), 127-132.

11074 _____. "Puddles," Diliman Review, XIV (January 1966), 40-42.

11075 Żukrowski, Wojciech. "The Wife," Edward Rothert, trans., Literary Review, X (Spring 1967), 365-379.

11076 Zwerenz, Gerhard. "The Cable Lift," Silas O Hughes, Jr., trans., Dimension, II, no. 2 (1969), 364-375 [in German and English on alternate pages].

11077 Zwerling, L. Steven. "A Victory Lost," Grande Ronde Review, II, no. 1 (1967), 33-36.

TRANSLATOR INDEX

TITLE INDEX